The Historical Atlas

of

World War II

A CARTOGRAPHICA PRESS BOOK

This edition published in 2007 by
Chartwell Books, Inc.
A division of BOOK SALES, INC.
114 Northfield Avenue
Edison, New Jersey 08837
USA

ISBN-10: 0-7858-2200-3
ISBN-13: 978-0-7858-2200-4

QUMHAOW

This book is produced by
Cartographica Press Ltd.
6 Blundell Street
London
N7 9BH

Design and cartography:
Malcolm Swanston
with
Jeanne Radford
Jonathan Young
Peter A. B. Smith
Alexander Swanston

Printed in Singapore by
Kyodo Printing Co. Pte. Ltd.

THE
HISTORICAL ATLAS
OF
WORLD WAR II

BY
ALEXANDER SWANSTON
AND
MALCOLM SWANSTON

CHARTWELL
BOOKS, INC.

CONTENTS

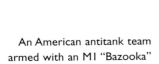

An American antitank team armed with an M1 "Bazooka" knock out a German Panther tank in Normandy, June 1944.

KEY TO MAPS

Military units/types

⊠ infantry

▬ armored

⌒ airlanding and Luftwaffe field

⊕ airborne

▪ artillery

Military units/size

XXXXX
☐ army group

XXXX
☐ army

XXX
☐ corps

XX
☐ division

X
☐ brigade

III
☐ regiment

II
☐ battalion

I
☐ company

Military unit colors

■ British / Canadian / U.S. / Polish

■ German

■ French

■ training

□ refitting

■ Chinese

■ Japanese

■ Finnish

■ Polish

■ Soviet Union

General military symbols

—XXXXX— army group boundary

—XXXX— army boundary

—XXX— corps boundary

⬭ pocket or position

☂ paratroop drop

⬐ sunken ship

╫ mobile gun

╪ antitank gun

⅄ light machine gun

⊥ heavy machine gun / other infantry weapon

⊞ gun emplacement

⊓ gun in casement

● heavy AA gun

○ light AA gun

⚔ 20mm antiaircraft gun

■ German strong points

⊓ pillbox for guns

□ concrete shelter

⊡ shelter with cupola

⬤ sea mine

◣ land mine

×××××× barbed wire

⌐⌐⌐ major defensive line

∿∿∿ entrenchment

◯ radar station

⚲ church

Military movements

➔ attack

▪▪➔ retreat

✛ bombers

✳ explosion

⊕ airfield

Geographical symbols

⋰⋱ buildings

▨ urban area

— road

┅ railroad

— river

--- seasonal river

⊟ canal

— border

⊰ bridge or pass

✶ marsh/swamp

▨ rocks and beach

■ woodland

MAP LIST

INTRODUCTION

At the Armistice of 11 November 1918, German armies were in retreat, beaten on the battlefield. While the Allies grew stronger by the day, Germany grew weaker. The massive contribution by the United States from April 1917 in materials and men, tipped the scales in the Allies' favor. Nevertheless the German Army still stood on foreign soil, Germany was not invaded and German industry still functioned almost undamaged by war.

World War I ended officially with the Treaty of Versailles, signed in 1919. Germany was not consulted about the terms, she was sent the details on the proposed treaty and allowed to comment but these were largely ignored. When the terms of the Treaty of Versailles became known, many Germans were astounded, war guilt and loss of territory all came as a shock, especially after President Wilson's "Fourteen Points" was grasped by Germany as a fair end to a terrible war. In these circumstances the myth of the "Stab in the back" by defeatists in Germany began to grow. With the rise of the Nazis, these myths were propagandized, demands for territorial restitution were soon realized. However, Hitler wanted more. Italy and Japan also developed their expansionist agendas. The World War began as a series of regional conflicts which, by the signing of the Tripartite Pact on 27 September 1940 between Germany, Italy, and Japan, created a full global military alliance. The Rome-Berlin-Tokyo Axis connected wars in Europe, in the Mediterranean, Africa, and Atlantic, to wars in Asia and the Pacific. It eventually drew in the majority of the sovereign nations that existed in 1939.

The Asian war began in 1933 with Japan's invasion of China from their puppet state of Manchuria (Manchukuo). The war in Africa began in 1936 with the Italian invasion of Abyssinia (Ethiopia). In Europe in 1939 with the invasion of Poland, which drew in Britain and France with both their empires. It began in the Pacific in 1941 with the Japanese attack on Pearl Harbor. This brought the United States into the war against Germany, with Hitler declaring war on the US in the aftermath of the Japanese attack. Over 60 million people would perish in this global conflict, making it the most cataclysmic event human history.

In this single volume it is our intention to bring all of the major events into focus, our maps throw spotlights onto crucial battles and campaigns—this was a total struggle of decency against darkness, as British Prime Minister Winston Churchill stated in 1940, "If the light of Freedom ... should be finally quenched, it might well herald a return to the Dark Ages, when every vestige of human progress during two thousand years would be engulfed." But as history demonstrated he was not just talking to Britain but the whole free world. It was a simple struggle between darkness and light. If our forefathers had failed, the consequences would have been unbearable for most—and certain death for many.

To those who saved our freedom, this book is respectfully dedicated.

The Authors, October 2006

Europe
11 November 1918

Central Powers

Allied

Neutral

Armistice lines

THE PEACE SETTLEMENTS 1919–20

"YOU HOLD IN YOUR HANDS THE FUTURE OF THE WORLD."

PRESIDENT POINCARÉ, JANUARY 1919

THE FOURTEEN POINTS

1 The abolition of secret treaties
2 The freedom of the seas
3 Free trade
4 Disarmament
5 Adjustment of colonial claims
6 Russia
7 The restoration of Belgium
8 Alsace-Lorraine
9 Italy
10 Austria-Hungary
11 Romania, Serbia, Montenegro and other Balkan states
12 Ottoman Empire
13 The Polish question
14 A general association of nations

On 28 June 1919 in the Hall of Mirrors, within the Palace of Versailles, the treaty was signed that ended the war to end wars. Between August 1914 and November 1918 a confident Imperial Europe tore itself to pieces. Four empires collapsed: Russian, Austro-Hungarian, Ottoman, and German. From their ashes emerged new states: Czechoslovakia and Yugoslavia. Old states, Poland, Lithuania, Latvia, and Estonia, reemerged from years of domination.

The peacemakers had gathered in Paris in January 1919 after the Armistice of 11 November 1918. President Wilson arrived in the port of Brest the previous December aboard the liner *George Washington* to cries of "Vive Wilson" and "Vive l'Amerique." He and the American delegation were greeted by the French foreign minister, before they caught the special night train to Paris. There they were met by the French government. Clemenceau, President Poincaré, and their ministers greeted Wilson; the crowds cheered, bands played, and flags waved. Amid wild cheering, the President and his wife were driven in an open carriage along the Champs-Elysées to their residence. The President, happy with his reception, also came armed with is "Fourteen Points." Many in Europe hoped he would bring a fair solution to their ancient and deeply-held prejudices.

Clemenceau's France was a sad place in the spring of 1919, a quarter of Frenchmen between the ages of 18 and 30 were dead, a further quarter were maimed, the northern industrial zone including the coal mines, the power for what was left of its industry, was in ruins. Thousands of square miles were pitted with shell holes, and scarred by lines of abandoned trenches. So bad was the damage to the land, especially around Verdun, that nothing would grow.

Fourteen Points or not, so much was at stake for France: Clemenceau's raison d'être was to make sure that Germany paid in full. France needed a secure future from a more populous Germany, whose industry was undamaged by war.

The British had already largely achieved almost all of its desires: the German High Seas Fleet was destroyed and Germany's colonies were now mostly in British and a few more in Allied hands. The Americans, however, were eager to get the job of peacemaking done and go home, protected by their powerful navy and the wide expanses of the Atlantic and Pacific Oceans.

The British Prime Minister, Lloyd George's view was clear; he wanted to achieve a balance of power in Europe. Germany must not be destroyed, leaving the way open for a strong and revolutionary Russia; it must be left with some kind of strength. Britain would then be free, with its unchallenged naval dominance, to pursue its trade and enjoy the benefits of its recently extended and already vast empire.

The day after his arrival in Paris, Lloyd George met Wilson, Clemenceau, and Vittorio Orlando, the Italian Prime Minister, at the French Foreign Ministry on the Quai d'Orsay. Each leader brought along his Foreign Minister and a small group of advisors. On 13 January, in line with British wishes, two representatives from Japan joined the group. This became known as the Council of Ten, although some referred to it as the Supreme Council, since smaller states and allies were not included. This group would meet more than 100 times. By March, as negotiations became more difficult, the Supreme Council met without the Foreign Ministers and the Japanese, to become the Council of Four: Wilson, Lloyd George, Clemenceau, and Orlando.

The Council of Ten was scrapped as too unwieldly, becoming the Council of Four. Speeding up the work of the Peace Conference, the more informal group met largely in President Wilson's private study. From left to right: Orlando, Italy; Lloyd George, British Empire; Clemenceau, France; and Wilson, United States.

The peacemakers had taken on, at least for a short term, the administration and feeding of much of Europe and the Near East. If they did not undertake the work it seemed no one would, or perhaps worse Socialist or right-wing revolutionaries might.

Apart from destroying human life, hope, and expectation on an immense scale, the war had disrupted the world economy. It would not be easy to repair this and deal with a host of problems created by emerging new states changing ownership of territory, populations, and raw materials.

The absentee in all of these deliberations was Russia, an ally from 1914 until March 1918. After the first revolution of February, Russia continued to fight alongside the Allies, though with decreasing effectiveness. By October 1917 the Bolsheviks had seized power. The Treaty of Brest-Litovsk ended the war between the central powers and Russia on 3 March 1918. The Armistice of 11 November 1918 between the Allies and Germany effectively ended the Treaty of Brest-Litovsk. When German and Austrian forces withdrew from occupied lands in the east a mixed bag of nationalists and revolutionaries claimed territory for their respective causes.

In January the American government sent William Bullitt, a self-confident, upper-class product of Yale, on a mission to the revolutionary government in Russia. He was to search out acceptable grounds upon which a peace might be made with the Western Allies. They had previously supported the counterrevolutionary governments by sending forces to support "the Whites," of whom there were quite a number. However, it was the "Reds," the Bolsheviks, that held the Russian heartlands.

After various communications and discussions with the Bolsheviks—or the Soviets, as they now styled themselves—came to nothing. On 23 May 1919, the Allies decided on partial recognition of the White, Kolchack government, but by June the Reds were defeating Kolchack's forces on all fronts. Nothing more could be done about Russia's possible interests. A clause was added to the treaty that was then being finalized, stating that in future any treaty made between the Allies and Russia, or any parts of it, would be binding on any future Russian government. After a few final days of discussion and last minute amendments, the final Treaty of Versailles, with its 440 clauses, went off to the printers. Two days later a final session was called to vote on the terms but, alas, no printed version was yet available. It had to be read out aloud to the gathering in French. The non-French speakers are reputed to have nodded off, while others voiced objections; China complained that the Japanese were given German holdings and concessions in China; other issues were raised but ignored. Then Marshal Foch, Head of the French Army, rose and asked to be heard. He pleaded, once again, that the River Rhine should be the frontier, a barrier between France and Germany. He said later to a *New York Times* reporter, "...remember, the next time the Germans will make no mistake, they will break through into northern France and capture the Channel ports and use these as a base of operations against England." The peacemakers ignored his pleas and seemed satisfied with their final draft. The German delegation was led by Ulrich von Brockdorff-Rantzau, the Foreign Minister, who put his faith in the Americans and in Wilson's Fourteen Points as, indeed, did most Germans.

On 7 May, the terms were handed over to the German delegation, with two weeks to reply. The Germans were soon at work on the treaty: translations were printed and distributed. The shock was instantaneous. Loss of land to Poland and France, all the overseas colonies, millions in gold to be paid, the final amount yet to be specified. Germany would not be allowed to join the newly-forming League of Nations, would face the loss of almost all of its merchant fleet, and almost complete disarmament.

Within the specified time the Germans replied, with page after page of carefully argued objections and proposals. They considered that the Treaty was not a fair one; by taking territory from Germany it denied the right of self-determination, as laid out in the Fourteen Points. Reparations were unsustainable, Germans would be turned into a nation of slaves. Brockdorff-Rantzau strenuously rejected Clause 251, believing that it implied Germany's war guilt. When the peacemakers read the terms in full some were uneasy. Herbert Hoover, then working as American Relief Administrator, recalled some years later, "many parts of the proposed Treaty would ultimately bring destruction."

After further discussions, the Allies ratified the final Treaty, with little changed. This was presented to the Germans on 16 June. They were informed they had three days to accept and this was later extended to six days. The Germans left immediately for Weimar, the seat of Germany's shaky coalition government. The German cabinet, which had been inclined to sign, became deadlocked and on 20 June resigned. Brockdorff-Rantzau resigned his position as head of the German peace delegation. President Friedrich Ebert was left high and dry, with no government and no spokesman. He almost resigned himself but was persuaded to stay. He cobbled together another government by 22 June and, after another debate in the National Assembly, a vote was taken in favor of signing, with the proviso that Germany would not accept Clause 251, articles on the surrender and trial of those responsible for the war and the war guilt. The reply from Paris was unequivocal: the German government must accept or refuse. Finally the Germans accepted. The formal signing was set for 28 June in the Hall of Mirrors at the Palace of Versailles and, without further delay, it was signed. Dignatories posed for the camera, a few speeches were made and crowds cheered. President Wilson left the same day for Le Havre and a ship home.

While the Allies cheered, Germany mourned, and flags flew at half-mast. The myth of Germany's "undefeated" army prospered; others blamed traitors at home who had "stabbed Germany in the back." In the beer halls of Bavaria an unemployed ex-soldier and would-be politician drew crowds with his speeches on the "peace of shame." Hitler was just beginning to make his mark.

Europe 1920–21
Postwar Settlements

THE DEPRESSION 1930S

"FINANCIAL STORM DEFINITELY PASSED."

BERNARD BARUCH, CABLEGRAM TO WINSTON CHURCHILL,

15 NOVEMBER 1929

"ALL SAFE DEPOSIT BOXES IN BANKS OR FINANCIAL INSTITUTIONS HAVE BEEN SEALED... AND MAY ONLY BE OPENED IN THE PRESENCE OF AN AGENT OF THE I.R.S."

PRESIDENT F.D. ROOSEVELT, 1933

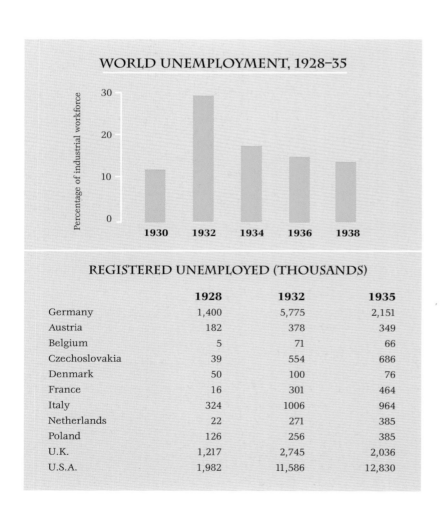

WORLD UNEMPLOYMENT, 1928–35

(Percentage of industrial workforce; years shown: 1930, 1932, 1934, 1936, 1938)

REGISTERED UNEMPLOYED (THOUSANDS)

	1928	1932	1935
Germany	1,400	5,775	2,151
Austria	182	378	349
Belgium	5	71	66
Czechoslovakia	39	554	686
Denmark	50	100	76
France	16	301	464
Italy	324	1006	964
Netherlands	22	271	385
Poland	126	256	385
U.K.	1,217	2,745	2,036
U.S.A.	1,982	11,586	12,830

After World War I industry in Europe rapidly recovered, production increased, especially in the traditional industries of coal mining, steel, and shipbuilding. The United States also developed new industries—motor vehicles and consumer goods—and its economic growth rate outstripped Europe, seizing a relatively larger share of world trade.

Such was the growth of the American automobile industry that by 1927, some 21,000 people had been killed in road accidents, but the United States' economy continued to boom. However, ominous signs began to appear during the autumn of 1929. The price of basic commodities began to fall. Russia reappeared as a major supplier of timber, cutting the price, affecting, in particular, countries such as Canada and Finland. At the beginning of October there was a drastic fall in the price of wheat, hitting hard not only farmers in America but also in Canada and Australia. On 23 October a massive sell-off of shares took place on the New York Stock Market. President Hoover made reassuring statements but it was

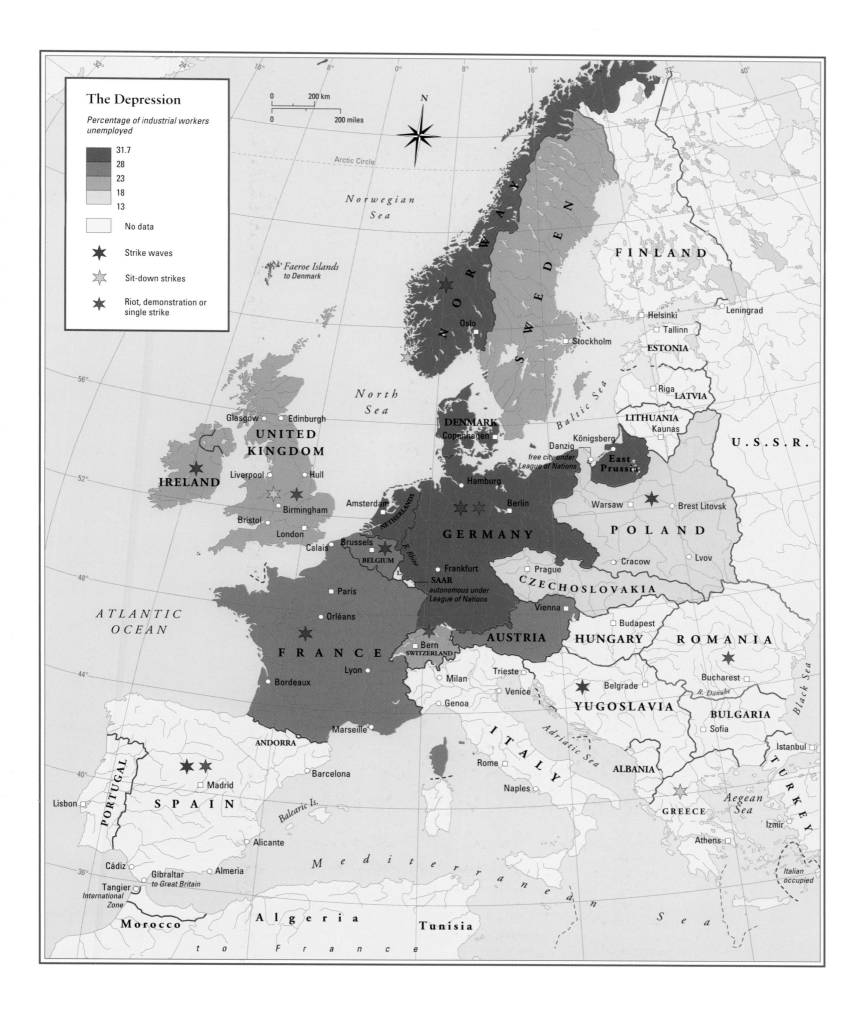

The Depression

Percentage of industrial workers unemployed

- 31.7
- 28
- 23
- 18
- 13

No data

★ Strike waves

☆ Sit-down strikes

★ Riot, demonstration or single strike

0   200 km

0   200 miles

N

Norwegian Sea

Arctic Circle

Faeroe Islands to Denmark

FINLAND

Helsinki
Leningrad
Oslo
Tallinn
Stockholm
ESTONIA

NORWAY
SWEDEN

North Sea

Baltic Sea

Riga
LATVIA

Glasgow
Edinburgh

UNITED KINGDOM

LITHUANIA
Kaunas

U.S.S.R.

DENMARK
Copenhagen
Königsberg
Danzig
free city under
League of Nations
East Prussia

IRELAND
Liverpool
Hull

Hamburg
Berlin
Warsaw
Brest Litovsk

Amsterdam
NETHERLANDS
GERMANY
POLAND

Bristol
Birmingham

London
Calais
Brussels
BELGIUM
R. Rhine
Frankfurt
SAAR
autonomous under
League of Nations
Prague
Cracow
Lvov
CZECHOSLOVAKIA

ATLANTIC OCEAN

Paris
Vienna
Budapest

Orléans
AUSTRIA
HUNGARY
ROMANIA

FRANCE
Lyon
Bern
SWITZERLAND
Milan
Trieste
Bucharest

Bordeaux
Venice
Belgrade
R. Danube

Genoa
YUGOSLAVIA
Black Sea

Marseille
BULGARIA
Sofia

ANDORRA
ITALY
Adriatic Sea
Istanbul

Barcelona
Rome
ALBANIA
TURKEY

Madrid
Naples
Aegean Sea

Lisbon
PORTUGAL
SPAIN
GREECE
Izmir

Balearic Is.
Athens

Alicante
Italian occupied

Cádiz
Almería
Gibraltar
to Great Britain
Mediterranean

Tangier
International
Zone
Sea

Morocco
Algeria
Tunisia
to France

By 1932 over 12 million Europeans were unemployed. Some states increasingly moved to the right hoping that centralized popular dictatorships would solve their problems.

too late. At first it was thought that only the very rich would be hit and that the economy would roll on, but it quickly became clear that millions who had set aside their savings and invested, would also be affected. The second downward lurch in the Stock Market hit on 19 November.

Across the world countries were importing American products and materials, financed by American loans. At the same time the U.S. maintained high import tariffs, which prevented customer nations a way of paying for these goods and loans. They were forced to balance their trade by payments in gold or by further loans.

World War I had created massive intergovernmental debts, partly owed by the victors to the U.S. and partly by Germany to its near neighbors in the form of reparations. After 1929, however, American loans to support their payments were no longer available. These loans had financed post-war trade and reconstruction. The end of this cashflow strangled European economies and the situation could not be worse. The Americans then raised their trade tariffs further by the Smoot-Hawley Act of 1930.

The U.S. and Europe, along with the rest of the world, struggled with agricultural overproduction, shrinking trade, increasing protective trade tariffs, inter-Allied debts and reparations. The U.S. recalled loans, particularly from Germany, but the Germans were paying war reparations to Britain and France; they, in turn, were required to pay interest due on their American war loans. Unable to meet these payments, industrial and commercial activity declined; unemployment grew rapidly and reached over 30 percent in Germany, 24 percent in France and 26 percent in Austria. Social disruption and distress was immense.

Desperate English workers set out on the Jarrow Crusade. Jarrow, a town in the north-east of England, where almost the entire workforce was unemployed, set out on a march to London. All along their route they were supported and aided by equally desperate people hoping that some sort of message would be carried to the national government. Unfortunately, government reactions to these situations sometimes exacerbated the distress. Import tariffs were increased or very strictly applied, and even Britain ended its 86 years of free trade and brought in trade tariffs with the 1932 Import Duties Act. The British also applied a preference system for trade from and to its Empire. France adopted a similar

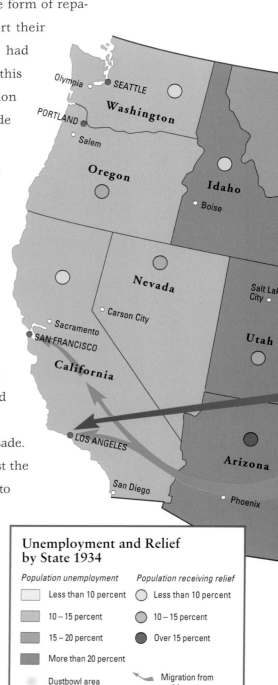

Unemployment and Relief by State 1934

Population unemployment	Population receiving relief
☐ Less than 10 percent	○ Less than 10 percent
☐ 10–15 percent	◐ 10–15 percent
☐ 15–20 percent	● Over 15 percent
☐ More than 20 percent	
▨ Dustbowl area	↘ Migration from prairie states
● DENVER Twenty largest cities	↘ Migration from Appalachians

system with its colonies. Germany, now with no overseas possessions, was in no place to use similar economic tactics. They led the way in deflationary policies. The German people in the street, and distinguished financial experts, already believed that they had been ruined by "reparations." To some extent Germany lost its faith in the multiparty system, they just wanted a solution to their problems. The Nazi Party, under Hitler, had all the solutions and more besides: investment in heavy industry and a massive public works program seemed to get things started.

Under the Presidency of Franklin D. Roosevelt a range of agencies were created to deal with unemployment. One of these was the Works Progress Administration (W.P.A.) launched in May 1935. When the W.P.A. finally came to an end, during World War II, it had spent some $11 billion creating part- and full-time work for 8.5 million people.

Montana
na
North Dakota
• Bismarck
Minnesota
Maine
• Augusta
Montpelier

South Dakota
• Pierre
MINNEAPOLIS St Paul
Wisconsin
Madison
DETROIT
Michigan
Lansing
Vt. N.H.
• Concord
New York
Albany
BUFFALO
Mass. BOSTON
Hartford Providence
Conn. R.I.

Wyoming

Cheyenne

DENVER •

Colorado

Nebraska
Lincoln

Iowa
• Des Moines

CHICAGO
Illinois
Springfield

Indiana
Indianapolis

CLEVELAND

Ohio
Columbus

CINCINNATI

Pennsylvania
PITTSBURGH
Harrisburg
BALTIMORE
Annapolis
WASHINGTON
D.C. Md.

N.J.
Trenton
PHILADELPHIA
Dover

NEW YORK

Delaware

Santa Fé

New Mexico

Topeka •

Kansas

Jefferson
City

KANSAS CITY
Missouri
ST LOUIS

West
Virginia
Charleston

Frankfort

Kentucky

Virginia
Richmond

Raleigh •

North Carolina

Oklahoma
• Oklahoma City

Nashville •

Tennessee

Arkansas
Little Rock •

Mississippi

Alabama

Georgia

Atlanta •

Columbia •

South
Carolina

• Dallas

Texas

Louisiana
Jackson

Montgomery

• Austin

Houston •

Baton
Rouge

NEW ORLEANS

Tallahassee •

Florida

Miami

0 300 km

0 300 miles

THE RISE OF FASCISM

"FASCISM ACCEPTS THE INDIVIDUAL ONLY INSOFAR AS HIS INTERESTS COINCIDE WITH THE STATE'S."

BENITO MUSSOLINI, ITALIAN DICTATOR

A poster from 1938 celebrating the Hitler-Mussolini Pact.

The aftermath of World War I, with its peace treaties created between 1919 and 1921, redrew Europe into a patchwork of small, precariously-viable states. President Wilson's Fourteen Points intended to create states based on ethnic-cultural identities. The reality of the Treaty of Versailles, however, was ethnic minorities in almost all of the new states. The resentment felt by the defeated powers manifested itself in the growth of new nationalist regimes. The economic crisis of the early 1930s persuaded ordinary men and women to look in new directions, leaving traditional leaders and institutions in favor of radical new movements and parties.

In Italy, as early as October 1922, Benito Mussolini marched on Rome and seized power, as the leader of *Fasci di Combattimento*—the Fascist Party. His authoritarian oratory and right-wing policies appealed to many in Italy and across Europe, especially those who feared the spread of Communism and detested the weakness and inability of multi-party, democratic governments to deal with this threat and the economic crisis of the early 1930s. This feeling ran deep in Germany where Communist groups tried to seize power as early as 1919.

In 1923 a little-known leader of the National Socialist German Workers' Party, Adolf Hitler, attempted a coup in Bavaria. It failed and he was imprisoned—in not too harsh conditions—since he enjoyed the support of some eminent figures. However, it did bring attention to his right-wing ideals and gave him time to write *Mein Kampf* (*My Struggle*). The emphasis of this book was the restoration of German "greatness," defying the terms of the

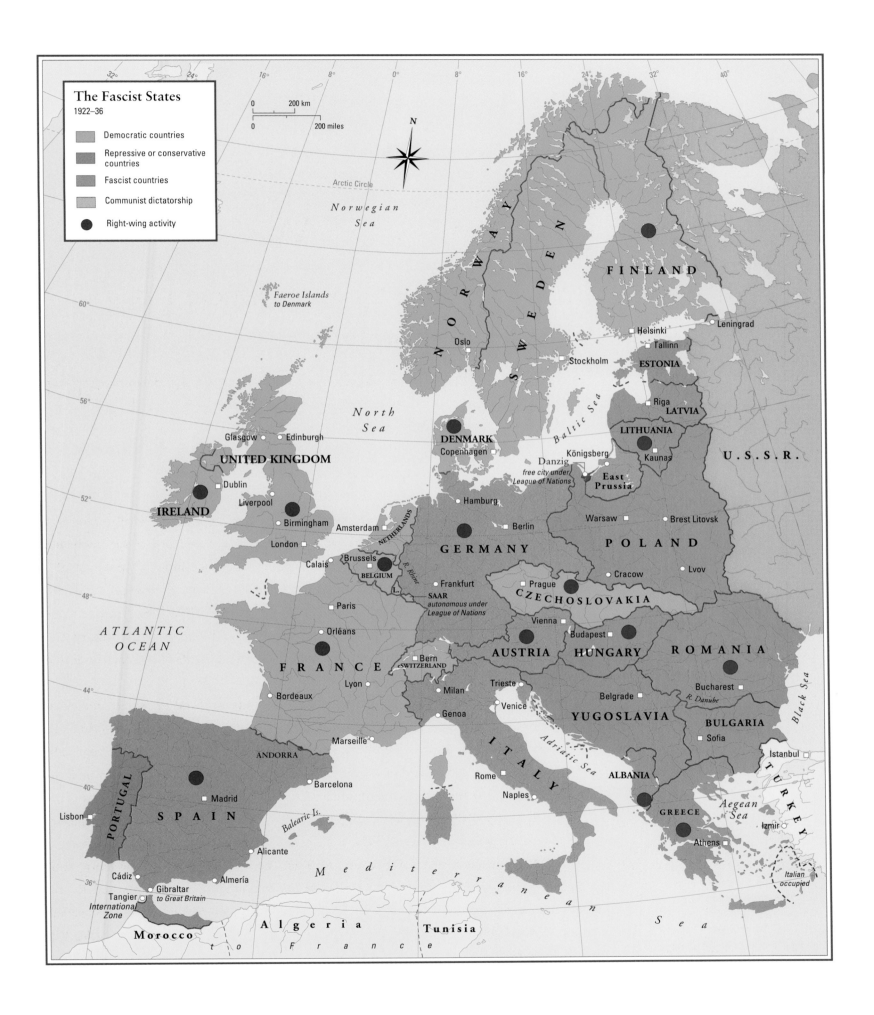

The Fascist States
1922–36

Democratic countries

Repressive or conservative countries

Fascist countries

Communist dictatorship

● Right-wing activity

A poster supporting the Hitler Youth in a march and rally to be held in Nuremberg, 1938.

FASCISM
The name derives from the Latin *fasces*, a ceremonial bundle of rods wrapped around an axe representing the power and unity of ancient Rome. Mussolini used the term to describe his National *Fascist* Party, which was the first fascist party to gain power.

Far right: Adolf Hitler addressing a rally of the SA (Sturmabteilungen or Storm detachment founded by Hitler in 1920) at Dortmund in 1933. Just one year later he sacrificed this organization in what became known as the "Night of the Long Knives."

Treaty of Versailles, ridding Germany of the detested Weimar Republic and what he regarded as the international troublesome non-aryan Jews.

Germany almost crumbled under the economic pressure of the 1930s. Ordinary Germans needed a solution to their woes, and the quicker the better. Hitler in his popular speeches offered such a solution, a strong united leadership, and an end to inter party squabbles. The Nazi Party won major gains in the 1932 elections, becoming the largest party in the Reichstag, and by 1933 Hitler was Chancellor of Germany.

Some years earlier Mussolini said "Fascism accepts the individual only insofar as his interests coincide with the state." By 1934, when Hitler assumed the title of Führer, the Nazis would take these sentiments much further than the founder of Fascism could ever imagine.

Investors left Europe in search of higher interest rates elsewhere and the cycle of indebtedness established around German reparations payments merely confused matters further. American loans were made to Germany to help reparations payments to France and Britain, who could then repay interest to the U.S. for their own wartime loans. In this situation the Wall Street crash caused severe hardship, especially with the recall of U.S. European loans, damaging Germany in particular. Many industrial countries incurred 25 per cent unemployment rates (Germany 30.1 percent, France 24.3 percent, Austria 26.1 percent, Denmark 31.7 percent); industrial production fell to 53 percent of the 1929 figure in Germany, and social distress was immense. In Germany malnutrition was rife, meat consumption fell and the death rate increased, while in England this despair is best exemplified by the hunger marches from the Jarrow shipyards to London. Government reactions to the Depression sometimes exacerbated the distress. Import tariffs were strictly applied all over Europe, and even Britain ended its eighty-six years of free trade by the 1932 Import Duties Act. The Ottawa Imperial Conference granted preferential treatment to Dominion agricultural products, while British manufactured goods received reciprocal treatment in Dominion markets. France adopted similar tactics regarding her own colonies. European states adopted deflationary policies, especially in Germany and France; budgetary control in Britain; and government intervention in Nazi Germany, concentrating on promoting heavy industry, a public works program and a secret rearmament program.

In Britain the revival of domestic consumer demand provided with cheap money helped private enterprise and gradually turned around the economy. The Depression had a significant impact on domestic and international politics. Democracies experienced unusual political tendencies. Ministerial crises in France and the development of Fascist leagues, the Croix de Feu, led in 1936 to Léon Blum's Popular Front government, a sister system to that in Spain. Britain ended the normal single-party government and switched to a multi-party national government in the face of international events and Oswald Mosley's British Union of Fascists. Support for right-wing extremist parties grew, from the Lapua movement in Finland to the Hungarian Arrow Cross and the Iron Guard in Romania. Ruined farming interests backed the right (Romania's League of the Archangel Michael) and many ruined and worried middle-class voters in Germany helped bring Hitler to power.

Tensions in the East 1920-40

"THE REVOLUTION HAS ESTABLISHED IN CHINA LIBERTY AND EQUALITY... FRATERNITY IS THE AS YET UNREALIZED IDEAL OF HUMANITY... IT MAY BE FOR CHINA, THE OLDEST OF NATIONS, TO POINT THE WAY TO THIS FRATERNITY."

SONG CHING-LING, WIFE OF SUN YAT-SEN

Chinese soliders drum up support in the early days of the 1911 Revolution.

The waning of Manchu power—the 250-year-old ruling Dynasty in China—in the early 1900s was largely caused by western colonial exploitation of this vast nation. This resulted in the social upheaval of the 1911 Revolution, which was exacerbated by the attempt of Yüan Shih-k'ai, President of the newly-formed Republic, to establish himself as Emperor in 1915. His bid for ultimate power destroyed the authority of the new government.

The new nationalist state was unable to control its domain, much as it tried. Russia, France, Britain, and most of all, Japan's treaties survived the Revolution and they sought to expand and consolidate their agreements with this hapless nation. However, the events of World War I greatly weakened the European colonial powers' grip on China. German holdings in the Shantung Peninsula were occupied by Japan. As an Allied power Japan had attacked and captured the German base at Tsingdao in 1916, and after the Treaty of Versailles, this territory's ownership formally passed from Germany to Japan.

Between 1918 and 1928 China was gripped by a long period of violent disputes—the Warlord Period—in which various groups fought and made alliances in a bloody struggle for national power. No one was quite sure who to back. Japan's interests lay largely in the north-east, in Manchuria: this area was under the control of Chang Tso-lin, who planned to extend his rule across northern China. Unfortunately for Chang Tso-lin his plans began to fade during the late 1920s. Partly as a result of this the Japanese became involved in expanding Japan's interests in China. This involvement inevitably spread in to adjoining territories as Japan sought to take advantage of China's disunity.

After 1921 emerged a new political force, the Koumintang, calling themselves Nationalists. Based in Canton and led by Sun Yat-sen, the Koumintang were determined to end the state of civil war in China and become a force for national unity. By 1926, after consolidating themselves, with Soviet support, they were ready for the offensive. The Great Northern Offensive was launched in 1926, in which Koumintang armies secured Changsha, Wuchang, Nanking, and Changhai but

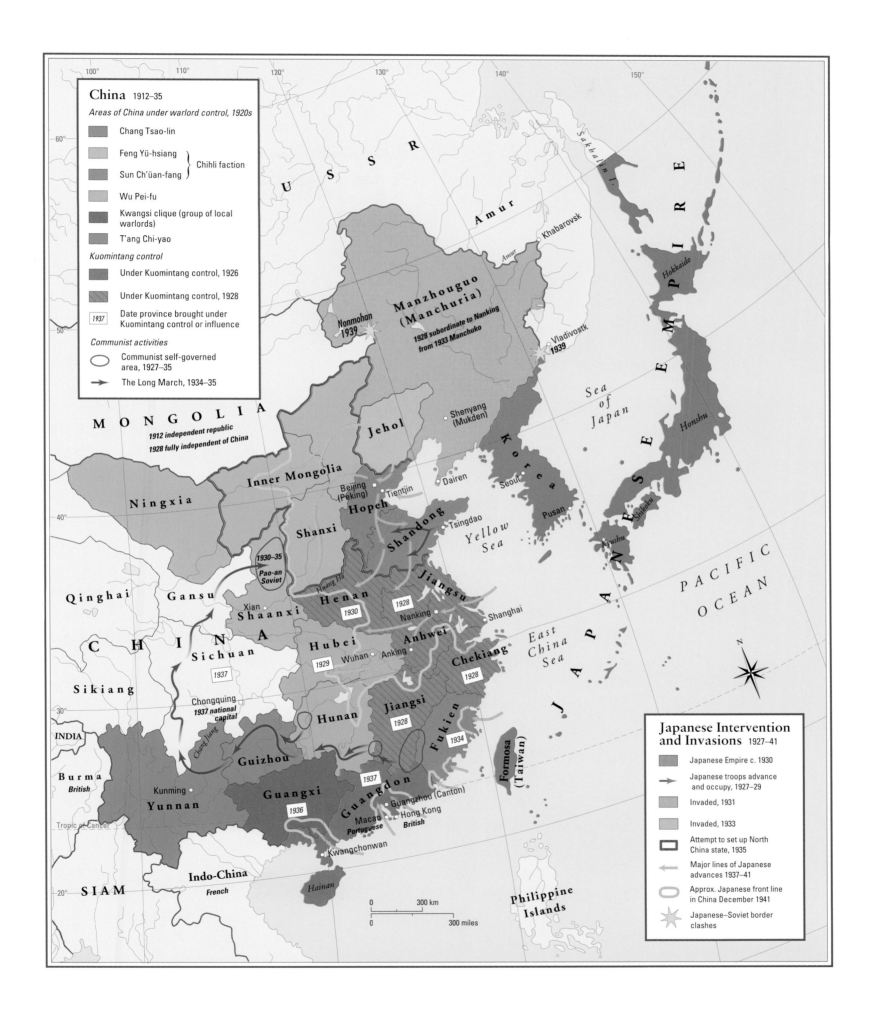

China 1912–35

Areas of China under warlord control, 1920s

Chang Tsao-lin

Feng Yü-hsiang
} Chihli faction
Sun Ch'üan-fang

Wu Pei-fu

Kwangsi clique (group of local warlords)

T'ang Chi-yao

Kuomintang control

Under Kuomintang control, 1926

Under Kuomintang control, 1928

1937 Date province brought under Kuomintang control or influence

Communist activities

Communist self-governed area, 1927–35

The Long March, 1934–35

Japanese Intervention and Invasions 1927–41

Japanese Empire c. 1930

Japanese troops advance and occupy, 1927–29

Invaded, 1931

Invaded, 1933

Attempt to set up North China state, 1935

Major lines of Japanese advances 1937–41

Approx. Japanese front line in China December 1941

Japanese–Soviet border clashes

MONGOLIA
1912 independent republic
1928 fully independent of China

U S S R

Amur
Khabarovsk
Amur

Nonmohan 1939

Manzhouguo (Manchuria)
1928 subordinate to Nanking from 1933 Manchuko

Vladivostk 1939

Sakhalin I.

Hokkaido

Honshu

Sea of Japan

Shigoku

Kyushu

J A P A N E S E   E M P I R E

Shenyang (Mukden)

Jehol

Inner Mongolia

Ningxia

Beijing (Peking)
Tientjin
Dairen

Korea

Seoul

Pusan

Hopeh

Shanxi

Shandong

Tsingdao

Yellow Sea

Qinghai

Gansu

1930–35 Pao-an Soviet

Huang Ho

Xian
Shaanxi

Henan
1930

Jiangsu
1928

Nanking

Shanghai

East China Sea

PACIFIC OCEAN

C H I N A

Sichuan

1937

Hubei
1929
Wuhan   Anking

Anhwei

Chekiang
1928

Sikiang

Chongquing
1937 national capital

Chang Jiang

Hunan

Jiangsi
1928

Fukien
1934

Formosa (Taiwan)

Burma
British

Kunming

Guizhou

Guangxi
1936

Yunnan

Guangdon
1937

Macao
Portuguese

Guangzhou (Canton)
Hong Kong
British

Tropic of Cancer

Kwangchonwan

SIAM

Indo-China
French

Hainan

Philippine Islands

0   300 km

0   300 miles

INDIA

N

Japanese troops march along a
village street in Manchuria
(Manzhouguo).

faced significant defeats at Hsüchow. At about this time the Koumintang leadership realized that their Communist allies also had an agenda of their own—planning a seizure of power. The Koumintang turned on their erstwhile allies and, to strengthen their position, sought agreements with northern and other warlords that would preserve, at least in a nominal sense, Koumintang authority across China. In 1927, Koumintang, riven with these uneasy alliances, split between a left-wing government in Hankow and a right-wing government in Nanking under Chiang Kai-shek, the latter styling themselves as the National Government of China, thereby presenting a vague prospect of bringing some sort of unity to the country. The Nationalists in Nanking were now free of Soviet assistance and sought further alliances with various warlords. The aim of these complex negotiations was to isolate both Chang Tso-lin in the north-east and the left-wing Hankow government in the south. Campaigns followed until mid-1928 when Chang Tso-lin was murdered by the Japanese.

In October 1928, the Nationalist government was formally inaugurated with its capital at Nanking, this gained at least a nominal allegiance of most of the warlords, though the Communists still remained independent and a threat. The Nationalists attempted to bring Manchuria into the fold in 1929, which led to a brief and unsuccessful war with the Soviet Union.

Foreign powers were alarmed by Chinese ambitions to regain some form of unity. Their position in China relied on weakness, not strength or unity on the part of China. By 1930 Japan decided it was time to act, firstly in Manchuria and then on into China itself. Japan and its armed forces prepared to take decisive action.

A five-month campaign completed effective Japanese control of Manchuria. On 18 February 1932, a Japanese-controlled puppet assembly proclaimed the independence of Manchuria—Manchuko—with the last Chinese Emperor as its head, Pu-yi, the successor to the Manchu throne. This declaration also included the province of Jehol, the territory annexed to Manchuria on 21 January 1933. The driving force behind Japanese aggression was the suspicion that China was possibly able to put an end to her domestic disunity and thereby become able to resist external aggression. Following the "Long March," when the Communists withdrew from their southern strongholds in 1934–35 to the north west, the Siam Agreement in December 1936 ended a decade of civil war between Communist and Nationalist.

In 1937, the Japanese began a massive offensive, a full-scale invasion of northern and central China. The Japanese made gains in the north but were bitterly resisted on the lower Yangtse River. Shanghai was not captured until November, with Nanking following a month later, among horrific scenes of rape and butchery perpetrated by the Japanese. Five months later the Japanese had captured Tungshan, linking the conquests in northern and central China. The Japanese advance continued along the Yangtse River, capturing Hankow and Wuchang, and exhibiting great brutality with every step.

Japan made various peace overtures to the Chiang Kai-shek Nationalist Government, but these were rejected. Attempts to form puppet regimes in Peking and Nanking both failed, unable to rival Chiang's new regime, now based in its new capital at Chungking.

The Japanese lacked the means to consolidate the areas they had already conquered. Further advances merely meant further complications. However, they occupied much of the north parts of the lower Yangtse Valley and many major coastal cities and were in a good position to isolate the Nationalist Chungking government from outside support. Then a gift arrived with the fall of France in 1940: the Japanese moved into Indo-China and, in July 1941, forced the Vichy Government to accept a joint protectorate over Indo-China. These developments prompted the United States to impose trade sanctions against Japan, which, in turn, set Japanese military minds problems that would lead to war in the Pacific. Meanwhile, the war in China took its own brutal course.

Soldiers of the Chinese 8th Army strike an heroic pose on the Great Wall. Japanese advances, from 1933-37, meant that the Wall itself was of no strategic value and this photograph was taken for purely patriotic reasons.

EUROPEAN POLITICAL AGREEMENTS 1933–39

"... THE EXISTENCE AND INCREASE OF OUR RACE AND NATION, THE SUSTENANCE OF ITS CHILDREN AND THE PURITY OF ITS BLOOD, THE FREEDOM AND INDEPENDENCE OF THE FATHERLAND, AND THE NATION'S ABILITY TO FULFILL THE MISSION APPOINTED TO IT BY THE CREATOR OF THE UNIVERSE."

ADOLF HITLER, MEIN KAMPF

On 30 January 1933 Adolf Hitler was appointed Chancellor by President Paul von Hindenburg. Hitler's first aim was to restore German power—to re-build the army, navy, and airforce, which in the opinion of many Germans had been humiliated and crippled by the Treaty of Versailles. With this rebuilt force he would take back the territories lost in 1918–20 and reshape the German lands in Europe as the new Third Reich. Hitler did not expect to win *Lebensraum* ("living space," fundamental to Nazi ideology's expansionist policies) without committing Germany to war that would, by its nature, deprive other peoples of their homelands.

Political Agreements
1934–35

■ German-Polish non-aggression pact, 1934

■ Rome protocols, March 1934

■ Franco–Soviet/Soviet–Czech. pact, May 1935 (see also 1936–37)

By 1933 Hitler had developed a plan by which he would achieve these aims. The German armed forces, however, were not as ready as the party and its membership may have been. Glittering rallies, however, together with a marching fever that seemed to have gripped Germany, held Europe mesmerized. These gave an impression of unified, unchallenged power. The propaganda film *Triumph of the Will* flickered on cinema screens across Germany and Europe.

In the West, Britain and France, the victors of 1918 were unsure how to deal with this restless new power. Hitler was quite clear in his view of them: France, after suffering massive human loss in World War I, remained a committed enemy to any kind of German expansion, with the prospect of any growth in German power an anathema to them. Italy, whose politics and dictatorship began to coalesce with Germany, would serve to

Political Agreements
1936–37

Axis, Nov. 1936

Declaration of neutrality, 1936

Anglo–Egyptian treaty, 1936

Franco–Soviet/Soviet-Czech. Pact, May 1935

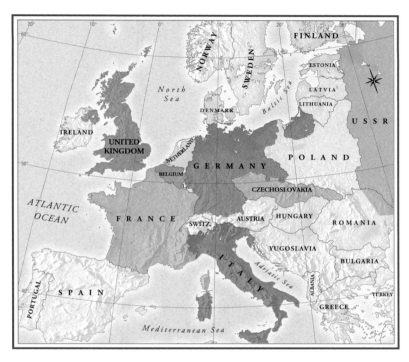

distract Britain and France in the Mediterranean. Hitler's view of the British was complex: they were successful imperial "Aryans" but their day was past. *Mein Kampf* assumed no military contest with Britain. German policy was to avoid a protracted war with Britain; they could keep their empire, as long as Germany had a free hand in Europe. Sir Neville Henderson, the British Ambassador in Berlin, urged British politicians to "look facts in the face ... We are an island people, the Germans a continental one. On that basis we can be friends without a clash of vital interests."

Russia was, according to Hitler, an inevitable enemy and source of Lebensraum. Soviet Russia's position was politically opposed to Fascist Germany. In reality, Soviet Russia needed German technical excellence and Germany needed somewhere to develop new equipment and tactics out of sight of the Versailles Treaty. In this way, Soviet Russia and Nazi Germany found a use for each other. It seemed that these totalitarian societies had more in common than most realized.

Between 1934 and 1939 Britain and France attempted to contain the threats posed by the Fascist states and the U.S.S.R. In 1934 the Franco-Soviet-Czech Pact was signed. In the same year the Rome protocols attempted to contain German expansion and to give Italy a greater say in European affairs. Smaller states made non-aggression pacts with Germany or signed the Declaration of Copenhagen in 1936 in an attempt to create a neutral bloc that would prove ineffective. In March 1938, Germany and Austria had affected a political union the "Aushluss." The Munich Agreement, reached on 29 September 1938, gave the predominantly German-speaking Sudetenland border regions of Czechoslovakia to Germany. This, it was proclaimed by the British Prime Minister, would bring "peace in our time".

In 1939 the British and French guaranteed the safety of Poland, Greece, Romania, and Turkey. Massive European rearmament was under way. On 23 August, perhaps the most extraordinary treaty was signed: the German-Soviet Non-Aggression Pact, ensuring almost immediate aggression.

Political Agreements
1938–39

British and French guarantees for Poland, Greece, Romania and Turkey, 1939

Copenhagen declaration of neutrality, July 1938

Axis, May 1939

German-Soviet Non-Aggression Pact, 23 August 1939

THE EXPANSION OF GERMANY 1933–39

"IT IS THE LAST TERRITORIAL CLAIM WHICH I HAVE TO MAKE IN EUROPE, BUT IT IS A CLAIM FROM WHICH I WILL NOT RECEDE AND WHICH, GOD WILLING, I WILL MAKE GOOD."

ADOLF HITLER, SPEECH CONCERNING THE SUDETENLAND, 1938

After being appointed Chancellor of Germany, Adolf Hitler mentioned to a newspaper editor, who opposed the Nazis, that he, Hitler, intended to come to power by winning seats in the Reichstag: after he had achieved this it might as well close its doors and become a museum. Four weeks later, on the morning of 27 February, the Reichstag went up in flames. Hitler at once blamed the Communists, many of whom blamed Hitler. Hitler's governmental position was less secure than may be imagined; he was head of a coalition government with only two other Nazis in the Cabinet. Much to his distaste, he needed other parties' support to win a majority in the Reichstag. The overthrow of Germany's parliamentary system began with the Reichstag Fire Decree, which gave Hitler or "the government" emergency powers that were used against the enemies of the Nazi Party, the Communists in particular.

The voters were given no rest, being called back to vote on 5 March. The Nazi Party won 43.9 percent of the vote, still short of a majority. Eighteen days later Hitler presented the Enabling Act, which would give the Chancellor permanent emergency powers. Enough of the center right representatives voted with the Nazi Party and the Act was approved on 24 March 1933. In effect, it gave Hitler permanent dictatorial powers.

The German economy was already recovering from the worst effects of the depression, its nadir reached in early 1932, but new measures speeded things up. The state funded a new motorway network—the *autobahnen*—which would connect the major cities to newly-created towns and under-developed areas. New industrial sites sprang up and flagging industries benefited from state support. The armaments industry, in particular, enjoyed full order books, especially now the cursed Treaty of

Hitler leads a motorcade from the Reichstag, a ceremony on a huge scale that was designed to hypnotize both foreigners and the German people alike. The overwhelming impression of a disciplined mass restored the belief of the German people in themselves and their country, throwing off the disunity of the Weimar years, and carefully binding their destiny to Hitler and his regime.

The German Army advanced and occupied Sudetenland on 1 October 1938 and were greeted by ethnic Germans *(above)*. However, when German forces entered the Czech capital, Prague, in the following March, they were greeted by silent crowds.

Versailles was cast aside. All of this activity created a massive boost to the German economy.

German foreign policy, even before Hitler came to power, was firmly nationalist in sentiment, directed at recovering German sovereignty and the restoration of German prestige. Hints of a new and more aggressive direction came when Hitler took Germany out of the League of Nations in October 1933. He also agreed to continue with secret plans to expand the armed forces, which were already in hand. However, Hitler remained prudent at this point. He knew that Germany must con-

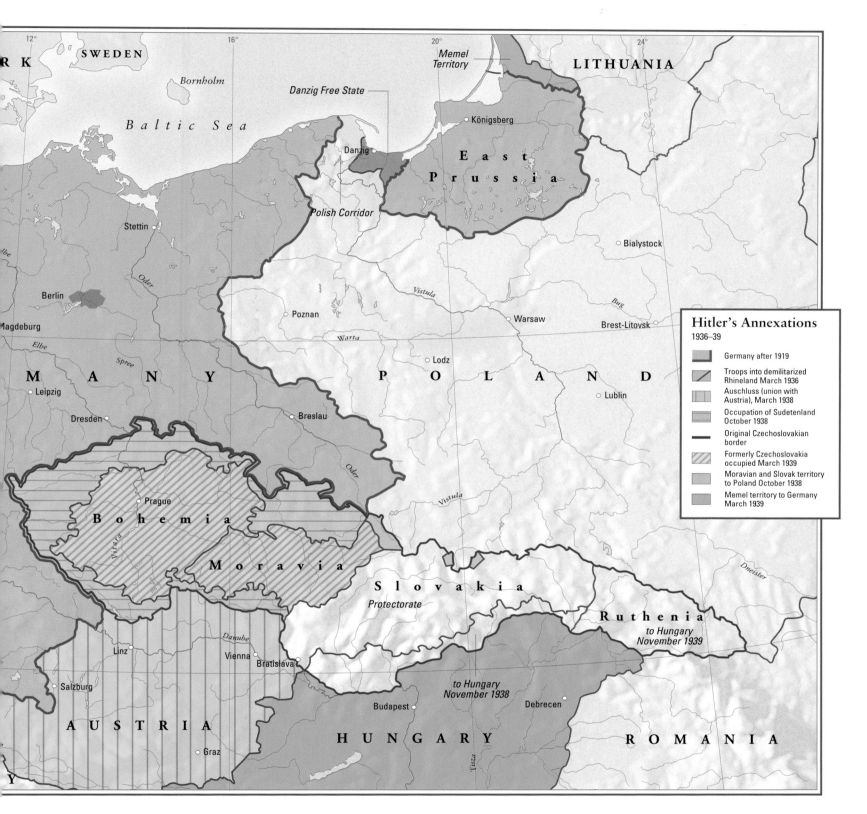

Hitler's Annexations
1936–39

- Germany after 1919
- Troops into demilitarized Rhineland March 1936
- Auschluss (union with Austria), March 1938
- Occupation of Sudetenland October 1938
- Original Czechoslovakian border
- Formerly Czechoslovakia occupied March 1939
- Moravian and Slovak territory to Poland October 1938
- Memel territory to Germany March 1939

tinue to recover before provoking any possible military reaction. In 1934, Germany signed a Non-Aggression Pact with Poland, an attempt to side-track the French security agreements and, for a period, Hitler persuaded Europe that he just wanted to negotiate a restitution of Germany's grievances.

In the vascilating scene of European politics it seemed, for a short while, that Germany could be held by an Anglo-French-Italian agreement, but Italy's own ambitions in Africa soon drove her firmly into the German fold.

INVASION OF POLAND 1939

"THE BATTLEFRONT DISAPPEARED, AND WITH IT THE ILLUSION THAT THERE HAD EVER BEEN A BATTLEFRONT. FOR THIS WAS NO WAR OF OCCUPATION, BUT A WAR OF QUICK PENETRATION AND OBLITERATION—BLITZKRIEG, LIGHTNING WAR."

JOURNALIST WORKING FOR TIME MAGAZINE, 25 SEPTEMBER 1939

With the rearmament of Germany, Poland realized the possibility of invasion. This caused major concern for the military for two main reasons. Firstly its army and air force were poorly equipped, the air force especially having very few modern types of aircraft, particularly interceptors essential to defending the cities and troop concentrations from bomber attacks. Worse was the state of the army, still reliant on the horse cavalry and with a severe lack of motorized transport for its infantry, though this did not mean that these units fought with any lack of conviction. The second problem facing the Poles was where and how to defend. Germany had annexed Czechoslovakia in 1938, thus allowing the Germans to enter from the south through Slovakia. There was also the problem of East Prussia, allowing the Germans to enter from the north. This effectively surrounded Poland, with the unsympathetic U.S.S.R. on the east. With such a huge front to cover and most of the important industry in the west of the country, the Poles would have to fight a holding battle on the borders for as long as possible in order to mobilize the maximum number of troops. The problem with this tactic was that forward formations could be easily surrounded and cut off but

Despite propaganda claims German infantry units bore the brunt of much of the fighting: here an infantry section moves into the suburbs of Warsaw.

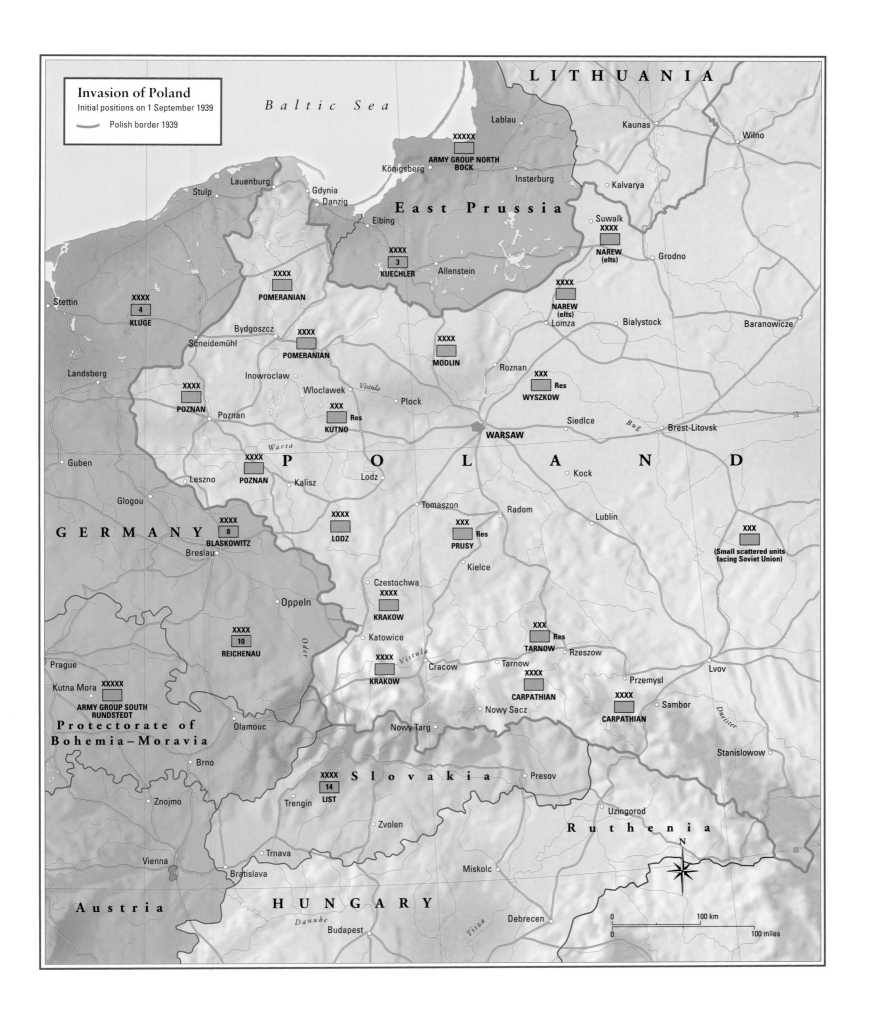

A group of German soldiers tear down a frontier barrier before advancing into Polish territory on the morning of 1 September 1939.

The Ju 87 Stuka dive-bomber proved extremely effective in the Polish campaign but still needed fighter protection against the largely outdated Polish fighters.

Invasion of Poland
1–28 September 1939

Polish border 1939
German advance
Russian advance
Polish retreat
German field work
Polish defensive lines
Polish positions
German-Russian demarcation line

Poland had hopes that France would intervene before this came about. They could then fall back onto a defense using the river system of Poland.

The Germans held all the advantages, having started a process of rearmament that had been running for many years, breaking the Treaty of Versailles and equipping its army and air force with the best weapons and vehicles available. They also had another advantage, a new tactic, Blitzkrieg. This entailed rapid control of the skies and comprehensive bombing of enemy lines of communication and transport. It was followed by a concentrated thrust by armored units on a small front to punch a hole in the defense allowing for mechanized troops to spill into the rear of the enemy's position. All these movements were covered by the air force preventing counterstrikes by the enemy, and by mobile artillery which could be called upon to destroy any strong defensive pockets. However, many German infantry units still depended on horse transport to consolidate captured positions.

Using this new technique from 1 September 1939, the Germans enjoyed rapid success. Dive-bombers wiped out much of the Polish Air Force while it was still on the ground, though some Polish pilots bravely succeeded in making a few effective sorties. The Luftwaffe could then concentrate on

In the preceding two centuries Poland had been steadily reduced from a once great empire to a Grand Duchy by 1812. At the end of the Napoleonic Wars the Duchy was finally shared out between Prussia, Russia, and the Austrian Empire. Poland, as an independent state, disappeared for over one hundred years. At the end of World War I Poland was reestablished as a state by the Treaty of Versailles. This Treaty granted sizeable areas to the new Poland from Germany, including a corridor to the Baltic Sea. Poland also acquired territories east of Brest-Litovsk from Soviet Russia, stabilizing its frontier at the end of 1921. As German and Soviet power expanded in the 1930s, Poland's position between these two states became increasingly difficult. Treaties with Britain and France meant very little in real terms. After the German and Soviet attacks in 1939, Poland once again disappeared from the map for over five years. After World War II, Poland was restored by the Allies. At Stalin's behest, the country's boundaries were moved westward, losing its eastern provinces but gaining large areas of German territory. Millions of Germans were displaced westward; millions of Poles, mostly from the eastern territories, took their place.

supporting the advancing divisions. Army Group North, commanded by the arrogant but ambitious General von Boch gave the order to take the ground between Pomerania and East Prussia, cutting off what became known as the "Polish Corridor." This maneuver was entrusted to General Heinz Guderian, a proponent of tank warfare, who quickly accomplished his goal. He then continued on through East Prussia and back into the north east of Poland in order to meet up with the advancing Army Group South. Meanwhile, the 3rd Army pressed south easterly towards Warsaw from East Prussia. The 8th, 10th, and 14th Armies, under the command of General von Rundstedt, who had recently been pulled out of retirement, pushed north-eastwards from Silesia and Slovakia creating a gigantic pincer movement.

By 6 September, the 3rd and 4th Armies from the north and the 8th and 10th from the south were advancing on Warsaw, while the 14th Army took Crakow. The Wehrmacht (Nazi armed forces) proceeded to make probing attacks on the outskirts of Warsaw, but were beaten back by a stubborn defense, the 4th Army losing nearly 60 tanks in action that showed the Poles had developed an effective anti-tank strategy. During these attacks the Poles attempted a risky counterattack on the flank of the advancing 8th Army, which took the Germans by surprise, incurring large casualties on both sides

before being beaten back, thanks in part to the Luftwaffe's control of the skies and the high degree of skill shown by the German artillery support.

On 15 September Warsaw was completely surrounded, as were many other cities and army units in western Poland. This was a grave time for the Poles, but they still refused to accept the German call to surrender. German commanders now sat back awaiting the capitulation of Warsaw, which was slowly being starved out. Hitler could not wait for this and ordered an extensive artillery and air bombardment of the city. On 17 September the Red Army entered eastern Poland against minimal resistance, since almost all available Polish forces were involved in the fight in the west. This action had been previously arranged between Germany and U.S.S.R. before the invasion, with Stalin proclaiming that Poland no longer existed as an independent state, therefore taking back what was rightfully the property of Soviet Russia.

Warsaw managed to combat the onslaught until 27 September, with other pockets of resistance managing to hold out until 2 October, this final surrender marking the end of the campaign. During a month of vicious fighting the Poles suffered over 200,000 casualties, with a further one million servicemen becoming prisoners of war. However, more than 100,000 men managed to escape through Romania and make the arduous journey to western Europe to carry on the fight against Fascism. The Germans suffered 40,000 casualties, killed and wounded—comparatively fewer than the Poles —demonstrating the success of the Blitzkrieg. Now Hitler looked to expand westward but first he had to secure his northern flank: Scandinavia.

THE WINTER WAR

"MEN WERE THROWN HEADLONG AT FINNISH GUNS. TANKS AND THEIR CREWS WERE SHELLED AND BURNED, WHOLE REGIMENTS OF INFANTRY ENCIRCLED. ENTIRE BATTALIONS OF TROOPS, THE SPEARHEAD OF THE RED ARMY, WERE CUT OFF FROM THEIR REINFORCEMENTS AND SUPPLIES." ANONYMOUS SOVIET SOLDIER

A Finnish patrol in the Lake Ladoga sector. The courage of the Finnish people won the admiration of the western democracies, as its tiny army took on the might of the Soviet juggernaut.

Soviet interest in Finland in 1939 was due to Stalin's desire to strengthen the Soviet Union's northern border. He also wanted to lease the port of Henko for a 30-year period but talks between Finland and Soviet Russia did not go to plan, even when the Soviet Union offered territorial compensation in Soviet Karelia. The Finns thought that any leeway towards the Soviets, after only gaining independence in 1917, would only lead to Stalin wanting more. After the bargaining failed, Stalin fell back on military intervention, thinking that it would be an easy conflict to conclude, even setting up an interim Finnish government before the invasion had begun. Stalin felt that the workers would welcome the Communists with open arms. This was not to be the case.

Defending Finland was an army of 10 divisions supplemented with a few specialist units. These divisions were poorly equipped, lacking automatic weapons, artillery and, most importantly, anti-tank weapons. Each division had only 30-odd pieces of pre-1918 artillery with a severe lack of ammunition. But what they lacked in equipment they made up for in training. They were particularly skilled in maneuvering in the heavily forested and snow-covered countryside, using ski troops to mount surprise attacks then quickly melting back

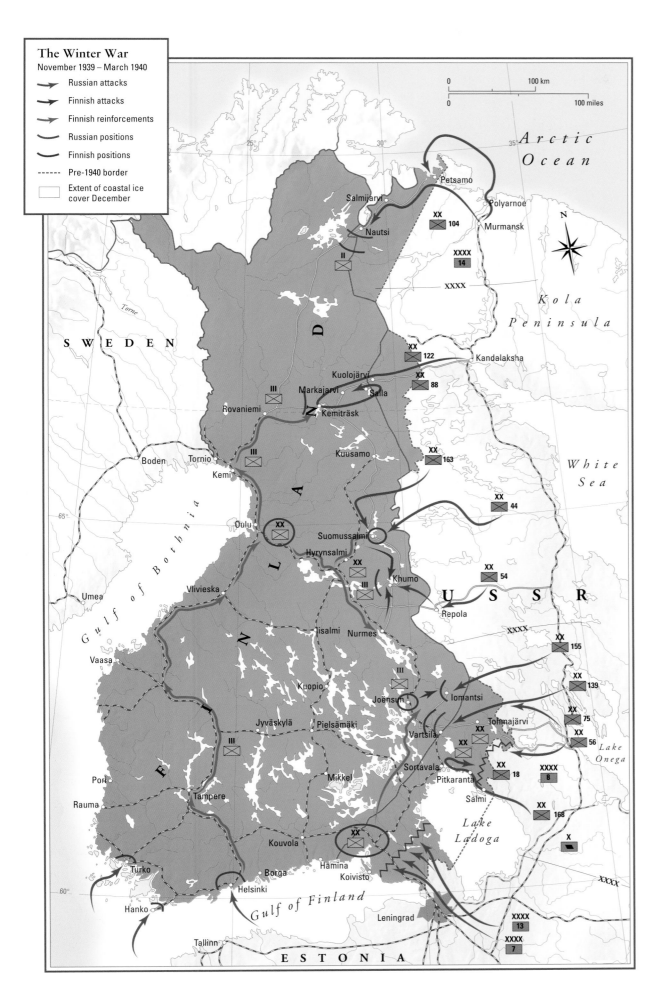

The Winter War
November 1939 – March 1940

→ Russian attacks
→ Finnish attacks
→ Finnish reinforcements
⌒ Russian positions
⌒ Finnish positions
---- Pre-1940 border
☐ Extent of coastal ice
   cover December

The first real test for Stalin's Army came at the end of 1939. On 30 November, Soviet troops invaded Finland. The campaign was a disaster, after initial Finnish successes. However, sheer numbers of men and heavy guns were ultimately reflected in the Soviets' favor.

into the forest. These troops were also highly motivated to retain the independence of Finland and were led by intelligent officers and N.C.O.s. The commander of the defense of Finland was Marshal Carl Gustaf von Mannerheim. He had begun constructing a defensive line earlier in the 1930s, based on a 40 mile front, blocking the main route for an attacking army hoping to take Finland's most populous region. This defensive line was made up of modern pill boxes and anti-tank ditches along the Karelian Isthmus. It was a strong position to defend but could, by no means, hold out indefinitely against the sheer numbers the Soviets could throw at it and was designed to give time for outside assistance to arrive.

Facing these defenses were 1.2 million men of the Soviet Army, comprising 26 divisions, supported by 1,500 tanks and 3,000 aircraft of all types. But with all this abundance the Soviets soon ran into problems with communication between men and machines, as well as the problem of supply. The Russian plan was to advance on all fronts and for the total occupation of Finland. This could not be possible as there was only room to maneuver in the south and the north. Mannerheim managed to check the advance of the Soviets on the Karelian Isthmus with relative ease and did not even have to

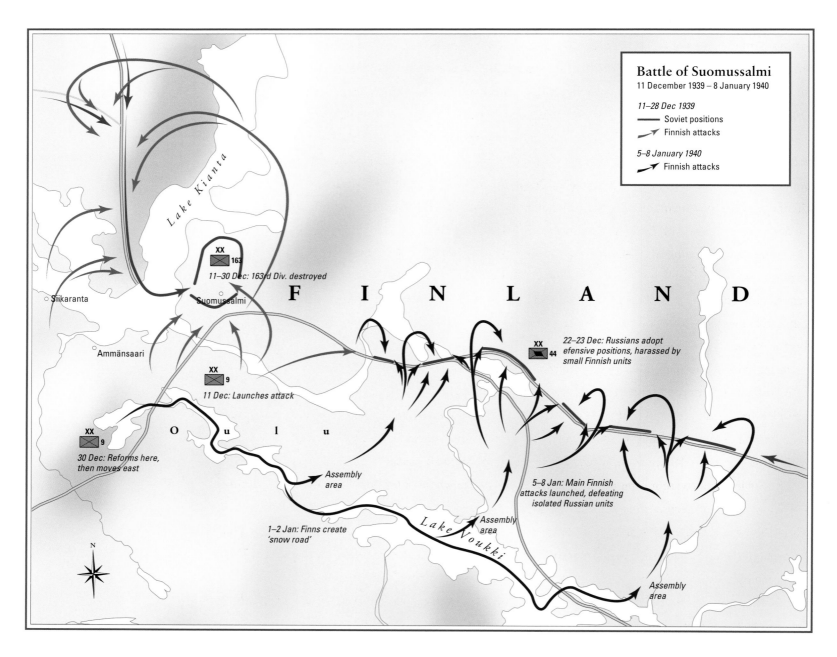

Battle of Suomussalmi
11 December 1939 – 8 January 1940

11–28 Dec 1939
—— Soviet positions
↗ Finnish attacks

5–8 January 1940
↗ Finnish attacks

Lake Kianta

XX 163
11–30 Dec: 163rd Div. destroyed

Siikaranta

Suomussalmi

F I N L A N D

Ammänsaari

XX 44
22–23 Dec: Russians adopt
defensive positions, harassed by
small Finnish units

XX 9
11 Dec: Launches attack

XX 9
30 Dec: Reforms here,
then moves east

O u l u

Assembly
area

5–8 Jan: Main Finnish
attacks launched, defeating
isolated Russian units

1–2 Jan: Finns create
'snow road'

Lake Noukki

Assembly
area

N

Assembly
area

Finnish soldiers walk and ski passed the remains of the Red Army's 44th Division, after the Battle of Suomussalmi in January 1940. The Red Army acquitted itself very badly against the tiny Finnish Army. This performance was not lost on the German High Command who would later be responsible for planning Operation Barbarossa.

deploy his strategic reserve. This was partly due to the lack of leadership on the Soviet side thanks to Stalin's earlier purges of the officer class. The advantage of having so many aircraft did not assist the Soviets either; the short winter days offered few daylight hours to fly, resulting in heavy losses and little strategic gain. The number of tanks facing the Finns could have created a huge problem: they had little or no anti-armor weapons and scant knowledge of armored warfare. This was soon learnt in the harsh conditions and the Finns employed many improvised weapons such as the Molotov cocktail, a bottle filled with petrol with a simple fuse, lit before throwing. The Soviets employed their tanks independently of their infantry so the Finns could sneak up on them at night and attack with relative ease. Up in the north the Murmansk troops had taken the port of Petsamo and began moving south towards Nautsi, cutting Finland off from the Arctic Ocean.

In late December the Finnish army counterattacked all along the Eastern Front, using ski troops to penetrate around and behind the Russians, who were having to use the road network. These attacks created isolated pockets of resistance, which were slowly destroyed one by one. The Soviets suffered heavy losses—almost four divisions—with the Finns using captured equipment against their former owners.

At the start of February, after intensive training in tank infantry cooperation, the Soviets launched a fresh attack against the Mannerheim Line, and broke through on 11 February. The Finns fell back to a second line of defense but this was again broken by the massive attacking force. The Soviets then launched an attack into the rear positions of the Finnish lines across the frozen sea west of Viipuri. With bleak prospects Mannerheim urged his government to make peace.

The Soviet terms were for the port of Hanko as well as the whole of the Karelian Isthmus including Viipuri and the northern portion of Lake Ladoga. The Finns hoped for Anglo-French intervention but when this was found lacking they eventually signed the Treaty of Moscow on 12 March 1940. The Russians lost over 126,000 men and almost 300,000 more were evacuated through injury and frostbite. Much material was lost, but more importantly it showed a lack of military competence in beating the tiny Finnish army. The Soviets credibility had been tarnished and set about a serious reorganization of the army. The lessons of this campaign were not lost on the German observers.

THE PHONEY WAR

"WE'RE GONNA HANG OUT THE WASHING ON THE SIEGFRIED LINE

HAVE YOU ANY DIRTY WASHING, MOTHER DEAR?

WE'RE GONNA HANG OUT THE WASHING ON THE SIEGFRIED LINE

'COS THE WASHING DAY IS HERE.

WHETHER THE WEATHER MAY BE WET OR FINE

WE'LL JUST RUB ALONG WITHOUT A CARE.

WE'RE GONNA HANG OUT THE WASHING ON THE SIEGFRIED LINE

IF THE SIEGFRIED LINE'S STILL THERE."

BRITISH "PHONEY WAR" HIT SONG

The day Poland capitulated, 27 September 1939, Hitler announced his intention to attack the Western powers. A blueprint for this attack—Plan Yellow—was submitted by Oberkommando des Heeres (O.K.H.) on 19 October. This called for a drive to Dutch and Belgian coastlines, creating a secure base for further operations against British and French forces in northern France. As far as Hitler was concerned this was completely inadequate. He required something much more decisive. Bad weather forced a series of postponements and O.K.H. gave in. Plan Yellow was cancelled when a small group of German officers, carrying copies of the plan, force-landed in Belgium on 9 January 1940.

A new plan was drawn up—"Sicklestroke"—produced by a critic of O.K.H., General Manstein, somewhat more in line with Hitler's own ideas. It became the master plan to encircle the French and British armies. The detailed plan was drawn up by O.K.H. and was ready by 24 February 1940.

The Allies, the French and British, depended on the Maginot Line to defend the Franco-German frontier. France had poured an enormous amount of its national wealth into the construction of this defensive line. The country's major problem with Germany was a demographic one; Germany's existing population and birth rates were substantially higher than France's. If these trends continued Germany could always field more troops than France. Therefore an essentially defensive war was the best hope for France. Belgium was to be covered, in the event of a German advance in that direction, by mobile forces advancing to the line of the River Dyle with its right flank in the Ardennes Forest, which the allies considered impassible by armored forces.

However, what the Allies considered impassable was the subject of extensive German exercises,

British Expeditionary Force soldiers march into Fort de Sainghain on the Franco–Belgium border. Inclement weather in the winter and early spring of 1940, placed considerable strain on the French and British troops awaiting the expected German onslaught.

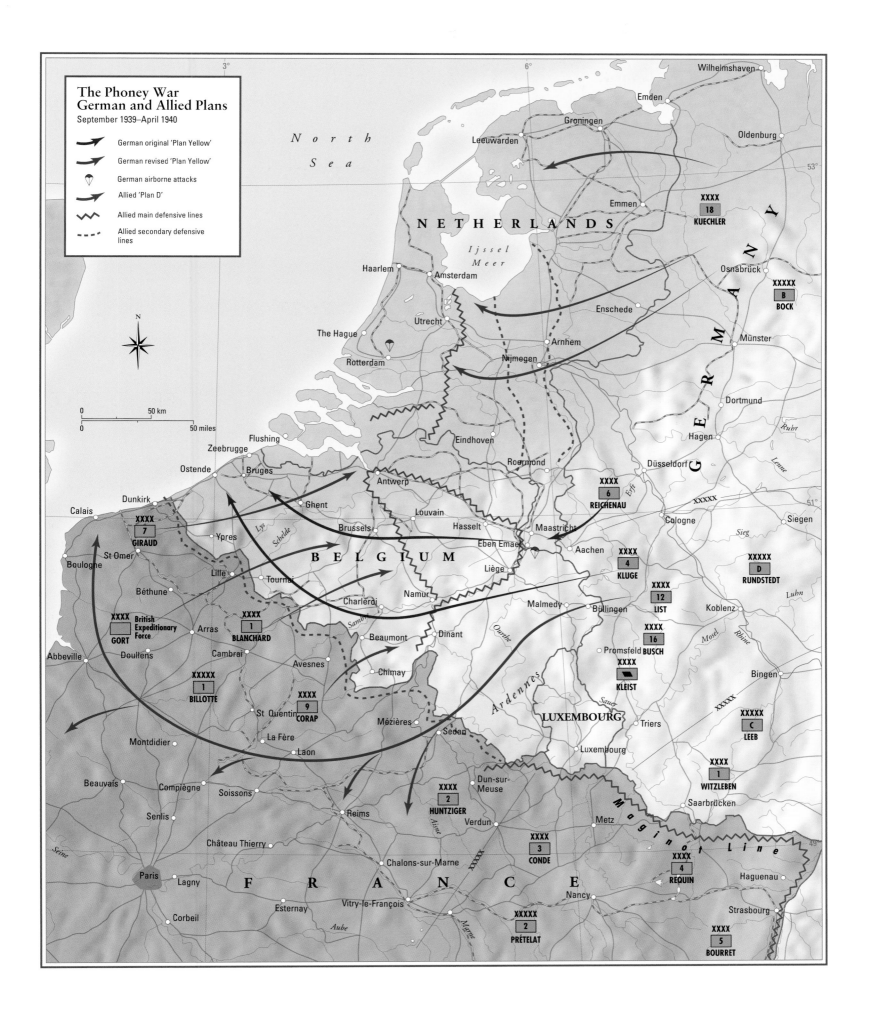

The Phoney War
German and Allied Plans
September 1939–April 1940

- German original 'Plan Yellow'
- German revised 'Plan Yellow'
- German airborne attacks
- Allied 'Plan D'
- Allied main defensive lines
- Allied secondary defensive lines

North Sea

NETHERLANDS

Ijssel Meer

GERMANY

Wilhelmshaven
Emden
Groningen
Oldenburg
Leeuwarden
Emmen
Osnabrück

XXXX
18
KUECHLER

XXXXX
B
BOCK

Haarlem
Amsterdam
Enschede
Münster
Utrecht
Arnhem
The Hague
Nijmegen
Rotterdam
Dortmund
Hagen
Ruhr

Eindhoven
Roermond
Düsseldorf
G

XXXX
6
REICHENAU

Erft
XXXXX
51°

Flushing
Zeebrugge
Ostende
Bruges
Antwerp
Ghent
Louvain
Hasselt
Maastricht
Cologne
Siegen

Dunkirk
Calais

XXXX
7
GIRAUD

Ypres
Lille
Lys
Schelde
Brussels
Eben Emael
Aachen
Sieg

XXXX
4
KLUGE

XXXXX
D
RUNDSTEDT

Luhn

Boulogne
St Omer
Tournai
Liège
Malmedy
Büllingen

XXXX
12
LIST

Koblenz

Béthune
Charleroi
Namur

XXXX
British Expeditionary Force
GORT

Arras

XXXX
1
BLANCHARD

Beaumont
Dinant
Ourthe

XXXX
16
BUSCH

Mosel
Rhine
Bingen

Abbeville
Doullens
Cambrai
Avesnes
Chimay
Ardennes

XXXX
KLEIST

XXXXX
1
BILLOTTE

St Quentin
XXXX
9
CORAP

Mézières
Sedan
LUXEMBOURG
Triers

XXXXX
C
LEEB

Montdidier
La Fère
Laon

Beauvais
Compiègne
Soissons
Reims

Dun-sur-Meuse
Luxembourg

XXXX
1
WITZLEBEN

Senlis
Aisne

XXXX
2
HUNTZIGER

Verdun
Metz
Saarbrücken

Château Thierry
Chalons-sur-Marne
XXXXX

XXXX
3
CONDE

Maginot Line
49°

Paris
Lagny
Vitry-le-François
Nancy
Haguenau

XXXX
4
RÉQUIN

F R A N C E

Corbeil
Esternay
Aube
Marne
Seine

XXXXX
2
PRÉTELAT

Strasbourg

XXXX
5
BOURRET

0   50 km
0   50 miles

N

Maginot Strongpoint

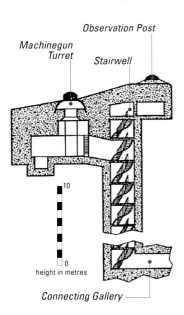

Observation Post

Machinegun Turret

Stairwell

10

0

height in metres

Connecting Gallery

France poured an immense amount of national wealth into the construction of the Maginot Line. Above is a typical combat block with turret and observation post, with an underground section extending down several floors. There would have been a staircase and an elevator leading to a connecting gallery to other supporting positions.

to drive an armored thrust and bypass the Maginot Line was a critical part of Manstein's plan. Sicklestroke planned to drive armored columns through the Ardennes Forest and cross the formidable River Meuse at Dinant, Sedan, and Monthermé. The columns would then turn northwest and drive as hard as possible for the Channel coast, trapping the British Expeditionary Force (B.E.F.) together with the French First Army Group and surviving Belgians. German Army Group B would attack in the Netherlands and eastern Belgium, backed by the specialist airborne forces, especially at the key Belgium fortress of Eben Emael. The southern Army Group C, under Leeb, was to engage the garrison of the Maginot Line and penetrate if possible. It was not allotted any tanks to achieve this.

Both sides were about equal in divisions: 94 French, 12 British, 9 Dutch, and 22 Belgian opposed 136 German. The Allies, however, had few dedicated tank formations. The Germans concentrated their tank force into ten dedicated divisions, so their 2,500 tanks were far more effectively controlled than the dispersed 3,000 Allied tanks. The Germans could also deploy over 3,200 modern aircraft in support of their armies. The Allies had around 2,000 aircraft, though many of them were of doubtful quality. Perhaps the most decisive part of the operation was the German doctrine of Blitzkrieg, while Allied forces practiced only defensive war and its High Command lacked a firm, clear structure of command and control, thinking in terms of a slightly updated war of 1918.

In September 1939, the British and French had mobilized their armies, approximately 3,000,000 for France and almost 450,000 for Britain, of which some 300,000 were sent to France as the B.E.F.. This was almost all of Britain's mobile army and all of its tank force. During September, October and the following months British forces took their places at the 'front' that stretched from Switzerland along the Maginot Line, the Belgian border and to the Channel coast.

During the winter of 1939 and spring of 1940, British and French troops expected to replay tactics of the last war, but on a more sensible defensive line, while the Germans would wear themselves out. But the enemy were not playing by the same terms. The Treaty of Versailles had removed the old plan, persuading the Germans to develop new tactics. On 10 May 1940 these tactics would be tested.

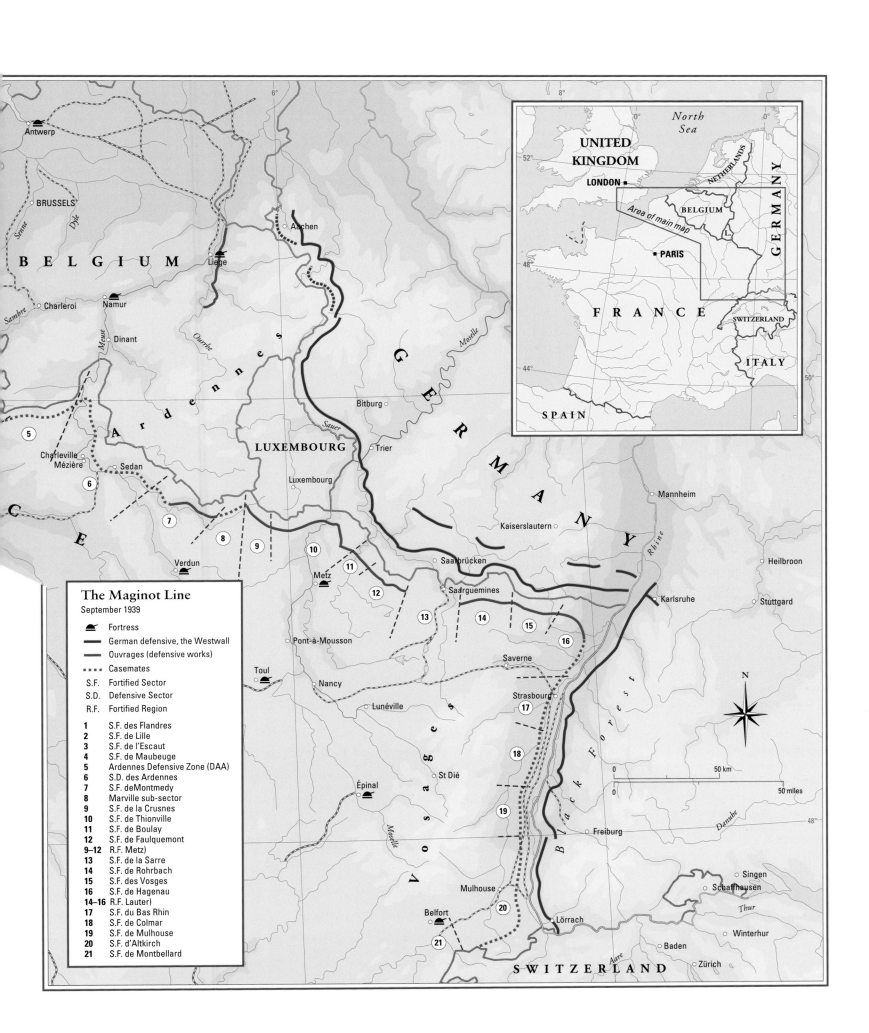

The Maginot Line

September 1939

🛡 Fortress

▬▬ German defensive, the Westwall

▬▬ Ouvrages (defensive works)

┈┈ Casemates

S.F. Fortified Sector

S.D. Defensive Sector

R.F. Fortified Region

1 S.F. des Flandres
2 S.F. de Lille
3 S.F. de l'Escaut
4 S.F. de Maubeuge
5 Ardennes Defensive Zone (DAA)
6 S.D. des Ardennes
7 S.F. deMontmedy
8 Marville sub-sector
9 S.F. de la Crusnes
10 S.F. de Thionville
11 S.F. de Boulay
12 S.F. de Faulquemont
9–12 R.F. Metz)
13 S.F. de la Sarre
14 S.F. de Rohrbach
15 S.F. des Vosges
16 S.F. de Hagenau
14–16 R.F. Lauter)
17 S.F. du Bas Rhin
18 S.F. de Colmar
19 S.F. de Mulhouse
20 S.F. d'Altkirch
21 S.F. de Montbellard

INVASIONS OF DENMARK AND NORWAY 1940

"THE WHOLE OF NORTHERN NORWAY WAS COVERED WITH SNOW TO DEPTHS WHICH NONE OF OUR SOLDIERS HAD EVER SEEN, FELT, OR IMAGINED. THERE WERE NEITHER SNOW-SHOES NOR SKIS—STILL LESS SKIERS. WE MUST DO OUR BEST. THUS BEGAN THIS RAMSHACKLE CAMPAIGN."

WINSTON CHURCHILL, 1940

In order to sustain Hitler's expansion of the Reich, Germany required the raw materials to fuel it. Most pressing was the iron ore that Germany imported from the neutral country of Sweden. The French and the British were well aware of the importance of this material and it became a race of who could control it first. The German plan would mean the invasion of Norway. In order for Germany to do this it first had to deal with Denmark.

Denmark was a pacifist state, with a tiny army and even smaller airforce and navy. This was not going to be the Wehrmacht's toughest assignment. In the early hours of 9 April, 1940 Germany invaded. It faced a small resistance in North Schleswig, but this was soon overpowered. The Danish navy, in charge of defending the numerous ports of Denmark, allowed German troop ships to simply enter Copenhagen at will. The very first airborne attacks occurred during this fleeting campaign, with the fort at Madneso and the airport of Aalborg north of Jutland being swiftly taken by the elite Fallschirmjager (German Parachute troops). With Copenhagen occupied by the morning, the Danish government ordered a ceasefire and the Danish invasion ended.

France and Britain had been planning to send an expeditionary force to the northern port of Narvik since the beginning of hostilities between the Finns and the Soviets. This was really a cover so they could secure the port and control the all important iron ore from Sweden. The Nazis beat them to it. As German forces were taking Denmark with relative ease another German combined force was on its way to Norway. Surprise was total with troops coming in by air and sea, the airborne troops taking the airports of Stavanger and Oslo, which were vital for the follow–up transports to land more troops and material. The coastal cities were also taken stretching from Kritiansand in the south

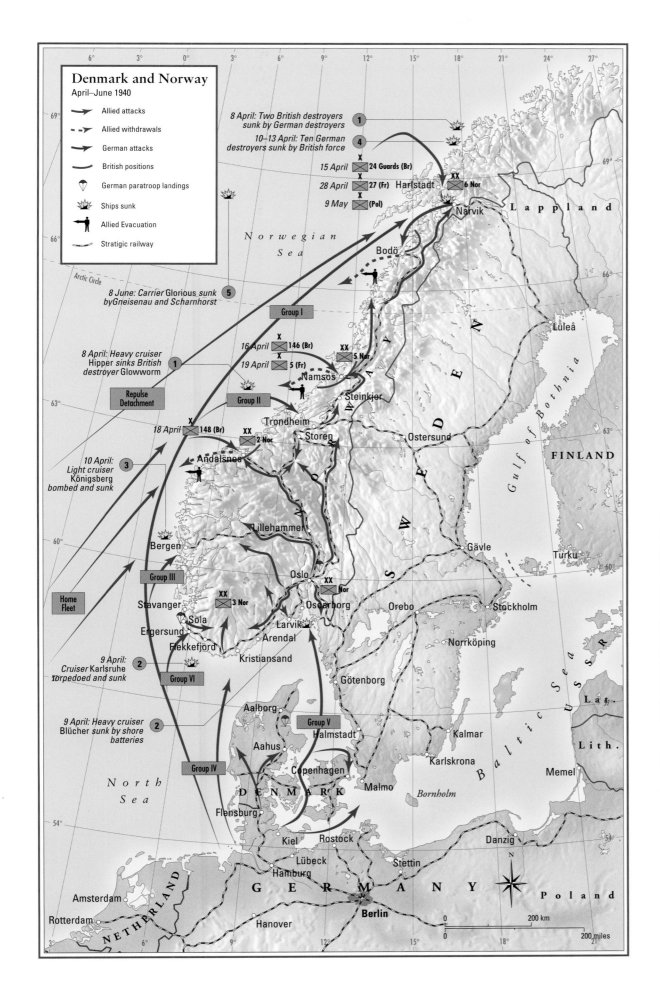

Denmark and Norway
April–June 1940

→ Allied attacks

⇢ Allied withdrawals

➤ German attacks

⌒ British positions

▽ German paratroop landings

✿ Ships sunk

🧍 Allied Evacuation

〰 Stratigic railway

8 April: Two British destroyers sunk by German destroyers ①

10–13 April: Ten German destroyers sunk by British force ④

15 April ⊠ 24 Guards (Br)

28 April ⊠ 27 (Fr)

9 May ⊠ (Pol)

⊠⊠ 6 Nor

Harlstadt

Narvik

Lappland

Norwegian Sea

Bodö

8 June: Carrier Glorious *sunk by*Gneisenau *and* Scharnhorst ⑤

Arctic Circle

Group I

8 April: Heavy cruiser Hipper *sinks British destroyer* Glowworm ①

16 April ⊠ 146 (Br)

19 April ⊠ 5 (Fr)

⊠⊠ 5 Nor

Namsos

Steinkjer

Repulse Detachment

Group II

Trondheim

18 April ⊠ 148 (Br)

⊠⊠ 2 Nor

Storen

Ostersund

Luleå

Gulf of Bothnia

FINLAND

10 April: Light cruiser Königsberg bombed and sunk ③

Andalsnes

Lillehammer

Bergen

Gävle

Turku

S W E D E N

Oslo

⊠⊠ Nor

Oscarborg

Orebo

Stockholm

Home Fleet

Group III

Stavanger

Sola

Ergersund

Flekkefjord

Kristiansand

⊠⊠ 3 Nor

Larvik

Arendal

Norrköping

9 April: Cruiser Karlsruhe *torpedoed and sunk* ②

Group VI

Göteborg

Baltic Sea

Lat.

Lith.

Memel

9 April: Heavy cruiser Blücher *sunk by shore batteries* ②

Aalborg

Group V

Halmstadt

Kalmar

Karlskrona

U.S.S.R.

Aahus

Copenhagen

Malmo

Bornholm

Group IV

North Sea

D E N M A R K

Flensburg

Kiel

Rostock

Danzig

Lübeck

Stettin

Hamburg

Amsterdam

Rotterdam

NETHERLAND

G E R M A N Y

Hanover

Berlin

P o l a n d

200 km

200 miles

N

German troops advance through a Norwegian town, set on fire by a previous Luftwaffe attack. British, French, and Norwegian forces were continuously at a disadvantage by the almost unchallenged German control of the air.

The intense seaborne campaign waged by both the British and the German navies resulted, inevitably, in the loss of many ships. he British destroyer *Gloworm* spotted the German heavy cruiser *Admiral Hipper* on April, immediately engaging it and, despite serious damage, she was lost with few survivors. The *Blücher*, one of Germany's new heavy cruisers, was the lead ship for Task Force 5 heading for Oslo. On board were a large number of Gestapo officers intended for the new administration and 900 men of the 163rd Infantry Division. The *Blücher* was engaged at short range by shore batteries in the Dröbak Narrows as she attempted to approach Oslo. She was also hit by two torpedoes fired from a shore battery. She sank with great loss of life. The *Glorious* operated as part of a British Task Force and was caught unawares by the German battlecruisers *Scharnhorst* and *Gneisenau* and sank within 70 minutes.

to Narvik in the very north of the country. The Norwegians defending these ports were soon overwhelmed but did manage to sink the German cruiser *Blücher* with torpedoes and artillery fire from the Oscarsborg fortress in the Oslofjord.

After these setbacks, the Norwegian government retreated into the interior of the country and King Haakon VII, gave command of the army to Major-General Otto Ruge, who quickly set up plans for a fighting retreat to slow down the German advance long enough for outside assistance to arrive. When this arrived in the form of a British Expeditionary Force south of the port of Trondheim they were sent to reinforce the Norwegian troops in that sector but were soon evacuated after a poorly attempted attack on the city. From this stage all Allied resistance was based in the north of the country.

In the north the Allied forces were trying desperately to eject German forces from the Narvik area. The Royal Navy had done its part well by driving off the German navy in the area. The port was eventually re-taken on 28 May by French and Norwegian troops. But the invasion of Belgium, Holland, and France now had the Allies looking elsewhere and suddenly Norway was not as important as originally thought. The British Royal Navy began to evacuate troops at the beginning of June, along with the Norwegian government and the King, who would sit out the rest of the war in exile in London. This was not to be the last large scale evacuation the Allies would have to cope with.

The Germans suffered the heaviest casualties, losing 5,500 men and 200 aircraft. Crucially they also lost two major modern warships that would never quite allow the German surface fleet to recover. The British lost about 4,000 men, including 1,500 men lost with the sinking of the carrier *Glorious*. The Norwegians lost 1,800 men and the French about 500.

BLÜCHER

Heavy Cruiser	launched 1937
Displacement	19,042 tons
Length	665 feet
Armament	8 x 8 inch guns
	12 x 5 inch
	20 light AA guns
	12 x 21 inch torpedoes
	3 aircraft
Crew	1,600

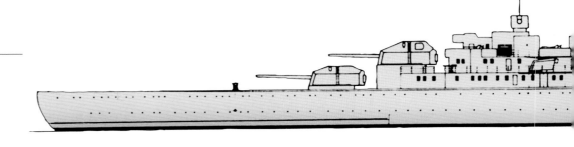

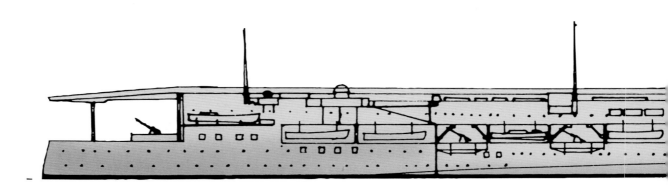

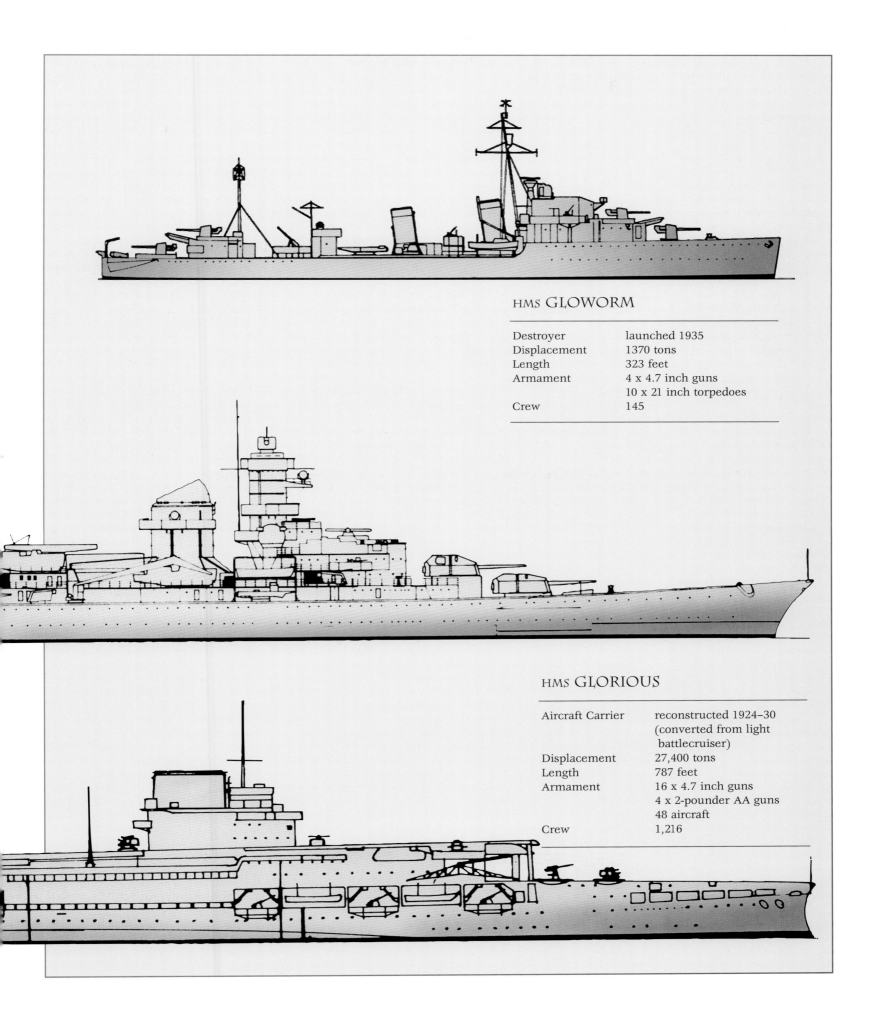

HMS GLOWORM

Destroyer	launched 1935
Displacement	1370 tons
Length	323 feet
Armament	4 x 4.7 inch guns
	10 x 21 inch torpedoes
Crew	145

HMS GLORIOUS

Aircraft Carrier	reconstructed 1924–30
	(converted from light
	battlecruiser)
Displacement	27,400 tons
Length	787 feet
Armament	16 x 4.7 inch guns
	4 x 2-pounder AA guns
	48 aircraft
Crew	1,216

Sedan—10 May 1940 The Panzer Breakthrough

"SCHÜTZENREGIMENT I HAS AT 22:40 TAKEN HIGH HILL JUST TO THE NORTH OF CHEVEUGES. LAST ENEMY BLOCKHOUSE IN OUR HANDS. A COMPLETE BREAKTHROUGH!"

LIEUTENANT-COLONEL HERMANN BALCK, NEAR SEDAN

The Panzer III was designed as a medium tank, armed with a small 37 mm high velocity gun. Despite the lack of firepower it performed well tactically. Large numbers used at specific points on the battlefield overwhelming the opposition.

The key to the German attack in the West was the advance through the "impassable" Ardennes Forest and the capture of the river crossings along the Meuse River. After the German attack on 10 May, a major consequence of the French theory of the 'impassable' Ardennes was that their failure to move the full compliment of men and guns assigned to this sector and to Namur, in Belgium, to link up with forces in Givet, in France, before the German Armored columns arrived.

Erwin Rommel and Heinz Guderian were given the task of making the initial breakthrough. Heinz Guderian stated that it was vital for his force to be on the Meuse within five days from the start of the campaign. In fact, both commanders' units were on the Meuse in two and a half days. The first attempt to cross was made just after 4:00 pm on 12 May at Dinant. Four tanks of the 7th Panzer rushed to seize the bridge. At least one of the group got within 33 feet of the bridge when it was blown up. German aerial reconnaissance revealed another bridge still standing almost four and a half miles to the north, near Yvoir. The commander of 31st Panzer Regiment, part of the 5th Panzer Division, immediately ordered armored vehicles forward to attempt to capture it. The column reached the bridge and the leading vehicle, an armored car, was about halfway across when a sole Belgian soldier manning a 47 mm antitank gun fired, hitting the armored car. It swerved sideways and burst into flames. French forces were in the process of taking over the defense of the bridge from their Belgian allies, but it was left to a Belgian Lieutenant to blow the bridge. In much confusion the bridge was blown up, taking two German armored cars with it. The Germans, for a moment, fell back.

Another attempt to cross the river on the remains of a blown railroad bridge between Houx and Yvoir by the German infantry was beaten back by Belgian infantry. After these initial failures the

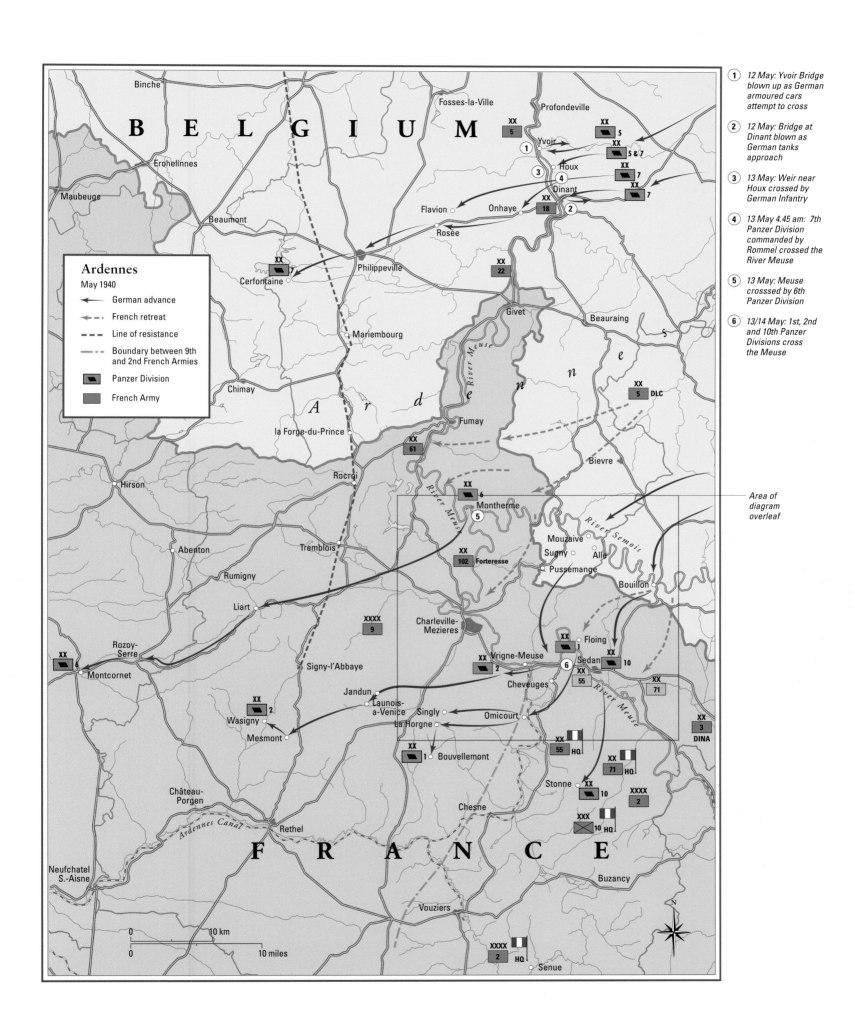

Binche

B E L G I U M

Fosses-la-Ville

Profondeville

Erohelinnes

① 12 May: Yvoir Bridge
blown up as German
armoured cars
attempt to cross

Yvoir

Maubeuge

Beaumont

Houx

② 12 May: Bridge at
Dinant blown as
German tanks
approach

Dinant

Flavion

Onhaye

③ 13 May: Weir near
Houx crossed by
German Infantry

Rosée

④ 13 May 4.45 am: 7th
Panzer Division
commanded by
Rommel crossed the
River Meuse

Cerfontaine

Philippeville

Beauraing

⑤ 13 May: Meuse
crosssed by 6th
Panzer Division

Givet

⑥ 13/14 May: 1st, 2nd
and 10th Panzer
Divisions cross
the Meuse

Ardennes

May 1940

→ German advance

French retreat

Line of resistance

Boundary between 9th
and 2nd French Armies

Panzer Division

French Army

Chimay

Mariembourg

A r d e n n e River Meuse

la Forge-du-Prince

Fumay

Area of
diagram
overleaf

Rocroi

Hirson

River Meuse

Montherme

Abenton

Tremblois

Mouzaive

Sugny

Alle

River Semois

Rumigny

Forteresse

Pussemange

Liart

Bouillon

Charleville-
Mezieres

Rozoy-
Serre

Floing

Montcornet

Sedan

Signy-l'Abbaye

Vrigne-Meuse

Cheveuges

River Meuse

Jandun

Launois-
a-Venice

Singly

Omicourt

Wasigny

La Horgne

Mesmont

Bouvellemont

DINA

Château-
Porgen

Stonne

Ardennes Canal

Rethel

Chesne

F R A N C E

Neufchatel
S.-Aisne

Buzancy

0 10 km

0 10 miles

Vouziers

N

Senue

Germans sent reconnaissance patrols to locate suitable crossing points. One of these patrols found an island connected by a weir and lock: the French had not been able to destroy this because the level of the river would have been lowered, making the sector fordable in many places. The Germans waited until nightfall then, around 11:00 pm, their infantry crossed and much to their surprise were not fired on; the immediate area on the west bank was undefended. The French had identified this weir as a possible problem but, such was the poor quality of their command and control, they had not reacted until it was too late. Eventually the French opened fire on the weir but despite this the Germans continued to feed soldiers across, gaining their first foothold on the west bank of the Meuse.

Meanwhile, on the night of 12 May, the French commanders of this sector, including General Gamelin, slept soundly in their respective headquarters believing all was well. German commanders were not so comfortable knowing the next 24 hours could be critical. Once again failures in the French command aided the Germans. General Huntziger, commander of the French 2nd Army, knew from reports coming from the 5th Division Légère de Cavalerie (D.L.C.), a French cavalry unit forming an advance screen about 18$\frac{1}{2}$ miles north east of Sedan, that the Germans were well on their way to the line of the Meuse. Huntziger ordered the 71st Division, held in reserve, north to support the 55th Division and 147th Fortress Regiment. The 71st, some 31 miles behind the first line, lacked

The Panzerkampfwagen was operated by many German tank units in 1940. Ordered and manufactured originally for the Czech army in 1938–39, after the German takeover of Czechoslovakia, they were delivered direct to the German army.

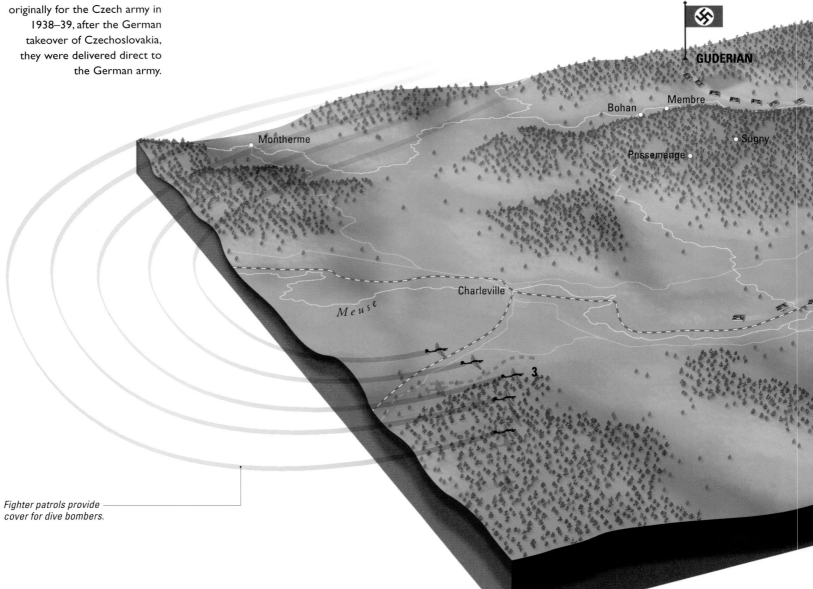

Fighter patrols provide cover for dive bombers.

transport and an order from Huntziger to make best speed to the front. Advance units of the 71st arrived on the night of 13/14 May, but too late for the 55th to redeploy and consolidate its positions. These second line French units, which were made up of elderly reservists who hoped to see out the war in a quiet sector, lacked equipment. They should have had 100,000 mines to defend the most exposed positions but only had 2,000, none of which worked. Planned equipment also called for over 100 antitank guns but by 10 May they had received just nine. Heading for the elderly reservists was one of the best-trained, most-determined armored forces yet created.

Some time after 7:00 am the first of many air attacks began. The bombers were joined by Stuka dive-bombers attacking out of a cloudless sky. The French line was cracked but not broken. At 3:00 pm German troops attempted to cross the river in rubber boats, and were met by a fierce artillery barrage. Of the 96 rubber boats setting out, only 15 made it to the Allied bank. After such loss the Germans launched smaller raiding parties, to some extent, were covered by the smoke of explosions and suffered a much lower rate of loss. These small parties of infantry pushed forward, capturing and destroying French positions and creating a gap in the French defenses. German units followed, exploiting and expanding the breach. By 5:45 am on 14 May, a bridge was built over the river, just south of the destroyed Pont de la Gare at Sedan.

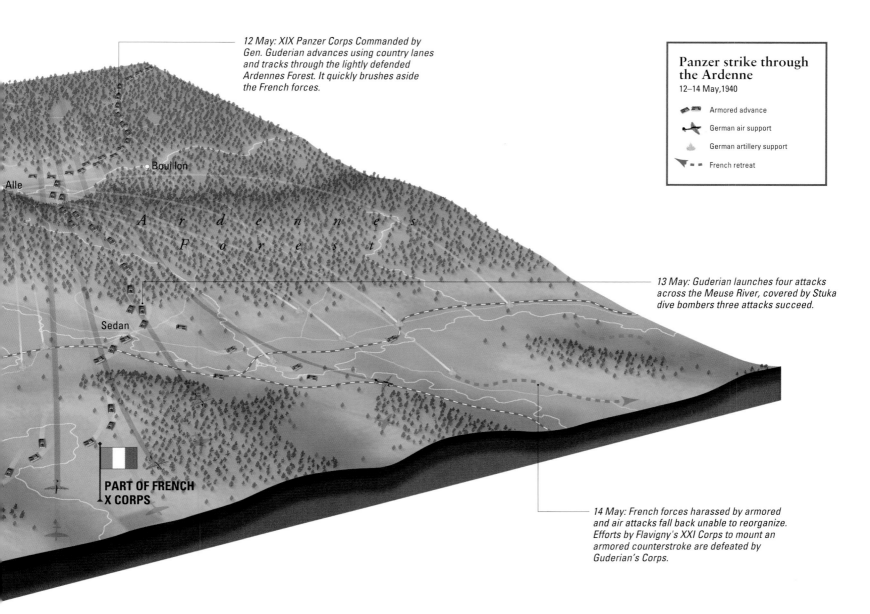

12 May: XIX Panzer Corps Commanded by Gen. Guderian advances using country lanes and tracks through the lightly defended Ardennes Forest. It quickly brushes aside the French forces.

Panzer strike through the Ardenne
12–14 May, 1940

🚙 Armored advance

✈ German air support

🔺 German artillery support

▼ - - French retreat

Boullon

Alle

A r d e n n e s F o r e s t

13 May: Guderian launches four attacks across the Meuse River, covered by Stuka dive bombers three attacks succeed.

Sedan

PART OF FRENCH X CORPS

14 May: French forces harassed by armored and air attacks fall back unable to reorganize. Efforts by Flavigny's XXI Corps to mount an armored counterstroke are defeated by Guderian's Corps.

BLITZKRIEG IN THE WEST

"GENTLEMEN, YOU ARE ABOUT TO WITNESS THE MOST FAMOUS VICTORY IN HISTORY."

ADOLF HITLER, 9 JUNE 1940

After many months of the Phoney War, Hitler was now ready to strike in the west. Predicting that the Allies would expect the main offensive through Belgium and northern France, General von Manstein drew up a plan that would entail a diversionary thrust through Holland and Belgium, drawing Allied strength and reserves north, while the main Panzer attack would drive through the "impassable" forests of the Ardennes and head for the coast, catching the main body of the Allied armies in an enormous pocket.

Von Bock was to lead Army Group B, consisting of 29 divisions of regular infantry, into Belgium and Holland drawing the main Allied defense force toward him. Meanwhile von Rundstedt's Army Group A had charge of 44 divisions, including almost all the Panzer divisions: sufficient to strike through the Ardennes. General Leeb had Army Group C, 17 divisions, between Switzerland and Luxembourg, holding the French on the Maginot Line.

The French army was similar in size to that opposing it, if not stronger. This advantage was to become void as the command structure, under General Gamelin, was poorly thought through and slow to respond to changing situations. They also had great confidence in the truly giant defenses of the Maginot Line, never expecting them to be merely bypassed. The British had sent over an expeditionary force consisting of ten divisions to bolster the French defense and under French command. The Allies always thought that the main German advance would come through Belgium, just as they had done in 1914, and based their defensive maneuvers on this. Together the British and French came up with the Dyle Plan, which entailed the main forces of the Allies advancing to a line drawn by the River Dyle to Wavre, just east of Brussels, the Belgian capital. In 1940 this line was extended to the River Maas in

Holland in order to create one long line from the channel coast to the Franco-Belgian border.

On the morning of 10 May the town of Eben Emael was attacked by an airborne force that landed on the roof of the fortress. Arriving in gliders the specialist engineers used shaped charges to destroy the gun cupolas that were placed commanding the approaches to the strategic bridges, where the Meuse met with the Albert Canal. While the engineers dealt with the fort, Fallschirmjäger troops landed next to these bridges and captured them quickly. Within 24 hours the 4th Armored Division arrived to consolidate the bridgehead; meanwhile the rest of the Belgian forces still trying to defend the fort capitulated. The Germans lost six troops in this outstanding maneuver, the most successful airborne attack of the entire war.

Von Manstein's plan to lure the Allied armies into a defensive line in northern Belgium achieved great success. Von Rundstedt proceeded to advance through the Ardennes with the bridge crossing the Meuse at Sedan his target. The Panzers rolled through the heavily forested area on extremely narrow roads and met only cursory opposition. Because of the German air superiority, the French and British had no chance of seeing the enormous traffic jam occurring before them. By the evening of the 12 May, seven Panzer divisions stretched from Dinant in the north to Sedan in the south, ready to forge ahead. On 13 May Guderian received the order to force a crossing of the Meuse, under a massive aerial umbrella, with Stukas dive-bombing any defenses and terrifying the French Second Army under the command of General Huntziger. By the end of the day 1st Panzer held a bridgehead three miles wide and four miles deep. The French were slow to attempt to counterattack, with the 3rd Armored Division keen to strike the weak flank of the German advance, but held back and spread along a thin defensive line. With the Allies now aware of the German bridgehead they attempted to destroy the pontoon that the 1st Panzer had used to force a crossing, sending out a force of obsolete Fairey Battles biplanes. Losses were catastrophic, and the bridge remained intact. With the point of the German advance on the boundary of two French armies the pace of the advance quickened, helped by command and control problems on the French side.

After this failure by the French to contain the Panzers on the Meuse, the German commanders exploited it for all its worth, turning westward toward the Channel. The French commanders were in complete disarray, not knowing what the enemy's main objective was: Paris or the Channel. No major counterattacks were mounted, except for a local offensive action near the town of Montcornet, led by the brilliant young tactician Colonel Charles de Gaulle. However this was soon beaten back by a superior German force.

Guderian's Panzers arrived at the Channel on 19 May ending an advance of nearly 200 miles in ten days. This meant that the majority of the Allies' best fighting units were now caught in a pocket in northern France and Belgium with little chance of escape and almost assured destruction.

The Allies attempted a counterattack on 24 May into the flank of the 2nd Panzer and achieved

German PzK III wIII with short-barrelled 50 mm gun. The Panzer troops wore a black uniform that served to hide oil stains. The campaigns in Poland and the West demonstrated the increased pace of operations generated by armored fighting vehicles with efficient radio communications, handled by quick-thinking commanders who led from the front.

some success before the Germans eventually beat them back to the start line by the end of the day. Then the shocking news came through to the Panzer commanders from the Führer himself for all armored advances to cease; he wanted to let the supply line catch up to the tanks and save them for the rest of France. Hitler preferred to leave the destruction of the B.E.F. to Goering's Luftwaffe, which would simply flatten the army from the air.

The evacuation of an army was a massive undertaking, with all arms playing vital roles. General Gort,

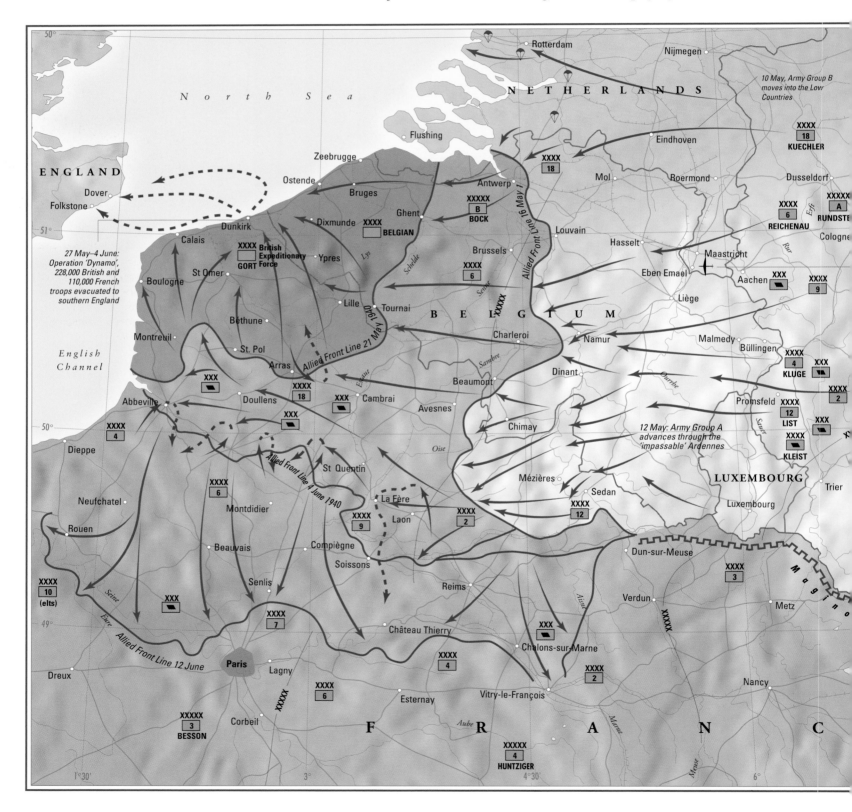

leading the B.E.F., set up a perimeter to stop any infantry from penetrating to the beach along the Aa, Scarpe, and Yser canals. Churchill placed Vice-Admiral Ramsey in charge of the naval evacuation and duly sent an order to scrape, borrow, and steal any vessels between nine and 30 feet long on the south coast. These boats, usually piloted by their owners, braved the bombing and strafing to go right into the beach to pick up the beleaguered troops, who had to stand in the sea sometimes up to their chests for many hours, often having to physically push back the desperate soldiers for fear of overloading and sinking. Over the

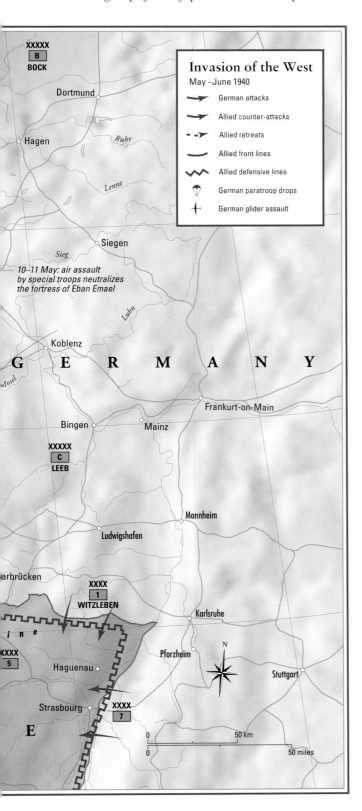

next eight days, with the R.A.F. vigorously trying to stave off the Luftwaffe and achieving many victories, although vastly outnumbered, the navy and its assorted craft managed to lift off 338,226 men, a third of these being of foreign services. The evacuation had been a success in bringing back the B.E.F.; all arms of the services had worked in unison and achieved an almost impossible task. But it did cost all of the B.E.F.'s equipment, from small-arms to artillery.

After the evacuation and the surrender of Belgium on 28 May, the French were on their own and in disarray. The Wehrmacht turned their attentions southward and to the rest of France, with the French digging in on the line of the Somme and the Aisne. The French fought heroically but against overwhelming odds and the Germans soon broke through and on 14 June entered Paris, proclaimed an open city by the French government for fear of aerial attack and annihilation. With nothing to hold them back the French were forced to agree to an armistice, signing it on 22 June in the same railroad carriage they had accepted the German surrender in 1918.

Within six weeks Holland, Belgium, and France were under Nazi control all for the cost of 30,000 dead German soldiers and airmen and casualties reaching 160,000. French losses were of an estimated 90,000 dead, 200,000 wounded and nearly two million missing or taken prisoner.

In this dramatic picture, German artillerymen take cover after destroying two British tanks, possibly of the 7th Royal Tank Regiment. The 88 mm gun was undoubtedly the most effective anti-tank weapon of World War II.

DUNKIRK 1940

"BY NOW DIVE-BOMBERS SEEMED TO BE ETERNALLY DROPPING OUT OF THE CLOUD OF ENEMY AIRCRAFT OVERHEAD. WITHIN HALF A MILE OF THE PIERHEADS A TWO-FUNNELED GRAY-PAINTED TRANSPORT HAD OVERHAULED AND WAS JUST PASSING UP TO PORT WHEN TWO SALVOES WERE DROPPED IN QUICK SUCCESSION RIGHT ALONG HER PORT SIDE. FOR A FEW MINUTES SHE WAS HID IN SMOKE AND I CERTAINLY THOUGHT THEY HAD GOT HER. THEN SHE REAPPEARED, STILL GAILY HEADING FOR THE PIERS AND ENTERED JUST AHEAD OF US."

COMMANDER C.H. LIGHTOLLER (RETIRED)

After the German attacks on 10 May 1940, the rapid advance, particularly of the Panzer divisions, made a nonsense of the Allied defense plan. By 15 May the British and the Belgians were being outflanked in the north by German advances in the Netherlands. Appearing out of the Ardennes Forest, German Army Group A crossed the River Meuse at Sedan and Dinant, French Resistance collapsed at these weakly-held points, allowing the Germans to advance into northern France. Trying to realign his armies, Gamelin, the French commander agreed to the withdrawal of the French First Army Group and the British Expeditionary Force from the line of the Dyle to the River Scheldt on 16 May. French armored attacks on the 17–19 May and British on 21 May gave the Germans a scare and a few temporary problems, their advance continued reaching Abbeville by 20 May and then the Channel coast on 22 May. A German attack separated most of the Belgian army from the British on 25 May, leading to Belgian capitulation on 28 May. The British and the French First Army were being squeezed into what would become the Dunkirk perimeter. By Hitler's direct command, the Panzer divisions were halted from 26 to 28 May. The Allies took this moment to draw breath and consider their position. The Germans could not believe their luck, they needed time for infantry to catch up and to service their tanks and transport. Meanwhile, on 27 May the decision to withdraw the Allied forces from Dunkirk was taken. A miracle of improvisation was about to begin.

Under the command of Admiral Ramsey a fleet of ships was assembled, which ranged from pleasure steamers, coasters, family riverboats, and fishing boats to Royal Navy warships. This fleet of all

Far right: French and British troops, some wounded, who failed to be rescued from the beaches of Dunkirk. They all faced the future as prisoners of war of the Germans.

shapes and sizes sailed across the Channel. The smaller craft picked men off the beaches and ferried them to larger vessels in the deeper water, the Royal Navy took men from the Mole, a long jetty in the port of Dunkirk. Above, the R.A.F. home-based fighter force battled to keep the Luftwaffe at bay. Despite their losses the Luftwaffe broke through the British fighter screen, sinking many ships and killing many soldiers on the beaches. But discipline and training held up: men formed up to take their place on the ships. Somehow they managed to get aboard under air attack, wounded and hungry. Between 26 May and 4 June 222 Royal Navy ships and 665 other commandeered vessels succeeded in bringing back 112,546 French and Belgian soldiers, and 224,585 British troops to British soil. Most of the B.E.F.'s equipment lay abandoned and smashed in France but the men escaped to form the cadre of a new and better army. Most of all, Britain's resolve not to give in was confirmed in the sight of enemy and friends alike.

The remaining British forces in France, mainly the 51st Highland Division, and units of the R.A.F., together with the French forces, were given little respite. On 5 June the German army renewed its attacks and on 20 June Italy attacked south-eastern France.

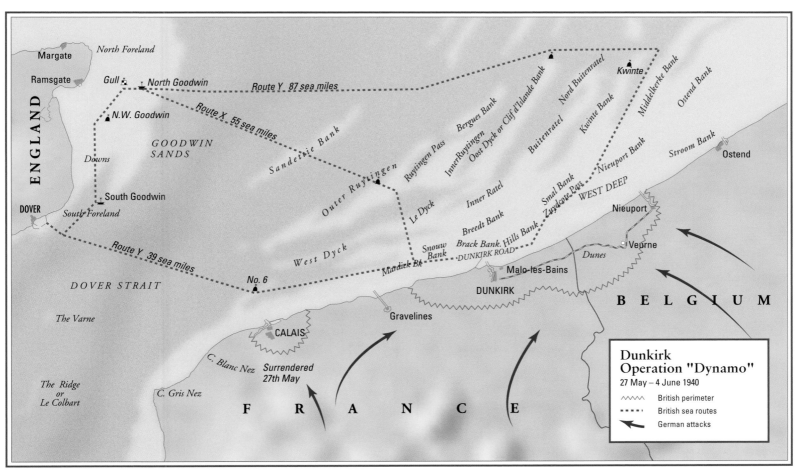

**Dunkirk
Operation "Dynamo"**
27 May – 4 June 1940

〰〰〰 British perimeter
- - - - British sea routes
⬅ German attacks

THE FALL OF FRANCE

"THERE IS NOTHING PREVENTING THE ENEMY REACHING PARIS.
WE WERE FIGHTING ON OUR LAST LINE AND IT HAS BEEN
BREACHED. I AM HELPLESS, I CANNOT INTERVENE ... "

GENERAL WEYGAND

Brit019 and French counterattacks on 17, 18, and 21 May 1940 failed to halt the German advance. Meanwhile, Weygand, the French Supreme Commander, had been organizing a new defensive line along the River Somme and River Aisne. Reinforcements and surviving units from the battles in northern France and Belgium were deployed in the new 4th Army Group formed under the command of General Huntziger which, together with the 2nd and 3rd Army Groups—a total of 50 divisions—held a front line of 230 miles facing a German strength of 120 divisions. Many other French troops manned the static defenses of the outflanked Maginot Line. The French airforce had received limited reinforcement from the British Royal Air Force and mustered over 1,000 aircraft to face the Luftwaffe's complement of almost 3,000 aircraft.

The Germans concentrated almost all of the Panzer divisions in Army Groups A and B to form armored spearheads commanded by Guderian and Kleist respectively. Kleist launched his attack on 5 June and Guderian launched his on 9 June. The French army, facing the onslaught launched by Army Group B, resisted with great valor. Among them was the British 51st Highland Division, the only part of the British Expeditionary Forces still fighting, apart from the R.A.F. However, by the night of 8 June units of Army Group B had broken through the French line and were heading for Paris. On 9 June Rundstedt's Army Group A launched a series of attacks towards Rheims, meeting fierce resistance. On 11 June the French units facing Boch's Army Group B attacks collapsed. This forced French units facing Rundstedt to retreat, falling back behind the River Marne. The continued pressure on the French was maintained by the German ability to drive the armored spearheads forward, protected and supported by the Luftwaffe. The French command structure was not

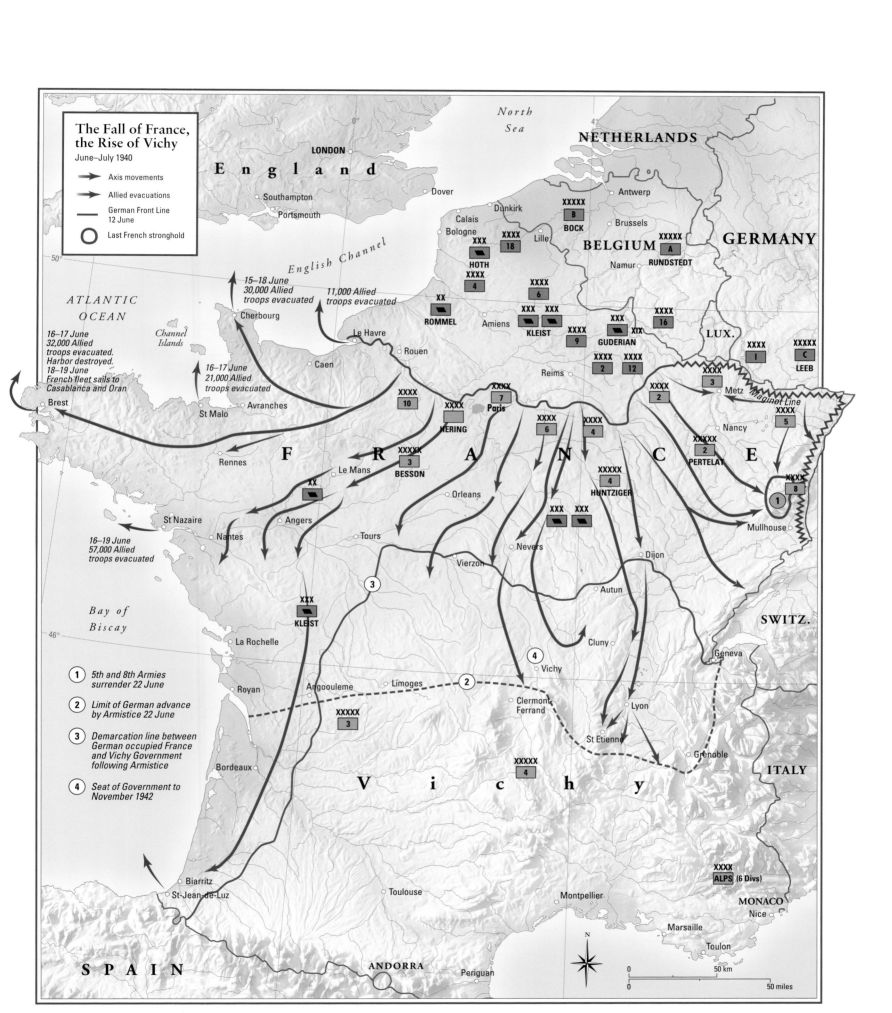

The Fall of France, the Rise of Vichy
June–July 1940

→ Axis movements

→ Allied evacuations

— German Front Line 12 June

◯ Last French stronghold

North Sea

NETHERLANDS

LONDON

E n g l a n d

Southampton
Portsmouth

Dover

English Channel

Calais
Bologne
Dunkirk

Antwerp

Brussels

BELGIUM

GERMANY

Namur

XXXXX B BOCK

XXX HOTH
XXXX 18
Lille

XXXXX A RUNDSTEDT

ATLANTIC OCEAN

Channel Islands

Cherbourg

16–17 June 32,000 Allied troops evacuated. Harbor destroyed.
18–19 June French fleet sails to Casablanca and Oran

Brest

15–18 June 30,000 Allied troops evacuated

11,000 Allied troops evacuated

Le Havre

Rouen

Caen

Avranches

St Malo

16–17 June 21,000 Allied troops evacuated

XXXX 4
XX ROMMEL

XXXX 6

Amiens

XXX XXX KLEIST

XXXX 9

XXX XIX GUDERIAN

XXXX 16

Reims

LUX.

XXXX 1

XXXXX C LEEB

XXXX 2 XXXX 12

XXX 3

Metz

Maginot Line

XXXX 2

Nancy

XXXX 5

Rennes

F   R   A   N   C   E

XXXX 10

XXXX NERING

XXXX 7 Paris

XXXX 6

XXXX 4

XXXXX 3 BESSON

Le Mans

XX

St Nazaire

Angers

16–19 June 57,000 Allied troops evacuated

Nantes

Orleans

Tours

XXXXX 4 HUNTZIGER

XXX XXX

Nevers

Vierzon

XXXX 2 PERTELAT

XXXX 8
①

Mullhouse

Dijon

Autun

Bay of Biscay

XXX KLEIST

La Rochelle

SWITZ.

Cluny

Geneva

③

④ Vichy

② Limoges

Clermont-Ferrand

Lyon

Royan

Angoouleme

XXXXX 3

St Etienne

Grenoble

ITALY

① 5th and 8th Armies surrender 22 June

② Limit of German advance by Armistice 22 June

③ Demarcation line between German occupied France and Vichy Government following Armistice

④ Seat of Government to November 1942

Bordeaux

V   i   c   h   y

XXXXX 4

XXXX ALPS (6 Divs)

MONACO
Nice

Biarritz
St-Jean-de-Luz

Toulouse

Montpellier

Marsaille

Toulon

S P A I N

ANDORRA

Periguan

N

0   50 km

0   50 miles

up to facing such a fluid situation and failed to organize defense lines effectively or organize any strategy that would defeat German tactics. On 12 June Guderian's Panzer Group, now joined by Kleist, broke through east of Paris. On the same day elements of the Tenth Army and surviving units of British forces surrendered at St. Valéry-en-Caux.

However, two days earlier on 10 June the French government under Paul Reynaud left Paris for Tours, leading a vast column of followers and refugees: *l'exode*. Reynaud was visited at Tours on 11 June by Churchill, who urged continued resistance. On Churchill's return to England, General

Panzer Grenadiers dismount from Sd Kfz 251 halftracks. This vehicle served the German army well and by the end of the war existed in 21 variants, ranging from command vehicle to mobile flak guns. During the French campaign, however, the majority of Panzer Grenadiers relied on trucks for transport. Not until 1941 were they fully equipped with these armored personnel carriers.

Charles de Gaulle had risen to his new position as Under-secretary for war, after his valiant effort to stop the German advance at Laon on 17–19 May. De Gaulle was an ardent supporter of the pro-war party in the French Cabinet and at his urging Churchill, on 16 June, made a remarkable proposal to the French government, an 'indissoluble union of Britain and France'. This, it was stated, would be a testimony of their joint determination to fight Germany to the end. It might also serve, should France fall—in a more cynical view—that it would be a way of saving a large portion of the French Army and especially the powerful French fleet, thus keeping them in a continued war with Germany from British and French colonial bases. By this time a large area of France containing over 30 percent of its industrial base was overrun. It was this industry that supplied the French Field Army. Another large portion lay under German gunfire. Many of the French army's supply depots were overrun. If the line could be stabilized, which was doubtful, how could a continued French army of 50–60 divisions be supplied? Equipment and men were being used faster than they could be replaced. The British could only just rearm the returned B.E.F. and could do little or nothing to help further. Any commitment from the United States was unlikely to be effective quickly enough. The French High Command realized this terrible reality very quickly. The British, mesmerized by the size of the French Army, were slower to come to terms with this horrific situation. Set against this situation the British proposal of union was unacceptable to the French government, now dom-

inated by their peace party which, on 16 June, appointed the hero of Verdun, Marshall Philippe Pétain, as its new Head of Government.

Pétain immediately formed a new government and that same evening sued through Spanish diplomatic connections for an armistice. The war dragged on for another six days. By 17 June the last British forces were withdrawn from France. There was talk of the French government moving to its colonies in North Africa but in the end no ministers went.

After Hitler and Mussolini, whose army invaded south-eastern France on 20 June, met in Munich, their terms were presented to the new French government on 22 June at Compiègne, on the same train that Germany had signed its armistice with the Allied powers in November 1918.

The 1918 signing had been a quiet, secret affair but this time it was done in the full glare of German propaganda—bands played, soldiers presented arms, photographs were

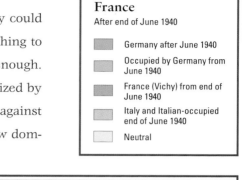

taken, cine films rolled—and amongst all this Hitler arrived to take the surrender. Two days later an agreement was signed with Italy confirming its possession of Nice and parts of Savoy. The zone of German occupation was somewhat smaller than the area conquered by the advancing army. The *zone libre* (free zone), its capital at Vichy, ran south of the River Loire, less its Atlantic and Alpine frontiers. The French empire and its fleet remained in the hands of the Vichy government. The provinces of Alsace-Lorraine were ceded to Germany. The French war was over. France would be drained of its productive resources and its young men sent to labor in Germany. However, it was not the end, many Frenchmen fought on at home and abroad with the hope that one day they would see a liberated France. It would take four long and bloody years.

THE BATTLE OF BRITAIN

"THE BATTLE OF FRANCE IS OVER. THE BATTLE OF BRITAIN IS ABOUT TO BEGIN. UPON THIS BATTLE DEPENDS THE FUTURE OF CHRISTIAN CIVILIZATION."

WINSTON CHURCHILL, JUNE 1940

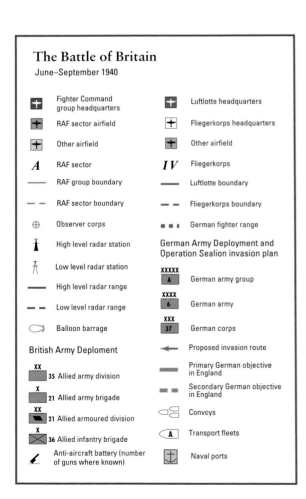

The Battle of Britain
June–September 1940

✠	Fighter Command group headquarters		✠	Luftlotte headquarters
✠	RAF sector airfield		✠	Fliegerkorps headquarters
✠	Other airfield		✠	Other airfield
A	RAF sector		*IV*	Fliegerkorps
—	RAF group boundary		—	Luftlotte boundary
– –	RAF sector boundary		– –	Fliegerkorps boundary
⊕	Observer corps		▪ ▪ ▪	German fighter range
⊤	High level radar station		German Army Deployment and Operation Sealion invasion plan	
⊤	Low level radar station			
—	High level radar range		xxxxx A	German army group
– –	Low level radar range		xxxx 6	German army
⬭	Balloon barrage		xxx 37	German corps
British Army Deploment			←	Proposed invasion route
xx 35	Allied army division		—	Primary German objective in England
x 21	Allied army brigade		– –	Secondary German objective in England
xx 21	Allied armoured division		⬭	Convoys
x 36	Allied infantry brigade		A	Transport fleets
⚓	Anti-aircraft battery (number of guns where known)		⚓	Naval ports

After the British withdrawal from Dunkirk and the fall of France, Hitler expected that Britain would sue for peace and end the war in Europe. However, Churchill, with the support of the British people, committed Britain and its commonwealth to see the war through to a victorious conclusion, no matter how desperate the circumstances seemed. On the 16 July Hitler ordered the directive for Operation Sealion as a prelude to a full cross-channel invasion, and the Luftwaffe was instructed to destroy the air defense of Great Britain.

"As England, in spite of the hopelessness of the military position, has so far shown herself unwilling to come to any compromise, I have decided to begin to prepare for, and if necessary to carry out the invasion of England. This operation is dictated by the necessity of eliminating Great Britain as a base from which the war against Germany can be fought, and if necessary, the island will be occupied."—Adolf Hitler.

The campaign would be decided for the first time by air power alone. German control of the air would be crucial in protecting German seaborne forces as they crossed the English Channel. The might of the British Navy would have to be defeated, or at least held at bay, by the Luftwaffe in order that the invasion fleet could land its troops without suffering a complete disaster.

Although the Luftwaffe was still recovering from its losses in the French campaign, it could still command 2,669 aircraft, of which 993 were single-engine fighters, 375 long-range twin-engine fighters protecting a force of 1,015 bombers and 346 dive-bombers. Facing this threat the R.A.F. had 704 fighters, mostly single-engine Hurricanes and

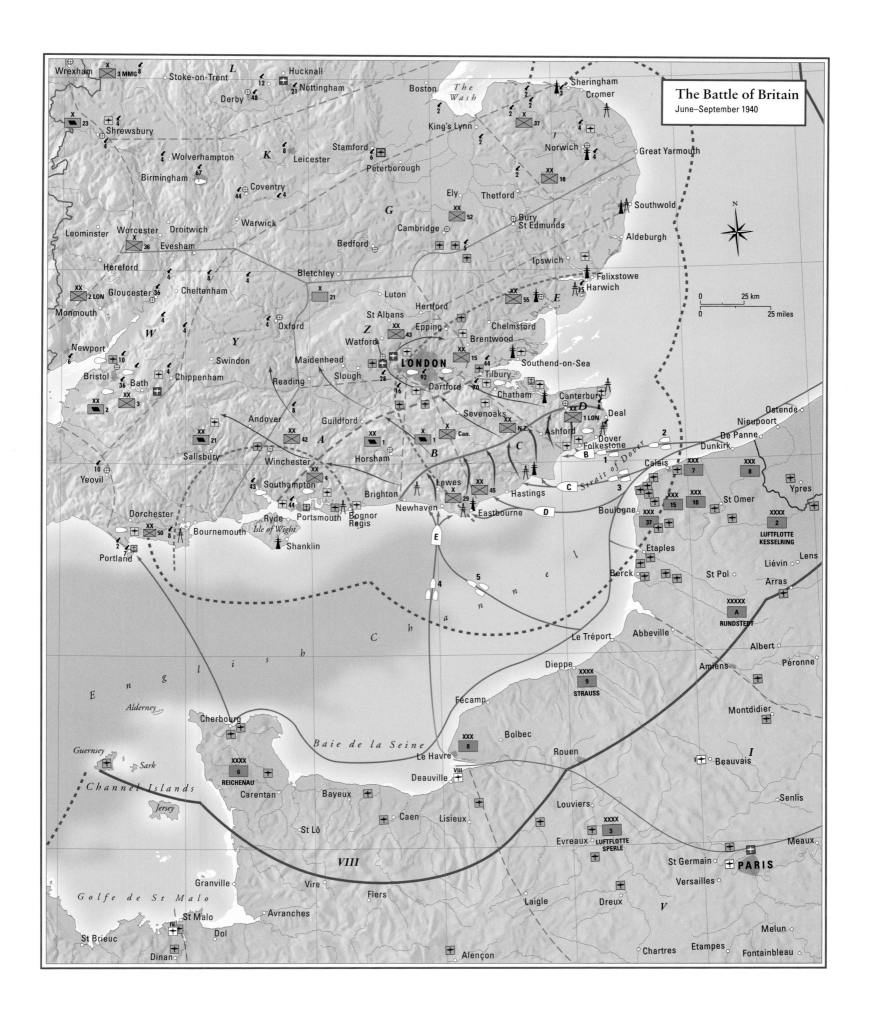

The Battle of Britain
June–September 1940

Spitfires and Hurricanes provided the mainstay of Royal Air Force fighter command, though among the 704 fighter aircraft available at the start of the Battle of Britain, there remained some older and slower aircraft. The Spitfire photographed above is the sole survivor of the Battle of Britain still flying.

Spitfires, but including some slower, older aircraft and around 440 bombers. The bombers would have to bomb German transport concentrations in the Channel ports and the invasion force, should it appear. The figures may seem to have been heavily in favor of the Luftwaffe, but the British had been preparing their air defense for a number of years. The key element was Radio Location (Radar) and the command and control structure based around it. This would allow the British to keep their fighters on the ground until directed against specific targets. Those targets were German formations "spotted" by radar forming up over northern France and tracked as they approached southern England. The Germans, however, were unprepared for long-range operations, since their airforce had been designed for the support of ground forces. Their fighter escort for the bomber formations had limited range and could only escort the bombers for some 20 minutes over England, leaving them at the mercy of British fighters. The Luftwaffe was operating over enemy territory and any aircraft shot down meant the loss of a trained crew, while the British crewman, if he survived, could rejoin his unit and be back in action, occasionally on the same day.

The first phase of the Battle of Britain opened in July with Luftwaffe attacks on Channel convoys, radar stations, and other targets, mainly along the south coast. German strategy was to draw the British fighter force into combat, destroying the aircraft by sheer force of numbers, competence, and the experience of their aircrews, together with the superiority of their aircraft. However, Britain's command and control system worked too well. Air Vice Marshal Hugh Dowding, the commander of Britain's air defense, was almost always able to concentrate his available aircraft. With the aid of radar, fighters were in the right place at the right time to intercept incoming German raids.

THE BRITISH AIR DEFENSE SYSTEM, SUMMER 1940

Fighter Command controlled its force of interceptors based on information supplied by radar and supported by the Royal Observer Corps. On receiving this information it ordered "scrambles" from sector airfields (see example right) to intercept incoming German formations. On the night of 24 August German bombers attacked London and other British provincial cities. This change of tactics provoked the British to attack Berlin, on the night of 25/26 August, diverting the Luftwaffe to defend its own cities, so began attacks on each others cities. Fighter Command's structure, its bases, and systems were no longer attacked, allowing it to rebuild, reinforce, and recover.

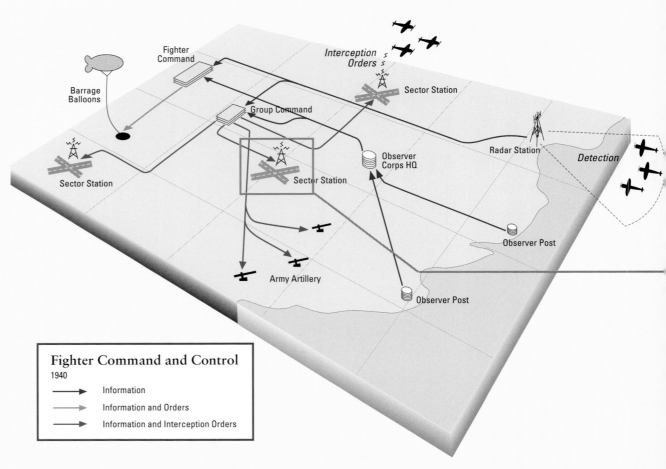

Fighter Command
Interception Orders
Barrage Balloons
Sector Station
Group Command
Radar Station
Observer Corps HQ
Detection
Sector Station
Sector Station
Observer Post
Army Artillery
Observer Post

Fighter Command and Control
1940

→ Information
→ Information and Orders
→ Information and Interception Orders

By early August, German raids had become focussed on British airfields and aircraft industry. On 1 August, Hitler issued First Directive No. 17, "for the conduct of air and sea warfare against England [meaning Great Britain]." Aerial battles, however, were already a daily occurrence over southern England. On 13 August—"Adler Tay" (Eagle Day)—approximately 1500 German aircraft were launched against England. Despite many previous attacks, the radar-directed air defense system was still intact. On 15 August this massive German force of 1,270 fighters and 520 bombers was directed at British air bases and the support structure that supplied air defense, airfields, repair depots, aircraft factories, and antiaircraft sites.

Thanks to radar, Dowding was able to concentrate his aircraft at crucial locations along the front of the enemy's approach. To the Germans it seemed as though the R.A.F. was always able to attack or at least disrupt their every move.

The He 111 provided the mainstay of the German bomber force. On targets beyond London, German bombers were obliged to fly without fighter protection and thus were increasingly vulnerable to British fighters.

The campaign to destroy the Royal Air Force continued for another month. By mid-August Luftwaffe intelligence had reported that the task was almost complete. However, German pilots reported the opposite. By now British industry was producing 400 fighters per month, against the German's 200. The real fact was the Luftwaffe was weakening while the R.A.F. was growing stronger, though its lack of trained pilots remained a real weakness. However, as the battle progressed, pilots from other commands of the R.A.F. were transferred to Dowding's fighter command. These, together with foreign contingents—French, Czechs, and particularly Poles—made a major contribution to the battle.

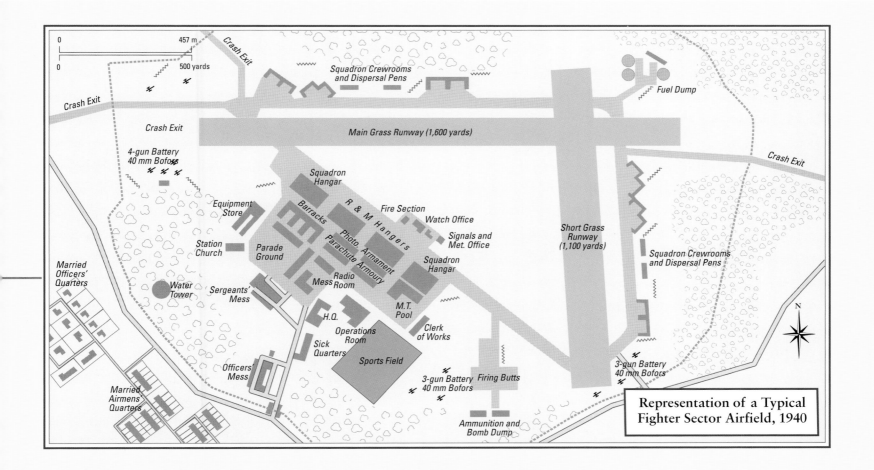

Representation of a Typical Fighter Sector Airfield, 1940

THE BLITZ 1940–41

"A STRING OF BOMBS FELL RIGHT BESIDE THE THAMES, THEIR WHITE GLARE WAS REFLECTED IN THE BLACK, LAZY WATER NEAR THE BANKS, AND FADED IN MIDSTREAM WHERE THE MOON CUT A GOLDEN SWATHE BROKEN ONLY BY THE ARCHES OF FAMOUS BRIDGES ..."   ED MURROW, AMERICAN REPORTER

The bombing campaign began on the night of 24/25 August 1940, known more by its popular name, "The Blitz" and was aimed at Britain's capacity to make war. Industrial targets of all kinds were repeatedly bombed: factories, shipyards, oil terminals, and any domestic homes that might be in their way. Urban centers were bombed without restriction from August 1940 to May 1941, after which large numbers of German bombers were transferred east in preparation for the attack on Russia.

This event was not unexpected, since Britain had prepared for the possibility, or probability, of air attacks. Most citizens had been issued with gas masks, trained air raid wardens patrolled every city street, and country lane enforcing the black-out that had been introduced. No chink of light must show from factory, home, or chicken shed, which might guide German bombers to their targets. Children and young mothers had been evacuated from major cities to the countryside in one of the largest movements of civilian population ever undertaken. Around key centers, barrage balloons, searchlights, and anti-aircraft guns were deployed. Most of this valuable and scarce equipment was deployed in the south-east and London, although 42 guns were still found to defend the provincial town of Derby, home to the Rolls-Royce Works producing Merlin engines for Spitfire and Hurricane fighters.

During August, the Luftwaffe concentrated its efforts on London, flying daylight raids. These proved so costly on aircraft that by mid-September night raids were to become the norm. Their attacks were therefore less precise and bombs aimed in the darkness fell on a much wider area, hitting homes as often as factories. Despite all the preparations, the weight of attacks shocked

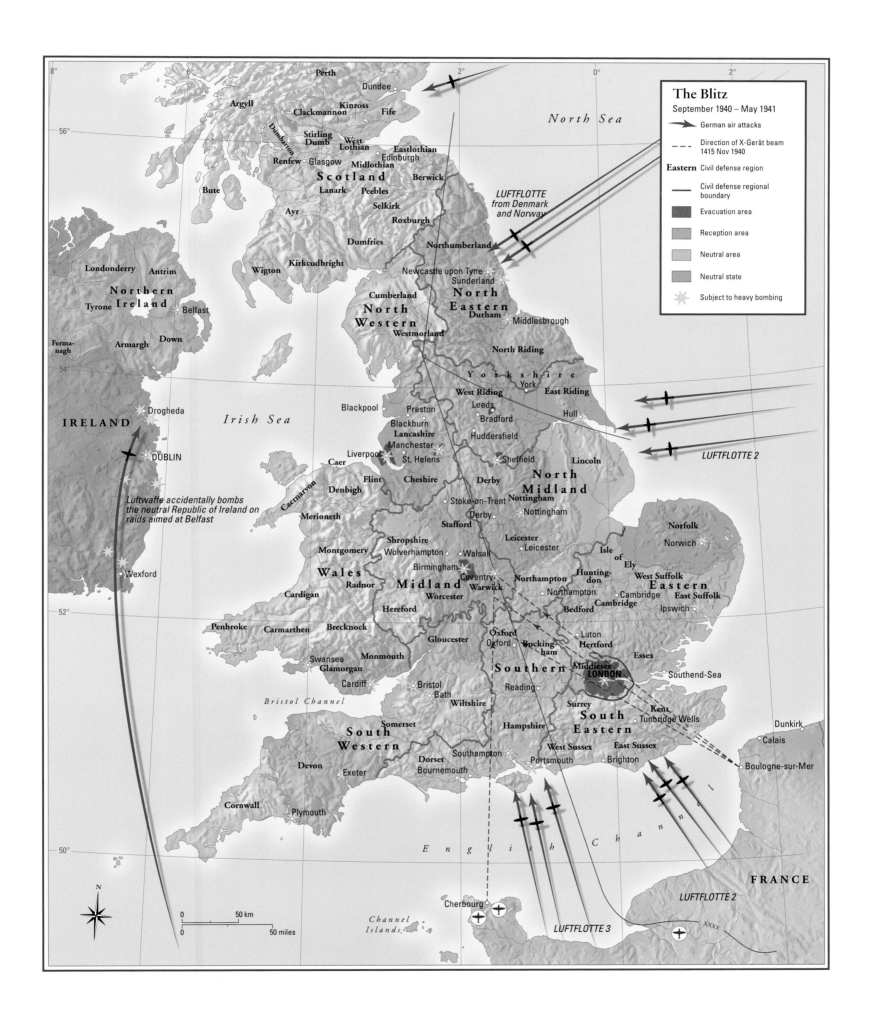

The Blitz
September 1940 – May 1941

→ German air attacks

- - - Direction of X-Gerät beam 1415 Nov 1940

Eastern Civil defense region

Civil defense regional boundary

Evacuation area

Reception area

Neutral area

Neutral state

✳ Subject to heavy bombing

LUFTFLOTTE from Denmark and Norway

LUFTFLOTTE 2

Luftwaffe accidentally bombs the neutral Republic of Ireland on raids aimed at Belfast

LUFTFLOTTE 3

LUFTFLOTTE 2

the civilian population and some people in provincial cities, such as Plymouth, migrated to the nearby countryside each night, camping to avoid the bombs. In London the Underground system became a haven each night for people sleeping on the platforms deep beneath the street, seeking shelter from the nightly raiders. Nevertheless, by the end of September almost 7,000 civilians were dead, thousands wounded, and tens of thousands homeless.

On the night of 14/15 November 1940, German "pathfinder" bombers flying along radio direction beams, known as "X-Gerät," hit Coventry, a provincial manufacturing city heavily involved in Britain's war effort. Following the pathfinders were over 400 bombers. Aiming at the fires already created, they dropped 503 tons of high explosive bombs and some 30,000 incendiary bombs. Hundreds were killed, over 1,200 badly wounded, and thousands more made homeless. Thousands of buildings were destroyed or badly damaged. Yet, despite all the horror, within a few days factories were back in production and morale had recovered quickly. It seemed that bombing could not destroy

Between July and December 1940 the Luftwaffe had dropped 27,486 tons of bombs on British cities, killing 23,002 British civilians and injuring a further 39,096.

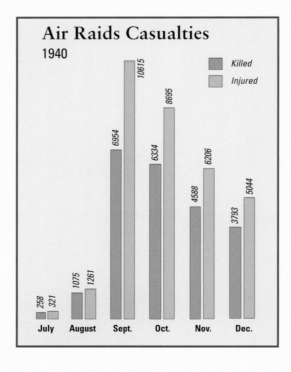

Air Raids Casualties
1940

- Killed
- Injured

Month	Killed	Injured
July	258	321
August	1075	1261
Sept.	6954	10615
Oct.	6334	8695
Nov.	4588	6206
Dec.	3793	5044

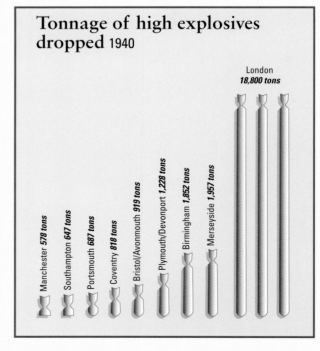

Tonnage of high explosives dropped 1940

- Manchester *578 tons*
- Southampton *647 tons*
- Portsmouth *687 tons*
- Coventry *818 tons*
- Bristol/Avonmouth *919 tons*
- Plymouth/Devonport *1,228 tons*
- Birmingham *1,852 tons*
- Merseyside *1,957 tons*
- London *18,800 tons*

a nation's will to fight and survive. It became a matter of pride, an indication of the national mood. Small signs displayed in broken shop windows defiantly announced "Business as usual."

By Christmas 1940, the raids covered most of Britain. Glasgow, Belfast, Liverpool, and Sheffield had all been badly hit, and London had not been spared. Just after Christmas, on the night of 29/30 December, more than 130 bombers attacked London. The area between the Guildhall and St Paul's Cathedral was ablaze; it seemed for a moment, that the great cathedral itself would be lost, until brave action by firewatchers saved the building. It was not the same for the homes and offices in the surrounding area; ancient dwellings and Wren churches were turned to ashes; hundreds of years of building, and history were lost. Despite this bleak time the country survived, new equipment came out of battered factories; including radar-directed guns that could predict the height and direction of bombers. Night fighters were now equipped with radar and began to intercept the night raiders with increasing success; fire and rescue teams became more expert; and bomb disposal units worked their lonely, dangerous tasks. It was now clear to all that Britain was not going to crack.

Far left: On the night of 14 November 1940, the English city of Coventry was devastated by a concentrated attack. Among the buildings destroyed was the city's medieval cathedral.

German Do 217 bombers approach their targets over the River Thames.

THE BOMBING OF GERMANY 1940–41

"THE SIRENS SUDDENLY SCREAMED OUT OVER THE CITY. IMMEDIATELY THERE WAS A DEAD SILENCE ALL AROUND. SHOPS CLOSED, BUSINESS PEOPLE AND GOSSIPING WOMEN STOPPED TALKING. THEY BEGAN TO RUN THROUGH THE STREET ... ALL OF THEM RAN, AND NO ONE SPOKE AT ALL."

ELSE WENDEL, HOUSEWIFE

The British Royal Air Force, the world's first air force independent of army or navy, had been formed around the proposition of taking the war to the enemy by bombing its industrial centers. The R.A.F. had done this in 1918, operating from bases in northern France. Its fleet of strategic bombers was just coming into meaningful service when the World War I ended.

Through to the 1920s and 30s, the R.A.F.'s main role had become a colonial one—bombing rebellious tribes with a fleet of light biplane bombers. Its strategic role relegated to theory and discussion in training schools. By the mid-30s rearmament was underway, which included new aircraft for R.A.F. Bomber Command. In September 1939 this Command was ready to operate from bases in eastern England, following its "Western Air Plans" (originated by the Combined Services Planning Section in 1936). These plans assumed immediate military operations by German forces in the west. From the beginning of a German offensive R.A.F. attacks would be mounted on Luftwaffe bases and supply depots. It was assumed as German attacks developed against France, that raids by the R.A.F. would be focussed on the German lines of supply. Following these attacks, raids would then be directed on German war industry, especially oil refineries and oil storage facilities.

Bomber Command lost part of its strength two days before Britain's declaration of war when, as planned previously, No. 1 Group, with ten squadrons of Fairey Battle light bombers, moved to France together with two Blenheim squadrons from another group to form the Advanced Air Striking Force. Five

R.A.F. Bomber crews deliver their post-raid reports.

more squadrons of Battles were left in England but were reduced to a training and reserve basis. The restricted nature of operations after the outbreak of war gave Bomber Command the opportunity to withdraw a further nine of its squadrons from the home-based groups and add these to the reserve, leaving only 23 front line squadrons that contained approximately 280 aircraft with trained crews. That part of Bomber Command which now stood ready to proceed with war operations was organized in the following manner:

Bomber Command Headquarters at Richings Park, Langley, Buckinghamshire (but due to move in March 1940 to a new location being prepared at High Wycombe). The Commander-in-Chief was Air Chief Marshal Sir Edgar Ludlow-Hewitt.

An R.A.F. Wellington bomber, the best medium bomber in the early part of the war, being prepared for a raid into Germany.

2 Group HQ: Wyton. Commander: Air Vice-Marshal C.T. Maclean. Squadrons: Nos. 21, 82, 107, 110, 114, and 139, equipped with Bristol Blenheims; 101 Squadron non-operational.

3 Group HQ: Mildenhall. Commander: Air Vice-Marshal J.E.A. Baldwin. Squadrons: Nos. 9, 37, 38, 39, 99, 115, and 149, equipped with Vickers Wellingtons; 214 and 215 Squadrons non-operational.

4 Group HQ: Linton-on-Ouse. Commander: Air Vice-Marshal A. Coningham. Squadrons: Nos. 10, 51, 58, 77, and 102, equipped with Armstrong-Whitworth Whitleys; 78 Squadron non-operational.

5 Group HQ: St Vincent's House, Grantham. Commander: Air Commodore W.B. Callaway (Air Vice-Marshal A.T. Harris from 11 September). Squadrons: Nos. 44, 49, 50, 61, 83, and 144, equipped with Handley Page Hampdens; 106 and 185 Squadrons non-operational.

The four types of aircraft in use were the Blenheim, Hampden, Wellington, and Whitley, all of reasonable design and without major mechanical drawbacks. Maximum bomb loads varied from 1,000 pounds for the Blenheim to 8,000 pounds for the Whitley. The Blenheim had only a restricted range but the other three types could reach any part of Germany except the extreme east. It had always been intended that the main bombing operations would be carried out by tight, self-defending daylight formations and only the Whitley squadrons of 4 Group were trained in night bombing.

On 1 September, the U.S. President Franklin D. Roosevelt called for restraint from bombing operations where civilians might be hit. France and Britain agreed at once. On 18 September, Germany also agreed, but only as the Polish Campaign drew to a close. Meanwhile, the R.A.F. was cleared to attack German shipping as long as it was not alongside a wharf or dock. Bombers could also fly over enemy territory for the purpose of dropping propaganda leaflets. Many R.A.F. Commanders felt this

THE BOMBING OF EUROPE
1939–41
The Ruhr area of Germany was particularly targeted by the RAF bombing campaign because this was the major industrial zone in western Germany closely connected with the supply of Germany's armed forces.

was a waste of time, but it did build up experience of operating over enemy territory before actually being committed to an all-out bombing campaign. It also bought time to build up aircraft numbers and train aircrews beyond the number immediately available.

After the fall of France, Germany controlled the Atlantic coast from the Spanish border to the north of Norway. During the Battle of Britain, the British Bomber Command's main task was to bomb barge concentrations along the occupied Channel coast. Their planned attack on German industry was secondary to the needs of that moment. Despite this, a small number of bombers were sent to Germany night after night; oil-related targets were still their priority. Virtually all night raids were carried out by small groups of aircraft directed to various targets, with each crew navigating its own way. Although navigation equipment and skills were lacking, on moonlit nights visual sightings of rivers or other identifiable landmarks helped the bomber crews to locate their targets. As German flak and searchlights became more effective, however, the bombers were forced to fly at higher altitudes, making identification of the target even more difficult. A small number of aircraft were fitted with bombing cameras and these were given to the best crews, since the interpretation between claims of the crews indicated massive discrepancies. Within Bomber Command the optimism prevailed.

On the night of 23/24 September a unique raid was launched against Berlin, 129 aircraft were dispatched to 18 targets within the city: railroad yards, factories, gasworks, and power stations. Of the 129 aircraft dispatched, 112 reported bombing the city, while three aircraft were lost. Very few details from the German side are available, possibly having been removed from the records for security purposes, although it is known that most of the bombs fell in the Moabit district, where the power stations were hit and the baroque palace, Schloss Charlottenburg, was damaged.

During the Battle of Britain and for many months after, Germany was visited by British bombers, but numbers were small, and sometimes the missions involved only the dropping of leaflets. However, during the winter of 1940 the raids became much larger. On the night 16/17 December 134 bombers—the largest raid sent to a single target—flew to Mannheim in retaliation for the devastating attacks on Coventry.

The R.A.F. raid began with eight chosen bomber crews attacking Mannheim city center with incendiary bombs. The bombers following would use the resulting fires as a target marker to drop high explosive bombs in order to cause maximum destruction. The raid, however, was not a success, with bombs being scattered all over the city rather than concentrated in the center as planned. For the first time the target was not primarily industrial or military in nature. The raid left 34 dead, 81 wounded, 476 buildings destroyed or severely damaged and 1,266 people lost their homes. Four aircraft failed to return.

Cities in Britain had been badly hit, including Liverpool, Manchester, Plymouth, and many others. The bombing of London was still an almost nightly occurrence. It was felt strongly by High Command that R.A.F. Bomber Command should take war to the heart of the German cities, what the R.A.F. would later call "area bombing." The concerted terror bombing of the Germans was about to begin.

BOMBING STATISTICS 1940–42

Bomber Production

	Germany	Britain	U.S.
1940	2,852	3,488	—
1941	3,373	4,668	—
1942	4,502	6,253	12,627

These figures include all bomber types.

Bomber Losses

	Germany	Britain	U.S.
1940	1,653	494	—
1941	1,814	914	—
1942	2,338	1,400	30

German losses are for all bomber types and from all causes. British and American losses are for aircraft involved in operations from only British bases against Europe, all causes.

Bombing Tonnage

	Luftwaffe on U.K.	R.A.F. on Germany and Occupied Europe	USAAF on Germany and Occupied Europe
1940	36,844	13,033	—
1941	21,848	31,704	—
1942	3,260	45,561	1,561

Figures for U.K. are for Bomber Command flying from British bases; figures from USA are for 8th Air Force flying from British bases.

The Bombing of Europe
1939–41

● Bomber Command Headquarters

• Bomber Group Headquarters

Weight of bombs

✳ 25 – 1000 tons

✴ 1000 – 3000 tons

✴ 3000 – 4000 tons

Wesel

Starkade   Bottrapp   Gielen-Kirchen   Lunen
Homberg   Dortmund
Huls   Wanne-Eickel
Duisberg   Essen   Schwerte
Krefeld   R h u r

Munchen-   Dusseldorf
gladbach   Reisholz

Norway

SWEDEN

Denmark

Copenhagen ☐

Irish
Sea

UNITED
KINGDOM

• York

North Sea

Sylt
Flensburg
Kiel
Warnemunde
Rostock
Lubeck
Wismar
Cuxhaven   Hamburg   Stettin
Wilhelmshaven   Bremerhaven
Emden   Bremen

• Grantham

Texel
Oldenburg

Berlin

Amsterdam ☐
Schipol
NETH.
Rotterdam   Soesterberg

Salzbergen
Osnabruck
Bielefeld

Brunswick

Magdeburg

Huntingdon • • Exning

Abingdon •   ● High Wycombe
London ☐

Haamstede
Flushing
Ostend
Dunkirk   Zeebrugge
Calais   Hazebrouck
Bologne
Merville

Eindhoven
Emmerich   Munster
Munchen-   Hamm
gladbach   Soest
Monheim
Cologne

Paderborn

See inset

Kassel

Merseburg

GERMANY

English Channel

Cherbourg   Dieppe
Le Havre

Brussels ☐

Belgium

Coblenze
Frankfurt

Prague ☐

Paris ☐

Mannheim
Nuremberg
Karlsruhe
Stuttgart

Brest

Lorient

F   r   a   n   c   e

Munich

St Nazaire

Austria

Bay of
Biscay

La Pallice/
La Rochelle

Royan

SWITZERLAND

Bern ☐

Geneva

Ambares

Bordeaux   Bordeaux
Airfield

Vichy
Occupied 11 Nov. 1942

Turin   • Milan   • Venice

I   T   A   L   Y

Genoa

SPAIN

WAR IN EAST AFRICA 1941

"WAR ALONE CAN CARRY TO THE MAXIMUM TENSION ALL HUMAN ENERGIES AND IMPRINT WITH THE SEAL OF NOBILITY THOSE PEOPLE WHO HAVE THE COURAGE TO CONFRONT IT; EVERY OTHER TEST IS A MERE SUBSTITUTE."

BENITO MUSSOLINI, c. 1930

The German invasion of France in May 1940 transformed the strategic situation in the Mediterranean and North Africa. Eager to profit from this new situation, Italy declared war on Britain and France on 10 June 1940, sending troops over the border into France on 21 June ensuring—Italian Prime Minister and dictator Benito Mussolini hoped—a say in the peace following a glorious victory. However, Hitler made peace without any reference to his erstwhile ally. The surrender of France seriously weakened the British position in the Mediterranean, the neutralization of the French fleet left Italy the dominating naval power. Added to this, Italian ground forces based in Italian Somaliland, Eritrea, Ethiopia, and Libya, formed the largest fighting force in Africa, some 300,000 Italian and a further 150,000 locally-recruited troops facing approximately 75,000 British troops scattered across north and eastern Africa.

Hoping to seize the initiative, Mussolini ordered attacks on Sudan and Kenya and an all-out attack to seize British Somaliland, which was occupied from 5–19 August. Along the North African coast a force of six Italian divisions marched 60 miles into Egypt, where it dug in, building a forward base at Sidi Barrani. General Sir Archibald Wavell, the British Commander-in-Chief, gave priority to the Italian invasion of Egypt, launching the first attacks on 9 December in a five-day operation. Its success encouraged Wavell to advance into Libya in early January 1941, capturing Tobruk on 22 January. He then divided his forces, one part following the coast road, the other part advancing across the desert, linking up at Beda Fomm. His force had advanced 500 miles, capturing 130,000 prisoners and most of their equipment.

Meanwhile, the British offensive in East Africa began. On 19 January the 4th and 5th Indian

Four cruisers of the Italian Fleet lay at anchor in Naples harbor. The Italian Fleet was built to turn the Mediterranean Sea into an Italian lake. However, three of these four cruisers were sunk by the British at the Battle of Matapan.

Africa in the Second World War

→ German and Italian advance from 1942

→ Allied movements

Colonial possessions

- British
- French
- Portuguese
- Spanish
- Italian
- Belgium

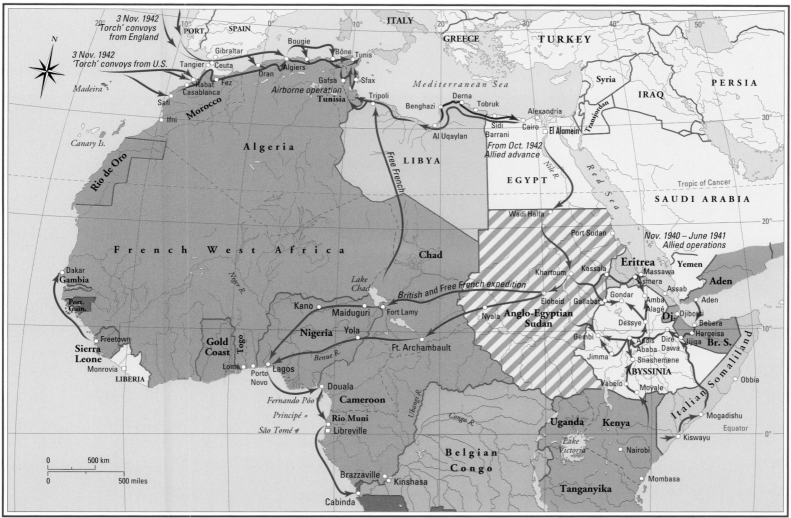

Divisions advanced into Eritrea from Sudan. Commanded by Major-General William Platt, this force slowly advanced through difficult terrain, oppressive heat, and bitter fighting. The vital port of Massawa fell to them on 8 April.

A new front had opened on 11 February. Three divisions, commanded by Lt-General Alan Cunningham, advanced into Italian Somaliland. Fourteen days later, Mogadishu, the capital, was captured. This force then pushed on, advancing across the Ogadem Desert deep into Ethiopia from the south, entering the town of Jijiga unopposed.

On 25 February, yet another British force landed at Berbera, recapturing British Somaliland. Part of this force advanced to Jijiga joining British Commonwealth units already there. This united force faced formidable Italian defenses at Harar. As it turned out, the Italian forces put up a token resistance before withdrawing. On 28 March Diredawa fell, opening the way to the capital city of Ethiopia, Addis Ababa. The city fell to British and Commonwealth troops on 6 April after an eight-week fighting advance covering over 1,700 miles.

The Italian defenders of Addis Ababa withdrew northward linking up with forces facing the British in and around Tigre province. Their commander concentrated his surviving forces at Amba Alagi, a mountain stronghold, and there the Italians would make their last stand. On 3 May attacks were launched by Indian troops from the north, joined by Cunningham's troops attacking from the south. By 19 May the Duke of Aosta, realizing his situation was hopeless, surrendered. Scattered resistance continued until 3 July and clearing-up operations were completed in November. This victory liberated the ancient state of Ethiopia and returned Emperor Haile Selassie to his throne. The end of this campaign ensured vital supply routes into and through the Red Sea were firmly under Allied control.

The British King's African Rifles accord the honors of war to the surrendering Italian garrison at Wolkefit near Gondar, Ethiopia, in 1941.

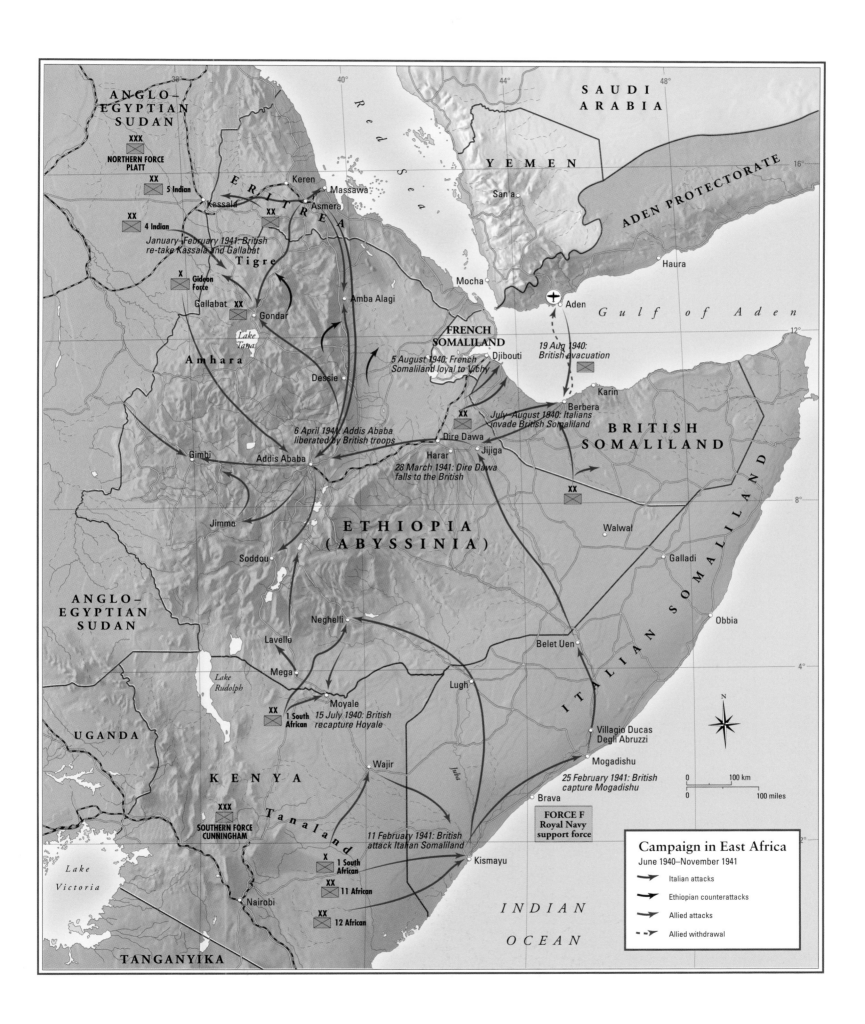

ANGLO-
EGYPTIAN
SUDAN

XXX
NORTHERN FORCE
PLATT

XX 5 Indian

Keren
Massawa

Kassala

XX
Asmera

XX 4 Indian

January–February 1941: British
re-take Kassala and Gallabat

ERITREA

Tigre

X Gideon
Force

Gallabat XX

Amba Alagi

Gondar

Lake
Tana

Amhara

Dessie

SAUDI
ARABIA

Y E M E N

San'a

ADEN PROTECTORATE

Haura

Mocha

19 Aug 1940:
British evacuation

Aden

Gulf of Aden

FRENCH
SOMALILAND

5 August 1940: French
Somaliland loyal to Vichy

Djibouti

XX

Karin

Berbera

July–August 1940: Italians
invade British Somaliland

BRITISH
SOMALILAND

6 April 1941: Addis Ababa
liberated by British troops

Gimbi

Addis Ababa

Dire Dawa

Harar

28 March 1941: Dire Dawa
falls to the British

Jijiga

XX

ETHIOPIA
(ABYSSINIA)

Jimme

Walwal

Galladi

Soddou

ANGLO–
EGYPTIAN
SUDAN

Neghelli

Lavello

Obbia

Belet Uen

ITALIAN SOMALILAND

Lake
Rudolph

Mega

Lugh

Moyale

XX 1 South
African

15 July 1940: British
recapture Hoyale

UGANDA

Villagio Ducas
Degli Abruzzi

Wajir

Mogadishu

25 February 1941: British
capture Mogadishu

K E N Y A

Tanaland

Juba

Brava

FORCE F
Royal Navy
support force

XXX
SOUTHERN FORCE
CUNNINGHAM

11 February 1941: British
attack Italian Somaliland

Lake
Victoria

X 1 South
African

Nairobi

XX 11 African

Kismayu

XX 12 African

I N D I A N

O C E A N

0   100 km
0   100 miles

N

Campaign in East Africa
June 1940–November 1941

Italian attacks

Ethiopian counterattacks

Allied attacks

Allied withdrawal

TANGANYIKA

Iraq, Syria, and Persia 1941

"YOU DO NOT NEED TO BOTHER TOO MUCH ABOUT THE LONG FUTURE IN IRAQ. YOUR IMMEDIATE TASK IS TO GET A FRIENDLY GOVERNMENT SET UP IN BAGHDAD, AND TO BEAT DOWN RASHID ALI'S FORCES WITH THE UTMOST VIGOR."

CHURCHILL TO WAVELL, 9 MAY 1941

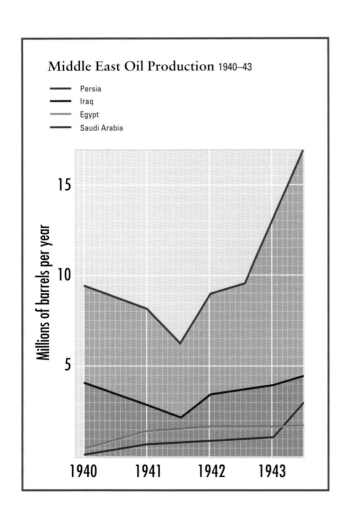

Middle East Oil Production 1940–43

— Persia
— Iraq
— Egypt
— Saudi Arabia

Millions of barrels per year

15

10

5

1940   1941   1942   1943

Despite victories in north-east Africa, the British position in the region remained precarious. The German invasion of Yugoslavia and Greece had forced the British to withdraw to the island of Crete, which was itself under threat of invasion. Rommel and his Afrika Korps had advanced from El Agheila, in Libya, to the western border of Egypt. The British garrison in the Libyan town of Tobruk was also besieged by the Axis forces.

In April 1941, in addition to all these separate campaigns faced by the British and Commonwealth forces, a new problem arose—Iraq—a British mandate until 1932 when it gained full independence. Under an agreement with Iraq, British garrisons still remained. The pro-British Regent, Emir Abdullah and his government wished to declare war on Germany but nationalist factions wanted concessions from the British first. On 3 April the Emir was overthrown in a coup led by the pro-Axis General, Rashid Ali. The General objected to the arrival of the 10th Indian Division sent to secure the vital oilfields around Basra. The British had treaty rights to the port of Basra and his objections were ignored, so he ordered his troops to surround the British airbase at Habbaniya, some 50 miles west of Baghdad. On 2 May British aircraft bombed Iraqi positions, the Iraqi forces replied with artillery fire bombarding the British base. After some intense pressure from London,

A British armored column drives through the Khyber Pass on its way to occupy Persia (Iran). Britain and Russia coerced Persia into excepting Allied protection.

Projected German Advances
Late 1941–1943

→ Line of advance

Territorial control November 1942

Axis

Allied

PROJECTED GERMAN ADVANCES
After the capture of Crete and Rommel's advance into Egypt, Hitler saw the strategic possibilities of taking control of, not only the Soviet oilfields in the Caucasus, but also of linking up with his forces advancing from the Mediterranean and north Africa and seizing the oilfields of the Middle East.

General Wavell, the area commander, agreed to send a relief force to Habbaniya.

"Habforce" was created out of the scarce troops available, mostly units of the 1st British Cavalry Division based in Palestine. This scratch force left on 13 May crossing the desert terrain in temperatures of 120°F, arriving at Habbaniya on 18 May in time to find the Iraqis already withdrawing. The British advance was attacked by Luftwaffe aircraft operating from bases in Syria and northern Iraq, but nevertheless they secured Habbaniya and continued on to take Baghdad, while in the south the 10th Indian Division pacified the area around Basra. Meanwhile General Rashid Ali and his pro-Axis clique fled to Persia (Iran) and Emir Abdullah was restored on 30 May.

Evidence of German involvement in the region caused British Prime Minister Churchill grave concern, anxious that the Germans should not be allowed the opportunity to develop a new front from the Vichy French-controlled Syria and Lebanon. Churchill overruled the reluctance of Wavell (commander of the Middle East) to become involved in a new campaign. Charles de Gaulle, leader of the Free French forces, also lobbied for the invasion of Vichy-held Lebanon and Syria.

Wavell reluctantly did agree to commit part of the British 1st Cavalry Division, most of the 7th Australian Division and the Free French units—a total of 34,000 troops—to Operation Exporter. This operation began on 8 June, advancing along the coast road towards Beirut and over the mountains into Syria. Initially the advance was successful, but by 13 June the advance had stalled allowing time for the Vichy French forces to launch a counterattack. Bitter fighting followed but British control of the air and 'Habforce' from Iraq, advancing toward Homs and Aleppo, as well as two extra British Brigades from Palestine, overwhelmed the Vichy French forces who fell back from Damascus. Supported by naval gunfire the Australians broke through into the outskirts of Beirut and, in a fierce five-day battle, captured the city. With Vichy French forces already surrendering in eastern Syria, Dentz, the Vichy commander, was in a hopeless situation and signed an armistice on 14 July. Of his surviving 38,000 men, despite his appeals, only 5,700 joined de Gaulle's Free French forces.

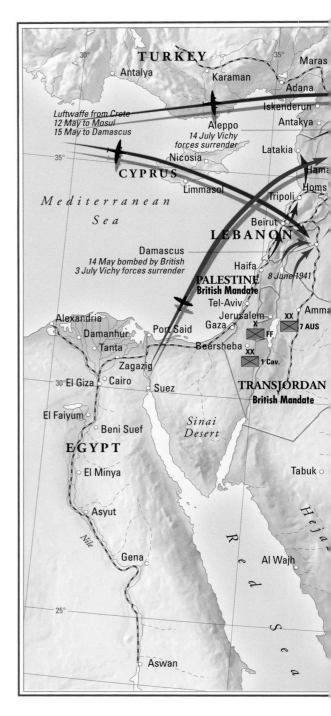

On 22 June Germany invaded the U.S.S.R. creating a new ally for the hard-pressed British. Determined to support its new ally, Britain in concert with the Soviets, entered the neutral country of Persia (Iran) on the night 24/25 August 1941. Soviet columns advanced southward from the Caucasus Mountains and from central Asia, east of the Caspian Sea. A British force advanced northward from the Persian Gulf and westward from Iraq and overland from India. Tehran was occupied on 17 September. The ruler of Persia, the Shah, put up only a token resistance and then ordered a ceasefire on 28 August. He abdicated and was taken by the British, firstly to a remote island in the Indian Ocean, and then to South Africa, where he died. Meanwhile his son, Mohammed Reza Pahlavi, had taken the throne. The strategic supply route to Soviet Russia and valuable oilfields were safely under Allied control.

Iraq, Syria and Persia
April – September 1941

→ Allied forces movements

→ Free French forces movements

→ Russian forces movements

↦ Allied bomber movements

↦ German bomber movements

- - → Allied supply routes

⛟ Oilfield

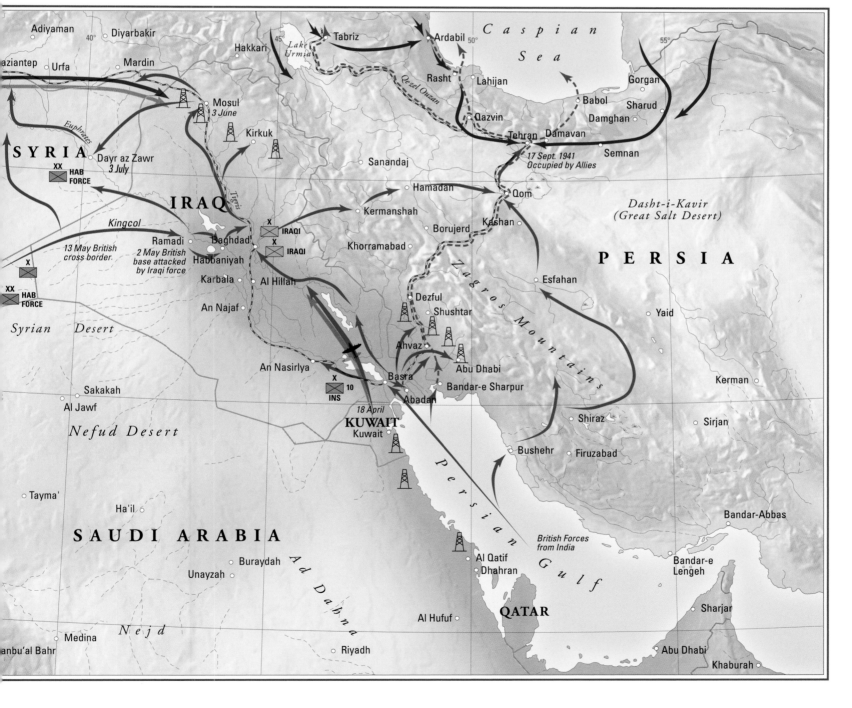

THE WESTERN DESERT 1940–43

"BEFORE ALAMEIN, WE HAD NO VICTORIES. AFTER ALAMEIN, WE HAD NO DEFEATS."

WINSTON CHURCHILL

With the insistence of Il Duce himself, Marshal d'Armata Rodolfo Graziani timidly pushed his troops over the border of Egypt with some five divisions of his 10th Army on 13 September. Facing these troops was the imaginative Lt-Gen Richard O'Connor who had under his command two very experienced and tough divisions, the 4th Indian Division and the tanks of 7th Armored Division. O'Connor's plan was to allow the Italians to advance up to the line of Mersa-Matruh and then using the 7th Armored that was in the south, punch north and cut their supply and command lines. However, the Italian advance halted at Sidi Barini, apparently having run short of fuel, and proceeded beginning to fortify its positions and stock up on food and wine, and await any counterattack.

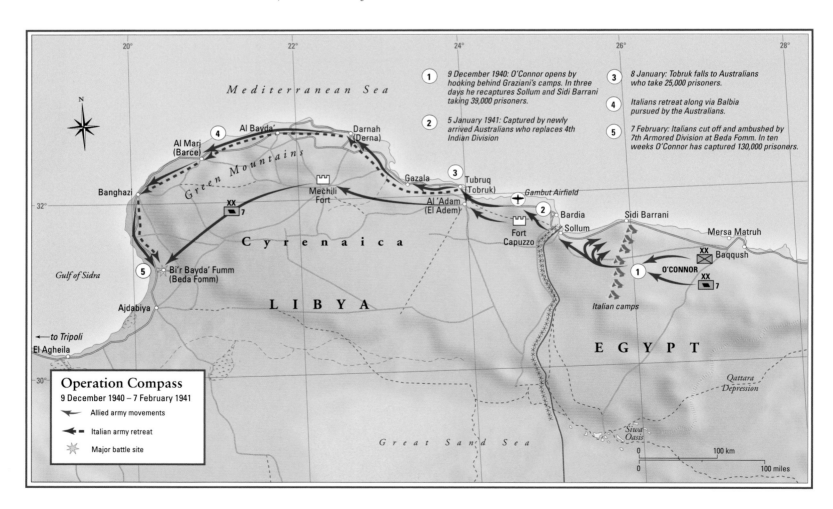

1. 9 December 1940: O'Connor opens by hooking behind Graziani's camps. In three days he recaptures Sollum and Sidi Barrani taking 39,000 prisoners.

2. 5 January 1941: Captured by newly arrived Australians who replaces 4th Indian Division

3. 8 January: Tobruk falls to Australians who take 25,000 prisoners.

4. Italians retreat along via Balbia pursued by the Australians.

5. 7 February: Italians cut off and ambushed by 7th Armored Division at Beda Fomm. In ten weeks O'Connor has captured 130,000 prisoners.

Operation Compass
9 December 1940 – 7 February 1941

- Allied army movements
- - Italian army retreat
- ✳ Major battle site

The counterattack came on 9 December when O'Connor launched Operation Compass, supposedly a five-day raid using both divisions at his disposal to attack the newly fortified Italian positions and to try and push them back to their original start line. They would then withdraw into the desert with as many prisoners as possible. The Royal Air Force and Royal Navy pounded the Italian positions prior to the attack as a diversionary tactic, while the forward elements of 7th Armored probed the Italian defenses for a weak spot to exploit. In the early hours of 9 December the attack began and surprise was total. Many of the Italians were still enjoying their breakfast as the tanks of 7th Royal Tank Regiment stormed past them and into their rear. The British were at Nibeiwa by noon, arriving at Sidi Barini soon after. Forward elements of 7th Armored arrived at the border wire on 10 December, which was an incredibly quick advance. Now the greatest problem facing the Allied advance was dealing with the 20,000 plus prisoners they had taken in such a short period of time. Camps were hastily erected. With this huge success, O'Connor realized that he could exploit the situation even further than he had originally anticipated, exploiting the reduction in Italian positions in Egypt. With 4th Indian Division having been taken out of the line in order to bolster forces in Ethiopia, the Australian 6th Division took its place, and 7th Armored were now circling north through the wire in order to cut the road between Bardia and Tobruk.

Bardia itself was assaulted by the newly-arrived Australians on 3 January, and within three days the Italian defenders had capitulated. Once again thousands of prisoners were taken by the Australian division, with elements of 7th Armored reaching El Adem to eventually seal off Tobruk. The Australians were ready to assault Tobruk on 21 January and within a day and a half the city had fallen. Once again, hordes of prisoners trudged off to the PoW camps. Encouraged by the rousing advances and enormous amount of prisoners taken, O'Connor once again saw that he could take even more ground and perhaps push Italy out of North Africa altogether. So he gave the order for the Australians to push on to take Derna and for 7th Armored to take Mechili, so they could both advance on Benghazi. Both these objectives were achieved by 2 February but the forces needed a serious over-haul to all their vehicles and for the men to take a hard earned rest. This would entail at least five days to refit all the tanks with new tracks and engines, to allow the infantry to restore some strength and to allow for supplies to catch up with them. But before any of this could happen the order came through for the men to advance yet again. The orders were for the Australians to push round the coastal road and to chase the Italians into a trap, which would be set by an armored force that would motor across the desert and cut the road from Benghazi to Tripoli at Beda Fomm. By 5 February a rifle brigade had established a road block with supporting artillery and armored cars, all with as much

Matilda tanks move forward. These tanks, though slow and carrying only a 2-pounder main armament, were the best available to the British in the early part of the war.

Area of operations 1940–43.

ammunition as they could carry. Just after the British had taken up their positions, the first elements of the Italian withdrawal came upon them without even realizing they were there. The Italians took many losses under intense and accurate rifle and artillery fire. Soon more Italian troops were piling up behind the devastated first elements and the British riflemen had to make every round count as they began to run low on ammunition. Then they heard the encouraging sound of tanks attacking the flanks of the enormous Italian column. White flags began to appear as night fell on the battle but there were still many Italian soldiers with fight left in them. In the morning the British were greeted by the sight of 13 Italian M13 tanks approaching the road block, but these were soon dispatched by fire from the British, with the artillery expending the last of their ammunition on the tanks. This was to be the climax of Operation Compass, for the length of the entire column was an ocean of fluttering white flags.

The victory was immense for the British army and fantastic for the morale of the fighting soldier, as well as the people on the home front. O'Connor's desert army had taken 500 miles of territory, destroyed the Italian 10th Army and captured 130,000 prisoners. Losses on the Allied side amounted to 550 killed and 1,300 wounded. O'Connor and his men felt that they could continue with the advance but Wavell and Churchill had other plans: they were looking towards Greece and the Balkans, thus the opportunity for O'Connor's advance was lost.

Hitler saw that the Italians were close to a humiliating defeat in the desert, so he took steps to reinforce the Axis armies. On 12 February the first units of the German army arrived in the port of Tripoli, consisting of the 5th Light Division and the 15th Panzer Division. These were to be under the command of Major-General Erwin Rommel, who had received orders to join forces with the Italian army and create a blocking force to curb the advance of the British in the area of Buerat. Rommel had specific orders telling him that he had to hold this line and to advance no further until told otherwise. However, Rommel disliked defensive actions and after hearing that Norfilia and El Agheila were unoccupied, he managed to persuade the Italian General Garibaldi to take and defend these places, which had the added benefit of allowing him to assess the quality of his allies.

On the British front things were not going to plan; 7th Armored had been pulled back to Cairo and 6th Australian had been transferred to the fighting now occurring in Greece. O'Connor was also out of the fighting due to illness and his replacement, General Philip Neame, lacked any real tactical understanding. Under his command was a brigade of the 2nd Armored Division, whose tanks were almost at the end of their tether, and a brigade of Australian Infantry that was placed on the plain between Benghazi and El Agheila. When General Wavell saw the state of these forces he quickly moved them into a better defensible position and, confident that the Germans would have to wait for an extended period of time in order to build up sufficient stocks of fuel and ammunition, left for Cairo to rethink his strategy.

Rommel was not a soldier who liked to sit around; he was a man of action and convinced that the positions opposite him were weak. He gave the order for the newly-arrived 5th Light Division to take the fort and landing strip at El Agheila on 24 March. A week later Rommel advanced even further and took Mersa el Brega. When he heard from his reconnaissance aircraft that there was no opposition at Agedabia he ordered 5th Light to advance up to the town, where he duly set up his head-

"The Desert Fox," the nickname given by British troops to General Erwin Rommel, was admired and respected by both his own troops, his Afrika Korps and the soldiers who made up the British 8th Army.

quarters. Even though he only had limited amounts of troops (his Panzer Division was yet to arrive), Rommel prepared to advance further. He was surprised to see that there was no sign of any British armor, which was being held back until the full extent of Rommel's intentions had been seen. This gave him even more reason to carry on the advance. Against orders from Berlin, Rommel sent elements of 5th Light Division on a right hook through the desert, taking the opposite route to that taken by 7th Armored. This took the British by complete surprise and all the forces started to withdraw toward Egypt rather than be trapped in the net the Afrika Korps was casting. Worse still, forward elements of the 5th Light captured O'Connor (now returned to the front) and Neame, as they were on their way to try control the disaster that was approaching the British. With Benghazi being taken on 4 April and Derna on 7 April, everything that Operation Compass had achieved was lost, and the British were back to their original start lines. Mechili fell on 8 April and by the evening of the next day, forward reconnaissance units of 5th Light were almost at the Egyptian border.

A large contingent of Allied forces had stayed behind the advancing Germans in the port of Tobruk and their number swelled as more and more ad hoc units stumbled in to the haven over the next few days. The forces were mainly made up of Australians who had previously been holed up in Benghazi, supplemented by random British and Indian units. Rommel wanted to take this vital port so as to shorten his supply lines. He attacked the town on 10 April but was easily repelled thanks to the accurate artillery and rifle fire of the defenders and a sandstorm. He tried again on 16 April with a mixed force

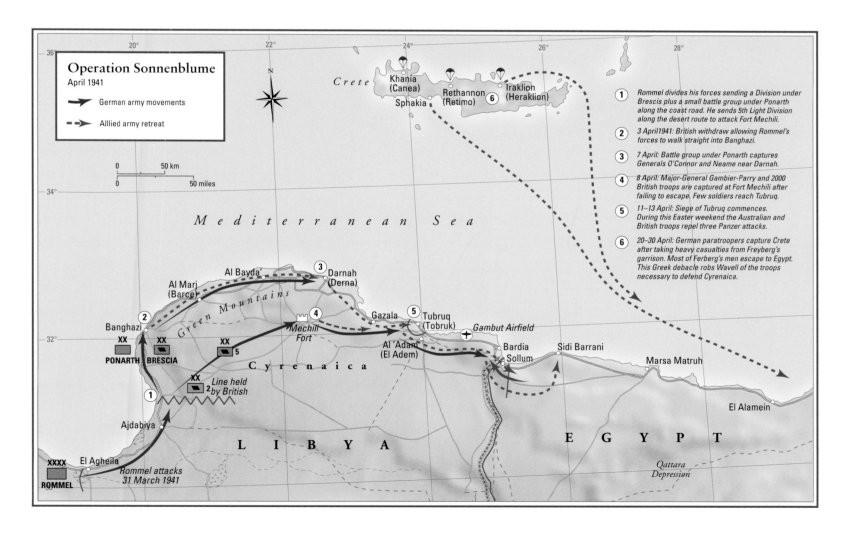

of German and Italian troops but, yet again, was repelled. After this Rommel decided to mop up any remaining opposing forces on the remainder of the battlefield and merely bypass Tobruk.

With all the Allied attention on the campaign in the Balkans it was difficult for the commander of 7th Armored to actually achieve anything against the rapidly growing Afrika Korps. The best he could do to halt their advance was by launching "Jock Columns," named after his second-in-command, Jock Campbell, which entailed mixed armored units probing the defenses of the Afrika Korps and generally making a nuisance. The British did, however, launch Operation Brevity which almost immediately failed as it was pitched against the newly-arrived 15th Panzer Division. Although still short of the majority of its armor, it had many anti-tank guns which ripped apart the British advance. On 27 May Rommel moved forward and took the Halfaya Pass with relative ease and proceeded to set up a massive anti-tank ring around the area using the formidable 88 mm cannon. The Allied position at this time was in a terrible state, both in the Balkans and in the western desert. Churchill promised that he would do all he could for the cause and promptly started stripping Britain of all the armor and aircraft that she could spare. In due course, 300 brand new tanks arrived along with 50 Hurricanes for the desert air force, ready for Operation Battleaxe to be launched.

A Crusader tank receiving tender, loving care from its crew. This tank was armed with a 2-pounder (40 mm) gun. The Crusader had a good turn of speed on the battlefield but its armor was relatively thin and needed careful maintenance to keep it in action.

The Allied tank formations swarmed ahead to do battle with the German tanks, but this was not how the German tankers fought; they merely withdrew from their original positions and drew the Allied tanks into a pre-arranged killing ground, enabling its anti-tank guns to tear them to shreds. This tactic was used by the Germans all along the front and within three days Wavell was issuing the order to call off the assault. When the Allied forces withdrew to their original start line they discovered that they had lost 50 percent of their tanks for absolutely no ground gained. This turn of events did not endear General Wavell to the Prime Minister, who expected results after stripping Britain of yet more of her defenses to aid him. Churchill could not just sack such a high-ranking officer, so he merely "swapped" Wavell with the commander-in-chief of India, General Auchinleck, who took command of the desert forces on 1 July 1941.

During Auchinleck's takeover Hitler had invaded Russia in Operation Barbarossa, and he felt this time would be well spent getting to know the men under his command and give to the soldiers a breather while Berlin's attention was elsewhere. This was not in accordance with the thoughts of Whitehall, who kept hassling Auchinleck to mount an offensive. But he stood his ground until he had accumulated sufficient troops and tanks to ensure success. This build up of troops was to become the 8th Army, which was made up of two Corps: the 8th and 30th. This Army was to be placed under the overall command of Lt-General Sir Alan Cunningham, who commanded more men and material than Rommel would in the entire desert campaign, and who had become obsessed with the capture of the besieged port of Tobruk.

On the morning of 19 November, Auchinleck was ready to unleash the power of the 8th Army. They crossed the wire with 8th driving north to attack the German and Italian garrisons from Sidi Omar all the way to the coast. The 7th Armored would advance north-west toward Bir el Gubi and to the relief of Tobruk, while 4th Armored Brigade held the ground between these two forces to the east of Gabr Saleh. By the end of the day 7th Armored were only ten miles from Tobruk but were not to get any closer, as the Italians defending this area were well dug in with anti-tank support. Rommel saw the purpose of the Allied attack, to relieve Tobruk, and personally led the counterattack against

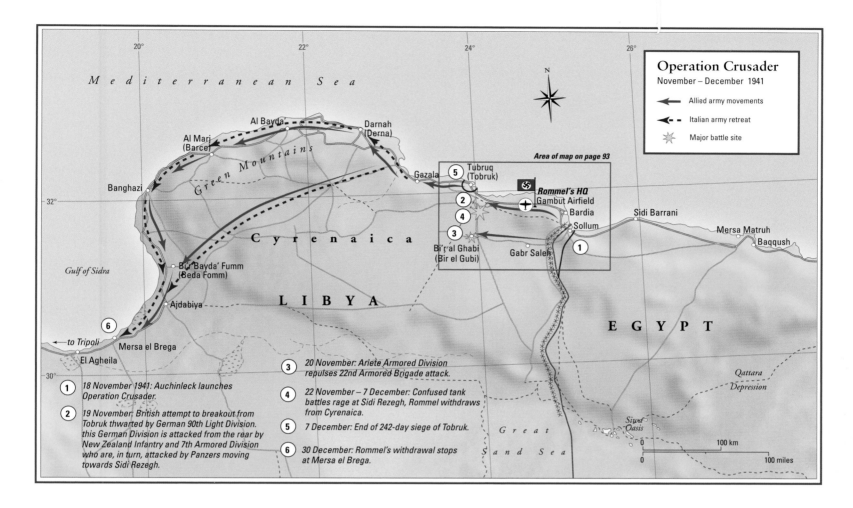

Operation Crusader
November – December 1941

←——— Allied army movements

◄- - Italian army retreat

✳ Major battle site

Area of map on page 93

Rommel's HQ
Gambut Airfield

① 18 November 1941: Auchinleck launches Operation Crusader.

② 19 November: British attempt to breakout from Tobruk thwarted by German 90th Light Division. this German Division is attacked from the rear by New Zealand Infantry and 7th Armored Division who are, in turn, attacked by Panzers moving towards Sidi Rezegh.

③ 20 November: Ariete Armored Division repulses 22nd Armored Brigade attack.

④ 22 November – 7 December: Confused tank battles rage at Sidi Rezegh, Rommel withdraws from Cyrenaica.

⑤ 7 December: End of 242-day siege of Tobruk.

⑥ 30 December: Rommel's withdrawal stops at Mersa el Brega.

the British at El Duda. He then ordered 15th Panzer and 21st Panzer to join up and strike the 4th Armored Brigade, sending them reeling back with many casualties. The Panzer Divisions then swung north-west to strike the 7th at Sidi Rezegh which the Germans retook on 22 November and left the 8th Army a shattered mess with small units isolated and left to their own devices to try to make it back to Allied lines. While the 8th Army was in disarray, Rommel took this chance to "race for the wire" with 21st Panzer in the lead and 15th Panzer in close support. These formations crossed the British lines with relative ease but the Allied formations that had been bypassed by Rommel were now reforming behind him and managed to link up with the defenders of Tobruk on 26 November. With the devastation in front of him, Cunningham could not cope so he was quickly replaced by Auchinleck with Major-General Neil Ritchie. Realizing that he had left the Allied army undefeated to his rear, Rommel gave the order for his two Panzer Divisions to make a general retreat as far as Gazala, but when he realized there was no suitable defense line he fell back to the Gulf of Sirte, thus bringing to an end what became known as "Operation Crusader."

The Afrika Korps were quick to dust themselves down after the rapid retreat it had just undertaken, and Rommel realized that the Allied supply lines were now the ones being stretched over the vast expanse of the desert. With the Korps retreating as far as El Agheila they soon regrouped and readied for a major counteroffensive. Over the Christmas period more vital Panzers had been delivered and, even more importantly, fuel. Rommel chose to strike in the early hours of 21 January and by the second day they had reached Agedabia, easily breaking through the Allied columns which were still dis-

Many Afrika Korps prisoners were taken during the course of Operation Crusader.

organized and used to chasing the retreating Germans. By 2 February Barce, Marawa, and Derna had been recaptured with Timini and Mechili falling on 6 February. The Afrika Korps took many prisoners and also enjoyed the contents of all the Allied stores that had been built up, restoring the honor of the Korps.

Rommel brought his advance to a halt in a line with Timini while he restocked his army with fuel, replacements, and ammunition for the final push into Egypt. While this was occurring he sent reconnaissance units to probe forward and test the Allied defenses. The Allies were digging in along a line running south from the Gazala inlet all the way to the Foreign Legion outpost at Bir Hakeim, with the main strength of the defense being placed in the center and north of the line. The Allies laid deep minefields in front of their positions and the Germans realized that it would take a major offensive to break the line, especially in the north and center sections. Auchinleck wanted the 8th Army to take an offensive movement again but he realized that this could not be done without vast stockpiles of men and material, so he started feeding these forward. He also began setting up a strong reserve force that could be utilized to repel any Afrika Korps attack. He felt this was best placed in the center of the defense, as this was where he thought Rommel would attack. Ritchie felt otherwise, considering that Rommel would try to bypass the defenses by swinging south into the open desert and striking their rear. He came up with a compromise so he could have reserves in the center as well as in the south, but this meant the reserves were kept in "boxes" behind the mainline of defense but in easy reach when called upon.

Just as Ritchie had predicted, Rommel launched his attack around the southern end of the defenses and was soon devastating the "boxes" of the reserve formations. Many were simply annihilated. These moves were made by 21st Panzer and 15th Panzer with the 90th Light and the Italian Ariete Divisions covering their flanks. Their successful attack was soon brought to a halt, not by the Allied defense, but yet again by lack of fuel and ammunition, although losses had been surprisingly light. The problem of supply to the forward elements was exacerbated by the bypassed troops of the 8th Army attacking the columns bringing up the important supplies. But this was not to hold for long as the Allied units retreated in disarray through Tobruk and then onto the Egyptian border, sometimes moving right through positions occupied by German troops.

General Auchinleck, looking at the situation on 15 June, decided to order a defensive line to be held from Tobruk through El Adem to El Gubi. This was not to be broken by the Germans and Tobruk was not to fall. But Rommel was obsessed with the capture of this port which had been denied him several times before; this time he must be victorious. He first needed supplies and saw the huge Allied supply dump near the R.A.F. airfield at Gambut in Belhammed. This would feed his hungry troops and thirsty tanks. Rommel ordered 21st, 90th Light, and the Ariete Divisions to move through the still scattered Allied defenses and attack the dump from the south, which was being defended by the 20th Indian Brigade. It was in German hands by the early afternoon, with counterattacks being easily fought off. With the airfield at Gambut also in his hands, Rommel was once again ready to assault Tobruk.

Tobruk had been reinforced by the arrival of the 2nd South African Division commanded by Major-General Klopper and was kept in reserve in readiness for yet another assault on the port. The attack came as dawn broke on 20 June in the south-eastern quarter of the defenses. This was lucky for Rommel, as this happened to be one of the weaker spots. The Allied commanders had expected any attack to come from the south-west. The Germans easily picked their way through the minefield that had been plundered to increase the strength of the defenses in the west and overran the 2nd/5th Mahrattas, who were completely wiped out. Rommel himself was in the center of the town by lunchtime and Klopper was on the back foot with no idea how to remedy the situation. Within 24 hours Klopper decided that it was not worth the slaughter of his men. He gave the order to hoist a white flag above the brigade headquarters, much to the disgust of the ordinary soldier who had been waiting for the order to counter that never came. The Allies were defeated with 30,000 surrendering, Rommel's success saw him promoted to the rank of Field Marshal.

The victory was not enough for Rommel, who now wanted to keep up his advance all the way to the River Nile and to complete the Allied defeat in the desert. He immediately ordered his units to continue pushing back the Allied units, and to his fortune, Rommel captured yet more supplies as 90th Light drove into Fort Capuzzo. Now Rommel had no fuel problems. The Allies tried to create a holding line south of Mersa Matruh but this did not hold the 90th Light for very long and the Allied soldiers began to lose faith, both in what they were fighting for and in their immediate superiors.

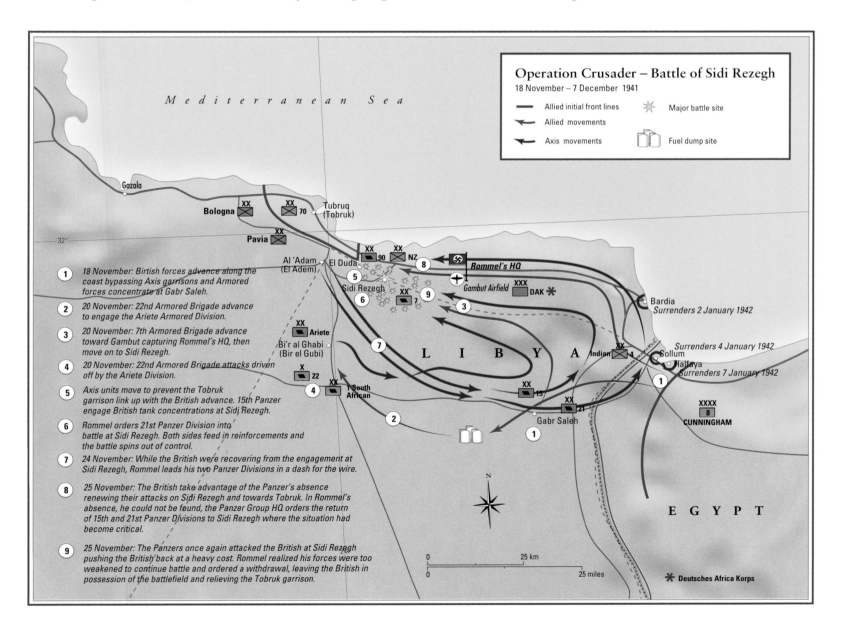

Operation Crusader – Battle of Sidi Rezegh
18 November – 7 December 1941

- Allied initial front lines
- Allied movements
- Axis movements
- ✳ Major battle site
- Fuel dump site

1. 18 November: British forces advance along the coast bypassing Axis garrisons and Armored forces concentrate at Gabr Saleh.

2. 20 November: 22nd Armored Brigade advance to engage the Ariete Armored Division.

3. 20 November: 7th Armored Brigade advance toward Gambut capturing Rommel's HQ, then move on to Sidi Rezegh.

4. 20 November: 22nd Armored Brigade attacks driven off by the Ariete Division.

5. Axis units move to prevent the Tobruk garrison link up with the British advance. 15th Panzer engage British tank concentrations at Sidi Rezegh.

6. Rommel orders 21st Panzer Division into battle at Sidi Rezegh. Both sides feed in reinforcements and the battle spins out of control.

7. 24 November: While the British were recovering from the engagement at Sidi Rezegh, Rommel leads his two Panzer Divisions in a dash for the wire.

8. 25 November: The British take advantage of the Panzer's absence renewing their attacks on Sidi Rezegh and towards Tobruk. In Rommel's absence, he could not be found, the Panzer Group HQ orders the return of 15th and 21st Panzer Divisions to Sidi Rezegh where the situation had become critical.

9. 25 November: The Panzers once again attacked the British at Sidi Rezegh pushing the British back at a heavy cost. Rommel realized his forces were too weakened to continue battle and ordered a withdrawal, leaving the British in possession of the battlefield and relieving the Tobruk garrison.

✳ Deutsches Africa Korps

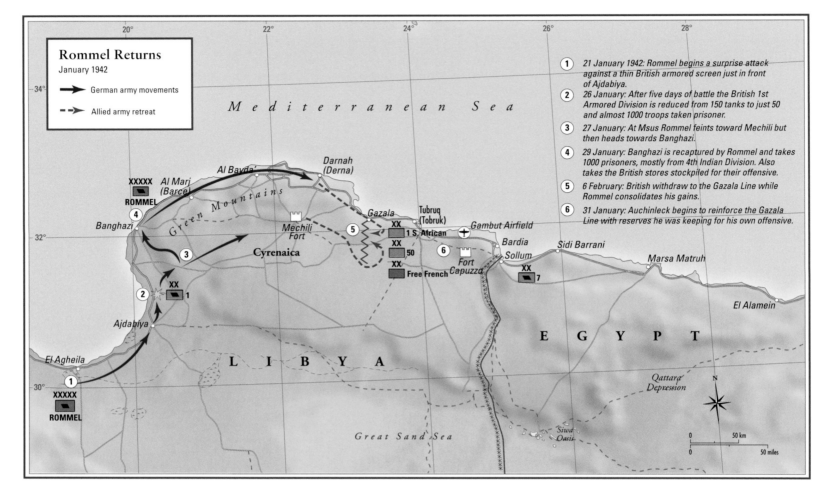

Rommel Returns
January 1942

→ German army movements

--→ Allied army retreat

① 21 January 1942: Rommel begins a surprise attack against a thin British armored screen just in front of Ajdabiya.

② 26 January: After five days of battle the British 1st Armored Division is reduced from 150 tanks to just 50 and almost 1000 troops taken prisoner.

③ 27 January: At Msus Rommel feints toward Mechili but then heads towards Banghazi.

④ 29 January: Banghazi is recaptured by Rommel and takes 1000 prisoners, mostly from 4th Indian Division. Also takes the British stores stockpiled for their offensive.

⑤ 6 February: British withdraw to the Gazala Line while Rommel consolidates his gains.

⑥ 31 January: Auchinleck begins to reinforce the Gazala Line with reserves he was keeping for his own offensive.

Auchinleck duly sent Ritchie home and took command of the battle himself, restoring some faith in the infantry soldier although not immediately stemming the German advance.

By 29 June, Italian and German forces were well past Mersa Matruh and the two Panzer Divisions were striking south-west toward El Quseir. The only thing between Rommel and certain victory was a wire defense line around a railroad station at El Alamein. Rommel saw no reason why the hungry and tired Afrika Korps could not push through one last defense and reach the coveted Nile delta and the promise of victory and spoils. As the 90th Light Division set off for this final push they were hit by bombs from the desert air force and then hit again by a massive bombardment from every artillery piece Auchinleck could draw on. This stopped the 90th in their tracks and panic began to filter through their ranks for the first time. Rommel came up to the line personally. After a few days of minor skirmishes the two sides withdrew a short distance to catch their breath, before the British artillery opened up again, tearing apart the Axis opposition followed by a sweep by the 9th Australian Division, which succeeded in pushing the Germans further back. Auchinleck had succeeded in stopping the Afrika Korps but it was by no means defeated.

The 3 August saw the arrival of Churchill himself, and he immediately held meetings with General Auchinleck and his staff to see for himself what plans were being put in place. He was not impressed by what he saw, and although he had great respect for Auchinleck, he sacked him. His replacement was to be General Sir Harold Alexander with Lt-General "Strafer" Gott taking command of the 8th Army, replacing Ritchie. But on his way to Cairo, Strafer's plane was attacked and shot down. As he tried to save his fellow passengers, he was killed by the returning fighters. He would be sorely missed by everyone in the 8th Army. In turn Gott's replacement was to be Lt-General Sir Bernard Law Montgomery. Perhaps a man with some character faults, he was a great soldier and soon busied himself by visiting as many of the front line units that he could. This was a great morale booster for the troops as they rarely, if ever, saw a General in their midst.

Montgomery was to predict that the Afrika Korps would try to attack and break the line of defense and was confident that this could be stopped. Then it would be the turn of the 8th Army to drive the Germans back. Rommel launched this attack on 30 August and immediately ran into trouble. The Germans were subjected to constant bombing from R.A.F. Wellington bombers and a wall of antitank and artillery fire laid down by the 25-pounders of the Royal Artillery. Also the British tanks were not being lured out into open ground for the German 88's to pick off and were, instead, used as mobile artillery to support any waning defense. With nightfall the Germans thought they would get some respite from the bombardment but this was not to be; it was to continue until 4 September, when Rommel gave the order for his troops to start a withdrawal to their original lines, leaving behind hundreds of destroyed vehicles of all types and thousands of dead. Now Rommel had to await the next move that would surely come from Montgomery, but ill health would force the German General to be airlifted back to the Fatherland for rest and recuperation, leaving the experienced General Stumme in charge of the Afrika Korps.

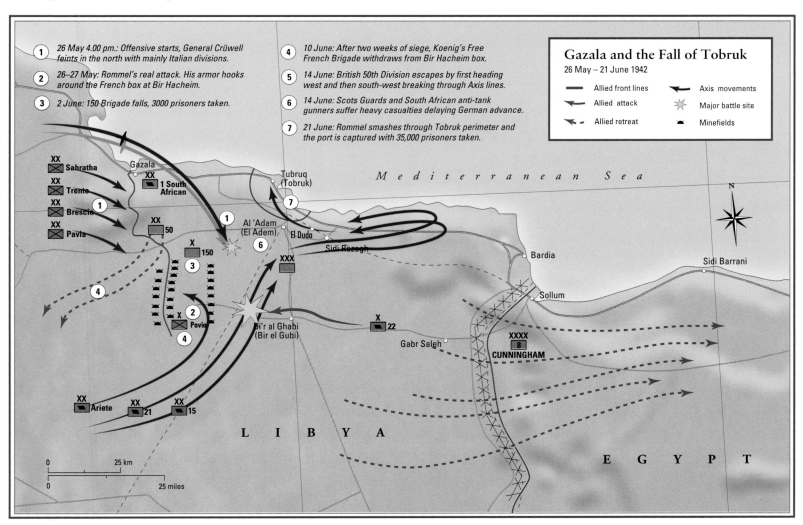

A German soldier laying land mines. By October 1942, the Germans had laid hundreds of thousands of mines, defending their positions facing Montgomery's 8th Army.

On the night of 23 October nearly 900 guns of the Royal Artillery of all calibers opened fire on the German and Italian rear echelon, hoping to cause maximum disruption to command and supply lines. Once this was accomplished the barrage fell back in front of the ready to advance Allied troops and then began to creep forward with them. On the right of the advance was 9th Australian Division and to their left were the Scots of the 51st Highland Division, then two brigades of New Zealanders with the 9th Armored Brigade. The Miteiriya Ridge was their main objective. The sappers were the first to go forward to clear paths through the extensive minefields that had been laid down by the enemy, sometimes two miles deep. This was not an easy task as the German counter barrage was stepping up. Through these paths, marked by white tape, the infantry advanced and started to clear positions of the enemy. By the morning of 24 October, most of the objectives had been taken, and they began to dig in and wait for the armor to move up and support them. But behind the infantry there was absolute chaos as the armor tried to advance up the narrow tracks through the minefields. If one was blocked by a damaged or destroyed vehicle this would cause massive bottlenecks, becoming easy prey for the German long-range artillery. With the armor still not able to reach the infantry in the front, the battle was beginning to stall. However, Montgomery still wanted them to advance to reach more defensible positions for the inevitable Axis counterattack. Rommel arrived back on 25 October and immediately ordered his 21st Panzer to move up north to try to hold the Allied advance, but they burnt up precious fuel doing so. Montgomery organized the armor he needed to draw in as many Axis tanks and infantry as possible, in order to wear them down in a war of attrition where he clearly outnumbered the opposition. He ordered the 9th Australian Division to break out towards Tel el Eisa, and this achieved his aim, as it drew many Axis tanks and infantry into that sector.

The 2nd Battalion, the Rifle Brigade, advanced to a forward position known as "Snipe" on the night of 26 October with the orders to hold a defensive position until relieved by advancing armor. This armor did arrive but attracted so much artillery fire that they were forced to retire. All around the Snipe position were advancing Axis armor and the 2nd Battalion were able to take a vicious toll on the enemy, thanks to the 19 6-pounders that were attached to the unit. After a hard engagement that lasted all day the Snipe position claimed 34 armored vehicles, damaging many more and causing the counterattack to falter.

Rommel began to prepare to fall back but first had to break his troops out of a salient holding out near Tel el Eisa. For this task he made an assault group from 21st and 90th Light Divisions, which were immediately attacked by bombers of the R.A.F. but still went forward into the attack. They took a heavy

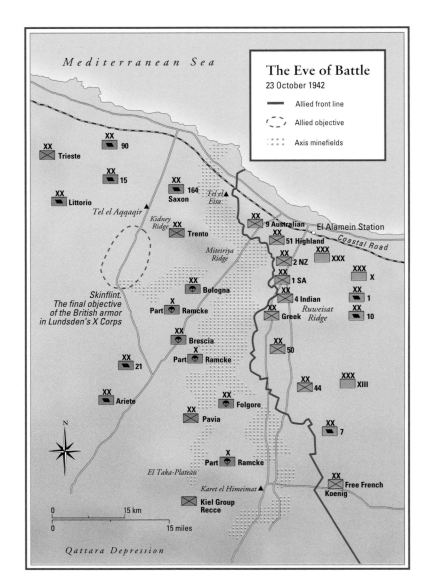

The Eve of Battle
23 October 1942

—— Allied front line
⌐ ⌐ ⌐ Allied objective
∶∶∶∶ Axis minefields

Mediterranean Sea

Trieste

90

15

164 Saxon

Littorio

Tel el Aqqaqir

Tel el Eisa

Kidney Ridge

Trento

9 Australian

El Alamein Station

51 Highland

Coastal Road

Miteiriya Ridge

2 NZ

1 SA

Bologna

Part Ramcke

4 Indian

Ruweisat Ridge

Greek

Skinflint.
The final objective of the British armor in Lundsden's X Corps

X

XXX

1

10

Brescia

Part Ramcke

50

21

44

XIII

Ariete

Folgore

Pavia

7

N

Part Ramcke

El Taka-Plateau

Free French Koenig

Karet el Himeimat

Kiel Group Recce

0   15 km
0   15 miles

Qattara Depression

toll on the defending Australians with the support of some Rhodesian Valentine tanks and they suc-ceeded in opening up a gap for their troops to escape. While this was occurring Montgomery was preparing for another massive thrust, again to be preceded by an enormous barrage. This was the opening of Operation Supercharge and was a smaller version of Operation Lightfoot. The infantry was to march forward, followed by an armored push to break out into the enemy's rear. But once again the armor had the same problems as before and were bogged down in the small tracks through the minefields. However, some units did get through and were led by the infantry through the night and over the Aqqaqir Ridge. By this time the sun was rising behind the tanks, silhouetting them and mak-ing easy prey for the German antitank gunners. But the advance had achieved what Montgomery required, as Rommel gave the order for the Afrika Korps to retreat just as Hitler's order to "Halt" came in. Rommel had no choice but to launch the 21st and 15th toward the enemy on 2 November and great losses were incurred on both sides. Montgomery had more reserves and Rommel now only had less than 40 serviceable tanks. The Afrika Korps had been beaten and by 4 November the Argyll and Sutherland Highlanders were at Tel Aqqaqir, the Battle of El Alamein was over and the tide of war was about to turn.

British tanks advance during Operation Supercharge, experiencing trouble passing through the dense minefields. Superior numbers swung the balance in favor of the British.

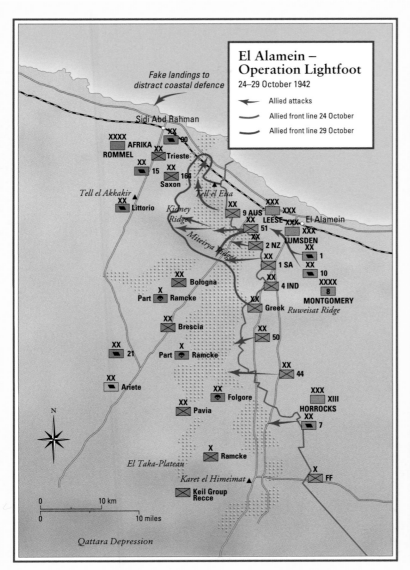

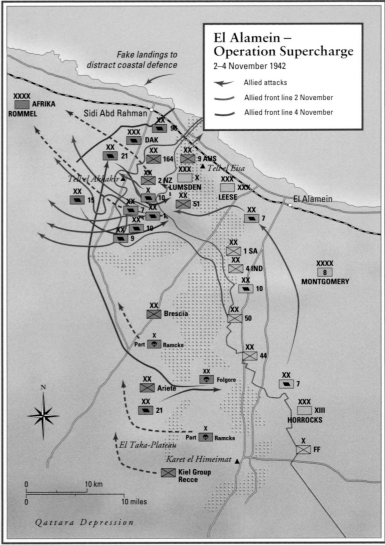

NORTHWEST AFRICA 1943

"EVEN WITHOUT THE ALLIED OFFENSIVE, I SHOULD HAVE HAD TO CAPITULATE BY 1 JUNE AT THE LATEST AS I HAD NO MORE FOOD TO EAT."

GENERAL OBERST VON ARMIN, MAY 1943,

AFTER AXIS SURRENDER IN TUNISIA

A fresh American army came into action for the first time in north Africa, 1943.

After the British victory at the Battle of El Alamein, British forces had pursued Rommel's Afrika Korps and their allies, the Italians, across north Africa from the Egyptian border, across Libya and into Tunisia. Rommel was organizing yet another defensive line when news arrived that an Anglo-American landing had been made along the northwest coast of Africa from Casablanca to Algiers, under the name Operation Torch.

The landing involved three Task Forces. The Western Task Force landed on the Moroccan coast between Safi and Mehdia, under the command of Major-General Patton. Center Task Force was landed at Oran under the command of Major-General Fredenhall; and finally the Eastern Task Force was landed at Algiers under the command of Lt-General Anderson. The Allies were unsure where the loyalties of the Vichy French troops lay and Major-General Mark Clark was smuggled ashore before the landings to clarify where the French stood. But in order to keep operational security, the information that Clark could give the French commanders was very vague. When the forces did land the French troops were unsure and sporadic firing did occur but caused minimum casualties. The French ended all resistance officially on 10 November.

British Bren-gunners holding a hilltop position at Mateur, in Tunisia, 1943.

The Allied advance across northwest Africa was rapid, even with the difficult terrain, and they linked up with the British and American paratroops that had been dropped to secure the airfields at Bone and Gafsa.

Hitler saw the new threat being posed in north Africa and immediately flew in reinforcements. By January there were over 100,000 German troops in western Tunisia. The Afrika Korps had now withdrawn behind the French-made defenses known as the Mereth Line, while Montgomery continued to regroup in Libya readying to outflank the position. But with the winter rains turning the desert into an almost impassable bog and the Allied supply lines being, in some places, over 200 miles long, the advance slowed.

While Montgomery built up his forces, Rommel turned his attention to the U.S. 1st Army at Kesserine Pass; it was to be a harsh introduction to the still unblooded troops of the American Army. Rommel left north Africa and his beloved Afrika Korps in secret, so as not to affect the morale of his troops. On 9 March the Afrika Korps came under the command of the Italian General Giovanni Messe's 1st Italo-German Panzer Army. The Germans, now under the command of General von Arnim, wanted to emerge in this sector in order to break apart the two ends of the pincer that was closing in on them. Faid was assaulted by the 21st Panzer and taken, then using the same trick that had fooled the British two years earlier, drew the U.S. tanks onto their antitank guns and destroyed over 100 tanks. What followed was an ugly retreat, with U.S., British, and French troops all intermingled. Then the Germans stopped the follow-up due to a disagreement between Rommel and his superiors. This allowed the Allies to regroup, enabling them to take up new positions, hold the renewed German assault and, within days, to recapture the ground they had lost.

On 20 March Montgomery opened up his attack on the Mereth Line and just over a week later the 1st Army took the offensive on the west and by early April elements of the U.S. 2nd Corps met with the 8th Army. With this link up the Germans and Italians were now trapped in an ever decreasing bridgehead with nothing on which to retreat. Even the Royal Navy was hampering any evacuation by sinking anything that sailed from the shores.

The final push of the Allied armies was all that was required to evict the enemy from Africa, with the armies now linked up, U.S. 2nd Corps in the north, the 1st Army in the center and the 8th Army in the southern sector. The battle commenced on 6 May with a massive artillery bombardment of the enemy positions in the center section, and the leading Indian division accomplished their task by the end of the day. With the road now open all the way to Tunis, von Arnim realized that the game was nearly up and, heavily outnumbered, he was captured on the 12 May. By then over 250,000 Axis troops had surrendered with the Allies and would take no further part in the fighting. After three hard years of fighting in extreme conditions the war in the north African deserts was finally at an end.

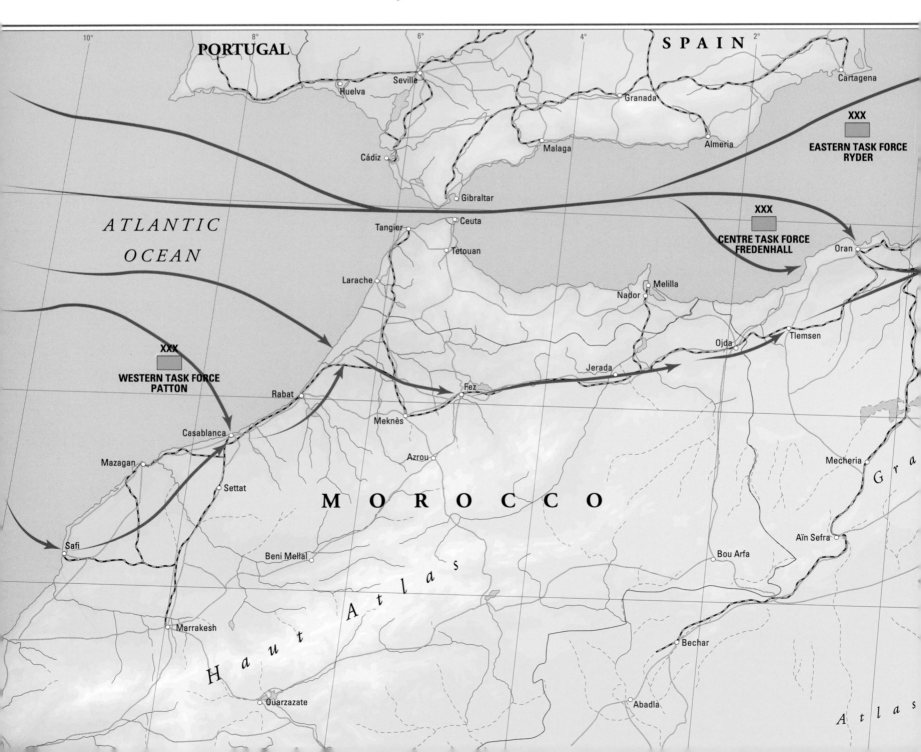

Abandoned by their German allies, thousands of Italians go into captivity near Tunis, 1943.

Operation 'Torch'
8 November 1942

⛛ Allied airborne dropping zone

→ Allied landings and attacks

→ German landings

〰 German defensive line

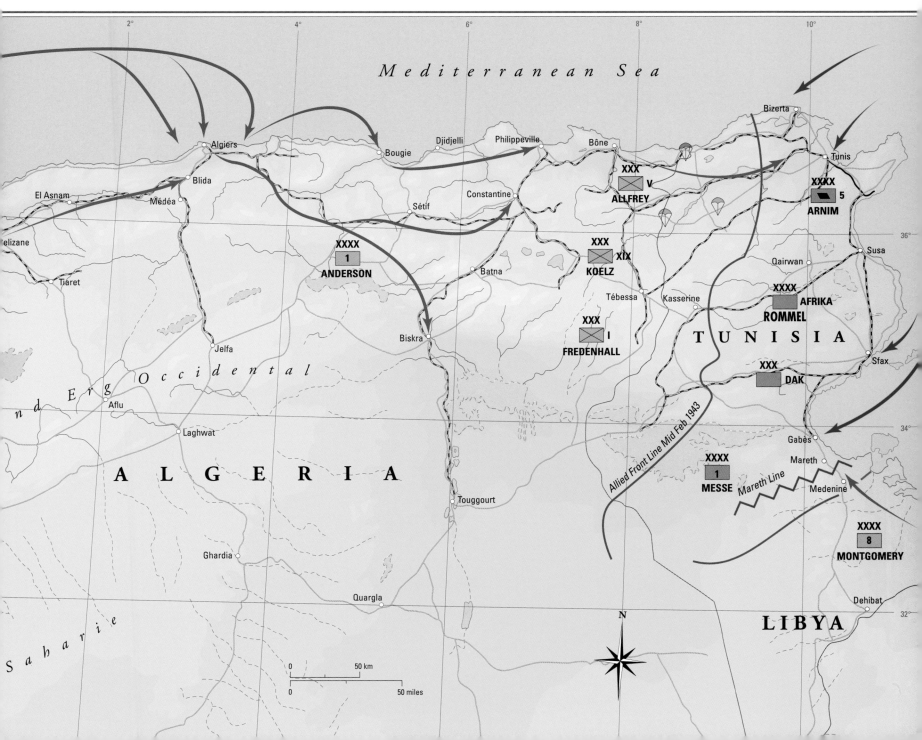

Mediterranean Sea

Bizerta

Algiers
Bougie
Djidjelli
Philippeville
Bône

Blida

El Asnam
Médéa

elizane
Sétif
Constantine

Tiáret

Batna

XXX
V
ALLFREY

XXXX
5
ARNIM

Tunis

XXXX
1
ANDERSON

XXX
XIX
KOÉLZ

Qairwan

Susa

Tébessa
Kasserine

XXXX
AFRIKA
ROMMEL

T U N I S I A

Jelfa

Biskra

XXX
I
FREDENHALL

XXX
DAK

Sfax

n d   E r g   O c c i d e n t a l

Aflu

Laghwat

Allied Front Line Mid Feb 1943

Gabès

Mareth

A L G E R I A

Touggourt

XXXX
1
MESSE

Mareth Line

Medenine

Ghardia

XXXX
8
MONTGOMERY

Quargla

Dehibat

S a h a r i e

LIBYA

N

0   50 km

0   50 miles

BATTLE OF THE ATLANTIC 1939–41

"AS THE BOWS WENT HIGHER SO DID THE SHRIEKS. I CLUNG TO A STANCHION FEELING SICK AND HELPLESS AS I HAD TO LOOK ON WHILE THE CHILDREN WERE SWEPT OUT INTO THE DARKNESS BELOW BY THE TORRENT OF WATER WHICH ROARED THROUGH THE SMOKING-ROOM."

ADMIRAL SIR K. CREIGHTON,
CONVOY COMMODORE

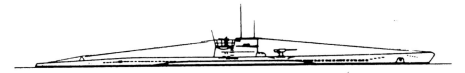

The Type VIIc U-boat was the mainstay of the German U-boat service throughout most of the war. They required a crew of 44 men and were armed with five 533 mm torpedoes, four bow tubes, one stern tube. They also carried one 88 mm gun and one 20 mm gun. The vessel was 220 feet long and had a displacement of between 750 and 850 tons. Though subject to various improvement as the war progressed, by 1943 they were out-classed by Allied submarine counter-measures. Five hundred and ninety-three units were completed and commissioned.

At the outbreak of the war in Europe, the German Navy began to apply the same war of attrition that had failed it in the First World War. This was based on the calculation that if 750,000 tons of Allied shipping, mostly British, could be sunk per month for twelve months then Britain would be forced into surrender by starvation.

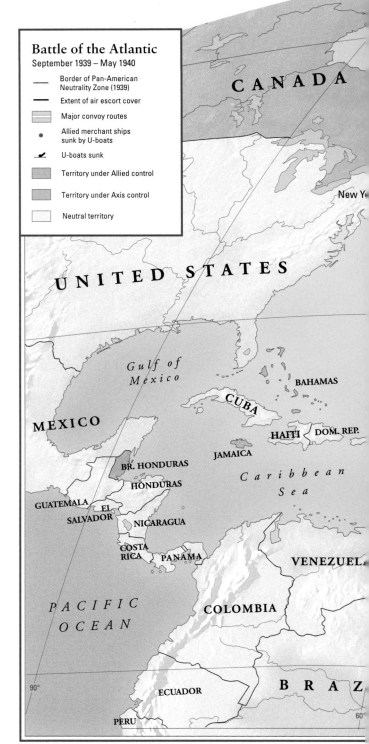

Battle of the Atlantic
September 1939 – May 1940

——	Border of Pan-American Neutrality Zone (1939)
▬	Extent of air escort cover
▤	Major convoy routes
•	Allied merchant ships sunk by U-boats
⬈	U-boats sunk
▨	Territory under Allied control
▨	Territory under Axis control
☐	Neutral territory

CANADA

New Y[ork]

UNITED STATES

Gulf of Mexico

BAHAMAS

CUBA

MEXICO

HAITI DOM. REP.

JAMAICA

BR. HONDURAS

Caribbean Sea

HONDURAS

GUATEMALA

EL SALVADOR

NICARAGUA

COSTA RICA PANAMA

VENEZUEL[A]

PACIFIC OCEAN

COLOMBIA

90°

ECUADOR

BRAZ[IL]

PERU

60°

Germany began the war with 57 U-boats. German naval planners required 350 but with the help of mines, aircraft, warships, and surface raiders, this total might be achieved. Against this force Britain could deploy 12 battleships and battlecruisers, six aircraft carriers, 58 cruisers and, most importantly, over 200 destroyers, and escorts with antisubmarine capabilities, as well as some 69 submarines. The

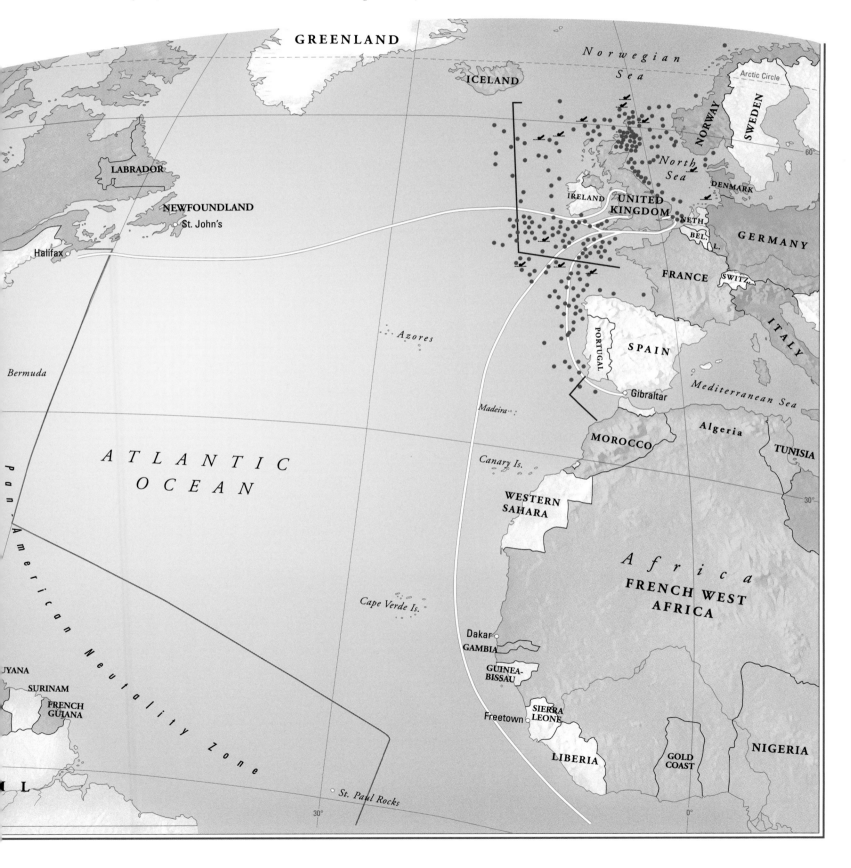

French navy could also help but its main task was to face the Italian Fleet in the Mediterranean.

In September 1939 the German navy, apart from two surface raiders out in the Atlantic, were unable to operate much further west than a few hundred miles off the British coast, an area known as the Western Approaches to the British Admiralty. The North Sea and the English Channel were about the limits of U-boat operations. Thus, the bulk of ships lost were in these areas. In the period from September 1939 to June 1940, 702 merchant ships were lost.

One of the raiders loose in the Atlantic Ocean was the *Admiral Graf Spee* commanded by Captain Hans Langsdorff. She had left her German port before war broke out and was well positioned to raid Allied commerce. She was supported by the supply ship the *Altmark*. During her cruise in the Indian Ocean and the South Atlantic, the *Graf Spee* sank nine merchant ships, then began to have problems with her engines. Captain Langsdorff planned a route back to Germany, but this would include a visit to the River Plate off the coast of South America where Langsdorff knew Allied convoys would gather. The British anticipated this and sent "Force G" (one of eight such groups formed to hunt down the surface raider). On sighting the three cruisers of "Force G" Langsdorff assumed they were merchant ships and steamed straight for them. Too late, he realized they were warships, although of inferior gun power. In the brief 80-minute battle all three cruisers were damaged but so was the *Graf Spee*. She sought the safety of Montevideo, in neutral Uraguay, to make repairs and bury her dead. The Uraguayans gave her permission for just 72 hours in port. Meanwhile the British reinforcements were on their way. Another cruiser arrived but Langsdorff was forbidden to intern his ship and, if he could not fight his way back to the Fatherland, was instructed to scuttle the ship. He was also misled by British radio signals into believing that a larger force awaited him. He scuttled the *Graf Spee* on 17 December and a few days later committed suicide. These events were greeted as a great victory by the British but the real threat to lines of supply and survival still lurked beneath the waves.

With the German conquest of Norway and later France in July 1940, the nature of the U-boat war in the Atlantic changed. In July at Lorient in western France the first U-boat base came into operation. Immediately the U-boats' route to their patrol area was reduced by some 450 miles. Not only could more of the available U-boats be on patrol for longer periods but a greater number of them could be kept in action. From the start of the war 25 U-boats had been lost but production had increased so, despite these losses, there were now 51 in service. In addition to the U-boats, the Germans possessed the first Focke-Wulf Condor, four-engine, long-range aircraft. These began operations from an airfield near Bordeaux in August 1940. Ranging far out into the Atlantic, they acted primarily as reconnaissance, reporting the positions and directions of Allied convoys. This task completed, they were then free to unload their bombs on any target of opportunity.

At this time most convoys had one or two escorts; these were primarily antisubmarine and could not perform any meaningful antiaircraft role. In the sky and

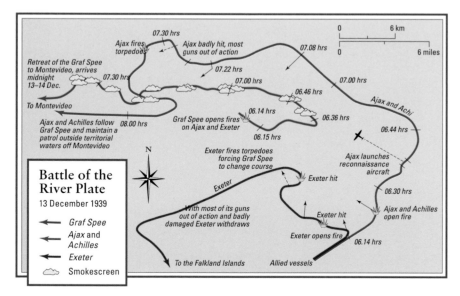

Battle of the River Plate
13 December 1939

Graf Spee
Ajax and Achilles
Exeter
Smokescreen

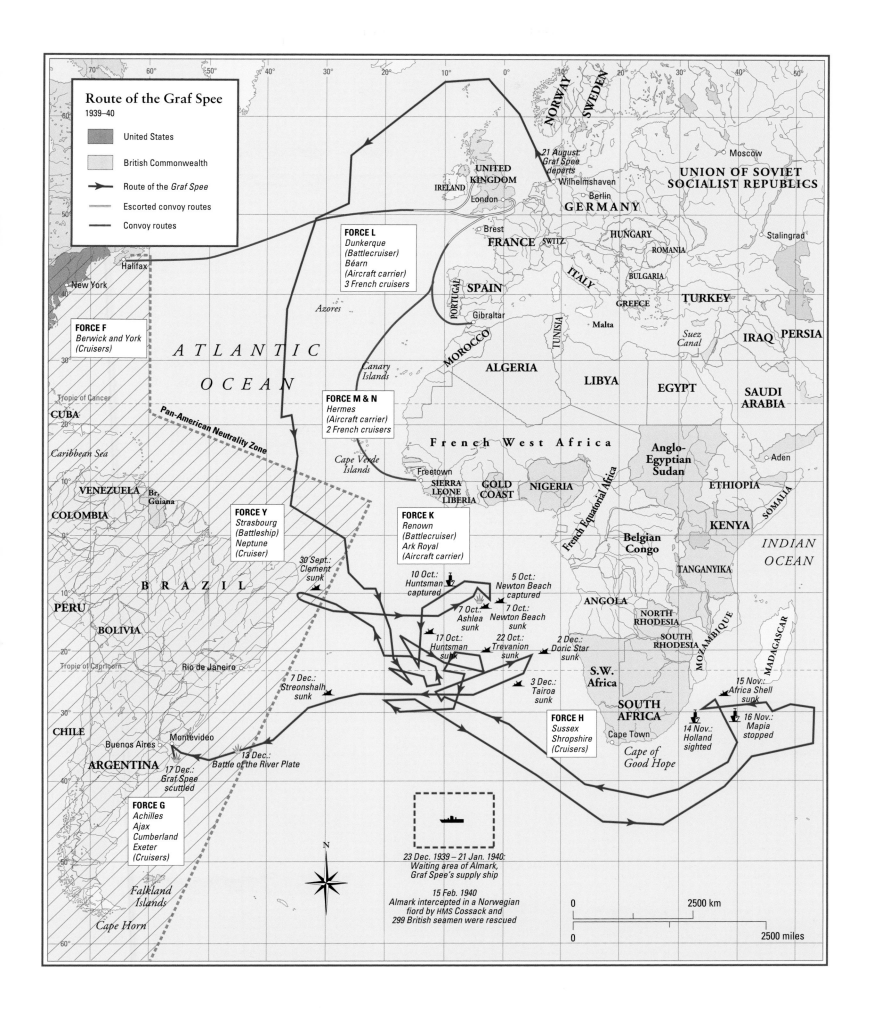

Route of the Graf Spee
1939–40

- United States
- British Commonwealth
- Route of the *Graf Spee*
- Escorted convoy routes
- Convoy routes

FORCE L
Dunkerque
(Battlecruiser)
Béarn
(Aircraft carrier)
3 French cruisers

FORCE F
Berwick and York
(Cruisers)

FORCE M & N
Hermes
(Aircraft carrier)
2 French cruisers

FORCE Y
Strasbourg
(Battleship)
Neptune
(Cruiser)

FORCE K
Renown
(Battlecruiser)
Ark Royal
(Aircraft carrier)

FORCE H
Sussex
Shropshire
(Cruisers)

FORCE G
Achilles
Ajax
Cumberland
Exeter
(Cruisers)

*21 August:
Graf Spee
departs*

*30 Sept.:
Clement
sunk*

*10 Oct.:
Huntsman
captured*

*5 Oct.:
Newton Beach
captured*

*7 Oct.:
Ashlea
sunk*

*7 Oct.:
Newton Beach
sunk*

*17 Oct.:
Huntsman
sunk*

*22 Oct.:
Trevanion
sunk*

*2 Dec.:
Doric Star
sunk*

*15 Nov.:
Africa Shell
sunk*

*3 Dec.:
Tairoa
sunk*

*14 Nov.:
Holland
sighted*

*16 Nov.:
Mapia
stopped*

*7 Dec.:
Streonshalh
sunk*

*13 Dec.:
Battle of the River Plate*

*17 Dec.:
Graf Spee
scuttled*

Pan-American Neutrality Zone

*23 Dec. 1939 – 21 Jan. 1940:
Waiting area of Almark,
Graf Spee's supply ship*

*15 Feb. 1940
Almark intercepted in a Norwegian
fiord by HMS Cossack and
299 British seamen were rescued*

0   2500 km

0   2500 miles

ATLANTIC OCEAN

INDIAN OCEAN

Caribbean Sea

NORWAY
SWEDEN
UNITED KINGDOM
IRELAND
London
Wilhelmshaven
Berlin
GERMANY
Brest
FRANCE
SWITZ.
Moscow
UNION OF SOVIET SOCIALIST REPUBLICS
Stalingrad
HUNGARY
ROMANIA
BULGARIA
PORTUGAL
SPAIN
Gibraltar
ITALY
GREECE
Malta
TURKEY
TUNISIA
MOROCCO
ALGERIA
LIBYA
EGYPT
Suez Canal
IRAQ
PERSIA
SAUDI ARABIA
Azores
Canary Islands
Cape Verde Islands
Freetown
SIERRA LEONE
LIBERIA
GOLD COAST
NIGERIA
French West Africa
French Equatorial Africa
Belgian Congo
Anglo-Egyptian Sudan
Aden
ETHIOPIA
SOMALIA
KENYA
TANGANYIKA
ANGOLA
NORTH RHODESIA
SOUTH RHODESIA
MOZAMBIQUE
MADAGASCAR
S.W. Africa
SOUTH AFRICA
Cape Town
Cape of Good Hope
Halifax
New York
CUBA
Tropic of Cancer
VENEZUELA
Br. Guiana
COLOMBIA
BRAZIL
PERU
BOLIVIA
Rio de Janeiro
Tropic of Capricorn
CHILE
Buenos Aires
Montevideo
ARGENTINA
Falkland Islands
Cape Horn
N

The U-47, *left*, commanded by Gunter Prien, returns from its successful sortie to Scapa Flow, where it sank HMS *Royal Oak*. U-47 was sunk on 7 March 1941 depth charged by HMS *Wolverine* with the loss of all hands.

The U-boats were joined briefly in the Atlantic by Germany's mighty new 42,000-ton battleship, the *Bismarck*, *above*. Although she sank the pride of the Royal Navy, HMS *Hood* in a short engagement in the Denmark Strait, she failed in her primary mission to intercept and destroy British convoys. The *Bismarck* was torpedoed and damaged by Swordfish aircraft flying from HMS *Victorious* and later sunk by ships of the British Home Fleet on 27 May 1941. This effectively ended the German Navy's use of its big ships on the Atlantic, though they remained a threat, especially to Arctic convoys sailing to Russia.

below the waves, the Germans seemed to hold the key to victory. Thousands of Allied merchant seamen lost their lives and cargoes which meant survival to Britain, ended up on the seabed.

German sinkings of Allied merchant ships reached a peak in April 1941, but as the convoy system became more widespread sinkings began to decline. The German naval code was now being read, thanks to the work of the cryptanalysts at Bletchley Park in England. The German plan to sink 750,000 tons of shipping per month was never consistently achieved. Britain also instituted careful rationing at home and a strict control of shipping space, reducing the country's import requirements by half during the course of the war. British escorts became more effective, now being joined by the growing Canadian Navy, forcing U-boats further out into the Atlantic beyond the range of patrol aircraft. As the U-boats moved west there was, however, the danger of meeting more U.S. merchant ships and warships which created the possibility of a clash with the U.S. Already U.S. warships were patrolling towards Britain and it was obvious that the Americans were deter-

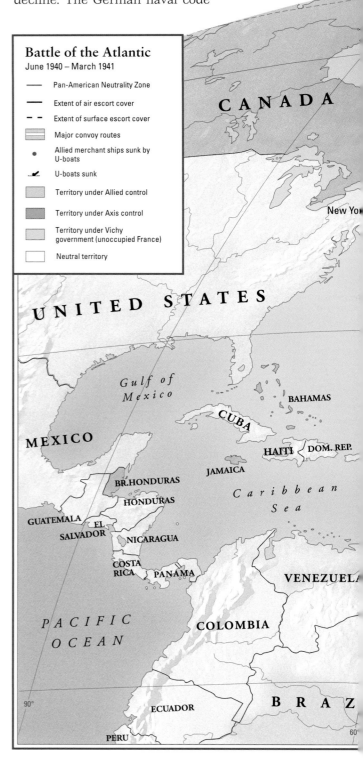

mined to aid Britain's survival. Hitler did not want to have any problems with the U.S.—not at this time—and with his armies gathering on the borders of the Soviet Union, he was happy for the U-boats to do their duty in the Atlantic. Hitler was looking eastward.

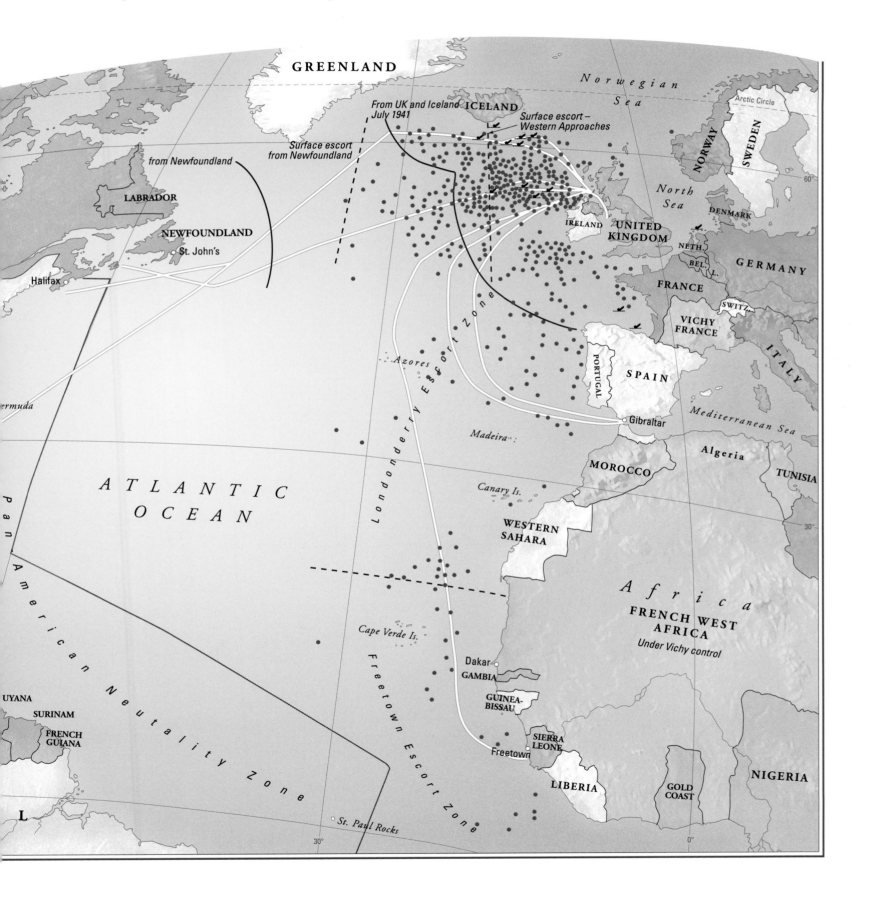

British, Allied, and Neutral Mercantile Losses
(from all causes) 1939–1941

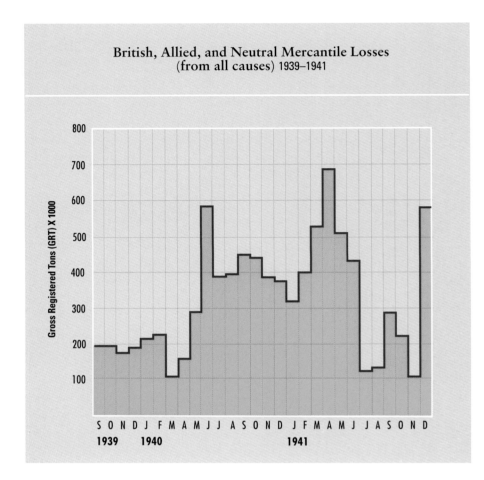

German plans called for the sinking of 750,000 tons of British or Allied ships supplying Britain per month, to force the country into starvation and surrender. In the period September 1939 to the end of 1941, the only time the U-boats came near this target was in April 1941. This recorded the fourth highest monthly loss rate of the entire war.

As the convoy system expanded and became better protected, sinkings by U-boats fell despite the fact that more U-boats were commissioned and available for action. The U-boats moved further westward, beyond the range of British patrol aircraft and where escorts were fewer, but the Battle of the Atlantic was by no means over.

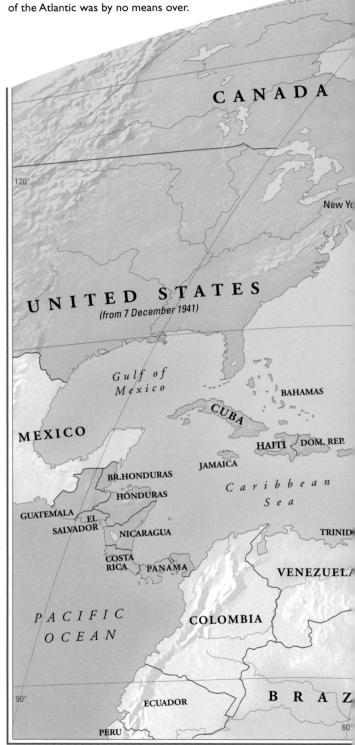

German U-boat Strength 1939–1941

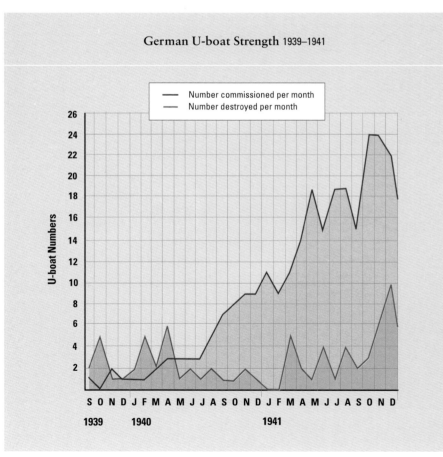

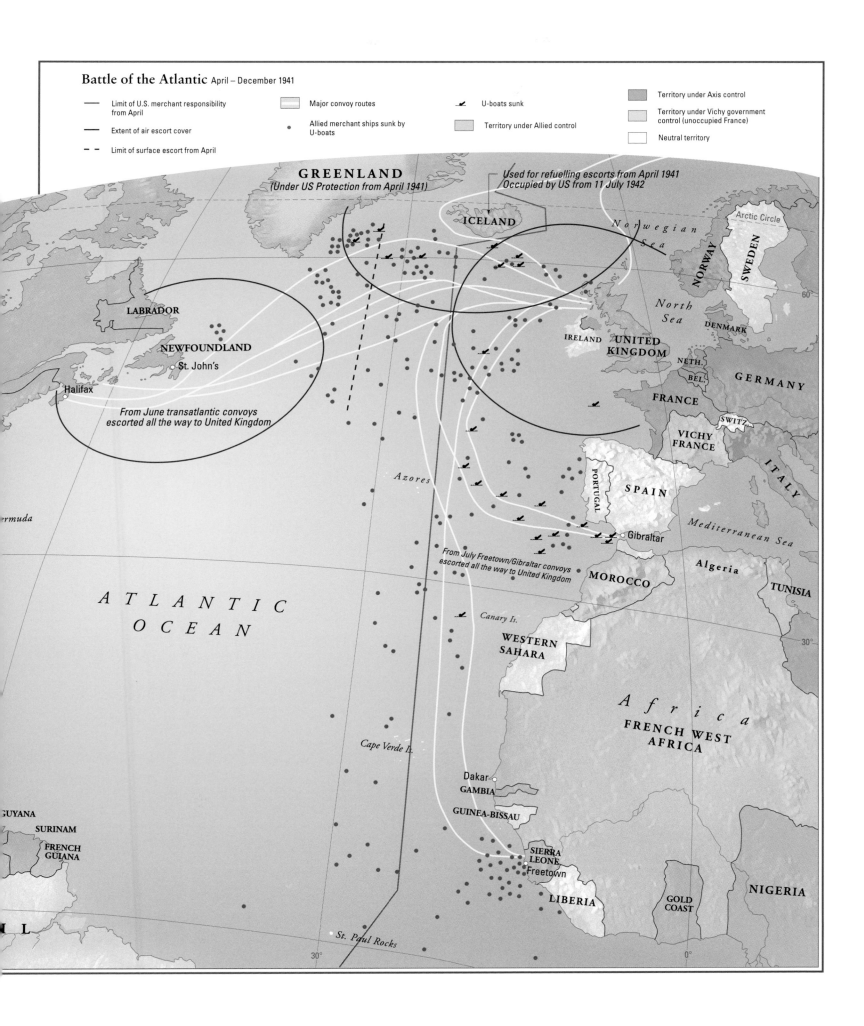

Battle of the Atlantic April – December 1941

--- Limit of U.S. merchant responsibility from April

— Extent of air escort cover

- - - Limit of surface escort from April

▭ Major convoy routes

• Allied merchant ships sunk by U-boats

⚓ U-boats sunk

▭ Territory under Allied control

▭ Territory under Axis control

▭ Territory under Vichy government control (unoccupied France)

▭ Neutral territory

GREENLAND
(Under US Protection from April 1941)

Used for refuelling escorts from April 1941
Occupied by US from 11 July 1942

ICELAND

Norwegian Sea

Arctic Circle

NORWAY

SWEDEN

LABRADOR

North Sea

DENMARK

NEWFOUNDLAND

St. John's

IRELAND

UNITED KINGDOM

NETH.

GERMANY

BEL.

Halifax

From June transatlantic convoys escorted all the way to United Kingdom

FRANCE

SWITZ.

VICHY FRANCE

ITALY

Azores

PORTUGAL

SPAIN

Mediterranean Sea

Gibraltar

From July Freetown/Gibraltar convoys escorted all the way to United Kingdom

MOROCCO

Algeria

TUNISIA

Bermuda

ATLANTIC
OCEAN

WESTERN SAHARA

Africa
FRENCH WEST AFRICA

Cape Verde Is.

GUYANA

SURINAM

FRENCH GUIANA

Dakar
GAMBIA

GUINEA-BISSAU

SIERRA LEONE
Freetown

LIBERIA

GOLD COAST

NIGERIA

St. Paul Rocks

THE INTELLIGENCE WAR

"THE KNOWLEDGE NOT ONLY OF THE ENEMY'S PRECISE STRENGTH AND DISPOSITION, BUT ALSO HOW, WHEN, AND WHERE HE INTENDS TO CARRY OUT HIS OPERATIONS BROUGHT A NEW DIMENSION TO THE PROSECUTION OF WAR."

FIELD MARSHAL SIR HAROLD ALEXANDER, ON ULTRA

Secure communications are a vital part of political and military organization; to meet this requirement, Germany invested in an encoding machine originally developed in the Netherlands. The original machine was intended for commercial use. However, with further development, this machine could be made "unbreakable," or so the Germans thought.

The "Enigma" machine was a kind of typewriter using notched rotors that utterly scrambled any message by the rotors' carefully selected settings and then could produce literally hundreds of millions of possibilities in any given message. This could only be unscrambled by another Enigma machine following the same series of rotor settings chosen for that particular day's messages. The settings could be changed as often as security required.

The French and Belgians knew a little regarding the military version of the Enigma machines and the breaking of the Enigma code began in Belgium, with some help from the French. With the aid of secret agents, the French began to read simple messages but the complexity of the machine daunted even their most gifted cryptographers.

The French tried to involve the British. However, they proved disinterested. The French then turned to their new allies, the Polish, passing on all they had learned to date. By 1932, the Poles had constructed a reproduction of the Enigma machine. French agents continued to supply information as the Germans worked to improve their machines. With the updated information, the Poles worked on the cracking of encoded messages and, by 1938, had constructed what they termed a "bombe"— this consisted of a number of linked Enigma machines. By the end of 1938 the French agents' supply of codes ceased but, by this time, the code-breakers had developed their own techniques and were capable of cracking a limited number of encoded transmissions.

With Europe on the brink of war the Poles held a meeting in Warsaw with their French and British Allies where they demonstrated their new methods of breaking the Enigma codes. Some of the most important work was carried out by a brilliant mathematician, Marian Rejewski, perhaps one of the most gifted cryptanalysts of the 20th Century. When the French and British left the meeting they were both presented with Polish-built replicas of the Enigma machine. Given the little preparation the British, in particular, had made for an "intelligence war" against Germany, this gift was of incalculable importance.

After the invasion of Poland, the Polish code-breakers escaped to France to continue their work. Following the invasion and fall of France the code-breakers again escaped and, for a time, worked in the Vichy zone of France, sending the results of their work—encoded on their Enigma machines—to London. By this time some French and Polish cryptographers had fallen into German hands. The captives, however, had been able to convince their German interrogators that the Enigma, with its millions of variables, was impossible to break, a story the Germans were eager to believe.

In Britain, at Bletchley Park, a country house situated in a quiet rural backwater, a codebreaking center had been established that continued the work that the French and the Poles had started. Academics were recruited and the establishment quickly expanded. By 1941 new, improved "bombes" were installed at Bletchley Park, ten feet tall electro-mechanical giants of their age. With amazing speed, the machines searched through the millions of possible rotor and key settings made by the German Enigma operators. The "bombe" came to a stop when it found the letter matches for which the cryptographer was searching. This could then be tried out on a British version of the Enigma machine. If these settings worked out they could lead to a group of messages being broken. It would then be sent to either the Navy, Army, or Air Force departments to turn into a meaningful message in English. The message was assessed for importance, and any person or unit mentioned was entered in a vast and growing archive. This gave a picture of events, people, places, and units, built up in detail.

Other information was gathered from German shortwave radio traffic and compared to Enigma decrypts. Perhaps the most important factor in intelligence gathering was German carelessness. The Luftwaffe provided the most intelligible signals simply due to lazy operators providing regular recognizable chains of letter codes. The German Navy proved much more difficult to break on a regular basis.

The Enigma machine, originally a commercial machine produced in the Netherlands, was further developed in Germany, becoming a more complex device for diplomatic and military use.

Bletchley Park and its team of academics still relied on captured material from the enemy. Such an incident occurred when the British destroyer HMS *Somali* engaged and damaged the German trawler *Krebs*. The sinking *Krebs* was beached and the *Somali*'s Signals Officer boarded and searched the German vessel, recovered spare rotors and the Enigma settings for February 1941. Further captures, especially the occasional German weather ship out in the Atlantic, provided more rotor settings and data. In May 1941 HMS *Bulldog* escorting Convoy OB318 was some seven days outbound from Liverpool when the convoy was attacked by U-110, commanded by Kapitünleutnant Lemp (the U-boat commander who sent the passenger liner *Athenia* to the bottom at the beginning of the war). Lemp fired three torpedoes at the convoy and two merchant ships were hit. The periscope of U-110 was spotted and a pattern of depth charges was immediately laid, this sent the U-boat downward but Lemp soon returned to periscope-depth in time to see another escort coming straight at him. The second depth charge damaged his U-boat, which started to sink. Lemp ordered the ballast tank to be blown, which brought the U-boat back to the surface. As she surfaced, the crew abandoned ship. Lemp should have set fuses which would have destroyed the U-boat, but either this was not done or the fuses were faulty. The U-110 remained on the surface. HMS *Bulldog* immediately sent a boarding party consisting

General Manstein conducts operations from the rear of a mobile command vehicle. Some of his communications staff can be seen using the Enigma coding machine.

of a young Sub-Lieutenant and five seamen. They boarded the abandoned and dark U-boat aware that charges had probably been set but calmly searched for any useful information. They found charts, code-books and a complete Enigma machine, which they carefully unscrewed from its mounting. It took some three hours to recover everything of potential value and get back on to HMS *Bulldog*. The British ship attempted to tow the damaged U-110 back to port but the attempt failed. However, the most valuable cargo got home to port. The Bletchley Park staff could hardly believe their luck: a new machine with all its codes for the length of the U-boat's cruise, some three months, plus material that would help read the German Navy's Hydra Code for the rest of the war.

In the Pacific, however, the American cryptographers working on Japan's diplomatic and military codes, known to the Americans as "Purple" codes, did not enjoy the benefit of captured machines. They were led in their endeavors by William Friedman, chief cryptanalyst of the United States Army Signal Intelligence Service. He was an expert in statistics and probability, and by 1941 he had over 20 years experience of code-breaking. With Friedman was a carefully gathered team who had worked on the "Purple" problem since 1939. The Japanese used a mechanical device to encode their messages: this consisted of two typewriter keyboards connected by switches, plugs, and circuits. The Japanese machine did not use rotors but "stepping switches" as used in the telephone systems of the day. It was the realization, by cryptanalyst Harry Clark, that ordinary telephone stepping switches could be used in this way that led to the American breakthrough in reading the "Purple" codes.

With agonizing slowness, separating encrypted text in segments representing possible key settings, looking for letters in known frequency of use, skilled translators could form a complete message. Though missing letters might lead to some educated guesswork on the part of the translator.

The first message was completed on 25 September 1940. With experience, the American cryptanalysts built a machine that would duplicate "Purple's" functions. By early 1941 four machines were at work, two in Washington, one in the Philippines and one was sent to Bletchley Park.

After the gift of this machine, the British began to intercept Japanese messages to their embassies in Europe and the Middle East. By June 1941, a second machine had been sent for British use in Singapore. So important had the decoding of Japanese messages become to the prosecution of the war that the information was distributed under the codename "Magic;" in Britain, the information from Enigma was known as "ULTRA." The information distributed under Magic and ULTRA had a remarkable impact, allowing the Allies to prepare their moves on all fronts, preempting Yamamoto's plans at Midway, Pacific, in June 1942 and also to enable General Montgomery to change his plans at Caen, Normandy, in June 1944 when it became known that the Second S.S. Panzer Corps was to be deployed in that area.

The Axis powers never enjoyed quite the same advantages as the Allies, probably because they placed such faith in their encoding machines. They did have their successes, however: German agents compromised the whole Special Operations Executive's operation in the Netherlands; Japanese spies were working many years before the Pacific War and could report on the state of Allied defenses in Singapore, Hong Kong, Manila, and Pearl Harbor. In the end it was the Allied ability to break the Axis codes and turn what was a slim chance to gain knowledge of enemy intentions and the ability to deploy growing Allied military power in the right place at the right time.

The Wireless War

- ■ Germany
- ■ Allied to Germany
- ■ German/Axis occupied
- ■ Allied states or under Allied control
- □ Neutral states
- — German Army wireless links using Enigma coding machine
- *Parr* British codename for penetrated German wireless link
- ⊼ German listening post
- ⊼ British listening post
- ☐ German Army, Navy, Luftwaffe HQ
- △ Geheimschreiber station (encryption-decryption station)

Narvik

Arctic Circle

Arkhangelsk

Luleå

Norwegian Sea

FINLAND

L. Onega

64°

L. Ladoga

60°

SOVIET
UNION

Helsinki

Leningrad

Moscow

Stockholm

Estonia

Mullet

Oslo

56°

Memel

Latvia

Riga

Whiting

Denmark

Trout

Lithuania

REICHKOMMISSARIAT
OSTLAND

to U-boat
wolf packs

Copenhagen

Königberg

Rastenburg *Messages received from Eastern Front*

North Sea

Baltic Sea

East
Prussia

Perch

Turbot

Dace

Dace

Dublin

UNITED
KINGDOM

Hamburg

52°

IRELAND

Grilse

Neth.

Wilhelmshaven

Warsaw

REICHKOMMISSARIAT
UKRAINE

Kiev

Amsterdam

Berlin

Parr

Gen. Gov.
of Poland

London

GERMAN EMPIRE

to Caucasus

Brussels

Prague

Vinnitsa

Octopus

Belgium

Roach

Shad

Jellyfish

Frankfurt

48°

Prot. of
Bohemia-Moravia

SLOVAKIA

Pollack

Paris

St. Cloud

Munich

Vienna

Tarpot

ROMANIA

*ATLANTIC
OCEAN*

Stuttgart

Salzburg

Budapest

Crimea

FRANCE

Bern

Austria

HUNGARY

44°

SWITZ.

Geneva

Sebastopol

Milan

Venice

Banat

Bucharest

Grayling

Danube

*Black
Sea*

Genoa

CROATIA

Belgrade

Marseille

Adriatic Sea

Serbia

Sofia

BULGARIA

Bream

Gurnard

ITALY

Mont.

Istanbul

40°

SPAIN

Rome

ALBANIA

PORTUGAL

Madrid

Corsica

Greece

*Aegean
Sea*

TURKEY

Lisbon

Taranto

Sardinia

Balearic Is.

Athens

to Italy

36°

Gibraltar
to Britain

Mediterranean

Sicily

Crete

Algiers

Bone

Tunis

Malta
to Britain

Sea

32°

French North Africa

Tripoli

Benghazi

LIBYA

Libya *to Italy*

BATTLE OF THE ATLANTIC 1942–45

"OUR LOSSES ... HAVE REACHED AN INTOLERABLE LEVEL."

GRAND ADMIRAL DONITZ, MAY 1943

From 7 December 1941 the United States was officially in the war, this presented the U-boats with rich pickings off the east coast of the U.S. The U.S. Navy was initially unwilling to instigate a convoy policy, then suffered difficulties in organizing them. This left their ships prey to U-boat attack and losses soared, reaching a peak in summer and fall of 1942. Surface escorts fought back and U-boat losses also increased in the same period. By September 1942, with New York as the focus and western terminus for transatlantic convoys, the U.S. now introduced convoys in the Gulf of Mexico and along the eastern seaboard, and the main battle zone swung back to the mid-Atlantic.

First introduced in the spring of 1941 "Wolfpacks"—U-boats organized into patrol lines across the usual convoy routes—grew larger. More U-boats than ever patrolled the airgap: the mid-Atlantic area beyond the range of Allied patrol aircraft. As the Germans concentrated their forces in the mid-Atlantic, they met better armed and equipped Allied escorts, who were using improved tactics. By August even the airgap itself was reduced by the introduction of V.L.R. (very long range) Liberator patrol bombers. Their patrols were now more carefully coordinated with the convoys themselves; instead of circling over the convoy or a suspected area, they flew just ahead or on either side: sightings and sinkings of U-boats increased.

The surface escorts' 10-centimeter radar, with a 360° sweep, for the first time made it possible to establish a radar watch completely around a convoy, day and night, in good weather. The assembly of Wolfpacks around the convoy could also be detected by high frequency direction finding sets, which picked up U-boats sending reports to each other and to their base. The convoy battles of late 1942 and early 1943 were positively affected by these developments. Major victories were scored over the Wolfpacks in May 1943, when 41 U-boats were sunk. The Allies, via ULTRA, were able to read the German naval code again after January 1943, except for a brief period in the first three weeks of March. During the March period half of all convoys located by the Germans were attacked and 22 percent were lost. By this time

Battle of the Atlantic
January 1942 – February 1943

⎯⎯ Change of operational control
UK to U.S., August 1942

▬▬ Extent of air escort cover

- - - UK Escort Stations to July 1942

▭ Major convoy routes

• Allied merchant ships sunk by U-boats

✄ U-boats sunk

▨ Territory under Allied control

▨ Territory under Axis control

▢ Neutral territory

Admiral Donitz, now head of the Kriegsmarine, had between 400 and 435 U-boats available for operations. Despite successes, the U-boat-arm was still losing U-boats at an alarming rate. ULTRA intelligence continued to penetrate the German codes.

At the Casablanca Conference between Roosevelt and Churchill in January 1943, the Allies gave the Atlantic first priority. By late March support groups had been established to assist convoy escorts, especially through the still existing airgap. More V.L.R. Liberators

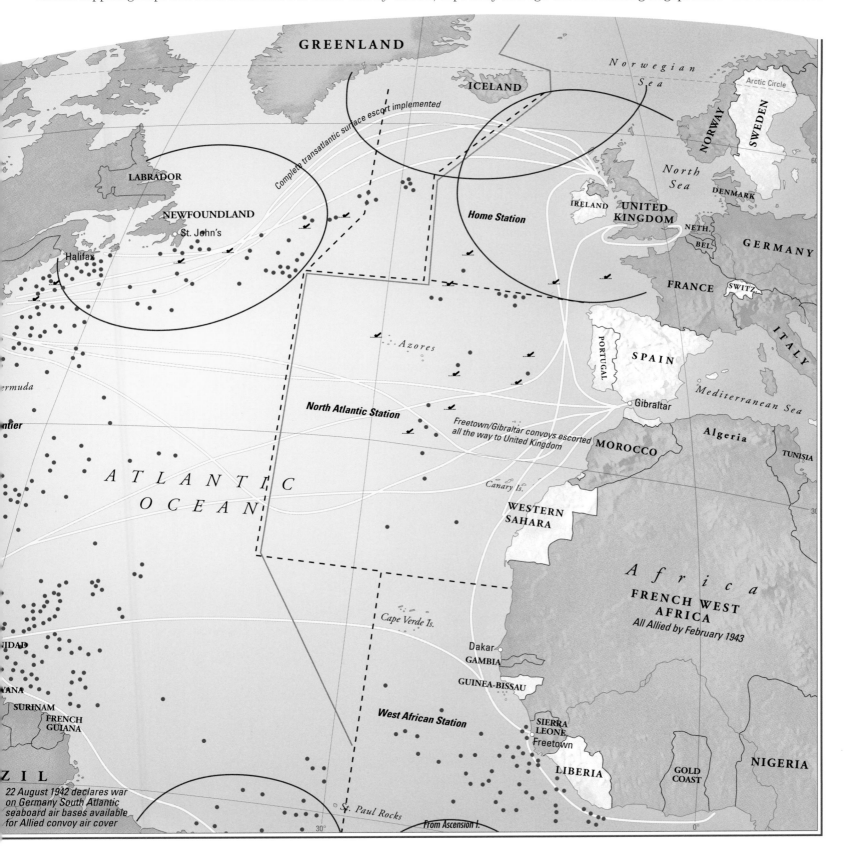

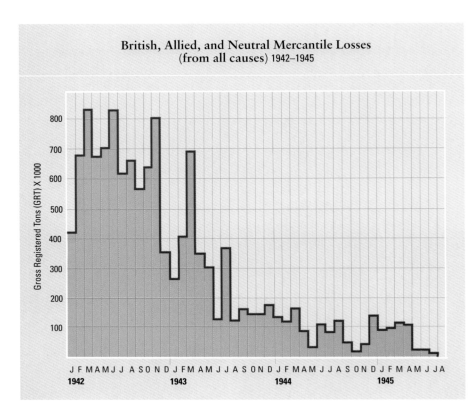

British, Allied, and Neutral Mercantile Losses
(from all causes) 1942–1945

In the early months of 1942, the Battle of the Atlantic swung in favor of the U-boats with the highest monthly losses ever recorded in March, June, and November. The U.S. had entered the war in December 1941, its merchant fleet was not organized into convoys and were largely unprotected, presenting a perfect target for the U-boats. After the convoy system was adopted by the U.S. and further patrol aircraft were introduced, the battle was forced back into the mid-Atlantic and despite more U-boats being available, sinkings declined.

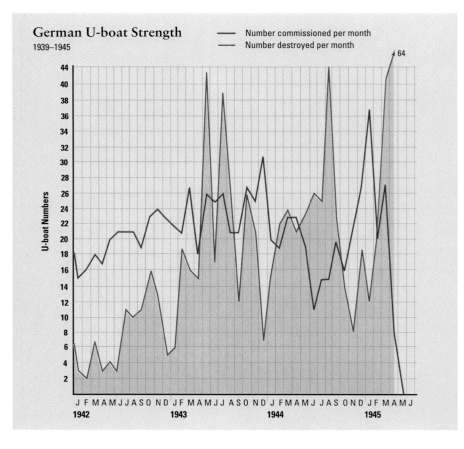

German U-boat Strength
1939–1945

— Number commissioned per month
— Number destroyed per month

finally closed the gap in May. ULTRA decrypts had a devastating effect at this point, routing convoys clear of U-boats patrol lines and diverting escort reinforcements into attack positions where it was possible to take an enormous toll. Almost 100 U-boats were sunk in the first five months of 1943. At the end of May, Admiral Donitz withdrew almost all of the mauled U-boat fleet back to base.

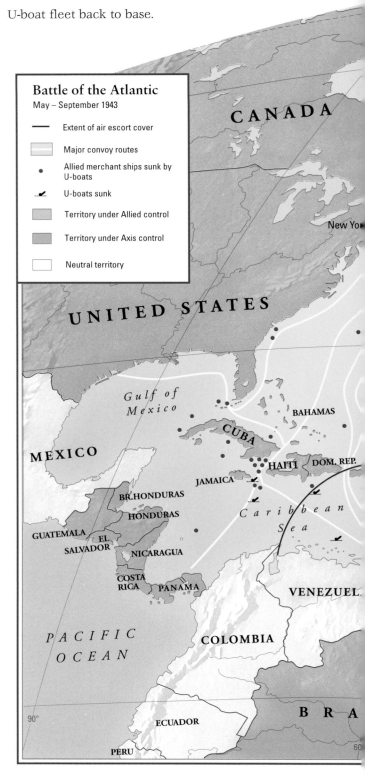

Battle of the Atlantic
May – September 1943

— Extent of air escort cover

Major convoy routes

• Allied merchant ships sunk by U-boats

⚓ U-boats sunk

Territory under Allied control

Territory under Axis control

Neutral territory

The Battle of the Atlantic had been won, almost; ships continued to be sunk until May 1945 but never would the supply of materials and food be threatened again. The U-boat force was now used to tie down the massive Allied naval escort force, while new and improved U-boats could be designed and built. It was not until 30 April 1945 that this new generation sailed on its first patrol, a Type 23 with high-speed underwater performance. On the same day in Berlin, Hitler committed suicide.

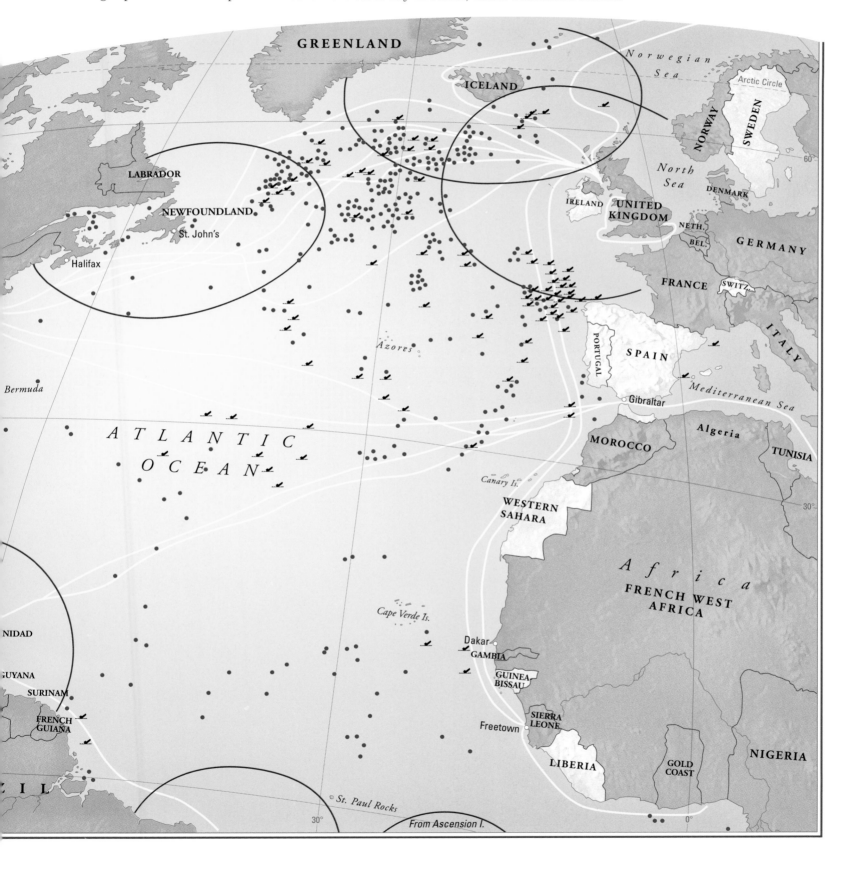

MEDITERRANEAN NAVAL WAR 1940–43

"THE MEDITERRANEAN WILL BE TURNED INTO AN ITALIAN LAKE."

BENITO MUSSOLINI

The Fairey Swordfish, the unlikely hero of the Royal Navy's night attack on the Italian Fleet anchored at Taranto.

The Mediterranean naval war was fought by the Allies and the Axis in order to keep open the supply routes they required to supply their efforts in the North African campaigns. Britain also had a major concern with keeping open the Suez Canal, which was their route to and from colonies in the east without having to navigate the long route around southern Africa.

When France capitulated in the summer of 1940, the British were aware that her formidable naval forces could be taken over by the Germans and used to seize the balance of naval power. This could not be allowed to happen. Two modern battleships, *Dunkerque* and *Strasbourg* along with two older battleships, were stationed in the port of Mes-el-Kabir on the coast of Algeria at Oran. Negotiations were attempted to persuade the French Fleet to surrender its ships to the Royal Navy, who would then sail them either to British bases or bases in the French Caribbean, where they would be out of reach of the German Navy. Alternatively they could face destruction. The negotiations were drawn out and muddled. Without further options the British Fleet opened fire on French ships on 3 July, damaging *Provence*, *Dunkerque* and a destroyer, but the battleship *Strasbourg* managed to escape to the French Base at Toulon. Two days later an air attack, using Fairey Swordfish (ancient biplanes nicknamed "stringbags"), was launched to finish off the stricken French ships, so severely damaging the *Dunkerque* that she ran aground. The attacks resulted in 1,297 French sailors losing their lives and led to extremely bad relations between the French and British, although it impressed upon the United States the determination of Britain to survive.

On the night of 11/12 November, the Royal Navy, using aircraft of the Fleet Air Arm, launched an attack that was considered impossible by many tacticians, against a large

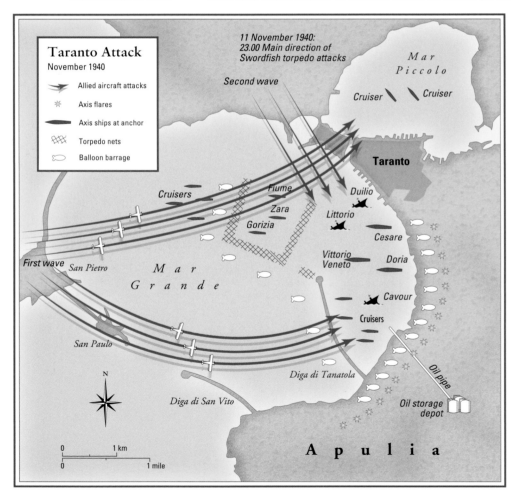

Taranto Attack
November 1940

- ✈ Allied aircraft attacks
- ✳ Axis flares
- ▬ Axis ships at anchor
- ▨ Torpedo nets
- ⬯ Balloon barrage

11 November 1940:
23.00 Main direction of
Swordfish torpedo attacks

Second wave

Mar Piccolo

Cruiser / \ Cruiser

Taranto

Cruisers
Fiume
Zara
Gorizia
Duilio
Littorio
Cesare
Vittorio Veneto
Doria
Cavour
Cruisers

First wave San Pietro

Mar Grande

San Paulo

Oil pipe

Diga di Tanatola

Oil storage depot

Diga di San Vito

N

0   1 km
0   1 mile

A p u l i a

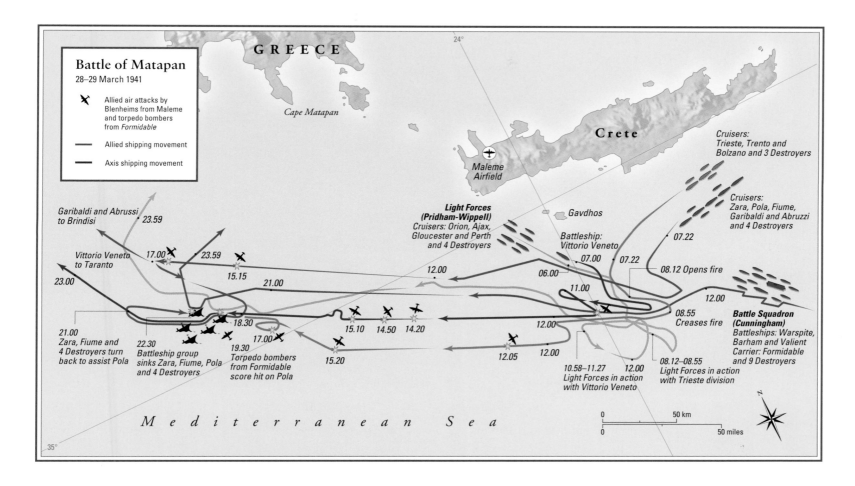

Battle of Matapan
28–29 March 1941

✈ Allied air attacks by
Blenheims from Maleme
and torpedo bombers
from *Formidable*

— Allied shipping movement

— Axis shipping movement

GREECE

Cape Matapan

Crete

Maleme Airfield

Gavdhos

Cruisers:
Trieste, Trento and
Bolzano and 3 Destroyers

Cruisers:
Zara, Pola, Fiume,
Garibaldi and Abruzzi
and 4 Destroyers

*Garibaldi and Abrussi
to Brindisi* 23.59

*Vittorio Veneto
to Taranto* 17.00 23.59

23.00

15.15 21.00

*Light Forces
(Pridham-Wippell)*
Cruisers: Orion, Ajax,
Gloucester and Perth
and 4 Destroyers

Battleship:
Vittorio Veneto

12.00 06.00 07.00 07.22

07.22

08.12 Opens fire

11.00 12.00

08.55
Creases fire

*Battle Squadron
(Cunningham)*
Battleships: Warspite,
Barham and Valient
Carrier: Formidable
and 9 Destroyers

21.00
Zara, Fiume and
4 Destroyers turn
back to assist Pola

22.30
Battleship group
sinks Zara, Fiume, Pola
and 4 Destroyers

18.30

17.00

19.30
Torpedo bombers
from Formidable
score hit on Pola

15.10 14.50 14.20

15.20 12.05 12.00

12.00

10.58–11.27 12.00
Light Forces in action
with Vittorio Veneto

08.12–08.55
Light Forces in action
with Trieste division

M e d i t e r r a n e a n   S e a

0   50 km
0   50 miles

part of the Italian fleet at Taranto harbor. In the harbor were six battleships, seven heavy cruisers, two light cruisers, and eight destroyers, a formidable force that could strike a blow at any time against British transports struggling to get supplies to the army in Egypt. Two waves of torpedo- and bomb-armed Fairey Swordfish flew in to attack the ships at anchor, using specially adapted torpedoes that could run in shallow water. They succeeded in hitting the battleship *Littorio* three times and hitting two more battleships with one apiece, all for the loss of two aircraft and crews. The success of the raid alarmed the Italians so much that they moved the remainder of the fleet to safer ports in northern Italy and the damaged *Littorio* remained out of action for four months. The Japanese Navy also took a great interest in the attack; it was influential in their developing plan to strike the American Fleet anchored at Pearl Harbor.

Between 27 and 29 March 1941, an engagement was fought off the Peloponnesian coast between a large force of Italian warships and the Royal Navy. Admiral Sir Henry Pridham-Wippell's force was based off the southern coast of Crete with three cruisers of the Royal Navy and one cruiser of the Royal Australian Navy, HMS *Perth* along with a covering force of destroyers. In Alexandria was Admiral Cunningham's force of a carrier HMS *Formidable* along with three battleships including his Flagship HMS *Warspite*. Cunningham received information, via ULTRA intercepts, that an Italian force, commanded by Admiral Angelo Iachino with the modern battleship *Vittorio Veneto*, was on its way east to intercept troop ships taking Allied soldiers to Greece. Pridham-Wippell's force spotted the Italians approach south of Crete, the Italians giving chase and opening fire from extreme range in the belief that the British were attempting to escape. The chasing Italian cruisers then gave up the pursuit,

The Fiume, one of three Zara-class cruisers lost at the Battle of Matapan. After this battle the Italian Navy were reluctant to commit their larger warships beyond the range of air cover from the Italian mainland.

returning to the *Vittorio*, with the British shadowing them. Cunningham's force, which had been steaming into the area, then launched an airstrike against the Italians, alarming the *Vittorio*, which turned back to the safety of Italian-based aircover. A second air attack was launched, this time damaging the *Vittorio*, although she was still able to proceed after some repairs. However, a third strike crippled the cruiser *Pola* and after leaving a force of cruisers and destroyers as protection for her, *Vittorio* continued on its route back to Taranto. During the night, the British were able to sneak up on the stricken ship and escort, opened fire at short range, quickly sinking the cruisers *Fiume* and *Zara*.

The Italian destroyers then tried to counterattack but two of these were also sunk. With the morning came the threat of Italian air attack and the British decided to torpedo the damaged cruiser *Pola*, rather than to tow her to Alexandria as a prize. After the loss of so many ships, the Italians never sailed into the eastern Mediterranean again.

Malta was an important strategic position between Italy and North Africa, and aircraft and ships based there had the potential to disrupt the supply lines of enemy forces. This fact was immediately

HMS Ark Royal, *below*, the first large, purpose-built aircraft carrier for the British Royal Navy. The ship served through two years of the war until sunk while operating east of Gibraltar by a single torpedo fired from U-81. The crew struggled for 14 hours to keep the ship afloat, but she finally capsized and sank. Despite terrible losses, the Royal Navy was never driven from the Mediterranean.

The Mediterranean
Late 1942

Under German or Axis occupation

Allied to Germany

Italian territory

Under Italian occupation

Allied or under Allied occupation

French, under Vichy control

Axis occupied

Neutral countries

→ Allied convoy route

→ Axis convoy route

⊕ Allied airfield

⊕ Axis airfield

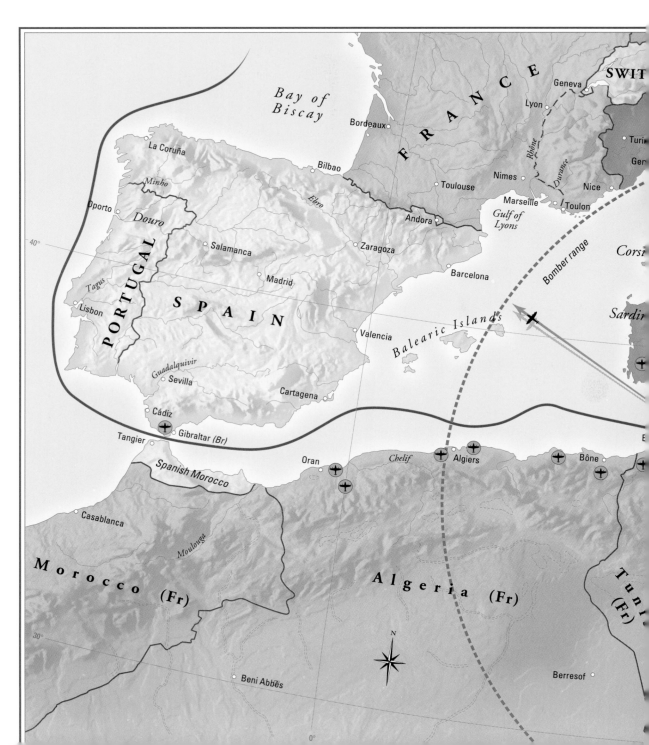

recognized by Italy who began a campaign of bombing the island as soon as it declared war on Britain. The island's original defense was down to outmoded Gloster Gladiator biplane fighters and antiaircraft guns. Surprisingly this weak defense still caused the Italians to be cautious and the British decided that Malta must be defended. In June 1941, the Luftwaffe arrived in the form of Fleigerkorps X, covering the Afrika Korps sailing to Tunisia. This increased the intensity of the bombing campaign and the island was almost cut off. Convoys continued to reach Malta but experienced horrendous losses. As a result, the island's population and garrison were surviving on limited rations. During a respite HMS *Furious* managed to fly in 61 Spitfires to aid the defense but supplies of food, oil, and medicine were also urgently required. During August 1942, Operation Pedestal was carried out: 14 merchantmen were escorted by a massive naval force including three carriers, two battleships, and 32 destroyers. Just five transports survived. One carrier, two cruisers, and a destroyer were lost in the defense of the convoy. As the war moved in the Allies' favor, the siege of Malta eased. In acknowledgement of their bravery, the island's inhabitants received the George Cross, the highest British decoration awarded to civilians.

THE BALKAN CAMPAIGN 1941

"FÜHRER, WE ARE ON THE MARCH!"

BENITO MUSSOLINI TO ADOLF HITLER, 28 OCTOBER 1940

Junkers-87, Stuka dive-bombers, over the Bosnian Mountains. The small and ill-equipped Yugoslav Airforce was almost useless against the highly-proficient, experienced and well-equipped German Luftwaffe.

On 7 April 1939 Italy annexed Albania, giving Mussolini a foothold in the Balkans, Italy's backyard. The Russo-German Non-Aggression Pact of 1939 also reorganized the Soviet Union's interest in the Balkans. This treaty assigned northern Bukovina and Bessarabia, parts of Romania, to the U.S.S.R..

In the Vienna Award of 30 August 1940 Germany and Italy recognized these annexations, and the treaty also awarded southern Dobruja to Bulgaria and northern Transylvania to Hungary. However, this vastly reduced Romania was to be guaranteed by Germany and Italy. Germany, in particular, was anxious to protect its main supply of oil from the Ploesti region of Romania. Hitler's plan to secure the region for the Tripartite Pact, as reliable satellites, was thrown off balance by Mussolini's attack on Greece from Albania. Mussolini expected Greece to fall within a few days of his attack but, much to his surprise, the Greeks resisted and forced the Italians back into Albania. The British sent an expeditionary force to aid the Greeks, which placed further pressure on the Italians. Hitler was infuriated by his Italian allies' incompetence, which provided the British with a reason to enter Greece and alarmed the Soviet Union. The Soviets were suspicious of Axis armies operating in the region, especially with regard to Bulgaria, already earmarked by them as a possible satellite of their own.

At a meeting in Berlin on 11–12 November 1940, Foreign Minister Molotov, announced the Soviet Union's intention of declaring a unilateral guarantee of the existing Bulgarian borders. Hitler was increasingly convinced that his plan to attack the Soviet Union was correct but first he must sort out the situation in the Balkans. He ordered the Army General Staff to prepare a plan for the invasion of Greece. The plan called for attacks to be launched from Bulgaria but he was far more unsure of Yugoslavia, which was wavering. Its ruler, Regent Paul, encouraged by the British and Americans, resisted German diplomatic pressure, but eventually gave in and signed up to the Tripartite Pact on 25 March 1941. Germany would enjoy transit rights for its troops for the planned attack on Greece, thus widening the front and outflanking Greek defenses north and west of Salonika. However, two days after Regent Paul signed, he was deposed by General Simovic, leader of an antiroyalist military coup. His supporters wanted nothing to do with pacts and wars, seeking to steer a neutral course. Hitler quickly resolved to include Yugoslavia in his plans for Greece, thereby ending any possibility of Britain, or any other power, interfering in his arrangements for the future of the Balkans.

On 6 April 1941, German forces launched their attack on Yugoslavia from the north and east. A massive air attack on Belgrade killed some 17,000 people. Four days into the campaign Yugoslavia's resistance began to fall apart when the predominantly Croatian 4th and 7th Armies mutinied. The semiautonomous Croatian government welcomed Axis forces in Zagreb the same day. The Serbian part of the country fought on for two more days before asking for an armistice.

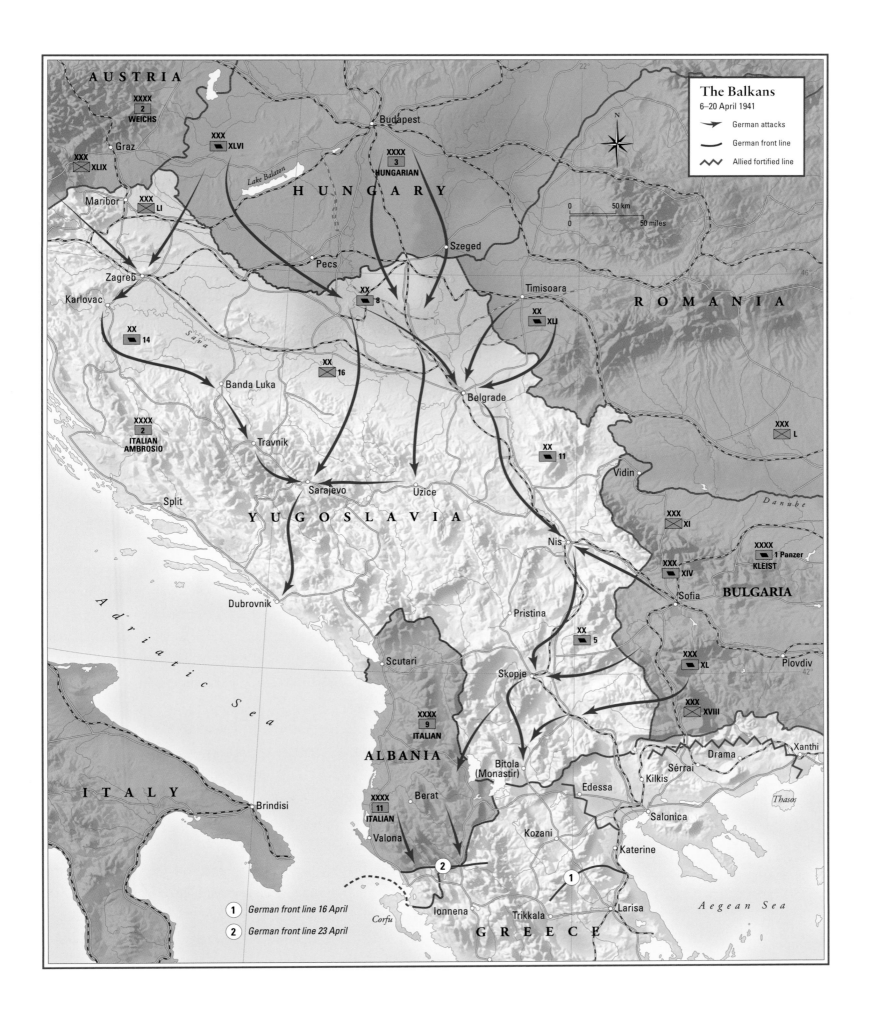

AUSTRIA

XXXX
2
WEICHS

Graz

XXX
XLIX

XXX
XLVI

Budapest

XXXX
3
HUNGARIAN

H U N G A R Y

Lake Balaton

Maribor

XXX
LI

Szeged

Pecs

Zagreb

XX
8

Timisoara

R O M A N I A

Karlovac

Sava

XX
14

XX
XLI

XX
16

Banda Luka

Belgrade

XXX
L

XXXX
2
ITALIAN
AMBROSIO

Travnik

XX
11

Vidin

Danube

Split

Sarajevo

Uzice

Y U G O S L A V I A

Nis

XXX
XI

XXXX
1 Panzer
KLEIST

XXX
XIV

A
d
r
i
a
t
i
c

S
e
a

Dubrovnik

Pristina

Sofia

B U L G A R I A

Scutari

XX
5

XXX
XL

Plovdiv

Skopje

XXX
XVIII

XXXX
9
ITALIAN

Bitola
(Monastir)

Drama

Xanthi

Sérrai

Thasos

I T A L Y

Brindisi

ALBANIA

XXXX
11
ITALIAN

Berat

Edessa

Kilkis

Salonica

Valona

Kozani

Katerine

2

Aegean Sea

1

Corfu

Ionnena

Trikkala

Larisa

G R E E C E

1 German front line 16 April

2 German front line 23 April

The Balkans
6–20 April 1941

→ German attacks

⌒ German front line

〰 Allied fortified line

N

0   50 km
0   50 miles

THE CONQUEST OF GREECE AND CRETE 1941

"WE HAVE TAKEN A GRAVE AND HAZARDOUS DECISION TO SUSTAIN THE GREEKS AND TRY TO MAKE A BALKAN FRONT."

WINSTON CHURCHILL

A propaganda photograph from the German magazine *Signal* shows "German bombers over the Acropolis, April 1931." In this case propaganda was not far from reality: throughout the Greek campaign the Luftwaffe enjoyed complete air superiority.

The planned German attack was preceded by a renewed Italian offensive launched in mid-March. A confident Mussolini was present at the beginning of the offensive but left abruptly when it became bogged down and came to nothing.

The German attack on Yugoslavia began on 6 April, 1941 with the 18th Corps also attacking north-eastern Greece, outflanking Greek defensive positions north-east of Salonika. Within three days German troops were within the city itself. The Metaxas Line, further south, manned by British and Commonwealth troops, was outflanked by the 40th Panzer Corps advancing south from Skopje, in southern Yugoslavia, over "impassible" mountains through the Monastir Gap. They also advanced to the east of the Greek 1st Army facing the Italians, partly cutting off their supply routes. The British forces fell back to an area around Mount Olympus. When these positions became untenable, they again fell back to the Thermopylae Line, protecting the roads leading to Athens. The Greek Army, facing the Italian 11th and 9th Armies now backed-up by advancing German units, began to disintegrate. Despite occasional local success, the Greeks held the 40th Corps at Ptolemais and the New Zealanders held part of the 18th Corps advancing near Mount Olympus. The die was cast. By 21 April the British decided to evacuate Greece.

The German invasion of Crete, the first major airborne invasion of World War II, took place on the morning of 20 May 1941 as part of Operation Mercury. Poor intelligence on the German side led them to believe that Crete was badly defended and the civilians would be nothing less than welcoming. This resulted in horrific losses, which determined that they would never again make another large-scale airborne assault. However, it showed to the Allies the potential of paratroop assaults and led them to creating and training units of their own.

The defense of Crete was made up of 9,000 Greeks of the 5th Division plus the Crete Gendarmerie and remnants of the 12th and 20th Divisions. Though these units were poorly armed with little ammunition, they would fight ferociously for their island. There was also an original garrison of some 14,000 British troops that were supplemented by the New Zealand 2nd Division, Australian 9th Division, and the British 14th Infantry Brigade. Commanded by Major-General

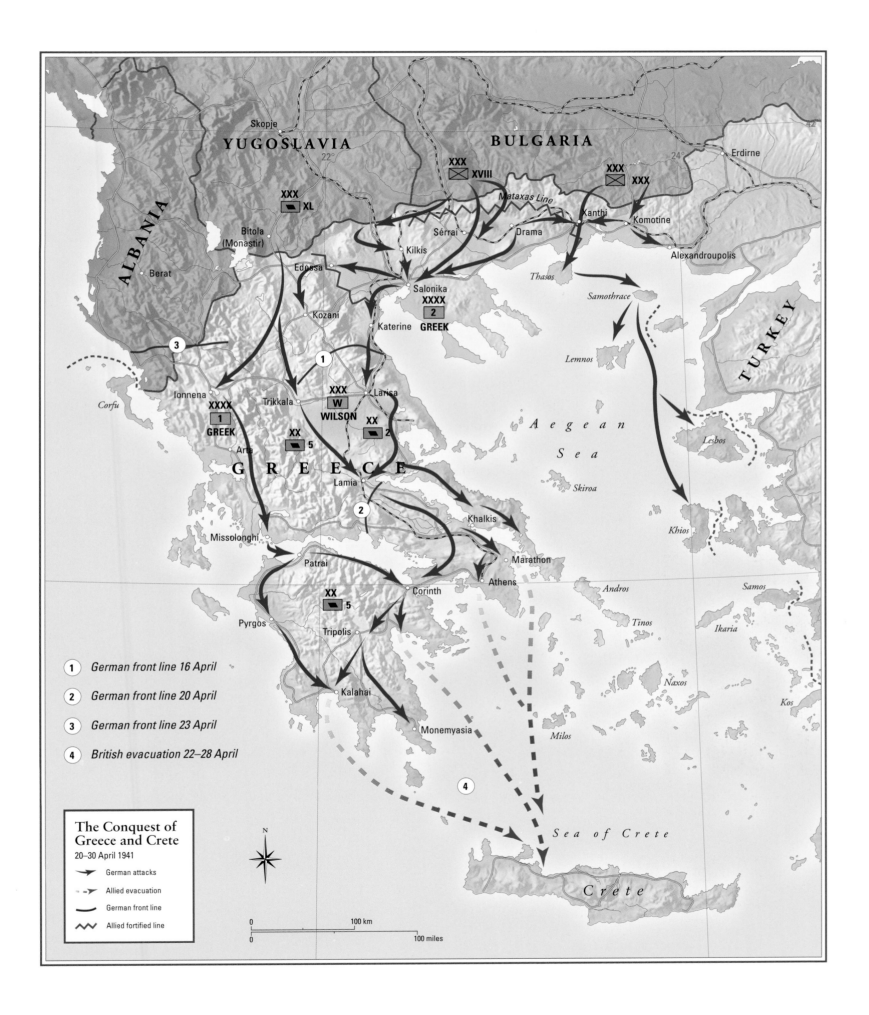

1 German front line 16 April

2 German front line 20 April

3 German front line 23 April

4 British evacuation 22–28 April

The Conquest of
Greece and Crete
20–30 April 1941

German attacks

Allied evacuation

German front line

Allied fortified line

0   100 km
0   100 miles

A Fallschirmjäger leaps from a Ju-52 transport plane over Crete. Losses sustained by this highly-trained and motivated division prevented them from being deployed in the airborne role again.

Freyberg, the defending force lacked any heavy equipment. The initial assault by the Germans was carried out by the Fallschirmjager of 7th Air Division and the 5th Mountain Division, numbering in all some 25,000 men.

The Germans planned to take the major airfields on the western side of the island, secure these to allow supplies and men to be ferried in, then to advance inland and take the rest of the island. At 08:00 am paratroops started to descend on the airfields around Maleme and Canea but were severely mauled, taking many casualties. Some units straying off the drop zone did, however, manage to set up strong positions off the airfields, which were continually attacked by the defenders and Allied troops, as well as civilians brandishing whatever weapons they could find. In the afternoon a second drop was made around the Rethiminon and Heraklion area, and again the paratroops took many casualties as they fell on units of the 14th Infantry Brigade supported by Australians and Greeks.

The Germans did manage to fight through to the docks of Heraklion but were beaten back by concerted Greek counterattacks. By the end of 20 May none of the German objectives had

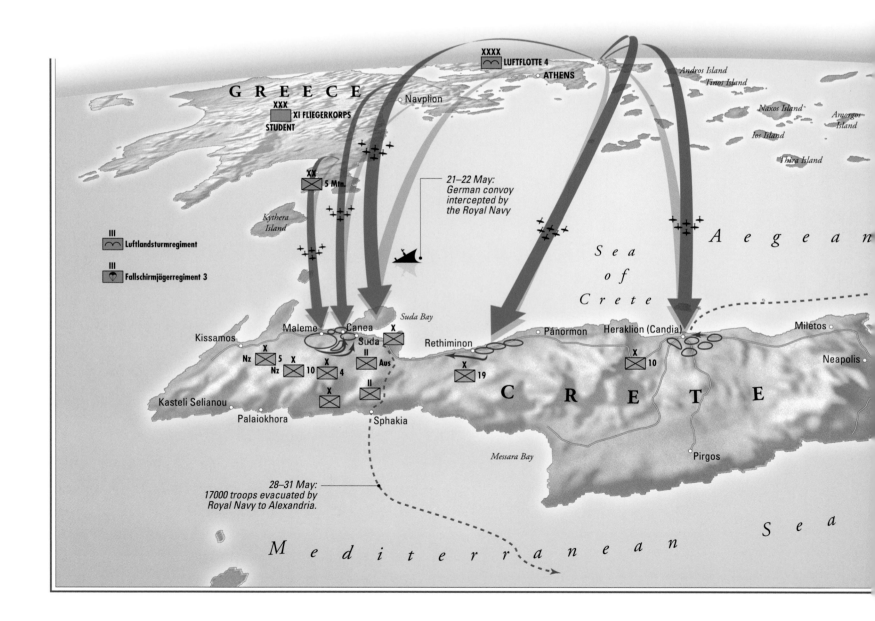

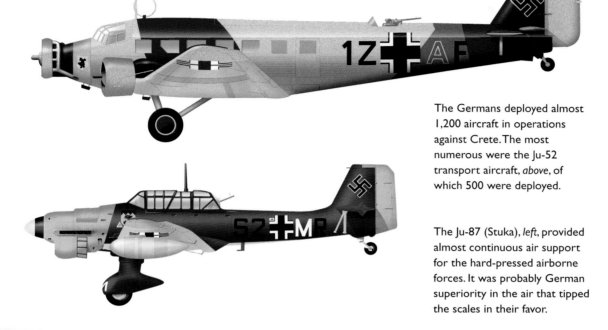

The Germans deployed almost 1,200 aircraft in operations against Crete. The most numerous were the Ju-52 transport aircraft, *above*, of which 500 were deployed.

The Ju-87 (Stuka), *left*, provided almost continuous air support for the hard-pressed airborne forces. It was probably German superiority in the air that tipped the scales in their favor.

A Ju-52 goes down in flames, caught by British anti-aircraft fire. Although the Germans enjoyed air superiority, they still lost heavily in aircraft involved in Operation Mercury, particularly in transport aircraft.

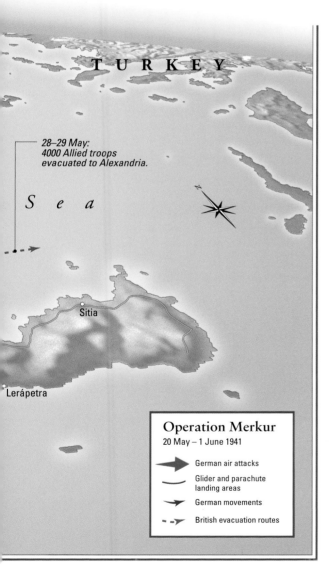

TURKEY

S e a

28–29 May:
4000 Allied troops
evacuated to Alexandria.

Sitia

Lerápetra

Operation Merkur
20 May – 1 June 1941

➡ German air attacks

⌣ Glider and parachute landing areas

➤ German movements

- - ➤ British evacuation routes

been seized. On the second day of fighting the Germans succeeded in capturing the airfield near Hill 107 and immediately started landing Ju-52 Transports bringing in the 5th Mountain Division, even though the airfield was under continuous artillery fire. An attempt to retake the airfield by a brigade of New Zealanders was beaten back and the Germans could start to establish a bridgehead on the island.

From that point onwards the Allies were fighting a rearguard action as they continued to fall back slowly to avoid flank attacks. The Greek 8th Regiment holding the village of Alikianos in "Prison Valley" successfully held back the Germans for seven days, allowing the Allies to fall back southward and avoid capture. Many brave rearguard actions were fought, including that of the 28th Mauri Battalion that held the road between Souda and Chania long enough for the main force to retreat before retreating themselves with the loss of only two men in the process. Layforce, a Commando unit given the task of covering the withdrawal, did the task before they were cut-off by the advancing Germans, many of them being captured or killed.

The Royal Navy evacuated many of the troops from Sphakia and Heraklion before the Germans closed in, making the island theirs. By the end of the fighting the Germans had captured 12,250 Allied troops with many of the Greek troops staying behind to blend in and continue the fight as guerrillas. The official German record states that losses were around 6,400 but this was probably altered for propaganda purposes, the number being probably nearer 16,000.

OPERATION BARBAROSSA 1941

"THE RED ARMY AND NAVY AND THE WHOLE SOVIET PEOPLE
MUST FIGHT FOR EVERY INCH OF SOVIET SOIL, FIGHT TO THE
LAST DROP OF BLOOD FOR OUR TOWNS AND VILLAGES ...
ONWARD, TO VICTORY!"

STALIN, JULY 1941.

A German infantryman advances while under fire through barbed wire entanglements surrounding a Soviet position in the opening stages of Operation Barbarossa.

B y the evening of 21 June, 1941, the largest invasion army in history had assembled on the western border of Soviet Russia. Approximately 10 percent of the adult male population of Germany was armed and waiting for the order to advance. Alongside them stood Finnish, Romanian, and Hungarian units; they would be joined by Italian, Bulgarian, and volunteer units from many countries including "neutral" Spain. This gigantic operation, codenamed Barbarossa, was launched by Hitler in violation of the German-Soviet Non-aggression Pact.

Meanwhile, in Moscow, Stalin consistently refused to believe the domestic and foreign intelligence arriving on his desk. His instructions to Army and Air Forces based along the border were to make no provocative moves that could be misunderstood or misinterpreted by German forces.

Axis forces amounted to almost 3.6 million men with some 3,600 tanks and almost 2,800 aircraft,

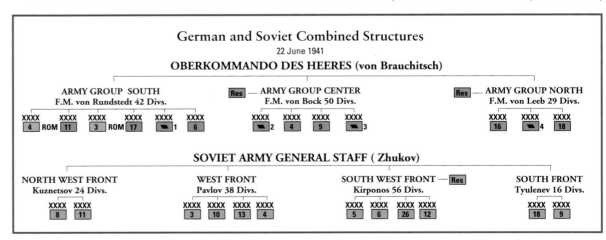

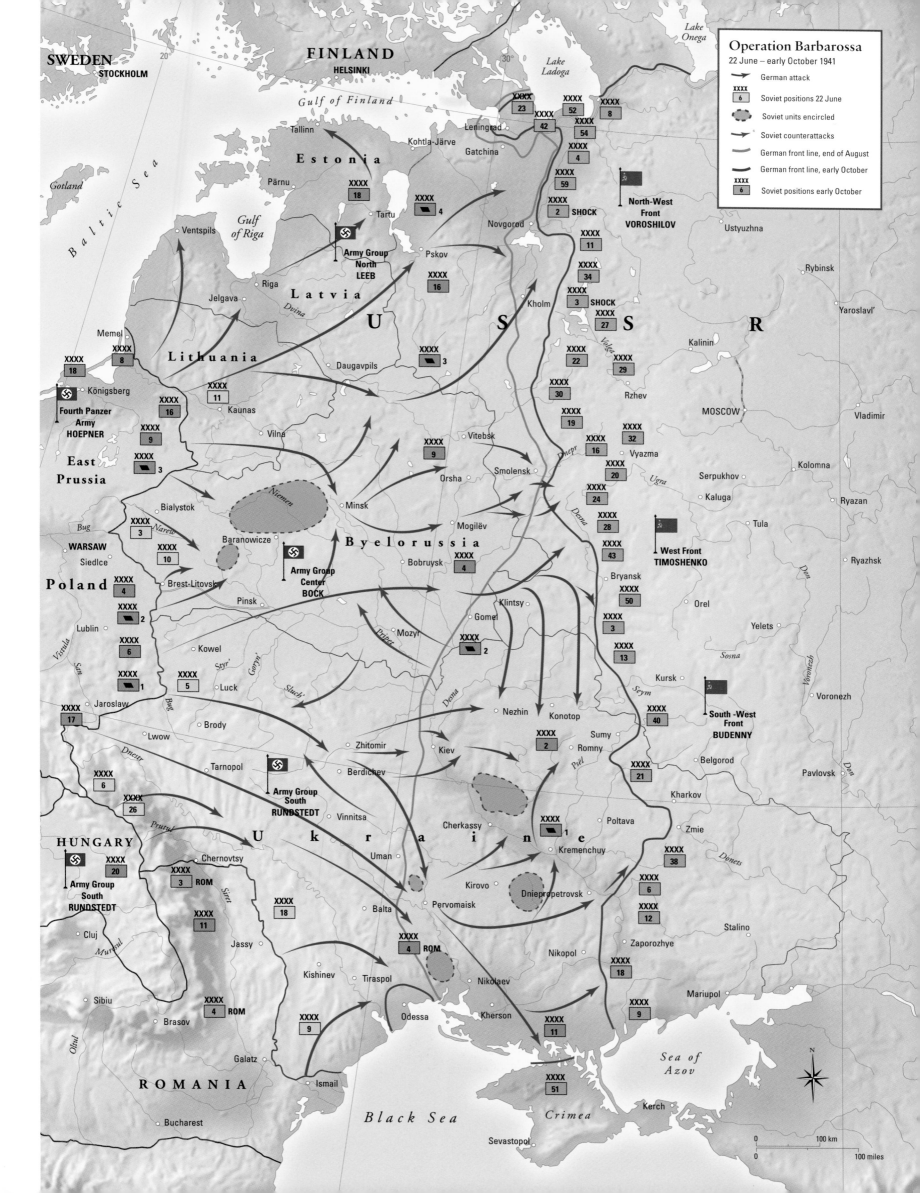

SWEDEN
STOCKHOLM

FINLAND
HELSINKI

Gulf of Finland

Lake Ladoga
Lake Onega

Operation Barbarossa
22 June – early October 1941

→ German attack

XXXX
6 Soviet positions 22 June

⬭ Soviet units encircled

→ Soviet counterattacks

〜 German front line, end of August

〜 German front line, early October

XXXX
6 Soviet positions early October

Baltic Sea

Gotland

Tallinn

Kohtla-Järve

Leningrad

Gatchina

Estonia

Pärnu

Tartu

XXXX
18

XXXX
4

XXXX
23

XXXX
42

XXXX
52

XXXX
54

XXXX
8

XXXX
4

Novgorod

XXXX
59

XXXX
2 SHOCK

North-West
Front
VOROSHILOV

Ustyuzhna

Ventspils

Gulf of Riga

Riga

Jelgava

Dvina

Latvia

Pskov

XXXX
16

U   S   S   R

XXXX
11

XXXX
34

XXXX
3 SHOCK

Kholm

XXXX
27

Rybinsk

Yaroslavl'

Memel

XXXX
18

XXXX
8

Lithuania

Daugavpils

XXXX
3

Volga

XXXX
22

XXXX
29

Kalinin

MOSCOW

Vladimir

Königsberg

Fourth Panzer
Army
HOEPNER

XXXX
16

XXXX
11

Kaunas

Vilna

XXXX
30

XXXX
19

Rzhev

XXXX
9

East
Prussia

XXXX
3

Niemen

Minsk

Vitebsk

XXXX
9

Orsha

Smolensk

XXXX
16

XXXX
32

Vyazma

XXXX
20

Ugra

Serpukhov

Kolomna

Ryazan

Bialystok

XXXX
3

Narew

Baranowicze

Army Group
Center
BOCK

Byelorussia

Mogilëv

Bobruysk

XXXX
4

Dnepr

XXXX
24

Desna

XXXX
28

Kaluga

Tula

Ryazhsk

WARSAW

Siedlce

XXXX
10

Brest-Litovsk

Pinsk

Pripet

Bug

XXXX
43

West Front
TIMOSHENKO

Poland

XXXX
4

XXXX
2

Klintsy

Gomel

Bryansk

XXXX
50

Orel

Lublin

XXXX
2

Kowel

Styr'

Goryn'

Mozyr

XXXX
3

Yelets

Vistula

XXXX
6

San

XXXX
1

XXXX
5

Luck

Sluch'

Desna

XXXX
13

Kursk

Seym

Sosna

XXXX
40

Voronezh

Jaroslaw

XXXX
17

Brody

Zhitomir

Kiev

Nezhin

Konotop

Sumy

South -West
Front
BUDENNY

Belgorod

Pavlovsk

Lwow

Dnestr

Tarnopol

Berdichev

XXXX
2

Romny

Psël

XXXX
21

Kharkov

Don

HUNGARY

XXXX
6

Army Group
South
RUNDSTEDT

Vinnitsa

Cherkassy

XXXX
1

Poltava

Zmie

Donets

XXXX
20

XXXX
26

Prut

U   k   r   a   i   n   e

Uman

Kremenchug

XXXX
38

Army Group
South
RUNDSTEDT

Chernovtsy

XXXX
3 ROM

Kirovo

Dniepropetrovsk

XXXX
6

Cluj

Siret

XXXX
18

Balta

Pervomaisk

Nikopol

XXXX
12

Stalino

Sibiu

Jassy

Kishinev

XXXX
4 ROM

Tiraspol

Nikolaev

Zaporozhye

Mariupol

Brasov

Mureş

XXXX
4 ROM

XXXX
9

Kherson

XXXX
18

XXXX
9

Olt

Galatz

XXXX
9

Odessa

XXXX
11

Sea of
Azov

ROMANIA

Ismail

Black Sea

XXXX
51

Crimea

Kerch

Bucharest

Sevastopol

0   100 km

0   100 miles

N

Right: Street fighting in the town of Zhitomir, east of Kiev in September 1941.

organized into three army groups: North, Center, and South. These groups were commanded respectively by Field Marshals von Leeb, von Bock, and von Rundstedt. Each group had its own tactical air-force in support. Facing them was the Red Army with 140 Divisions and other brigade-size units numbering approximately 2.9 million men and 10–19,000 tanks; though many were obsolete, some were still serviceable. The Red Air Force with some 8,000 aircraft was in the process of being reequipped.

The invasion began shortly after Hitler's Barbarossa Jurisdiction Decree, which exempted German soldiers from prosecution if they committed crimes against Soviet citizens. This, together with unrelenting German propaganda, set the bloody style of what would develop into an unrelentingly brutal campaign. Following the advance of the Wehrmacht came the Einsatzgruppers, whose mission was to murder the Jewish and any other "undesirable" elements in the conquered population.

After Stalin recovered from the shock of German invasion, he called on all Soviet citizens to commit themselves to a "relentless struggle" against the invaders. On 3 July he announced, in a famous radio broadcast, a "Patriotic War," a scorched earth policy: nothing of use was to fall into the hands of the invaders and a partisan war must be carried on in occupied territories. What was not destroyed in the fighting was destroyed by retreating Russians. German killing squads were at large and partisan groups began to emerge. Killing on an epic scale spread across western Russia. Attack, counterattack, ambush, annihilation: over 6 million soldiers locked in combat. Millions of civilians fled their homes, or hoped they might just, somehow, survive.

The German advance was met by a confused and disorganized resistance. The Red Army responded slowly and ineffectively to the massive tasks facing it. This was partly down to Stalin's purges of the late 1930s and to his instructions to take no "provocative" action. German High Command knew they had to destroy the bulk of the Red Army before it could fall back into the vast Russian interior, where it would await its greatest friend, General Winter. The early days and weeks of the German campaign witnessed massive advances, led by the four main Panzer groups, sometimes averaging advances of more than $18\frac{1}{2}$ miles per day. It seemed, for a time, like the conquest of France and the Low Countries all over again. But the marching columns of infantry with their horse-drawn transport could not keep up with the Panzers. The Panzer units themselves became increasingly committed to holding objectives and could no longer push eastward as they had done in the early days of the offensive. They were also outrunning their lines of supply. Destroyed railroads needed repair; the Russian road network was inadequate to the task the Germans required of it. Despite all of its problems, the German army achieved in the first weeks of the war vast encirclements, capturing hundreds of thousands of prisoners.

However, there was no Russian collapse. Despite massive losses, they created new replacements. One month after the German attack, the Soviet Army had risen from 170 to 212 Divisions, although many were under strength. German planners had assumed that the inferior Slav could not withstand the German military machine. Hitler had said to one of his Generals, "you just have to give the Russian state a good kick and the whole rotten regime will collapse." His soldiers advancing deeper into Russia were coming to grips with much tougher problems, ones that race and politics would not explain.

The bulk of the German offensive was concentrated north of the Pripyat Marshes with the

Army Groups North and Center. After crushing Soviet forces in Byelorussia, Army Group Center was to assist Army Group North, driving along the Baltic coast and turning toward Leningrad near Smolensk. Meanwhile, Army Group South would push into the Ukraine. Among the units marching eastward was the German 6th Army, which would later meet its nemesis at Stalingrad.

Army Group North made good progress but still suffered delays waiting for marching columns of infantry to catch up. Army Group Center advanced closely to plan, with a massive battle of encirclement at Minsk capturing 280,000 prisoners. This battle delayed the intended advance on Smolensk. However, by 17 July the city was in German hands. At this point Hitler intervened personally, overruling his generals who, according to the second phase of the plan, intended to head for Moscow. Instead he ordered Panzer Group 2 southward to support von Rundstedt's Group South Amy. On its way it met with unexpected armored counterattacks and other heavy resistance, causing it to fall behind schedule. Hitler then redirected Panzer Group 3 north to support the advance on Leningrad.

As the Red Army retreated, a massive effort to move industry eastward began. Approximately 50,000 factories and workshops were systematically dismantled, placed on railroad wagons, and

Vast numbers of Russian prisoners fell into German hands during Operation Barbarossa. By the end of the Russo-German war the total missing and prisoners of war for the Red Army reached 4,559,000. Of those that became prisoners of the Germans over 80 percent did not survive their captivity.

sent eastward, whenever possible with their workforce, under the watchful eye of the ruthless People's Commissariat for Internal Affairs, the Narodnyi Kommissariat Vnutrennikh Del (N.K.V.D.). This military organization also rounded up any suspected of defeatism, and they were marched into captivity, or simply shot on the spot. Major General Kopets, commander of the Soviet Western Air District, saved the N.K.V.D. the trouble by committing suicide on the first day of the invasion.

The crew of an SdKfz 10/5 flakwagon drive their vehicle under cover of trees. Armed with a 20 mm cannon, this was one of the vehicles developed to support the Blitzkreig tactics.

The N.K.V.D. were also responsible for labor camps and exercised control over a vast labor force, which was used in the construction of fortifications. They also supplied "elite" forces to support Red Army formations at critical points, similar to the German use of S.S. troops. In July 1941, they were used to defend the approaches to Kiev while the 21st N.K.D.V. Division was

Right: Soviet Infantrymen entrenched not far from German positions. As the Germans approached Leningrad, the Soviets constructed defensive trench systems to defend the city. The Germans decided against a frontal attack on the city with all the expensive cost in lives that street fighting would entail. Instead they tried encirclement and siege tactics, intent on starving the population into surrender. However, the Soviets refused to give in and fought on tenaciously, despite hunger and shortages.

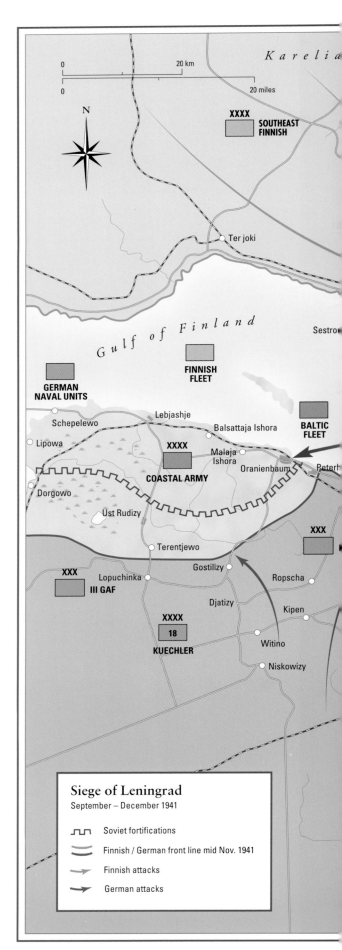

used in Leningrad's defense. However, they cast a far more sinister shadow in their apparent willingness to torture and slaughter large numbers of prisoners.

Meanwhile, Army Group North was advancing through the Baltic States and northern Russia, and by 21 August Panzer Group 4 had reached the area of Novgorod. A Soviet counterattack just south of Lake Ilmen temporarily caught Southern Corps off balance, but by 8 September advance elements of Army Group North captured Schlüsselburg, a small town on the shores of Lake Ladoga. With Germany's allies, the Finnish Army moved from the north along the Karelian isthmus, which effectively cut off the city of Leningrad.

Hitler decided not to advance into the city but to reduce it by artillery and air attack. So began one of the greatest sieges of modern times. The Soviets would hold on, defending the city of the October Revolution to the last. Leningrad's long, painful siege had begun.

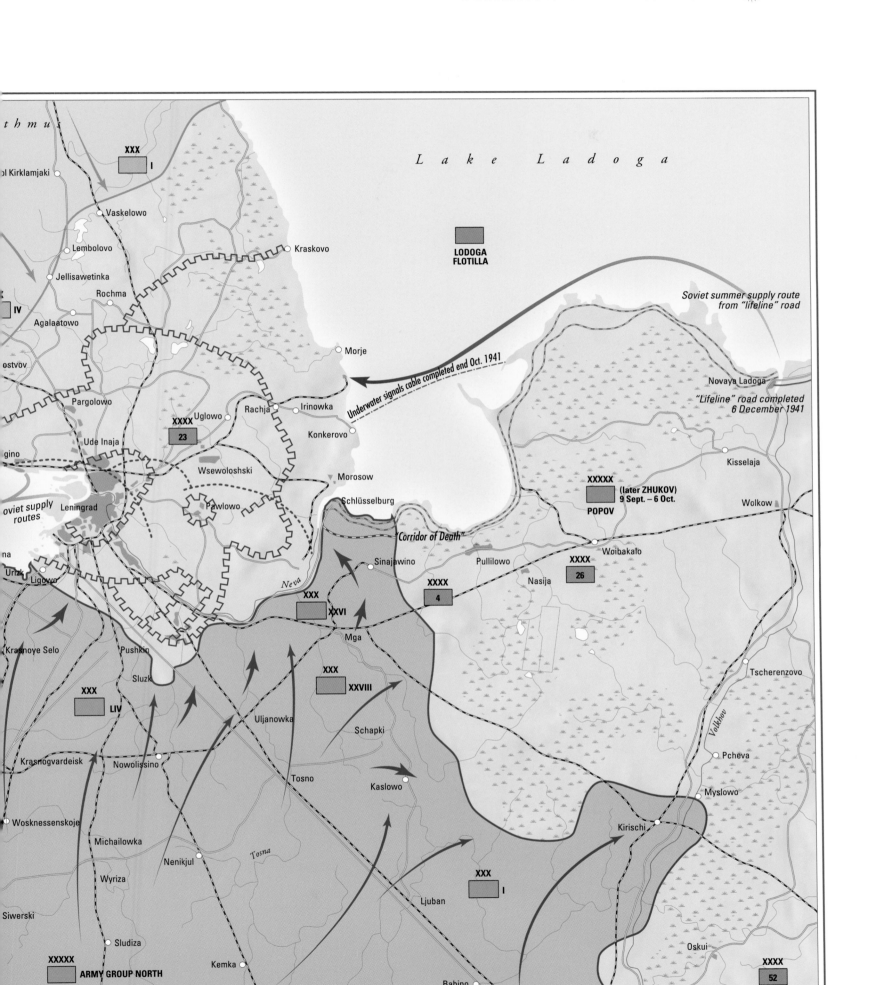

Lake Ladoga

XXX I

ol Kirklamjaki
Vaskelowo
Lembolovo
Jellisawetinka
Rochma
Kraskovo
Agalaatowo
IV
ostvov
Pargolowo
Morje
Ude Inaja
XXXX 23 Uglowo Rachja Irinowka
gino
Wsewoloshski
Konkerovo

LODOGA
FLOTILLA

Soviet summer supply route
from "lifeline" road

Underwater signals cable completed end Oct. 1941

Novaya Ladoga

"Lifeline" road completed
6 December 1941

Kisselaja

Morosow
Schlüsselburg

XXXXX POPOV (later ZHUKOV)
9 Sept. – 6 Oct.

Wolkow

oviet supply
routes
Leningrad
Pawlowo

"Corridor of Death"

na
Urizk
Ligowo

Neva
XXX XXVI

Sinajawino
Pullilowo
Nasija
XXXX 4

Woibakalo
XXXX 26

Krasnoye Selo
Pushkin
Sluzk

Mga

XXX XXVIII

Tscherenzovo

XXX LIV
Uljanowka
Schapki

Krasnogvardeisk Nowolissino
Tosno
Kaslowo
Pcheva

Wosknessenskoje
Michailowka
Nenikjul
Wyriza
Tosna
Ljuban
XXX I
Myslowo

Kirischi

Siwerski
Sludiza
Kemka
Oskui

XXXXX ARMY GROUP NORTH
LEEB
Babino
XXXX 52

Volkhov

OPERATION TYPHOON 1941

"THE RUSSIAN COLOSSUS ... HAS BEEN UNDERESTIMATED BY US ...
WHENEVER A DOZEN DIVISIONS ARE DESTROYED THE RUSSIANS
REPLACE THEM WITH ANOTHER DOZEN."

GENERAL FRANZ HALDER

GERMAN ARMY CHIEF OF STAFF, AUGUST 1941

One of the many problems faced by German infantry when the temperature dropped well below freezing was that the oil used to lubricate their weapons froze, jamming the action.

Intelligence information from guerrilla groups fighting behind the lines around Leningrad, reported seeing tanks and armored vehicles loaded onto trains and heading south away from the city. They were moving to the area west of Moscow leaving Leningrad—at least for now— to survive while preparing to attack Moscow. Stalin went with Zhukov, commander of the Leningrad Front, to Moscow. On arrival Zhukov was ordered by Stalin to oversee conditions on the Front personally. There he found chaos: units had lost touch with each other; stragglers from destroyed units wandered the countryside; and no one seemed to know where the Germans were, or had any idea of appropriate action to take. Within 24 hours of his arrival Zhukov sacked the commanders of the Western Front and Reserve Front and within another 48 hours he had assumed command of all forces around Moscow himself.

Zhukov inherited 90,000 beaten and hungry men, all that remained of the 800,000 who had begun the battle a few weeks earlier. He immediately set about strengthening Moscow's defenses, especially the Mozhaisk defense line 60 miles from the center of Moscow and the new defense line built in a semi-circle some 10 miles from the city center. It was constructed by hundreds of thousands of forced and volunteer

Operation Typhoon
September – December 1941

➤ German advances

➤ Soviet counterattacks

- - - German front line, 30 September

⎯ German front line, 15 November

⎯ German front line, 5 December

⊓⊔ Soviet defensive lines

◯ Soviet troops surrounded

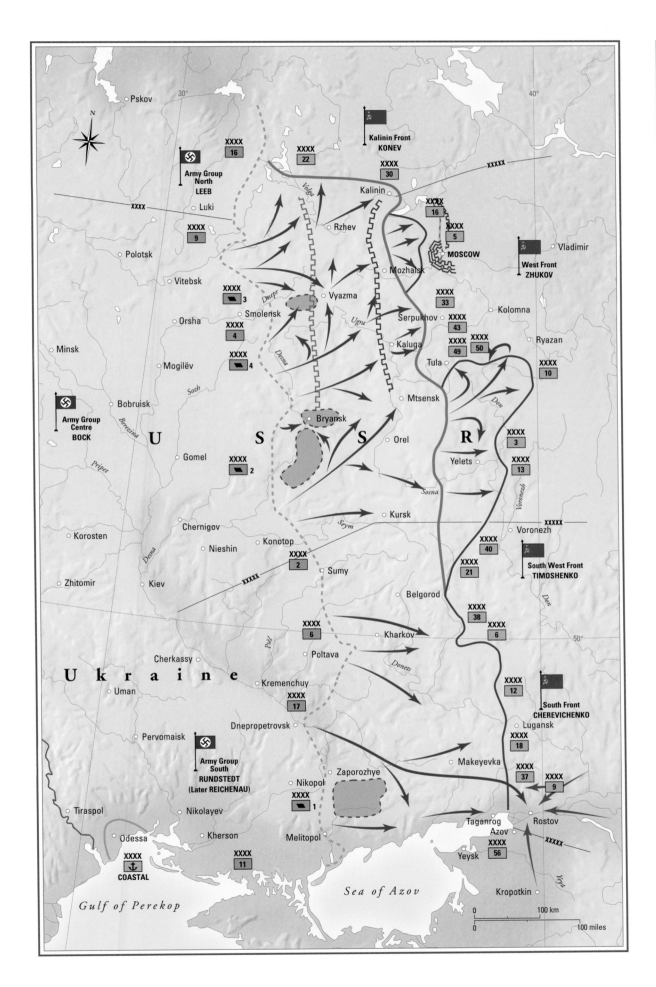

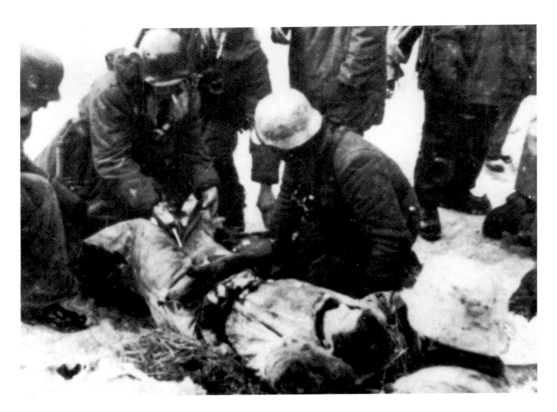

The original German plan called for Moscow to be captured before winter set in and had, therefore, not supplied its soldiers with sufficient winter clothing. In this dressing station near Moscow, medical orderlies dealt, not only with the wounded, but also severe cases of frostbite.

laborers, many of whom were women and children. They dug anti-tank ditches, built strong points and laid miles of barbed wire entanglements.

Meanwhile, reinforcements arrived in the form of six Soviet armies, some surviving veterans of earlier battles, and callow youths, fresh from the farm and the factory, whose first experience of all-out war this battle would be. On the other side of the wire, Hitler's Directive 35 of 6 September, made the capture of Moscow the primary objective of the 1941 Campaign.

Army Group North would continue to envelop Leningrad and Army Group South would head for Rostov-on-Don. Army Group Center, however, was to head for Moscow, combining with the bulk of German armor. After a period of regrouping, the mission would follow the familiar German pattern of deep armored thrust enveloping the Soviet forces, while the following infantry would consolidate and mop up, before moving on.

The assault began on 30 September, as the 2nd Panzer Group commanded by Heinz Guderian broke through the Soviet 13th Army, forcing two Soviet armies—the 50th and the 3rd—to attack eastward to avoid encirclement. Two days later, on 2 October, the 3rd and 4th Panzer Groups attacked, shattering Soviet defenses and surrounding elements of six Soviet armies west of Vyazma, taking 700,000 prisoners as they advanced.

On 6 October the first snow fell, earlier than usual; a day or so later it melted, turning the roads into an impassable state, the *rasputitsa*, meaning the "time without roads." The German armies' advances slowed down, not just for reasons of weather but also to consolidate the area already conquered and to round up numbers of leaderless Soviet soldiers roaming the landscape.

Although the German Army had made significant advances, the casualty figures were beginning to worry German High Command. At the end of August they stood at 389,924 killed, wounded, or missing—or 10 percent of the entire field army. By the end of September the figure was 551,039, over 16 percent of the field army. Replacements, however, were not being sent to the front at the same rate; the German Army on 1 October 1941 was over 200,000 men below strength.

The cities of Kalinin, north of Moscow, and Kaluga, to the south, had been captured by 18 October. It was beginning to look like another battle of encirclement but only very slow progress was made. The Soviets fought with bravery, driven mercilessly by Zhukov; there were some successes and some disasters but little by little the Soviets were getting to grips with German tactics and finding ways to defeat them.

A German sentry, on the front line before Moscow, keeps a careful look out for Russian counterattacks, while his comrade takes shelter from the freezing weather.

THE BATTLE OF MOSCOW 1942

"OH MERCIFUL LORD... CROWN OUR EFFORT WITH VICTORY ... AND GIVE US FAITH IN THE INEVITABLE POWER OF LIGHT OVER DARKNESS, OF JUSTICE OVER EVIL AND BRUTAL FORCE ... OF THE CROSS OF CHRIST OVER THE FASCIST SWASTIKA ... SO BE IT, AMEN." SERGEI, ARCHBISHOP OF MOSCOW, 27 NOVEMBER 1941

German soldiers fight their way through a town in central Russia. Despite the lowering temperatures these soldiers are still wearing their summer uniforms.

The German armies had made massive advances by October 1941, but crucially they were unable to make good all of their losses in manpower. Despite much higher losses, the Soviets had been able to raise reinforcements; new armies were formed and moved westward to threaten areas of the front. Special attention was paid to the line west of Moscow. While "the time of mud" continued, Zhukov could order, demand and harangue all sources of supply and men.

Stalin, meanwhile, decided to go ahead with the usual celebrations of the October Revolution. A meeting was held in the hall of the Mayakovsky Square subway station. Stalin rose and spoke to the audience, "If they want a war of extermination they shall have it!" and "Death to the German invaders!" He received tumultuous applause. The next day Red Square witnessed the usual parade, but this time the troops marched, not back to their barracks but straight to the front, now only 40 miles away.

To the north, the Germans waited for the mud to freeze and during November final plans for the encirclement and capture of Moscow were made. By mid-November the ground had frozen and the 3rd and 4th Panzer Groups attacked toward Klin, which fell on 24 November. Leading reconnaissance units pushed on and were just 12 miles from Red Square. South of the city, the 2nd Panzer Group attacked toward Tula; this time the Soviets were not going to give way. General Boldin, by now a tough veteran, had his men prepare defenses in depth so they would be better prepared than in previous battles. His men held their positions despite savage fighting. The southern thrust of the German attack ground to a halt.

At this point, Moscow was defended by the 240,000 men Zhukov had scraped together, with some

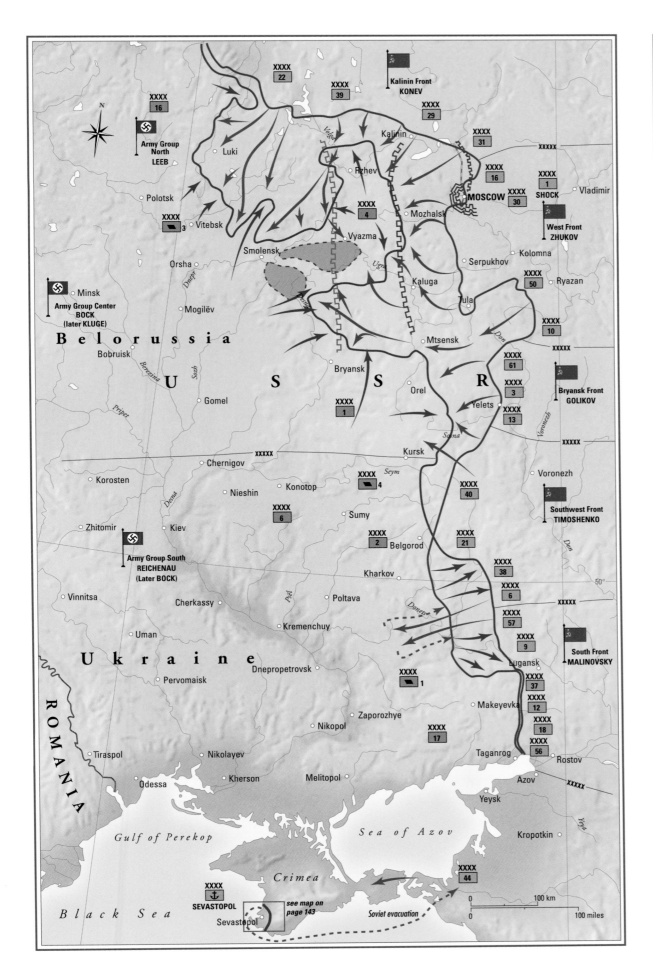

Battle for Moscow
January – June 1942

➤ German advances

➤ Soviet counterattacks

— German front line end May

— German front line June

⌐⌐ Soviet defensive lines

Soviet Partisans operating behind enemy lines

German soldiers warm themselves around a fire not far from the Moscow Front. The Wehrmacht was poorly equipped to face the harsh Russian winter.

A German tank moves into action on the Moscow Front with Infantry in support. The tank wears a swastika flag on its turret to help identify it for the Luftwaffe supporting aircraft, especially when in close action with the enemy.

500 tanks, many old and light, and of little use on the battlefield. He had concentrated his best troops in shock formations so that they could be rushed to any threatened sector. The bulk of Soviet soldiers defending Moscow at this stage were made of survivors from shattered units, men from rear areas, the most rudimentary trained Moscow militia, and men from the streets of Moscow and the surrounding villages. Zhukov maintained a tight control over this ragged force, and never lost contact with men at the front; he treated them all equally, but he drove them hard.

Around the middle of November, Stalin rang Zhukov asking, "Are you sure we can hold Moscow?" He replied, "We'll hold without a doubt." Privately, he admitted later, he was not so sure. However, little by little the German effort began to fade. By the end of November a quarter of the German army were casualties; their uniforms and equipment were not designed to stand up to the Russian winter. Soviet equipment was, and the men were also mentally ready for Russia's winter. The Soviets had somehow survived the worst. Since June almost 2,700,000 of their troops had been killed in action and 3,350,000 taken prisoner. Twenty Soviets had died for every German killed.

At the end of November, Stalin demanded a Soviet offensive to clear the German threat. Meanwhile, the Germans, exhausted and cold as they were, concluded that the Soviets were a spent force: they were to be proved wrong.

Zhukov explained to Stalin that he did not have the resources to launch an offensive but Stalin would have none of this and ordered Zhukov to get on with it. Zhukov drew up his plans and presented them to Stalin. His plan was simple: to hit the German pincers around Moscow. The force Zhukov assembled was about the same as the German forces it planned to attack but now, unknown to the Germans, the Soviet Stavka (General Headquarters of the armed forces) had carefully built a reserve for just such a plan. Some were already deployed before Moscow, with 58 new divisions ready, some withdrawn from the far east. They were tough Siberians boys, who arrived in December. They were equipped to fight in the deepest winter conditions; unlike the Germans who, in order to start a tank engine, had to light a stove placed beneath it.

The offensive began on the morning of 5 December 1941 at 03:00 am. In bitter weather both sides fought to the death, but slowly the Soviets gained more ground, recapturing Klin. In the south Stalinogorsk was liberated and the Soviet attack pushed forward. German Army Group Center was faced with the possibility of encirclement. German commanders asked Hitler for permission to fall back to more defensive positions. Hitler greeted the petition by sacking them all, and on 19 December took over command of the army himself. The battle went on into January, both sides fighting with tenacity and skill. Soviet units infiltrated the German front, while isolated German units were supplied by air or fought their way out.

Rasputitsa, "the time of mud" or "the time without roads." Here, a German supply wagon negotiates the rudimentary Russian road network. Much of the German Army's supply system still relied on horse-drawn wagons.

The sight of Germans on the defensive encouraged Stalin to order offensives along the front. Despite representations by Zhukov that the Red Army was not yet ready, the offensives were forced through. All failed and almost 450,000 Soviet troops were lost. It would be another 18 months before the Red Army would beat the Germans in an all-out summer offensive. Meanwhile, the army fought its dogged battles defending the Caucasus oilfields and in Stalingrad. The isolated Soviet garrison at Sevastopol finally succumbed to the German siege that had lasted from 6 June to 2 July 1942.

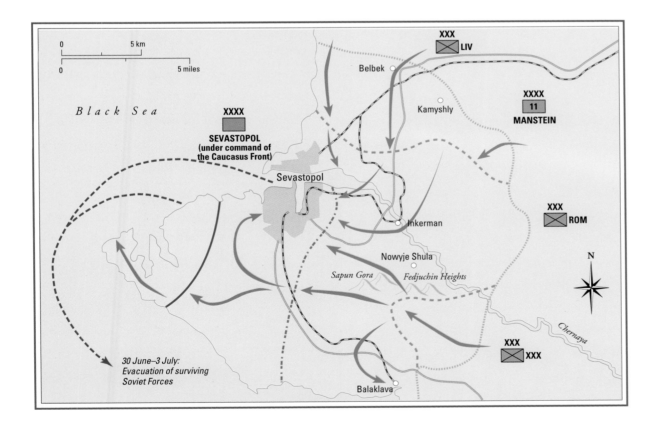

The Siege of Sevastopol
6 June – 2 July 1942

....	Front line 6 June
– – –	Front line 18 June
–·–·–	Front line 30 June
———	Front line 1 July
←	German attack
– –►	Soviet retreat

PEARL HARBOR 1941

"I CONTINUED TO WATCH THE SKY OVER THE HARBOR AS WELL AS THE ACTIVITIES ON THE GROUND. NONE BUT JAPANESE PLANES WERE IN THE AIR, AND THERE WERE NO INDICATIONS OF AIR COMBAT. SHIPS IN THE HARBOR STILL APPEARED TO BE ASLEEP."
CAPTAIN MITSUO FUCHIDA, COMMANDER FIRST AIR FLEET

THE HAWAII OPERATION
The operational units deployed were divided into two groups. The Task Force, responsible for the air attacks, and the Submarine Force, responsible for intercepting American ships leaving or entering Pearl Harbor and its surrounding area. At 6:00 pm. local time the Task Force sailed from Hitokappu Bay into the northern Pacific en route for Pearl Harbor. Meanwhile, the Submarine Force headed for the Hawaiian Islands via three converging routes.

With expansion of the Japanese empire into China during the 1930s and early 1940s, the U.S. Navy decided to start developing its assets in the Pacific area to defend America's interests. Japan's Navy and the U.S. Navy were almost identical in size, but Japan could not afford to fight a prolonged war with the U.S., limited by its severe lack of natural resources, especially oil. With the West's oil embargo forced upon Japan after her invasion of French Indo-China the situation was becoming desperate. Japan looked upon Malaya and the Dutch East Indies as the answer to her fuel crisis and with the European war holding down most of Britain's available forces and with the capitulation of the Dutch and French to Germany, Japan's only threat in the Pacific was the U.S. Navy. A preemptive strike on the U.S. fleet would ensure enough time for the Japanese to grab the assets they so desperately needed and achieve their aims before the U.S. could recover.

The planning of the attack was given to Admiral Yamamoto, even though he thought that making war with America was a grave mistake. Many of the military commanders thought

USSR

Manchukuo

Departure from Hitokappu Bay
Tokyo time 06.00 26 Nov
Hawaii time 10.30 25 Nov
Washington time 16.00 25 Nov

Fleet concentrates 22 Nov 41.
Sortie begins 26 Nov 41

Korea

Sea of Japan

2nd Submarine Gro
Sailed 16 November and proceeded ur
29 November when it turned for the Hawaii
Islands. This was a formation commanded
Rear Admiral Yamazaki Shigeaki and
consisted of the I-1, I-2, I-3, I-4, I-5, I-6 and

Honshu

JAPAN

Bonin Islands

Tropic of Cancer

N

3rd Submarine Group
Sailed 11 November. This was a formation
commanded by Rear Admiral Shigeyoshi Miwa
and consisted of the I-8, I-68, I-69, I-70, I-71,
I-72, I-73, I-74 and the I-75

0   1000 km
0   1000 miles

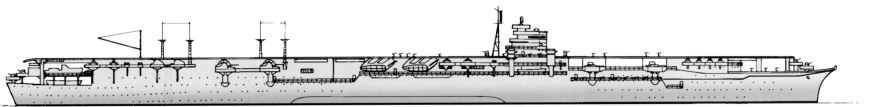

it impossible to attack a fleet at anchor, especially with torpedoes which would simply lodge into the mud of a relatively shallow harbor. This was proven wrong by 21 outmoded British Swordfish biplanes of the Fleet Air Arm, which attacked Taranto Harbor on 11 November 1940, sinking many of the Italian fleet and reversing the balance of naval power in the Mediterranean. The Japanese trained its pilots extensively on the attack and modified their torpedoes with wooden fins to prevent them going below a certain depth. It was to be a massive operation involving the fleet's six best aircraft carriers under the command of Vice-Admiral Nagumo with over 430 aircraft to be deployed in the attack.

After intense training in the secluded Kurile Islands, the fleet left for Hawaii, taking a northern route so as not to be easily detected by the U.S. Navy. Accompanying the six carriers were two battleships, numerous escort vessels, and eight support ships that would refuel the main force south of the Aleutian Islands before the task force steamed towards Hawaii. There would also be a force of

The aircraft carrier *Zuikaku*, launched in November 1939 and weighed in at 32,000 tons, was capable of carrying more than 72 aircraft. She was one of six carriers that took part in the Hawaii Operation.

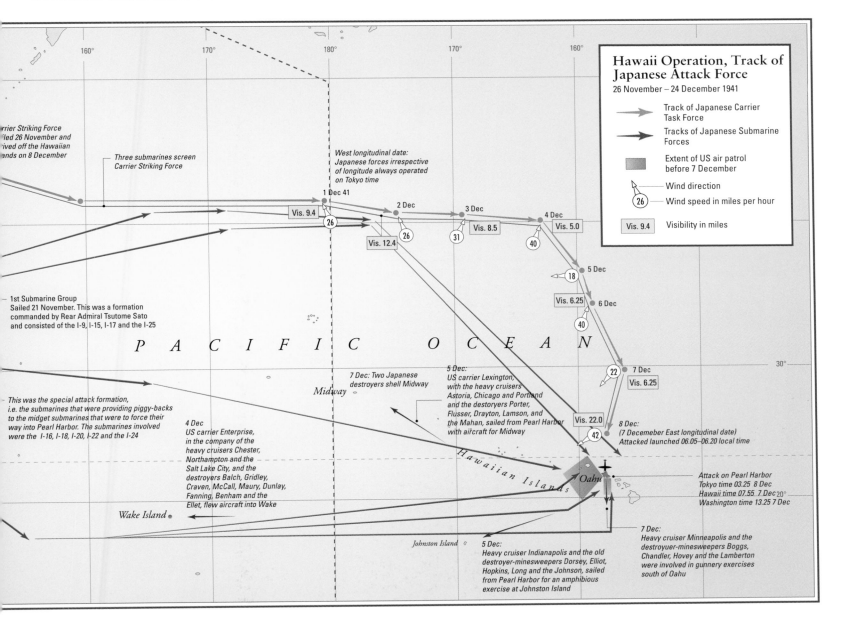

Midget submarine deployment

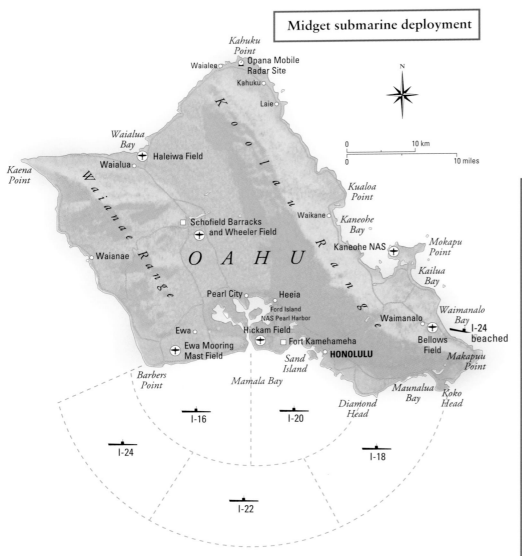

Map below: The first air strike deployed at 07:40 am, with the attack run ordered at 07:50 am, as the air group passed just off Keana Point. This first wave, of 190 aircraft, began their attacks. The first targets were airfields, in order to suppress possible interception by the few American fighters that could be made ready for take-off, followed by the crowded anchorage of Pearl Harbor.

The Japanese General Staff considered the successful outcome of an air attack on Pearl Harbor to be about 50 percent. Therefore a submarine operation was also launched, involving 18 submarines, five of which carried midget subs to be deployed in Manila Bay and the entrance to Pearl Harbor. The Submarine Force arrived according to plan, before the Task Force. Having time to reconnoiter ships entering and leaving the harbor, it was in a position to attack ships at anchor, or in the immediate area, should the air attack fail.

Below: One of the Japanese midget submarines that was located by the destroyer USS *Helms* and forced to beach.

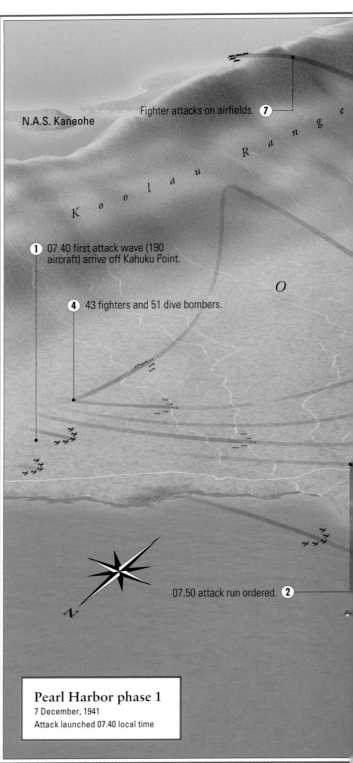

N.A.S. Kaneohe

Fighter attacks on airfields. ⑦

① 07.40 first attack wave (190 aircraft) arrive off Kahuku Point.

④ 43 fighters and 51 dive bombers.

07.50 attack run ordered. ②

Pearl Harbor phase 1
7 December, 1941
Attack launched 07.40 local time

midget submarines that would infiltrate the harbor and cause as much damage as possible, once launched from its larger parent submarine.

Even though the American intelligence expected an attack at some point from the Japanese, they concluded it would occur in the Philippines. The only sort of attack that was to be thought possible at Pearl Harbor was minor sabotage missions, but nothing on the scale that was en route to meet them. The Commander-in-Chief of the Pacific Fleet, Rear-Admiral Kimmel, looked toward the Marshall Islands, the closest Japanese territory to Hawaii, and it was from here that he expected any

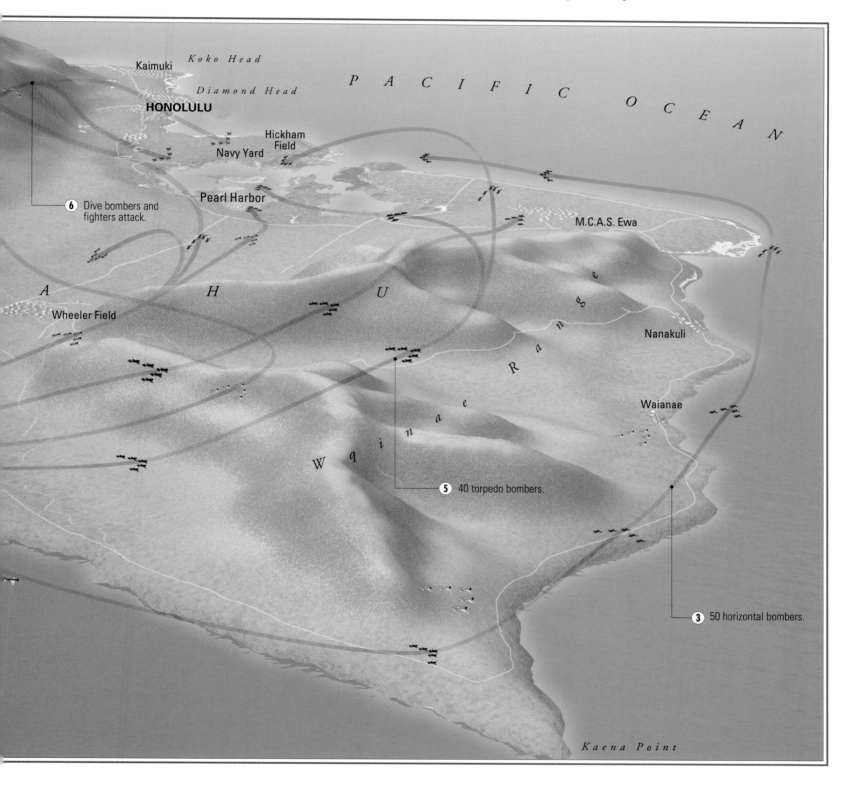

operation to be launched. The War Office in Washington, based on best available intelligence assessments, sent a final war warning to all military commanders in the Pacific, including the Army commander Lt-General Walter Short at Oahu. He assumed that this was to prepare for sabotage attacks and did not even authorize the deployment of ammunition to antiaircraft batteries. Aircraft designated to the defense of the islands were not dispersed properly and lined up on the runways like ducks in a shooting gallery. After some consideration, the Japanese took the decision to attack on a Sunday, since the maximum amount of naval crews would be ashore on leave and would not be able

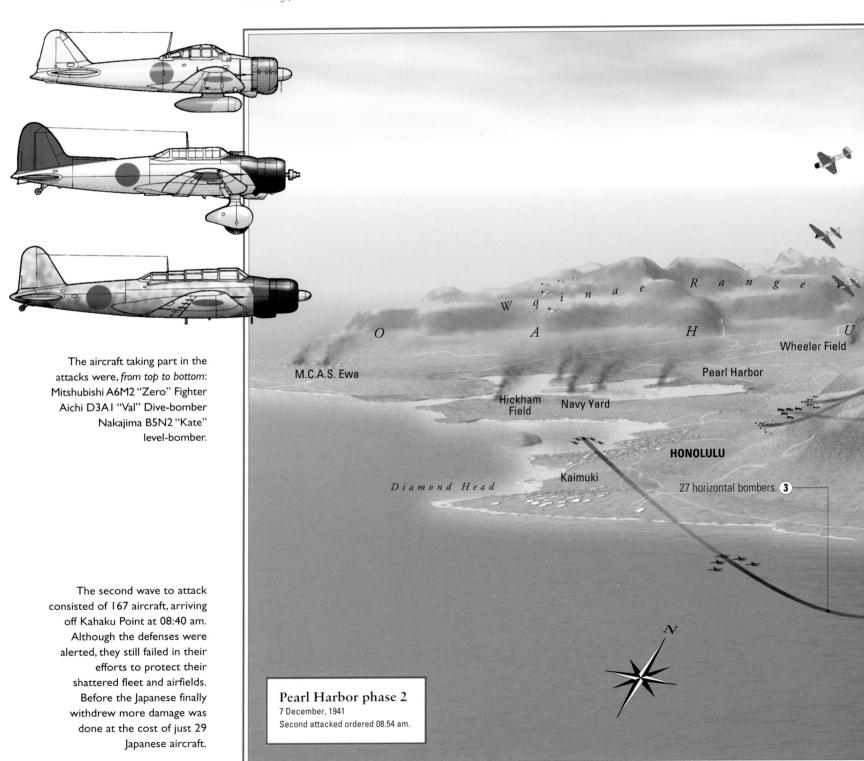

The aircraft taking part in the attacks were, *from top to bottom*: Mitshubishi A6M2 "Zero" Fighter Aichi D3A1 "Val" Dive-bomber Nakajima B5N2 "Kate" level-bomber.

The second wave to attack consisted of 167 aircraft, arriving off Kahaku Point at 08:40 am. Although the defenses were alerted, they still failed in their efforts to protect their shattered fleet and airfields. Before the Japanese finally withdrew more damage was done at the cost of just 29 Japanese aircraft.

27 horizontal bombers. **3**

Pearl Harbor phase 2
7 December, 1941
Second attacked ordered 08.54 am.

to assist in the defense of their ships or the harbor. With the Japanese strike force now 250 nautical miles north of Hawaii, Nagumo was disappointed to hear from a forward reconnaissance unit that there were no carriers in the harbor. They were in fact delivering aircraft to Midway Island. Nevertheless he gave the order for the first wave to take to the air at 6:00 am and were in formation and on their way in 15 minutes. The first wave consisted of 51 "Val" dive-bombers, 49 "Kate" level-bombers, 40 "Kate" torpedo-bombers, and 43 "Zero" fighters. This created a serious blip on the radar screens of a training unit on Kahuku Point, but when they reported to the duty officer he shrugged it

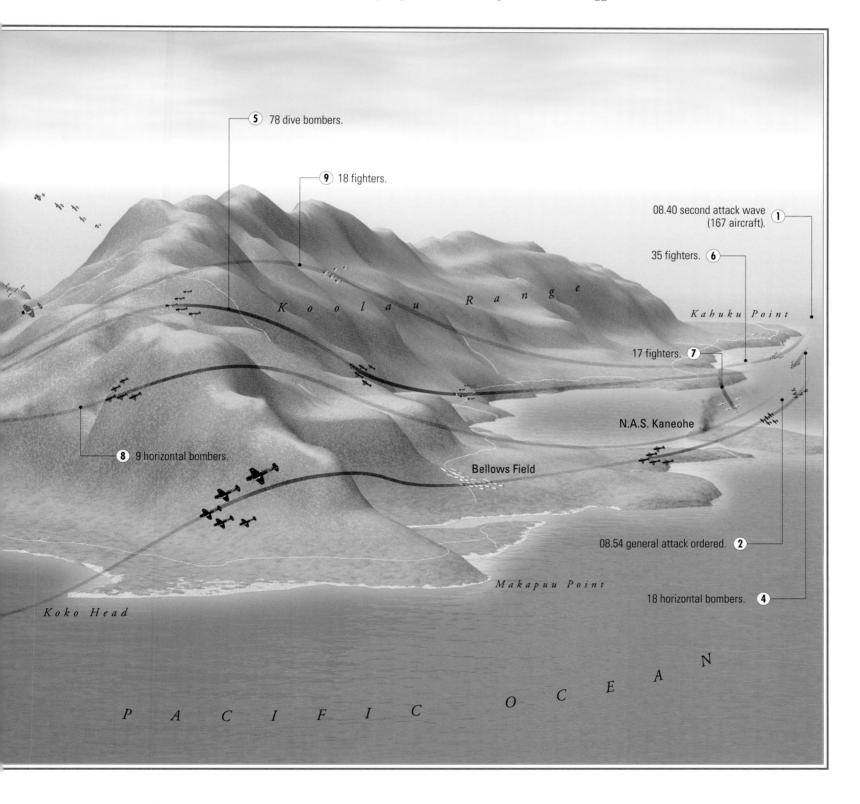

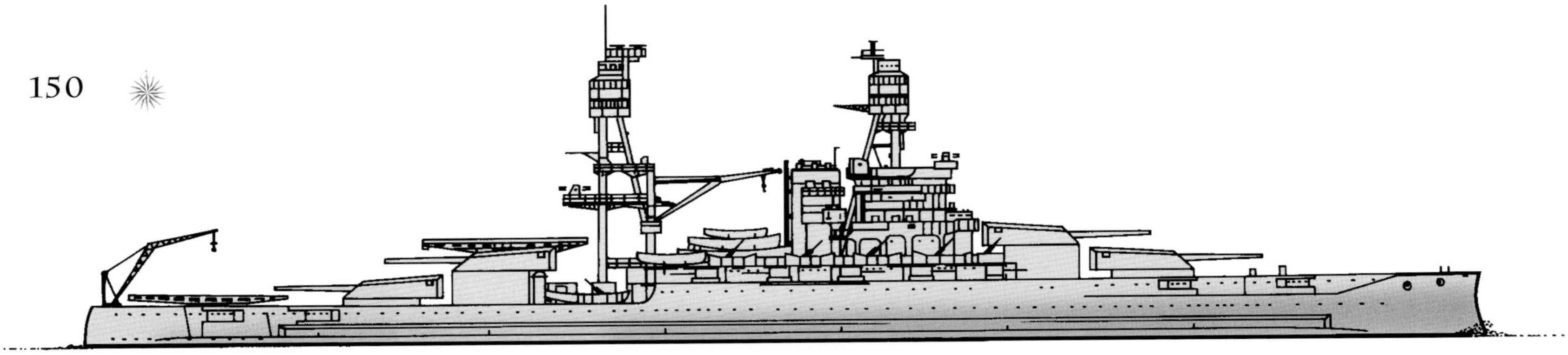

The USS *Arizona as* she appeared in 1941. She was destroyed with the loss of almost 1,200 men.

① Tender *Whitney* and destroyers *Tucker, Conyngham, Reid, Case,* and *Selfridge*
② Destroyer *Blue*
③ Light cruiser *Phoenix*
④ Destroyers *Aylwin, Farragut, Dale,* and *Monaghan*
⑤ Destroyers *Patterson, Ralph, Talbot,* and *Henley*
⑥ Tender *Dobbin* and destroyers *Worden, Hull, Dewey, Phelps,* and *Macdough*
⑦ Hospital Ship *Solace*
⑧ Destroyer *Allen*
⑨ Destroyer *Chew*
⑩ Destroyer-minesweepers *Gamble,* and *Montgomery,* and light-minelayer *Ramsey*
⑪ Destroyer-minesweepers *Trever, Breese, Zane, Perry,* and *Wasmuth*
⑫ Repair vessel *Medusa*
⑬ Seaplane tender *Curtiss*
⑭ Light cruiser *Detroit*
⑮ Light cruiser *Raleigh*
⑯ Target battleship *Utah*
⑰ Seaplane tender *Tangier*
⑱ Battleship *Nevada*
⑲ Battleship *Arizona*
⑳ Repair vessel *Vestal*
㉑ Battleship *Tennessee*
㉒ Battleship *West Virginia*
㉓ Battleship *Maryland*
㉔ Battleship *Oklahoma*
㉕ Oiler *Neosho*
㉖ Battleship *California*
㉗ Seaplane tender *Avocet*
㉘ Destroyer *Shaw*
㉙ Destroyer *Downes*
㉚ Destroyer *Cassin*
㉛ Battleship *Pennsylvania*
㉜ Submarine *Cachalot*
㉝ Minelayer *Oglala*
㉞ Light cruiser *Helena*
㉟ Auxiliary vessel *Argonne*
㊱ Gunboat *Sacramento*
㊲ Destroyer *Jarvis*
㊳ Destroyer *Mugford*
㊴ Seaplane tender *Swan*
㊵ Repair vessel *Rigel*
㊶ Oiler *Ramapo*
㊷ Heavy cruiser *New Orleans*
㊸ Destroyer *Cummings,* and light-minelayers *Preble,* and *Tracy*
㊹ Heavy cruiser *San Francisco*
㊺ Destroyer-minesweeper *Grebe,* destroyer *Schley,* and light-minelayers *Pruitt* ,and *Sicard*
㊻ Light cruiser *Honolulu*
㊼ Light cruiser *St. Louis*
㊽ Destroyer *Bagley*
㊾ Submarines *Narwhal, Dolphin,* and *Tautog,* and tenders *Thornton,* and *Hulbert*
㊿ Submarine tender *Pelias*
(51) Auxiliary vessel *Sumner*
(52) Auxiliary vessel *Castor*

off as a flight of B-17s expected from the U.S. mainland. As the strike force neared the harbor they were assisted by listening to the local radio broadcasts. First to press home their attack were the dive-bombers, early by five minutes at 7:55 am, then shortly after, the torpedo bombers started their run at battleship row. Meanwhile the Zero fighters were strafing all the nearby airfields and destroying the majority of U.S. aircraft neatly lined up on the ground. With the element of surprise, hardly any anti-aircraft fire and no fighter interceptors to worry about, the Japanese pilots could completely concentrate on the job in hand. Ten minutes after the attack had begun there was an almighty eruption as USS *Arizona*'s ammunition magazine was penetrated by an armor-piercing bomb, immediately sinking, taking 1,200 sailors down with her. Behind her mangled stern, USS *West Virginia* and USS *California* were also torpedoed and sunk. USS *Nevada* actually got underway and tried in desperation to get to the relative safety of the open sea. The Japanese pilots concentrated fire upon her and she was eventually beached. With the harbor covered in burning oil and stricken and sinking craft, the first wave headed back to the carriers.

There was to be no respite for the servicemen at Pearl Harbor: as soon as the first wave left the second wave of attack planes arrived. However, the defenders by now were starting to get themselves in order and were throwing up a ferocious amount of antiaircraft fire and, with the smoke from fires started in the first attack, the Japanese could not cause as much damage as the initial assault.

By the end of the attack, the Japanese forces had lost 29 aircraft but created total havoc below them, sinking six battleships, three destroyers, and three light cruisers, and damaging two. Having received reports, Nagumo decided his luck had been pushed far enough and did not give the order for the third wave to attack. This vital decision was a grave mistake, since none of the harbor installation had been destroyed and Pearl Harbor could still be used as a serviceable base.

Although this was a massive blow to the American psyche, the country was united in defeating a deceitful and vicious enemy, something Yamamoto had always feared: instead of weakening the beast they had only succeeded in making it angry. Nagumo had also missed the opportunity to destroy the U.S. carrier fleet, which was much more important than sinking six outmoded battleships. It may have been a tactical victory for the Japanese but they would soon lose the initiative they needed.

Left: The USS Nevada managed to get underway and was moving down battleship row when she attracted the attention of the second attack. She was repeatedly hit and finally was beached.

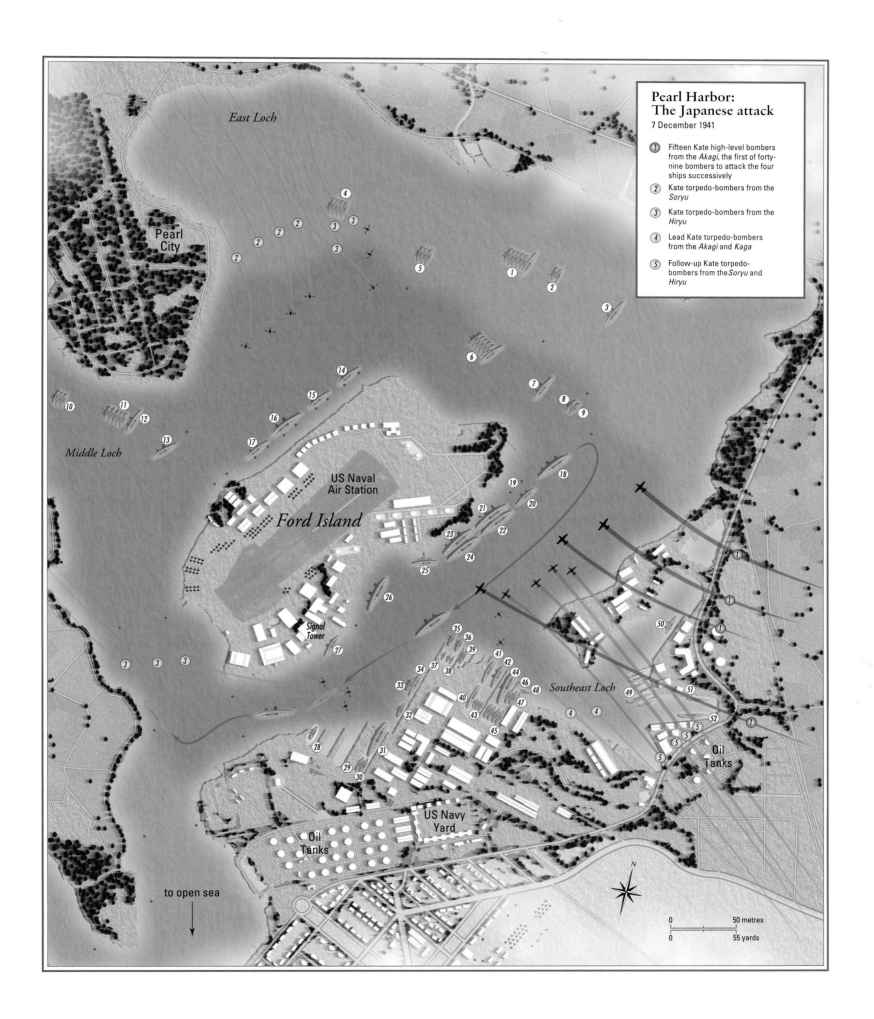

**Pearl Harbor:
The Japanese attack**
7 December 1941

① Fifteen Kate high-level bombers from the *Akagi*, the first of forty-nine bombers to attack the four ships successively

② Kate torpedo-bombers from the *Soryu*

③ Kate torpedo-bombers from the *Hiryu*

④ Lead Kate torpedo-bombers from the *Akagi* and *Kaga*

⑤ Follow-up Kate torpedo-bombers from the *Soryu* and *Hiryu*

East Loch

Pearl City

Middle Loch

US Naval Air Station

Ford Island

Signal Tower

Southeast Loch

US Navy Yard

Oil Tanks

Oil Tanks

to open sea

0   50 metres
0   55 yards

CHINA 1942–43

"THE CHINESE SOLDIER WAS TOUGH, BRAVE, AND EXPERIENCED. AFTER ALL HE HAD BEEN FIGHTING ON HIS OWN WITHOUT HELP FOR YEARS. HE WAS A VETERAN AMONG THE ALLIES."

GENERAL BILL SLIM

Chinese troops go into action in the defence of Nanking.

After Japan's attack on Pearl Harbor, the Sino-Japanese War merged into World War II. The Japanese in China had been consolidating their positions and a virtual stalemate existed. Now the war picked up again in an engagement called the Battle of South Shanxi (7–27 May 1941). Later, Japanese forces attempted to take Changsha (6 September–8 October 1941) with over 120,000 troops but were repulsed by Chinese units under General Xue Yue, sustaining 10,000 dead.

Another attempt against Chagsha began at the end of 1941 (24 December 1941–15 January 1942). While marching from Yueyang, four Japanese divisions pushed aside three Chinese divisions, and stormed Changsha on 31 December. The city had been evacuated of civilians while Chinese forces still held on. The Japanese broke the first lines of defense but were held up by the second line when the Chinese launched a counterattack. Meanwhile, the original three divisions returned to assault Japanese supply lines, the combined Chinese onslaught forcing the Japanese to retreat suffering heavy losses. The victory was a much needed boost to Allied morale coming just one month after Pearl Harbor, though little was heard of the battle in the west.

Other major engagements took place during the Battles of the Yunnan–Burma Road. The Chinese intervened under Lt. General Joseph Stilwell to help their British Allies in the 1942 Burma campaign. Fourteen engagements took place between 20 March and 23 May 1942, though the British and Chinese were pushed out of Burma. The most publicized battle took place at Yenangyaung (17–19 April 1942) when the Allies lost control of the oilfields there.

On 18 April, the United States launched an attack by B-25 Mitchell bombers from USS *Hornet* on Tokyo, Nagoya, and Yokohama. The planes were to land in China but crash-landed in Zhejiang and Jiangxi provinces after they ran out of fuel. Sixty-four airmen parachuted into Zhejiang after which the Japanese mounted a huge search operation destroying any settlement thought to be harboring these men. The two provinces were devastated and an estimated 250,000 civilian deaths resulted.

Elsewhere, the Koumintang forces under the command of Chaing Kai-shek established an economic blockade of Communist-held Yan'an. The Communists constantly used small night-time guerrilla actions to attack isolated Japanese positions and communications. These successes resulted in brutal reprisals. During this period, the Communists gained more party members and built up their forces to over 900,000 men and women. Although these forces could not confront heavily-armed Japanese troops in battle, their control of the countryside at night soon tied down some one million Japanese soldiers. Meanwhile, the Nationalists press-ganged the population for military recruits, and this, added to the massive corruption in the political and military elite, created gross inequalities between officers and men. Little fighting against the Japanese took place, Chiang preferred to save his best units for a confrontation against the Communists.

Meanwhile, Major-General Claire Lee Chennault's "Flying Tigers" mercenary force, operating in China, was achieving a superb combat record and later became part of the U.S. 14th Air Force. By 1942, U.S. transport planes flew supplies over the Himalayas, "the Hump," to help the Nationalists after the Burma Road running between Lashio and Kunming had been cut by the Japanese seizure of Burma.

During the course of World War II the bulk of the Japanese army was deployed in China.

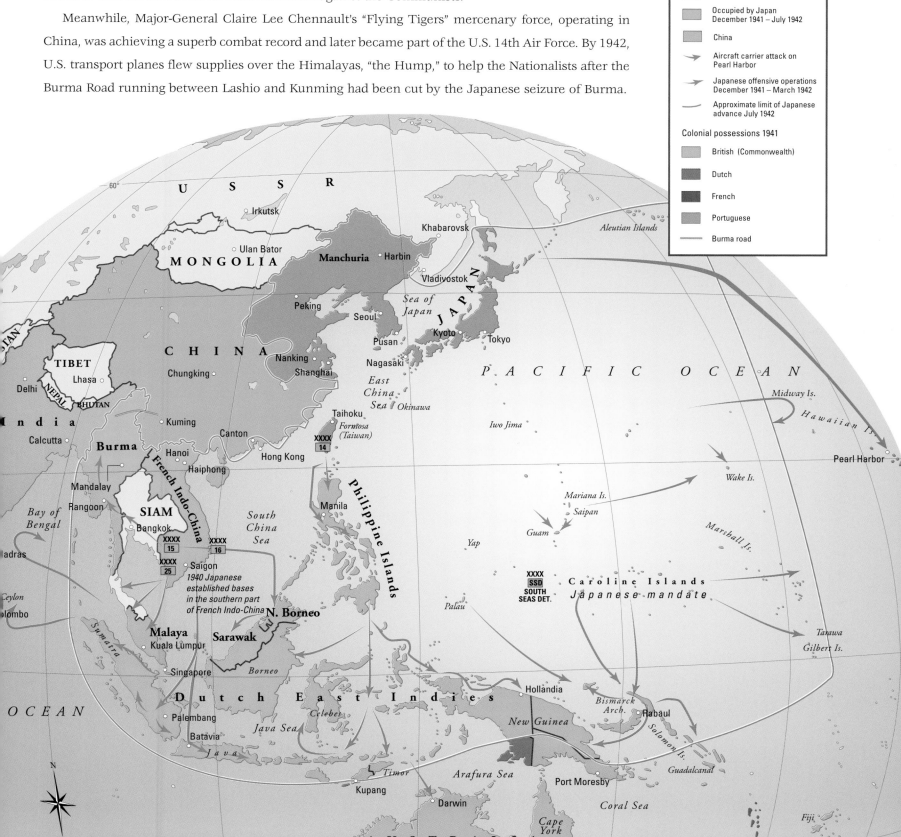

Japanese Expansion
December 1941 – July 1942

▨	Japanese Empire early 1941
▨	Occupied by Japan December 1941 – July 1942
▨	China
→	Aircraft carrier attack on Pearl Harbor
→	Japanese offensive operations December 1941 – March 1942
⌒	Approximate limit of Japanese advance July 1942

Colonial possessions 1941

▨	British (Commonwealth)
▨	Dutch
▨	French
▨	Portuguese
—	Burma road

Malaya, Singapore, the Philippines, and the Dutch East Indies 1941–42

"IN THIS HOUR OF TRIAL THE GENERAL OFFICER COMMANDING CALLS UPON ALL RANKS OF MALAYA COMMAND FOR A DETERMINED AND SUSTAINED EFFORT TO SAFEGUARD MALAYA AND THE ADJOINING BRITISH TERRITORIES. THE EYES OF THE EMPIRE ARE UPON US."

LT.-GENERAL ARTHUR E. PERCIVAL

The Japanese invasion of Malaya was carried out with skill and incredible speed and was to be a decisive blow to British prestige and power in the east. Many of the British units facing the Japanese onslaught were untried in battle, some only half-trained and recently arrived in the region, whereas most of the Japanese forces facing the British had been "blooded" in the savage fighting in Manchuria and China. It was not going to be an equal contest.

On 8 December Japanese forces from the 25th Army, led by Lt-General Tomoyuki Yamashita, invaded northern Malaya and parts of southern Thailand. Yamashita's aim was to take Malaya as quickly as possible and not give the British forces any chance to set up a viable line of defense. He could then attack and capture Singapore from the lightly defended north. Almost all of the British heavy guns faced east, west, and south, covering the seaward approaches to Singapore. After a heavy bombardment from the warships of Vice-Admiral Kondo, Japanese forces swarmed ashore at Koto Bharu in northern Malaya while other forces landed at Singora and Petani in southern Thailand. The defenders on the beach cut down many of the Japanese, but by sheer weight of numbers and determination they were soon overwhelmed.

Yamashita sent his 5th Division heading south toward Singapore, down the west coast of Malaya from Thailand, while elements of 18th Division, known as Koba and Takumi detachments, headed down the east coast. Takumi detachment quickly took the British airbase at Kota Bharu and immediatly made use of it as a forward base. The Japanese also began daily bombing raids on Singapore itself, and with the R.A.F. flying just a few obsolete aircraft, they were unable to put up much resistance.

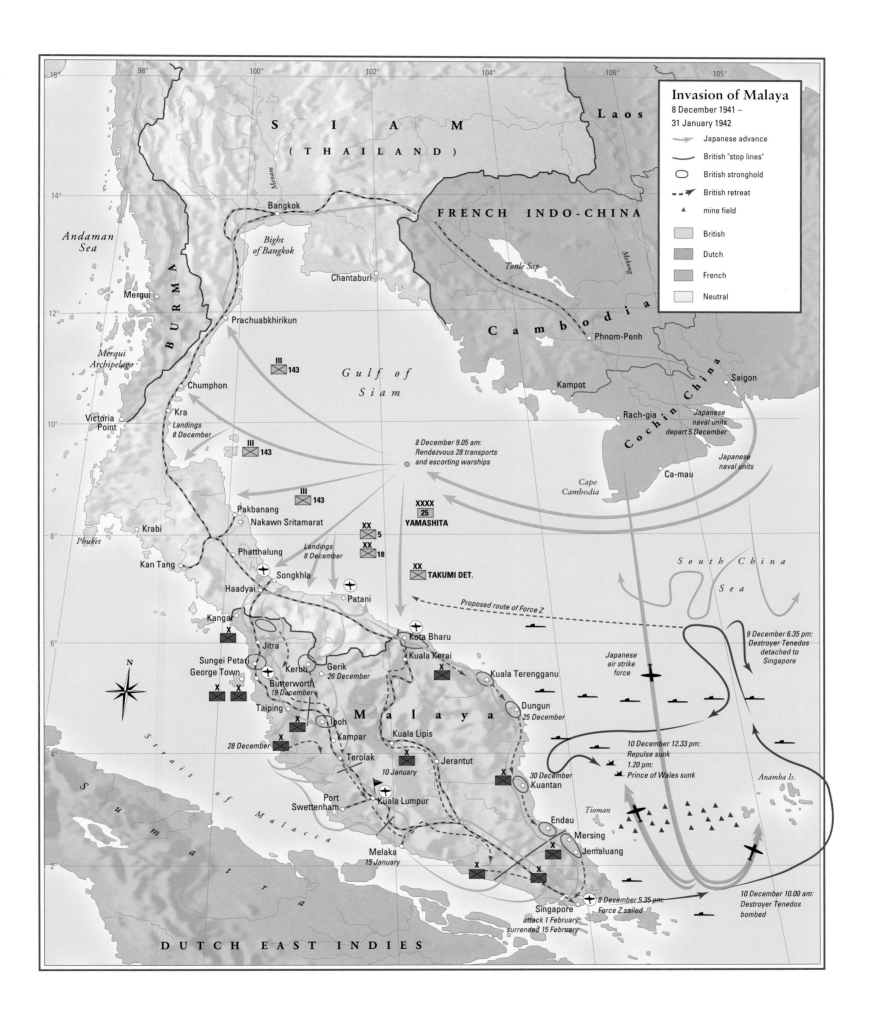

Invasion of Malaya
8 December 1941 –
31 January 1942

→ Japanese advance
⌒ British "stop lines"
◯ British stronghold
- -▸ British retreat
▲ mine field

British
Dutch
French
Neutral

S I A M

(T H A I L A N D)

Laos

FRENCH INDO-CHINA

Andaman
Sea

Bight
of Bangkok

Bangkok

Chantaburi

Tonle Sap

B U R M A

Mergui

Prachuabkhirikun

Cambodia

Phnom-Penh

Kampot

Saigon

Mergui
Archipelago

Chumphon

III 143

Gulf of
Siam

Rach-gia

Japanese
naval units
depart 5 December

Cochin China

Kra
Landings
8 December

Victoria
Point

III 143

Ca-mau

Japanese
naval units

Pakbanang

III 143

Cape
Cambodia

Krabi

Nakawn Sritamarat

XXXX 25 YAMASHITA

Phuket

Phatthalung

Landings
8 December

XX 5
XX 18

South China
Sea

Kan Tang

Songkhla

XX TAKUMI DET.

8 December 9.05 am:
Rendezvous 28 transports
and escorting warships

Haadyai

Patani

Proposed route of Force Z

Kangar

Kota Bharu

9 December 6.35 pm:
Destroyer Tenedos
detached to
Singapore

Jitra

Kuala Kerai

Japanese
air strike
force

Sungei Petani
George Town

Keroh
Gerik
26 December

Kuala Terengganu

Butterworth
19 December

X
X

Taiping

Ipoh

Malaya

Kuala Lipis

Dungun
25 December

Kampar
28 December

X

Terolak

Jerantut

10 December 12.33 pm:
Repulse sunk
1.20 pm:
Prince of Wales sunk

10 January

30 December
Kuantan

Anamba Is.

Port
Swettenham

Kuala Lumpur

Tioman

Strait of Malacca

Endau

Mersing

Melaka
15 January

Jemaluang

X

X
X

Singapore
attack 1 February
surrendered 15 February

8 December 5.35 pm:
Force Z sailed

10 December 10.00 am:
Destroyer Tenedos
bombed

D U T C H   E A S T   I N D I E S

Sumatra

Lieutenant-General Sir Arthur Percival with his staff officers are escorted by Japanese officers to sign the British surrender of Singapore on 15 February 1942.

The British dispatched two battleships, HMS *Prince of Wales* and HMS *Repulse*, to attack the Japanese invasion fleet still moored off Kota Bharu on 8 December. However, local commanders failed to provide air cover for these major warships and they were soon spotted by Japanese aircraft, attacked, and quickly sunk. This was a massive blow to Allied sea power in the area, since they were two of the Royal Navy's most powerful warships, the only capital ships based in Singapore.

The Japanese rapidly advanced to the south, thanks to the simple employment of bicycles, although they also had at their disposal 80 tanks and 40 armored cars with which the British forces had nothing to combat. The British did manage to set up defensive lines on the west coast but the Japanese simply outflanked them by sea or through the dense jungle. The British forces, thus outflanked, continued falling back. The capital, Kuala Lumpur, was captured by the Japanese on 11 January. The British decided to set up a holding line north of the Jahore Strait using 8th Australian and 9th Indian Divisions, which became known as Westforce, with a similar group, Eastforce, made up from 22nd Australian Brigade. When these still failed to stem the Japanese advance, all of the surviving Allied units were withdrawn to the island of Singapore.

Singapore was supposed to be an island fortress, known as the "Gibraltar of the east," but all its defenses were situated to face a seaborne attack and not from the jungle on the mainland to the north. The man in charge of the defense was Lt-General Percival, who quickly opted to place his forces thinly around the whole perimeter after blowing up the causeway connecting Singapore to the

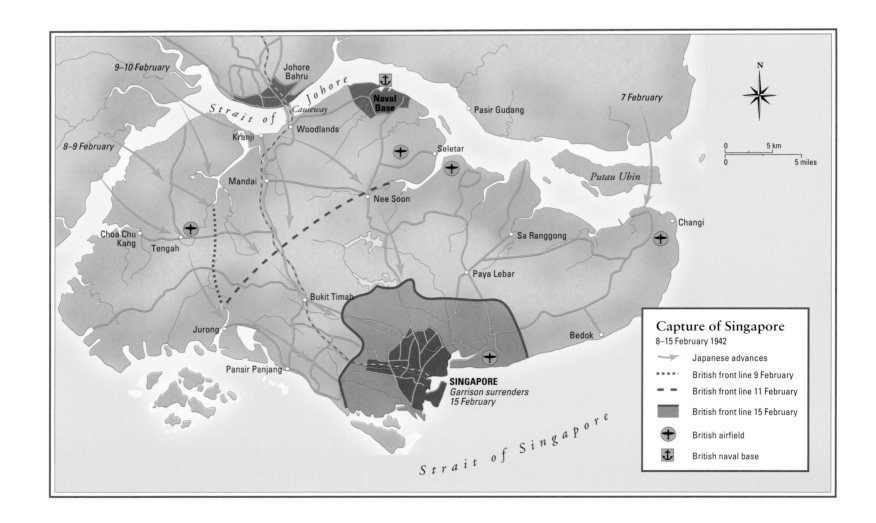

Capture of Singapore
8–15 February 1942

→ Japanese advances
····· British front line 9 February
– – – British front line 11 February
▬ British front line 15 February
✛ British airfield
⚓ British naval base

mainland. The forces that would be facing the Japanese onslaught were made up of Indian, Australian, and British troops, totaling about 70,000. However, they did not add up to a determined force, with many of the soldiers demoralized after fighting on the mainland, and others having just arrived with little training behind them.

On the night of 8 February Yamashita's 25th Army attacked Singapore with 35,000 troops accompanied by tank and air support. They attacked in great strength along the northern shoreline of Singapore with the Allied army putting up a solid defense for a short while. However, this soon began to show weaknesses from poor planning, leadership, and low morale. On 12 February Percival ordered the formation of a perimeter around Singapore town, which did little for the troops left to fend for themselves outside the perimeter. With lack of food and the water supply damaged, the situation went from bad to worse. In desperation Percival held a conference with his commanders suggesting they take the offensive, or surrender. Percival favored the former but his lackluster commanders the latter. In the afternoon Percival led the surrender of over 62,000 Allied troops, some having just arrived and not even shot at the enemy. This was to be one of the worst defeats in the history of the British Army. It was, however, a great victory for Yamashita and the Japanese Army, who managed to take Singapore through an effort that had stretched his supply line, and his men, to the maximum.

With the expansion of Japanese influence, including the takeover of French-Indo China, the U.S. set about strengthening their positions on the vital strategic islands of the Philippines. They also called back into U.S. service General Douglas MacArthur, who had been serving as military advisor to the Philippine government. With the Japanese advancing southward, their ambitions set on the oil-rich Dutch East Indies, it became obvious that they were not going to overlook the Philippines, especially being aware of the force of Americans based there on the eastern flank of their advance. Roosevelt ordered that MacArthur make the islands more defensible and to integrate the two U.S. and Philippine armies together and to be jointly under his command, these were made up of 30,000 U.S. soldiers and 110,000 Filipino soldiers. The U.S. also had a force of three cruisers and 13 destroyers in the area, as well as a number of submarines. The air defense was made up of 40 bombers and 80 fighters, under the command of Major General Brereton.

When Japan attacked Pearl Harbor on the morning of 7 December MacArthur was aware of this by 03:00 am. Manila time, having time to alert his officers and men to expect an imminent attack. At 07:00 am. MacArthur received a telegram from Roosevelt confirming that a state of war existed between the U.S. and Japan and to start implementing war plans against them. With this information Brereton, the air commander, was keen to send a force of bombers to the island of Formosa, where a major part of the Japanese bomber force was based. Unfortunately this action was delayed, and by noon Japanese bombers were sighted approaching northern Luzon. U.S. bombers and fighters were still on the ground, which made them easy targets for the Japanese air attack, and the U.S. lost much of its air strength in the attack. Over the next few days the U.S. suffered intense air attacks. The Japanese had all but wiped out the U.S. Air Force in the Philippines, before switching their attacks to the U.S. naval yards. With the U.S. air cover destroyed, the naval commander Admiral Hart, had no choice but to withdraw his remaining forces to the southern group of islands in the archipelago beyond the range of Japanese bombers but chose to leave U.S. submarines operating to the north, since they could run air blockades more easily than surface vessels.

The first landings began on 8 December on Bataan Island to the north of the main Philippine archipelago, and they faced little or no resistance. Two days later the Japanese landed on northern Luzon itself, again encountering little opposition and making a rapid advance southward. With the Japanese using the island of Palau to the east of the Philippines, as a staging post, they dispatched troops to land on the southern island of Mindinao on 20 December, in order to secure forward air-bases ahead of the main invasion, achieving immediate air superiority. The main invasion began on 22 December with two divisions landing on the Lingayen Gulf, consolidating their positions, then immediately striking for Manila. A smaller force landed to the east of Manila at Lamon Bay, and these forces immediately began advancing on the capital as well. The Japanese plan was to capture the U.S. forces in a classic pincer movement and to totally destroy them. On the central Luzon plain were troops under the command of Major General Wainwright, who gave orders to resist the Japanese advance southward. MacArthur soon realized that Wainwright's soldiers were heavily outgunned and gave the order for them to start falling back to the prepared defenses of the Bataan peninsula and the island fortress of Corregidor situated at the mouth of Manila Bay. As this was happening MacArthur gave the command that Manila be declared an open city and then continued with its evacuation, including his own headquarters and a large part of the Philippine government.

MacArthur was desperate for Roosevelt to send more troops and equipment to help in the fight against the Japanese advance, but with America's "Germany First" policy this just could not be done. There was a certain amount of embarrassment on the part of the U.S. government that they hadn't defended the islands properly. They had witnessed the expansion of Imperial Japan and should have expected and prepared for a move such as this aimed at their interests in the Philippines.

The order given to the troops on the Bataan Peninsula and Corregidor was to hold out as long as possible and to keep occupied in fighting as many Japanese units while doing so. But there was to be no rescue mission for the troops on the mainland and their outlook was bleak. These forces held on until 9 April at the Bataan garrison and until the 6 May at Corregidor. MacArthur was ordered to escape via PT boat on 12 March, which took him to an airfield in Mindanao where he boarded a plane to Australia, promising to return.

The Dutch East Indies included Java, Sumatra, Dutch Borneo, Dutch New Guinea, Celebes, Western Timor, and Moluccas. These islands were extremely important to the income of the Dutch Government, which still enjoyed control over the region after the Netherlands had been overrun in 1940. The most vital product was oil, and this is what Japan was most interested in, along with the country's production of rubber, bauxite, and coal, as well as its food production of rice, sugar, and tea. The Dutch Government had stopped the supply of oil to Japan in August 1941, so it was immensely important that the Japanese seize the area.

On 20 December 1941, units of the 16th Army, under the command of Lt-General Imamura Hitoshi, attacked Dutch Borneo, Celebes, and the Moluccas simultaneously, taking the airfields at Kendari and Amboina. On 16 February, Japanese paratroops landed ahead of the amphibious assaults on southern Sumatra in order to secure the massive oil refineries. They then moved on to invade Dutch Timor on the 19th. Initially the advance was contested by the Dutch East Indies Army, assist-

Japanese troops land on a Pacific Island. The Japanese intentions were to seize as large an area as possible in the early days of the Pacific War before the American industrial machine could gear up for war.

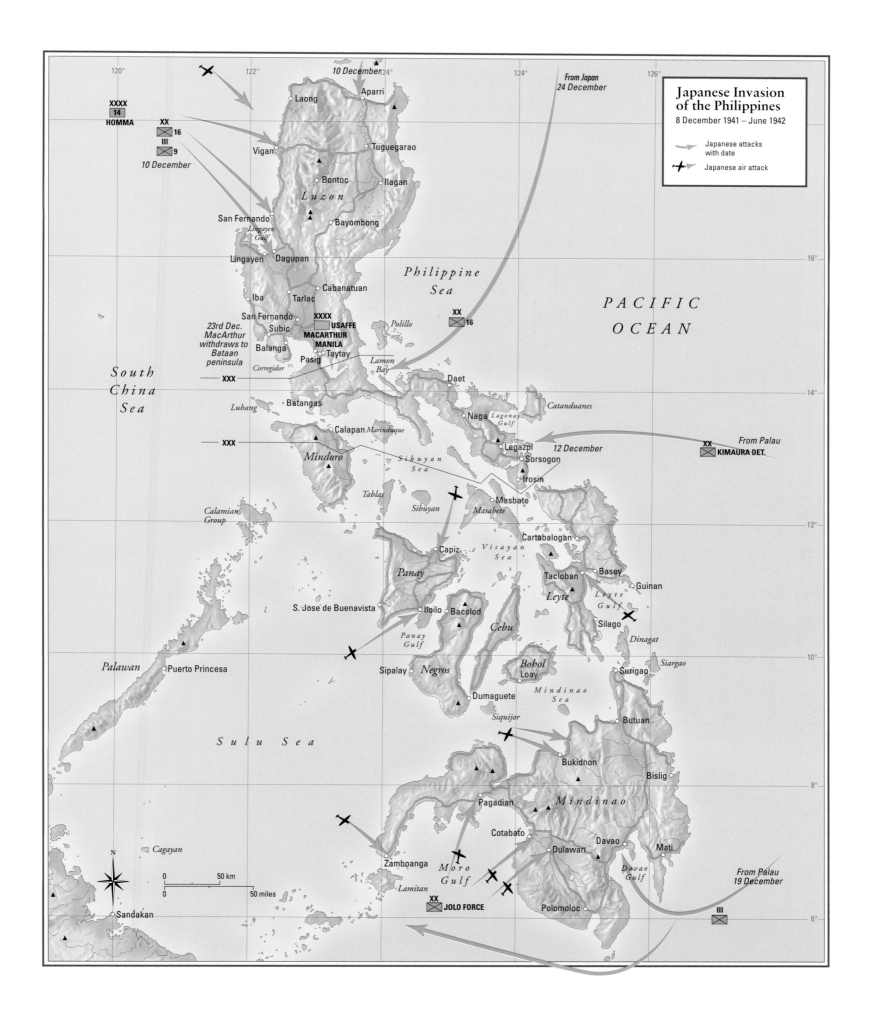

120°

10 December

124°

From Japan
24 December

126°

**Japanese Invasion
of the Philippines**
8 December 1941 – June 1942

→ Japanese attacks
   with date

✈ Japanese air attack

XXXX
14
HOMMA

Laong

Aparri

122°

XX **16**
III **9**
10 December

Vigan

Tuguegarao

Bontoc

Ilagan

Luzon

San Fernando

Bayombong

*Lingayen
Gulf*

Lingayen Dagupan

Cabanatuan

16°

Iba Tarlac

San Fernando

23rd Dec.
MacArthur
withdraws to
Bataan
peninsula

Subic

XXXX
□ USAFFE
MACARTHUR
MANILA

Balanga

Pasig Taytay

Corregidor

XXX

Polillo

XX **16**

*Philippine
Sea*

*PACIFIC
OCEAN*

Daet

*South
China
Sea*

Lubang

Batangas

XXX

Naga

*Lagonoy
Gulf*

Catanduanes

14°

Calapan *Marinduque*

Mindoro

*Sibuyan
Sea*

Legazpi
Sorsogon

Irosin

12 December

XX
KIMAURA DET.

From Palau

Tablas

Sibuyan

Masbate

Masabete

12°

*Calamian
Group*

Capiz

*Visayan
Sea*

Cartabalogan

Panay

Tacloban Basey

Leyte

Guinan

S. Jose de Buenavista

Iloilo Bacolod

Cebu

*Leyte
Gulf*

Palawan Puerto Princesa

Sipalay *Negros*

Bohol
Loay

Silago

Dinagat

10°

*Panay
Gulf*

Dumaguete

*Mindinao
Sea*

Surigao

Siargao

Siquijor

Butuan

Sulu Sea

Bukidnon

Bislig

8°

Pagadian

Mindinao

Cagayan

Cotabato

Davao Mati

Sandakan

Zamboanga

*Moro
Gulf*

Dulawan

*Davao
Gulf*

From Palau
19 December

Lamitan

XX
JOLO FORCE

Polomoloc

III

6°

0   50 km
0   50 miles

N

ed by British, American, and Australian troops under the command of General Wavell. However, their air support was virtually wiped out in the attacks on 19 and 27 February, which destroyed many of the Allied aircraft while still on the ground.

As the Japanese approached Java with another invasion force the Allied navies did attempt to take the fight to the enemy in the Battle of Java Sea. The two Japanese invasion forces were attacked by a mixed force of American, British, Australian, and Dutch ships under the overall command of Rear-Admiral Karel Doorman, of the Dutch Navy. His force comprised of five cruisers and nine destroyers, and they fought a night action against Vice-Admiral Tekeo's force of four cruisers and 14 destroyers. Allied communication and control was poor between the multinational fleet that Doorman commanded. This, added to the fact that he had no experience of a fleet action, led to the sinking of two

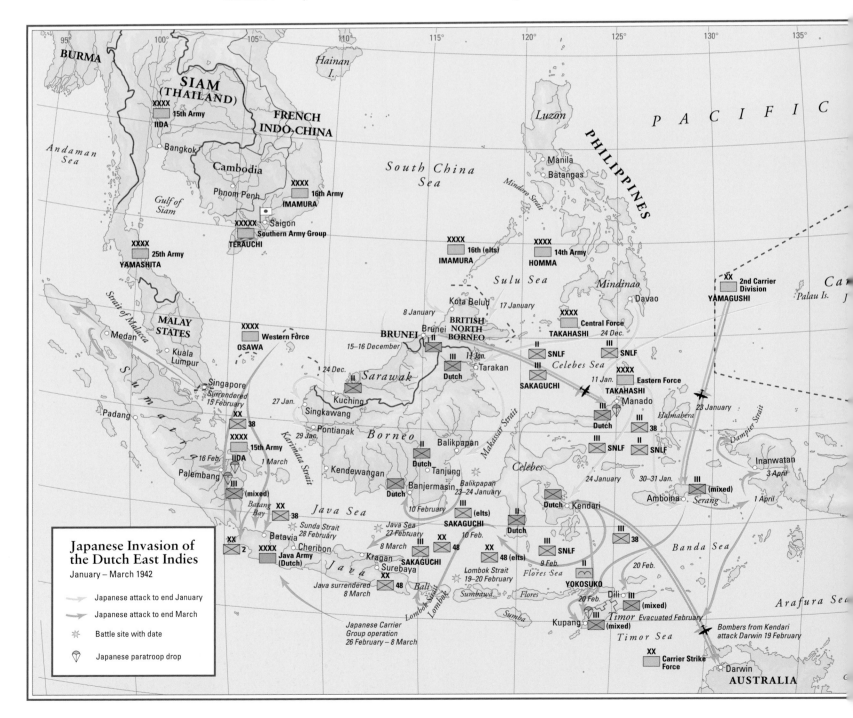

Japanese Invasion of
the Dutch East Indies

January – March 1942

→ Japanese attack to end January

→ Japanese attack to end March

✷ Battle site with date

⬙ Japanese paratroop drop

Dutch cruisers and three destroyers. Doorman himself was killed, and the British cruiser *Exeter* limped off to Surabaya badly damaged. The Royal Australian Navy cruiser *Perth* and the U.S. cruiser *Houston* beat a hasty retreat, stumbling upon the transports delivering the Japanese troops onto Java, and proceeding to sink two and damage a further three, before being intercepted by the covering force and themselves sunk. As the *Exeter* tried to escape to Ceylon, she was spotted by Japanese reconnaissance planes, attacked by Japanese ships and also sunk. The only surviving ships of the debacle were four U.S. destroyers that sailed through the Bali Straits to Australia.

On 1 March the Japanese troops began landing on Java with the aim of capturing Bandung, and on 8 March the Dutch surrendered, leaving the Japanese to continue their occupation. By the end of the month they were moving on to to Dutch New Guinea, having taken Sumatra with little difficulty.

A Japanese artist captures the drama of an air battle.
Air power was vital to cover the Japanese advance, and in the southeast Asia campaign this was largely provided by capturing airfields and the use land-based aircraft.

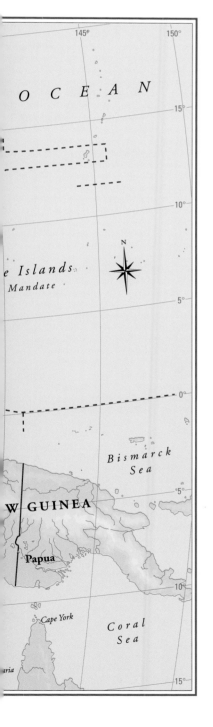

BURMA 1942

"I CLAIM WE GOT A HELL OF A BEATING. WE GOT RUN OUT OF BURMA AND IT IS AS HUMILIATING AS HELL. I THINK WE OUGHT TO FIND OUT WHAT CAUSED IT, GO BACK AND RETAKE IT."

GENERAL JOSEPH W. STILWELL, MAY 1942

Burma was not considered vital in the priorities facing the Allied Command and, as a result, the Japanese swept all before them. Most military personnel and material was sent for the defense of Malaya, Singapore, and the East Indies. However, as soon as it became clear that these could not be saved, Burma became the only area to stop the Japanese driving all the way into India. The Japanese saw Burma as an opportunity to cut lines of communication between China and the Allies in India, and denying the Chinese lines of supply. It would also provide a defensive "buffer zone" for the new Japanese empire. There were few natural resources apart from some agricultural pro-

A Japanese tank moves across the Siamese-Burma border early January 1942.

duce that was not of any great importance to the Japanese war effort.

The 15th Japanese Army was to be used for the invasion. In early January they captured the airfields at Tavoy and Mergui, allowing fighters a forward base from which to operate escort missions to the bombers raiding Rangoon and over much of southern Burma. The port at Rangoon became unusable by the end of January.

Facing the Japanese advance was the 17th Division of the Indian Army, which executed a series of holding actions using the rivers Salween, Bilin, and Sittang as natural barriers. The commander of the 17th, Major-General Smyth, took the decision in the chaos created by the rapid Japanese advance to destroy the bridge over the Sittang River while two of his three brigades were still on the eastern side. This caused the Japanese a ten-day delay in the capture of Rangoon

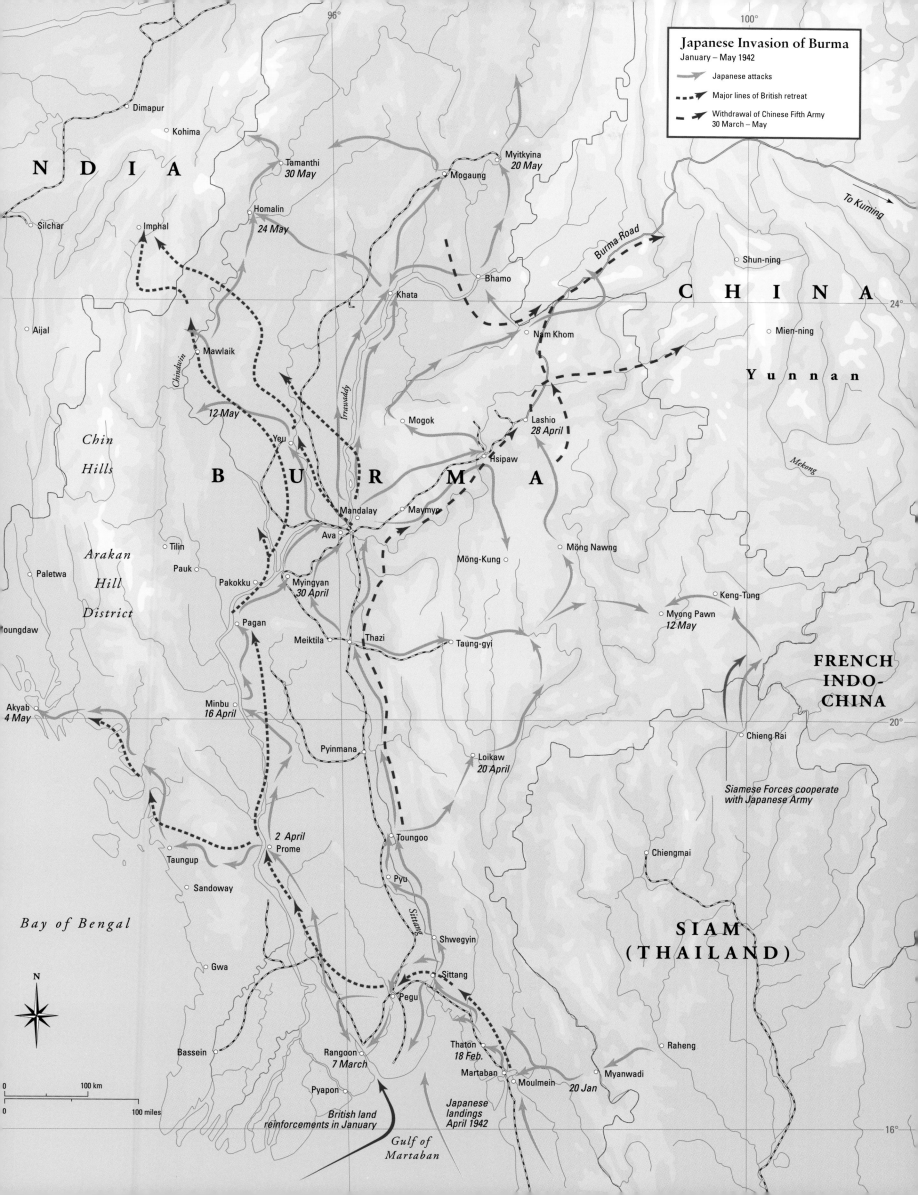

Japanese Invasion of Burma
January – May 1942

Japanese attacks
Major lines of British retreat
Withdrawal of Chinese Fifth Army
30 March – May

To Kuming

I N D I A

Dimapur
Kohima
Tamanthi
30 May
Homalin
24 May
Silchar
Imphal
Aijal
Mawlaik
12 May
Yeu

Chindwin

C H I N A

Myitkyina
20 May
Mogaung
Bhamo
Khata
Nam Khom
Shun-ning
Mien-ning

Y u n n a n

Mekong

Mogok
Lashio
28 April
Hsipaw

B   U   R   M   A

Chin
Hills

Tilin
Pauk
Pakokku

Arakan
Hill
District

Paletwa
oungdaw

Mandalay
Ava
Maymyo
Möng Nawng

Myingyan
30 April
Pagan
Meiktila
Thazi
Möng-Kung

Keng-Tung
Myong Pawn
12 May

F R E N C H
I N D O -
C H I N A

Minbu
16 April
Pyinmana
Loikaw
20 April

Chieng Rai

Akyab
4 May

Taungup
Sandoway

2 April
Prome

Toungoo
Pyu

*Siamese Forces cooperate
with Japanese Army*

Chiengmai

Bay of Bengal

N

Gwa

Sittang

Shwegyin
Sittang

S I A M
(T H A I L A N D)

Bassein
Pegu

Raheng

Thatôn
18 Feb.
Martaban
Myanwadi

Rangoon
7 March
Pyapon

Moulmein
20 Jan

*Japanese
landings
April 1942*

British land
reinforcements in January

*Gulf of
Martaban*

0 _____ 100 km
0 _____ 100 miles

Indian troops move forward cautiously down a jungle track in Burma. The soldier in the right foreground provides cover, armed with the British Army's standard light machine gun, universally known as the "Bren."

but also led to the dismissal and enforced retirement of Smyth. Rangoon fell to the Japanese 33rd Division on 8 March.

The Chinese 38th Division moved south to assist the 1st Burma Division around Yenangyuang but these forces were soon forced into retreat, marching though Imphal to India. Later in March, General Slim took command of 1st Burcorp, which consisted of what remained of the British Forces left in Burma, and led them in the longest fighting retreat in the history of the British Army, back to the Indian frontier. Of the Chinese forces committed, the 5th, 6th, and 66th Armies were forced back by Thai forces entering the Shan States in early May, Kengtung being captured on 27 May. The Chinese forces then fell back to the Yunnan Province.

Meanwhile Admiral Nagumo had sailed from Staring Bay in the Celebes on 26 March at the head of a fleet consisting of five aircraft carriers, four battleships, two heavy cruisers, one light cruiser, and eight destroyers. His mission was to drive the Royal Navy from the Bay of Bengal. Opposing the Japanese was the Royal Navy's Eastern Fleet, a fast division of one battleship, two carriers, and six destroyers, plus a slow division of four older battleships, three cruisers, and five destroyers. British patrol aircraft spotted the Japanese force approaching Ceylon, giving time to clear the local ports of shipping. On 5 April Japanese carriers launched a raid on Colombo and on the same day they found and sank two British Heavy cruisers: the Dorsetshire and Cornwall. Four days later Nagumo's force raided Tricomalee and also found the carrier Hermes sailing without an escort; she was attacked and sunk. Nagumo failed to find the major part of the British fleet or their anchorage at Addu Atoll, contented himself with his success and left the Bay of Bengal.

Another Japanese strike force under Admiral Ozawa raided the upper area of the Bay of Bengal during the first week of April, sinking almost 100,000 tons of Allied shipping, with Japanese submarines sinking a further 40,000 tons.

Allied operations in Burma for the rest of 1942 and into 1943 were frustrated by the Government giving priority to the fighting in the Middle East; they could only afford to properly supply one battle front. Matters were not improved by civil disorder in India, a large element of the population protesting for independence from British rule. However, small actions were carried out such as the first Arakan Campaign. Arakan was a small coastal strip along the Bay of Bengal and crossed by several rivers. An attempt was made, using the 14th Indian Infantry Division, to capture the Mayu Peninsula and Akyab Island, home to an important airfield. After initial success the division was thrown back when Japanese reinforcements arrived over the supposedly impassable ranges on their flank, pushing them back all the way to the Indian frontier.

There was also an operation with the 77th Indian Infantry Brigade led by Major General Orde Wingate, or the "Chindits" as they came to be known, which entailed 3,000 men penetrating deep behind the enemy lines in order to disrupt or sabotage the north–south railroad line. They achieved this objective by putting the railroad out of operation for some two weeks. This was, however, at the cost of a third of the Brigade's men. Many of the survivors were also wracked with disease on their return, although it did prove that the Allies could take the war to the Japanese in the jungle.

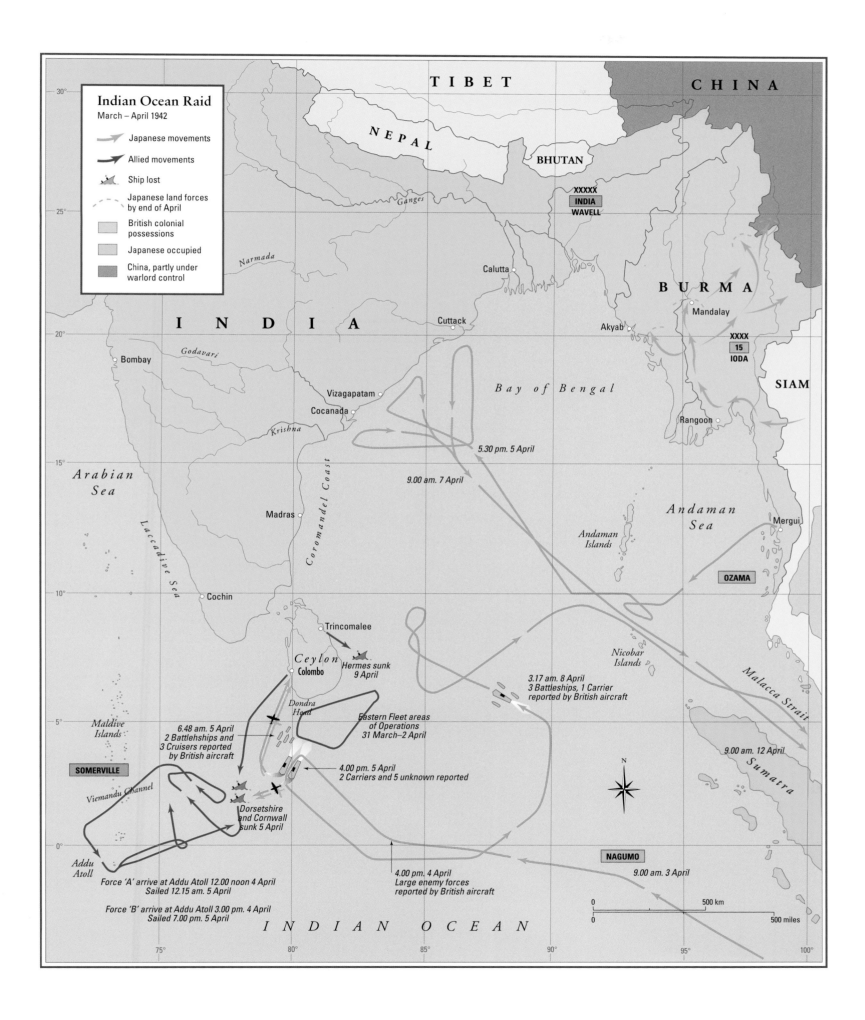

Indian Ocean Raid
March – April 1942

→ Japanese movements

➤ Allied movements

✴ Ship lost

⤍ Japanese land forces by end of April

British colonial possessions

Japanese occupied

China, partly under warlord control

TIBET

CHINA

NEPAL

BHUTAN

XXXXX
INDIA
WAVELL

Ganges

Calutta

BURMA

Mandalay

Akyab

XXXX
15
IODA

SIAM

I N D I A

Cuttack

Narmada

Bombay

Godavari

Vizagapatam

Cocanada

Krishna

Coromandel Coast

Bay of Bengal

Rangoon

Arabian Sea

Madras

5.30 pm. 5 April

9.00 am. 7 April

Andaman Sea

Andaman Islands

Mergui

OZAMA

Laccadive Sea

Cochin

Trincomalee

Nicobar Islands

3.17 am. 8 April
3 Battleships, 1 Carrier
reported by British aircraft

Malacca Strait

Ceylon
Colombo

Hermes sunk
9 April

Dondra Head

6.48 am. 5 April
2 Battleships and
3 Cruisers reported
by British aircraft

Eastern Fleet areas
of Operations
31 March–2 April

4.00 pm. 5 April
2 Carriers and 5 unknown reported

9.00 am. 12 April

Maldive Islands

SOMERVILLE

Sumatra

Viemandu Channel

Dorsetshire
and Cornwall
sunk 5 April

N

Addu Atoll

Force 'A' arrive at Addu Atoll 12.00 noon 4 April
Sailed 12.15 am. 5 April

Force 'B' arrive at Addu Atoll 3.00 pm. 4 April
Sailed 7.00 pm. 5 April

4.00 pm. 4 April
Large enemy forces
reported by British aircraft

NAGUMO

9.00 am. 3 April

0   500 km

0   500 miles

I N D I A N   O C E A N

CORAL SEA

"AUSTRALIA AND NEW ZEALAND ARE NOW THREATENED BY THE MIGHT OF THE IMPERIAL JAPANESE FORCES, AND BOTH OF THEM SHOULD KNOW THAT ANY RESISTANCE IS FUTILE."

GENERAL HIDEKI TOJO

PRIME MINISTER OF JAPAN

The Battle of the Coral Sea was to be the first sea battle where neither of the combatant fleets saw each other, and was to be one of the first major naval engagements between two carrier forces. The Japanese planned to capture Port Moresby, the capital of New Guinea, in order to provide a forward operating base for attacks aimed at the Australian mainland. Under the command of Vice-Admiral Shigeyoshi were three invasion convoys that were to steam out of Truk and Rabaul, then head to three different locations, the largest heading to Port Moresby and the others to set up sea-plane bases on the island of Tulagi and in the Louisiades. Protecting these convoys was a covering force commanded by Rear-Admiral Goto Aritomo. Under his command were four heavy cruisers, one destroyer, and one light carrier, the *Shoho*. There was also a strike force comprised of the two carriers *Shokaku* and *Zuikaku* along with two heavy cruisers and a number of destroyers. This force was to be commanded by Vice-Admiral Takagi Takeo. The Japanese expected the Allies to attempt to destroy the invasion convoy, but with this concentration of offensive seapower, the Japanese would strike first.

However, the Commander-in-Chief of the Pacific Fleet was fully aware of the Japanese intent and their strength in the area, thanks to the ULTRA decrypts, and assembled two task forces based around the carriers *Yorktown* and *Lexington*, with a third task force under the command of Australian Rear-Admiral John Crace. All these forces were then placed under the command of Rear-Admiral "Black Jack" Fletcher.

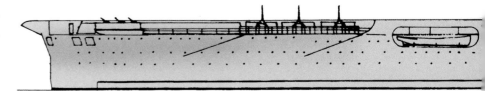

The Japanese forces sent to take Tulagi landed without incident on 3 May, but the next day were attacked by aircraft from the *Yorktown*, which inflicted considerable damage. On 5 May, the U.S. strike forces rendezvoused 400 miles south of Guadalcanal where they then sailed north-west to intercept the main Japanese invasion fleet bound for Port Moresby. Fletcher then ordered Crace to intercept the transports converging on Port Moresby, while his force of carriers went to face Takagi. Fletcher's force themselves then came across the transports, causing the Japanese convoy to retreat until the outcome of the battle had been decided. While this was happening a strike force from *Lexington* had located the escort carrier *Shoho* and duly sank her, a promising start for the Allies. When Crace heard that the convoy had been forced to retire, he also waited in reserve.

Fletcher then learned that Takagi's force was somewhere to the stern of him, and on the 8 May the two sides located each other with spotter planes. As soon as the sightings were confirmed they both launched massive airstrikes against each other. Both sides had a similar amount of aircraft but the Japanese were flying superior machines with better training and tactics. The Americans, however, reached the carrier *Shokaku* first and inflicted enough damage for her to retire north with black smoke trailing from her deck, and therefore unable to land the aircraft she had launched earlier.

Meanwhile the Japanese strike force had sighted *Lexington* and *Yorktown* and were beginning to press home their attack. *Yorktown* took a bomb hit on her flight deck but was still serviceable after the Japanese failed to follow up and finish her off. However, the *Lexington* took several bombs hits and a torpedo and began burning badly. After an hour fighting the flames, a spark set off the aviation fuel below decks making her beyond saving, and she was scuttled shortly afterwards.

There seemed to be no clear victory in the battle, with the Japanese exacting a vicious blow on U.S. naval power with the sinking of the *Lexington* and severely damaging *Yorktown*. But U.S. and Allied forces stopped the invasion convoy reaching Port Moresby and inflicted enough damage on *Shokaku* and destroyed so many planes from *Zuikaku* that they were unable to take part later in the Battle of Midway.

U.S. sailors leap for their lives from the burning USS *Lexington*. The ship had been hit by three bombs and one torpedo, the crew fought for over an hour to save the ship but the heat, or perhaps the spreading fires, ignited aviation fuel stored on lower decks.

USS *Lexington*, launched in October 1925, was reconstructed from the hull of a battlecruiser. *Lexington*, along with USS *Saratoga*, were the first fleet carriers operated by the U.S. Navy. When commissioned, the *Lexington* was equipped with a main battery of eight 8-inch guns. In 1941, the 8-inch guns were removed, intending to be replaced with modern 5-inch dual-purpose guns. However, she sailed into action before these guns could be fitted.

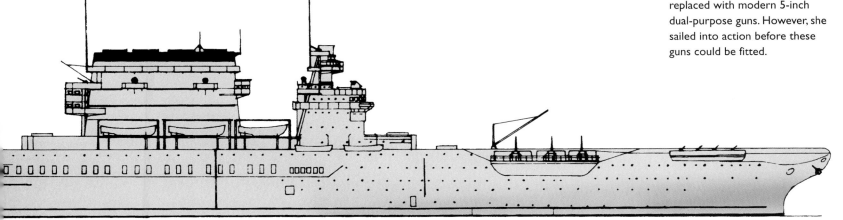

BATTLE OF THE CORAL SEA
This battle was crucial in that it denied the Japanese a forward base at Port Moresby which, in turn, would have threatened Australia and New Zealand.

Battle of the Coral Sea
28 April – 11 May 1942

→ Japanese movement

→ Allied movement

✠ Japanese air strikes

✚ Allied air strikes

⤙ Japanese sinking ship

⤙ Allied sinking ship

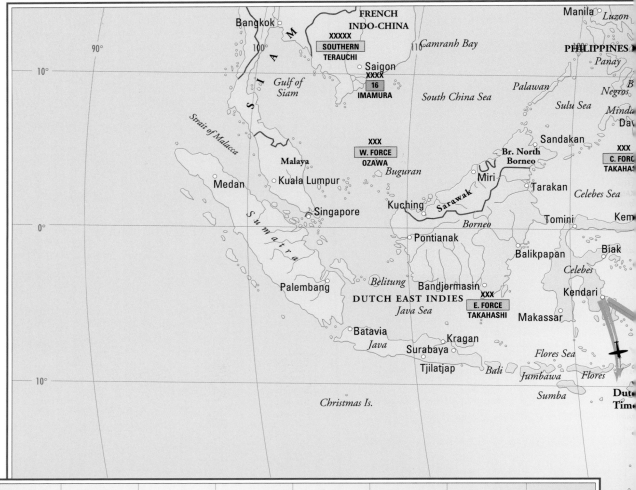

FRENCH INDO-CHINA

Bangkok

Manila

Luzon

XXXXX
SOUTHERN
TERAUCHI

Saigon

Camranh Bay

PHILIPPINES

Panay

Palawan

B.

Negros

XXXX
16
IMAMURA

South China Sea

Sulu Sea

Minda

Da

Sandakan

XXX
C. FORC
TAKAHAS

Gulf of Siam

S
I
A
M

XXX
W. FORCE
OZAWA

Buguran

Miri

Br. North Borneo

Tarakan

Celebes Sea

Strait of Malacca

Malaya

Kuala Lumpur

Kuching

Sarawak

Tomini

Kem

Medan

Singapore

Borneo

Balikpapan

Biak

Sumatra

Pontianak

Celebes

Palembang

Belitung

Bandjermasin

Kendari

Java Sea

Makassar

DUTCH EAST INDIES

XXX
E. FORCE
TAKAHASHI

Batavia

Kragan

Java

Surabaya

Flores Sea

Tjilatjap

Bali

Sumbawa

Flores

Christmas Is.

Sumba

Dut
Time

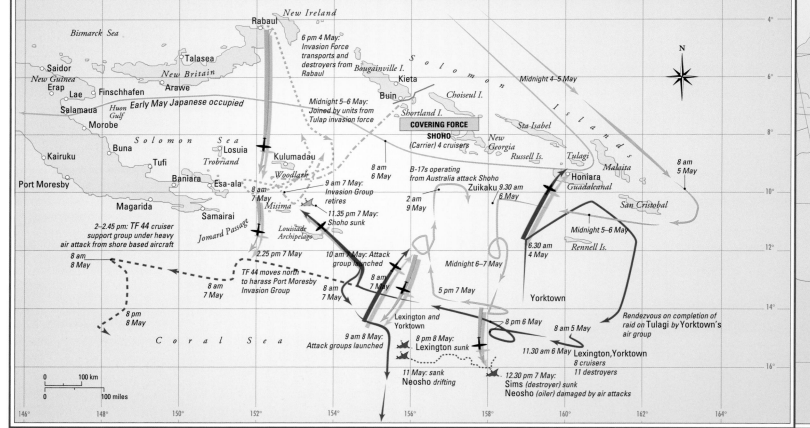

New Ireland

Rabaul

Bismarck Sea

Talasea

New Britain

6 pm 4 May:
Invasion Force
transports and
destroyers from
Rabaul

Bougainville I.

S
o
l
o
m
o
n

Midnight 4–5 May

N

Saidor

New Guinea

Erap

Lae Finschhafen

Arawe

Kieta

Choiseul I.

Salamaua

Huon Gulf

Early May Japanese occupied

Midnight 5–6 May:
Joined by units from
Tulap invasion force

Buin

Shortland I.

I
s
l
a
n
d
s

Morobe

COVERING FORCE
SHOHO
(Carrier) 4 cruisers

Sta. Isabel

Kairuku

Solomon Sea

Buna

Losuia

Trobriand

Kulumadau

8 am
6 May

B-17s operating
from Australia attack Shoho

New Georgia

Russell Is.

Tulagi

Malaita

8 am
5 May

Tufi

Woodlark

9 am 7 May:
Invasion Group
retires

Zuikaku 9.30 am
6 May

Honiara

Guadalcanal

Port Moresby

Baniara

Esa-ala

8 am
7 May

Misima

2 am
9 May

San Cristobal

Magarida

Samairai

11.35 pm 7 May:
Shoho sunk

Louisiade Archipelago

Midnight 5–6 May

2–2.45 pm: TF 44 cruiser
support group under heavy
air attack from shore based aircraft

Jomard Passage

6.30 am
4 May

Rennell Is.

2.25 pm 7 May

10 am 7 May: Attack
group launched

Midnight 6–7 May

8 am
8 May

TF 44 moves north
to harass Port Moresby
Invasion Group

8 am
7 May

8 am
7 May

5 pm 7 May

Yorktown

8 pm
8 May

Coral Sea

8 pm 6 May

8 am 5 May

Rendezvous on completion of
raid on Tulagi by Yorktown's
air group

Lexington and
Yorktown

9 am 8 May:
Attack groups launched

8 pm 8 May:
Lexington sunk

11.30 am 6 May Lexington, Yorktown
8 cruisers
11 destroyers

11 May: sank
Neosho drifting

12.30 pm 7 May:
Sims (destroyer) sunk
Neosho (oiler) damaged by air attacks

0   100 km

0   100 miles

146°   148°   150°   152°   154°   156°   158°   160°   162°   164°

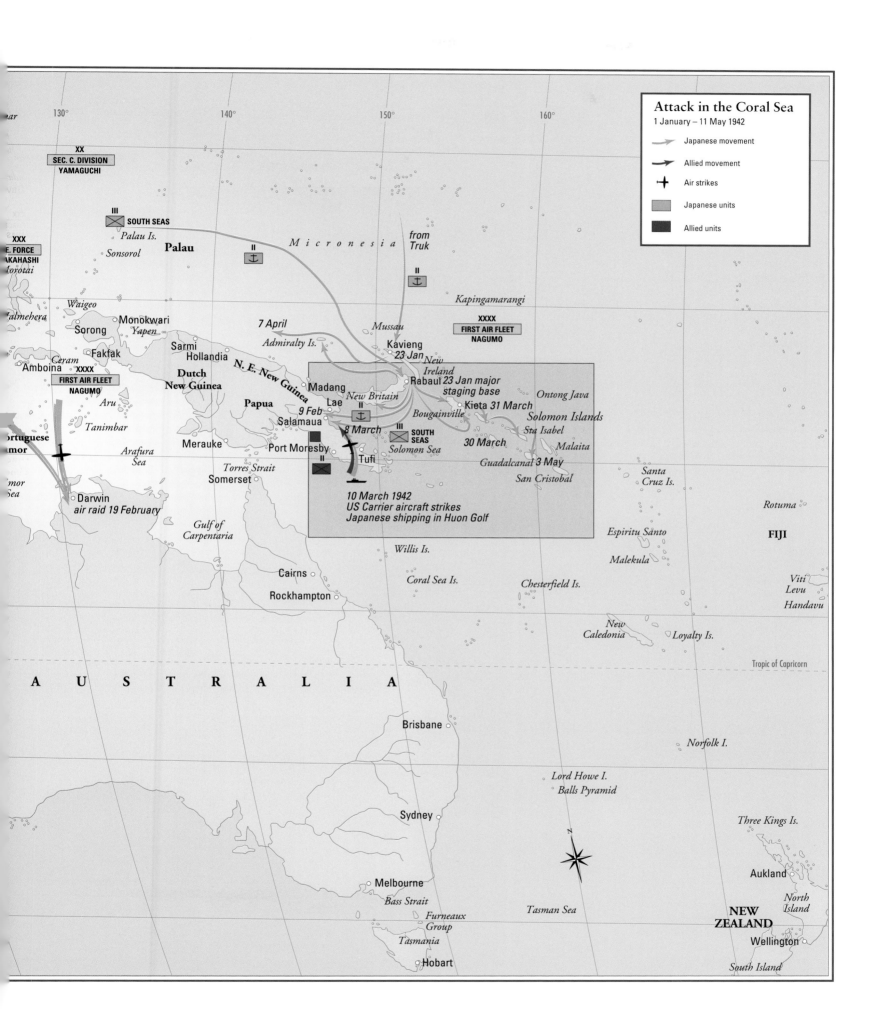

Attack in the Coral Sea
1 January – 11 May 1942

→ Japanese movement

→ Allied movement

✛ Air strikes

▧ Japanese units

▪ Allied units

130°   140°   150°   160°

XX
SEC. C. DIVISION
YAMAGUCHI

III SOUTH SEAS

Palau Is.

XXX
E. FORCE
AKAHASHI
Morotai

Sonsorol   **Palau**

II ⚓

Micronesia   from
Truk

II ⚓

Kapingamarangi

Waigeo

Halmahera   Monokwari

Sorong   *Yapen*

Ceram   Fakfak

Amboina   XXXX

FIRST AIR FLEET
NAGUMO

Aru

Tanimbar

Portuguese
Timor

*Timor
Sea*

Darwin
air raid 19 February

Sarmi   Hollandia

Dutch
New Guinea

Papua

Merauke

*Arafura
Sea*

Torres Strait

Somerset

*Gulf of
Carpentaria*

Cairns

Rockhampton

7 April

Admiralty Is.

N. E. New Guinea

Madang

Lae

9 Feb
Salamaua

8 March

Port Moresby

Tufi

10 March 1942
US Carrier aircraft strikes
Japanese shipping in Huon Golf

Willis Is.

Coral Sea Is.

Mussau

Kavieng
23 Jan *New
Ireland*

Rabaul 23 Jan major
staging base

New Britain   II ⚓

Bougainville

III SOUTH
SEAS

Solomon Sea

XXXX
FIRST AIR FLEET
NAGUMO

Ontong Java

Kieta 31 March
Solomon Islands

Sta Isabel

30 March   *Malaita*

Guadalcanal 3 May

San Cristobal

Chesterfield Is.

*Santa
Cruz Is.*

Espiritu Santo

Malekula

Rotuma

FIJI

*Viti
Levu*
Handavu

*New
Caledonia*   *Loyalty Is.*

Tropic of Capricorn

A U S T R A L I A

Brisbane

Sydney

Norfolk I.

Lord Howe I.
Balls Pyramid

Three Kings Is.

Melbourne

Bass Strait

*Furneaux
Group*

Tasmania

Hobart

Tasman Sea

Aukland

*North
Island*

**NEW
ZEALAND**

Wellington

South Island

BATTLE OF MIDWAY

"I WAS HORRIFIED AT THE DESTRUCTION THAT HAD BEEN
WROUGHT IN A MATTER OF SECONDS. THERE WAS A HUGE HOLE
IN THE FLIGHT DECK JUST BEHIND THE AMIDSHIP ELEVATOR.
THE ELEVATOR ITSELF, TWISTED LIKE MOLTEN GLASS, WAS
DROPPING INTO THE HANGAR. DECK PLATES REELED UPWARD
IN GROTESQUE CONFIGURATIONS. PLANES STOOD TAIL UP,
BELCHING LIVID FLAME AND JET-BLACK SMOKE."

MITSUO FUCHIDA, AIR COMMANDER,

CARRIER AKAGI

Admiral Yamamoto's plan to
eliminate the United States'
Fleet as Japan's major opponent
led to the Battle of Midway in
June, 1942. The outcome of the
battle resulted in the loss of
Japanese naval initiative and
superiority in the Pacific.

In May 1942, Admiral Yamamoto drew up plans to occupy the United States' outpost on the island of Midway, the most westerly point under U.S. command. In order for his plan to work he first needed to lure part of the U.S. fleet away towards the Aleutian Islands. If Yamamoto was successful in this deception he could easily overwhelm the U.S. forces on Midway, then carry on steaming towards Hawaii. But to draw the Americans north toward the Aleutians he would have to separate his attack force, therefore already putting himself at a disadvantage. Yamamoto also made the mistake of assuming the USS Yorktown had been sunk in the Coral Sea; this was not to be the case and the carrier had, in fact, steamed back to Pearl Harbor, where she was repaired and made ready in an amazing 48 hours. If there were any more carriers in Pearl Harbor Yamamoto planned to deploy a screening force of submarines to ambush any making for Midway.

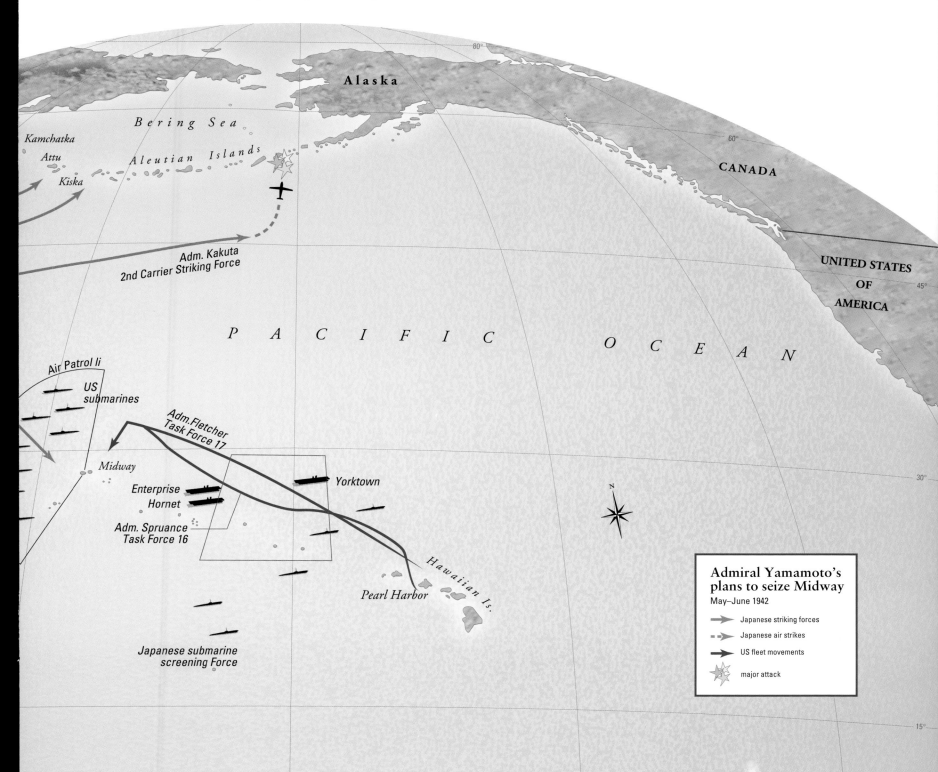

Alaska

Bering Sea

Kamchatka
Attu
Aleutian Islands
Kiska

CANADA

Adm. Kakuta
2nd Carrier Striking Force

UNITED STATES
OF
AMERICA

P A C I F I C   O C E A N

Air Patrol li
US submarines

Adm. Fletcher
Task Force 17

Midway

Enterprise
Hornet

Yorktown

Adm. Spruance
Task Force 16

Hawaiian Is.

Pearl Harbor

Japanese submarine
screening Force

Admiral Yamamoto's plans to seize Midway
May–June 1942

→ Japanese striking forces
∎∎➤ Japanese air strikes
➤ US fleet movements
✳ major attack

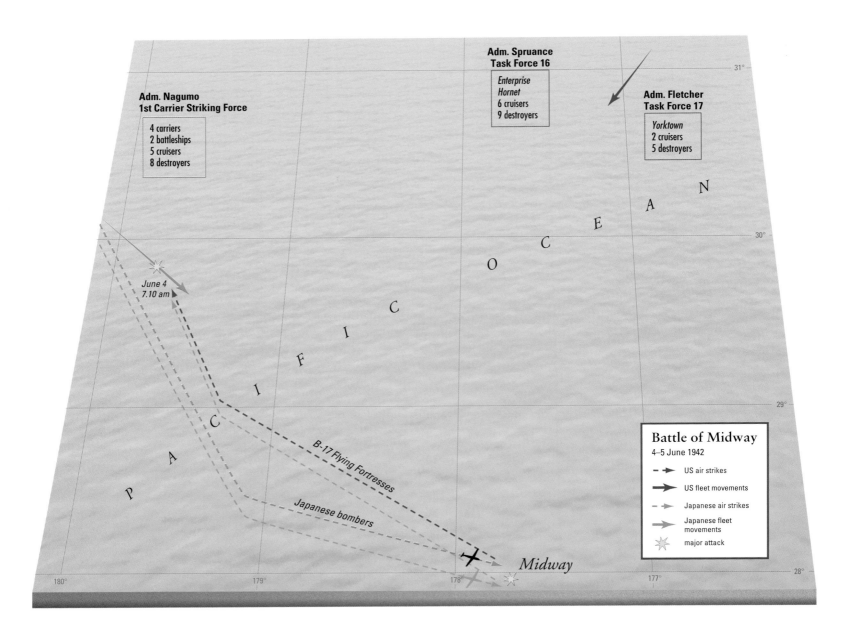

**Adm. Nagumo
1st Carrier Striking Force**

4 carriers
2 battleships
5 cruisers
8 destroyers

**Adm. Spruance
Task Force 16**

*Enterprise
Hornet*
6 cruisers
9 destroyers

**Adm. Fletcher
Task Force 17**

Yorktown
2 cruisers
5 destroyers

June 4
7.10 am

B-17 Flying Fortresses

Japanese bombers

Midway

Battle of Midway
4–5 June 1942

– ▸ US air strikes
➤ US fleet movements
– ▸ Japanese air strikes
➤ Japanese fleet movements
✳ major attack

All Yamamoto's carefully constructed plans were to no avail, thanks to the Allies breaking the Japanese code using the ULTRA decrypts. Therefore the Pacific Commander-in-Chief, Admiral Nimitz, was able to deploy his sea power in an advantageous position. He sent two carrier groups with a heavy escort comprising the USS *Hornet*, *Enterprise*, and the recently repaired *Yorktown*. This was placed under the overall command of Rear-Admiral Fletcher, who would be aboard the *Yorktown* with the other carrier group commanded by Rear-Admiral Spruance. Nimitz also placed his own submarine screening force to the west of Midway. All this was achieved and in place before the Japanese submarines arrived on their planned station to the west of Pearl Harbor.

The Japanese force was separated into three main groups. The first comprised the Invasion Group supported by a powerful escort, under Yamamoto's command. The strike force was made up of four carriers—*Hiryu*, *Kaga*, *Akagi*, and *Soryu*—two battleships and other smaller craft, under the command of Vice-Admiral Nagumo, the main group made up of three battleships and support craft. With all these vessels the Japanese heavily outweighed the U.S. forces.

The invasion force was first sighted on 3 June and was attacked by a force of bombers flying off

Midway, although they did little to stop it, or damage it. This highlighted the shortcomings of high level bombing on naval targets taking evasive action. At dawn the next day Nagumo launched a force of aircraft to attack Midway, and after this successful raid decided to use the aircraft he had held as reserve in case of any U.S. surface vessels intervening as a second wave. This was to be a grave mistake, for Spruance's forces spotted Nagumo's carriers and immediately ordered his torpedo and dive-bombers to attack. The torpedo bombers were the first to arrive at the target, but the dive-bombers became lost on the way and suffered horrendous casualties, with only one out of the 41 launched making it back. As this attack faltered and failed, the dive-bombers found the target and, with the torpedo bombers drawing the Japanese fighter cover down to sea level, they were more or less unopposed. The Japanese carriers' decks were covered in ordnance and aircraft being refuelled were soon

The Douglas SBD Dauntless proved to be the most effective dive-bomber developed by the United States in World War II. A total of 5,936 were built in all, and this tough and reliable aircraft remained in front line service until the end of 1944. The Dauntless excelled in everything expected of it and at the Battle of Midway, sank the Akagi, the Kagi, and the Soryu, and so badly damaged the Hiryu that she was later scuttled.

set ablaze by the bombs raining down on them. *Hiryu* managed to escape the attack thanks to a squall hiding her from view of the American aircraft. *Kaga*, *Akagi*, and *Soryu* were left as burning hulks and

Akagi circles, avoiding the high-altitude bombs dropped by B-17s operating from Midway. The early, unsuccessful attacks by the high-level bombers served to point out that in order to successfully attack ships at sea, dive-bombers, or torpedo bombers, were likely to be far more successful.

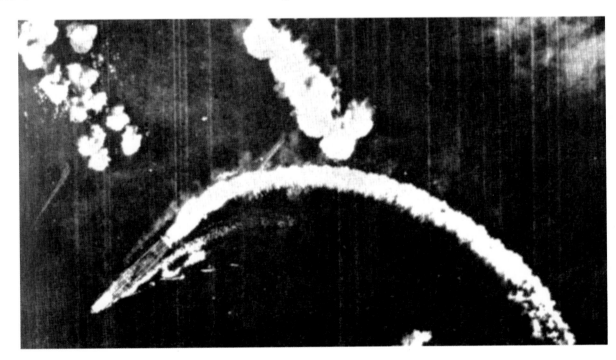

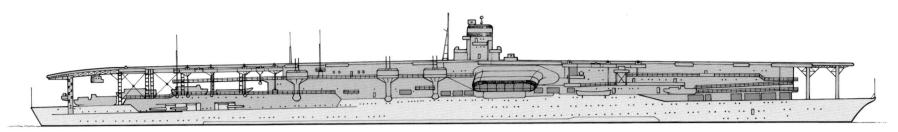

Above: The *Akagi* was originally laid down in 1920, as a battle cruiser. However, in 1922 construction was suspended and conversion to an aircraft carrier began in 1923. She entered service in 1927 and was again reconstructed between 1935 and 1938, producing a modern aircraft carrier capable of carrying a maximum of 91 aircraft.

unable to be saved. *Hiryu* launched an attack on *Yorktown*, the only carrier the Japanese thought was in the area; she was hit by three bombs and torpedoed twice, but was still able to stay afloat thanks to the valiant effort of her crew. Launching attacks on the *Yorktown* revealed *Hiryu*'s position and she was severely damaged in the following strike launched by Spruance's aircraft from *Enterprise* and she would eventually have to be scuttled.

With the loss of four carriers Yamamoto conceded defeat and withdrew east, harassed by U.S. dive- and torpedo bombers. However, the Japanese did reap revenge when a Japanese submarine sighted *Yorktown*, torpedoed, and sunk her. Despite this, the battle was a massive defeat for the Japanese and they would never regain their strength in the Pacific. The Americans now held the advantage.

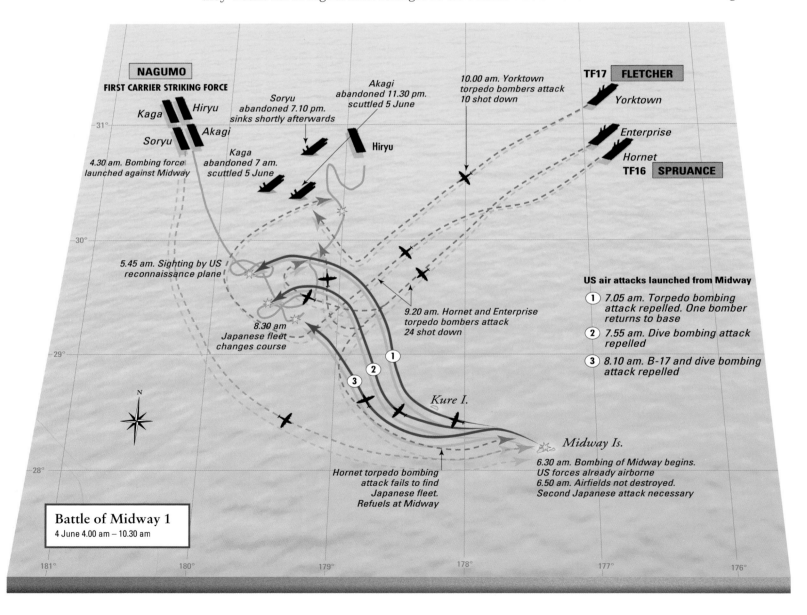

NAGUMO
FIRST CARRIER STRIKING FORCE

Kaga   Hiryu
Soryu   Akagi

4.30 am. Bombing force launched against Midway

Soryu abandoned 7.10 pm. sinks shortly afterwards

Akagi abandoned 11.30 pm. scuttled 5 June

Kaga abandoned 7 am. scuttled 5 June

Hiryu

10.00 am. Yorktown torpedo bombers attack 10 shot down

TF17   FLETCHER

Yorktown

Enterprise

Hornet

TF16   SPRUANCE

5.45 am. Sighting by US reconnaissance plane

8.30 am Japanese fleet changes course

9.20 am. Hornet and Enterprise torpedo bombers attack 24 shot down

US air attacks launched from Midway

① 7.05 am. Torpedo bombing attack repelled. One bomber returns to base

② 7.55 am. Dive bombing attack repelled

③ 8.10 am. B-17 and dive bombing attack repelled

N

Kure I.

Midway Is.

Hornet torpedo bombing attack fails to find Japanese fleet. Refuels at Midway

6.30 am. Bombing of Midway begins. US forces already airborne
6.50 am. Airfields not destroyed. Second Japanese attack necessary

Battle of Midway 1
4 June 4.00 am – 10.30 am

The surviving Japanese aircraft carrier the *Hiryu* launched two air attacks aimed at the U.S. aircraft carrier *Yorktown*. Despite putting up a fierce antiaircraft barrage, the *Yorktown* was heavily damaged by Japanese air attacks and was finally torpedoed by a Japanese submarine. The Japanese lost four aircraft carriers, a cruiser, 332 aircraft and over 3,500 men. Perhaps most significantly was the loss of their most experienced carrier pilots. They had failed in their objective of capturing Midway. Meanwhile the Americans lost one aircraft carrier, one destroyer, 150 aircraft, and 307 men. The Battle of Midway marked the turning point in the Pacific War.

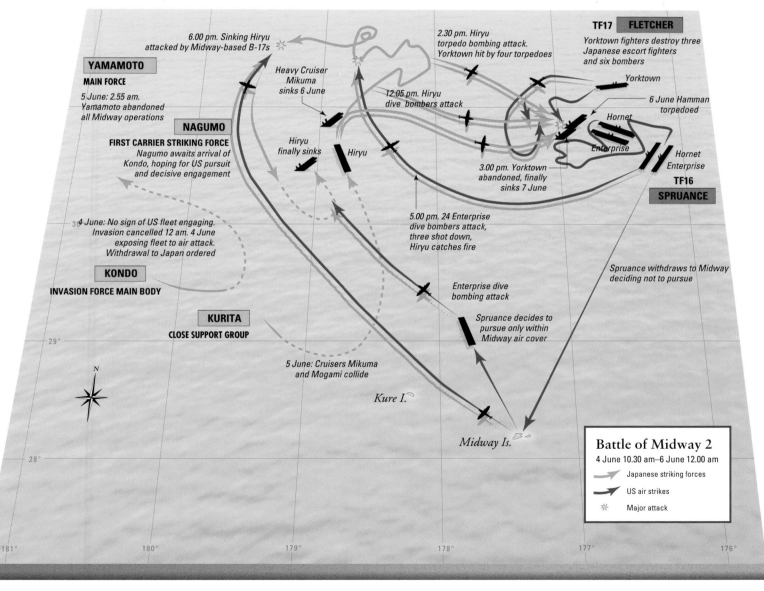

6.00 pm. Sinking Hiryu attacked by Midway-based B-17s

YAMAMOTO
MAIN FORCE
5 June: 2.55 am. Yamamoto abandoned all Midway operations

Heavy Cruiser Mikuma sinks 6 June

NAGUMO
FIRST CARRIER STRIKING FORCE
Nagumo awaits arrival of Kondo, hoping for US pursuit and decisive engagement

Hiryu finally sinks   Hiryu

4 June: No sign of US fleet engaging. Invasion cancelled 12 am. 4 June exposing fleet to air attack. Withdrawal to Japan ordered

KONDO
INVASION FORCE MAIN BODY

KURITA
CLOSE SUPPORT GROUP

5 June: Cruisers Mikuma and Mogami collide

Kure I.

2.30 pm. Hiryu torpedo bombing attack. Yorktown hit by four torpedoes

12.05 pm. Hiryu dive bombers attack

3.00 pm. Yorktown abandoned, finally sinks 7 June

5.00 pm. 24 Enterprise dive bombers attack, three shot down, Hiryu catches fire

Enterprise dive bombing attack

Spruance decides to pursue only within Midway air cover

TF17   **FLETCHER**
Yorktown fighters destroy three Japanese escort fighters and six bombers

Yorktown

6 June Hamman torpedoed

Hornet

Enterprise

Hornet Enterprise

TF16
SPRUANCE

Spruance withdraws to Midway deciding not to pursue

Midway Is.

Battle of Midway 2
4 June 10.30 am–6 June 12.00 am

Japanese striking forces

US air strikes

Major attack

N

181°   180°   179°   178°   177°   176°

30°

29°

28°

Convoys to Russia 1941–45

"THE COLD WAS HARDENING NOW, CLOSING ON THEM WITH STEELY FINGERS, FEELING FOR THE BLOOD IN THEIR VEINS; IT TOOK THE WIND FOR AN ALLY AND CAME SHRIEKING DOWN FROM THE NORTH POLE, FROM THE REGIONS OF ETERNAL ICE. SNOW CAME WITH IT TOO, AND THE SHIPS BECAME PALE GHOSTS, MOVING ON UNDER THE IRON DOME OF THE SKY INTO A WORLD OF DEATH AND DARKNESS."

JAMES PATTINSON, MERCHANT SEAMAN

Sailors observe the massive explosion of a depth charge dropped from the stern of their destroyer. Depth charges were the major anti-submarine weapon.

The Arctic convoys sailed from August 1941 to the end of the war in Europe. Initially they were of the utmost importance in maintaining Soviet resistance to the German invasion as the Soviets moved most of their surviving industry to the east. Britain and the U.S. supplied vast amounts of fighting vehicles and aircraft as well as the fuel, munitions and clothing for them to remain effective. In order for these supplies to reach the Russian Front, they had to be by the only sea route available to the Allies, through the treacherous waters of the Arctic Circle to the northern ports of Murmansk and Archangel. These waters were well within range of land-based German aircraft flying from occupied Norway, as well as being patrolled by U-boats and surface vessels of the Kreigsmarine.

The first convoys sent to Soviet Russia managed to make the ports with little trouble but by mid-July 1942 the Germans were beginning to intercept Allied convoys and sinkings rapidly increased. Convoy PQ-17, after suffering losses to Luftwaffe bombers, was forced to scatter after encountering a large German surface fleet, including *Tirpitz* and *Admiral Hipper*, that had been sent to intercept them. The German capitol ships were only changing berth however, and the scattered convoy was easy prey for the German U-boats and aircraft, the convoy losing 25 of the 36 ships that had set out for Russia.

At the end of 1942, Convoy JW51B set sail for Russia, with 14 merchant ships escorted by 6 destroyers, 2 Flower class Corvettes, 1 minesweeper, and 2 armed trawlers. Two crusiers, HMS *Sheffield* and *Jamaica* which formed Force 'R' were patrolling the Barents Sea and provided cover for the convoy should it meet any trouble. The convoy was duly sighted by U-354 and a report was immediately sent to the German surface fleet to intercept. This fleet included the heavy cruiser *Admiral Hipper* and the pocket battleship *Lutzow* along with 6 destroyers. In the early morning of 31 December HMS

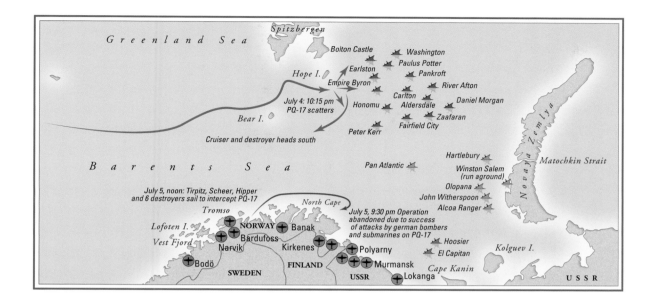

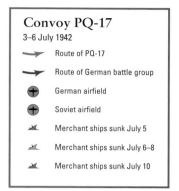

Of the 39 Allied convoys sent to Soviet Russia, made up of a total of 533 escorted ships, 69 were lost to enemy action. Convoy PQ-17 was the most heavily attacked with 22 of its 37 merchant ships sunk.

Obdurate, one of the escort destroyers, spotted a force of German destroyers and moved in order to engage with the other escorts, leaving HMS *Achates* to lay smoke to cover the convoy. The Germans retreated when faced with the approaching British destroyers, but *Hipper* returned for another attack, badly damaging the *Onslow* before moving to the north of the convoy where it engaged *Achates* and another escort, sinking *Achates*. The firing drew Force "R" into the battle, which immediately started firing on *Admiral Hipper* causing extensive damage, before both sides broke off the engagement. Force 'R' shadowed the German vessels until it was obvious that they were returning to base as the convoy continued to its destination. The outcome of the raid so incensed Hitler that he ordered the Surface Fleet to be scrapped so the Kreigsmarine could concentrate on U-boat warfare. The head of the Kreigsmarine resigned to be replaced by Admiral Donitz.

The Arctic Convoys' importance was reluctantly recognized by Stalin. It supplied Soviet Russia with armaments at its time of greatest need and helped swing the balance in that theater. It also drew German surface and U-boat resources away from other areas where they could have caused more extensive damage to the Atlantic lifeline.

A convoy bound for Soviet Russia. As well as facing attack from submarines, the convoys also faced attack from the Luftwaffe, which had a force of almost 300 aircraft in northern Norway. The air threat from these aircraft was sufficient enough to halt the flow of convoys to the Soviet Union during the perpetual daylight period of the Arctic summer.

THE CAUCASUS 1942–43

"WIPE OUT THE ENTIRE DEFENSE POTENTIAL REMAINING TO THE SOVIETS."

DIRECTIVE NUMBER 41, ADOLF HITLER

German troops at a street barricade in Rostov-on-Don. This major city was captured relatively easily compared to the vicious struggles in other major Soviet cities.

With the arrival of spring 1942, German High Command looked forward to attacking toward Moscow once again, driving back Zhukov's gains of the previous winter and completing the capture of Moscow, the Soviet Union's capital. The High Command were convinced that its capture would demoralize the Soviet war effort and bring a swift end to the war.

Hitler disagreed. He had a greater vision: the army would drive to Stalingrad and toward the Caucasus oilfields. With Rommel and the Afrika Korps driving the British back toward the Suez Canal, it could be possible to affect a link up from the Caucasus into the Middle East, making a massive final sweep northward behind Moscow and on to the Ural Mountains. The plan—Operation Blue—was launched on 28 June. The Germans pushed forward their usual combination of tanks supported by aircraft and infantry following along behind to clear up. They bypassed strong points and collected prisoners by the thousands.

By 9 July, German units reached Voronezh then turned south to link up with armies moving from the Crimea through southern Ukraine. Rostov-on-Don was abandoned by the Soviets on 23 July almost without a fight. As in the summer of 1941, panic seemed to have spread amongst the Red Army. By the end of the month Hitler was so confident of a massive victory that, instead of concentrating his forces on the capture of the oilfields, he split them into two parts. Army Group B, under the command of General Maximilian von Weichs, was sent eastward with orders to capture the city of Stalingrad. Meanwhile, Army Group A and the 1st Panzer Army, under von Kleist, continued on its mission to the oilfields.

These setbacks the Red Army suffered could not be hidden from the Soviet population and rumors of failure and defeat soon spread. After Rostov-on-Don was lost anger amongst the general population also spread, especially when people recalled the sacrifice before Moscow and Leningrad. The army was, once again, in headlong retreat, abandoning equipment and ignoring the orders of their officers. Stalin, in some desperation, issued Order 227, Ne Shagu Nazad! (Not a step back!).

Ignoring Stalin's order to hold their position, the army continued to fall back, but little by little resistance did grow. The dreaded N.K.V.D. rounded up cowards and deserters, but many Soviet soldiers fought on for reasons others than terror and coercion. In the summer of 1942, Stalin called for the Soviet Union to become a single "War Camp" with the resources and people of the country to become focussed on one agenda: the defeat of the invader and saving "Mother Russia." Religion was allowed to flourish once again in an atheist state, since it was what the people wanted, or perhaps needed, in order to

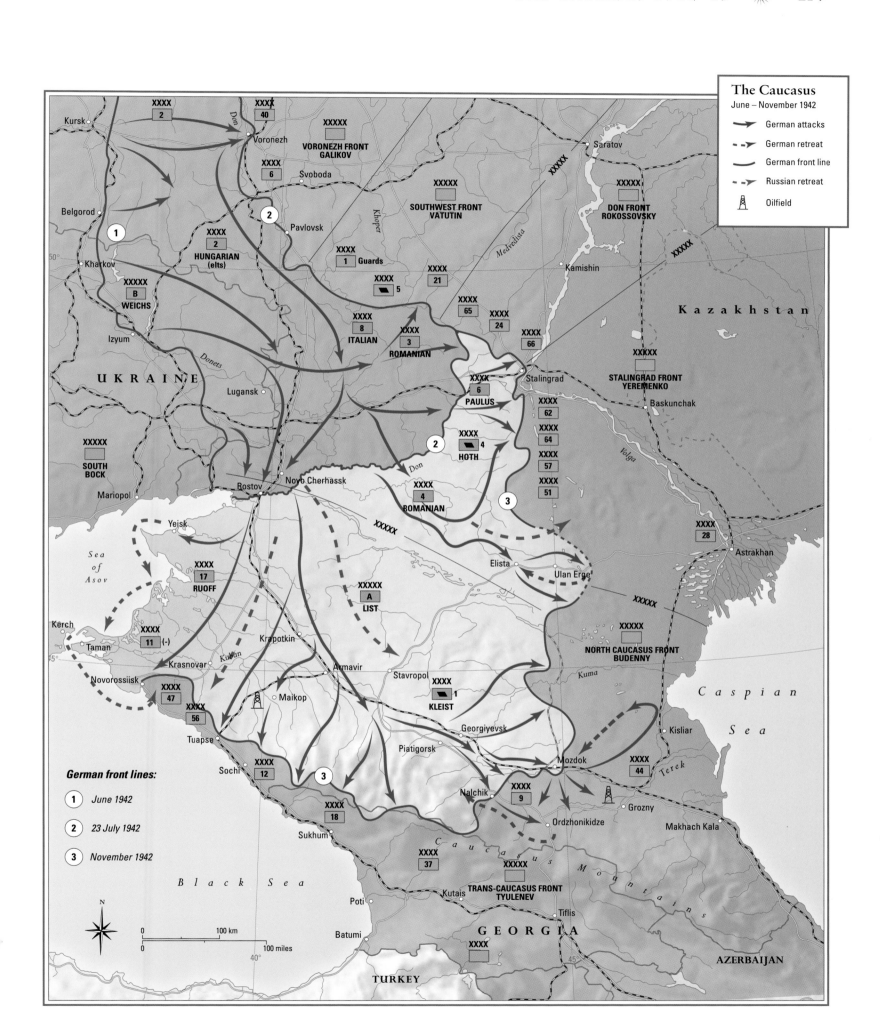

The Caucasus
June – November 1942

→ German attacks
⇢ German retreat
— German front line
⇢ Russian retreat
⛏ Oilfield

XXXX
2

XXXX
40

XXXXX
VORONEZH FRONT
GALIKOV

XXXX
6

XXXXX
SOUTHWEST FRONT
VATUTIN

XXXXX
DON FRONT
ROKOSSOVSKY

Kursk

Voronezh

Svoboda

Saratov

Pavlovsk

2

Belgorod

1

Kharkov

XXXX
2
HUNGARIAN
(elts)

XXXX
1 Guards

XXXX
21

Kamishin

Kazakhstan

XXXXX
B
WEICHS

Izyum

XXXX
5

XXXX
65

XXXX
24

XXXX
66

XXXXX
STALINGRAD FRONT
YEREMENKO

Baskunchak

UKRAINE

Donets

Lugansk

XXXX
8
ITALIAN

XXXX
3
ROMANIAN

Stalingrad

XXXX
6
PAULUS

XXXX
62

XXXX
64

XXXXX
SOUTH
BOCK

Mariopol

Rostov

Novo Cherhassk

Don

2

XXXX
4
HOTH

XXXX
4
ROMANIAN

XXXX
57

XXXX
51

Volga

XXXXX

3

XXXX
28

Astrakhan

Yeisk

Sea
of
Asov

XXXX
17
RUOFF

XXXXX
A
LIST

Elista

Ulan Erge

Kerch

Taman

XXXX
11 (-)

Krapotkin

Kuban

XXXXX

XXXXX
NORTH CAUCASUS FRONT
BUDENNY

Kuma

Caspian

Krasnovar

Novorossiisk

XXXX
47

XXXX
56

Armavir

Stavropol

XXXX
1
KLEIST

Kisliar

Sea

Tuapse

Maikop

Georgiyevsk

Mozdok

XXXX
44

Terek

Sochi

XXXX
12

Piatigorsk

German front lines:

① June 1942

② 23 July 1942

③ November 1942

XXXX
18

Nalchik

XXXX
9

Ordzhonikidze

Grozny

Makhach Kala

Sukhum

XXXX
37

XXXXX
TRANS-CAUCASUS FRONT
TYULENEV

Caucasus

Mountains

N

0   100 km
0   100 miles

Black Sea

Poti

Kutais

Tiflis

Batumi

GEORGIA

XXXX

40°

45°

AZERBAIJAN

TURKEY

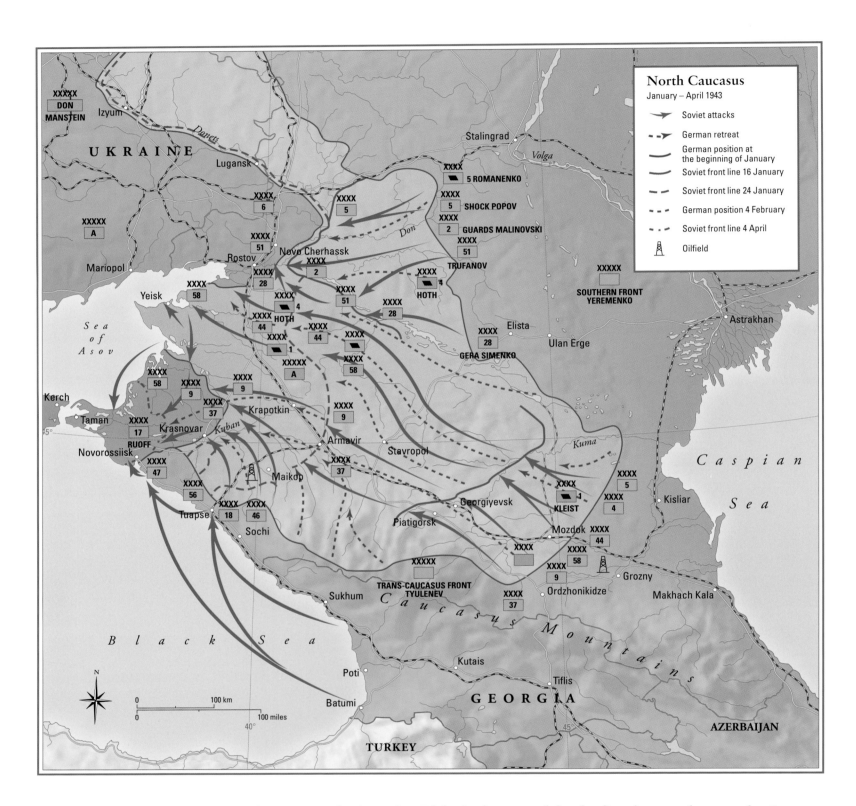

North Caucasus
January – April 1943

→ Soviet attacks
- - → German retreat
—— German position at the beginning of January
—— Soviet front line 16 January
- - - Soviet front line 24 January
- - - German position 4 February
-·-· Soviet front line 4 April
⛴ Oilfield

survive. On 25 July Operation Edelweiss began, and for the first three weeks or so the Germans advanced between 20 and 30 miles per day. But slowly the Soviets recovered, fresh troops arrived and as German resources on the Caucasus Front were re-directed to Stalingrad, especially the 4th Airfleet, which was now ordered to send all of its aircraft to support the Stalingrad attacks.

As Army Group A drove further south their progress slowed; by mid-August average progress was a little over one mile per day. On the Soviet side fresh troops and new commanders arrived. Amongst these troops were the internal security NKVD division, sent to keep an eye on the local non-

Russian nationalists and to stiffen resistance at the front.

The German 17th Army, with the Romanian 3rd Army, faced the Soviet Trans-Caucasus Front, struggling to gain control of the coast road running from Novorossiisk to Sukhumí. The 17th Army reached the outskirts of Novorossiik on 6 September, but stubborn Soviet resistance prevented further progress. Attacks on the coast road also made little further progress before winter set in and made any further meaningful advance impossible. To the east of the 17th Army, the 1st Panzer Army advanced with apparent ease, skirting the northern foothills of the Caucasus Mountains. The River Terek was crossed at Mozdok on 2 September. Facing Soviet counterattacks the German advance faltered, finally coming to a halt in November on a front from Nalchik to Ordzhonilidze. Snowfalls prevented further advances and the German line of supply was, by now, long, thin, and at its maximum extent.

Through the winter both sides dug in and made the best arrangements possible for defense. During the early winter Soviet supplies of men and equipment strengthened the North Caucasus and Trans-Caucasus fronts.

The Soviet winter offensive developed in Moscow, largely at Stalin's behest, was devised to trap Army Group A, and this needed cooperation between the Southern Front and Trans-Caucasus Front. Trans-Caucasus attacked along an axis from Taupse to Krasnovar; unfortunately they made slow progress in freezing weather. Meanwhile, the 1st Panzer Army managed a fighting withdrawal. The Southern Front, under Yeremenko, failed to close the bottleneck and the German Panzers escaped to rejoin Manstein and recently formed Army Group Don. At the same time, the German 17th Army were, with the Romanians, left holding the Taman Peninsula.

For most of the summer attention was focussed on Rostov-on-Don and northward; the Caucasus Front remained a quiet sector. This changed on 9 September, when a seaborne assault was launched on Novorossiisk, directly into the harbor area. Pressure from the Soviet 58th, 9th, 56th, and the 18th Armies, plus further landings along the coast, cleared the peninsula of German forces by 9 October.

The liberation of the Caucasus ended Hitler's dream of capturing and exploiting the region's valuable oilfields.

German Infantry fighting in the foothills of the Caucasus Mountains. Between August and the end of December they advanced toward the precious oilfields. However, by the winter they had been thrown onto the defensive.

The Taman Offensive
9 September – 9 October 1943
- German movements
- Russian movements
- Russian front lines
- German strongholds

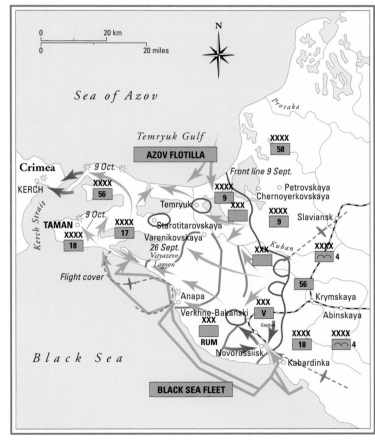

THE NEW ORDER

"GREATER GERMANY—THE DREAM OF OUR FATHERS AND
GRANDFATHERS—IS FINALLY CREATED."

GUSTAV KRUPP VON BOHLEN,

GERMAN ARMAMENTS MAGNATE

H itler had a vision for Germany: at the head of the European nations, this new Germany would be the political, economic, cultural, and racial hub of the continent. In his vision this power would radiate outward across Europe, eastward to the Ural Mountains, south to the Mediterranean and westward, to the Atlantic Ocean.

By 1941, German rule extended over 15 European states. In Hitler's new racial order the Nordic peoples were accorded the most privileged position, while the Slavic peoples of the east were to be treated as inferior, educated only to the most basic level, fit only to labor for their superiors. The peoples inhabiting the Balkans and the "Latins" of southern Europe held a questionable place in the hierarchy: they were allied to Germany but not quite as equals.

The economic structure for the New Europe matched the racial structure that Germany had started to put into practice following its conquests between 1939 and 1942. Germany planned a compulsory economic union, with the Reichsmark as the reserve or, eventually, the only currency. Berlin was already the emerging financial center of this new system, supported by Vienna extending its traditional trade contacts in central, eastern, and southwestern Europe. These two cities would serve as the financial twins overseeing the commercial and industrial activity of Europe.

German businesses, state and private, were encouraged to take over European businesses whenever possible. By 1942–43 German domination and exploitation of Europe's productive capacity became almost complete. Occupied Europe provided huge amounts of materials, labor, and food. Manufactured goods poured into the Greater German Reich amounting to a total of 90 billion Reichsmarks by 1944, a massive contribution toward the German war effort.

The huge, state-owned Reichswerke Holding Company planned industrial development on a massive scale, reaching out from central Germany toward Kiev and beyond in the Ukraine. This giant corporation had already taken over most of the captured heavy industry. All this effort was to be bound together by a vast new continent-wide autobahnen (motorway) system. There would also be a new wide-gauge railroad stretching out from Berlin to Kazan in the east, to Paris in the west, and Istanbul in the south-east. The Führer, always an enthusiast for air travel, planned airports in all major cities, connected, of course, by comfortable German-built aircraft. Hitler's chosen elite would, at least, travel in style.

The political future of this new Europe was less defined, although some kind of sovereignty might

THE GREATER GERMAN REICH was divided into *"gaus,"* each administered by a *gauleiter*, who enjoyed dictatorial powers over his district.

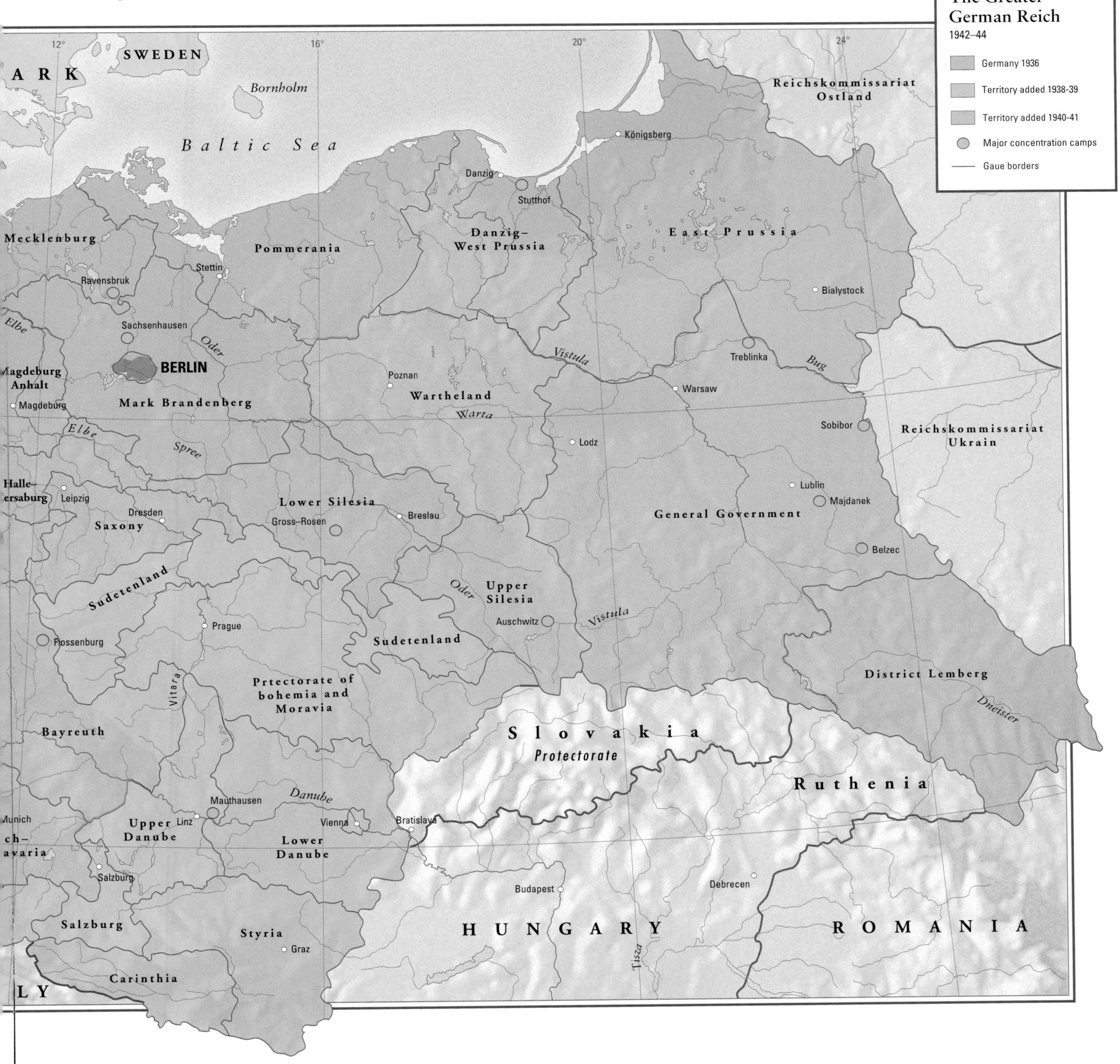

The Greater German Reich
1942–44

- Germany 1936
- Territory added 1938-39
- Territory added 1940-41
- Major concentration camps
- Gaue borders

The German Empire
Late 1942

- Germany
- Allied to Germany
- German/Axis occupied
- Allied states or under Allied control
- Neutral states

be tolerated in the Nordic states of the north and west. The Balkans and the southern countries would be seen as allies, though under some supervision. Only for the east were any concrete plans created, with two main options discussed by Nazi high command. Hitler's preference was to annex to the Reich vast areas of western Russia, parts of the Ukraine, and the Baltic States. These would become areas of settlement, the living space he had written about in *Mein Kampf*. He had stated many times to his acolytes, "the British have India, we shall have the vast spaces of Russia." All the way to the Ural Mountains would be open to settlement and exploitation. The population of the region would be "Germanized," driven eastward beyond the Urals, or exterminated.

There was another view of the east put forward by Alfred Rosenberg, Minister for the Eastern Areas: he wanted to develop national states in the east, the product of German liberation from the Communists. There was enthusiasm for this idea among the nationalist groups in the east, most of whom had suffered woefully under Stalin's rule. However, as the cruel and ruthless rule of the Germans asserted itself, this opportunity was lost. Local identities and interests were summarily swept aside, as conquered areas became part of the Nazi Empire.

The conquest of vast new territories also had a major effect on the Reich's racial policy, as huge numbers of Jews fell under German rule. There was a move from discrimination and brutality to a deliberate policy of genocide. At the dark heart of the Nazi State, it was decided that the extermination of the Jews, and any other "undesirables," should be carried out in a systematic program of annihilation. This was carried out by the building of a series of special extermination camps under the control of the Reichssicherheitshauptamt (R.S.H.A.). At these camps the majority of victims were gassed on arrival: those incapable of work; children; the elderly; or those deemed to be too weak. The rest were to be worked to death at sites adjacent to these special camps.

A recruiting poster for the Waffen-SS. The translation reads: "You can join them on your 17th birthday." The Waffen-SS started as a very undisciplined group and were guilty of many battlefield crimes. But later they became a very effective combat organization.

The killing went on until the last weeks of the Reich, when trains were used to transport hundreds of thousands of people to the death camps despite the need to move supplies to the front and the wounded back to Germany. The death trains still rolled, given priority by the political hierarchy of the Reich.

Germany had been transformed by the demands of the war. Young Germans had marched off to the battlefields and to police the occupied territories. They, in turn, had been replaced by foreign workers, volunteered, conscripted, and enslaved from across Europe, especially from the east. Germany had become a multiracial slave state, far from the Nordic haven that Hitler and the Nazis originally planned.

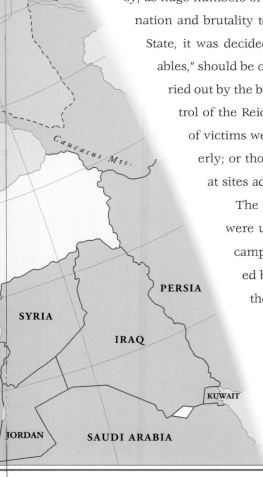

BOMBING OF GERMANY 1942–43

"THEY SOWED THE WIND, AND NOW THEY ARE GOING TO REAP THE WHIRLWIND."

AIR MARSHAL "BOMBER" HARRIS

The bombing campaign against Germany increased in intensity in the years after 1942, with the introduction of long-range, four-engined bombers that could take an increased bomb load further into enemy territory. The newly-arrived U.S. 8th Air Force also took part in planning a combined bombing offensive. By 1942 the R.A.F., having learned that daylight precision bombing was costly on aircraft and crew, decided on a policy of nighttime area bombing, in the hope of destroying the chosen target and lowering the morale of the enemy.

The U.S. 8th Air Force felt that they could achieve precision bombing with their Norden bomb sights during daylight and be able to defend their more heavily-armed aircraft by flying in mutually-supporting formation. It was also important for the Allies to continue the bomber offensive. It was seen as a "Second Front" for Stalin that kept resources that could be used against Russia, such as antiaircraft artillery and fighters, in Germany to protect its industry.

1942 was a period for the bomber commanders to learn new tactics and train the crews that would be required to fly against the Reich. Time was also spent building up the 8th Air Force in Britain. However, the Germans developed a new and more effective defense system against the Allied bombers that were flying daily and nightly missions into German airspace. They deployed new direction finding and radar to control fighters and antiaircraft guns as well as improving their tactics. By May the new Commander-in-Chief of Bomber Command, Sir Arthur Harris, was ready to launch his first "1000 bomber raid" on Cologne. This raid was intended to prove that area-bombing could devastate targets better than attempting precision bombing, and with fewer losses of aircraft. After launching two more raids on a similar scale, they were discontinued in order to concentrate on the build up of bombers and trained crews. A new tactic was developed with the Pathfinder Force that would be directed to the target using "Oboe," a radio navigation aid, after which they would then mark the target for the following main force.

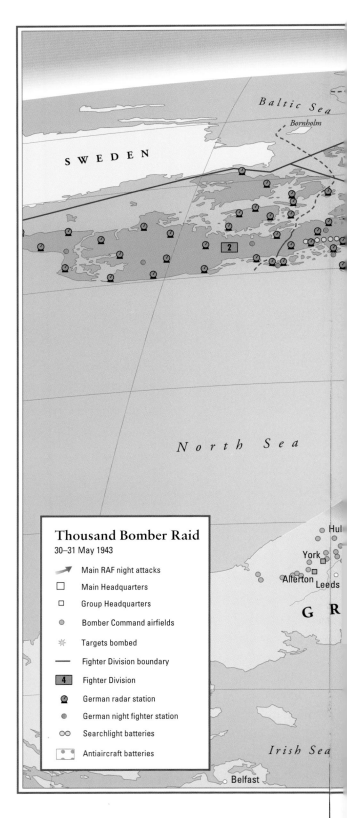

Thousand Bomber Raid
30–31 May 1943

↗ Main RAF night attacks

□ Main Headquarters

□ Group Headquarters

● Bomber Command airfields

✳ Targets bombed

— Fighter Division boundary

[4] Fighter Division

⊕ German radar station

● German night fighter station

◯◯ Searchlight batteries

▱ Antiaircraft batteries

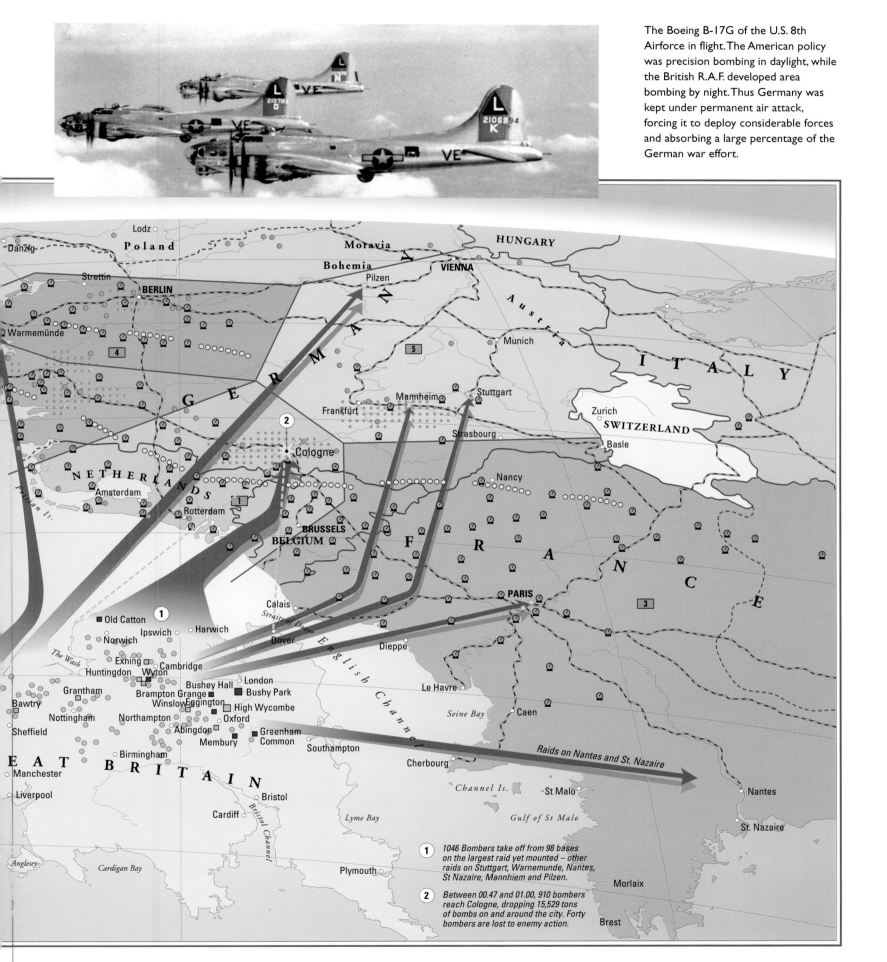

The Boeing B-17G of the U.S. 8th Airforce in flight. The American policy was precision bombing in daylight, while the British R.A.F. developed area bombing by night. Thus Germany was kept under permanent air attack, forcing it to deploy considerable forces and absorbing a large percentage of the German war effort.

1 1046 Bombers take off from 98 bases on the largest raid yet mounted – other raids on Stuttgart, Warnemunde, Nantes, St Nazaire, Mannhiem and Pilzen.

2 Between 00.47 and 01.00, 910 bombers reach Cologne, dropping 15,529 tons of bombs on and around the city. Forty bombers are lost to enemy action.

STALINGRAD 1942–43

"NOW WE KNOW THE GERMANS ARE NOT HUMAN. NOW THE WORD "GERMAN" HAS BECOME THE MOST TERRIBLE SWEAR WORD. LET US NOT SPEAK. LET US NOT BE INDIGNANT. LET US KILL. IF YOU DO NOT KILL THE GERMAN, HE WILL KILL YOU ... IF YOU HAVE KILLED ONE GERMAN KILL ANOTHER."

ILYA EHRENBURG IN THE "RED STAR"

Exhausted German troops advance through the ruins in the factory district of Stalingrad.

After continuous campaigning ended in defeat before Moscow, German Army Group Center was now totally exhausted, suffering the combined effects of the Soviet counteroffensive and the Russian winter. Hitler's sights moved south to the southern Russian Steppe and the vast oilfields and wide agricultural lands that would fuel his country's war machine. Operation Blue was put into action, an advance using Army Group South that would drive into the Caucasus in two massive groups. The 6th Army, commanded by General Freidrich Paulus, along with General Huth's 4th Panzer Army, would strike toward Stalingrad. The capture of the city would be a massive propaganda coup for the Nazis as well as denying northern Russia its link to the Caspian Sea and the Caucasus oilfields. The remainder of Army Group South would move southward to the Caucasus and the precious oilfields.

By the end of July 1942, the 6th and 4th Armies had reached the banks of the River Don and set about establishing a defensive line using their allies, the Romanian, Hungarian, and Italian troops, while the majority of the German units advanced on toward Stalingrad itself.

The battle for the city began with the usual German preemptive airstrikes flown by bombers and the Luftwaffe, decimating the city. Stalin ordered that no civilians were to leave the city. Thousands were employed by the many factories that were now part of a gigantic Soviet industrial effort producing as many tanks and artillery pieces as humanly possible in order to beat off the German invaders. The sight of the population staying in the city would also help to boost the morale of the troops defending them. By the height of the air attack 80 percent of the city was reduced to rubble. Firestorms swept through the city's wooden buildings, leaving many dead and many more homeless.

The initial German advance was met by a mostly female unit, the 1077th Antiaircraft Regiment, who had to level their guns in order to engage the Panzers approaching the city. They only ceased fire when their positions were overrun or destroyed, but still managed to inflict a heavy toll on the Panzers. As the Germans advanced further into the city, the Russians threw absolutely everything possible in their path, tanks were rolling off the production lines straight into the thick of battle, sometimes being driven by volunteers from the factory itself. By 23 August, the Germans had advanced up to the line of the Volga in the north and south of the city, bringing up their allies to protect their flanks.

The Soviets now clung on to a pocket close by the River Volga. This was their only supply route and it came under constant bombardment and strafing attacks from artillery and Stuka dive bombers. With the city about to fall, Stalin issued his "Not a step back" order, the officers pushing Soviet infantry as close as possible to the Germans to frustrate their artillery and air support. With Soviet troops so close, the Germans could not attack with artillery or air strikes for fear of hitting their own men.

Every street, house, and cellar was now bitterly contested, with vicious hand-to-hand fighting with any lethal object the combatants could lay their hands on, sometimes the Germans winning the living room while the Russians still held the kitchen. On the hill that dominates Stalingrad, Mamayev Kurgan, horrific casualties were incurred by both sides. The hill changed possession several times, the Russians losing almost a division in one counterattack alone. However, the ruined city now favored the defender and was a perfect hunting ground for the talented Russian snipers who stalked the Germans incessantly, notching up hundreds of kills and severely affecting the morale of the German soldier. The Germans were still stronger in manpower and had succeeded in splitting the pocket on the west bank of the Volga in two, but the Russians stoically held on

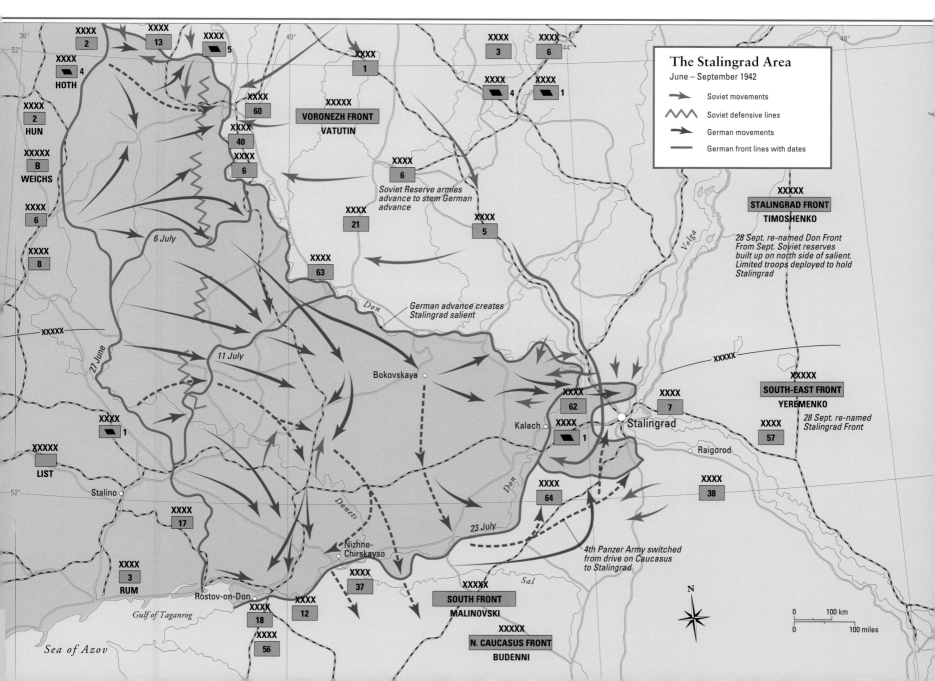

The Stalingrad Area
June – September 1942

→ Soviet movements
︿︿ Soviet defensive lines
→ German movements
— German front lines with dates

STALINGRAD FRONT
TIMOSHENKO

28 Sept. re-named Don Front
From Sept. Soviet reserves
built up on north side of salient.
Limited troops deployed to hold
Stalingrad

SOUTH-EAST FRONT
YEREMENKO

28 Sept. re-named
Stalingrad Front

Soviet Reserve armies
advance to stem German
advance

German advance creates
Stalingrad salient

4th Panzer Army switched
from drive on Caucasus
to Stalingrad

VORONEZH FRONT
VATUTIN

SOUTH FRONT
MALINOVSKI

N. CAUCASUS FRONT
BUDENNI

HOTH
HUN
WEICHS
LIST
RUM

Bokovskaya
Kalach
Stalingrad
Raigorod
Stalino
Nizhne-Chirskayso
Rostov-on-Don
Gulf of Taganrog
Sea of Azov

6 July
11 July
27 June
23 July

0   100 km
0   100 miles

A Panzergrenadier officer takes
cover in a shell hole near the
Krasny Oktyabr (Red October)
steel works.

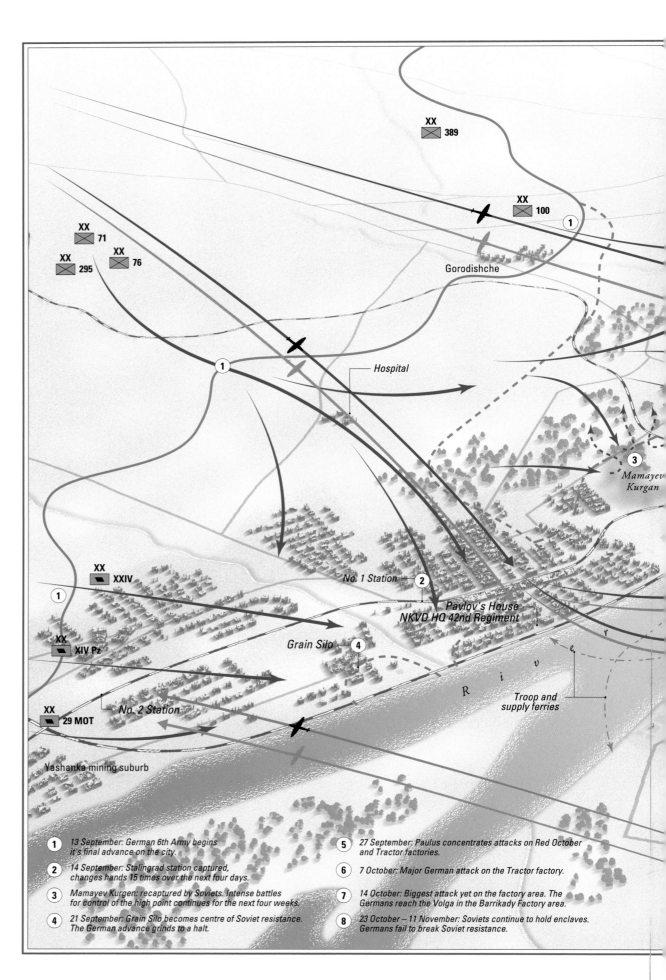

XX 389

XX 100

1

Gorodishche

XX 71

XX 295

XX 76

1

Hospital

3

Mamayev
Kurgan

XX XXIV

1

No. 1 Station

2

Pavlov's House
NKVD HQ 42nd Regiment

Grain Silo

4

XX XIV Pz

R   i   v   e   r

No. 2 Station

XX 29 MOT

Troop and
supply ferries

Vashanka mining suburb

1. **13 September:** German 6th Army begins it's final advance on the city.

2. **14 September:** Stalingrad station captured, changes hands 15 times over the next four days.

3. **Mamayev Kurgen:** recaptured by Soviets. Intense battles for control of the high point continues for the next four weeks.

4. **21 September:** Grain Silo becomes centre of Soviet resistance. The German advance grinds to a halt.

5. **27 September:** Paulus concentrates attacks on Red October and Tractor factories.

6. **7 October:** Major German attack on the Tractor factory.

7. **14 October:** Biggest attack yet on the factory area. The Germans reach the Volga in the Barrikady Factory area.

8. **23 October – 11 November:** Soviets continue to hold enclaves. Germans fail to break Soviet resistance.

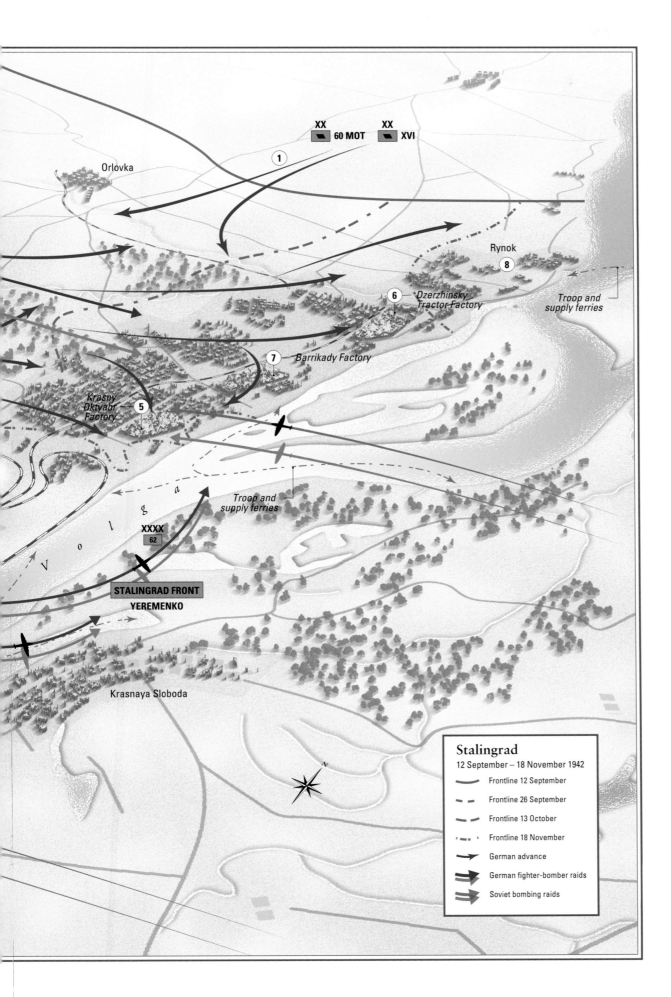

XX 60 MOT

XX XVI

①

Orlovka

Rynok

⑧

⑥ Dzerzhinsky Tractor Factory

Troop and supply ferries

⑦ Barrikady Factory

Krasny Oktyabr Factory ⑤

Troop and supply ferries

V o l g a

XXXX 62

STALINGRAD FRONT
YEREMENKO

Krasnaya Sloboda

Stalingrad
12 September – 18 November 1942

⎯⎯ Frontline 12 September

- - - Frontline 26 September

⎯ ⎯ Frontline 13 October

-·-·- Frontline 18 November

→ German advance

⇒ German fighter-bomber raids

⇒ Soviet bombing raids

A patriotic Soviet soldier waves the red flag after recapturing the city center of Stalingrad. The bitter fighting from street to street and from building to factory would ultimately cost almost 2,000,000 Axis and Soviet lives.

The German 6th Army battled its way in to Stalingrad's western suburbs, after months of severe fighting, Stalingrad, named after the leader of the Soviet state, lay in utter ruins. Violent, merciless, and bitter struggles had contested every street and cellar. Despite fearful losses, the single-minded determination of the Soviets, regardless of the casualties, won the day.

around the factory district that was home to the Red October and Dzerzhinsky factories. Of vital importance, it was here that tanks and heavy weaponry were repaired and sent straight back onto the battlefield. While hand to hand, street by street, struggles had been fought, the Soviets had been building up forces from across the Volga River opposite the Romanian positions to the north and south

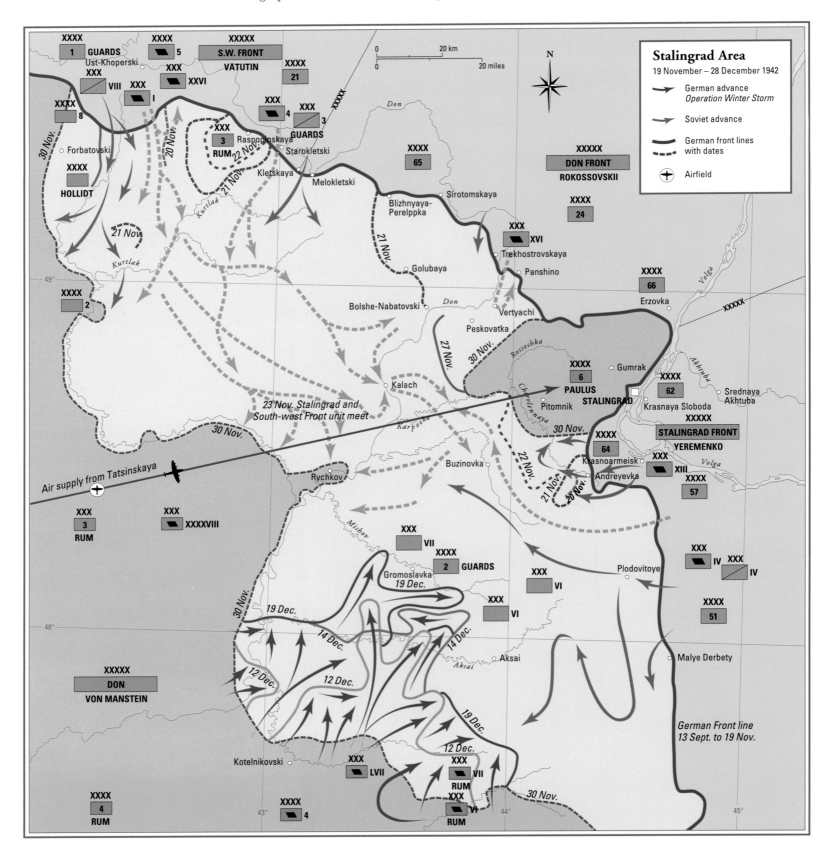

Stalingrad Area
19 November – 28 December 1942

→ German advance
Operation Winter Storm

→ Soviet advance

⌒ German front lines with dates

⊹ Airfield

of Stalingrad. The Romanians were less well equipped and trained than the German army, and were of low morale, especially when their commanders pleaded for reinforcements only to be abruptly turned down. Every available man and machine was being pressed into the capture of the center of Stalingrad. Hitler's obsession with capturing Stalingrad was about to cost him one of the largest and best-equipped German armies deployed in Russia, the 6th. Stalingrad was about to be surrounded by a massive Soviet maneuver that would change the course of the war on the Eastern Front.

On 19 November three Russian armies, under General Vatutin, engaged the Romanians defending the northern flank. This was the start of Operation Uranus. Poorly-equipped Romanians gave a good account of themselves but could not hold the weight of the Russian attack for long, their line broken by the end of the day. In the south the following day, another assault was launched against the Romanians; again this line broke after some initial resistance. The Russians now raced around Stalingrad and met at the small town of Kalach, in a pincer movement that was finally completed two days later. Now more than 250,000 German troops—along with thousands of Romanian soldiers—were now trapped inside an area that would become known by the men as "Der Kessel," the Cauldron.

German Infantrymen armed with an MG-34 set up a defensive position in Stalingrad.

The Soviets immediately set about preparing lines facing inward and outward to protect against enemy breakout or a relief force attempting to break in. German command immediately saw the need to plan for a breakout or witness the slow destruction of the 6th Army. However, Hitler, after conferring with Goering, Head of the Luftwaffe, agreed that the army could be resupplied by air and ordered the 6th Army to stand fast. This task of resupply was given to Wolfram von Richthofen's 4th Air Fleet. He argued that the entire Luftwaffe did not have enough transports to attempt to resupply the 400-plus tons that they would require each day, let alone the aircraft immediately available to him or within useful range of Stalingrad. Hitler and the German High Command had been encouraged by the Luftwaffe's ability to supply the men that had been trapped in the Demyansk Pocket in early 1942, though this was on a far smaller scale. Shortly after the air supply mission began its shortcomings were immediately obvious; the Soviet antiaircraft guns and interceptors took a heavy toll of the transports, only a small percentage of the supplies getting through to keep the army fighting. The troops inside Der Kessel were beginning to go hungry and were increasingly short of ammunition, but Hitler reissued the order of "no surrender."

The 4th Panzer Army, with the assistance of the the 17th and 23rd Panzer Divisions diverted from the Caucasus Front, attempted to advance into the south of the Russian encirclement around Stalingrad. Operation Winter Tempest, launched on 12 December to aid a planned breakout by Paulus' 6th Army, was beaten back. Paulus was not given the order to break out from Hitler himself, thousands of miles away from the front and still obsessed that not a single German soldier should retreat. Then the harsh Russian winter really started to hit the trapped Germans, with the frozen Volga helping the supply route to the Russians in the city. As the Russians continued to attack, the Germans inside the

Vengeful Soviet soldiers close in and mop up isolated German units, after the encirclement of Stalingrad.

pocket fought back doggedly, many of them falling to frostbite and disease rather than enemy action.

January saw the Russians launch a fresh offensive in the Caucasus. Operation Saturn aimed to completely cut off the remainder of the German forces in the south. However, the Germans fought an excellent mobile defense and they fell back to positions 200 miles short of Stalingrad. There was definitely no chance of reprieve and the 6th Army was beyond salvation, although the men were not told of this predicament and continued to fight in the hope of relief or extraction. The Germans were being pushed up against the banks of the Volga, fighting desperately for every inch. They feared surrender, expecting to be executed on the spot by the vengeful Russians.

On 30 January, Hitler promoted Paulus to First Colonel General then to Field Marshal, safe in the knowledge that no German Field Marshal had ever surrendered or had been taken prisoner. Soon after, the new Field Marshal did surrender as Russian troops closed in on his headquarters. All German troops surrendered on 2 February 1943. A total of 91,000 starving and exhausted troops marched into captivity, although only 6,000 would ever see their homeland again; most would succumb to the harsh conditions in Soviet labor camps.

The Battle for Stalingrad was truly horrific in scale and magnitude, estimates of casualties are hard to compile but it is thought that the Germans and their allies suffered close to 850,000 casualties and the Russians 1,128,000, making it the highest number of casualties in a single battle in human history.

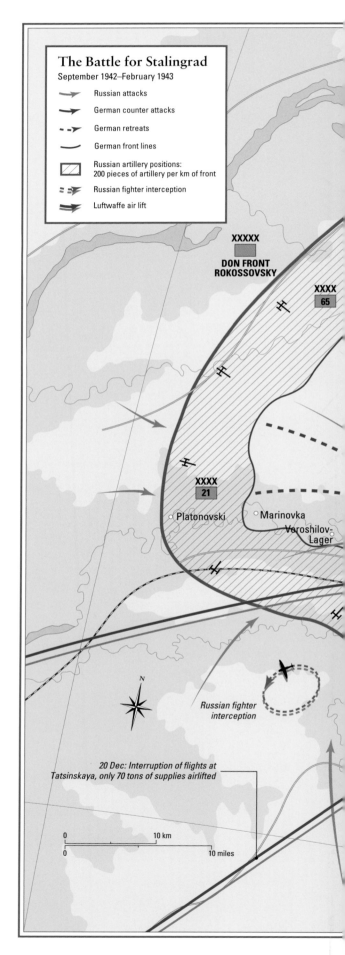

The Battle for Stalingrad
September 1942–February 1943

→ Russian attacks

➤ German counter attacks

- -➤ German retreats

⌒ German front lines

▱ Russian artillery positions: 200 pieces of artillery per km of front

═ ═➤ Russian fighter interception

➤ Luftwaffe air lift

XXXXX
DON FRONT ROKOSSOVSKY

XXXX
65

XXXX
21

Platonovski   Marinovka
Voroshilov-Lager

Russian fighter interception

N

20 Dec: Interruption of flights at Tatsinskaya, only 70 tons of supplies airlifted

0   10 km
0   10 miles

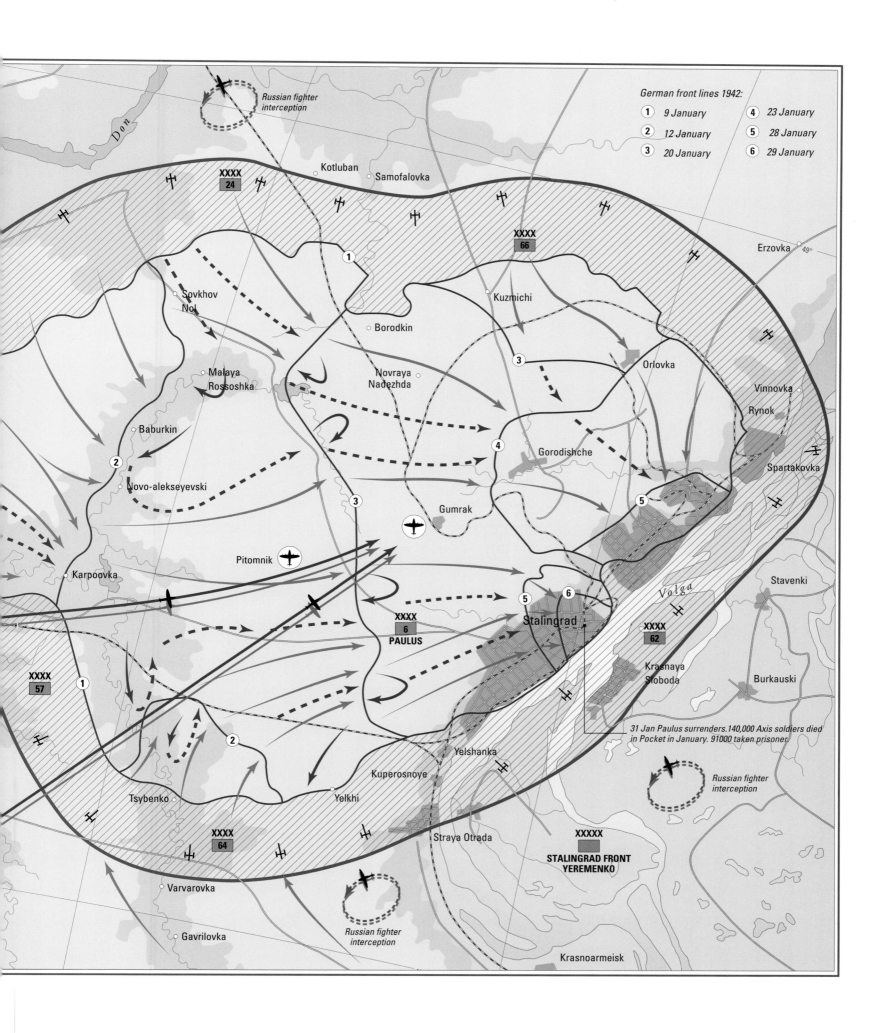

German front lines 1942:
① 9 January ④ 23 January
② 12 January ⑤ 28 January
③ 20 January ⑥ 29 January

Russian fighter interception

Don

Kotluban

Samofalovka

XXXX 24

XXXX 66

Erzovka 49°

Sovkhov Nol

Kuzmichi

Borodkin

Orlovka

Malaya Rossoshka

Novraya Nadezhda

Vinnovka

Rynok

Baburkin

①

Gorodishche

Spartakovka

Novo-alekseyevski

②

④

⑤

③

Gumrak

Karpoovka

Pitomnik

Volga

Stavenki

⑤ ⑥

Stalingrad

XXXX 57

①

XXXX 6 PAULUS

XXXX 62

Krasnaya Sloboda

Burkauski

②

Yelshanka

31 Jan Paulus surrenders. 140,000 Axis soldiers died in Pocket in January. 91000 taken prisoner.

Kuperosnoye

Russian fighter interception

Tsybenko

Yelkhi

XXXX 64

Straya Otrada

XXXXX STALINGRAD FRONT YEREMENKO

Varvarovka

Russian fighter interception

Gavrilovka

Krasnoarmeisk

THE SIEGE OF LENINGRAD 1941–44

"THE ENEMY IS AT THE GATE. IT IS A QUESTION OF LIFE

AND DEATH."

ANDREI ZHDANOV,

HEAD OF THE LENINGRAD PARTY COMMITTEE

The German and Finnish armies close in around Leningrad. The city would face a lengthy siege of some 900 days.

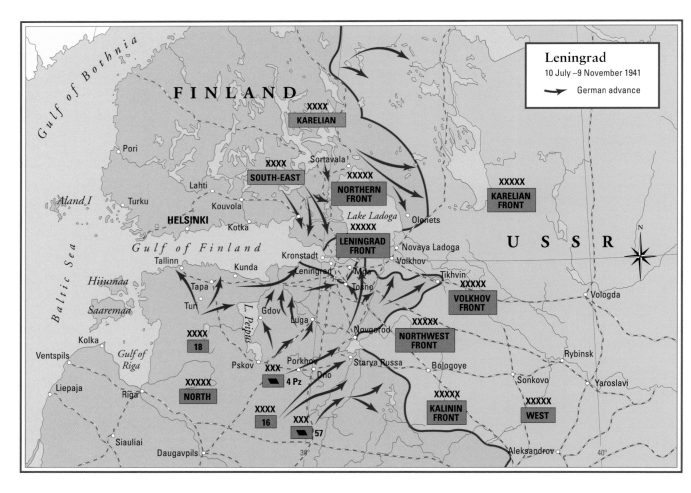

Leningrad
10 July –9 November 1941
→ German advance

L eningrad stood between the south-western shore of Lake Ladoga and the Gulf of Finland and was politically significant, being named after the hero and leader of the October Revolution, Lenin. Militarily it was important because it lay across the path of the German's advance into the north of Russia. Therefore, unless captured or isolated, the Germans would be unable to sweep deep into northern Russia and around to the east of Moscow. There were over 200,000 troops stationed in the second city of Soviet Russia, protecting a population of over three million, many of whom did not heed the dangers and stayed in their city as the German war machine approached.

Field Marshal von Leeb's Army Group North severed Leningrad's communications with the rest of Russia within weeks of the start of Operation Barbarossa and, with the aid of the Finnish army in the north, was confident of taking this highly-prized city. This was not to be, since the Finnish army refused to advance any further than the prewar boundary with Russia, which was some 40 miles to the north. The Germans assaulted the city from the south but their initial attack faltered on the hastily-constructed but stoutly-defended antitank ditches that covered the approaches to the city, which had been dug by Leningrad's citizens.

With tanks and men needed in other sectors of the Eastern Front, von Leeb decided to lay siege to the beleaguered city. Following this, Hitler issued a directive for the city to be completely destroyed by all means necessary and on no account to accept any form of surrender should one ever be offered. Leningrad's fate was sealed. It now faced ceaseless aerial and artillery bombardments that threatened to reduce the population and their city to dust.

Two Finnish snipers taking aim at their Russian enemies. The Finnish Army formed part of Operation Barbarossa, taking back the area they had lost to the Soviet Union in the war of 1939–40. Having regained this lost territory, they dug in and refused to advance any further. They had, however, effectively cut Leningrad off from the north.

Trucks loaded with supplies cross the temporary "ice road" during the winter of 1941-42. It is estimated that 365,000 tons were brought into the city over the frozen lake. Only just enough to keep the city fighting and prevent total starvation.

Stalin sent General Georgi Zhukov to investigate the crisis developing around Leningrad. The city was under the control Kliment Voroshilov, a devoted Communist but regarded by many as militarily incompetent, with the day-to-day work carried out by Andrei Zhdanov. The latter was a competent leader and popular with the people of the city. Stalin ordered Zhukov to replace Voroshilov and defend the city to the last citizen, and this he organized with the help of Zhdanov.

The German encirclement of the city had been completed by 8 September 1941, cutting all land communication to the outside world. There was, however, one lifeline left: supply boats across Lake Ladoga. Leningrad was completely dependent on outside sources for fuel, food, and oil, and only held in its warehouses enough food stocks to last a month, maybe two. The prospects were bleak. As winter closed in the population began to die of malnutrition and exposure. There was little water, heating, or electricity for many, and the basic ration for individuals sank to 4.4 ozs. (125 grams) of bread a day. Measures were taken as winter set in to try to resupply the city by sending trucks loaded with supplies across the "ice road" built over the frozen Lake Ladoga. This was constantly under artillery bombardment and not an ideal solution, since demand always outstripped supply. As the supply trucks returned across the lake they often carried evacuees, especially children, but many still chose to stay amongst the starving and defend their city. Mass graves were dug but many just fell in the street with the snow covering their bodies, remaining unburied. With the spring thaw came the threat of disease, which there would be no way to combat.

In the early days of January 1942, Stalin, encouraged by the defeat of the German forces before Moscow, gave orders for the siege of Leningrad to be broken, handing the task to General Meretskov, who attacked and achieved a small salient into the German lines north of Lake Ilmen. But this was soon slowed, bogged down into stalemate during the spring thaw as roads and tracks turned to deep mud.

When Lake Ladoga's ice melted, the "ice road," which had been so useful to the Russians, vanished. In order to keep supplies running into the city, the Leningrad garrison used any vessel they could lay their hands on. These boats were, like the trucks on the ice, under constant shelling and air attack.

The Leningrad Symphony Orchestra under their leader Dimitri Shostokovich. He composed the first drafts of his 7th Symphony while under siege in Leningrad, which later became known as the Leningrad Symphony. Orchestras and theaters were kept going as long as possible to keep up morale.

The city's garrison had been slowly gaining strength and, by the early autumn of 1942, the Soviets were ready to launch an attack on the Leningrad Front. With General Govorov attacking eastward and Meretskov driving to the west, the two forces met on 19 January near Shlüsselburg, thus lifting the siege. Soon after, trains were streaming through the small corridor that had been created but the Germans, far from being defeated, kept up a constant artillery barrage.

The situation around Leningrad was static for some considerable time, with neither side making any significant gains. Fighting on other fronts had drained men and material from the

Civilians leave a recently shell-damaged or possibly bombed building. Shelter as well as food became a priority as more buildings were damaged or completely destroyed.

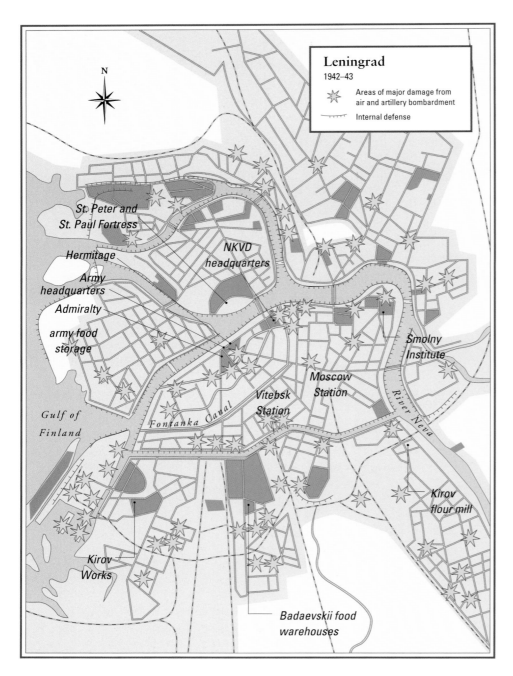

Leningrad
1942–43

✳ Areas of major damage from air and artillery bombardment

⌢⌢⌢ Internal defense

St. Peter and
St. Paul Fortress

Hermitage

Army
headquarters

Admiralty

army food
storage

NKVD
headquarters

Smolny
Institute

Moscow
Station

Vitebsk
Station

River Neva

Gulf of
Finland

Fontanka Canal

Kirov
flour mill

Kirov
Works

Badaevskii food
warehouses

The city of Leningrad remained within range of German heavy artillery throughout the siege. As well as targeting the Soviet defenses built around the city, the Germans made every attempt to shell food warehouses, distribution centers, and the limited lines of supply the Soviet commanders could keep open.

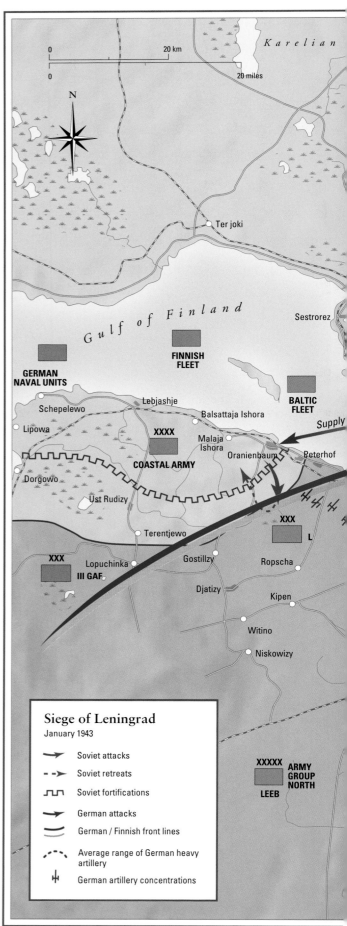

Karelian

0   20 km
0   20 miles

Ter joki

Gulf of Finland

Sestrorez

GERMAN
NAVAL UNITS

FINNISH
FLEET

BALTIC
FLEET

Schepelewo

Lebjashje

Balsattaja Ishora

Supply

Lipowa

XXXX

Malaja
Ishora

COASTAL ARMY

Oranienbaum

Peterhof

Dorgowo

Ust Rudizy

Terentjewo

XXX

L

XXX

Lopuchinka

Gostillzy

Ropscha

III GAF

Djatizy

Kipen

Witino

Niskowizy

Siege of Leningrad
January 1943

→ Soviet attacks

- -► Soviet retreats

⊓⌐⊓ Soviet fortifications

➤ German attacks

⌣⌣ German / Finnish front lines

•••• Average range of German heavy artillery

╫ German artillery concentrations

XXXXX
ARMY
GROUP
NORTH

LEEB

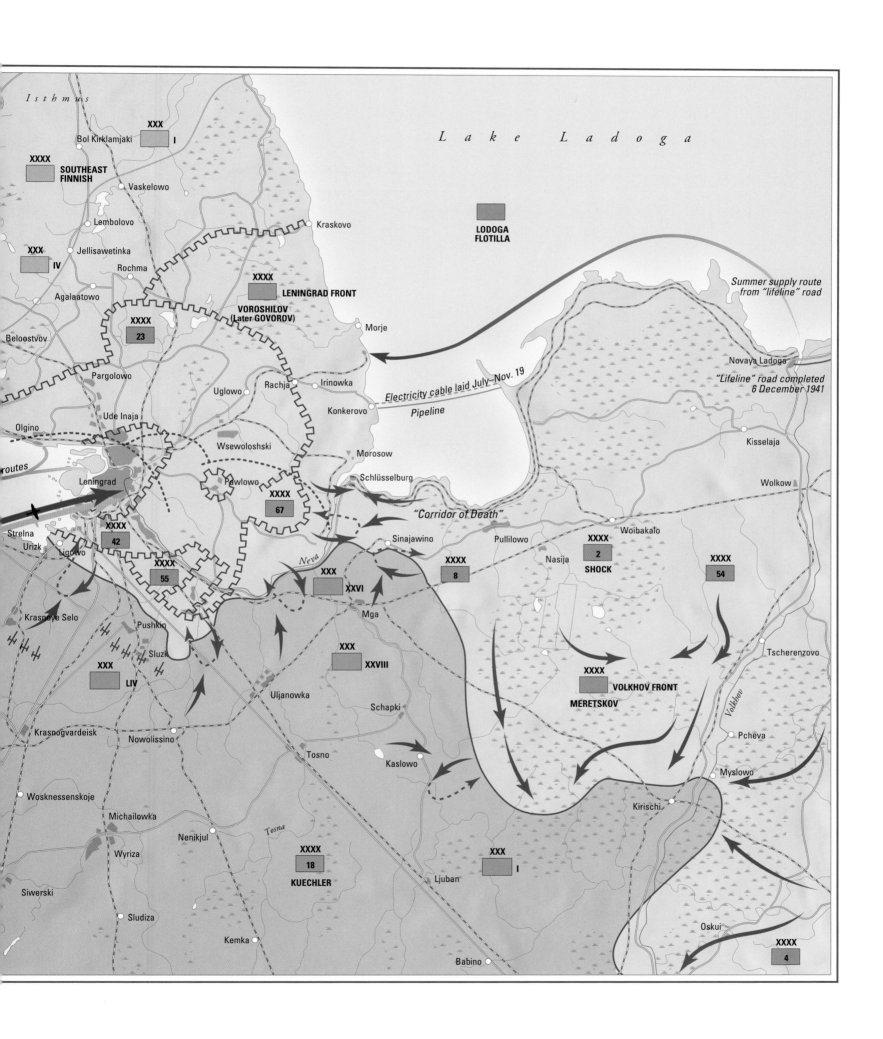

Isthmus

L a k e   L a d o g a

Bol Kirklamjaki

XXX
I

XXXX
SOUTHEAST FINNISH

Vaskelowo

Lembolovo

XXX
IV

Jellisawetinka

Rochma

Agalaatowo

Beloostvov

XXXX
23

Pargolowo

Kraskovo

LODOGA FLOTILLA

XXXX
LENINGRAD FRONT

VOROSHILOV (Later GOVOROV)

Morje

Summer supply route from "lifeline" road

Novaya Ladoga

"Lifeline" road completed 6 December 1941

Uglowo

Rachja

Irinowka

Konkerovo

Electricity cable laid July–Nov. 19

Pipeline

Kisselaja

Olgino

Ude Inaja

Wsewoloshski

Morosow

Wolkow

routes

Leningrad

Pawlowo

Schlüsselburg

XXXX
67

"Corridor of Death"

Strelna

XXXX
42

Urizk

Ligowo

Sinajawino

Pullilowo

Woibakalo

XXXX
2
SHOCK

Neva

XXX
XXVI

XXXX
8

Nasija

XXXX
54

XXXX
55

Krasnoye Selo

Pushkin

Mga

Sluzk

XXX
XXVIII

Tscherenzovo

XXX
LIV

Uljanowka

Schapki

Volkhov

XXXX
VOLKHOV FRONT

MERETSKOV

Krasnogvardeisk

Nowolissino

Pcheva

Tosno

Kaslowo

Kirischi

Myslowo

Wosknessenskoje

Michailowka

Tosna

Nenikjul

Wyriza

XXXX
18

XXX
I

Ljuban

KUECHLER

Siwerski

Sludiza

Oskui

Kemka

XXXX
4

Babino

Leningrad siege. Despite years of local bitter fighting, the city still remained within range of German artillery positions. However, when Meretskov and Govorov were happy that they had a superiority in manpower in early 1944, they gave the order to renew the attack and finally drive the Germans from Leningrad. Hitler, as always, gave the order that no ground was to be given up. This was a battle the Wehrmacht did not really have to fight, with pressure on their limited resources all along the Eastern Front. Soviet forces advanced from the outskirts of Leningrad liberating Luga and Novgorod during January, and finally restoring the main railroad line to Moscow.

The total numbers lost during the siege will almost certainly never be known. The official total given by the Soviet authorities was 632,253 civilian dead; 16,700 were killed by shelling and bombing and over 1,000,000 were evacuated, leaving a total civilian population by early 1943 of 639,000. From a prewar population of over 3,000,000, this left over 1,000,000 unaccounted for. Some fell into German hands and were never heard of again but most died in the terrible siege of the winter of 1941–42. The Leningrad siege remains one of the greatest examples of defiance in the history of World War II.

Soviet infantry advance on the Leningrad Front, part of the offensive to drive the German forces away from the city.

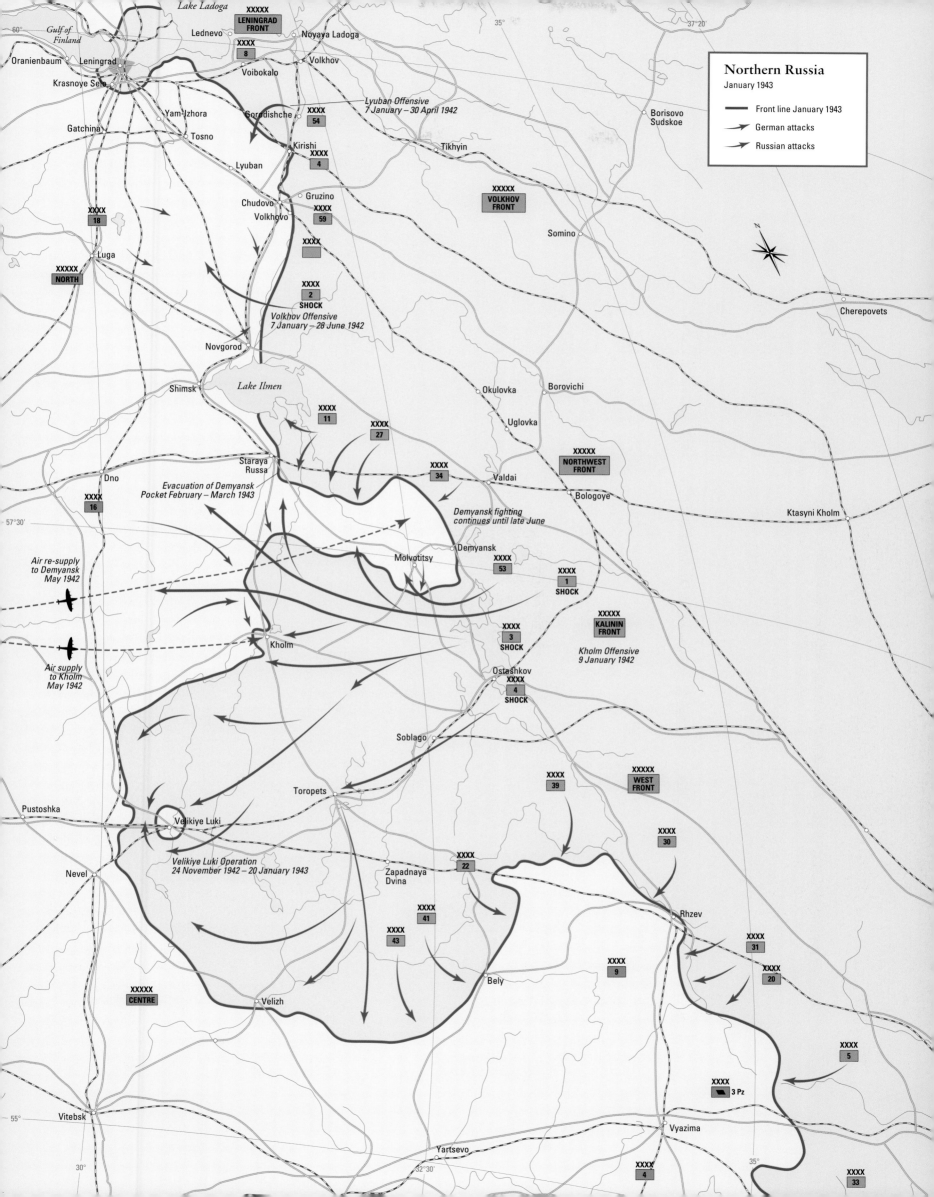

Lake Ladoga

Gulf of Finland

Oranienbaum Leningrad
Krasnoye Selo

Lednevo

XXXXX LENINGRAD FRONT

Noyaya Ladoga

XXXX 8

Volkhov

Voibokalo

Gatchina

Yam-Izhora

Tosno

Lyuban

Gorodishche

XXXX 54

Lyuban Offensive 7 January – 30 April 1942

Tikhvin

Kirishi

XXXX 4

Borisovo Sudskoe

Chudovo
Volkhovo

XXXX 59

Gruzino

XXXXX VOLKHOV FRONT

Somino

XXXX 18

XXXX

Luga

XXXXX NORTH

XXXX 2 SHOCK

Volkhov Offensive 7 January – 28 June 1942

Novgorod

Shimsk

Lake Ilmen

Okulovka

Borovichi

Cherepovets

Uglovka

XXXX 11

XXXX 27

Staraya Russa

XXXX 34

Valdai

XXXXX NORTHWEST FRONT

Bologoye

Dno

Evacuation of Demyansk Pocket February – March 1943

Ktasyni Kholm

XXXX 16

Demyansk fighting continues until late June

Air re-supply to Demyansk May 1942

Molvotitsy

Demyansk

XXXX 53

XXXX 1 SHOCK

Air supply to Kholm May 1942

Kholm

XXXX 3 SHOCK

XXXXX KALININ FRONT

Kholm Offensive 9 January 1942

Ostashkov

XXXX 4 SHOCK

Soblago

XXXX 39

XXXXX WEST FRONT

Toropets

Pustoshka

Velikiye Luki

XXXX 30

Velikiye Luki Operation 24 November 1942 – 20 January 1943

Nevel

Zapadnaya Dvina

XXXX 22

Rhzev

XXXX 41

XXXX 31

XXXX 43

XXXX 9

Bely

XXXX 20

XXXXX CENTRE

Velizh

XXXX 5

Vitebsk

XXXX 3 Pz

Vyazima

Yartsevo

XXXX 4

XXXX 33

Northern Russia

January 1943

—— Front line January 1943

→ German attacks

→ Russian attacks

N

THE BATTLE OF KURSK 1943

"SOLDIERS OF THE REICH! THIS DAY YOU ARE TO TAKE PART IN AN OFFENSIVE OF SUCH IMPORTANCE THAT THE WHOLE FUTURE OF THE WAR MAY DEPEND ON ITS OUTCOME."

ADOLF HITLER, 5 JULY 1943

The tough and reliable T-34 tanks move into action making the best use of the terrain to cover their advance toward German positions. The T-34 was simple, easy to produce, mechanically sound, and probably the best all round tank of World War II.

The battle for the Kursk salient was to be on a massive scale, involving millions of men from both sides, as well as employing thousands of armored vehicles, aircraft, guns, and mortars. The Front Line between the Soviets and the Germans ran from Leningrad, in the north, to Rostov-on-Don, in the south, with a salient 120 miles wide and protruding 75 miles into the German sector between Orel, in the north, and Kharkov, in the south. There were three armies in the bulge and the German plan was to attack at each flank and capture these armies, thereby reducing Russian manpower. The "pinching" of this salient would also reduce the length of the front line, allowing the defense to be more heavily manned. This would also mean the capture of the important rail hub at Kursk itself, helping the line of supply.

The German plan was for Model's 9th Army to strike south from the Orel district and Hoth's 4th Panzer Army to strike north from the Kharkov area, meeting in the middle. If all went to plan, they would move east to establish a line along the River Don. This plan was to be originally launched at the beginning of May but was postponed to allow time for the further buildup of tanks arriving from Germany, including Tiger 1's and the new Panther, which was designed to combat the ubiquitous Russian T-34. Ironically, this allowed the Russians to build up their own forces more quickly, and soon Russian armament was outstripping that of Germany.

To the Russian commanders it was quite obvious where the next offensive would come from but Stalin, overjoyed with the success at Stalingrad, was keen to push on. Zhukov succeeded in convincing him that it would be to their advantage to prepare a solid defense in depth and allow the Germans to attack, then counterattack once they were worn down. Stalin agreed and they immediately set about

preparing the area around Kursk into a massive fortress lined with thousands of miles of trenches and wire, built by the people of the area as well as the troops that would be defending the salient. Almost a million mines, antipersonnel, and, more importantly, antitank, were laid and to a great depth, with some trenches being almost 100 miles behind the front line. Twenty thousand pieces of artillery were placed, covering the likely German line of approach and carefully camouflaged with dummy gun positions placed to attract German fire away from the real positions. By the time of the impending attack, the

The Panzer VI "Tiger" formed a large part of the massive armored force the Germans threw at the Kursk salient. This new tank, mounted with an 88 mm high velocity gun, made it the most powerful tank on the battlefield to date.

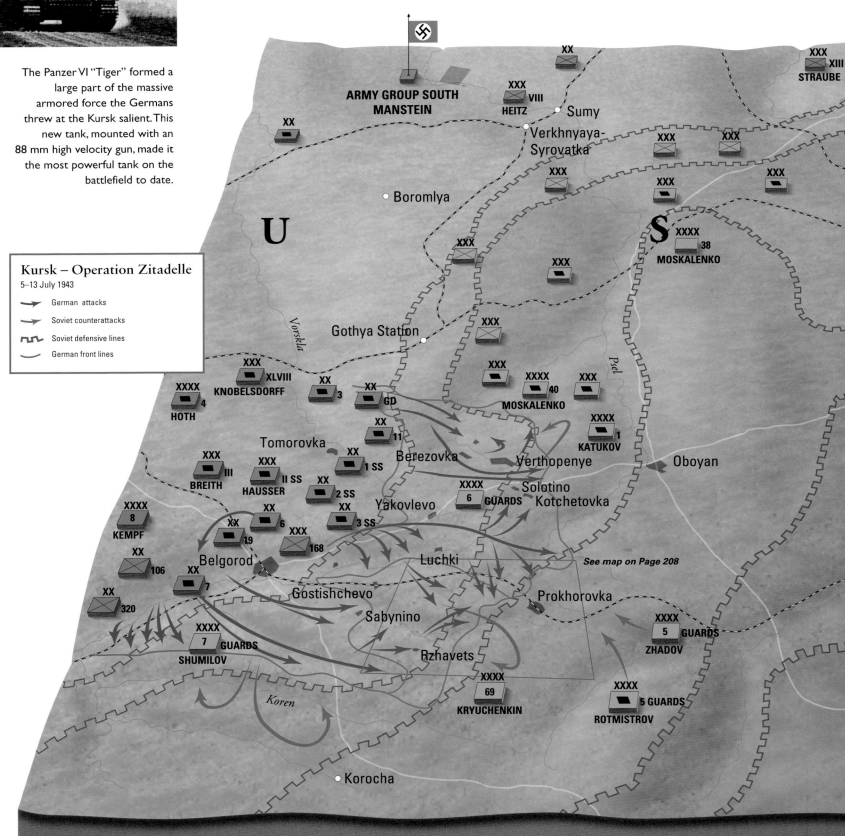

Kursk – Operation Zitadelle
5–13 July 1943

→ German attacks
→ Soviet counterattacks
⌐⌐ Soviet defensive lines
⌒ German front lines

See map on Page 208

Soviets were fully prepared with 1,300,000 men and 3,600 tanks waiting to meet 800,000 men and 2,700 tanks of the German Army, which mirrored the German/Soviet position from two years previously.

The Germans made a few tentative probing attacks on 4 July in order to try and destroy any forward observation posts so that they could preserve the element of surprise. Before the main German advance, Stuka dive bombers bombarded the area in front of the assaulting forces, followed by artillery fire. The Russians were quick to react with their own artillery fire. In the north concentrating on the German

A KV-1 advances into battle at Kursk. Although outnumbered by the T-34, the KV-1s still played an important part in the battle.

THE BATTLE OF KURSK
The Soviet forces had time to prepare for the impending German attack, Operation Zitadelle. They constructed defense in depth, defensive line after line of ditches, antitank obstacles, and minefields.

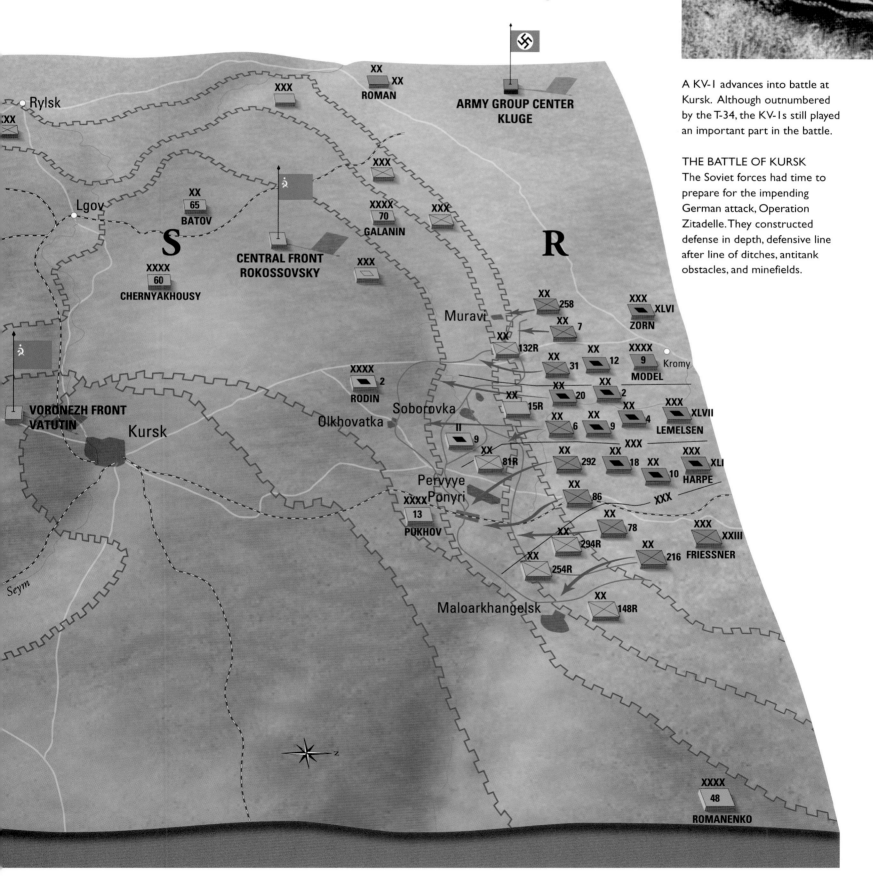

German SS Panzergrenadiers wait to move into action. They were to come up against Soviet defense in depth, which proved too much even for these tough, battle-hardened troops.

Battle of Prokhorovka
12 July 1943

→ German tanks formation
→ Soviet tanks formation

artillery positions, which were to support the main assault. In the south, their fire concentrated on the buildup of tank and infantry forces preparing to assault. Both caused enough havoc and confusion to slow up the German advance. With this loss of momentum it was clear that Blitzkreig was no longer working. The Soviets also launched preemptive strikes against any known Luftwaffe airfields in the area in an attempt to seize the air over the battlefield. However, many of the Luftwaffe aircraft were already airborne and one of the largest air battles seen in World War II developed as the ground forces were beginning to engage.

In the north, the Germans soon ran into a thick minefield and had to call up engineers, who worked under constant shell fire, the mines killing men, disabling tanks, and again slowing advance. The Soviets had correctly identified this as a likely sector where the German attack would come and had prepared defenses accordingly. The numerous antitank guns then started to take their toll on the Germans. By the end of the day the attackers had advanced a mere 4 miles into the Soviet lines.

After the initial Soviet counterstrike was fought off in the south, progress was much better than in the north. The advance frontage was smaller than in the north and was against a much thinner line of defense, but again the Soviets took their toll on the German tanks and, when threatened with being overrun, the Soviets fell back in good order, taking their equipment with them to carry on the fight. These delaying actions also helped to give the Soviets enough time to push reserves to threatened

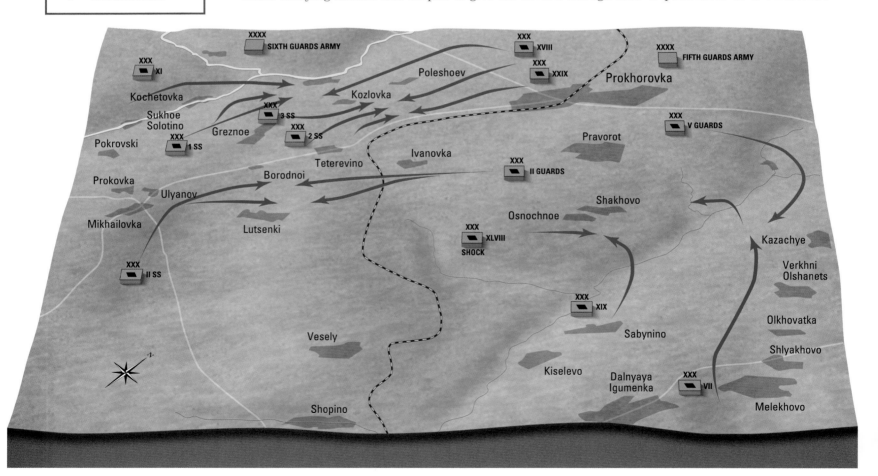

A wounded Soviet officer refuses to leave his position and continues to direct his unit. By this period in the war, the Soviet Army had become a force to be reckoned with and the defeats of the past were well behind them.

areas. At the end of the first day the 4th Panzer had managed to penetrate about 12 miles into the Soviet lines. This penetration was an obvious threat to the whole outcome of the battle. Recognizing this, the 5th Guards Tank Army was rushed to the southern front to counter the Panzers.

After heavy fighting and immense losses on both sides, the Germans, losing a particularly high number of tanks, many to breakdowns rather than enemy action, had still not managed to penetrate far into the Soviet lines, the defense in depth working wonders. By the night of 11 July the 5th Tank Army and 5th Guards Army were in place around Prokhorovka to strike at the leading elements of the Panzers—SS Adolf Hitler Panzerkorps—which were trying to drive between the 69th Army and the 1st Tank Army. On the morning of 12 July, the Totenkopf Division was forming up for another assault when they were rushed by the tanks of 5th Tank Army. The Soviets surprised and managed to get up close to the German tanks in order to readdress the balance in firepower, which favored the Germans. Although initially shocked by this attack, the Germans reacted quickly and soon took a heavy toll on the Soviet tanks, which lost two thirds of its strength by midday. By the evening, the Soviets, moved back to the defensive, had lost the ground they had gained in the morning, and had also lost around 300 tanks in the process. Losses on the German side were significant but the Soviets lost more.

After these immense battles, the German commanders had little to show for their sacrifice and started to withdraw forces in order to shorten their defensive lines. Also there had been the Anglo-American landings on Sicily, making Hitler look to other fronts that might require reinforcement, eventually sending the Liebstandarte Adolf Hitler Division. Within two weeks the Soviets had recovered enough to move onto the offensive, starting with Operation Kutuzov in the north that pushed the Germans back to their original start lines. On 3 August Operation Polkovodets Rumyantsev began, pushing the Germans out of Kharkov by 11 August. This was the decisive point where Soviet defense moved to the offensive, and the Germans began their slow retreat to the borders of Germany. Soviet High Command had developed ways of defeating the German war machine and they now held the advantage.

THE BATTLES FOR KHARKOV

"IN RUSSIA THE MORAL COMFORT OF MANSTEIN'S LATEST
VICTORY COULD NOT OBSCURE THE FACT THAT THE WHOLE
BALANCE OF POWER HAD CHANGED."

GENERAL VON MELLENTHIN

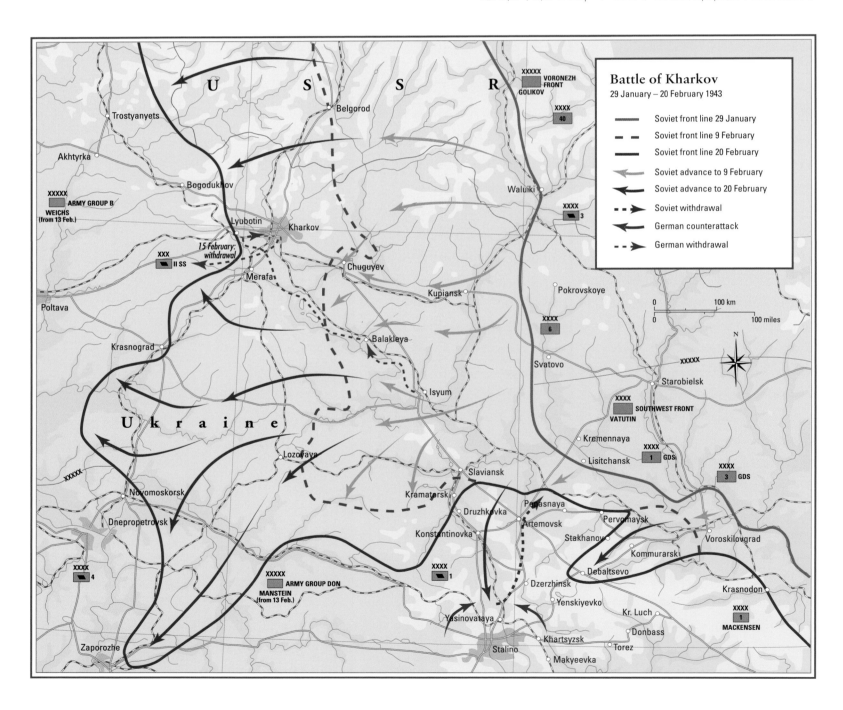

Battle of Kharkov
29 January – 20 February 1943

— Soviet front line 29 January
- - - Soviet front line 9 February
━━ Soviet front line 20 February
← Soviet advance to 9 February
← Soviet advance to 20 February
⇢ Soviet withdrawal
← German counterattack
⇠ German withdrawal

Kharkov was the largest city in terms of population in the Ukraine and the hub of the railroad system for the region as well as the administrative center. This meant that it was a highly prized city for both sides and would be the scene of no less than five bloody battles between 1941 and 1943, with the city changing hands four times. The German advance was beginning to meet tougher resistance on the part of the Red Army after their initial successes at the opening stage of Operation Barbarossa. The Germans approached the city limits of Kharkov on 24 October 1941, but this was to be the limit of the 6th Army's advance before the winter closed in and halted any chance of rapid advance. The Germans dug in 40 miles east of the city on the River Donets and prepared for the freezing winter weather.

As General Paulus was preparing his 6th Army for the spring offensive that would take them deeper into Russian territory, Soviet forces attacked his front in a preemptive strike to try to save the city. The Soviet advance achieved a certain amount of surprise but the Germans soon recovered and started throwing in concerted local counterattacks that took a heavy toll on the attackers, so much so that the rear-echelon troops were kept just behind the main line in case they needed to be put in themselves. Within two days Timoshenko's troop advance was beginning to falter under the weight of the counterattacks and the increased bombing by the Luftwaffe. But as the attack ground to a halt, the Soviet offensive to the south of the city had taken a reasonable amount of land, creating a massive bulge on the German front.

On 17 May Kleist's 1st Panzer Army plunged into the Soviets in a pincer movement on the Barvenkovo area. With this Kleist was trying to catch as many Russians as possible in a pocket. By the 24 May the Russian forces that had made the attack were completely surrounded, after Stalin had stalled the order for the retreat. Nearly a quarter of a million men were trapped in the salient along with nearly a thousand tanks. What had started off as a possible Russian victory in its time of need, had finished as yet another German victory. What was highlighted most here was the lack of experience of the newly-conscripted Soviet army and the serious problems in supplying them. It also showed the need for more concentrated planning of such offensives.

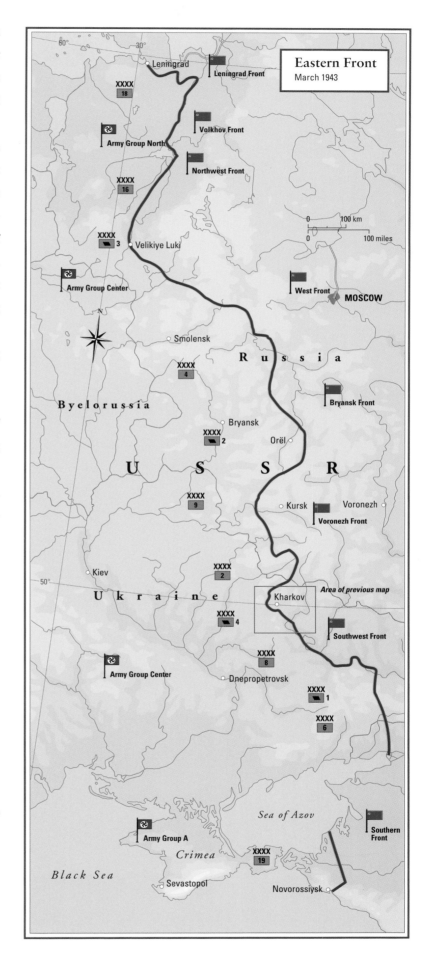

A German Fallschirmjäger at
Kharkov defends a position.
These elite soldiers were moved
around the battlefront to
bolster threatened defenses.

THE BATTLE OF KHARKOV
Army Group Don
counterattacked the Soviet
positions before Kharkov on 5
March. In an extremely hard-
fought battle German forces
succeeded in recapturing
Kharkov and its surrounding
area.

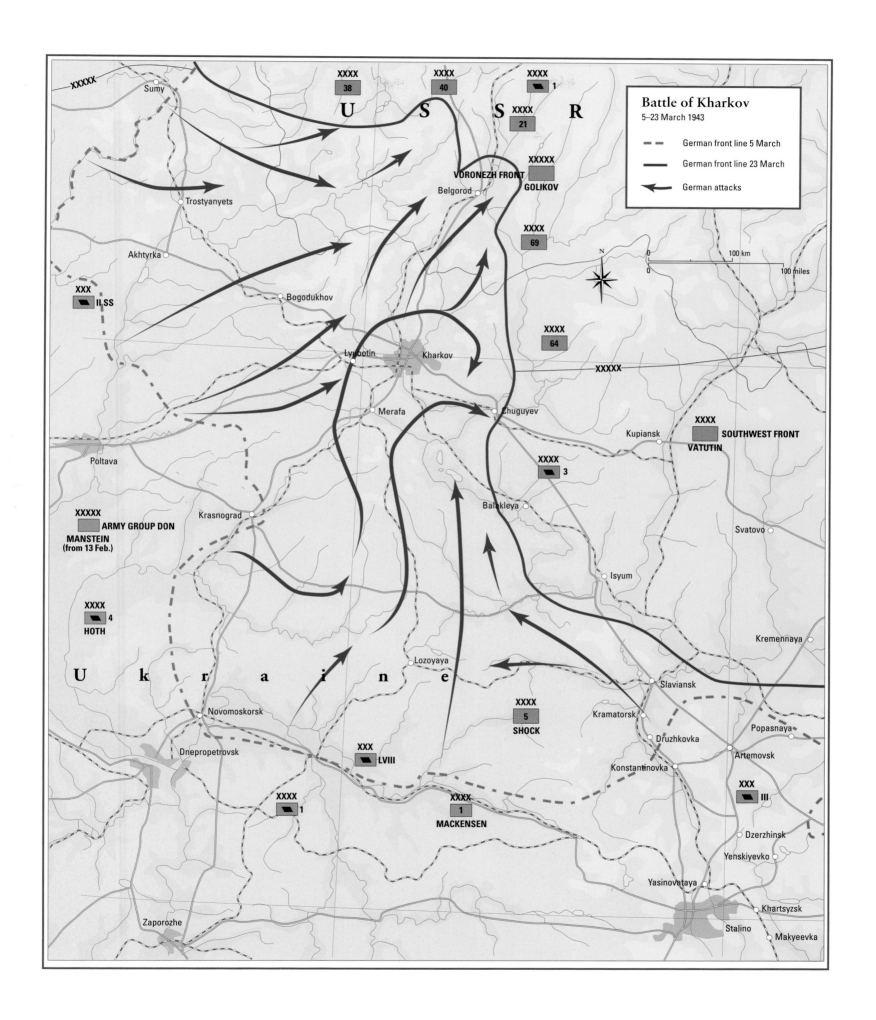

XXXXX

Sumy

U S S R

XXXX
38

XXXX
40

XXXX
1

XXXX
21

Trostyanyets

XXXXX
GOLIKOV

VORONEZH FRONT

Belgorod

Akhtyrka

XXXX
69

XXX
II SS

Bogodukhov

N

0   100 km
0   100 miles

Lyubotin   Kharkov

XXXX
64

XXXXX

Merafa

Chuguyev

Kupiansk

XXXX
SOUTHWEST FRONT
VATUTIN

Poltava

XXXX
3

XXXXX
ARMY GROUP DON
MANSTEIN
(from 13 Feb.)

Krasnograd

Balakleya

Svatovo

Isyum

XXXX
4
HOTH

Kremennaya

Lozoyaya

Slaviansk

U k r a i n e

Novomoskorsk

XXXX
5
SHOCK

Kramatorsk

Popasnaya

Dnepropetrovsk

XXX
LVIII

Druzhkovka

Artemovsk

Konstantinovka

XXX
III

XXXX
1

XXXX
1
MACKENSEN

Dzerzhinsk

Yenskiyevko

Yasinovataya

Zaporozhe

Khartsyzsk

Stalino   Makyeevka

Battle of Kharkov
5–23 March 1943

– – – German front line 5 March

—— German front line 23 March

← German attacks

After the defeat, the Russians waited for nearly a year to attack Kharkov again; this came in mid-Febuary 1943. Defending the city against the Russian onslaught was the veteran II SS Panzer Corps, having been recently equipped with the new, heavy Tiger tank. When the Soviets attacked, the Germans were heavily outnumbered but still managed to hold on for a time. However, the sheer numbers involved in the Soviet attack became too much and the Commander, Hausser, was refused the chance to retreat and ordered to make the city a fortress and fight to the death. This order, straight from the Führer himself, Hausser chose to disregard and ordered his troops to pull back. These units were later attached to Manstein's counterattack and Kharkov was quickly retaken in a masterful example of mobile warfare.

German troops armed with hand grenades storm a Soviet position.

Soon after, the city would be used by the Germans as the springboard for their offensive on the Kursk salient to the north. This offensive would be beaten back by a massive Russian force of over one and a half million men, and Kharkov would be their first objective. On the morning of 23 August, the Russians approached the city and engaged the Germans. By lunch time of the same day the Germans were given the order to retreat out of the city, and what was left of Kharkov now belonged to the Soviets again—this time for good.

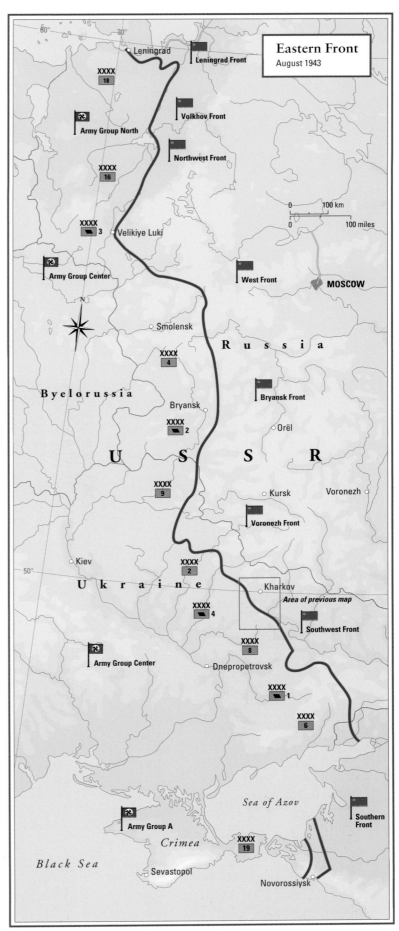

GUADALCANAL 1942

"IT IS A SORRY THING THAT WE MUST LEAVE THE BODIES OF OUR COMRADES AND THE GROUND WE HAVE WON SO DEARLY. SLEEP PEACEFULLY, MY FRIENDS. FAREWELL! WE SHALL MEET AGAIN IN HEAVEN!"

LIEUTENANT SAKAMOTO, OFFICER AT GUADALCANAL

Guadalcanal was to be the first major offensive against the Imperial Japanese forces in the Pacific war. The U.S. decided to start their fight back by securing the southern Solomon Islands. This would isolate the Japanese forward base at Rabaul on New Britain island that threatened northern Australia, and it would also deny the Japanese a base on Guadalcanal island to attack lines of supply and communication between the U.S., New Zealand, and Australia. The plan laid out by Admiral Ernest King involved Marines assaulting the two islands of Florida and Tulagi, while the main part of the force landed on Guadalcanal itself, which had become strategically important following U.S. intelligence reports that the Japanese were building an airfield there. The overall command of all forces during the campaign would be given to Vice-Admiral Robert Ghormley while the Marines would be led by Major-General Alexander Vandegrift. This campaign would not be fought on just one front but would include all arms of the services, all dependent on each other.

The landings took place on the morning of 7 August, 1942, the invasion fleet splitting into two; the smaller force of Marines heading toward Tulagi and Florida Islands, while the main force of 11,000 Marines sailed toward Guadalcanal itself. Two battalions of Marines landed on Tulagi unopposed and immediately advanced inland, where they met resistance in the form of prepared

U.S. Marines land on Guadalcanal island. This would be their first major action of the Pacific war.

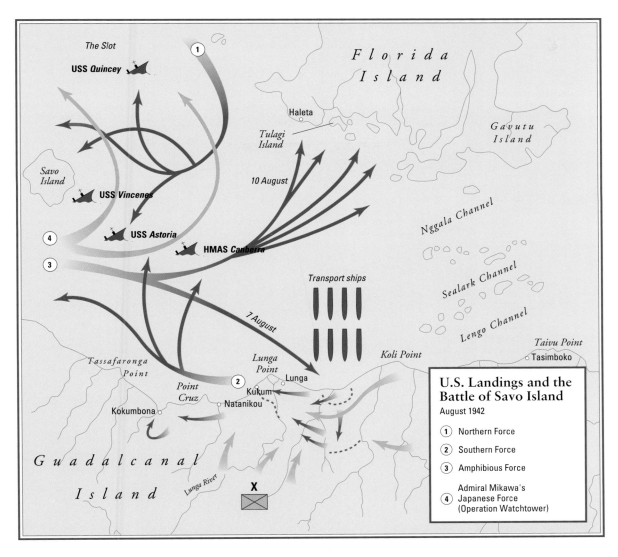

The Slot

USS *Quincey*

Savo
Island

USS *Vincenes*

④

③

USS *Astoria*

HMAS *Canberra*

Haleta

Tulagi
Island

10 August

F l o r i d a
I s l a n d

G a v u t u
I s l a n d

Nggala Channel

Sealark Channel

Lengo Channel

Transport ships

7 August

Tassafaronga
Point

Point
Cruz

Kokumbona

②

Lunga
Point

Lunga

Kukum
Natanikou

Koli Point

Taivu Point

Tasimboko

**U.S. Landings and the
Battle of Savo Island**
August 1942

① Northern Force

② Southern Force

③ Amphibious Force

④ Admiral Mikawa's
Japanese Force
(Operation Watchtower)

G u a d a l c a n a l

I s l a n d

Lunga River

X

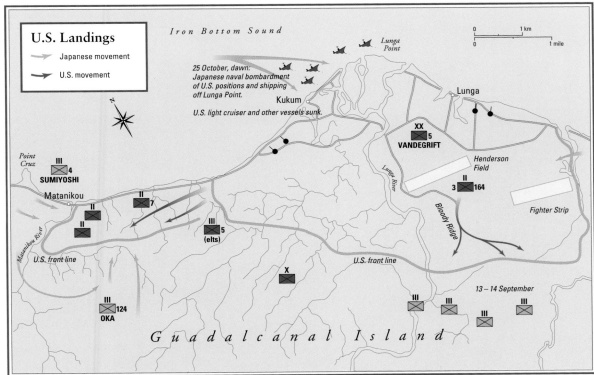

U.S. Landings

→ Japanese movement

→ U.S. movement

Iron Bottom Sound

Lunga
Point

0   1 km
0   1 mile

25 October, dawn:
Japanese naval bombardment
of U.S. positions and shipping
off Lunga Point.

U.S. light cruiser and other vessels sunk.

Kukum

Lunga

N

XX
VANDEGRIFT 5

Point
Cruz

III
SUMIYOSHI 4

Matanikou

II

II
7

III
5
(elts)

Matanikou River

U.S. front line

Henderson
Field

II
3 164

Lunga River

Bloody Ridge

Fighter Strip

X

U.S. front line

III

III

III

13 – 14 September

III
OKA 124

G u a d a l c a n a l   I s l a n d

machine-gun positions. Having survived numerous Japanese counterattacks during the night the Marines cleared the rest of the island by the end of 8 August. The same was to happen on the smaller islands taken by the Marines, where Japanese resistance was held almost until the last man, with few prisoners being taken.

As the minor islands were being cleared of their Japanese garrisons, the main force landed on Guadalcanal completely unopposed. The Marines quickly consolidated their position then began to

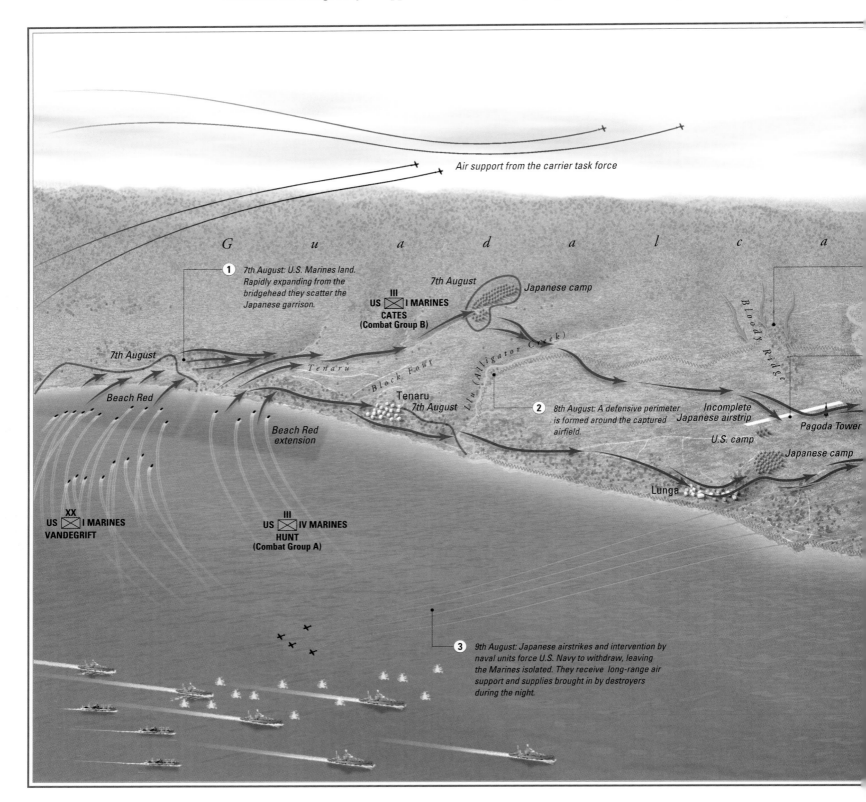

Air support from the carrier task force

G   u   a   d   a   l   c   a

1 *7th August: U.S. Marines land. Rapidly expanding from the bridgehead they scatter the Japanese garrison.*

7th August

Japanese camp

III
US ☒ I MARINES
CATES
(Combat Group B)

7th August

Bloody Ridge

7th August

Tenaru

Block Four

Ilu (Alligator Creek)

Beach Red

Tenaru
7th August

2 *8th August: A defensive perimeter is formed around the captured airfield.*

Incomplete Japanese airstrip

Pagoda Tower

Beach Red
extension

U.S. camp

Japanese camp

XX
US ☒ I MARINES
VANDEGRIFT

III
US ☒ IV MARINES
HUNT
(Combat Group A)

Lunga

3 *9th August: Japanese airstrikes and intervention by naval units force U.S. Navy to withdraw, leaving the Marines isolated. They receive long-range air support and supplies brought in by destroyers during the night.*

move off into the dense undergrowth, meeting only sporadic resistance. By the end of the first day the invasion force was just a mile short of the Lunga Airfield. On the following day the Marines again managed to advance without much hindrance and captured the airfield, along with much useful Japanese construction equipment. They began to lay a defensive perimeter around the airfield. Meanwhile, on the assault beaches, the transport and accompanying escort had been under constant air attack from land-based bombers flying from Rabaul. This caused enough concern for the commander of the escort,

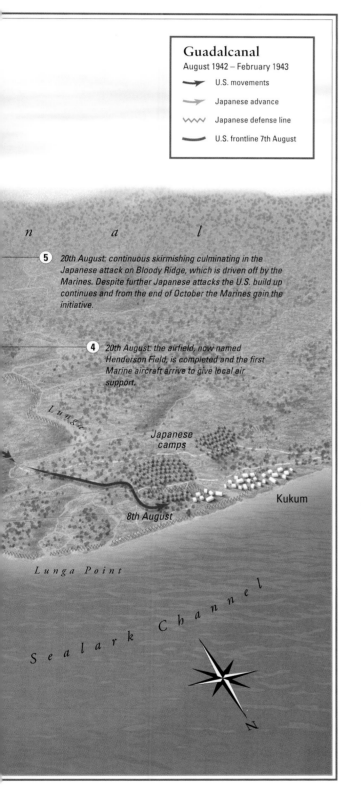

Guadalcanal
August 1942 – February 1943

➤ U.S. movements

➤ Japanese advance

〰 Japanese defense line

◡ U.S. frontline 7th August

n a l

5 *20th August: continuous skirmishing culminating in the Japanese attack on Bloody Ridge, which is driven off by the Marines. Despite further Japanese attacks the U.S. build up continues and from the end of October the Marines gain the initiative.*

4 *20th August: the airfield, now named Henderson Field, is completed and the first Marine aircraft arrive to give local air support.*

Lunga

Japanese camps

Kukum

8th August

Lunga Point

Sealark Channel

N

Vice-Admiral Fletcher, to withdraw his carrier force. This meant the transport had to leave as well, as it could not stay without air cover. The night before the withdrawal, the convoy attempted to land as much material as possible, but while this was in hand, a strong force of Japanese cruisers and destroyers arrived and engaged the American and Australian escorts. The Japanese force succeeded in sinking three

U.S. Marines at Hell's Corner, part of the perimeter defenses for Henderson Field. It was the successful defense of this vital airstrip that allowed U.S. forces air superiority over Guadalcanal and the lower Solomon Islands.

A U.S. Marine picks off a Japanese sniper in the trees opposite his position. American soldiers fighting on Guadalcanal rapidly mastered the techniques of fighting in dense jungle.

U.S. cruisers and one Australian before quickly withdrawing, wary of air attack at daybreak. Little did they know that Fletcher's carrier had already pulled out of the area: had they known they could have caused havoc amongst the transports, which then pulled out on 9 August not having completed unloading all the necessary troops or stores.

Having set up a defensive perimeter around the airfield and with construction begun on the half finished runway, Vandegrift set about moving all the supplies from the beaches into the perimeter. After a patrol returned from the Matanikau River area severely mauled, Vandegrift sent in a three-company attack. After successfully attacking the Japanese, driving them from the area, the Marines returned to the perimeter.

On 20 August, the first squadrons of aircraft began to arrive on the island, which proved a major factor in the development of the campaign. These fighters immediately got to work intercepting the Japanese bombers that constantly bombed the strip and U.S. perimeter. On 21 August the Japanese Ichiki Regiment attempted to assault the perimeter during the night at "Alligator Point" with 900 men. Underestimating the Marines' strength, something the Japanese command did through out the campaign, the attackers were annihilated with few surviving the withering machine-gun fire and the Marines' counterattacks.

Again the Japanese attacked in mid-September, this time using a force of 6,000 troops, but after savage fighting they were again beaten back. After this attack, U.S. forces attempted to increase the perimeter and thereby push the Japanese artillery out of range of the newly-named Henderson Field, but this move was stopped by the Japanese. The battleships *Kongo* and *Haruma* also bombarded Henderson Field, although these ships were chased off by U.S. fighter bombers and the airstrip was quickly repaired and returned to action.

While the struggle to control the airfield was fought out, the naval actions were also fought for the control of the sea approaches to the island of Guadalcanal, particularly around Savo Island and

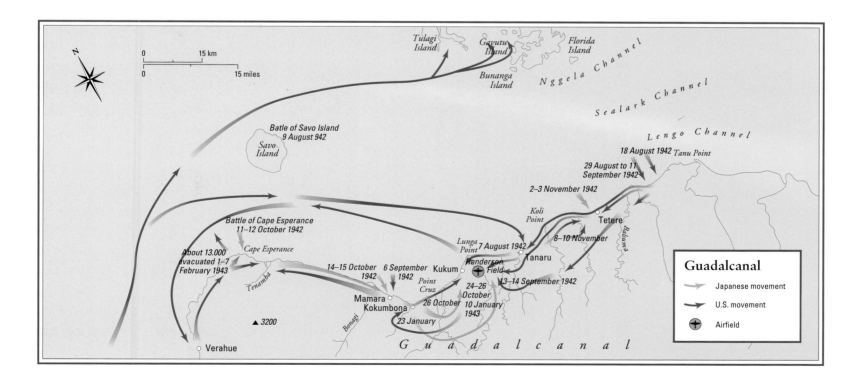

Ironbottom Sound. On 24 and 25 August an action between Japanese and U.S. carriers ended in a stalemate, as both withdrew from battle with the Americans incurring heavy damage to the fleet carrier *Enterprise*. However, they did succeed in interfering with Japanese troop reinforcements. On the night of 11/12 October the U.S. Navy successfully intercepted a force on the way to bombard Henderson Field and the resulting engagement ended as a tactical victory for the Americans. Even though they lost a destroyer, they managed to prevent the bombardment of the vital airfield. Despite heavy American casualties, all these naval actions meant that they were able to outnumber the Japanese troops on the island. By November, the Japanese made a concerted attempt to land the 38th Division on Guadalcanal. The transports were heavily escorted and met a quick but terrible engagement on the night of 12/13 November. The U.S. Navy lost six ships and the Japanese three in just half an hour. While the Japanese Navy was attempting to unload the Division, fighter bombers from Henderson sank six out of seven of the transports and a cruiser.

The remains of a Japanese transport ship that formed part of the 'Tokyo Express' that attempted to reinforce the Japanese garrison on Guadalcanal on the night 13/14 November. Out of ten transports dispatched with 7,000 troops, only four arrived, landing just 2,000 men.

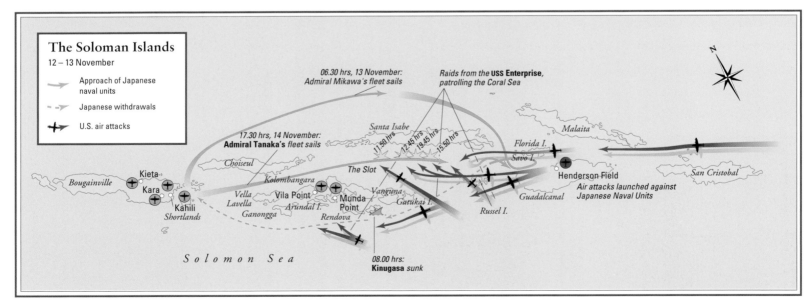

The Soloman Islands
12 – 13 November

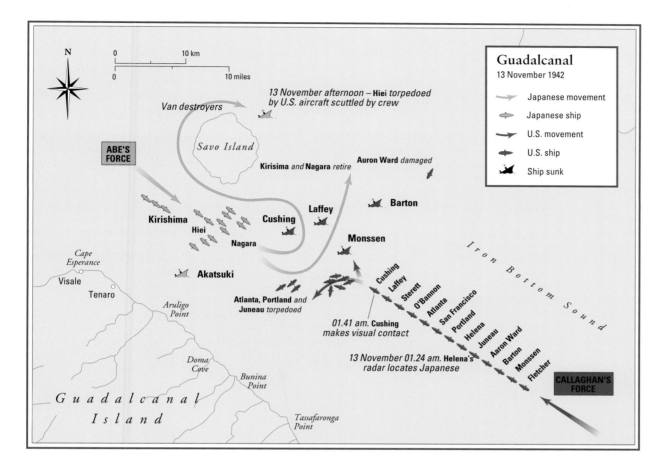

Guadalcanal
13 November 1942

→ Japanese movement
→ Japanese ship
→ U.S. movement
→ U.S. ship
× Ship sunk

13 November afternoon – Hiei torpedoed by U.S. aircraft scuttled by crew

Van destroyers

Savo Island

ABE'S FORCE

Kirisima and Nagara retire

Auron Ward *damaged*

Barton

Kirishima

Hiei

Cushing

Laffey

Nagara

Monssen

Akatsuki

Cape Esperance

Visale

Tenaro

Aruligo Point

Atlanta, Portland and Juneau torpedoed

Cushing
Laffey
Sterett
O'Bannon
Atlanta
San Francisco
Portland
Helena
Juneau
Aaron Ward
Barton
Monssen
Fletcher

01.41 am. Cushing makes visual contact

13 November 01.24 am. Helena's radar locates Japanese

CALLAGHAN'S FORCE

Iron Bottom Sound

Doma Cove

Bunina Point

Guadalcanal Island

Tassafaronga Point

Below left: From left to right Major General Alex Vandegrift, Colonel Gerald Thomas and Colonel Merrit Edson discuss the situation just after the Japanese had been driven from their positions on the Matanikau River.

By this time essential supplies were not getting through to the Japanese soldiers on the island, who were already on starvation rations. This caused the turn of the tide as the U.S. forces slowly took the tactical and numerical advantage, and after the Marines had been replaced by the 25th Army Division, the Japanese were forced to retreat to Cape Esperance. As the Americans pushed forward, the Japanese evacuated their remaining troops in a nightime operation that succeeded in getting more than 13,000 soldiers off the island. This would be a defeat from which the Japanese would never recover, although they felt far from defeated at this time.

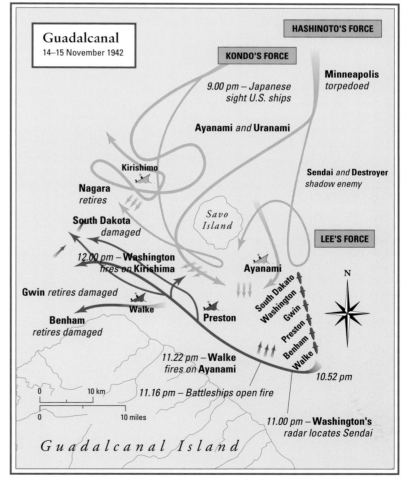

Guadalcanal
14–15 November 1942

HASHINOTO'S FORCE
KONDO'S FORCE

9.00 pm – Japanese sight U.S. ships

Minneapolis *torpedoed*

Ayanami *and* **Uranami**

Sendai *and* **Destroyer** *shadow enemy*

Kirishimo

Nagara *retires*

South Dakota *damaged*

Savo Island

LEE'S FORCE

12.00 pm – **Washington** *fires on* **Kirishima**

Ayanami

Gwin *retires damaged*

Walke

Preston

South Dakota
Washington
Gwin
Preston
Benham
Walke

Benham *retires damaged*

11.22 pm – **Walke** *fires on* **Ayanami**

11.16 pm – Battleships open fire

10.52 pm

11.00 pm – **Washington's** *radar locates Sendai*

Guadalcanal Island

New Guinea and Cartwheel 1942–43

"In times of peace a package of used razor blades might be—in terms of barter—a reasonable price to pay for a native hut in Buna village. But Buna cost dearly in war, because possession of the north coast of New Guinea was vital to future Allied operations."

LT.–GENERAL ROBERT L. EICHELBERGER

On 8 March 1942, two Japanese battalions landed at Lae and Salamaua on the Houn Gulf with the aim of striking south to capture Port Moresby, from where they could launch further attacks on the Australian mainland. Opposing these troops were two small Australian units, one at Wae—which was known as Kanga Force—and the other based at Kokoda. These units were severely depleted because of the overseas commitments of the Australian Army. Many troops were fighting the Germans and Italians in the Western Desert and many had been captured as a result of the fall of Singapore. After the Battle of Midway the initiative in the Pacific was with the Allies, and MacArthur authorized limited operations on Papua New Guinea in order to assist the Australians in forcing the Japanese back. Before any reinforcements for the Australians had arrived, Major-General Horii Tomitaro's South Seas Detachment landed on the north coast of Papua. The Japanese force intended to advance down the Kokoda Trail over the Owen Stanley Range and capture Port Moresby. The Australians moved up the trail to meet them but were badly mauled, retreating into the jungle as the Japanese continually harassed them with flanking attacks. As they fell back into the jungle, many were wounded or suffering from malaria, which would be a recurring problem throughout the campaign; some simply succumbed to their wounds. By 14 August the Japanese detachment was at Isurava, with plenty of reinforcements constantly landing on the northern beachheads. The Australians surviving the Kokoda engagement fell back on positions at Ioribaiwa, with the chances of the Allies holding on to Papua New Guinea looking

Australian troops move up to the front line near Milne Bay, September 1942.

slim. Thanks to ULTRA decrypts the Allies secured information about the Japanese submarine screen that was being prepared off Milne Bay to the southeast of the island. This meant the Allies had time to prepare defensive positions, using the 18th Australian Brigade supplemented by a contingent of U.S. engineers and two squadrons of Australian fighters. On the night of 25/26 August, 2,000 Japanese troops landed and were immediately engaged by the Australians. During the course of the action a further 600 troops were landed but by 4 September the Japanese force withdrew with only 1,200 survivors.

An Australian machine gun team in action north of Port Moresby. Many of the Australians fighting in New Guinea had been recalled from North Africa to defend their homeland from the Japanese advance.

By 17 September, on the Kokoda Trail, the Australians had been beaten back to their final defensive positions at Imata Ridge. MacArthur, losing faith in the Australians and not realizing the conditions they were fighting under, sacked the commander and put General Blamey, another Australian staff officer, in charge. By the time this was implemented Horii's troops had overextended their supply line and were now under constant air attack by the 5th USAAF. This all conspired, along with Japanese troops being transferred to the fighting on Guadalcanal, to cause Horii to withdraw to his original beachhead on the northern coast. In doing so, Horii ordered the fortification of this beach-

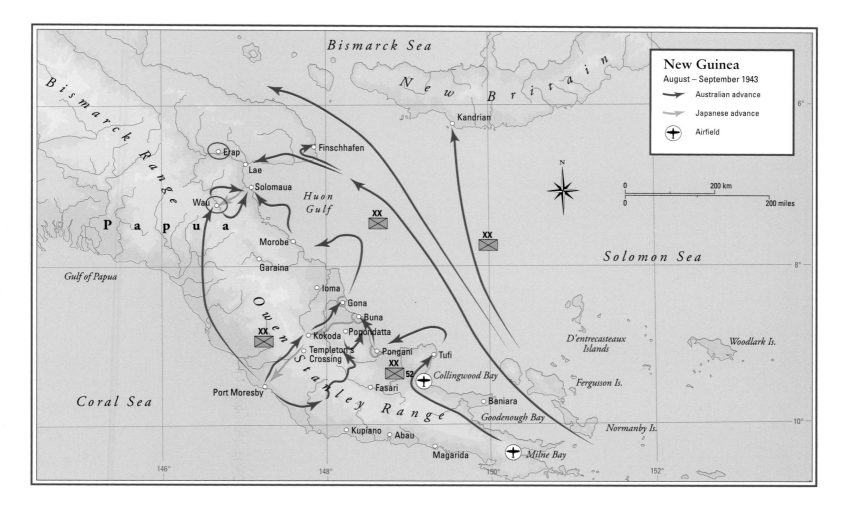

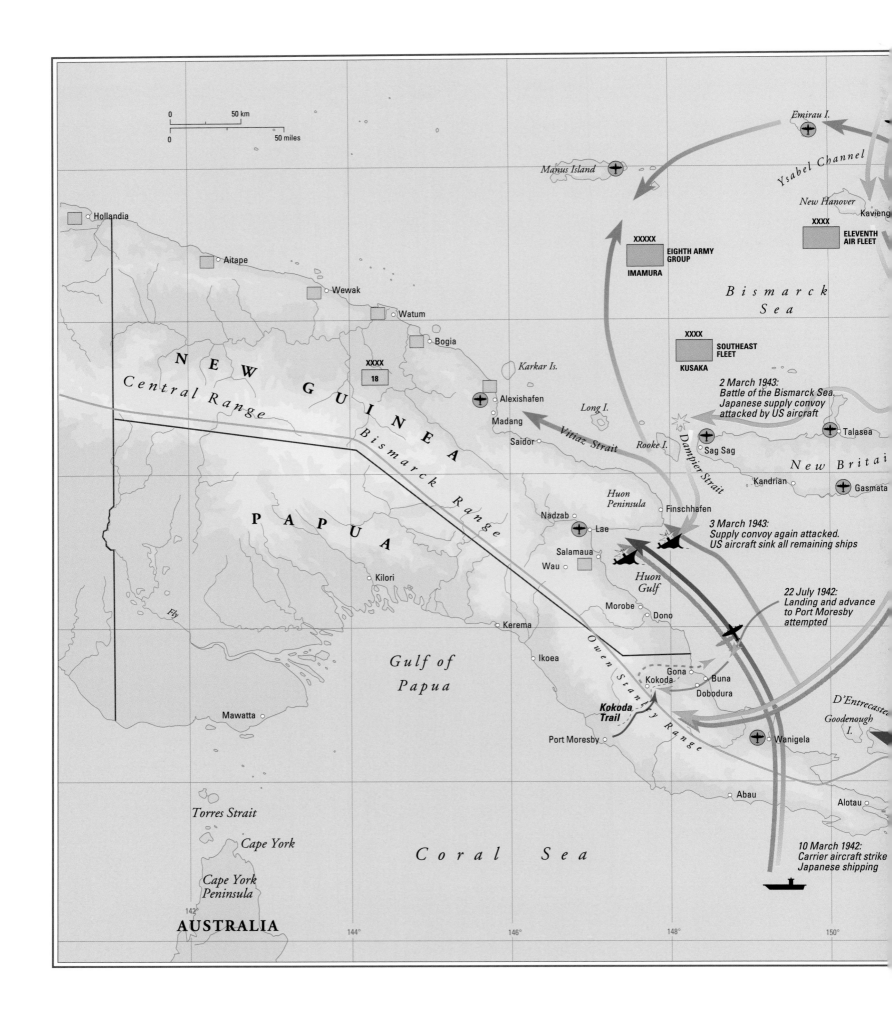

0   50 km

0   50 miles

Emirau I.

Manus Island

Ysabel Channel

New Hanover   Kavieng

XXXX
ELEVENTH
AIR FLEET

XXXXX
EIGHTH ARMY
GROUP
IMAMURA

*B i s m a r c k
S e a*

Hollandia

Aitape

Wewak

Watum

Bogia

XXXX
SOUTHEAST
FLEET
KUSAKA

N E W   G U I N E A

Central Range

XXXX
18

Karkar Is.

2 March 1943:
Battle of the Bismarck Sea.
Japanese supply convoy
attacked by US aircraft

Alexishafen

Long I.

Talasea

Madang

Bismarck Range

Saidor

Vitiaz Strait

Rooke I.

Sag Sag

Dampier Strait

N e w   B r i t a i

Kandrian

Gasmata

P A P U A

*Huon
Peninsula*

Nadzab

Lae

Finschhafen

3 March 1943:
Supply convoy again attacked.
US aircraft sink all remaining ships

Kilori

Salamaua

Wau

*Huon
Gulf*

22 July 1942:
Landing and advance
to Port Moresby
attempted

Morobe

Dono

Fly

Kerema

Owen Stanley Range

Ikoea

Gona

Buna

D'Entrecaste

*Goodenough
I.*

Kokoda

Dobodura

*Gulf of
Papua*

**Kokoda
Trail**

Mawatta

Port Moresby

Wanigela

Abau

Alotau

Torres Strait

Cape York

C o r a l   S e a

10 March 1942:
Carrier aircraft strike
Japanese shipping

*Cape York
Peninsula*

142°

AUSTRALIA

144°   146°   148°   150°

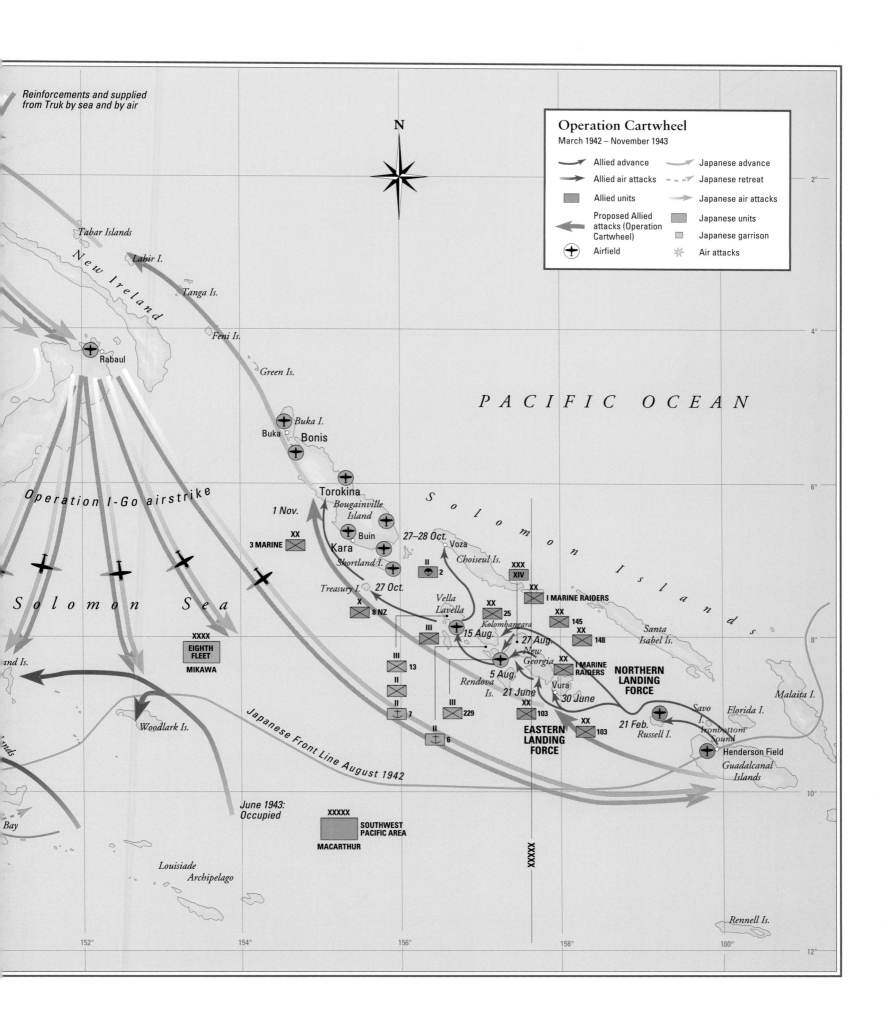

Reinforcements and supplied
from Truk by sea and by air

N

Operation Cartwheel
March 1942 – November 1943

→ Allied advance   → Japanese advance
→ Allied air attacks   ⇢ Japanese retreat
▭ Allied units   → Japanese air attacks
⬅ Proposed Allied
    attacks (Operation   ▭ Japanese units
    Cartwheel)   ▫ Japanese garrison
⊕ Airfield   ✳ Air attacks

Tabar Islands

New Ireland

Labir I.

Tanga Is.

⊕ *Rabaul*

Feni Is.

Green Is.

PACIFIC   OCEAN

⊕ *Buka I.*
Buka ▫ **Bonis**

⊕ **Torokina**
*Bougainville
Island*

1 Nov.   *S*
                        o
⊕ *Buin*   *l*
3 MARINE ⊠   ⊕ **Kara**   *o   27–28 Oct.*
                            m   ◦ *Voza*
Shortland I. ⊕   ⊠ **2** *Choiseul Is.*   ⊠ **145**
Treasury I. *27 Oct.*   **XXX**   ⊠ **148**
                        Vella   XIV
Operation I-Go airstrike   *X* ⊠ **8 NZ**   *Lavella*   ⊠ **25**   **I MARINE RAIDERS**
                                                ⊕   ⊠ **145**
✚   ✚   ✚   ✚   *III* ⊠   *15 Aug.* *Kolombangara* ⊠ **148**
                                                              *Santa
Solomon Sea   *III* ⊠ **13**   ⊕   Isabel Is.*
                                                27 Aug.
XXXX   *II* ⊠   *5 Aug. New
**EIGHTH   Georgia*   ⊠ **I MARINE
FLEET**   *II* ⊞ **7** *Rendova* *RAIDERS*   **NORTHERN
MIKAWA**   *Is. 21 June* *Vura* **LANDING
                                    III ⊠ **229**   *30 June* **FORCE**
                                                 ⊠ **103**
Woodlark Is.   *II* ⊞ **6**   **EASTERN** ⊠ **103**   ⊕ *Savo Florida I.*
                                                 LANDING   *21 Feb. Russell I.* *I.
                                                 FORCE   Ironbottom
            Japanese Front Line August 1942   Sound*
                                                                    Malaita I.
*June 1943:
Occupied*
                    XXXXX   ⊕ **Henderson Field**
Bay   ▭ **SOUTHWEST
            PACIFIC AREA**   *Guadalcanal
MACARTHUR**   Islands*

            XXXXX
*Louisiade
Archipelago*
                                                              Rennell Is.

152°   154°   156°   158°   160°

head with an 11-mile perimeter that would be hard to break. During this time the U.S. 32nd Division was landed on the island and sent into the offensive without proper equipment or appropriate jungle training. On 19 November, they were thrown into an attack on Buna and Cape Endaiadere while the Australians advanced up the Kokoda Trail to Gona and Sanananda. Casualties were enormous for the Americans, while the Australians were suffering through exhaustion and disease. When the Australians captured Gona after terrible fighting, the Americans entered Buna on 2 January 1943, eventually pushing the Japanese from the area three weeks later.

The fighting now moved to the Australian-mandated New Guinea, where the Allies now faced a force of Japanese that had been recently reinforced by Lt-General Adachi Hatazo's 18th Army. Again the Japanese aim was to secure Port Moresby and send 2,500 troops down the Bulolo Valley with the aim of destroying Kanga Force and to capture the airbase at Wau. This force was held back on the perimeter of the airbase until an additional Brigade of Australian troops could be flown in to push the Japanese back to Mubo. By this time, the situation on Guadalcanal had become worse for the Japanese, so holding onto New Guinea was imperative. The 4th Air Army was moved to the area to reinforce the ground troops and a new Japanese offensive was planned.

Adachi continued to build up his forces with the 20th Division at Wewak, the 41st Division at Madang, and elements of the 51st Division in the Huon Peninsula. To oppose this threat, MacArthur created two groups: Alamo Force, which consisted of U.S. troops; and New Guinea Force, which was made up of Australian troops. These troops were to be used as part of Operation Cartwheel with the aim of isolating the forward base of Rabaul on New Britain. The Allies also set about constructing a forward airbase for its fighters, which were until now out of range of the Japanese bomber bases around Wewak. On 17 August, raids were launched against these strips, which succeeded in decimating Japanese air power in the theater, leaving only 40 serviceable aircraft at their disposal and only one out of four airstrips in use. This attack meant that the Allied ground forces could continue their advance almost unhindered by air attack. The Australian 7th Division was then moved by air to the areas of Nadzab and a feint was launched to draw the Japanese from Lae to Salamaua. Once this had succeeded, the 7th advanced northward while the 9th Division landed, via the sea, east of Lae. The Japanese were being forced from the area by mid-September, but not before successfully evacuating over 7,000 troops from the peninsula. The 7th Division then proceeded to advance up the Dompu Valley and another amphibious assault allowed the Australians to capture Finschhafen by early October. Fighting also continued in the Huon Peninsula until all resistance was cleared by mid-December.

Attempts were made to cut the line of retreat of the Japanese 20th and 51st Divisions by the U.S. 32nd Division as they landed at Saidor, but this failed. A landing at Hollandia and Ataipe on 22 April 1944 cut Adachi's retreat. In October, after Wakde and Baik Islands had been cleared of the enemy, U.S. troops handed over full responsibility for the New Guinea campaign to the Australians, because they were needed in the up and coming invasion of the Philippines. The Australians continued to pursue the Japanese up the coast, where they eventually took Wewak in May 1945. After this, the Japanese withdrew into the Prince Alexander Ranges, where they continued to fight on until the end of the war.

THE ITALIAN CAMPAIGN— SICILY TO ROME 1943

"BETTER TO FIGHT FOR SOMETHING THAN LIVE FOR NOTHING."

GENERAL GEORGE SMITH PATTON

General George S. Patton (center, foreground) wades onto the Sicilian shore.

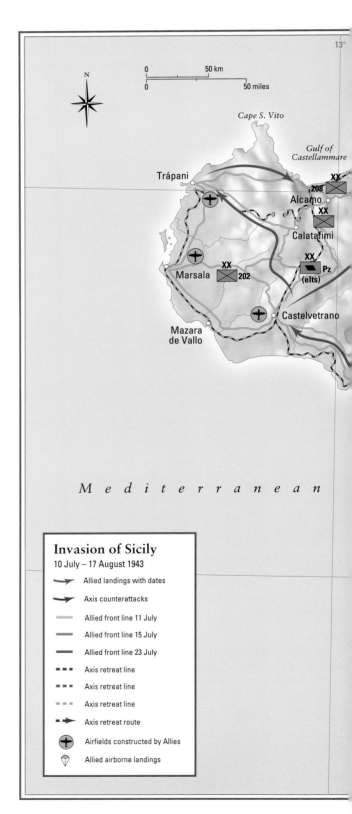

Invasion of Sicily
10 July – 17 August 1943

Allied landings with dates	
Axis counterattacks	
Allied front line 11 July	
Allied front line 15 July	
Allied front line 23 July	
Axis retreat line	
Axis retreat line	
Axis retreat line	
Axis retreat route	
Airfields constructed by Allies	
Allied airborne landings	

The invasion of Sicily was to be the largest amphibious assault to date, incorporating two armies, Lt-General Patton's U.S. 7th Army and Montgomery's British 8th Army. The operation was planned to bring the war in the Mediterranean to a swift conclusion but caused many interservice problems and rivalries later on in the campaign, particularly between "Monty" and some of the American Generals. This was partly Montgomery's fault for not working closely enough with the U.S. forces.

The amphibious landings were preceded by parachute and glider landings by men of the U.S. 82nd Airborne Division and the British 1st Airlanding Brigade. The airborne units were severely compromised by the adverse weather on the night of 9/10 July and many came down in the sea or turned back to base in Tunisia. Those that did manage to land safely caused chaos behind the lines, ambushing convoys, and holding onto strategic objectives. One such occurrence was successfully achieved by troops of the British Brigade (although only numbering 100 when there should have been 1,500). They managed to hold the bridge to Siracusa at Ponte Grande against overwhelming odds. They were eventually beaten off the bridge with only eight men escaping. While two men fired at the enemy engineers who were trying to lay demolition charges, the other men went in search of reinforcements and found the newly-landed British 5th Division and were duly able to win back the bridge.

The amphibious landings, although again affected by the adverse weather, went relatively well against little opposition. The British landed to the east between Pozallo and Siracusa with the aim of advancing north towards Messina, while the Americans landed between Cape Scaramia and Licata and would cover the left flank of the 8th Army's advance. The British made a swift advance

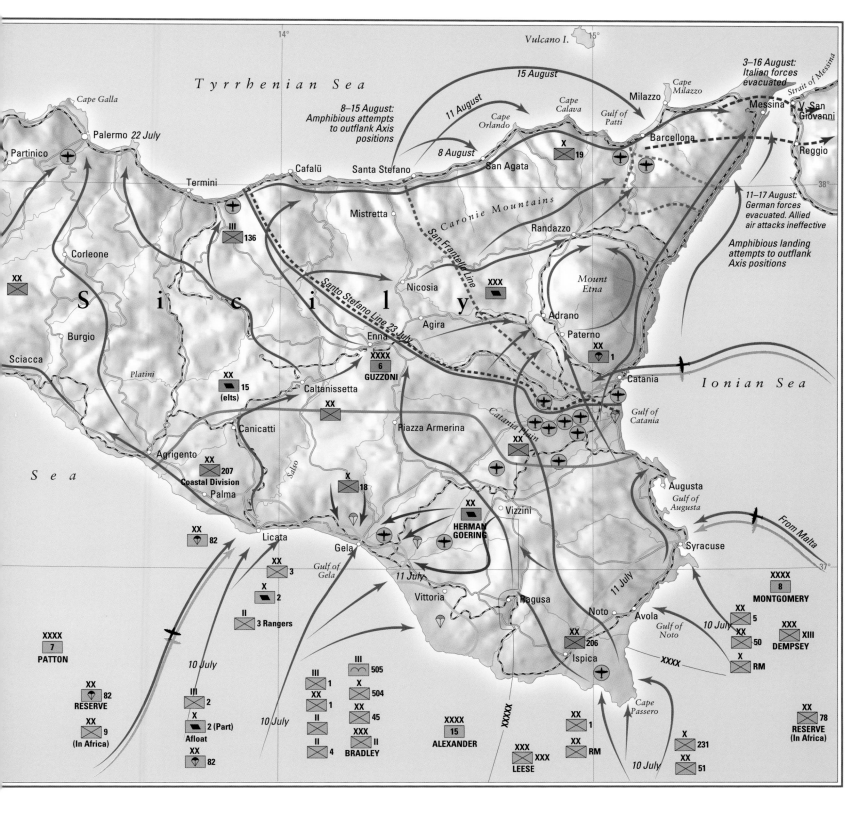

British medium artillery in action in southern Italy, 1943.

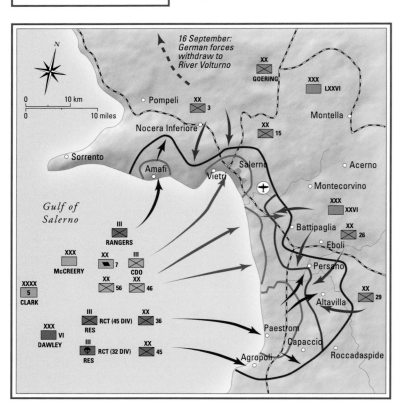

Landings at Salerno
9–16 September 1943

— German Frontline 14 Sept.
— Allied Frontline 11 Sept.
— Allied Frontline 9 Sept.
→ German movement
→ British movement
→ U.S. movement

and took control of Siracusa on the day of the landings, whereas the Americans faced a strong counterattack by elements of the Hermann Goering Division. The Germans were eventually beaten back, however, with the aid of naval gunfire from the invasion fleet offshore.

After this setback the advance continued well. Within two weeks Patton's 7th Army had reached Palermo on the northern coast, but the British hit a strong line of defense in the rugged terrain of eastern Sicily. A problem lay in the fact that General Omar Bradley, Commander of the 2nd U.S. Corps, had to safeguard Monty's flank rather than dashing north, trapping the 15th Panzer Division on the west of the island and denying them an escape route to the Italian mainland. Monty's troops made slow progress advancing north, faced by a capable enemy in excellent defensible positions and, because of the rugged terrain, their tanks had to keep to the small mountain roads; this soon caused bottlenecks and they became easy prey for the German antitank gunners. Patton, frustrated by Monty's slow advance, suggested he go for Messina in a big push along the north coast but this was held back by General Alexander.

Hitler did not want any form of planning to be made for the evacuation of his troops, although the situation changed when Mussolini fell from power on 25 July. Hitler authorized an evacuation. The Allies tried to outflank the defenders by launching small amphibious assaults, but these failed; the Germans had already retreated to another line of defense. Hube, the commander of the German forces, managed to hold open the Messina Strait with little air and naval support, but he did have a powerful antiaircraft defense. He pulled back his troops to a shorter defensive line and thinned out his men, doing this several times before the total evacuation on the night of 11/12 August, when the last troops crossed unimpeded by any Allied attacks. Hube took with him nearly all the garrison of Sicily with supplies and vehicles. Patton won the race to Messina when he entered the city on 16 August. The next step for the Allies was to assault the Italian mainland.

The Italian campaign was marred by tactical difficulties from the start. Being a mountainous country it would be unsuitable for massed armored advances yet perfect for the Germans to defend. On learning of Mussolini's downfall, German High Command wasted no time, disarming the Italian Army and reinforcing their own positions. A plan was drawn up for the British 8th Army to land at the toe of the Italian peninsula followed by an amphibious landing by the 5th Army at the Bay of Salerno. The first landing incurred relatively few casualties and achieved its aim, if a little slowly and cautiously, whereas the second landing was to be a near disaster for the Allies, but it did enable them

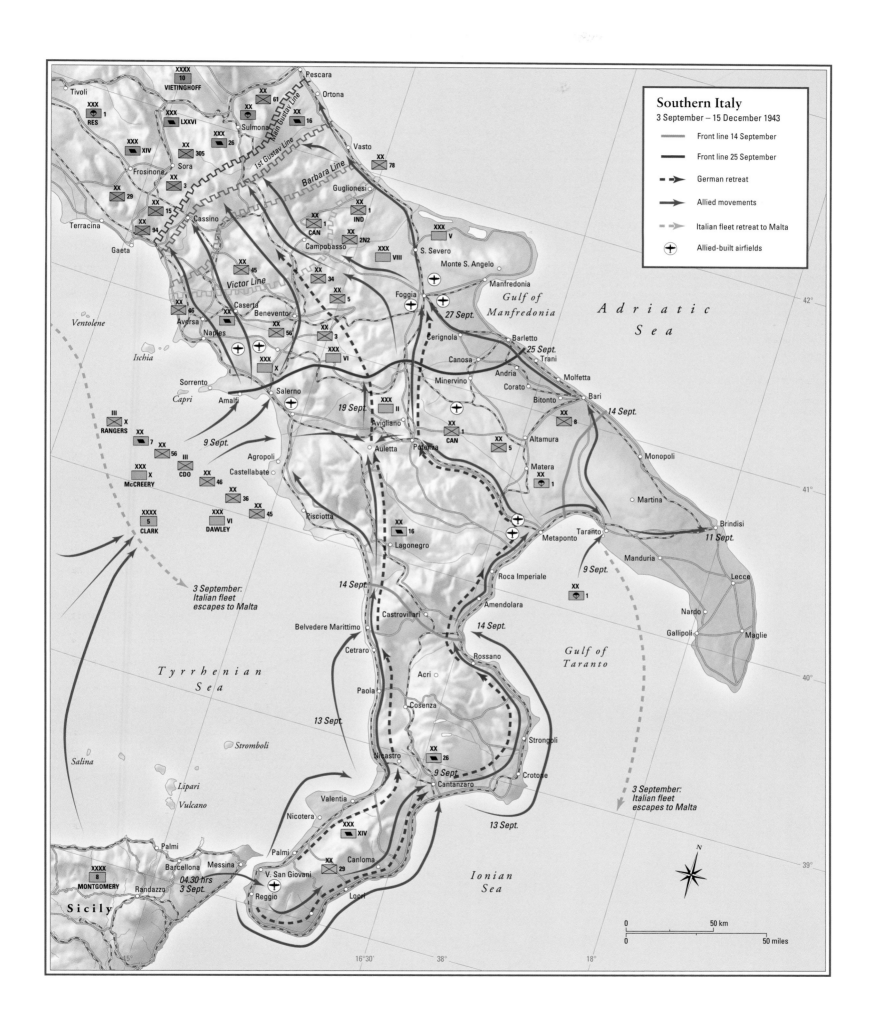

Southern Italy
3 September – 15 December 1943

Front line 14 September
Front line 25 September
German retreat
Allied movements
Italian fleet retreat to Malta
Allied-built airfields

XXXX
10
VIETINGHOFF

XXX
1
RES

XXX
LXXVI

XXX
XIV

XX
61

XX
16

XX
26

XX
305

XX
3

XX
29

XX
15

XX
94

XX
78

Pescara
Tivoli
Ortona
Sulmona
Vasto
Sora
Frosinone
Main Gustav Line
1st Gustav Line
Barbara Line
Cassino
Terracina
Gaeta

XX
45
Victor Line
Caserta
Benevento

XX
34

XX
5

XX
56

XX
3

XX
46
Aversa
Naples

XXX
X
Salerno
Sorrento
Capri
Amalfi

Guglionesi

XX
1
IND
CAN

XX
1

XX
2N2
Campobasso

XXX
V

XXX
VIII
S. Severo
Monte S. Angelo
Manfredonia
Gulf of Manfredonia
A d r i a t i c
S e a
Foggia
27 Sept.
Cerignola
Barletto
25 Sept.
Trani
Canosa
Andria
Corato
Molfetta
Minervino
Bitonto
Bari
14 Sept.

Ventolene
Ischia

III
X
RANGERS

XX
7

XX
56
III
CDO

XXX
X
McCREERY

XX
46

XX
36

XXXX
5
CLARK

XXX
VI
DAWLEY

XX
45

XXX
II
19 Sept.
Avigliano
Auletta
9 Sept.
Agropoli
Castellabate
Pisciotta

XX
1
CAN

XX
5

XX
8

XX
1
Altamura
Matera
Monopoli
Martina

XX
16
Lagonegro
14 Sept.

XX
1
Metaponto
Taranto
9 Sept.
Manduria
Brindisi
11 Sept.
Lecce
Nardo
Gallipoli
Maglie

Roca Imperiale
14 Sept.
Amendolara
Gulf of Taranto

3 September:
Italian fleet
escapes to Malta

Castrovillari
Belvedere Marittimo
Cetraro
Acri
Rossano
Tyrrhenian Sea
Stromboli
Salina
Lipari
Vulcano
Paola
13 Sept.
Cosenza
Strongoli

3 September:
Italian fleet
escapes to Malta

XX
26
Nicastro
9 Sept.
Cantanzaro
Crotone
13 Sept.

XXX
XIV
Valentia
Nicotera

XX
29
Canloma
Palmi
V. San Giovani
Reggio
Locri
Ionian Sea

XXXX
8
MONTGOMERY
Palmi
Barcellona
Messina
04.30 hrs
3 Sept.
Randazzo
Sicily

N

0   50 km
0   50 miles

to learn many lessons for the eventual invasion of western Europe.

The 8th Army crossed the Strait of Messina on 3 September with some elements sailing to the port of Taranto, which fell with ease on 9 September. The landings on Salerno began the morning after the official surrender of Italy, and the troops were expecting few problems. However, the Germans had been quick to take over the old Italian positions and were prepared for the assault. The British landed to the north of the bay and initially faced little opposition, since the German units were still dig-

German Fallschirmjäger make use of the ruins of the monastery of Monte Cassino.

ging in. This was not to last as the 14th Panzer Division soon began to assault the initial advance. The U.S. elements landed further south in the bay and were soon pinned down and unable to break out from the beachhead. The German commander, von Vietinghoff, quickly coordinated a strong counterattack, achieving enough success to panic the Allied commanders into almost evacuating their beachhead. This attack was eventually beaten back but only after every available person who could fire a weapon was thrown into the line, and elements of the 82nd Airborne Division were dropped onto the beachhead as reinforcements. By 16 September, the Germans had begun a steady withdrawal to a defensive line north of Naples. This same day the leading units of the 8th Army joined up with the Salerno beachhead, the Allies eventually entering Naples on 1 October.

The campaign reached a stalemate as the Italian countryside and mountains were perfect defensive positions and the Allies could not sweep forward because their armor was confined to the small mountain roads. Supplies were blighted by the winter rains, which soon caused everything to be clogged in mud. The only route for an advance on Rome was through the Gustav Line, which involved fighting through the Liri Valley, dominated by Monte Cassino. Any movement could be seen clearly by German observers and artillery directed onto any assault. General Mark Clark, in command of the U.S. 5th Army gave the task

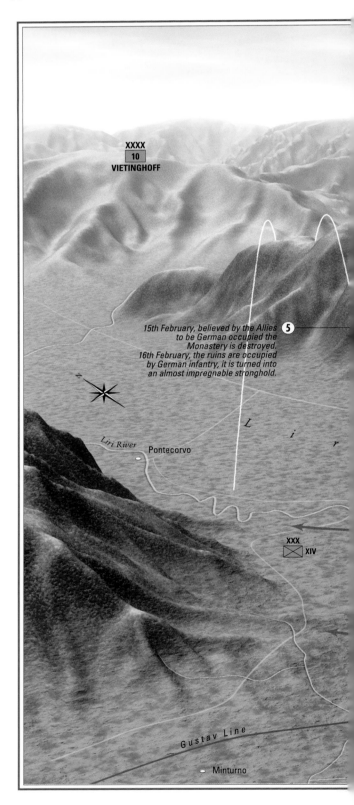

of taking the mount to 2nd U.S. Corps. This attack was beaten off with appalling losses. Clark decided on an improvised amphibious assault with the aim of outflanking the defenders and catching them in a pincer movement.

Major-General Lucas' 6th Corps landed on the Anzio beachhead on 22 January and, rather than break out quickly, he decided to consolidate his beachhead position. Even though the landing had achieved complete surprise, Lucas was wary of advancing until he felt he had adequate reserves. This

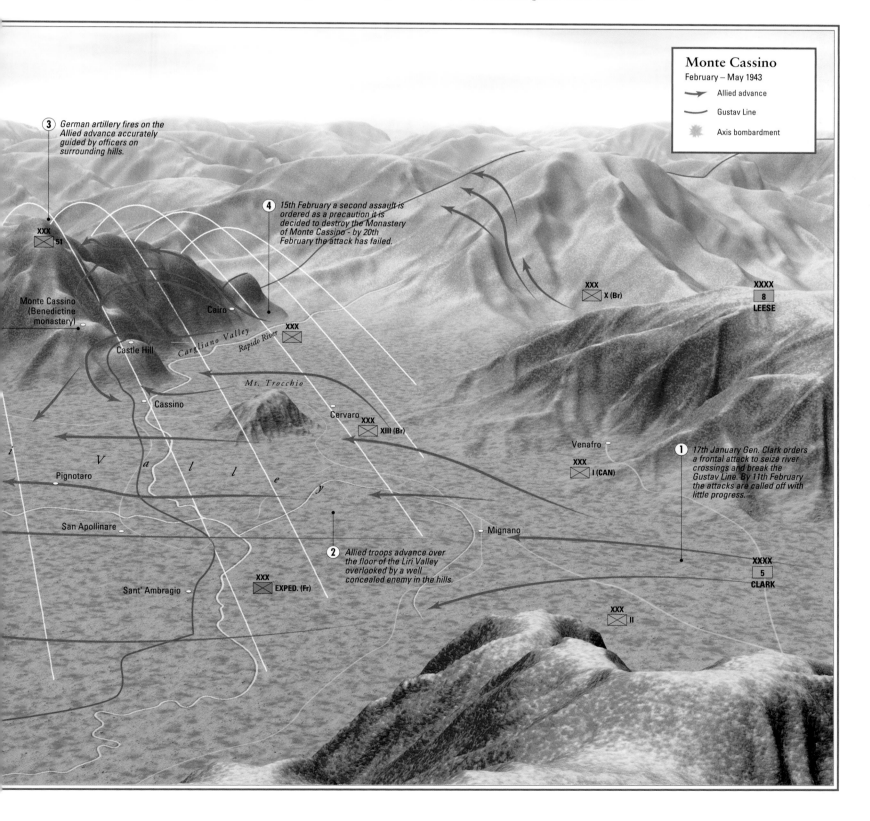

Monte Cassino
February – May 1943

→ Allied advance

⌒ Gustav Line

✳ Axis bombardment

3 German artillery fires on the Allied advance accurately guided by officers on surrounding hills.

4 15th February a second assault is ordered as a precaution it is decided to destroy the Monastery of Monte Cassino - by 20th February the attack has failed.

XXX 51

Monte Cassino (Benedictine monastery)

Cairo

Castle Hill

Cargliano Valley

Rapido River

XXX

Mt. Trocchio

Cassino

Cervaro XXX XIII (Br)

Venafro

XXX I (CAN)

Pignotaro

V a l l e y

XXX X (Br)

XXXX 8 LEESE

1 17th January Gen. Clark orders a frontal attack to seize river crossings and break the Gustav Line. By 11th February the attacks are called off with little progress.

San Apollinare

Mignano

2 Allied troops advance over the floor of the Liri Valley overlooked by a well concealed enemy in the hills.

Sant' Ambragio

XXX EXPED. (Fr)

XXX II

XXXX 5 CLARK

Free French machine-gun team in action, part of the massive multinational force that made up the Allied armies in Italy inlcuding New Zealanders, British, American, Indian, Brazilian, Polish, and Canadian.

Landings at Anzio
17 January – 26 May 1944

- → German attacks
- → Allied attacks
- → French attacks
- ▬ German front line 16 February
- ▬ Allied front line 22 May
- ▬ Allied front line end of May

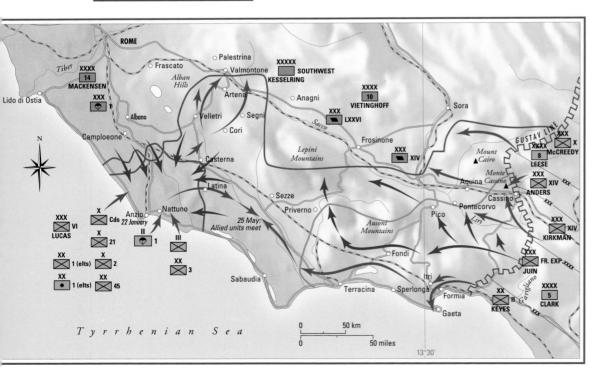

hesitation allowed the German Field Marshal Albert Kesselring to organize and move six divisions, under the command of General von Mackenson, to surround the beachhead. When Lucas' troops were ready to advance from his line they suffered heavy losses and immediately went back onto the defensive. A German counterattack came on 16 February, but was beaten back, thanks to ULTRA decrypts enabling the Allies to coordinate air, naval, and artillery bombardments. Shortly after this attack, Lucas was replaced by Major-General Truscott, who had formerly been his deputy commander.

Several more assaults on Monte Cassino using the New Zealand Corps had failed, again with appalling losses and few lessons being learned. Preceding these attacks had been enormous aerial and artillery bombardments, reducing the 6th-Century monastry astride the mountain to rubble. This, ironically, created a much more defensive position for the German Fallschirmjäger defending the mount. The fourth attack, which was part of Alexander's spring offensive, involved both the 5th and 8th Armies. Its aim was for the 13th Corps of 8th Army and 2nd Polish Division to advance on Cassino, along with the Free French Corps advancing to the east down the Liri Valley, while the bridgehead at Anzio broke out in the direction of Valmontone. On 11 May the artillery laid down a massive barrage which, when lifted, enabled the 13th Corps and the Poles, who had suffered enormous losses, to break through and eventually capture Monte Cassino from the crack Fallshirmjäger. The French also made a rapid advance and breached the Hitler Line, behind the Gustav Line, with relative ease. The 23 May saw the breakout of the Anzio beachhead and the encirclement of the German forces seemed inevitable. But before this movement could be successfully concluded, Mark Clark's gaze fell on Rome. He was adamant that he and his 5th Army would be the one to liberate the first major European city and did not want to share the glory. He ordered Trusscott to alter his advance even before his objective was complete, much to Trusscott's annoyance. This change of advance opened up a salient big enough for the German army to slip through yet again and fight another day. A great decisive maneuver was lost. Rome fell on 4 June to Clark's 5th Army, as planned, with no shots fired. There was, however, to be many more months of fighting left in Italy and Clark's "glory" was to be eclipsed by a great undertaking on the shores of northern France two days later.

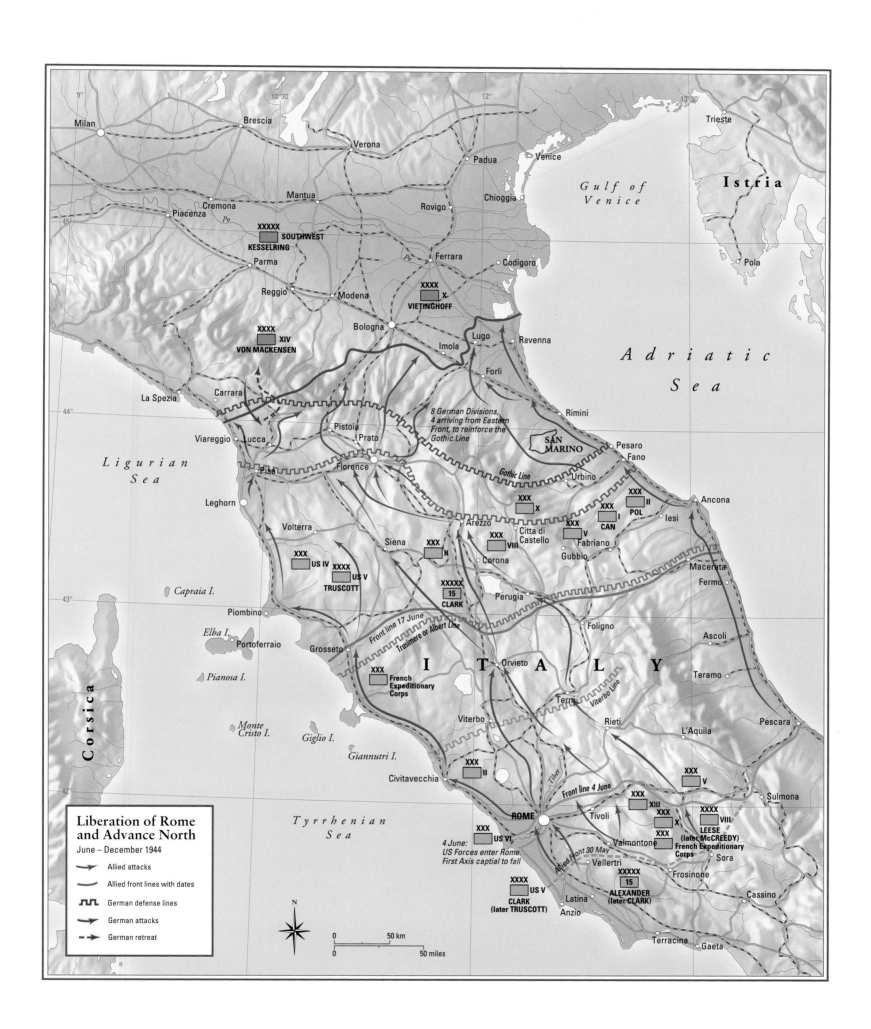

Milan
Brescia
Trieste
Verona
Padua
Venice
Gulf of Venice
Istria
Cremona
Mantua
Piacenza
Po
Rovigo
Chioggia
Pola
XXXXX
SOUTHWEST
KESSELRING
Parma
Ferrara
Codigoro
Reggio
Modena
Po
XXXX
X.
VIETINGHOFF
Bologna
Lugo
Ravenna
XXXX
XIV
VON MACKENSEN
Imola
Forli
A d r i a t i c
S e a
La Spezia
Carrara
Pistoia
8 German Divisions,
4 arriving from Eastern
Front, to reinforce the
Gothic Line
Rimini
Viareggio
Lucca
Prato
SAN MARINO
Pesaro
L i g u r i a n
S e a
Pisa
Florence
Gothic Line
Fano
Urbino
Ancona
Leghorn
XXX
X
XXX
POL
II
Volterra
Citta di
Castello
XXX
CAN
I
Iesi
Siena
Arezzo
XXX
V
Fabriano
XXX
XXX
VIII
Gubbio
Macerata
Capraia I.
XXX
US IV
XXXX
US V
TRUSCOTT
XXX
H
Corona
Perugia
Fermo
XXXXX
15
CLARK
Foligno
Piombino
Elba I.
Portoferraio
Front line 17 June
Trasimere or Albert Line
Orvieto
Ascoli
Grosseto
XXX
French
Expeditionary
Corps
I T A L Y
Teramo
Pianosa I.
Terni
Viterbo Line
Rieti
L'Aquila
Pescara
Monte
Cristo I.
Giglio I.
Viterbo
Giannutri I.
XXX
V
Sulmona
XXX
II
Tiber
Civitavecchia
Front line 4 June
XXX
XIII
XXX
XXXX
VIII
Tivoli
X.
LEESE
(later McCREEDY)
French Expeditionary
Corps
T y r r h e n i a n
S e a
XXX
US VI
4 June:
US Forces enter Rome,
First Axis captial to fall
ROME
Valmontone
Sora
Allied Front 30 May
Vellertri
Frosinone
XXXX
US V
CLARK
(later TRUSCOTT)
XXXXX
15
ALEXANDER
(later CLARK)
Latina
Cassino
Anzio
Terracina
Gaeta

**Liberation of Rome
and Advance North**

June – December 1944

→ Allied attacks

⌐ Allied front lines with dates

⊓⊓ German defense lines

→ German attacks

- -→ German retreat

N

0   50 km
0   50 miles

Corsica

THE UKRAINE 1943–44

"TO A DISTANT LAND IS OUR COMRADE DEPARTING,

HIS NATIVE WINDS A SAD FAREWELL ARE PIPING,

HIS BELOVED TOWN, HIS HOME, HIS LOVER'S TENDER GAZE,

VANISH WITH HIS NATIVE FIELDS IN A DEEP BLUE HAZE."

POPULAR RUSSIAN WARTIME SONG

The five months from August to December 1944 witnessed one of the great battles of the Soviet–German war: the Battle of the River Dnieper. The Soviet plan involved five fronts or army groups, over 2,600,000 men, 50,000 heavy mortars and guns, 2,400 tanks (and mobile assault guns) supported by almost 2,800 aircraft. Facing this huge force was the German 2nd Army, part of the Army Group Center commanded by Field Marshal von Kluge; the 4th Panzer; and the 1st, 6th and 8th Armies from Army Group South, commanded by von Manstein. Total German forces available were 1,240,000 men, 12,600 guns, 2,100 tanks and assault guns, and 2,100 aircraft. The Soviets enjoyed an advantage in men and guns but the balance was about even in tanks and aircraft.

Planning and implementation for this huge campaign began as the Battle for Kursk developed in July 1943, and finally ended in defeat for the German offensive Operation Citadel. The initial aim was to liberate the eastern Ukraine, with its valuable industrial areas of the Donbass, then to advance and liberate Kiev. This would take place on a 400-mile front, involving many separate operations. The distinctive feature of these would be numerous river crossings. As usual, the Red Army soldiers were driven hard by their commanders. At river crossings they were sent over on anything that could float: timbers lashed together, oil drums, or whatever came to hand to gain a bridgehead, before engineers came to build a sturdy structure capable of supporting tanks and trucks.

On 13 August, the right wing of the Soviet Steppe Front, under General Ivan Konev, launched its attack in the direction of Krasnograd. Three days later another attack began from a bridgehead on the northern Donets River, all as part of the Donbass Offensive that lasted until 22 September.

The Southwest Front, supported by the 17th Air Army, attacked German Army Group South and

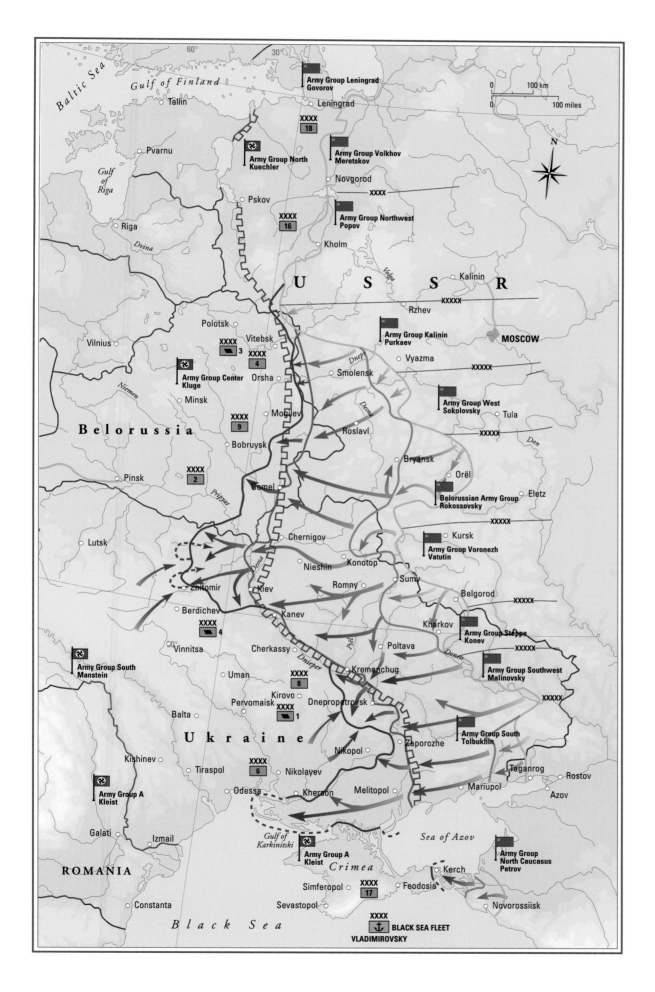

Baltic Sea

Gulf of Finland

Tallin

Pvarnu

Gulf of Riga

Riga

Dvina

Leningrad

Army Group Leningrad
Govorov

XXXX 18

Army Group Volkhov
Meretskov

Novgorod

Army Group North
Kuechler

Pskov

XXXX 16

Army Group Northwest
Popov

Kholm

Volga

Kalinin

U S S R

Rzhev

MOSCOW

Polotsk

Vitebsk

XXXX 3

XXXX 4

Army Group Kalinin
Purkaev

Vyazma

Dnepr

Smolensk

Vilnius

Army Group Center
Kluge

Orsha

Niemen

Minsk

XXXX 9

Mogilev

Desna

Roslavl

Army Group West
Sokolovsky

Tula

B e l o r u s s i a

Bobruysk

XXXX 2

Pinsk

Gomel

Bryansk

Orël

Eletz

Don

Belorussian Army Group
Rokossovsky

Pripat

Lutsk

Chernigov

Kursk

Army Group Voronezh
Vatutin

Desna

Nieshin

Konotop

Zhitomir

Kiev

Romny

Sumy

Belgorod

Berdichev

Kanev

XXXX 4

Vinnitsa

Cherkassy

Psel

Kharkov

Army Group Steppe
Konev

Poltava

Army Group South
Manstein

Uman

Dnieper

Kremenchug

Donets

Army Group Southwest
Malinovsky

XXXX 8

Kirovo

Pervomaisk

XXXX 1

Dnepropetrovsk

U k r a i n e

Balta

Nikopol

Zaporozhe

Army Group South
Tolbukhin

Kishinev

Tiraspol

XXXX 6

Nikolayev

Melitopol

Taganrog

Rostov

Azov

Odessa

Kherson

Mariupol

Galati

Izmail

Gulf of
Karkinitski

Sea of Azov

Army Group A
Kleist

R O M A N I A

Army Group A
Kleist

C r i m e a

Army Group
North Caucasus
Petrov

Kerch

Feodosia

Simferopol

XXXX 17

Sevastopol

Novorossiisk

Constanta

B l a c k S e a

XXXX ⚓ **BLACK SEA FLEET**

VLADIMIROVSKY

60° 30°

N

Soviet infantry move forward, supported by a gun team moving a Model 42 45 mm antitank gun into position. This weapon was also a very effective infantry support gun capable of firing high explosive as well as armor-piercing shells.

Luftflotte (Airfleet) 4. By December they had reached the Dnieper River just south of the city of Dnepropetrovsk.

Meanwhile, on 26 August in the north, the Soviet Center Front had attacked German Army Group Center, under the command of von Kluge, who had appealed to Hitler for permission to fall back to a more defensible line along the Dnieper River. Hilter refused, and ordered the Germans to hold their ground at all costs. Hitler did give permission, however, for General von Manstein's Army Group South to fall back to a line of Melitpol-Dnieper River. The Führer also sent four divisions of reinforcements from the hard-pressed Army Group Center.

Army Group South's withdrawal to its new line was in the face of massive odds, a bold maneuver. Three armies withdrew, fighting to keep the enemy at bay each step of the way, and converging on just five crossing points of the Dnieper River. Safely across, they fanned out to redeploy west of the river, all accomplished without the pursuing Soviets gaining a foothold.

There was no let up for the Germans, however, since the Soviets immediately ordered men across the river and successfully seized small bridgeheads on the west bank at Bukrin and Rzhischev. On the night of 24/25 September they attempted an airborne landing in support, which was not entirely successful. However, the surviving airborne troops from this operation fought on behind German lines. The main Soviet group of fronts now approached the Dnieper River line on a front of almost 500 miles. Early in October, Soviet forces reached Zaporozhye, and once there they found abandoned river barges, which they used to cross the river. Two weeks later, another bridgehead was established to the north, at Lyutezh. Kiev was finally liberated after fierce fighting on 6 November. By

This German infantry soldier clearly shows the strain of the continuos fighting in the Ukraine during the summer of 1943.

that time there were numerous bridgeheads across the river and Hitler's defense line, although stubbornly defended, did not hold. In the north, Smolensk had also been liberated. In the south a massive group of Soviet forces attacked out of the Zaporozhye bridgehead and along the northern shore of the Sea of Azov, trapping the German 17th Army, part of Army Group A, in the Crimea.

By the end of 1943, the Soviet forces on the Southern Front had consolidated their gains and were ready for further offensive operations. The German hope that winter would slow them down, giving time for replacements and new equipment to arrive, was dashed. On 24 December attacks were launched toward Zhitomir and Korosten by the 1st Ukrainian Front, and on 5 January 1944, Kirovgrad was captured by Konev's 2nd Ukrainian Front. The advances threatened the positions of the German 8th and 1st Panzer Armies, but as usual, Hitler forbade withdrawal: they were encircled, trapping 60,000 Germans at Zvenigorodka. Von Manstein counterattacked, almost reaching the surrounded troops, then, after bitter fighting on the night of 16/17 February, the cut-off troops attempted a breakout. Some 20,000–30,000 escaped, although Soviet sources claim that a lot less survived.

On 4 March, the 1st Ukrainian Front, commanded by Zhukov, attacked through the mud of an early spring thaw, then was joined 24 hours later by the 3rd Ukrainian Front. In the face of this massive onslaught, there was little the German commanders could do; it seemed likely that the 2nd Ukrainian Front, in the north, would meet up with the 1st Ukrainian Front from the southwest of Vinnitsa. This time they could trap the remains of the 1st Panzer Army at Kamenets-Podolsky. Meanwhile, the 2nd Ukrainian Front moved into Moldavia, threatening Army Group A and forcing the Germans to fall back to the line of the River Bug.

Von Manstein pleaded with Hitler for reinforcements and the Führer gave way, sending the 2nd Panzer Corps from France. This newly-arrived Corps launched an attack linking up with 1st Panzer Army near Tarnopol. After all his efforts von Manstein lost his command. It was renamed Army Group North Ukraine and given to Field Marshal Walter Model. Further south, Army Group A was renamed Army Group South Ukraine, von Kleist dismissed and replaced by General Ferdinand Schornër. By the time these changes were made, the River Bug Line was breached and Odessa liberated. Soviet troops crossed the border into Romania on 10 April. The Ukraine was free, or at least in Soviet hands.

Further east, in the Crimea, the German 17th Army was still cut off. Hitler, following his usual approach, refused any suggestion of withdrawal. Instead he had dispatched reinforcements and, by April 1944, there were 76,000 German and 46,000 Romanian troops facing three Soviet armies of 500,000 men. The Soviets attacked on 8 April and in 18 days the Germans and Romanians had been pushed back into the fortress city of Sevastopol. This, in turn, fell on 5 May, with less than 1,000 survivors escaping by sea to Romania. The Crimea was Soviet again.

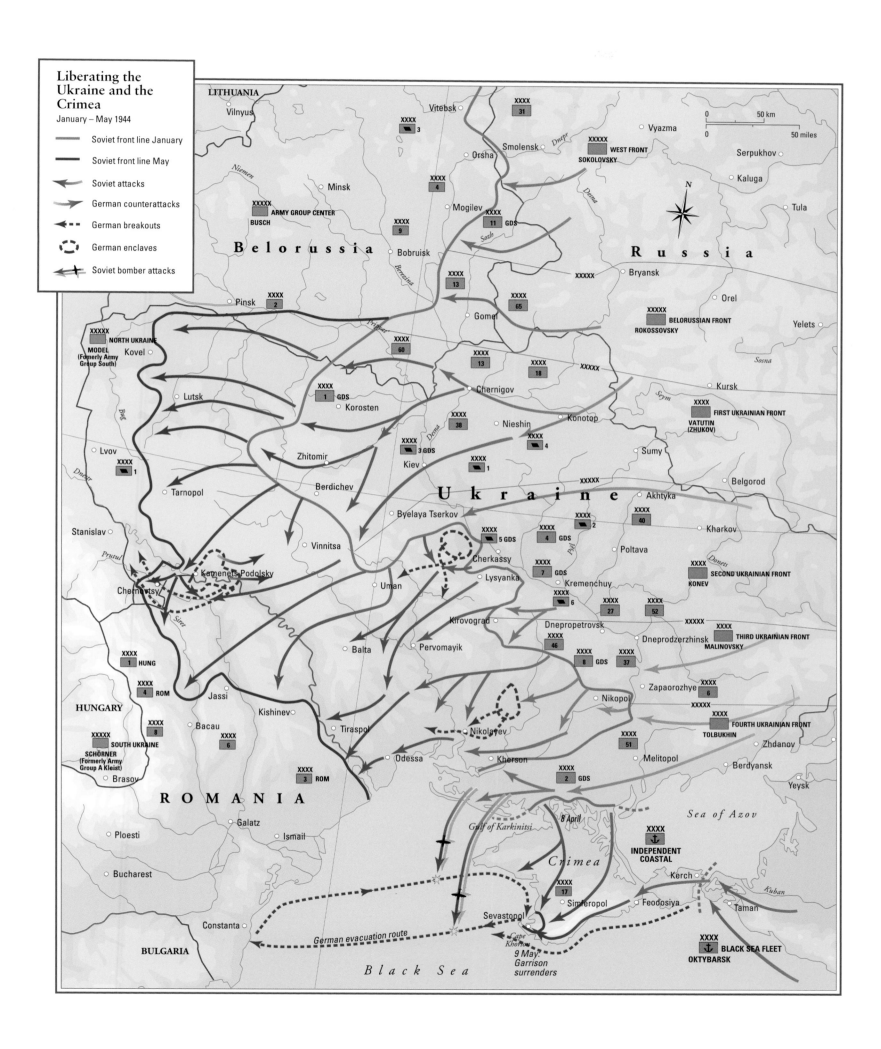

Liberating the Ukraine and the Crimea

January – May 1944

——	Soviet front line January
——	Soviet front line May
←	Soviet attacks
←	German counterattacks
◄--	German breakouts
⬭	German enclaves
✈	Soviet bomber attacks

LITHUANIA

Vilnyus

Vitebsk

XXXX 31

XXXX 3

Smolensk

Orsha

XXXXX WEST FRONT SOKOLOVSKY

Vyazma

Serpukhov

Kaluga

Tula

Minsk

XXXX 4

Mogilev

XXXX 11 GDS

R u s s i a

B e l o r u s s i a

XXXX 9

Bobruisk

XXXXX ARMY GROUP CENTER BUSCH

XXXX 13

XXXX 65

Bryansk

Orel

Yelets

Pinsk

XXXX 2

Gomel

XXXXX BELORUSSIAN FRONT ROKOSSOVSKY

Sosna

XXXXX NORTH UKRAINE MODEL (Formerly Army Group South)

Kovel

XXXX 60

XXXX 13

Chernigov

XXXX 18

XXXXX

Kursk

Lutsk

XXXX 1 GDS

Korosten

Zhitomir

XXXX 38

Nieshin

Konotop

Sym

XXXX 4

Sumy

XXXXX FIRST UKRAINIAN FRONT VATUTIN (ZHUKOV)

Bug

Lvov

XXXX 1

Tarnopol

Berdichev

XXXX 3 GDS

Kiev

XXXX 1

Belgorod

Dnepr

Stanislav

Byelaya Tserkov

XXXX 5 GDS

XXXX 4 GDS

XXXX 2

XXXX 40

Kharkov

Vinnitsa

Cherkassy

XXXX 7 GDS

Lysyanka

Kremenchuy

XXXXX SECOND UKRAINIAN FRONT KONEV

Donets

Kamenets Podolsky

Chernovtsy

Uman

XXXX 6

Poltava

Prutul

Balta

Pervomayik

Kirovograd

Dnepropetrovsk

XXXX 27

XXXX 52

XXXXX

Sira

XXXX 1 HUNG

XXXX 46

Dneprodzerzhinsk

XXXXX THIRD UKRAINIAN FRONT MALINOVSKY

XXXX 4 ROM

Jassi

Kishinev

XXXX 8 GDS

XXXX 37

HUNGARY

XXXX 8

Bacau

XXXX 6

Tiraspol

Nikolayev

Zapaorozhye

XXXX 6

XXXXX SOUTH UKRAINE SCHÖRNER (Formerly Army Group A Kleist)

Brasov

Odessa

Kherson

Nikopol

Melitopol

XXXXX FOURTH UKRAINIAN FRONT TOLBUKHIN

Zhdanov

R O M A N I A

XXXX 3 ROM

XXXX 2 GDS

XXXX 51

Berdyansk

Yeysk

Galatz

Ismail

Sea of Azov

Ploesti

8 April

Gulf of Karkinitsi

XXXX ⚓ INDEPENDENT COASTAL

C r i m e a

Kerch

Kuban

Bucharest

XXXX 17

Simferopol

Feodosiya

Taman

Constanta

Sevastopol

German evacuation route

Cape Khorsov

9 May: Garrison surrenders

XXXX ⚓ BLACK SEA FLEET OKTYABRSK

BULGARIA

B l a c k   S e a

0 —— 50 km
0 —— 50 miles

RESISTANCE 1941–44

"WHATEVER HAPPENS, THE FLAME OF FRENCH RESISTANCE MUST NOT BE EXTINGUISHED AND WILL NOT BE EXTINGUISHED."

GENERAL CHARLES DE GAULLE

R esistance networks were set up in all occupied territories to some degree, with each country reacting in their own unique way to counter Axis occupation, although these forces never unified to form a single national force. The majority of occupied countries aided resistance in some form or other, be it passively or actively. Resistance also helped the morale and self-respect of the occupied countries and helped them feel they were contributing to the war effort and to retain some national pride.

Active resistance involved gathering intelligence, which could be used locally and then sent via radio messages to Britain and other Allied countries, the aiding of escaped prisoners of war, sabotage of enemy installations, or ambush of enemy troops. Passive resistance could include strikes at important war production facilities, working at a slower rate, or demonstrating against the occupiers.

In order to resist effectively secrecy had to be complete; those who bragged, or were loose with their tongues, were soon found, arrested and, quite often, turned against their own side. Winston Churchill, recognizing that Britain might need a resistance network should she be invaded, gave a directive for the Special Operations Executive (S.O.E.) to be set up. This agency set about recruiting and training men and women, especially those who had escaped from occupied countries. They would then be returned to their native country to raise and lead resistance movements, as well as sending back vital information. The S.O.E. also equipped these resistance groups and armies, which ranged from the Maquis in France to the Partisans in Yugoslavia.

The United States also saw the need to create a clandestine operations unit and set up the Office of Strategic Services (O.S.S.). This unit operated, like its British counterpart, all over the globe and

---

**French Resistance:
Industrial Sabotage**
1942–44

☀ Sabotage location

Targets

F Fuel

P Power

A Aviation

M Military

I Industrial

T Transport

E Electrical

C Metals and chemicals

Date of Operation

● 1942

● 1943

● 1944

UNITED
KINGDOM

LONDON

*North
Sea*

HOLLAND

English Channel

50°

BELGIUM

Roubaix I

I Lille   Willems F

T Fives-Lille

F Liéven   Douaï
                 (Corbehem) F

GERMANY

Rouen
(Dieppedalle) E

I Déville-les-Rouen

Montataire T ● ●

Beaumont-sur-Oise I

I Asnières

Choisy-au-Bac T ●

Bar P

St. Georges P

T Mantes
C ● ● Mantes-Gassicourt

Levallois-Perret
M

Sevran T

Luneville T

A Courbevoie

Aubervilliers I

Ivry-sur-Seine I
Boulogne-sur-Seine I ● ● M

F R A N C E

E Blois

Orléans (Chaigny) E

Belfort ●

M ● ● Monbéliard (Sochaux)

A Bourges

Prémery C ● ●

Fourchambault A ●

Le Creusot P ●

SWITZERLAND

46°

*Bay of
Biscay*

Montluçon M T ●

Limoges (St. Marc) P

Lyons
(St. Fonds)   Lyons
Villeurbanne I ●   Annecy I

P Limoges
(Des Cassaux)

Ussel I ● ● ●

Clermont-
Ferrand

I A ● Lyons

Lyons
Venissieux

A T ●

Ugine P ● ●

M Tulle
A T

Tulle (Virevialle) P ● ●

I ●
St. Etienne

Grenoble
C I

P Mauzac

Brive-la-Gaillarde E ● ●

N

Figeac A ●

P ● ● Briançon

Garonne   *Lot*

Decazeville F ● ●

Salindres C ●

Carmaux I ●

Montbartier C ●

Teillet (Argenty) E ●

Adour

I Pau

Tarbes A M ● ●

M Bagnières de Bigorre

Lannemezan C ●

L'Estaque C ●

Gardanne C ● ●

ITALY

MONACO

P Laruns

P Gripp

Sarrancolin

I St. Lary P

T Béziers

T St. Marcel

Bordères-
Loudon

Lavelanet P

C

Gulf of Lion

Tarascon-sur-Ariège C

Escouloubre P

SPAIN

Usson P

ANDORRA

0   50 km

0   50 miles

Resistance fighters spring an ambush in the French countryside, armed with the British-supplied Sten machine-gun, a rudimentary but effective weapon.

particularly aided the forces of Chiang Kai-shek in China, as well as forces in northern France before and after the Normandy landings.

During the period between May 1941 and August 1944 over 400 S.O.E. agents were dropped into occupied France, setting up many new networks and coordinating attacks so they fitted in with the overall Allied plan. The most effective of these attacks was staged before D-Day in the sabotage of railroad lines and communications, severely disrupting German lines of supply. As well as direct sabotage, railroad workers either worked extremely slowly or not at all, effectively bringing the rail system to a halt. But reprisals could be harsh, as witnessed when the population of the French village of Oradour-sur-Glane were massacred for the resistance activities.

The S.O.E. supported resistance movements in eastern Europe, particularly Greece and Yugoslavia. In Yugoslavia, the Republican Chetnik movement was at first supported with arms and radios, but when they were found to be ineffective and often collaborated with the enemy, S.O.E. aided the pro-Communist Partisan movement led by Josip Broz, known as "Tito," forming groups deep in the mountains, well hidden from the enemy. They formed an effective resistance force and Tito soon became a target of the German occupying forces, narrowly avoiding capture and certain death several times. Although mainly supplied by the western Allies, Tito often fell out with U.S. and British liaison officers because of his close links to Stalin and the Communist cause. After the war Tito was

Rail supplies from German industrial centers to the soldiers manning the Atlantic Wall were of vast importance. Denying the Germans this vital link was just one of the many contributions made by the French Resistance.

to rise to become the Prime Minister of the country but later broke his links with the Communist-run eastern Europe.

In Norway there were many active resistance groups but perhaps the most famous was the group that attacked the German Heavy Water Plant, essential to Nazi ambitions to produce an atomic weapon. The operation entailed dropping S.O.E.-trained Norwegians with detailed knowledge of the area by parachute, to make a reconnaissance of the plant at Vemork. After this was completed they were to be joined by Royal Engineers landing in two gliders on a frozen lake. However, poor weather caused the gliders to crash land and the survivors were captured, tortured, and shot. The Norwegians managed to survive the horrific winter in hiding, living on lichen and moss, and eventually, on the point of starvation, killing a reindeer. As spring approached the S.O.E. dropped in more Norwegian Commandoes, who succeeded in breaking into the plant, setting explosive charges and making their escape. The Heavy Water stocks were destroyed in the explosion and all ten of the Commandoes successfully escaped, six skiing for Sweden and the remaining four staying to continue the fight with the local resistance.

The German occupation of the Soviet Union was brutal in the extreme with villagers hanged, entire village populations exterminated, and arbitrary machine-gunning of men, women, and children. As the Germans advanced, many villagers fled into the forests, often becoming partisans engaged in

Russian partisans played an important part in the liberation of their country. As well as loyal Soviet groups, the partisans were also formed by national minorities, notably Ukrainians, who had little sympathy for their former Soviet masters and continued to fight them after liberation from the Germans.

guerrilla warfare against the invaders. The experience of this cruelty and suffering motivated ordinary people to fight back, even though German army orders were to shoot captured partisans or bury them alive to increase their agony and as an example to the local population. The story of partisan school girl, Zoya Kosmodemyanskaya, who was tortured and hanged, became widely known. Elsewhere in Russia a woman partisan pretending to be a housemaid blew up a German commander, known as the "Butcher Of Belorussia." The partisans were especially effective operating out of the

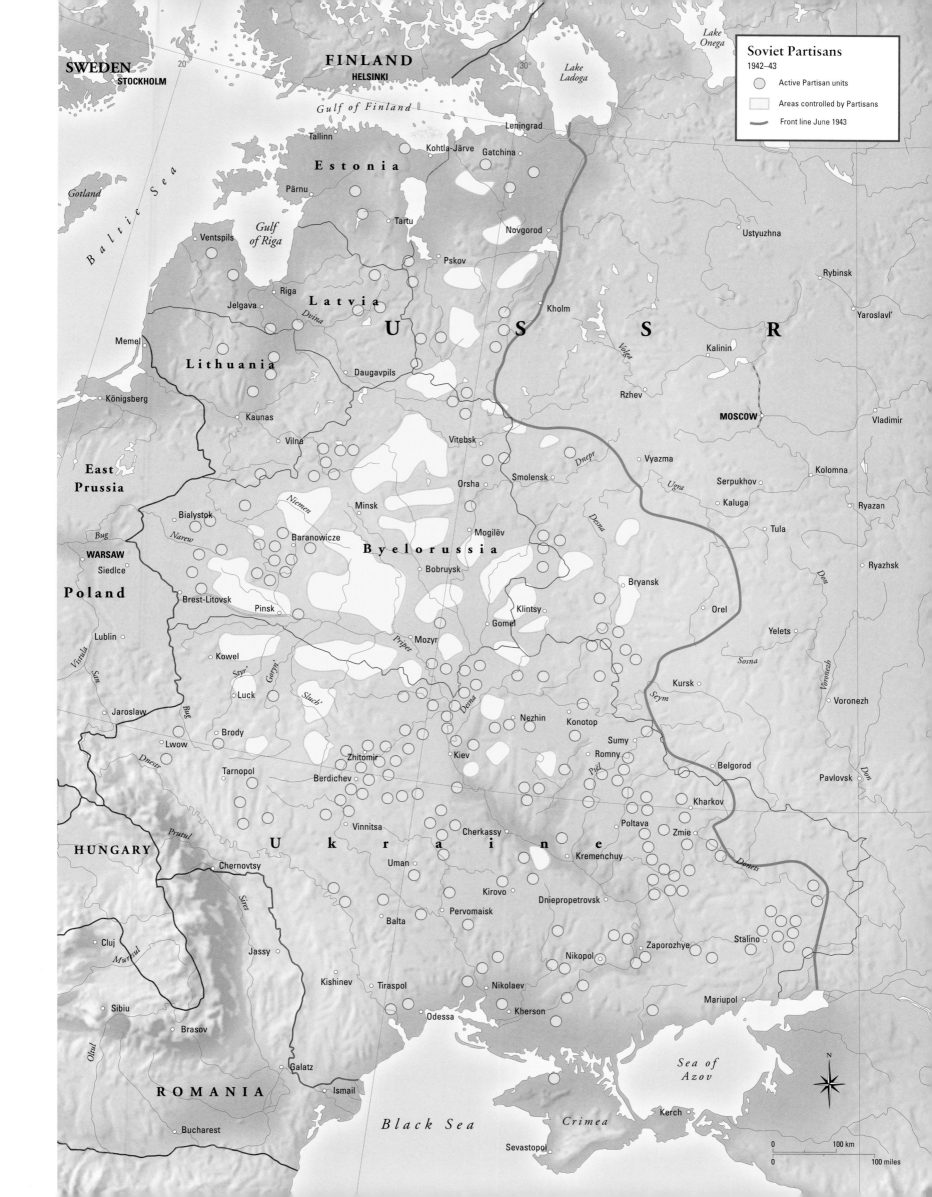

SWEDEN
STOCKHOLM

FINLAND
HELSINKI

Lake Onega

Lake Ladoga

Gulf of Finland

Baltic Sea

Gotland

Gulf of Riga

Tallinn
Kohtla-Järve
Gatchina
Leningrad

Estonia

Pärnu

Tartu

Novgorod

Ventspils

Pskov

Ustyuzhna

Riga

Rybinsk

Latvia

Jelgava

Dvina

Kholm

U   S   S   R

Yaroslavl'

Memel

Volga

Kalinin

Lithuania

Daugavpils

MOSCOW

Vladimir

Königsberg

Kaunas

East
Prussia

Vilna

Vitebsk

Vyazma

Serpukhov

Kolomna

Dnepr

Smolensk

Ugra

Kaluga

Ryazan

Orsha

Niemen

Minsk

Mogilëv

Desna

Tula

Bialystok

Byelorussia

Bug

Baranowicze

Ryazhsk

WARSAW

Narew

Bobruysk

Bryansk

Don

Siedlce

Orel

Ryazhsk

Poland

Brest-Litovsk

Pinsk

Klintsy

Yelets

Lublin

Pripet

Mozyr

Gomel

Sosna

Kowel

Styr'

Horyn'

Kursk

Luck

Sluch'

Desna

Seym

Voronezh

Vistula

San

Brody

Nezhin

Konotop

Belgorod

Lwow

Dnestr

Zhitomir

Kiev

Sumy

Romny

Bug

Pavlovsk

Jaroslaw

Tarnopol

Berdichev

Psil

Kharkov

Don

Prutul

Vinnitsa

Cherkassy

Poltava

HUNGARY

Uman

Ukraine

Kremenchuy

Zmie

Chernovtsy

Kirovo

Pervomaisk

Dniepropetrovsk

Siret

Balta

Zaporozhye

Stalino

Cluj

Jassy

Nikopol

Mursul

Kishinev

Tiraspol

Nikolaev

Kherson

Mariupol

Sibiu

Odessa

Brasov

Olul

Galatz

Ismail

Sea of Azov

ROMANIA

Black Sea

Crimea

Kerch

Bucharest

Sevastopol

Soviet Partisans

1942–43

◯ Active Partisan units

▭ Areas controlled by Partisans

〜 Front line June 1943

N

0   100 km

0   100 miles

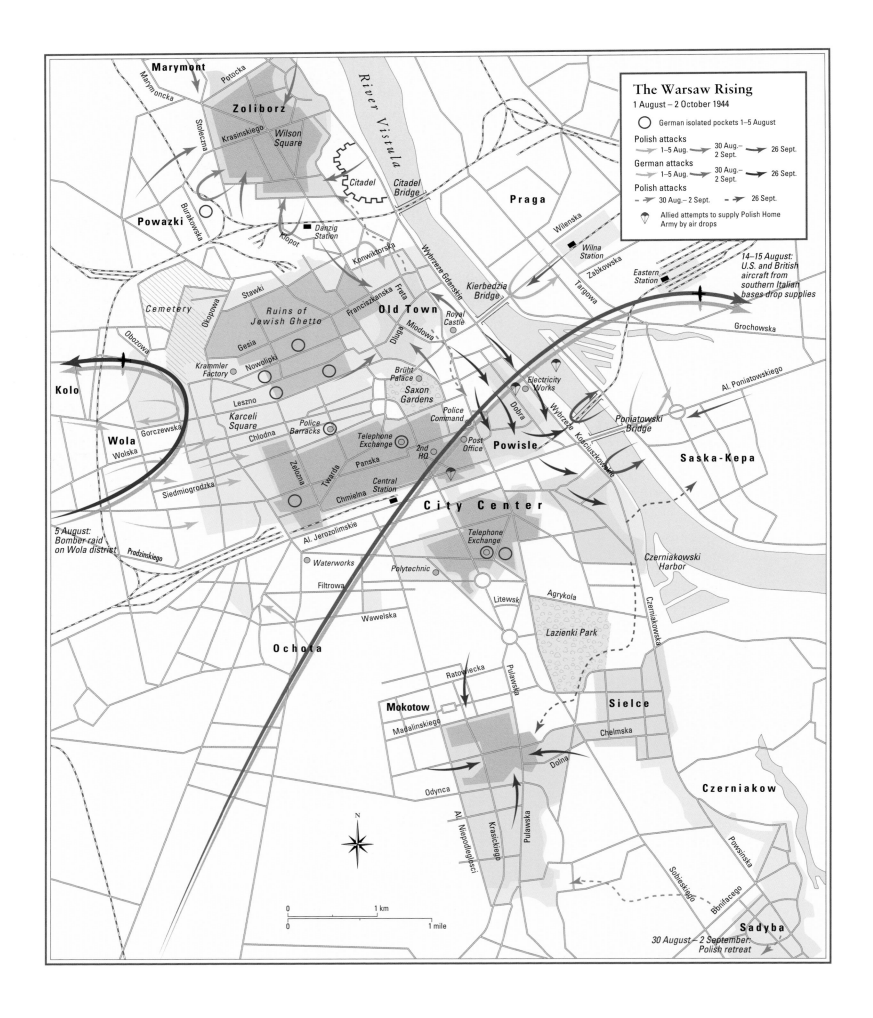

Marymont

Potocka

Maryjoncka

Zoliborz

Krasinskiego

Wilson
Square

Stoleczna

Burakowska

Powazki

Citadel

Citadel
Bridge

River Vistula

Praga

Wilenska

Danzig
Station

Klopot

Konwiktorska

Wybrzeże Gdanskie

Wilna
Station

Zabkowska

Targowa

Eastern
Station

14–15 August:
U.S. and British
aircraft from
southern Italian
bases drop supplies

Cemetery

Okopowa

Stawki

Ruins of
Jewish Ghetto

Gesia

Franciszkanska

Freta

Old Town

Miodowa

Dluga

Royal
Castle

Kierbedzia
Bridge

Grochowska

Obozowa

Krammler
Factory

Nowolipki

Brühl
Palace

Saxon
Gardens

Electricity
Works

Al. Poniatowskiego

Kolo

Leszno

Police
Command

Dobra

Poniatowski
Bridge

Wola

Gorczewska

Karceli
Square

Chlodna

Police
Barracks

Telephone
Exchange

2nd
HQ

Post
Office

Powisle

Wybrzeże Kosciuszkowskie

Saska-Kepa

Wolska

Zelazna

Twarda

Panska

Central
Station

Chmielna

City Center

5 August:
Bomber raid
on Wola district

Siedmiogrodzka

Pradzinskiego

Al. Jerozolimskie

Telephone
Exchange

Czerniakowski
Harbor

Waterworks

Polytechnic

Filtrowa

Litewsk

Agrykola

Czerniakowska

Wawelska

Lazienki Park

Ochota

Ratowiecka

Pulawska

Mokotow

Madalinskiego

Sielce

Chelmska

Dolna

Odynca

Al. Niepodleglosci

Krasickiego

Pulawska

Czerniakow

N

Sobieskiego

Powsinska

Bonifacego

Sadyba

30 August – 2 September:
Polish retreat

0   1 km
0   1 mile

The Warsaw Rising
1 August – 2 October 1944

○ German isolated pockets 1–5 August

Polish attacks
→ 1–5 Aug.   → 30 Aug.–
2 Sept.   → 26 Sept.

German attacks
→ 1–5 Aug.   → 30 Aug.–
2 Sept.   → 26 Sept.

Polish attacks
--→ 30 Aug. – 2 Sept.   --→ 26 Sept.

Allied attempts to supply Polish Home
Army by air drops

vast Pripet Marshes near Pinsk. The partisan group, the Young Guard of the Donbass—teenagers and students—sabotaged army positions around the German garrisons until they were all eventually captured, tortured, and buried alive in their local coal mines. The courageous stand of the partisan movement generated hope, but the Soviet military did little to support them because they feared and distrusted armed locals, especially from the non-Russian minorities.

Large scale resistance took place in Poland, occupied since September 1939 by both Germany and the U.S.S.R., and after 1941 by Germany alone. The country became a center for repression and extermination. The Polish resistance collected information to send to London and attacked German supply lines and garrisons. Perhaps, therefore, it is no surprise that the greatest uprising in occupied Europe happened in Poland.

Polish resistance fighters bring in a captured German soldier for questioning during the Warsaw Uprising.

The Warsaw Uprising began in August 1944, lasting until 2 October, after 63 days of combat. By 1944, Warsaw was the center of Polish resistance carried out by the Polish Home Army. This force was supported by and was loyal to the anti-Communist Polish government in exile. Led by General Tadeusz Komorowski, known as General Bor, the Home Army sought to expel the German Army before Soviet forces reached Warsaw. During the German siege, Red Army General Rossokovsky reached the outskirts of the city but failed to cross the River Vistula. The Russians refused to aid the Home Army and sat back watching German air raids pulverizing the city, while Stalin refused to let U.S. airplanes use Soviet airstrips as bases to parachute supplies to the Polish resistance fighters. Finally, on 18 September, one flight was allowed, comprising 110 B-17s, but it was too little too late.

Between 150,000 and 180,000 citizens of Warsaw died in the uprising and its aftermath, with the Germans sending many surrendered resistance fighters to concentration camps and then systematically destroying the city. Now, with all independent Polish resistance having been eradicated by the Germans, the Red Army entered Warsaw and established a Soviet-sponsored Committee of National Liberation, which imposed a Communist provisional government on Poland on 1 January 1945. Soviet control of Poland was recognized by the Allies at the 1945 summer Potsdam Conference.

In the Far East there were many resistance units. The most significant were the Hukbalap, or "The People's Army Against the Japanese," based in the Philippines. They grew to 20,000 active combatants, who often fought the Americans as well as the Japanese in order to throw out any occupying power. In Malaya and Burma there were also active guerrilla movements, but these were not as well supported by the Allies, mainly because of their Communist leanings.

THE BALKANS 1941–44

"INTO BATTLE AGAINST THE FASCIST OCCUPATION HORDES WHO ARE STRIVING TO DOMINATE THE WHOLE WORLD."

TITO, PARTISAN LEADER

CALLING ON THE PEOPLE OF YUGOSLAVIA, 4 JULY 1941

Hitler, having been drawn into the Balkans largely in support of his ally Italy, now wished to exploit the area without committing large numbers of troops. These would be needed for his planned invasion of Russia. Therefore, with little time to spare, he organized a new arrangement for the Balkans. Yugoslavia was quickly broken up, and in its place, based on old divisions, the following states were established: Croatia, largely pro-German; Serbia, occupied by Germany; Bosnia, occupied by Germany; Herzegovina, occupied by Italy; Montenegro, under Italian administration; Kosovo and western Macedonia, under Italian control and joined administratively to Albania. The rest of Macedonia was administered by Bulgaria. Other smaller areas were transferred to Hungary.

In Greece, Thrace was administered by Bulgaria while the area immediately adjacent to the Turkish border, Demotila, was occupied by Germany, as were the areas around Salonika, Athens, and some of the major Greek islands. The rest came under Italian occupation. Even before the invasion of Soviet Russia, the Communist movements in the Balkans and especially Yugoslavia were called upon to launch a partisan war in support of their Soviet brothers in the U.S.S.R.

Meanwhile, after the German conquest, remains of the Yugoslav Army took to the mountains, led mostly by Serb officers, who became known as the Chetniks, under the command of Drage Mihailovich. His plan was to restore the Serb-dominated monarchy, then, when the Allies returned, to take revenge on their Communist enemies. In Croatia, however, under the Ustasas resistance group, a campaign of genocide was launched against the region's Serbs, with the Jews, gypsies, and Communists also marked out for extermination. The aim was to produce a "pure" Croatia, ridding itself of its oriental minorities. In the Bulgarian-occupied lands to the south the locals soon lost faith in the heavy-handed style of

Vienna
Bratislava
**GREATER
GERMANY**
Graz
Varazdin

H U N G A R Y
Nyiregyhaza
Debrecen
Oradea
Dej
Cluj
Szegek
Arad
Subotica

Carpathians

Botosani
Jassy
Chisinau
Sibiu
Brasov
Bocau
Galati
R O M A N I A
Buzau
Tulcea
Pitesti
Ploesti
Bucharest
Craiova
Constanta

Zagreb
Karlovac
Gudovac
Prekopa
Blagaj
Jasenovac
Sava
Stara Gradiska
Banda Luka
CRAOTIA
Jajce
Travnik
Sarajevo

Banjika
Belgrade
Uzice
S E R B I A
Nis
Turnu-Severin
Vidin
Giurgiu
Ruse
Danube

B U L G A R I A
Sofia
Stara Zagora
Plovdiv
Khaskovo
Erdirne
Varna
Burgas
Black Sea

MONT
Dubrovnik
Mitrovica
Pristina
Kyustendil
Skopje
Macedonia

Adriatic Sea

ITALY
*Allied to Germany until
September 1943*
Brindisi

ALBANIA
Monastir
Berat
Edessa
Kilkis
Salonica
Kozani
Katerine
Thasos
Sérrai
Drama
Xanthi
Komotine
Alexandroupolis
Lemnos
Samothrace

*Sea of
Marmara*
Istanbul
Erdirne

Ionian Sea
Corfu
Ionnena
Trikkala
Larisa
Arta
G R E E C E
Lamia
Missolonghi
Patrai
Corinth
Khalkis
Marathon
Athens
*Aegean
Sea*
Andros
Tinos
Pyrgos
Tripolis
Kalahai
Monemyasia

Izmir
Khios
Lesbos
T U R K E Y
Naxos

Balkans

1941–44

▪ Massacre sites

● Concentration camps

▥ Occupied by Germany

☐ Allied to Germany

▨ Pro Axis. Occupied by
Italy and Germany

▨ Occupied by Italy, with limited
German support

N

0   100 km
0   100 miles

Bulgarian occupation. Hitler's reordering of the country was a major reason for the creation of an armed resistance and the civil war that followed in Yugoslavia. Amongst all of this developing situation emerged Josip Broz Tito, who took his Communist partisans to war. Firstly, he contested western Serbia with Mihailovich and his Chetniks, before moving into any area he could extend his influence. Mihailovich appealed to the Germans for arms in order to crush the Communists, but they refused. He then went to war with the partisans, almost throwing them out of Serbia. A civil war broke out in Serbia, spreading to the rest of the country, but the Communist partisans still held on, surviving until the German-led offensives of Weiss and Schwarz in the first half of 1943. By April, Tito's forces were also receiving aid from the British. After September, with the Italian surrender, Tito claimed the right to recognition as the future ruler of post-war Yugoslavia. He also stated that, by 1944, his forces—300,000-strong—were tying down as many Axis forces as the western Allies were in Italy. He was also busy destroying his Chetnik rivals in Serbia. To help toward this end, he asked Stalin to divert part of the advancing Red Army. Stalin agreed and Belgrade fell on 20 October 1944. The partisans were left to pursue the fleeing Germans out of Yugoslavia.

Albania had organized a pro-Communist National Liberation Movement in 1942. They faced a pro-Axis Republican Movement, the Balli Kombëtar. When the Axis forces withdrew in 1944, the Communists overcame their republican rivals, forming the ruling government in the fall of 1944.

In Greece, Communists were the first group to form an effective resistance movement, and by 1942–43 the National Popular Liberation Army (E.L.A.S.) was well-organized. As the Germans withdrew E.L.A.S. failed to fill the vacuum quickly enough, allowing the British-backed government to assume control. They did not know that Stalin had abandoned them under a deal with Churchill, in which Greece came under the British sphere of influence.

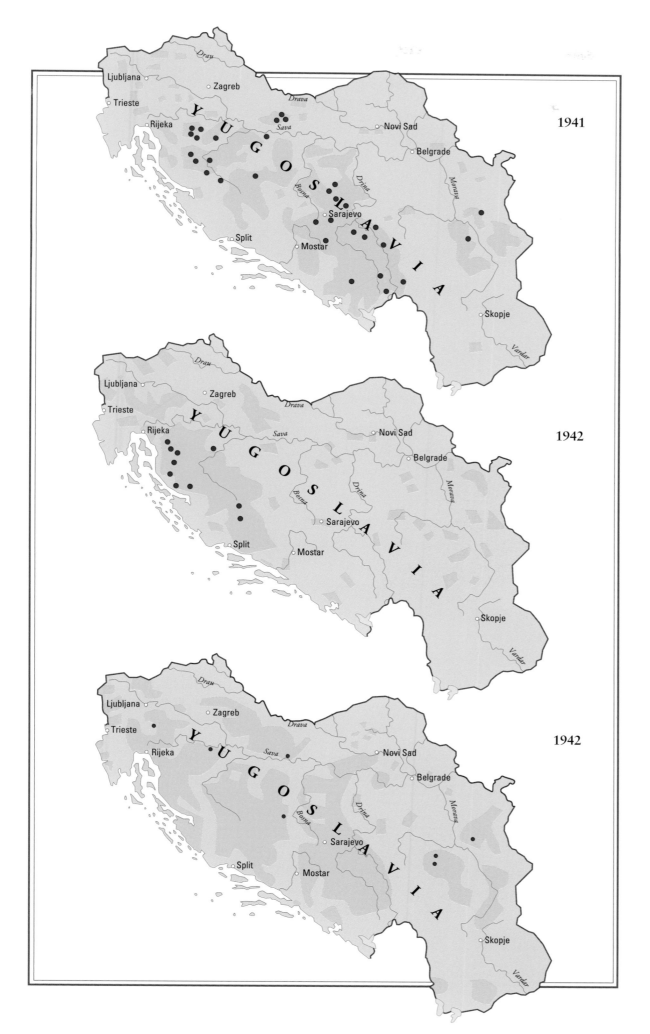

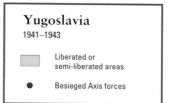

Yugoslavia
1941–1943

Liberated or semi-liberated areas

● Besieged Axis forces

Between 1941 and 1943 the partisan groups, after a period of fluctuating fortunes, became dominated by Tito's Pro-Communist Partisans. He managed to attract men of Yugoslavia's national groups into his command. The partisans almost always controlled the mountains, while the Germans and Italians controlled the valleys and the towns.

Far left: Josip Broz, born near Klanjec, Croatia, in 1892. He was a Communist revolutionary, spending a considerable time in Moscow working for the Comintern, an organization that represented international communist parties. He was chosen to take over the Communist Party in Yugoslavia. By the time Yugoslavia was attacked in April 1941, Tito, as he was now known, had successfully reorganized the Communist Party and increased its membership to over 8,000. In June the same year, he issued his call to arms responding to an appeal made by the U.S.S.R. He also seized the opportunity to promote a pro-Communist revolution in Yugoslavia.

BOMBING OF GERMANY 1943–44

"AFTER HAMBURG IN THE WIDE CIRCLE OF POLITICAL AND MILITARY HIGH COMMAND COULD BE HEARD THE WORDS 'THE WAR IS LOST.'"

COLONEL ADOLF GALLAND, LUFTWAFFE

Air Chief Marshal "Bomber" Harris chose to bomb specific areas of Germany and opened his new strategy with the Battle of the Ruhr, the industrial heart of the country, which lasted six weeks. This battle also included the Dambusters raid, led by Guy Gibson, flying modified Lancasters to drop the "bouncing bomb," a cylindrical mine that skimmed along the reservoir then sank to the base of the dam before exploding. The Mohne and Eder dams were breached using this method.

Next came the bombing of Hamburg with Operation Gomorrah, four raids that decimated 60 percent of the city with firestorms, killing nearly

P-51 Mustangs of the U.S. 375th Fighter Squadron patrol above the clouds. The P-51 could carry under-wing drop tanks to extend its range, allowing it to fly all the way to Berlin and back.

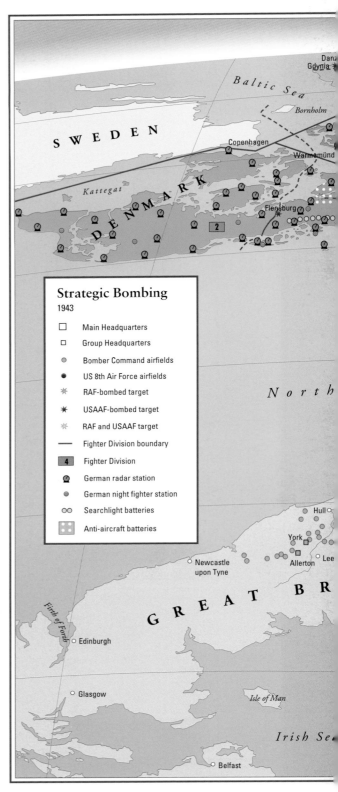

Strategic Bombing
1943

☐   Main Headquarters

☐   Group Headquarters

●   Bomber Command airfields

●   US 8th Air Force airfields

✳   RAF-bombed target

✳   USAAF-bombed target

✳   RAF and USAAF target

—   Fighter Division boundary

4   Fighter Division

⊕   German radar station

●   German night fighter station

∞   Searchlight batteries

⊞   Anti-aircraft batteries

50,000 people. By this time the U.S. 8th Air Force was well into its offensive against the Reich. Flying in large formations, which were intended to be mutually-supporting, the B-17 carried 13 0.5-inch machine guns for defense against fighter attack. Nevertheless, the Luftwaffe still managed to penetrate this defensive screen, shooting down large numbers of bombers. Despite this, by mid-May the intensity of the raids increased and the 8th Air Force started to penetrate deeper into the Reich. They attacked the Messerschmitt factory at Regensberg and the ball bearing plant at Schweinfurt, but as

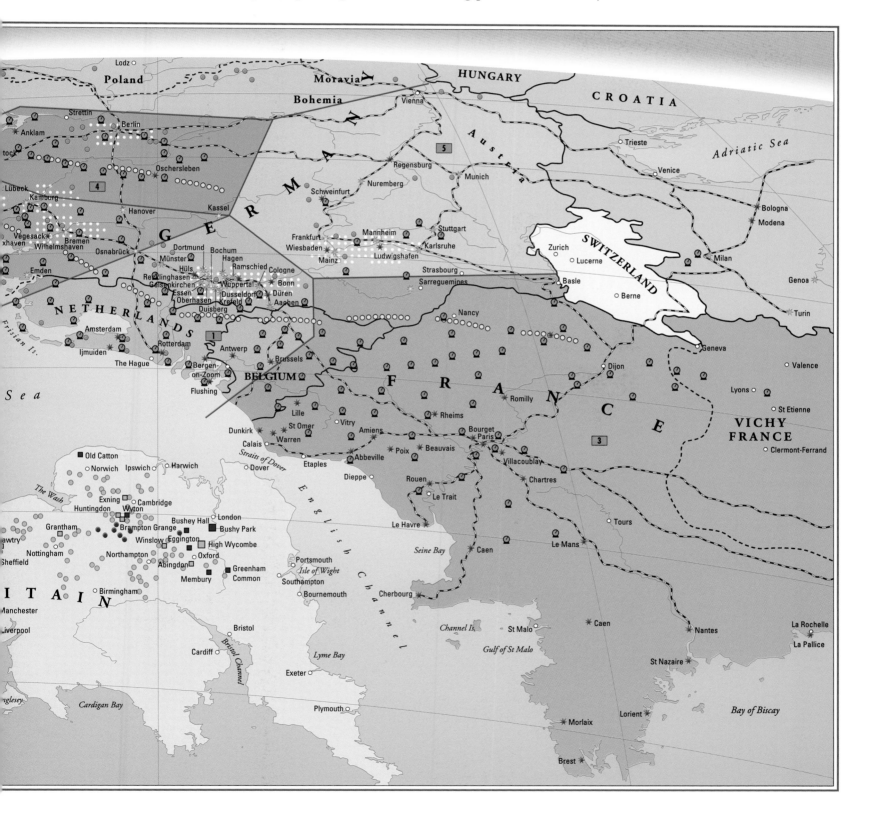

these targets were out of range for the protecting fighters losses were heavy. By early 1944, the range of the escort fighters had been increased with the introduction of drop tanks that allowed the fighters to fly all the way to the targets and back. The Mustang proved to be the best all round fighter of World War II. For the first time U.S. bombers enjoyed real protection.

Bomber Command was also attacking deep into enemy territory, flying a series of raids on Berlin in a campaign running

The mightly Avro Lancaster bore the brunt of the RAF nighttime bombing offensive. Powered by four Rolls-Royce Merlin engines, it could carry a load of up to 22,000 lbs.

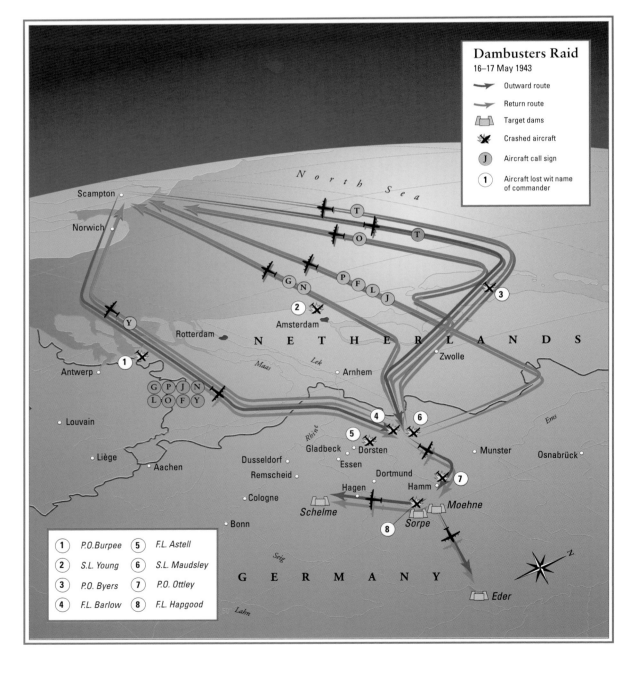

Dambusters Raid
16–17 May 1943

⟶ Outward route

⟶ Return route

Target dams

Crashed aircraft

Ⓙ Aircraft call sign

① Aircraft lost wit name of commander

① P.O. Burpee	⑤ F.L. Astell
② S.L. Young	⑥ S.L. Maudsley
③ P.O. Byers	⑦ P.O. Ottley
④ F.L. Barlow	⑧ F.L. Hapgood

from November 1943 to March 1944. These raids had a high price for the relatively small damage incurred, with 587 aircraft being lost and most of the crews killed or taken prisoner. To Harris's annoyance the Allied air offensive against Germany ended as the resource of Bomber Command and the U.S. 8th Air Force was required to help in the D-Day invasion of France and to attack the new German terror weapon, the V1 flying bomb, or "Doodlebug," being launched from northern France against the south of England.

American B-24Ds bombers on their way to a mission over Germany. There were more B-24s built during the war than any other variant.

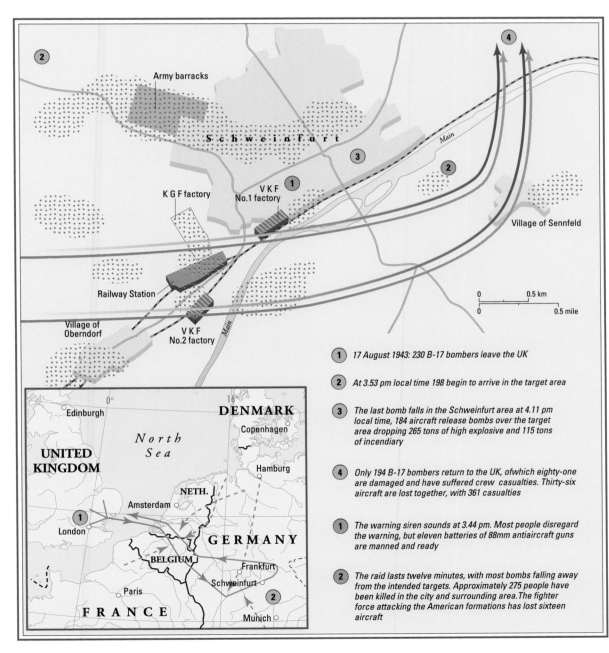

① 17 August 1943: 230 B-17 bombers leave the UK

② At 3.53 pm local time 198 begin to arrive in the target area

③ The last bomb falls in the Schweinfurt area at 4.11 pm local time, 184 aircraft release bombs over the target area dropping 265 tons of high explosive and 115 tons of incendiary

④ Only 194 B-17 bombers return to the UK, ofwhich eighty-one are damaged and have suffered crew casualties. Thirty-six aircraft are lost together, with 361 casualties

① The warning siren sounds at 3.44 pm. Most people disregard the warning, but eleven batteries of 88mm antiaircraft guns are manned and ready

② The raid lasts twelve minutes, with most bombs falling away from the intended targets. Approximately 275 people have been killed in the city and surrounding area. The fighter force attacking the American formations has lost sixteen aircraft

Schweinfurt Bombing Results

Bombing areas

Ball-bearing factories

Planned approach flights

Inset

Major German interceptions

Bombers route

OPERATION OVERLORD 1943–44

"THE ENEMY MUST BE ANNIHILATED BEFORE HE REACHES OUR MAIN BATTLEFIELD... WE MUST STOP HIM IN THE WATER."

FIELD MARSHAL ERWIN ROMMEL, APRIL 1944

An ambitious plan for the cross-Channel invasion of Continental Europe was presented at the Allied conference held in Quebec, Canada, in August 1943. The plan—Operation Overlord—had been devised by C.O.S.S.A.C., an organization headed by Lt.-General Frederick Morgan, the Chief of Staff to the Supreme Allied Commander. The object of the plan was

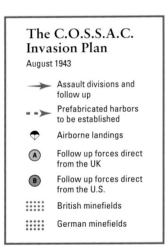

The C.O.S.S.A.C. Invasion Plan
August 1943

→ Assault divisions and follow up

- - -> Prefabricated harbors to be established

⊕ Airborne landings

(A) Follow up forces direct from the UK

(B) Follow up forces direct from the U.S.

⁝⁝⁝ British minefields

⁝⁝⁝ German minefields

COSSAC

An acronym derived from the title *Chief of Staff to the Supreme Allied Commander*, a position held initially by Lt.-General Frederick Morgan, and commonly used as the name for the organization headed by Morgan. It was instigated for planning an invasion of Continental Europe.

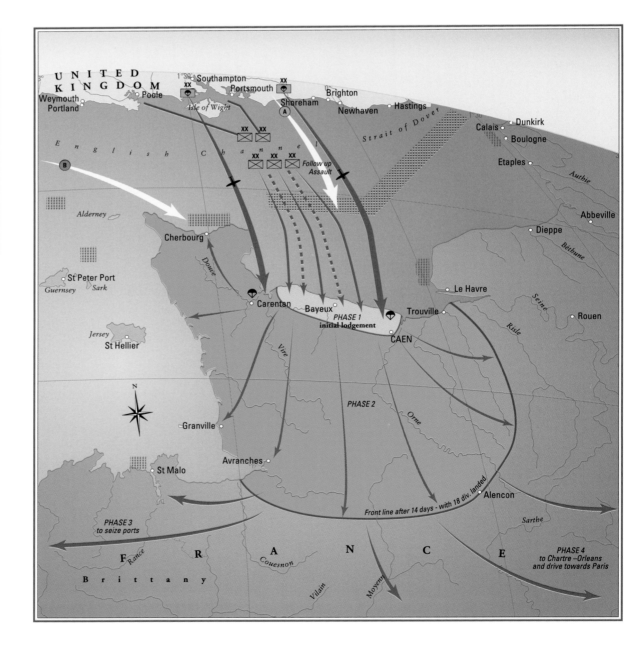

to utilize forces and equipment established in the UK to secure a lodgement area on the Continent, from which further offensive operations would be developed. The operation would be part of a concerted assault upon German-occupied Europe from the UK, the Mediterranean, and Russia. Two preliminary proposals had been previously drawn up and submitted: Operation Sledgehammer, an invasion in 1942; and Operation Roundup, a larger attack in 1943. The latter plan had been adopted and developed in Operation Overload, although it would not come to fruition until 1944.

Overlord relied upon resources that were not readily available at the time; the Sicily landings had taken place the month before the conference and, with Italy near to collapse, it was decided that landings should take place on the Italian mainland. This meant that landing craft that would need to be returned to Britain for the propsed invasion of France, and others that were to be redeployed to Burma, would be retained in the Mediterranean. The conference also accepted a U.S. proposal for landings in the south of France, as a diversion and an adjunct to Overlord. C.O.S.S.A.C. was instructed to proceed with the detailed planning and preparation for the invasion.

Eisenhower and Montgomery attend a U.S. exercise in early 1944. Both men made a great effort to be seen by and provide inspiration to their troops.

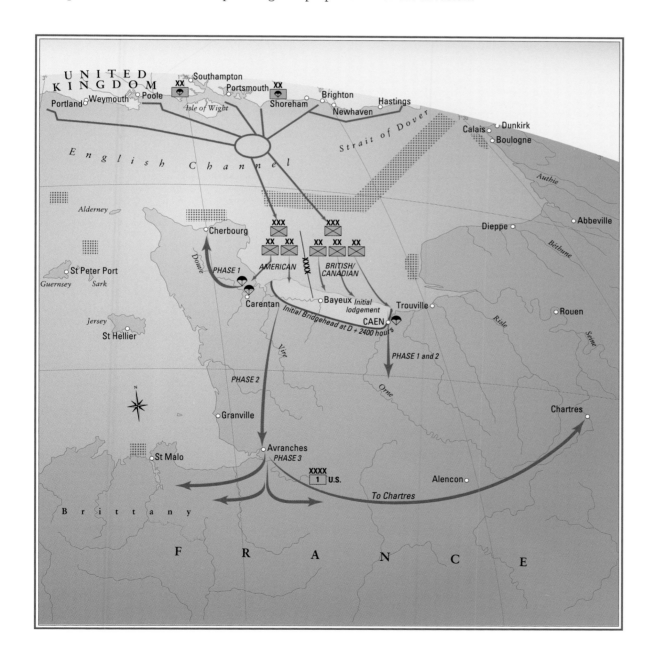

Revised C.O.S.S.A.C. Invasion Plan

April 1944

→ Assault divisions and follow up

Airborne landings

Initial bridgehead at 24.00 hrs

British minefields

German minefields

U.S. troops embark in landing craft for one of the early rehearsals for D-Day.

Ground forces, in the shape of the British 21st Army Group and U.S. 1st Army Group, were allocated to the operation. Two commanders had been appointed. The Overlord air commander was to be Sir Trafford Leigh-Mallory, whose Allied Expeditionary Air Force (A.E.A.F.) of fighters and day bombers was made up of the U.S. 9th Air Force and British 2nd Tactical Air Force, together with transport aircraft, had already been created. The naval commander was to have been the Commander-in-Chief Portsmouth, Admiral Sir Charles Little, but Churchill objected to this on the grounds that he lacked the necessary capacity to deal with such a major undertaking. Instead, he proposed Sir Bertram Ramsay, the man who had masterminded the evacuation from Dunkirk, and had then been the deputy naval commander for the "Torch" landings in north Africa and in charge of the naval forces supporting the British landings on Sicily. Ramsay had also served as a member of the Combined Command. This proposal was accepted by the Combined Chiefs of Staff, although Ramsay would not return to Britain until December 1943. A land commander had yet to be chosen.

Meanwhile, other Allied landings went ahead. The British made virtually unopposed landings on the toe of Italy on 3 September 1943. In Lisbon, Portugal, on the same day, an Italian representative signed an armistice agreement with the Allies, kept secret until the second landing. This took place at Salerno on 8 September in the face of fierce and unexpected German opposition. There was also a serious flaw in the planning in that the beachhead was too wide for the available amphibious landing force, making it difficult to defend. Even so, the Germans eventually withdrew, enabling the Allies to break out. The Germans reacted quickly, pouring in reinforcements through northern Italy and taking advantage of the hilly and mountainous terrain. The fall rains slowed the Allied progress still further, and by the end of the year they were held up by the formidable Gustav Line in the mountains south of Rome. This was to have a bearing on the planning of Overlord.

Allied relations in the Mediterranean became strained in the fall of 1943. In the immediate aftermath of the Italian surrender, Churchill gave orders for the Greek Dodecanese islands in the Aegean to be occupied. It was part of his desire to bring Turkey into the war on the Allied side, and develop a campaign in the Balkans. The problem was that the British garrisons on the islands lacked air support and the Americans were not prepared to divert any from Italy. The German forces in Greece took advantage of this and overran the British garrison on the Dodecanese islands at the beginning of October.

Meanwhile, the question over who would be the overall commander for Overlord was finally resolved. It had been agreed that he should be an American, while his subordinate single-service commanders were to be British. After some discussion in Washington, President Roosevelt appointed Eisenhower, who now had over a year's experience as an Allied coalition commander and the diplomatic skills to bind the Allies together, even if he had no combat experience at lower level. As for the ground commander, Montgomery was the obvious choice. In spite of his bumptious character, which did, at times, irritate the Americans, he had clarity of mind and drive, and had proved himself the most successful British General of the war so far.

At the beginning of January, Montgomery arrived back in Britain, while Eisenhower flew back to the States for a short break. Eisenhower had already seen a copy of the C.O.S.SA.C. plan for Overlord at the end of October 1943, well before he was given overall command of it, and commented that there was insufficient "punch" in the initial attack. Montgomery had his first sight of the plan when he was shown a copy by Churchill during a stopover at Marrakesh, on his way back to Britain. He agreed with Eisenhower's view, and also stated that the landing front was too narrow and would inevitably lead to congestion on the beaches, as follow-up forces were landed. He wanted each corps to have a dedicated group of beaches so that its follow-up divisions could land on them. On 3 January 1944, he convened the first of many meetings at St Paul's School, London. The C.O.S.S.A.C. staff presented their revised plan, which Montgomery immediately criticized, pointing out all of its shortcomings. Four days later, he produced his own plan. The landing frontage had been greatly extended and now stretched from the east coast of the Cotentin peninsula to the west bank of the River Orne. Five divisions would now make the initial assault, two from the U.S. 1st Army in the west, and three from the British 2nd Army in the east. The task of the Americans would be to seize Cherbourg and then advance south and west into Brittany, and east towards Paris, while the British provided a shield for them. It was, in many ways, remarkably similar to the C.O.S.S.A.C. version of August 1943. But General Morgan's plan had been constrained by likely amphibious shipping availability, and doubts remained whether there would be sufficient to support a five-division landing.

Eisenhower arrived in Britain on 12 January. Two days later, Morgan held his last weekly staff meeting, and on 17 January Eisenhower took over, with the H.Q. becoming Supreme Headquarters, Allied Expeditionary Force (S.H.A.E.F.). He had brought his own Chief of Staff, Walter Bedell Smith, and Morgan stepped into the background, although he remained on the S.H.A.E.F. staff. At the same time, a Deputy Supreme Allied Commander was appointed, the British Air Marshal Arthur Tedder, with whom Eisenhower had worked closely in the Mediterranean. On 21 January, Eisenhower held his first conference and approved Montgomery's plan. He was, however, very conscious of the shipping problem. In order to ensure that there was enough for the revised Overlord, he asked the Combined Chiefs of Staff if the invasion could be postponed until June. They eventually agreed, grudgingly, stipulating that D-Day—the date for the Normandy landings—must now be 31 May or a few days either side. There was also the question of the simultaneous landings in the south of France, codenamed "Anvil." The British, who had never really been in favor of them, pointed out that this operation merely served to aggravate the shipping problems and pressed for its cancellation.

Detailed beach reconnaissance was carried out by specialist teams. There was particular concern over the types of obstacle that the Germans were placing on the beaches. It would also be necessary to find beaches in Britain which were similar to those that would be encountered in Normandy, so that the assaulting troops could train on them. The U.S. assault divisions were the 1st Infantry Division, veterans of Tunisia and Sicily, and the unblooded 4th Infantry Division, which arrived in Britain in January 1944. The British contribution was much the same in terms of experience. The 50th (Northumbrian) Division had fought in North Africa from 1941 onwards, while the 3rd Infantry Division had not seen combat since France in 1940. The 3rd Canadian Division had been in Britain since arriving from Canada in July 1941. Of the airborne divisions, the U.S. 82nd had served in North Africa and Sicily, but the 101st was without combat experience, as was the British 6th Airborne Division. Those divisions which had not seen recent combat did, however, have some veterans posted in. Now, while the ground forces intensified their training, other elements of Operation Overlord were already being put into effect.

German soldiers preparing beach obstacles run for cover as a low-flying, Allied photograph reconnaissance aircraft passes over. The obstacles shown were designed to impale landing craft and would be hidden at high tide. Some defenses had explosive devices attached.

Poole

Assault
force 'O'

Weymouth
Portland

Force 'O'
Force 'U'

anti-submarine
support group
in reserve

Destroyer screen

Escort screen

UNITED KINGDOM

4°30'

6°

Follow up forces

Brixham

Follow up force 'B'   Plymouth
Dartmouth

Salcombe

Falmouth

Follow up forces

Penzance

English Channel

Destroyer screen

Alderney

50°

2 submarine support groups

E   n   g   l   i   s   h   C   h   a   n   n   e   l

Antisubmarine patrol

82nd

Guernsey
St Peter Port

Sark

101st

Antisubmarine patrol

Jersey

St Hellier

Antisubmarine patrol

Destroyer patrols

Antisubmarine patrol

49°

Lannion

Trieux

St Malo

Morlaix

St Brieuc

Dinan

F

R

A

B   r   i   t   t   a   n   y

Aulne

Brest

Blavet

Oust

Rance

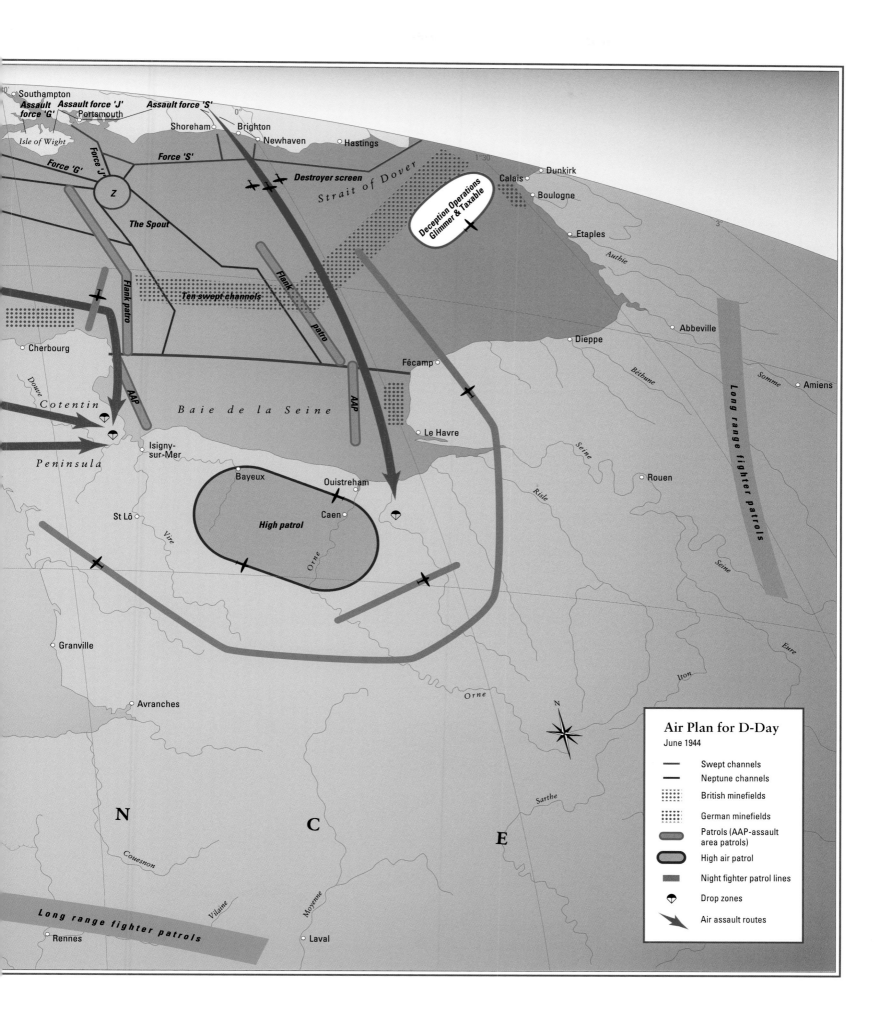

Southampton

Assault force 'G' **Assault force 'J'** **Assault force 'S'**

Portsmouth

Shoreham

Brighton

Isle of Wight

Newhaven

Hastings

Force 'S'

Force 'G' **Force 'J'**

Z

Destroyer screen

Strait of Dover

Deception Operations Glimmer & Taxable

Calais

Dunkirk

Boulogne

The Spout

Etaples

Flank patro

Ten swept channels

Flank patrol

Authie

Cherbourg

Cotentin

AAP

Baie de la Seine

AAP

Fécamp

Abbeville

Dieppe

Béthune

Somme

Amiens

Le Havre

Isigny-sur-Mer

Doue

Peninsula

Bayeux

Ouistreham

Caen

High patrol

St Lô

Vire

Orne

Risle

Seine

Rouen

Long range fighter patrols

Eure

Granville

Orne

Iton

Avranches

N

Sarthe

Seine

N

C

E

Couesnon

Long range fighter patrols

Vilaine

Moyenne

Rennes

Laval

Air Plan for D-Day

June 1944

——	Swept channels
——	Neptune channels
▦	British minefields
▦	German minefields
▬	Patrols (AAP-assault area patrols)
⬭	High air patrol
▬	Night fighter patrol lines
⬦	Drop zones
➤	Air assault routes

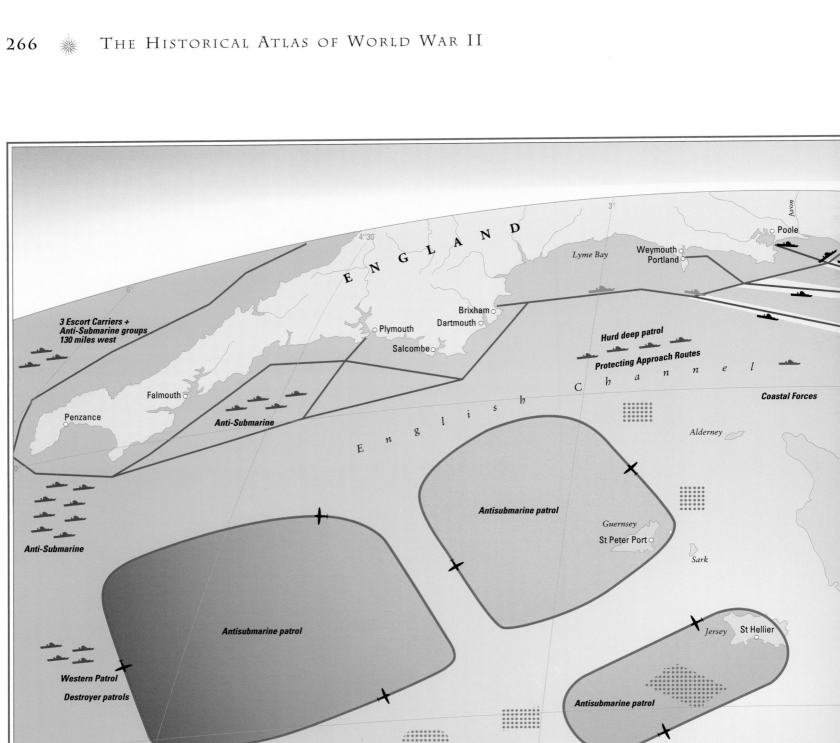

ENGLAND

Poole

Lyme Bay

Weymouth
Portland

Brixham
Dartmouth

Plymouth

Salcombe

**3 Escort Carriers +
Anti-Submarine groups
130 miles west**

Hurd deep patrol

Protecting Approach Routes

Coastal Forces

Falmouth

Penzance

Alderney

Anti-Submarine

English   C h a n n e l

E n g l i s h

Antisubmarine patrol

Guernsey
St Peter Port

Sark

Anti-Submarine

Antisubmarine patrol

Jersey   St Hellier

Antisubmarine patrol

Western Patrol

Destroyer patrols

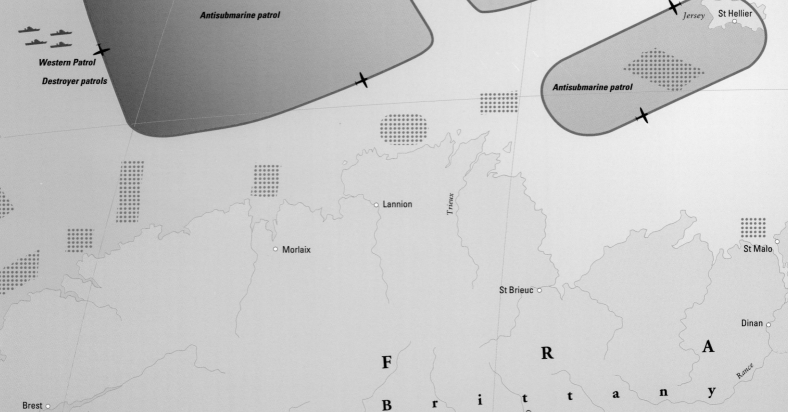

Lannion

Trieux

Morlaix

St Malo

St Brieuc

Dinan

F   R   A

Rance

B   r   i   t   t   a   n   y

Brest

Oust

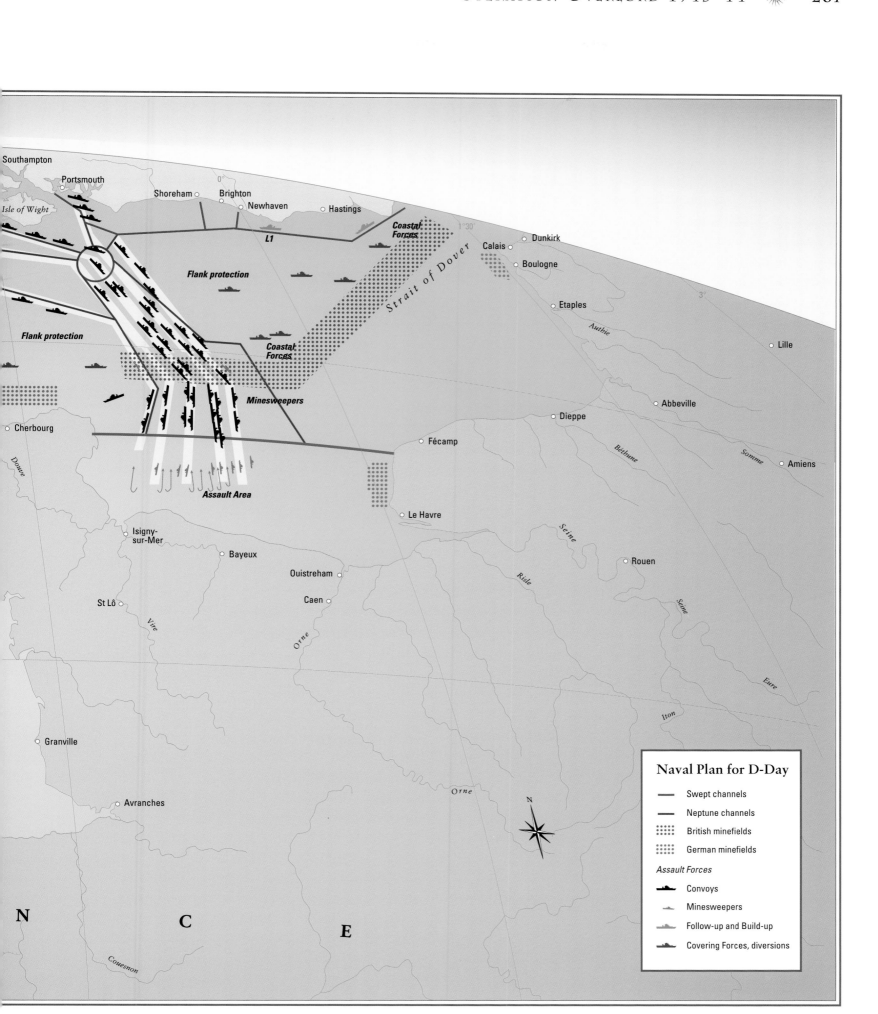

Southampton
Portsmouth
Shoreham
Brighton
Newhaven
Hastings
Isle of Wight
Coastal Forces
0°
Dunkirk
Calais
Boulogne
L1
Flank protection
Etaples
3°
Flank protection
Coastal Forces
Lille
Minesweepers
Authie
Cherbourg
Abbeville
Dieppe
Assault Area
Fécamp
Béthune
Somme
Amiens
Douve
Le Havre
Rouen
Isigny-sur-Mer
Bayeux
Seine
Ouistreham
Risle
St Lô
Caen
Vire
Orne
Seine
Eure
Granville
Orne
Iton
Avranches

N   C   E

Couesnon

Strait of Dover

Naval Plan for D-Day

——— Swept channels
——— Neptune channels
⋮⋮⋮⋮ British minefields
⋮⋮⋮⋮ German minefields

Assault Forces

🚢 Convoys
🚢 Minesweepers
🚢 Follow-up and Build-up
🚢 Covering Forces, diversions

BATTLE OF NORMANDY 1944

"YOUR TASK WILL NOT BE AN EASY ONE ... YOUR ENEMY IS WELL TRAINED, WELL EQUIPPED, AND BATTLE HARDENED. HE WILL FIGHT SAVAGELY."

GENERAL DWIGHT D. EISENHOWER

Below: The landing beaches on the French coast were codenamed Utah, Omaha, Gold, Juno, and Sword, which were mirrored along the British coast on the other side of the channel, so revealing the starting point and goal of attacking forces.

Concentration of Allied Invasion Forces in the United Kingdom

- First line of troops
- Second line of troops
- Third line or reserves
- Areas of restricted access

On 6 June 1944, after years of meticulous planning, Allied forces mounted a full-scale invasion of German-occupied northern France. A precursor to "D-Day" had begun at dusk on 5 June, when a series of airborne deception operations were mounted by the R.A.F. Lancaster bombers of 617 Squadron, known as the "Dambusters." They overflew the Strait of Dover in an elliptical course, dropping strips of aluminum foil known as "Window." Below them 16 small ships towed balloons fitted with reflectors. The idea was to present to the German radars a picture of a convoy crossing the channel towards the Pas-de-Calais.

Stirling aircraft of 218 Squadron carried out a similar exercise off Boulogne, while other Stirlings and Halifaxes dropped dummy parachutes and various devices to represent rifle fire, simulating airborne landings well to the south of the drop zones (D.Z.s) of the two U.S.

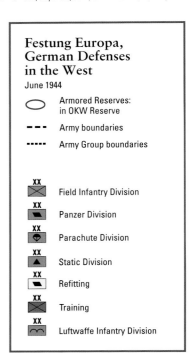

Festung Europa, German Defenses in the West
June 1944

⬭	Armored Reserves: in OKW Reserve
– – –	Army boundaries
-----	Army Group boundaries

XX	Field Infantry Division
XX	Panzer Division
XX	Parachute Division
XX	Static Division
XX	Refitting
XX	Training
XX	Luftwaffe Infantry Division

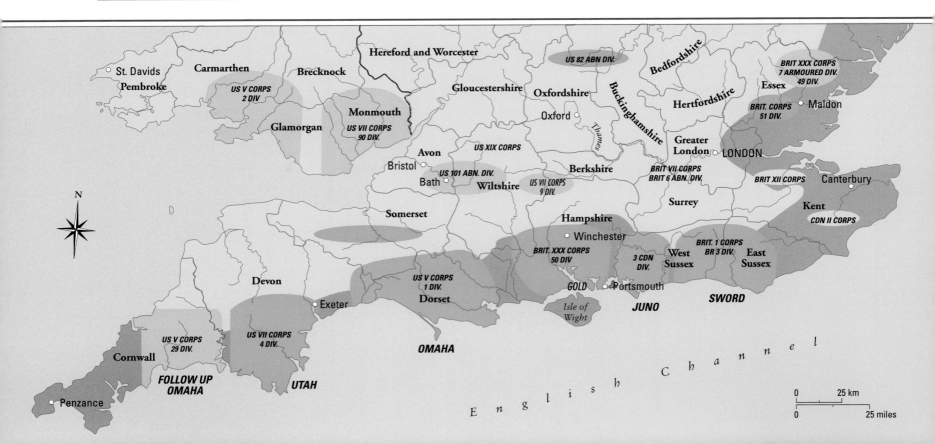

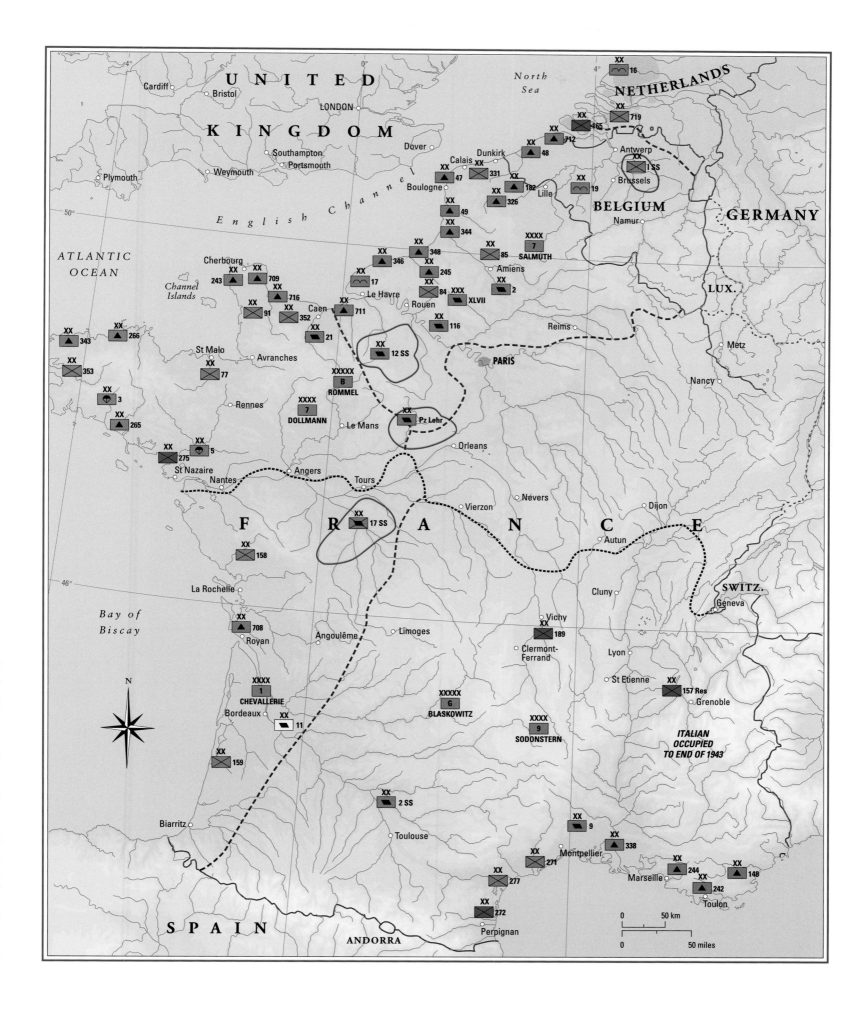

British Commandos move inland from Sword beach to relieve the Airborne troops on the bridges over the Caen Canal and the River Orne.

Five beaches had been code-named on each side of the Caretan Estuary: their names were, from west to east, Utah, Omaha, Gold, Juno, and Sword. The U.S. 7th Corps was to come ashore at Utah; the U.S. 5th Corps at Omaha; while in the east the British 30 Corps would land at Gold; and the British 1st Corp at Juno and Sword beaches (this Corp comprised the Canadian Infantry Division, coming ashore at Juno, and the British 3rd Infantry Division landing at Sword).

airborne divisions, whose vital task was to block the approaches to the landing beach that had been codenamed "Utah."

The first of the airborne troops to land, at 1:30 am on 6 June, was Major-General Maxwell Taylor's 101st Airborne Division, the "Screaming Eagles." Its task was to drop two miles behind Utah beach and secure the causeways leading to it. The landings were very scattered, with some men being dropped as much as ten miles from their D.Z. It took time for small groups of men to orientate themselves in the darkness. To help them identify one another, each man had been issued with a small metal object, which when pressed made a noise like a cricket. General Taylor parachuted with the 501st Regiment, whose D.Z. was just west of St-Marie-du-Mont. Luckily,

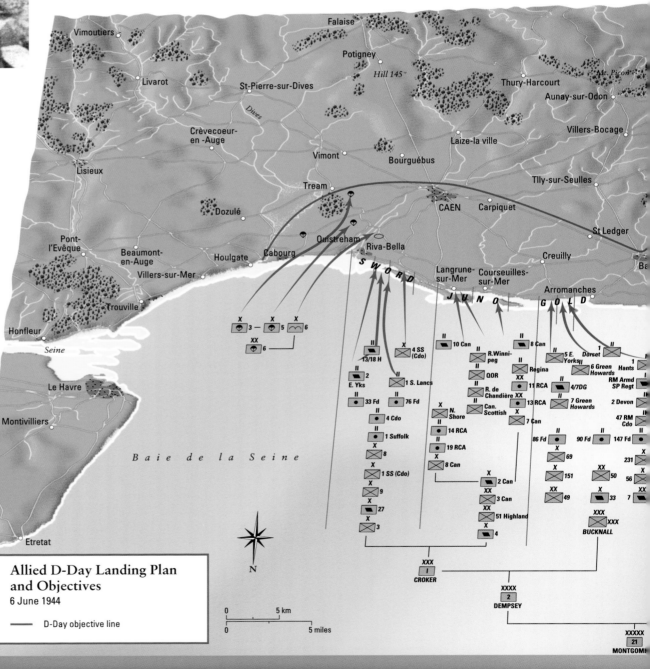

Allied D-Day Landing Plan and Objectives
6 June 1944

——— D-Day objective line

the regimental commander landed roughly in the right place. His key objective was the lock on the Douve River at La Barquette, since it was feared that the Germans might use it to flood the surrounding area. Major-General Matthew Ridgway's 82nd Airborne Division suffered much the same confusion. His D.Z.s were to the west of the 101st Airborne's and his overall task was to clear from the River Merderet east to the coast and to establish a bridgehead on the west bank of the river.

Far to the east, at the other end of the Allied landing beaches, the British 6th Airborne Division had experienced similar problems to the Americans. General Richard "Windy" Gale had the mission of landing between the Rivers Dives and Orne, securing bridges over both

U.S. paratroops moving towards their rendezvous in Normandy. They had numerous minor clashes with Germans on D-Day and had to be always on the lookout for surprise attack.

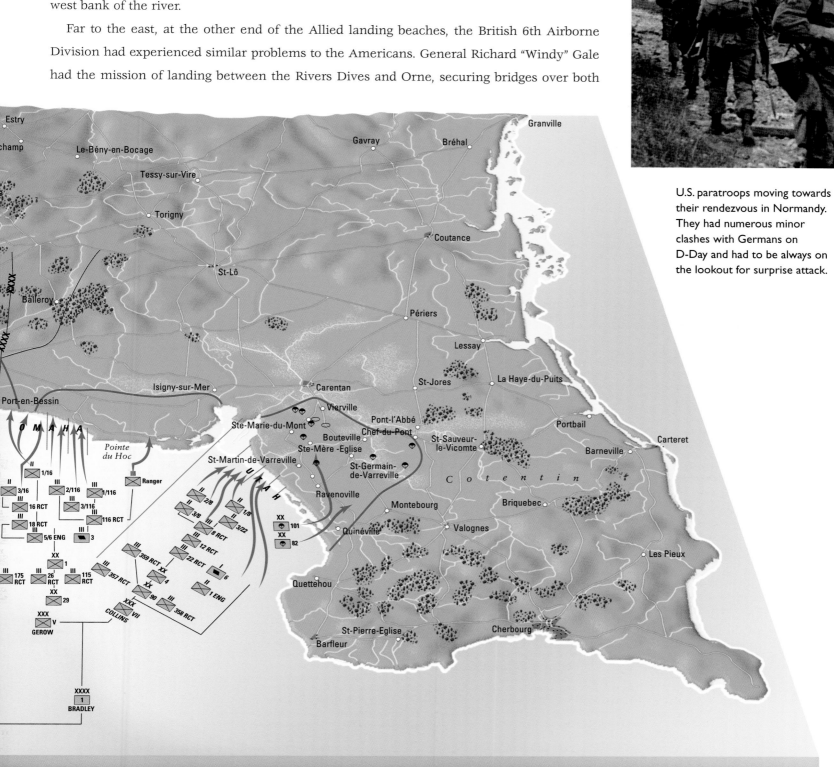

and providing a shoulder for the landings on Sword beach so that German reserves approaching from the east and south-east could be blocked. He also had to capture and destroy a coastal battery at Merville, which would otherwise be able to fire into the flank of the Sword landing.

The next phase of the plan was a daring glider operation. A company of the 2nd Oxfordshire and Buckinghamshire Light Infantry, under the command of Major John Howard, took off in six gliders, their objective the bridges over the River Orne and Caen Canal at Bénouville. Three gliders had been allocated to each bridge and all would land on the narrow strip between the two waterways.

There were other necessary preliminaries to the actual beach landings. First, bombers of R.A.F. Bomber Command attacked the coastal batteries, dropping almost 5,000 tons of bombs, including those used against the Merville Battery, mostly through heavy cloud. The bombers overcame this to a degree

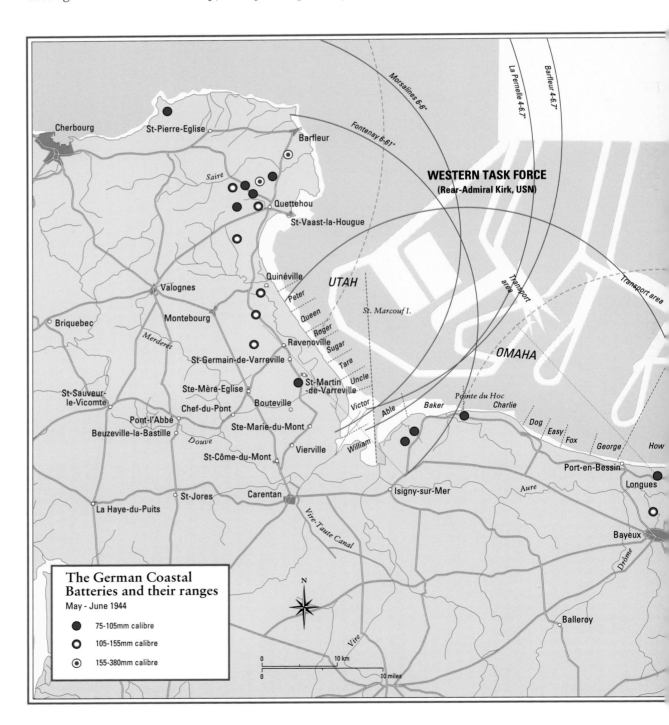

The German Coastal Batteries and their ranges

May - June 1944

● 75-105mm calibre

○ 105-155mm calibre

◉ 155-380mm calibre

through the use of "Oboe," a radar system fitted to Mosquitoes, the fast, light bombers that would mark the target for the heavier bombers. With the coming of daylight, the U.S. 8th and 9th Air Forces would join in, together with medium bombers, fighter-bombers, and fighters of the British 2nd Allies Tactical Air Force. The results of the campaign over the past few months to destroy the Luftwaffe in northern France and the Low Countries were now to be revealed. During D-Day the Allies flew almost 15,000 air sorties, while the Germans were able to manage only 319.

It was now the turn of the Allied navies. Each of the five task forces was preceded by minesweepers. Such was the success of their operations in clearing mines in the Channel that only two vessels were sunk in it on D-Day, a destroyer and an LST (Landing Ship Tank). By 2:00 am on 6 June the minesweepers were off the beaches. They had two tasks: to clear the approaches of mines and also

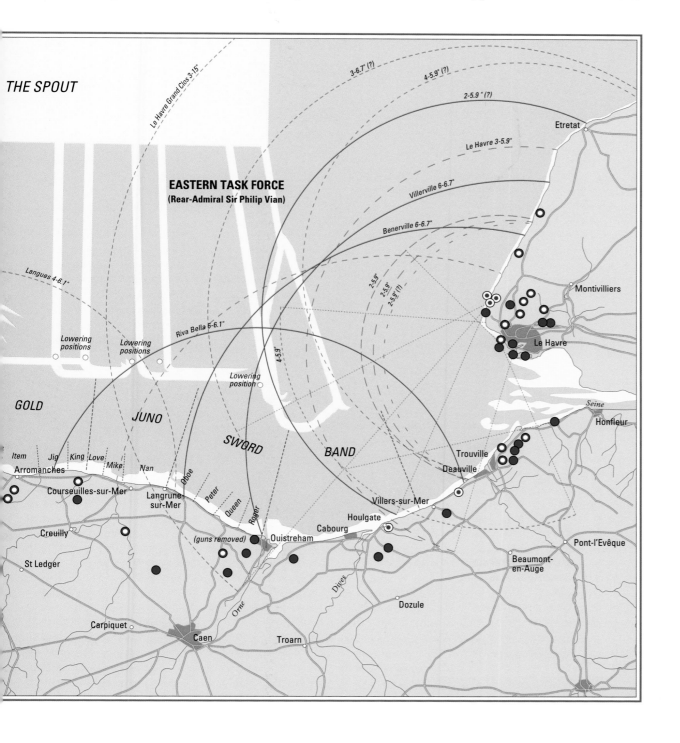

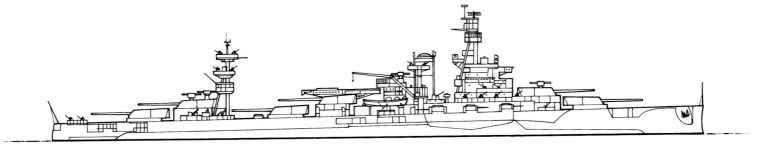

Launched in 1911, the USS *Arkanas* was the oldest U.S. battleship to serve in World War II. Her primary armament was twelve 12-inch guns and she supported the Omaha landings and the assault on Cherbourg.

the lanes that the bombarding ships would use. They faced a problem in that the Germans had laid several delayed-action mines, which remained on the sea bottom until activated. Consequently, continual sweeping was required and no stretch of water could be guaranteed totally free of mines. This was, in fact, the major cause of loss of Allied ships off Normandy.

The bombarding ships' task was to silence the German coastal batteries and they were organized in three groups. The heavier vessels in each task force—battleships, monitors, and cruisers—were positioned some 11,000 yards from the coast and operated in lanes parallel to the shoreline, in which they could maneuver. The destroyers, on the other hand, had to approach within 5,500 yards and then anchor. Although this made them more vulnerable to German fire, they would be less prone to falling victim to the delayed-action mines.

It was the Germans who opened fire first. With the coming of dawn, they began to spot ships through

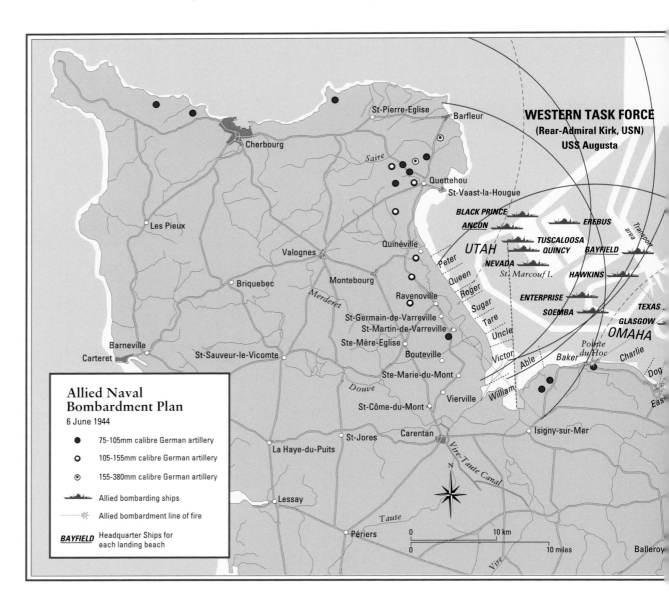

Allied Naval Bombardment Plan
6 June 1944

● 75-105mm calibre German artillery

○ 105-155mm calibre German artillery

◉ 155-380mm calibre German artillery

⎯⎯ Allied bombarding ships

········✳ Allied bombardment line of fire

BAYFIELD Headquarter Ships for each landing beach

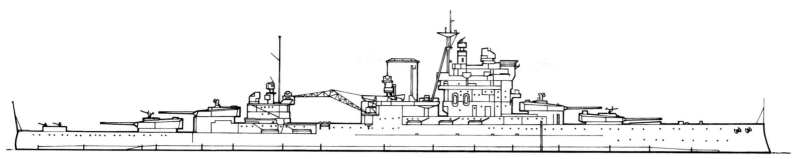

the murk. At 5:05 am a battery opened fire on the destroyers USS *Fitch* and USS *Corry* off Utah beach. Utah was the responsibility of General J. Lawton Collins' U.S. 7th Corps. He was a veteran of the Pacific campaigns on Guadalcanal and New Georgia, now tasked with cutting off the Cotentin peninsula and securing Cherbourg. Utah itself was less than a mile and a half long and characterized by gently sloping sand backed by a sea wall, between four and twelve feet high. Behind the beach there was some flooding, which made the causeways leading inland from the beach vital. Because the beach was relatively narrow, Collins decided that the initial landing would be made by just one reinforced Regimental Combat Team (R.C.T.) of the 4th Infantry Division. This was to advance off the beach to the River Merderet and link up with the airborne troops. Eighty-five minutes after H-hour (the time of the actual first attack), a second R.C.T. would land and move north to secure the high ground around Quinéville. The 4th Division's final R.C.T. would land at H + 4 hours, advance northwest and

The battleship HMS *Warspite*. A veteran of Jutland in May 1916, she also saw extensive service in World War II, including Norway in 1940 and the Mediterranean. On D-Day her eight 15-inch guns were used to silence German batteries at Villerville.

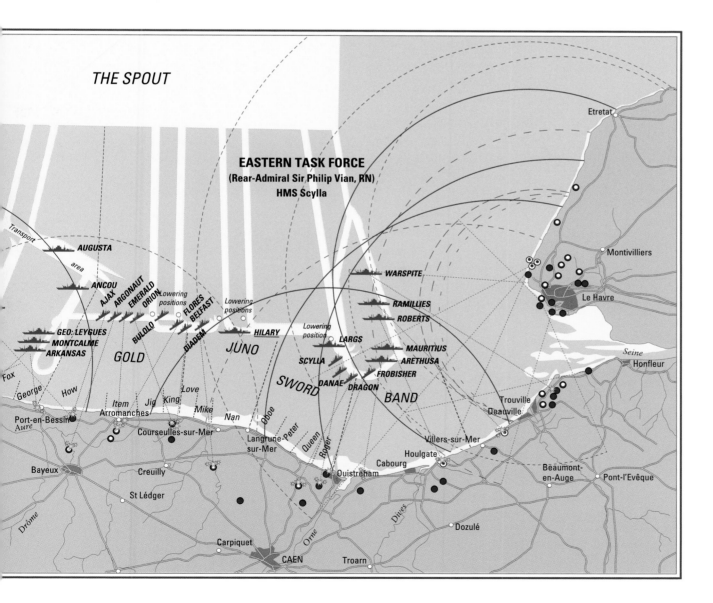

THE SPOUT

EASTERN TASK FORCE
(Rear-Admiral Sir Philip Vian, RN)
HMS Scylla

seize a crossing over the Merderet. Finally, a Reserve R.C.T., from 90th Division, would also land. Amphibious Sherman D.D. tanks would also float ashore to support the first wave of troops landing.

The landings for Utah began at 6:30 am, with the amphibious tanks supporting 116th R.C.T. launched. Almost immediately, some tanks began to founder in the rough sea and only five out of thirty-two reached the shore. Three survived only thanks to the L.C.T. commander pulling up his ramp when the first of the tanks he was carrying submerged. Those carrying the tanks to support the other R.C.T. also ran into the shore and landed them one minute before H-hour. Some of the landing craft in the leading waves were swamped during the run-in and as a result, almost all their supporting field artillery was lost. Poor visibility and the current played its part, as on Utah, with troops landing in the wrong place and being disorientated. Many landed shoulder-

British medical orderlies tend a badly-wounded German officer, Normandy 1944.

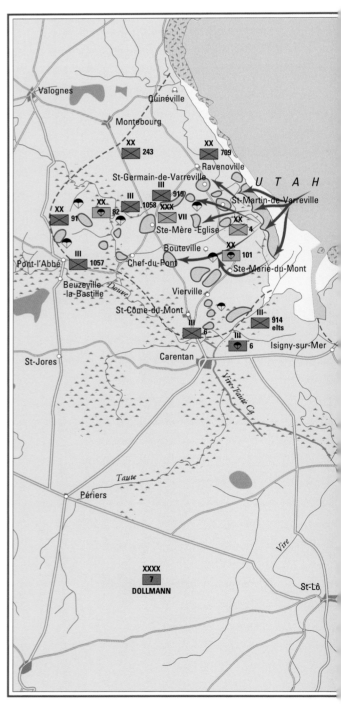

deep in water and struggled to get ashore with all the equipment they were carrying. Under intense German fire, many fell. Those who did make it onto dry land sought shelter under the sea wall or among the beach obstacles, but found that many of their radios did not work. Officers running between groups to try to restore cohesion were shot down, and confusion reigned.

Some six miles east of Omaha was the westernmost of the British beaches, Gold. The terrain here was somewhat different to Omaha. The beach was fringed merely by low sand dunes and behind it lay somewhat boggy ground intersected by dykes. One problem was that much of the foreshore was made up of blue clay, which made it difficult for vehicles to traverse. Gold beach lay in the eastern part of 352nd Division's sector and was covered by two battalions, supported by the Division's mobile reserve, which consisted of a further three battalions. The beaches had both underwater and exposed obstacles, which included mines attached to posts. There were also plenty of strongpoints overlooking the beach and the villages were well fortified.

The Royal Marine Commando was given a special task of landing on the extreme right flank of 231st Brigade and then advancing west to seize Port-en-Bessin and link up with the Americans who were battling their way up Omaha. Sword beach presented many of the same problems as Juno when it came to suitable landing points. It was divided into four sub-sectors—Oboe, Peter, Queen, and Roger.

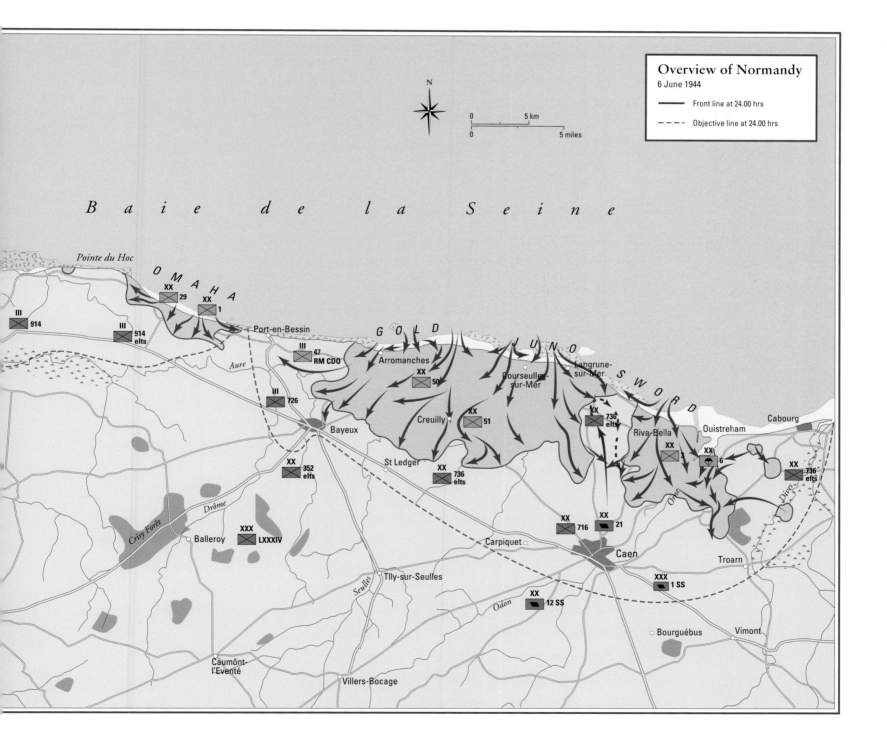

Overview of Normandy

6 June 1944

——— Front line at 24.00 hrs

- - - - Objective line at 24.00 hrs

Rocks prevented access to Oboe, Peter, and the western end of Queen. Roger, too, was beset by shoals. Queen was the only possible landing beach and only one brigade could land at a time. Behind the beaches the ground was generally low-lying, apart from the high ground that ran to Caen on the east flank.

The Allies had fought their way ashore in reasonable order, except for Omaha where bloody fighting had taken place. The U.S. 1st and 29th Divisions, despite all odds, had fought through terrible obstacles and intense small arms fire to seize the heights beyond the beach. While they had failed to secure many of their objectives, the Allies could feel content. They had succeeded in landing 150,000 men in Normandy at a cost of 9,000 casualties, less than many had feared. The experience gained during the previous years of amphibious operations had proved invaluable. But much still needed to be done. The five beachheads had to be linked up and expanded. Follow-up forces needed to be landed quickly so that the initial success could be exploited. At the same time, while a major German counterattack had not materialized on D-Day itself, it was certain to come soon. As for the Germans, the day had been bewildering, catching many by surprise. Yet they were still unconvinced that Normandy was the invasion area. An assault elsewhere was still possible. They were cheered to learn that, having driven back from Germany, Rommel had returned to his headquarters on the evening of D-Day. With a significant armored force now gathering, there was still time to defeat the Allies.

The main concern was still Omaha beach, one that General Omar Bradley, commanding the U.S. 1st Army, shared. Apart from the fact that its beachhead was the shallowest of the five, there was a yawning gap between it and the British 2nd Army, which could be easily exploited by Rommel. Montgomery therefore decided that he would have to postpone U.S. 7th Corps' advance to Cherbourg from Utah beach. Instead, it was to link up with Omaha. To keep the Germans

U.S. Infantrymen fight their way through a ruined French village.

distracted, the British and Canadians were to continue to advance inland. To Rommel, sitting in his headquarters at the La Roche Guyon château, on a loop in the Seine near Bonnières, Caen and Cherbourg were the two principal areas of interest. As long as both were held, the Allies would have neither a firm left flank nor a useful port.

Meanwhile, the Allies continued to grind on. West of Caen, the Canadians attacked on 3 July, their objective Carpiquet airfield. They managed to secure the village of the same name but their old adversary, 12th S.S. Panzer Division, denied them the airfield. This, however, was a mere preliminary to the main assault on Caen. General Miles Dempsey, commanding the British 2nd Army, decided that maximum firepower was the key that would unlock the door.

That night 450 heavy bombers blasted the northern outskirts. At 11:00 pm the artillery opened fire, pounding the German positions. At 4:20 am on 8 June, 90 minutes before sunrise, the D-Day veterans of 3rd Infantry Division and the newly-arrived 59th Division attacked. Numbed by the ferocity of the preparatory bombardment, the Germans in the forward defenses succumbed quickly. The 3rd Canadian Division now began to attack from the west. By the end of the day it and the British 3rd Division had advanced two and a half miles, but 59th Division's progress was not as good, resulting in a two-mile gap between the former two formations. But the pressure on 12th S.S. Panzer Division had become almost unbearable and that night General Heinrich Eberbach agreed that all German forces around and in the city could withdraw to the south bank of the Odon.

The Americans, too, had begun to press south. Montgomery's concept was for them to now swing south and east from Caumont and then attack into Brittany as well as breaking out eastward. To Bradley the crucial first objective to enable all this to happen was the road communications center at St-Lô. With his 14 divisions now in place, outnumbering the Germans opposite 1st Army by at least three to one, it appeared straightforward. The terrain, however, was against him. Along the 50 miles of American front there were no open areas where he could deploy armor en masse. In the east the deep valley of the River Vire and the tenacious German hold on St-Lô itself gave him few options. The center of the sector

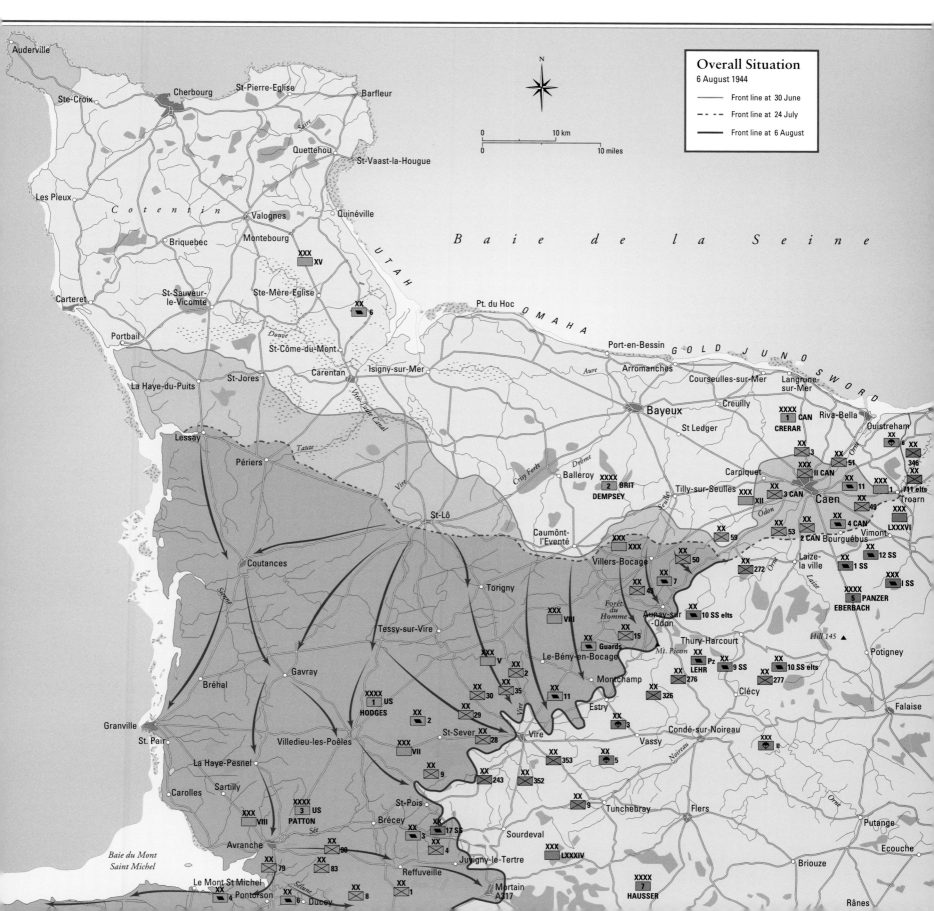

Overall Situation
6 August 1944

Front line at 30 June
Front line at 24 July
Front line at 6 August

was dominated by flooding with just one decent road, running from Carentan to Périers, while the west was covered with thickly-wooded hills and ridges. Nevertheless, to Bradley the right flank seemed to offer the best prospects, and it was here that the U.S. 8th Corps kicked off the offensive on 3 July. Its opponent was the German 84th Corps, formerly commanded by one-legged General Erich Marcks, who had been killed by a U.S. fighter-bomber on 12 June, and now under General Dietrich von Choltitz. He took maximum advantage of the terrain to make the American advance slow and costly. The U.S. 19th and 7th Corps experienced much the same frustration and by 10 July Bradley was forced to call a halt,

French inhabitants return to their shattered homes after the fighting had passed on. In the liberation of Normandy over 12,000 civilians lost their lives in the battle for freedom.

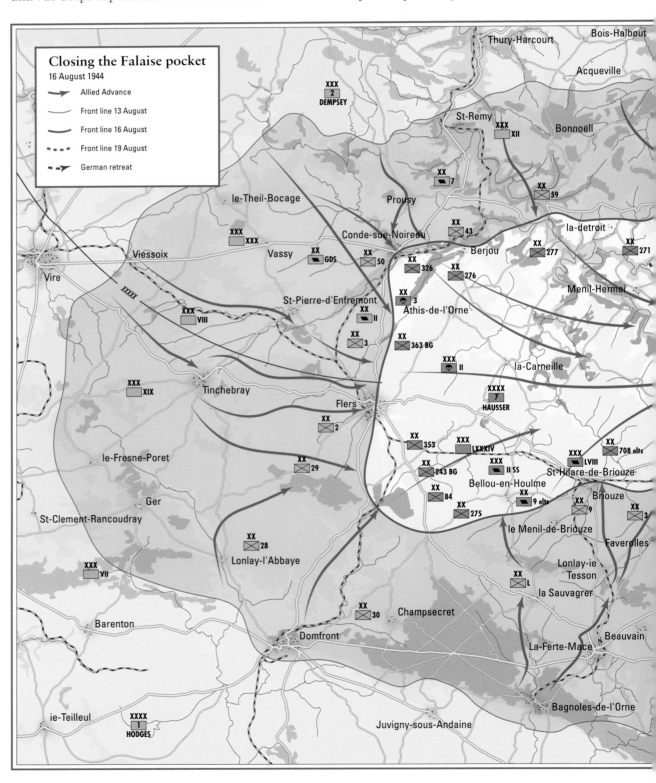

Closing the Falaise pocket
16 August 1944

→ Allied Advance

— Front line 13 August

— Front line 16 August

••• Front line 19 August

- ◄ German retreat

with St-Lô still firmly in German hands. But the attrition was having its effect. The German 88th Corps warned: "The struggle cannot be maintained with the present forces for any length of time."

The American forces broke through by launching Operation Cobra, sweeping south and west into Brittany. Other elements of the U.S. forces headed to Rennes, then turned east sweeping all before them heading for Le Mans, then turning north to Alençon and Argentan. Here they were to meet the British and Canadians heading south from the battles around Caen. Despite disagreements, the Allies closed in on the retreating Germans at Falaise. Falaise marked the final phase in the Battle for Normandy.

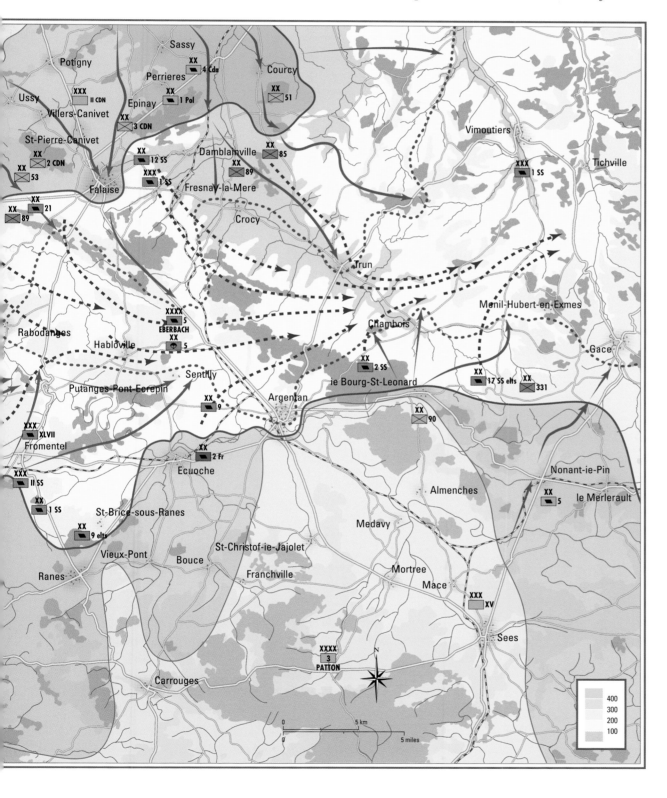

The bloody remains of the retreating German army in the Falaise pocket at the end of the battle of Normandy.

ASSAULT OF SOUTHERN FRANCE

"WHERE ARE WE GOING? WE ARE GOING TO HOLD TILL HELL FREEZES OVER OR WE ARE RELIEVED, WHICH EVER COMES FIRST."

LT.-COLONEL WILLIAM P. YARBOROUGH, COMMANDER OF 509TH PARACHUTE BATTALION

The planning for the invasion of southern France went through many drafts before the final concept was born. Churchill was keen for a landing to be made in the Balkan region so as to place British troops on the eastern front and achieve a presence there before Soviet Communism brought the region under its control. However, U.S. commanders only saw this as Churchill trying to stake a colonial claim and dismissed the plan. Originally the idea was for a simultaneous assault with that of Operation Overlord, the invasion of Normandy, but this was not to be as the Allies did not have the necessary amount of landing craft to support both ventures.

The plan was to land the U.S. 6th Corps, under the command of Trusscott, made up of three divisions on the French Riviera, between the Golfe de Napoule and the Baie de Cavalaire, flanked by French Commandoes and the U.S. 1st Special Service Force. There was also to be an airborne landing made up of Anglo-American forces, combining to form the 1st Airborne Task Force, which was to be dropped near Le Muy in order to cause havoc behind the lines. Following up these assaulting Corps was French Army B, comprising seven divisions under the command of General de Lattre de Tassigny. The air support was to be supplied by the 12th Tactical Army Air Force flying from bases on Corsica and Sardinia, which itself was to be supplemented by fighter aircraft from seven Royal Navy and two U.S. carriers.

Opposing the Allied Task Force were around ten German divisions under the command of General Blaskowitz with only three divisions in the immediate area of the assault beaches. Air superiority was enjoyed by the Allies, since the Germans could only muster 200 aircraft to the 2,000 Allied.

The landings were, as usual, preceded by a massive aerial and naval bombardment. Underwater demolition teams of sappers were also sent in to clear paths through the extensive underwater obstacles. The 3rd Division landed with relative ease on the western beach known as Alphe Beach, thanks to the bombardment neutralizing the defenders, with a similar landing for the 45th Division on Delta Beach. On Camel Beach, where the 36th Division landed, they encountered thick enemy minefields

U.S troops arrive in the old port of Marseilles at the beginning of Operation Dragoon. As the invasion developed it became clear the Germans would offer less resistance than anticipated and, indeed, they began a fighting withdrawal to the north. It became known to the men as the "Champagne Campaign."

as well as dug in machine gun posts that took a serious toll on the soldiers assaulting. By the end of the day a strong bridgehead had been achieved. The following day saw the link up of troops moving inland from the beach with the airborne units.

Once through the main line of defense on and around the shoreline, the strategy was one of pursuit and entrapment, so Truscott struck northwest toward Avignon and north toward Sisteron. The French II Corps turned toward the two ports of Toulon and Marseilles and expected a strong fight as Hitler had given the order for them to become "fortresses" and hold out in order to deprive the Allies of any useful port. The French attacked to the rear of Toulon, which was protected by three fortified hills, with the port protected from the sea by massive guns taken from a scuttled French Battleship *La Provence*. The hills were taken by 23 August and the French began to assault the port itself, with bombardments from the sea aiding them. These bombardments took a heavy toll on the German defenders and Allied ships sailed into the harbor on the 26th, with the formal surrender of the German defenders on 28 August.

By the beginning of September the American forces had swept northward, giving chase to the German division past Grenoble and Valence, though the strong resistance of 11th Panzer Division aided in Blauskowitz's Armys' escape north before it could be trapped. Lyon fell on 3 September shortly followed by Dijon on 11 September, only a day after Truscott's forces had joined up with elements of Patton's 3rd Army. Then on 15 September all the Dragoon forces were placed under the command of Eisenhower, with their advance slowing because it was outstretching its supply columns coming up from the south, the Dragoon forces had managed to advance some 400 miles in 40 days.

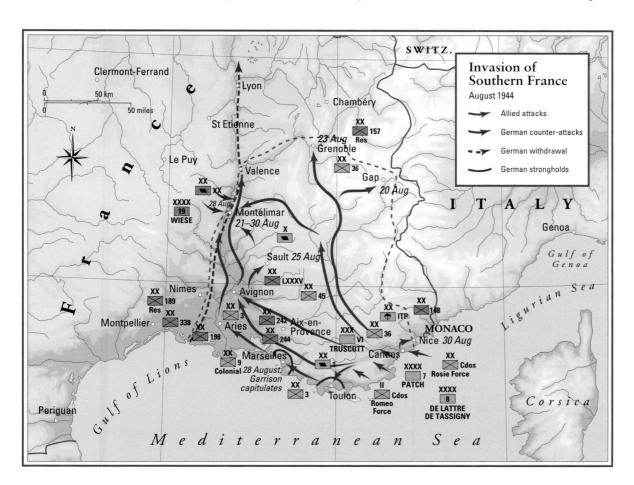

LIBERATION OF PARIS AND BRUSSELS

"ATTENDED A THANKSGIVING SERVICE ... FOR THE LIBERATION OF PARIS ... HEARING THE MARSEILLAISE GAVE ME A GREAT THRILL. FRANCE SEEMED TO WAKE AGAIN."

GENERAL SIR ALAN BROOKE, CHIEF OF IMPERIAL GENERAL STAFF

With the Allied forces beginning to break out from the Battle of Normandy, the population of Paris began to feel that liberation was almost upon them, the railroad workers and the police going on strike on 10 and 15 August respectively. This was to be followed by a general strike of all the capital's workers on 18 August. In reality, Eisenhower wanted to delay the liberation of Paris for as long as possible. It would divert vital supplies that were still coming ashore over the beachheads to feeding the population of a major city instead of feeding and fueling his troops in the headlong pursuit of the Germans. But as the civil population grew bolder and began to build barricades in the streets and attack at the German garrison, Eisenhower had no choice but to divert forces for the liberation.

De Gaulle insisted that the forces to liberate Paris were to be French and for this task he chose elements of General leClerc's 2nd Armored Division. This unit was fighting with the U.S. 5th Corps under General Gerow at the time, and he was ordered to send a force of ten armored cars and a similar number of tanks to drive for the capital immediately. Fighting in the capital between the Germans and the civilian population had reached a critical point by the time the French force entered Paris. General Choltitz, the commander of the garrison, had been given explicit orders from the Führer to fight for

General Charles de Gaulle walks along the Champs Elysées in Paris, the city of his youth, amongst scenes of great jubilation from the crowd.

every brick and stone of Paris. This was one order he was not to carry out: no one would want to be known in history as the destroyer of such art and architecture. Choltitz signed the surrender document on the afternoon of 25 August. Many of his troops did put down their arms, although not immediately, for fear of attacks of retribution from the population of the city, eager for revenge after years of exploitation and occupation. A victory parade was organized hastily for the next day down the Champs Elysées, with the crowd under occasional sniper attack. Another parade was held for the U.S. liberators on 28 August.

Meanwhile, the Allied forces were flooding across the Seine and

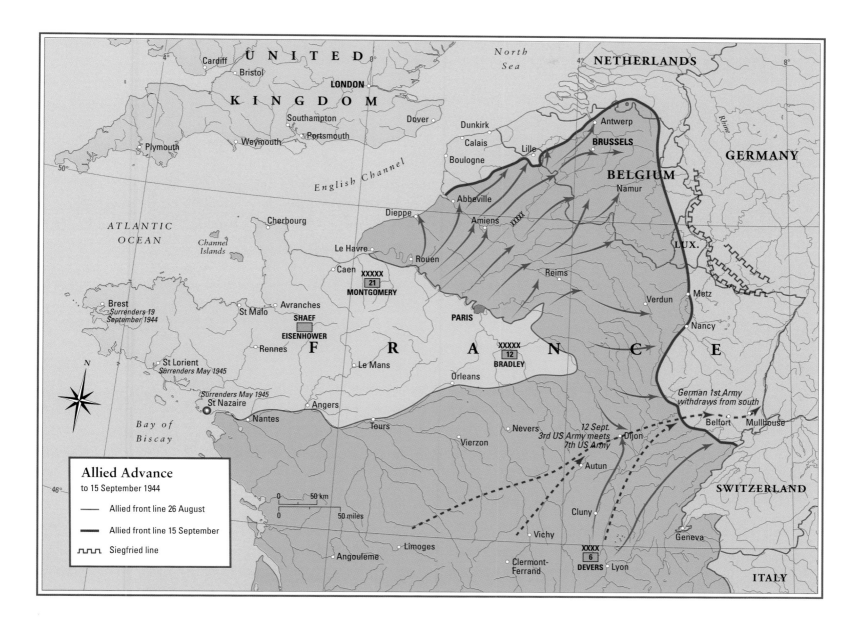

any useable bridge, with pontoon bridges being built at any appropriate point. The Allied pursuit gained momentum, fighting only small skirmishes, trying not to let the enemy use any of the rivers on the line of its retreat as a defensive position. Montgomery's 21st Army Group advanced on the left, the Canadians captured the ports of Le Havre, Dieppe, Boulogne, and Calais, while British 2nd Army drove onto Amiens and Lille. South of Montgomery's group was Hodge's 1st Army, which had taken Mons and Tournai on 2 September, and was now heading toward the Meuse and the German border. Further south was Patton's 3rd Army, which was advancing at an astonishing rate. However, by the end of August, the enemy was not to be the Germans but a severe lack of fuel, and the Allied advance came to a standstill.

When the British heard of the capture of Tournai they felt confident that nearby Brussels could be taken with just as much ease. The Guards Armored Division, which was in the vanguard of the British advance, was ordered to race ahead and capture the city. This they did within 24 hours of receipt of the order, to be greeted, not by the enemy, but by a throng of joyous Belgians, lining the streets in their thousands. Yet another city had been liberated from the dying Nazi empire.

OPERATION MARKET GARDEN

"HAND GRENADES FLEW IN EVERY DIRECTION. EACH HOUSE HAD TO BE TAKEN THIS WAY. SOME OF THE BRITISH OFFERED RESISTANCE TO THEIR LAST BREATH."

GERMAN SOLDIER, ARNHEM

Operation Market Garden becomes a reality. Airspeed Horsa gliders are unloaded as more troops arrive by parachute.

Operation Market Garden was a plan conceived by Field Marshal Montgomery as a means of flanking the German defensive line known as the West Wall, or Seigfried Line, and driving down into the industrial heartland of Germany—the Ruhr—from the Netherlands, bringing the war in the west to a close. It would also secure a crossing point for the mighty Rhine River, which the Germans regarded as their strongest defensive line. The mission was to use the First Allied Airborne Army under the tactical command of Lt-General Browning, made up of two American divisions, the veteran 82nd and 101st, and the British 1st. These divisions were to be dropped behind the lines to seize the bridges over eight waterways in Holland for the 30th Corps to utilize, as it broke through the lines to eventually meet up with the 1st Division dropped around Arnhem. The 30th Corps only had one narrow road to advance up and would be very susceptible to flanking attacks, these were to be contained by the 43rd and 50th Divisions covering the flanks.

The "Market" part of the plan involved the airborne forces, the 101st Division, under the command of Major-General Maxwell Taylor, which would drop nearest to the 30th Corps start line at Eindhoven. To the north would be the 82nd Division, under Major-General Gavin, taking the bridges at Grave and Nijmegan. Just to the northeast would be the 1st Airborne Division, taking the final bridge at Arnhem over the Lower Rhine, under General Roy Urquart. This massive undertaking was to be the largest Airborne Operation of World War II, even eclipsing those of Operation Overlord the previous June. Nearly 35,000 men were to be dropped in the operation, but due to lack of air transport for them all they would have to be dropped over several days.

The "Garden" part of the plan would concern the 30th Corps' rapid advance up the single highway, through all towns and bridges captured by the airborne troops for an eventual link up with the 1st Airborne at Arnhem. To cover the 60-odd miles to Arnhem, General Horrocks, commander of 30th Corps, said they would have three days. Battles, however, tend not to run to strict timetables. Intelligence from the Dutch Resistance also indicated that there were two German Panzer Divisions refitting in the area north of Arnhem, although these were deemed not to be strong enough to pose any real threat to the operation. In fact, these forces were up to strength and full of veteran soldiers who had spent time fighting bloody battles on the Eastern Front, as well as being augmented by the crack troops of 1st Parachute Army under the command of Kurt Student.

In the early afternoon of 17 September the 2,800 troop-carrying aircraft and 1,600 gliders also packed with troops, Jeeps, and artillery, droned their way over the Dutch countryside, protected by over 1,200 fighter escorts. All the troops managed to hit their respective drop zones with ease and with surprisingly few casualties, mostly down to jump injuries. The 101st Division achieved all their objectives bar one: the bridge over the Wilhelmina Canal at Son was blown up as elements of the division were approaching. However, this could be easily solved by a Bailey Bridge that the 30th Corps were bringing with them. The 82nd managed to secure the bridge at Grave but could not force a crossing of the two main spans in Nijmegan. In the British drop zone, the troops had landed safely but were over seven miles from the bridge at Arnhem. This, coupled with the loss of the majority of their Jeep transportation in crashed gliders, meant that only the leading battalion, the 2nd Battalion—under Lt-Colonel John Frost—reached the northern end of the bridge by the end of the day and consolidated their positions. However, because only half the British force had been flown in, the other half already in Holland had to stay and defend the drop zones. This meant that Frost's battalion would not be

Operation Market Garden – The Air Lift
17 September 1944

▭	Allied-held territory
▭	German-held territory
▦	German flak concentrations
⬭	52nd Troop Carrier Wing Bases USAAF
⬭	53rd Troop Carrier Wing Bases USAAF
⬭	38 and 46 Groups RAF

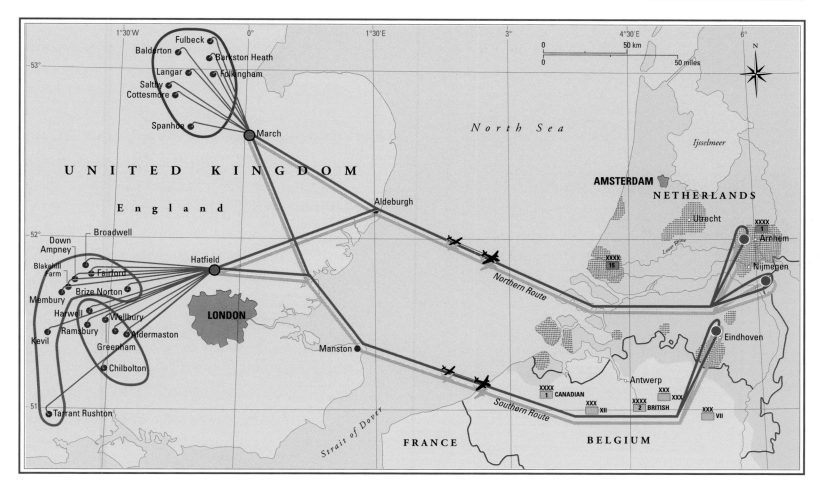

The U.S. 82nd "All American" descend on their drop zones near Nijmegen.

reinforced for a further 24 hours. Frost's men did attempt a crossing of the bridge twice that afternoon but were repelled both times. With the 2nd Battalion on the northern end of the bridge and the other two battalions of the brigade fighting in the outskirts and Oosterbeek, problems arose with communication. The radio sets that had been issued were not working well, or at all, and others were destroyed in the fighting. This meant that commanders could not keep in contact with each other. Urquart could not, therefore, have a clear view of the outcome of the battle and the Division could not communicate with fighter bombers for support. This led Urquart to try and reach the bridge himself. Having to dodge German patrols and hiding in a Dutch loft for many hours, he was out of touch with his troops, while the German defense was getting more organized and stronger.

The 30th Corps advance did not begin until after the Paratroops had landed, their advance soon ran into dug-in antitank positions on either side of the road. The armored column made an easy target for the German gunners, the only road being on a raised embankment above the surrounding countryside. This slowed the advance considerably, because the enemy guns had to be systematically destroyed before the Corps could move on. They had not reached Eindhoven by dusk.

The following day, the second half of the lift brought in three more battalions of paratroops into the Arnhem area, as the two other battalions tried in vain to reach Frost's men on the bridge. In the 82nd sector the drop zone defenders were beaten off by a vicious German counterattack. However, the paras countered and cleared the drop zone half an hour before the reinforcements arrived. In the 101st area the troops were still waiting for a Bailey Bridge to be bought up, which eventually arrived at dusk.

On the morning of the third day, the British paras again attempted to break through to the bridge but took a severe mauling and were forced to fall back to Oosterbeek. Frost's men on the northern end of the bridge, having fended off infantry attacks successfully, were being heavily mortared and shelled. Many houses were demolished and heavy casualties were taken, but still they hung onto that small part of Holland. That morning, on the American front, 30th Corps arrived and joined with 82nd Division, immediately assaulting the bridge. This was beaten back, so a plan was drawn up for another attack to go in while a battalion of paras crossed the river in boats about a mile upstream and attacked the bridge from the rear. However, the troops had another long wait while the assault boats were bought up from the rear. All this time the situation was getting worse for the men in Arnhem. In the 101st sector enemy tanks attempted to fire on the Bailey Bridge, but this attack was soon beaten off.

These American paratroopers move rapidly along a Dutch street, dodging ever-present sniper fire.

During the fourth day, things went from bad to worse for Frost's men. Because they lacked antitank ammunition the Germans could enter the British positions and open fire at point blank range on them and the houses they were sheltered in, causing many buildings to catch fire, with high casualties, including Colonel Frost himself. A truce was held so the injured could be evacuated to German care. Out of ammunition and without hope of reinforcement, the men defending the bridge had no choice but to surrender. Many tried to escape and some were taken in by the Dutch townsfolk to hide until an opportunity came for escape. The men in the Oosterbeek area continued to resist German attacks, successfully thwarting an attempt to cut them off from the Rhine, their only route of escape. In Nijmegen the assault boats eventually arrived in the afternoon and a hasty attack was laid on using the 3rd Battalion of the 504th Paratroop Infantry Regiment to paddle over the river in boats. This attack was to become known by the men as 'Little Omaha' in reference to the high losses taken at both actions. About half the battalion made it across and then had to fight over 218 yards of ground with no cover, eventually forcing back the Germans from both ends of the bridge. The 101st Division was having problems with repeated attacks by German Panther tanks attempting to cut the road, denying any supplies to the forward elements, but these attacks were beaten back with ferocious bravery.

The men in the Oosterbeek pocket continued to wait for the 30th Corps to arrive but to no avail. Lt-General Brian Horrocks, Commander of 30th Corps, although across the Waal at Nijmegen, refused

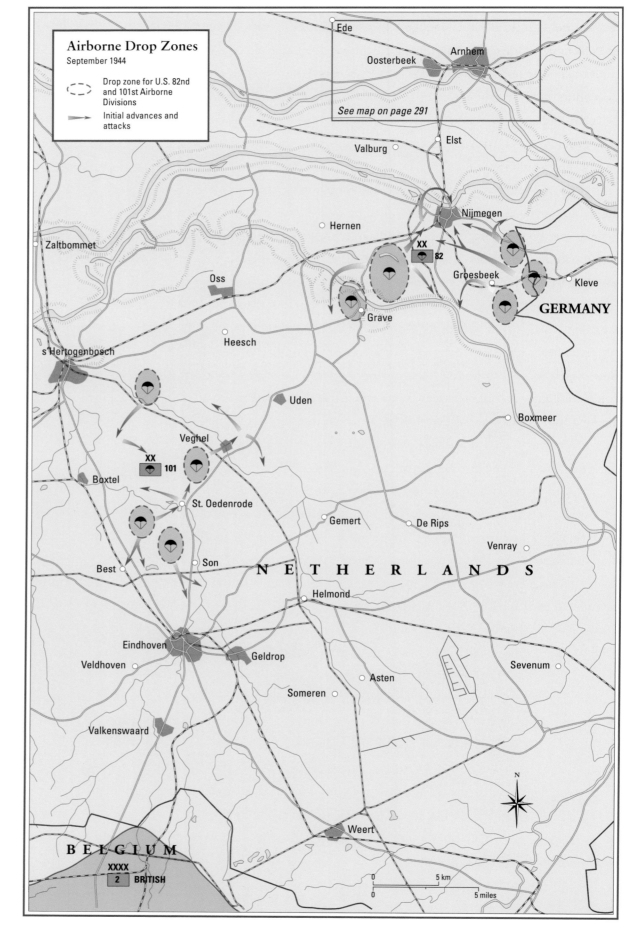

Airborne Drop Zones

September 1944

- - - Drop zone for U.S. 82nd and 101st Airborne Divisions

→ Initial advances and attacks

See map on page 291

Ede

Oosterbeek   Arnhem

Valburg   Elst

Nijmegen

Hernen   XX 82

Zaltbommet

Oss   Groesbeek   Kleve

Grave   **GERMANY**

Heesch

s'Hertogenbosch

Uden   Boxmeer

Veghel

XX 101

Boxtel   St. Oedenrode

Gemert   De Rips

Venray

Best   Son   **N E T H E R L A N D S**

Helmond

Eindhoven

Veldhoven   Geldrop   Sevenum

Asten

Someren

Valkenswaard

N

Weert

B E L G I U M

XXXX
2 **BRITISH**

0   5 km
0   5 miles

Two paratroopers of the 1st British Airborne Division advance cautiously through the ruins of a schoolhouse in the town of Arnhem

to go forward while his troops were in such a confused state, as over half the Guards Armored Division were engaged elsewhere, including helping the 82nd clear the town of Nijmegen. The Polish 1st Parachute Infantry were dropped opposite the British at Dreil, but could not find a place to cross to aid the beleaguered force, so had to resign themselves to digging in around Dreil town. The 101st also continued to fend off attempts to cut the road southeast of Arnhem with bravery and skill.

The next day the British Airborne Division, despite facing less men, was being constantly pounded by artillery. The Germans had pulled some men out to face the Poles on the other side of the river, fearing they would try to assault the southern end of the bridge, cutting off the 10th S.S. Panzer facing 30th Corps. Attempts were made to cross troops over to the north bank of the Rhine, but this was under German observation and heavy casualties were incurred and the attempt called off.

Over the weekend, fighting continued, with the Germans again trying to cut off the British paras from the Rhine with heavy losses on both sides. Also an attempt to put across a battalion of the Dorset Regiment ended in disaster when only 75 of the 315 that crossed managed to reach the paras. After this attempt the decision was made to evacuate the paras from the north shore and establish the new front line south of Nijmegen.

Having managed to hold off a major attack by the German S.S. (Schutzstaffel) on Monday, that same night the remnants of the 1st Airborne were ferried over by engineers under the cover of darkness. Out of the 10,000 men sent into Arnhem about 2,500 managed to make it back across the Rhine. Nearly 1,500 had died in the undertaking and the rest were captured, of which half were wounded.

The road bridge at Arnhem, the famous 'Bridge too Far', in a photograph taken shortly after the battle.

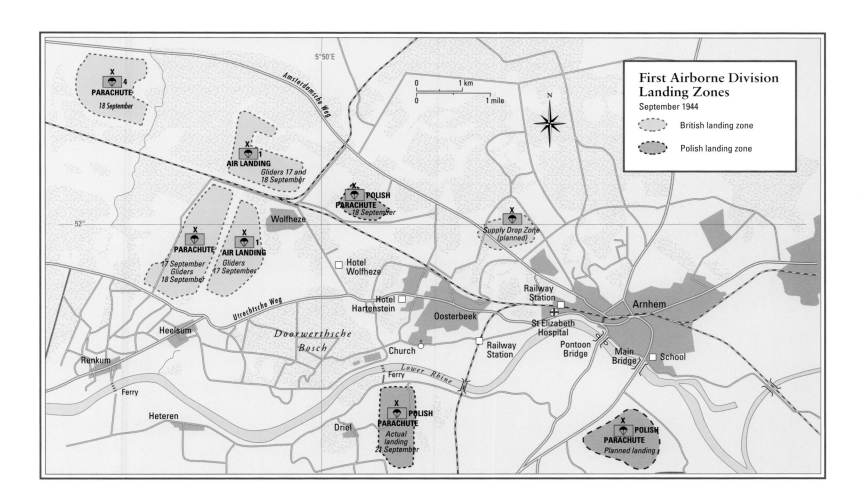

First Airborne Division Landing Zones

September 1944

British landing zone

Polish landing zone

CARRIERS IN THE PACIFIC 1941–45

"THE UNITED STATES POSSESSES TODAY CONTROL OF THE SEA MORE ABSOLUTE THAN WAS POSSESSED BY THE BRITISH. OUR INTEREST IN THIS CONTROL IS NOT RICHES AND POWER AS SUCH. IT IS FIRST THE ASSURANCE OF OUR NATIONAL SECURITY, AND, SECOND, THE CREATION AND PERPETUATION OF THAT BALANCE AND STABILITY AMONG NATIONS WHICH WILL INSURE TO EACH THE RIGHT OF SELF-DETERMINATION UNDER THE FRAMEWORK OF THE UNITED NATIONS ORGANIZATION."

FLEET ADMIRAL CHESTER W. NIMITZ, U.S. NAVY

O f the world's major navies involved in World War II only four possessed aircraft carriers: the United States, Great Britain, Japan, and France. Only two of these—the United States and Japan—had developed the striking power of these ships beyond the role of supporting the heavy guns of the battle fleet.

In the Washington Naval Treaty, signed in 1922, Britain, the United States, and Japan agreed to a 5:5:3 ratio with the U.S. allowed 525,000 tons. Existing aircraft carriers would be classed as experimental but could be replaced at any time, yet limited to 27,000 tons. Under the same Treaty, Japan was prohibited from fortifying her Pacific territories and island possessions. Therefore, the Japanese were obliged to study and develop an aircraft carrier force to protect its battle fleet. The U.S. regarded Japan as its major threat in the Pacific and decided to develop seaborne air power. Capital ship hulls, which would have been scrapped under the Treaty, were converted into aircraft carriers. Both the U.S. and Japan therefore acquired large carriers with well-equipped air groups and quickly gained an understanding of their potential by the late 1920s.

In the early phases of the war, British fleet carriers were in short supply and were equipped with

Epitomizing the "New Order" in the U.S. Navy, carriers lead a line of battleships and cruisers. Nearest the camera is a C.V.L., converted from a cruiser hull and with funnels characteristically cranked out to starboard. Next in line is an Essex-class C.V. The large aircraft "deck-parks" were typical of American ships.

Far right: The Essex-class aircraft carriers formed the core of the U.S. Navy's Fast Carrier Task Force. The illustration shows USS *Randolph* built at Newport News and commissioned on 9 October 1944, one of 24 examples of her class. They could carry over 90 aircraft, steam at over 30 knots, and were crewed by 2,682 men.

Above: A Grumman F6F Hellcat approaches the USS *Lexington*, an Essex-class Carrier.

Map, far right: CARRIER RAIDS IN THE CENTRAL PACIFIC These raids were usually formed around one or two large carriers with, perhaps, two escort carriers and cruisers in support. They sailed well behind the Japanese outer ring of defenses, hitting supply convoys and bases that were previously thought by the Japanese to be beyond the range of any potential threat.

low performance aircraft. They were seen as the "eyes" of the fleet and to some extent its air defense. The strike role, while understood, never received the investment required to create a meaningful attack force. Despite this failure, in 1940, the Royal Navy managed to attack the Italian fleet anchored in the Italian harbor of Taranto, sinking two and damaging one battleship, an event carefully observed and considered by both Japan and the U.S.

By 1941 the Japanese had ten carriers at their disposal. With six of these ships, they perfected and carried out the Pearl Harbor attack plan. Ironically, when their attack was launched, the U.S. ships they failed to sink were the American carriers, which were absent from Pearl Harbor engaged on maneuvers. These very ships became the core of the American fight back in the Pacific.

In 1941, the U.S. Navy had seven fleet carriers and one escort carrier in service. With these ships the vital battles of the Coral Sea and Midway were fought and won. As American industry got into gear major new warships, especially the Essex-class carriers, were added to the U.S. Navy. With the delivery of these new ships, the U.S. fleet was able to launch carrier raids deep into enemy territory to attack Japanese island bases across the central Pacific, and this paved the way for the great seaborne offensives that followed.

By the end of 1944, the U.S. Navy could count on 18 fleet carriers and 76 other light and escort carriers giving an immense offensive air power equipped with some 3,800 aircraft. All this power was carefully backed up with an immense fleet "train" of supply ships reaching from the supply centers of the U.S. west coast to the theater of operations. A feat unequalled before or since.

The epitomy of American carrier design incorporating all the lessons of the Pacific War was the immense USS *Midway*, laid down in October 1943, launched in March 1945 and commissioned on 10 September 1945, just missing involvement in the war. She could carry over 130 aircraft, with a displacement of 60,000 tons and a crew of 4,104 men. She served until being decommissioned in April 1992.

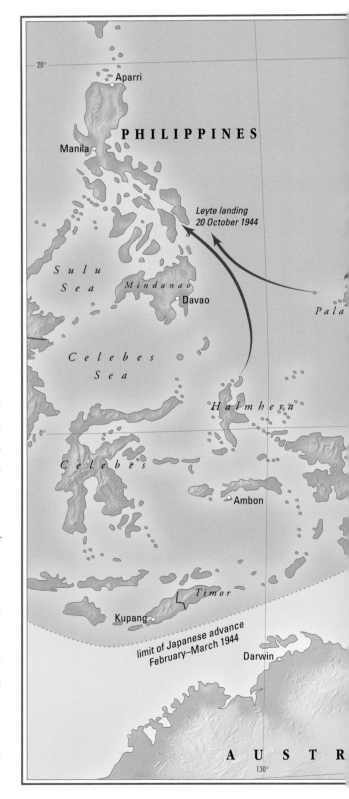

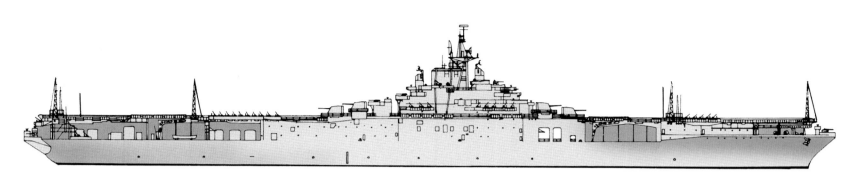

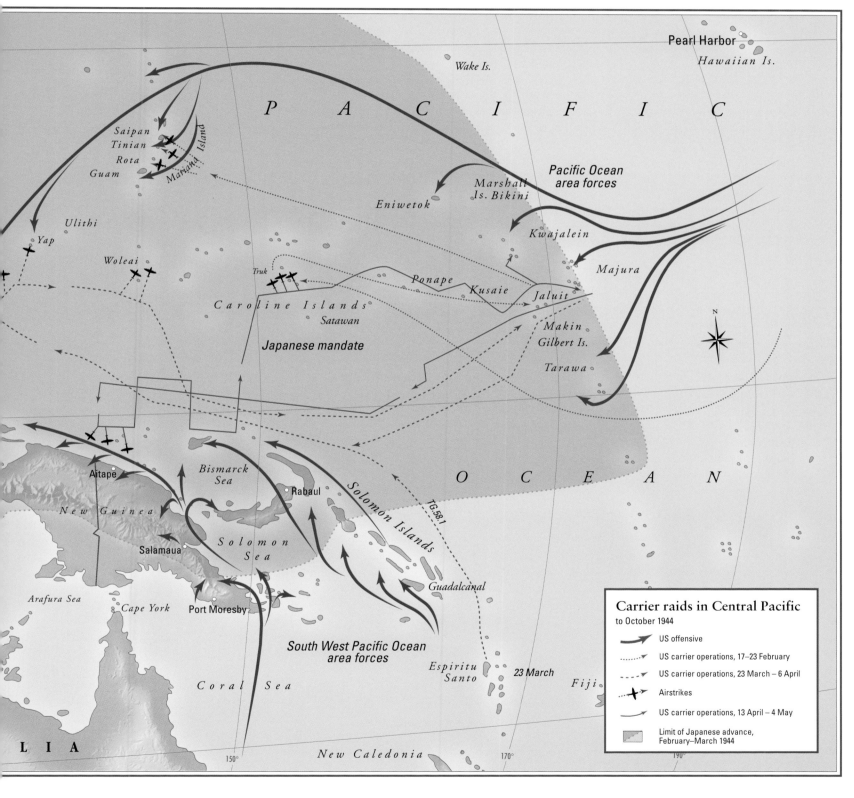

Pearl Harbor

Wake Is.

Hawaiian Is.

P A C I F I C

Saipan
Tinian
Rota
Guam

Mariana Island

Pacific Ocean
area forces

Marshall
Is. Bikini

Eniwetok

Ulithi

Yap

Kwajalein

Woleai

Majura

Truk

Ponape
Kusaie

Caroline Islands

Satawan

Jaluit

Japanese mandate

Makin
Gilbert Is.

Tarawa

N

Bismarck
Sea

Aitape

Rabaul

O C E A N

New Guinea

Solomon Islands

Solomon
Sea

Salamaua

TG 58.1

Arafura Sea

Cape York

Port Moresby

Guadalcanal

South West Pacific Ocean
area forces

Espiritu
Santo

23 March

Fiji

Coral Sea

L I A

New Caledonia

150°

170°

190°

Carrier raids in Central Pacific
to October 1944

— US offensive

········▸ US carrier operations, 17–23 February

– – –▸ US carrier operations, 23 March – 6 April

–✈–✈– Airstrikes

——▸ US carrier operations, 13 April – 4 May

▢ Limit of Japanese advance,
February–March 1944

THE GILBERT AND MARSHALL ISLANDS 1943

"THE 2ND MARINE DIVISION HAS BEEN ESPECIALLY CHOSEN BY THE HIGH COMMAND FOR THE ASSAULT ON TARAWA ... WHAT YOU DO HERE WILL SET THE STANDARD FOR ALL FUTURE OPERATIONS IN THE CENTRAL PACIFIC AREA."

MAJOR-GENERAL JULIAN C. SMITH,

COMMANDER 2ND MARINE DIVISION

On 10 November 1943, U.S. Task Force 52 set sail for the Gilbert islands in the Pacific and on arrival split into two, the northern force going to assault Makin Atoll, the southern to Tarawa. First to attack was the northern force, taking the Makin Atoll that included a Japanese flying boat base. On 13 November aerial attacks began bombing the defenses of the tiny atoll. The total Japanese garrison numbered only 800 men under the command of Seizo Ishikawa.

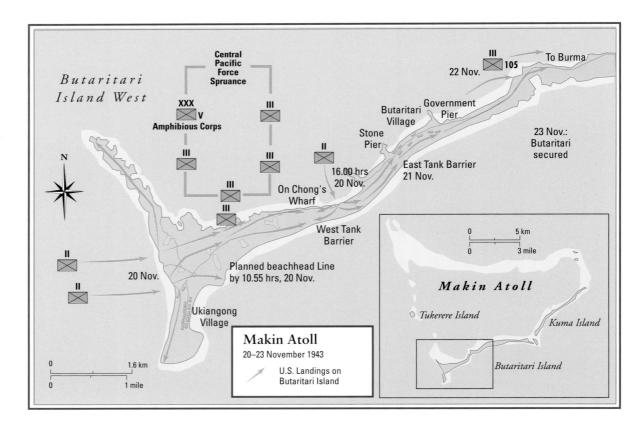

The 27th Division landed on 20 November, suffering few casualties; the Japanese defenders had retired inland to previously constructed strongpoints and resistance was cleared after two days with only half of the defenders surviving.

Next in line to be attacked was Tarawa, which was made up of 38 tiny atolls, the main defense being sited on the atoll that was home to the only airfield, Betio. This was much more strongly defended than Makin, with 5,000 men under the command of Rear-Admiral Shibasaki Keiji, although many were Korean construction engineers. Also at Keiji's disposal were 14 massive coastal defense guns captured from the British after the fall of Singapore in 1942 along with over 50 other guns. The preliminary bombardment by the U.S. did little to affect the carefully prepared defenses, which were strongly con-structed from logs and layers of coral along with concrete pillboxes. The bombardment also carried on for too long, delaying the assault until low tide. The assault boats became stranded on the reef surrounding the island, leaving the Marines and soldiers to wade through 700 yards of surf before they reached the beach. Seeing the Americans' dilem-ma the Japanese took full advantage and covered the area with mortar fire and small arms, causing many casualties. When the soldiers eventually reached the beach they found themselves pinned down and were obliged to wait for support. This arrived in the form of a lone tank, which quickly broke into the defenses. Following the tank were men armed with flamethrowers specifically to deal with bunkers. The Marines eventually succeeded in splitting the defenders into two groups. The Japanese commander, Keiji, was killed in one of numerous counterattacks and the last 150 Japanese soldiers took part in a final Banzai charge—a last-ditch bayonet charge—that left most of the original garrison dead.

A U.S. Marine runs forward under fire. The initiative and bravery of individual soldiers frequently decided the outcome of an engagement.

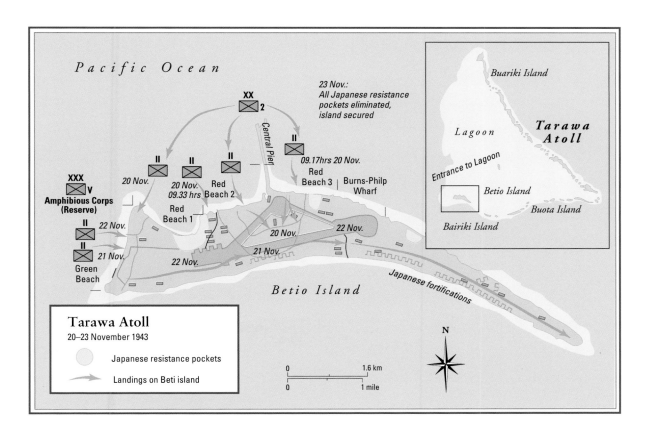

When the island was declared secure, only 17 wounded Japanese and 129 Koreans were all that remained of the Japanese force. Due to the mistakes the U.S. forces had made in the execution of the landing, Admiral Nimitz made sure that more intensive training and planning went into future assaults.

The next target, the Marshall Islands, were bombed continuously for seven weeks before the invasion forces' landing. The 7th Infantry Division headed for Kwajalien, and the 4th Marine Division to the atoll of Roi-Namur. The Marines were first to carry out their objective with naval and air support. Resistance was light and the island was taken with relative ease, although some logistical problems caused difficulties for the troops on the front line.

On Kwajalien the troops and stores were delivered with efficiency and speed, but the men faced a tougher defense. The Japanese commander of the island led several charges in person, trying to dislodge the Americans' bridgehead. These attackers then fell back on a strong line of trenches supported by concrete bunkers. However, after six days of hard fighting the island was in U.S. hands.

The last island series to be taken was Eniwetok, defended by about 4,000 Japanese troops. Invaded by 8,000 U.S. Marines and 2,000 Army personnel, the island was taken again with relative ease and with almost total annihilation of the defenders, most of whom preferred death to surrender.

With the Gilbert and Marshall islands in U.S. hands, they could look to the next strategic group of islands to invade. Ahead of schedule, the only problems being highlighted from the recent campaign were the need for more organization in getting troops and stores off the beach in order not to create a supply problem, and to allow for the fanatical resistance of the Japanese. This could only mean that it would not get any easier the closer the Americans got to the Japanese home islands.

Left: Soldiers of the 165th U.S. Infantry wade ashore on Makin Island in the Gilbert chain of islands. The smoke rising from among the trees is a result of the preliminary bombardment.

Above: Two U. S. soldiers come under sniper fire. A favored tactic of the Japanese was to infiltrate behind their enemy and snipe from the rear, which was a considerable problem for the troops consolidating their positions.

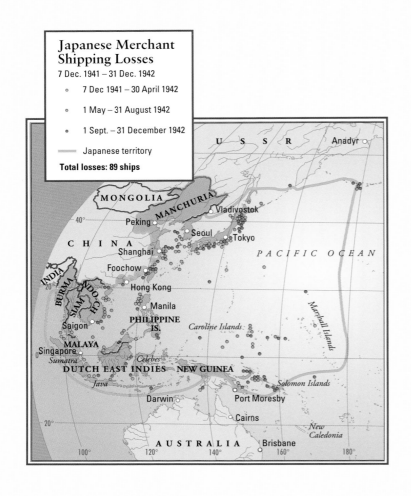

Japanese Merchant Shipping Losses
7 Dec. 1941 – 31 Dec. 1942
- 7 Dec 1941 – 30 April 1942
- 1 May – 31 August 1942
- 1 Sept. – 31 December 1942
— Japanese territory
Total losses: 89 ships

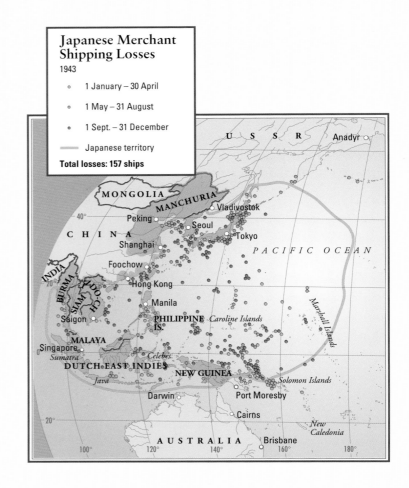

Japanese Merchant Shipping Losses
1943
- 1 January – 30 April
- 1 May – 31 August
- 1 Sept. – 31 December
— Japanese territory
Total losses: 157 ships

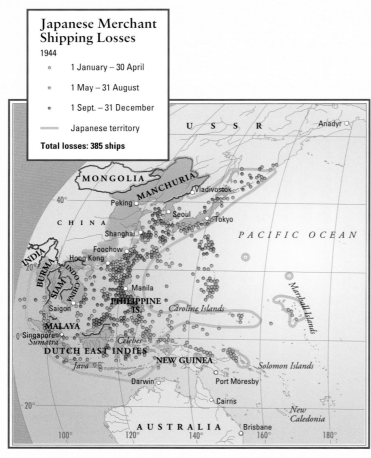

Japanese Merchant Shipping Losses
1944
- 1 January – 30 April
- 1 May – 31 August
- 1 Sept. – 31 December
— Japanese territory
Total losses: 385 ships

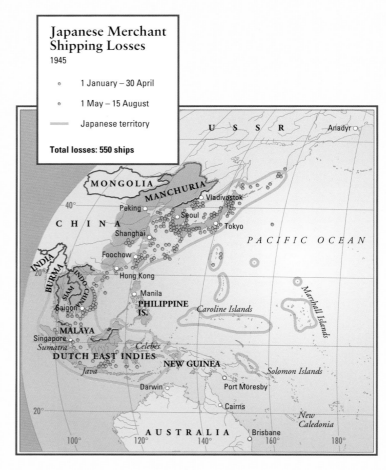

Japanese Merchant Shipping Losses
1945
- 1 January – 30 April
- 1 May – 15 August
— Japanese territory
Total losses: 550 ships

THE WAR AGAINST JAPAN'S SUPPLY LINES

The reason Japan had gone to war and extend its empire was to secure itself the vital resources it considered necessary for future security. The United States High Command had recognized that the destruction of Japan's merchant fleet would render this policy meaningless.

With the U.S. now firmly on the offensive, it became possible to increase the pressure on the Japanese shipping routes. Japan needed to import raw materials on a considerable scale to keep its war industries producing weapons and munitions for the war effort. The Japanese were slow to introduce the convoy system, which they finally introduced in September 1943. Unlike the Allies they only allotted a mere 59 ocean-going escorts for trade defense for the entire eastern Pacific. For this oversight the U.S. submarines would make Japan pay dearly. Japan began the war with 6,000,000 tons of merchant shipping under their flag. By January 1945, just 2,750,000 tons were left, and by August it was down to just 1,500,000 tons.

In the Pacific, the American and Allied forces had achieved what the U-boats had failed to do to in the Atlantic. Japan's industry and population had been starved of raw materials and food.

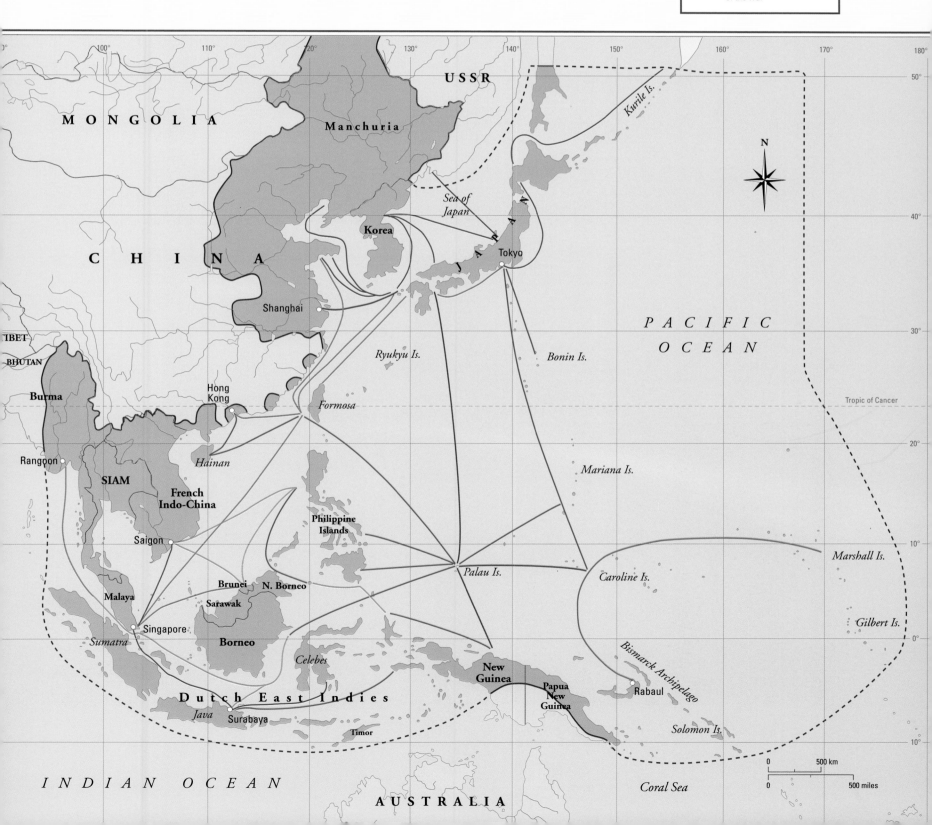

Japanese Merchant Shipping Routes
1941 – 45

——	Maximum extent of Japanese occupation
- - -	
——	1 January 1944
——	1 May 1944
——	1 September 1944
——	1 January 1945
——	1 May 1945
——	15 August 1945
——	Still in operation at the end of the war

THE MARIANA AND PALUA ISLANDS 1944

"I HAVE ALWAYS CONSIDERED SAIPAN THE DECISIVE BATTLE OF THE PACIFIC OFFENSIVE ... IT WAS THE NAVAL AND MILITARY HEART AND BRAIN OF THE JAPANESE DEFENSE STRATEGY."

LT.-GENERAL HOLLAND–SMITH, JULY 1944

The Mariana Islands had been occupied by the Japanese since the end of World War I, so were heavily defended and garrisoned, especially as it formed part of the main defensive line in the Pacific. Saipan, Tinian, and Guam had to be taken by U.S. forces, since the islands would provide the airfields required for the new B-29 Superfortess that would bring the Japanese homeland within bombing range.

The first of the islands to be assaulted was Saipan, using the 2nd and 4th Marine Divisions on the first day, and the 27th Infantry Division on the second day. Defending the island was the Japanese 43rd Division commanded by Lt-General Yoshitsuga Saito. U.S. aerial and naval bombardment continued for three days before the assault was launched, but when the Marines came ashore on 15 June the Japanese artillery had carefully zeroed in on the beach and took a terrible toll on the landing forces. However, a beachhead of some seven miles wide was established and all Japanese counterattacks successfully beaten off. The 27th Division advanced on Aslito Airfield and, after initial fighting, this valuable real estate was abandoned by Saito and his men on 18 June. When Saito realized that the Japanese fleet was not going to arrive and attack the U.S. fleet, he ordered his men to fall back into the mountainous central region of the island around Mount Tapotchau and stall

While under fire, U.S. troops plant the Stars and Stripes on the beach at Saipan after disembarking from their Amtrak (amphibious tractor) that had carried them ashore.

the Americans for as long as possible. The U.S. 27th Division was ordered to attack this rugged area, which became known as "Purple Heart Ridge," but failed to make any progress. This led the Marine commander, General Holland Smith, to relieve the division's commander. On 7 July, with nowhere to go, Saito ordered his men to make an all out infantry charge, before he committed suicide. This was to be the war's largest Banzai charge, with some 3,000 Japanese troops being killed in this traditional response, after which all organized defense collapsed. The result of the battle led to the Japanese Prime Minister, Hideki Tojo, being relieved as head of the Army and he resigned with all of his Cabinet.

Tinian was assaulted on 24 July, after a successful feint drew the defenders away from the actual landing site on the north coast. The 2nd and 4th Marine divisions came ashore with relative ease, but at night their positions would be counterattacked and Japanese soldiers would infiltrate the lines and attack from the flanks and rear, lowering morale considerably. Again the Japanese retreated into the central part of the island in an attempt to forestall the Americans. However, the terrain on Tinian was more conducive

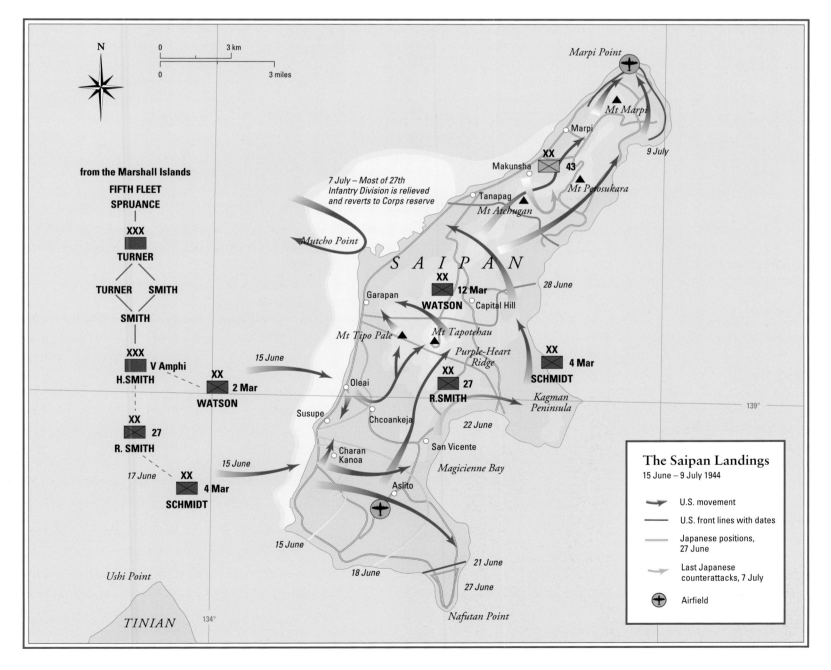

U.S. Marines move fast and low during street fighting in Angana, Saipan.

to tank warfare and the island was made secure within nine days of the assault. Construction battalions soon got to work on the airfields, which would be used to support further planned landings, as well as air attacks on the Japanese mainland.

Guam was the largest of the Mariana Islands and was assaulted on 21 July by 3rd Marine Division and 77th Infantry Division on each side of the Orote Peninsula. The Marines made good progress, but the Infantry Division—which was short of amphibious vehicles—had to wade in over the coral while under heavy fire. Again the Japanese used the tactic of counterattack and infiltrating troops

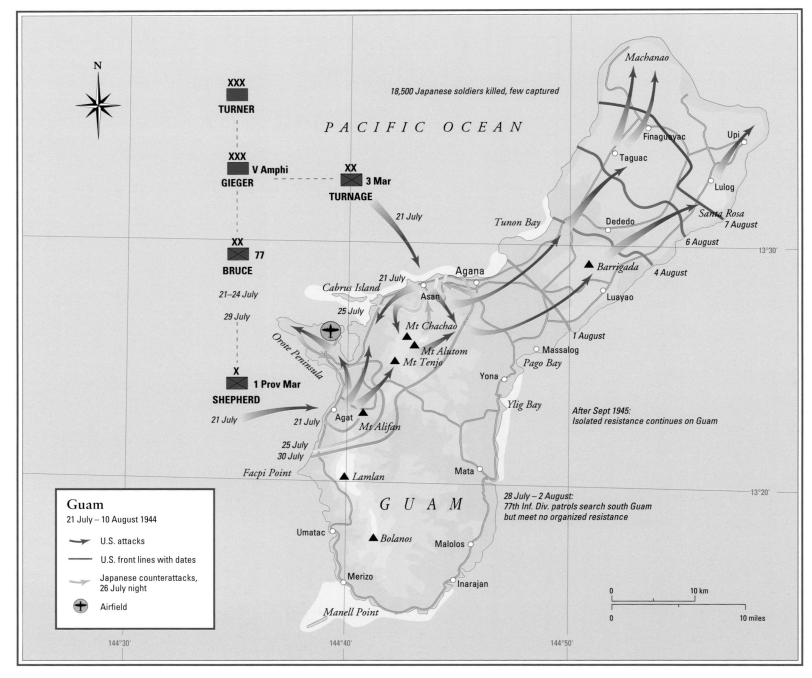

N

XXX
TURNER

XXX
V Amphi
GIEGER

XX
3 Mar
TURNAGE

XX
77
BRUCE

21–24 July

29 July

X
1 Prov Mar
SHEPHERD

21 July

21 July

25 July
30 July

Facpi Point

PACIFIC OCEAN

18,500 Japanese soldiers killed, few captured

Machanao

Finaguayac

Upi

Taguac

Lulog

Santa Rosa
7 August

Tunon Bay

Dededo

6 August

13°30'

21 July

Cabrus Island

Agana

Barrigada

4 August

Asan

Luayao

25 July

1 August

Mt Chachao

Massalog

Mt Alutom

Pago Bay

Mt Tenjo

Yona

Ylig Bay

After Sept 1945:
Isolated resistance continues on Guam

Agat

Mt Alifan

Mata

Lamlan

GUAM

13°20'

28 July – 2 August:
77th Inf. Div. patrols search south Guam
but meet no organized resistance

Umatac

Bolanos

Malolos

Merizo

Inarajan

Manell Point

Guam
21 July – 10 August 1944

→ U.S. attacks

— U.S. front lines with dates

→ Japanese counterattacks,
26 July night

⊕ Airfield

0   10 km

0   10 miles

144°30'   144°40'   144°50'

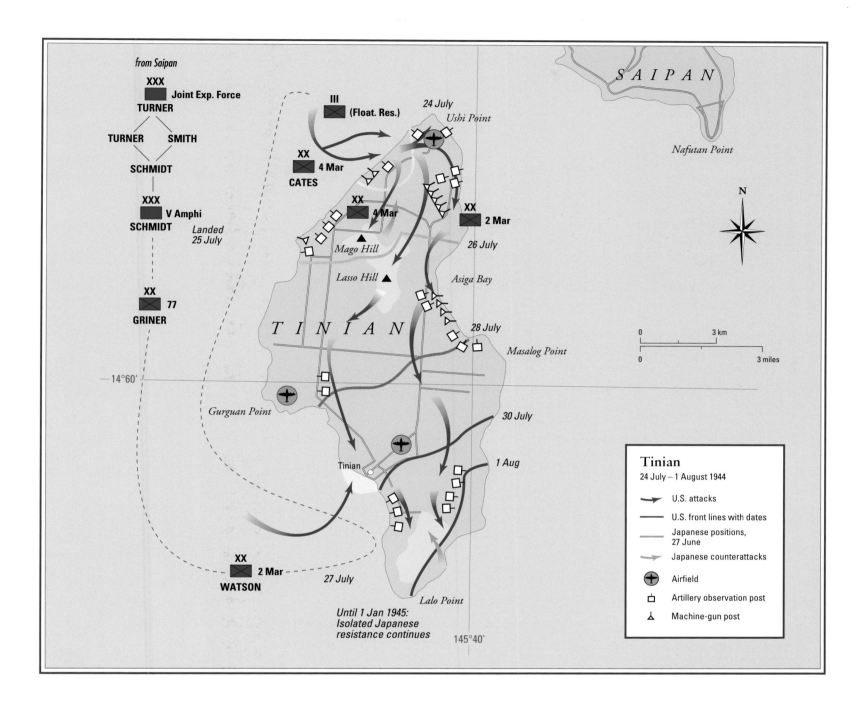

behind the U.S. advance to fire from the rear, the frontal attacks were always driven off with heavy

losses. Orote Airfield was captured on 30 July, shortly after the death of the Japanese commanding

officer, Takashima, with Lt-General Obata taking over command. The constant counterattacks by the

Japanese soon exhausted even the hardiest of the soldiers, and they fell back into the interior of the

island, retreating to an area around Mount Barrigada. Eventually the U.S. forces broke this final line

and pursued the remaining enemy to the north of the island, where few surrendered.

Finally, the 1st Marine Division and the 81st Infantry Division assaulted Peleliu, where the

Japanese had made use of the many caves on the island, this time defended against flamethrower

and explosive attack, which made the U.S. advance far more difficult. The Americans had to devel-

op new tactics to defeat the enemy's new methods. After immensely difficult fighting and intense

attacks led by tanks, the Marines and Infantry overcame all of these difficulties.

CHINA 1944–45

"EVERY COMMUNIST MUST GRASP THE TRUTH THAT POLITICAL POWER GROWS OUT OF THE BARREL OF A GUN."

MAO TSE-TUNG

Japan continued its expansion in China, seizing the provinces of Henan, Hunan, and Guangxi, but it only managed to disrupt the U.S. 14th Air Force's operations, not halt them.

The war gathered momentum in China in 1944, when the Japanese attempt to invade India was stopped at the Battle of Kohima-Imphal. In northern Burma, U.S. General Stilwell's Chinese troops approached Mogaung and Myitkyina. Chiang-Kai-Shek was threatened by the U.S. that Lend-Lease would be suspended if he failed to use the 12 divisions of his Yunnan Army in Burma. These subsequently began crossing the Salween River, moving on Myitkyina, Bhamo, and Lashio. Myitkyina Airfield was seized by Stilwell's forces, with Merrill's Marauders on 17 May, while Mogaung was taken by Britain's Chindits. Myitkyina fell to Stilwell's Chinese forces on 3 August.

In China, by 1944, U.S. 14th Air Force bombers operating from Chinese bases were pulverizing Japanese supply lines in northeastern China and plans were almost complete for deploying B-29 Superfortress bombers, capable of targeting Japan itself, to airfields around Chengdu in Sichuan. This air campaign caused the Japanese to launch a series of attacks, known together as Ichi-go "the last throw." This Japanese strategy sought to control the railroad from Beijing, through Hankou, to Guangzhou, and to Indo-China, together with an attempt to capture the American airbases around Chongqing on the River Chang Jiang (River Yangtze). This offensive began in April, when 150,000 Japanese marched towards Zhengzhou from the east and south. The city fell on 22 April, allowing the advance to push westward taking Lo-yang in May, and Lingbau in June. Simultaneously, more Japanese forces moved south from Zhengzhou, attempting to link with a thrust north from Xinyang. By mid-June, the Japanese held the railroad from Beijing to Hangzhou, leaving the Chinese to retreat.

Elsewhere, a southward assault from Hangzhou moved toward the city of Chang-sha where the Chinese put up a stiff defense. Despite losing Chang-sha on 5 June and Hengyang (where the rail-

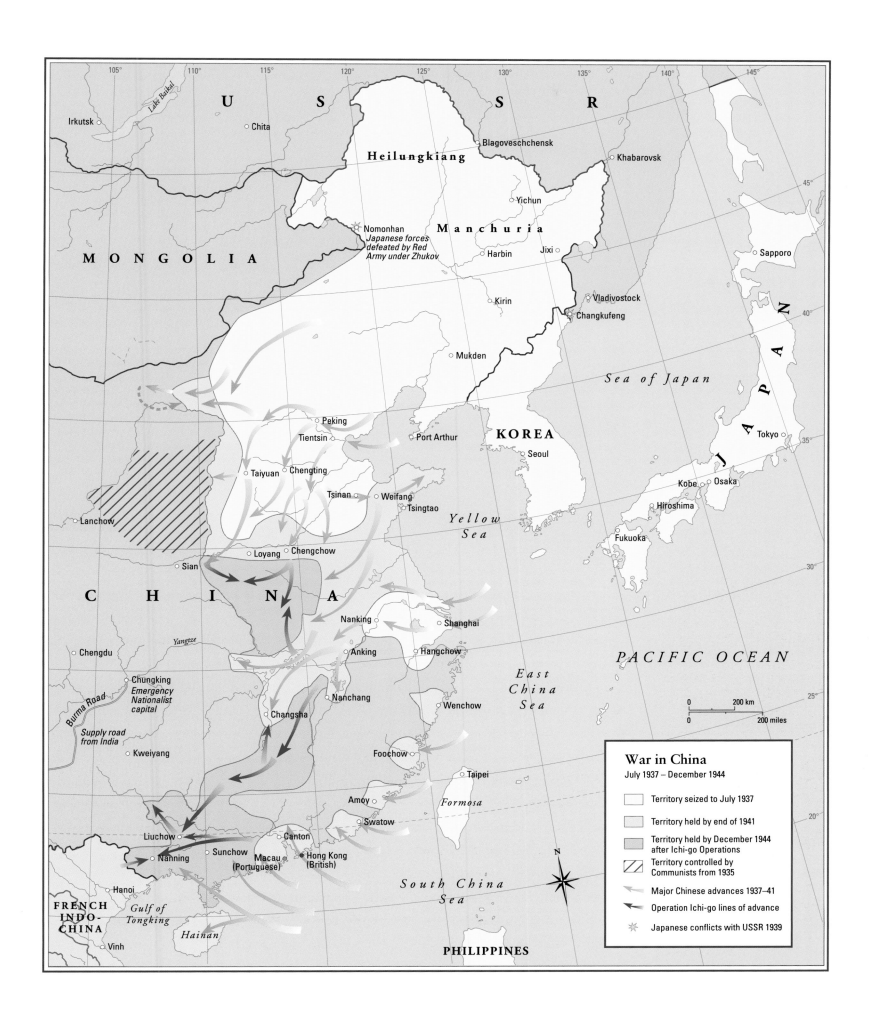

Irkutsk

Chita

Lake Baikal

U S S R

Blagoveschchensk

Khabarovsk

Heilungkiang

Yichun

Nomonhan
Japanese forces
defeated by Red
Army under Zhukov

Manchuria

Harbin

Jixi

Sapporo

MONGOLIA

Kirin

Vladivostock

Changkufeng

Mukden

Sea of Japan

J A P A N

Peking

Tientsin

Port Arthur

KOREA

Seoul

Tokyo

Taiyuan

Chengting

Tsinan

Weifang
Tsingtao

Yellow
Sea

Kobe
Osaka

Hiroshima

Lanchow

Loyang
Chengchow

Fukuoka

Sian

C H I N A

Nanking

Shanghai

Chengdu

Yangtze

Anking

Hangchow

PACIFIC OCEAN

Chungking
Emergency
Nationalist
capital

Nanchang

Wenchow

East
China
Sea

Burma Road

Changsha

Supply road
from India

Kweiyang

Foochow

Taipei

War in China

July 1937 – December 1944

Liuchow

Nanning

Sunchow

Canton

Macau
(Portuguese)

Hong Kong
(British)

Amoy

Swatow

Formosa

Territory seized to July 1937

Territory held by end of 1941

Territory held by December 1944
after Ichi-go Operations

Territory controlled by
Communists from 1935

Hanoi

FRENCH
INDO-
CHINA

Gulf of
Tongking

South China
Sea

N

Major Chinese advances 1937–41

Operation Ichi-go lines of advance

Vinh

Hainan

PHILIPPINES

Japanese conflicts with USSR 1939

Chiang Kai-shek addresses the people of China, urging them to keep up their brave resistance against the Japanese, to defend their country and the U.S. air bases in China.

America supplied vehicles to keep the Chinese Army on the move.
The United States provided an immense amount materials of all kinds to Chinese forces. Whenever possible via the Burma Road, but when this was cut by the Japanese advance of 1942–43, supplies were flown in over the Himalayan Mountains by U.S. transport aircraft flying from bases in India.

road forked towards Indo-China) in August, Chiang Kai-shek's forces, supported by the U.S. 14th Air Force, inflicted heavy casualties and bought valuable time. Nevertheless, when another Japanese advance commenced in late August, attempting to clear the railroad down to Guangzhou, huge areas of territory were abandoned to the Japanese. By November, Guilin, Liuzhou, and Yongning, plus the neighboring airfields, were captured and Chongqing was threatened. In December, a Japanese force moved out of northern Indo-China, making contact with other forces near Longzhou. The railroad was now clear along the entire length from Hanoi to Beijing.

Throughout their campaigns, the Chinese Nationalist Army adopted the tactic of so-called "magnetic warfare" in which Japanese troops would be offered a target, such as Chansha, then ambushed, outflanked, and encircled. During the subsequent major engagements the Japanese would suffer from attrition. This offensive-defensive tactic worked successfully. Out of about 57 major engagements between 1931 and 1945, the Chinese were victorious in 20 and even when suffering defeat inflicted severe casualties on the enemy.

The Japanese were severely stretched and their supply lines were thin; the Ichi-go campaigns had incurred tremendous casualties, leaving reduced numbers to hold the newly captured territories. The link between Indo-China and Hengyang could not be held for long, especially after Chiang's forces began to rebuild themselves, with American aid, after the recent losses. By November 1944, Chiang

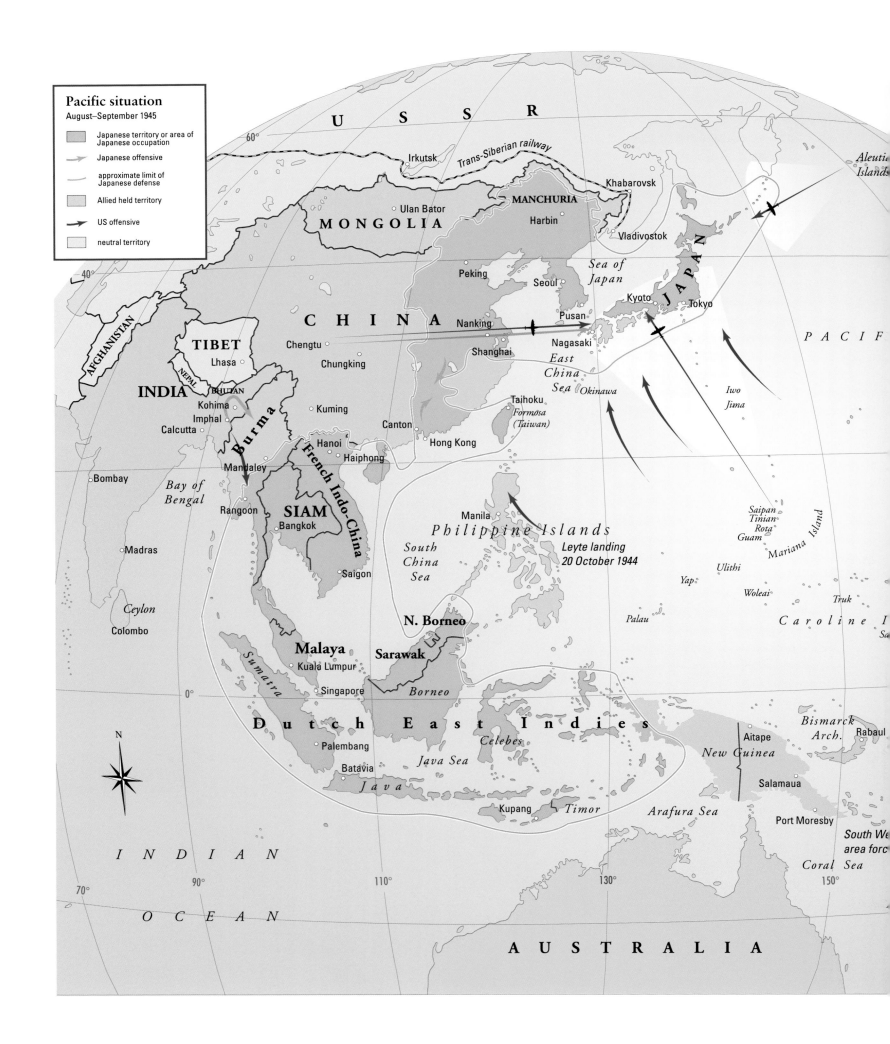

Pacific situation

August–September 1945

Japanese territory or area of Japanese occupation

Japanese offensive

approximate limit of Japanese defense

Allied held territory

US offensive

neutral territory

U S S R

Irkutsk

Trans-Siberian railway

Khabarovsk

MANCHURIA

Ulan Bator

Harbin

MONGOLIA

Vladivostok

Aleutian Islands

Sea of Japan

Peking

Seoul

Kyoto

JAPAN

Tokyo

CHINA

Nanking

Pusan

PACIFIC

Chengtu

Nagasaki

AFGHANISTAN

TIBET

Chungking

Shanghai

East China Sea

Okinawa

Iwo Jima

Lhasa

INDIA

NEPAL

BHUTAN

Kohima

Kuming

Taihoku

Formosa (Taiwan)

Imphal

Calcutta

Burma

Canton

Hong Kong

Bombay

Hanoi

Mandaley

Haiphong

French Indo-China

Bay of Bengal

Manila

Philippine Islands

Saipan

Tinian

Rota

Guam

Mariana Island

Rangoon

SIAM

Bangkok

South China Sea

Leyte landing 20 October 1944

Ulithi

Woleai

Truk

Madras

Saigon

Yap

Ceylon

N. Borneo

Palau

Caroline I

Colombo

Malaya

Sarawak

Kuala Lumpur

Sumatra

Singapore

Borneo

Dutch East Indies

Bismarck Arch.

Rabaul

Palembang

Celebes

Aitape

New Guinea

Batavia

Java Sea

Salamaua

Java

Kupang

Timor

Arafura Sea

Port Moresby

N

INDIAN

South West area forc

Coral Sea

70°

90°

110°

130°

150°

OCEAN

AUSTRALIA

Chinese soldiers prepare for action. The Chinese armies, both Nationalist and Communist, for the period from 1940 to 1946 cooperated against the common enemy, Imperial Japan. After Japan's surrender, civil war broke out between the two factions. By 1949 the Communists had succeeded in driving the Nationalists from mainland China to the island of Formosa (Taiwan).

was reequipping and training, this campaign being masterminded by his new American advisor, Major-General Wedemeyer, Stilwell having been recalled at Chiang's request. Thirty-nine new divisions were planned and although they were not fully effective by the end of the war in nine months time, their threat tied up more than 500,000 Japanese, some of whom could have been used elsewhere in the Pacific theater.

The conflict in China caused divisions between China, the U.S., and Britain. Winston Churchill did not want to commit his defeated troops to re-open the Burma Road, while General Stilwell saw that target as being a prime concern. Chiang Kai-shek also distrusted the British, who he thought were using Chinese troops in their Burma campaign to hold together Britain's imperial holdings in Asia. Chiang wanted to use his forces in eastern China to protect U.S. airbases, a ploy which delighted Claire Lee Chenault and his "Flying Tigers" mercenary force. A further complication was Chiang's vocal support for Indian independence, including a meeting with Gandhi. Britain was not happy. However, on 6 and 9 August respectively, Hiroshima and Nagasaki were atom-bombed, while the Soviets entered Manchuria. The Japanese surrendered on 2 September 1945.

Chinese Communist Party propaganda expressed the view that Mao Tse-Tung's armies, which grew from nothing to 1.7 million soldiers, were the victors. The view of many in the West was that they seemed more intent on planning for events after the war than in hard campaigning against Japan. General Chiang's Kounikang forces fought in 24 major battles involving more than 100,000 men on each side, 1,171 minor engagements (most of which with 50,000 men on each side), and nearly 39,000 skirmishes. They lost some 3.22 million troops while the Japanese losses were at least 1.1 million. The generally held view is that Chiang's Kounikang, which included many warlords who fought the enemy under the Kounikang banner, made the major contribution against the Japanese in China.

BATTLE OF THE BULGE 1944

"THAT WHOLE ARDENNES FIGHT WAS A BATTLE FOR ROAD JUNCTIONS, BECAUSE IN THAT WOODED COUNTRY IN DEEP SNOWS, ARMIES DO NOT MOVE OFF ROADS."

GENERAL MATTHEW B. RIDGWAY, 101ST AIRBORNE DIVISION

The Ardennes Offensive, known as the "Battle of the Bulge" (referring to the bulge in the Allied line), was Hitler's last major offensive in World War II. Its aim was to cut the Allied advance on the West Wall (a prewar defensive line on the western borders of Germany) in two and destroy the U.S. divisions caught in the resulting pocket, then capture the port of Antwerp, splitting the Allied armies. Antwerp was strategically important to the Allies, as most of their supplies still came via the road network all the way from Mulberry Harbor and Cherbourg on the Normandy coast. This, Hitler hoped, would catch the Allies napping. For the Germans the Ardennes—heavily forested with few major roads—was the best place to strike, as this was the weakest area where recuperating or new Allied units were placed.

Loaded down with weapons, ammunition and an entrenching tool, a German soldier looks on anxiously before going into combat in the Ardennes Forest.

The plan for the offensive was much like the one used for the summer offensive against France in 1940, except that, instead of passing through the Ardennes before attacking, the battle lines would be within the forest. The plan called for a bridgehead to be secured over the Meuse River, then for the major part of the force to swing north west toward Antwerp. For this attack there would be four armies: the newly-formed 6th S.S. Panzer Army commanded by Josef 'Sepp' Dietrich in the north; the 5th Panzer under Hasso von Manteuffel in the center; and Erich Brandenberger's 7th Army in the south. The 15th Army would be kept in reserve toward the northern sector. These forces would be overseen by Field Marshals Walter Model and Gerd von Runstedt, who strongly disagreed with the plan and tried to seek a less ambitious one. This was seen as defeatist by Hitler. For the plan to work the Germans would need complete surprise, and security was tight. Von Rundstedt did not even hear of the plan until the attack was close. In addition, poor weather would be required to stave off any chance of Allied air attack. Most important would be a rapid advance to overwhelm the defenders and capture as much enemy fuel as possible to feed the thirsty panzers. In order to create as much panic and uncertainty as possible in the U.S. ranks, teams of English-speaking troops were infiltrated behind the American lines wearing U.S. uniforms in order to disrupt troop movements and spread rumors.

At 05:30 on 16 December the German artillery opened fire and blasted the U.S. troop positions for nearly an hour before all the three assaulting armies moved off their start lines. The 6th S.S. drove on toward Liege while 5th Panzer drove to secure the vital road junctions at St. Vith and Bastogne. The 7th Army would push on steadily across the border into Luxembourg in order to establish a strong flank defense. Surprise was total, with some entire U.S. regiments surrendering to the sudden

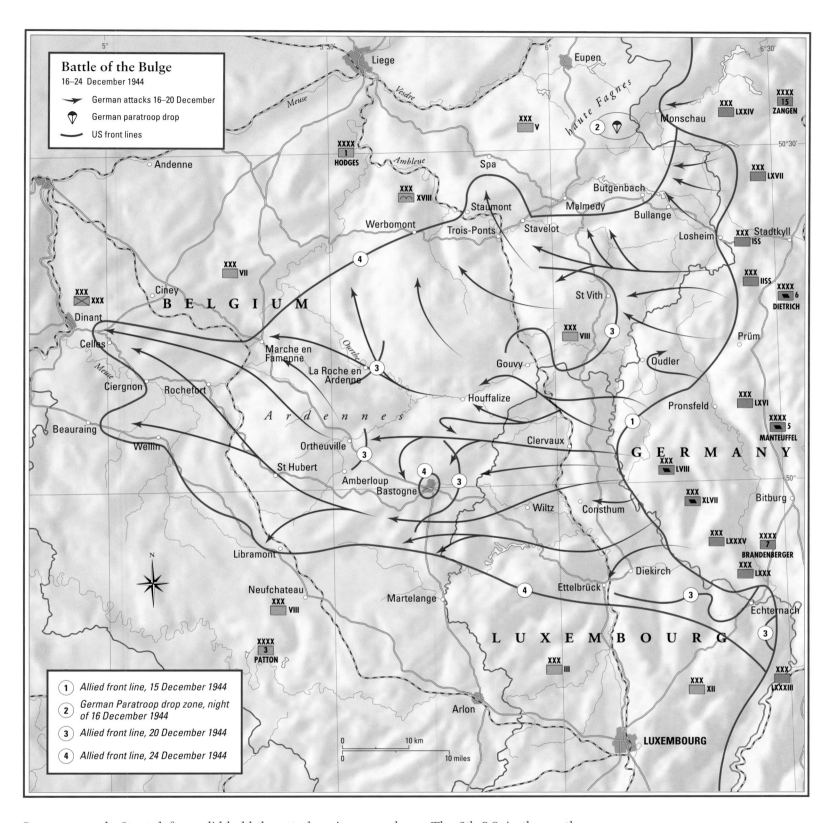

Battle of the Bulge
16–24 December 1944

➤ German attacks 16–20 December

⬇ German paratroop drop

⌒ US front lines

① *Allied front line, 15 December 1944*

② *German Paratroop drop zone, night of 16 December 1944*

③ *Allied front line, 20 December 1944*

④ *Allied front line, 24 December 1944*

0 ————— 10 km
0 ————— 10 miles

German assault. Stout defense did hold the attackers in some places. The 6th S.S. in the north were held up by the 2nd Infantry Division, and the 99th Division. The Allied High Command was caught by surprise, both Montgomery and General Omar Bradley believing that the Germans were all but finished and definitely not capable of a major offensive. The German advance slowed by the end of the day as the weather got steadily worse, creating the mixed blessing of keeping the Allied air forces on the ground, but also causing major traffic jams on the narrow woodland roads. As part of the

An exhausted trooper of General Matthew "Bunker" Ridgway's 101st Airborne Division reflects on the heroic defense of Bastogne.

A captured German soldier of the Waffen S.S. is photographed here being interrogated by members of the U.S. 82nd Airborne Division .

offensive, there was also an airborne operation, codenamed "Stösser," which involved dropping over a thousand Fallschirmjäger behind the lines just north of Malmedy to secure an important crossroads 'Baraque Michel'. Due to poor weather the drop was delayed until the early hours of 17 December and even this was affected by bad conditions, low cloud causing the paratroops to be badly scattered. Only 300 paras made the rallying point. The commander, Friedrich von der Heydte, who won the Iron Cross leading a battalion during the invasion of Crete, realized that the small force would not be able to hold the junction, and decided instead, to use his troops as a harassing force. This created enough chaos that U.S. commanders redirected troops on the way to the front to secure rear areas.

By the end of the day, General Eisenhower had taken the decision to send the 101st Airborne Division to Bastogne, to be joined by a combat team from the 10th Armored Division. This movement was carried out with incredible speed and would prove to be a vital course of action. The 82nd Airborne Division was also thrown into the fray, taking up positions defending the approach to Liege.

The spearhead of the 6th Panzer Army, Kampfgruppe Peiper—commanded by Joachim Peiper—struck out for Stavelot and reached it on 18 December. On the journey the day before, elements of Peiper's force captured 150 U.S. troops, who had surrendered when taken by surprise. The prisoners were then herded into a field and, according to eyewitness reports, an S.S. officer began to indiscriminatly shoot them, his men following suit with machine guns. Some men managed to escape but 84 were murdered in scenes common on the Eastern Front, but rarely seen on the Western. As reports started to spread of the 'Malmedy Massacre' U.S. troops took revenge on German prisoners and no quarter would be given in the fighting for the bulge from then on. Peiper was faced by strong defense at Stavelot and decided to reach the bridge at Trois Ponts, only to find that it had been blown earlier by U.S. engineers. Peiper moved his force onto Stoumont, where again the bridge had been blown and was heavily defended. Stavelot was completely retaken by U.S. soldiers on 19 December, cutting off Peiper. He had no choice but to give the order to abandon his tanks and half-tracks so his men could break through to the main German force. This he achieved with most of his men.

In the 5th Panzer sector, advance was severely hampered by the defenders of Bastogne. This was a major road junction with seven roads leading to it and was essential to the speedy advance of the German plan. The defenders, 101st Airborne Division and a combat command of 10th Armored Division, held onto the perimeter even though they were critically short of ammunition and winter clothing. Conditions inside the perimeter were harsh, with medical supplies and personnel to apply them very short, but the troops held and, when offered a chance to surrender, the commander of the beseiged town, General McAuliffe, simply answered "Nuts!." By 23 December the tide had begun to turn, with the weather breaking enough for aircraft to fly sorties to attack the long columns of German tanks confined to the narrow woodland roads, and to destroy their supplies in the rear. This caused an even worse shortage of fuel for the leading Panzers and the advance effectively ground to a halt, the Germans not even managing to reach the Meuse. On 26 December elements of Patton's 3rd Army broke through the perimeter of Bastogne and lifted the siege, bringing in much needed support and firepower.

On 1 January 1945, the Germans launched two simultaneous, but different, attacks. The first was launched by the Luftwaffe with the aim of destroying as many Allied aircraft on the ground as possible in Belgium and the Netherlands. This it succeeded in doing but caused heavy loss to itself in the process, partly from antiaircraft flak from both sides (German antiaircraft batteries not being told about the operation) and Allied interceptors. The Luftwaffe lost 300 aircraft, from which it would never recover. In the south opposite the U.S. 7th Army, German Army Group B launched an attack into the Alsace. This achieved initial success pushing the Americans back to the south bank of the Moder River. Again this attack failed due to lack of supplies and another determined defense by U.S. forces.

While this was happening, Eisenhower had ordered Montgomery in the north, and Patton, into the Bastogne area, toward the south of the bulge to advance toward each other and pinch out the salient. Patton proceeded immediately and took heavy casualties in a slow advance. Monty stalled for three days waiting out heavy snowstorms. The Germans put up a dogged rear guard action, and was able to save many of its troops at the cost of most of its heavy equipment, which had to be left behind because of a shortage of fuel. The two Allied forces eventually met on 15 January, effectively bringing to an end the last major offensive by the Germans in the West.

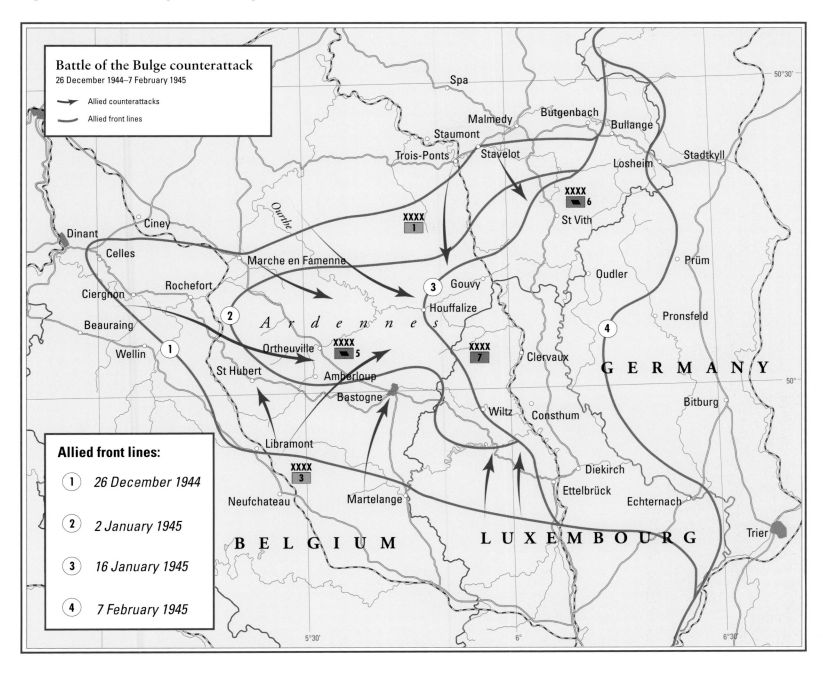

BOMBING OF GERMANY 1944–45

"...WE WALKED TOWARD THE GROSSE GARTEN. I FELT RAIN TRICKLING OUT OF THE SKY, THIN AND COLD, AND THEN I HEARD THE HUM OF AIRCRAFT ENGINES ..."

BRUNO WERNER, CITIZEN OF DRESDEN

By the beginning of 1944 Bomber Command and the U.S.A.A.F. had built up a massive bomber force that could carry a vast tonnage to German factories, marshalling yards and oil refineries under the control of the Third Reich. Their task was also aided by the introduction of radio detection equipment that allowed the bombers to more acurately identify their desired target, and the arrival of the long-range P-51 Mustang and P-47 Thunderbolt fighters that could escort the bombers all the way to the target and back. All this, combined with the advantage of experience, would show the true potential and the terrifying force of air power.

In February of 1944, the Allied bomber offensive targeted the German aircraft industry in what was known as "Big Week," which resulted in German factories having to be moved into more dispersed areas, slowing down production considerably and allowing the airforces a freer reign over the skies of Germany. The bombers were then thrown into the tactical role of bombing targets in aid of Operation Overlord, much to the consternation of the bomber commanders, who believed that their real task should be bombing the German homeland into

Top right: The B-17 bombers, along with the P-51 fighter escorts now became masters of the skies over Nazi Germany.

A Lancaster bomber is loaded with a variety of ordnance, including a massive 4000-lb. "Blockbuster" bomb.

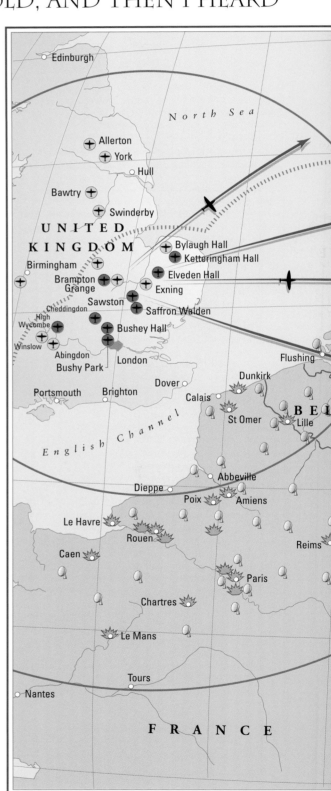

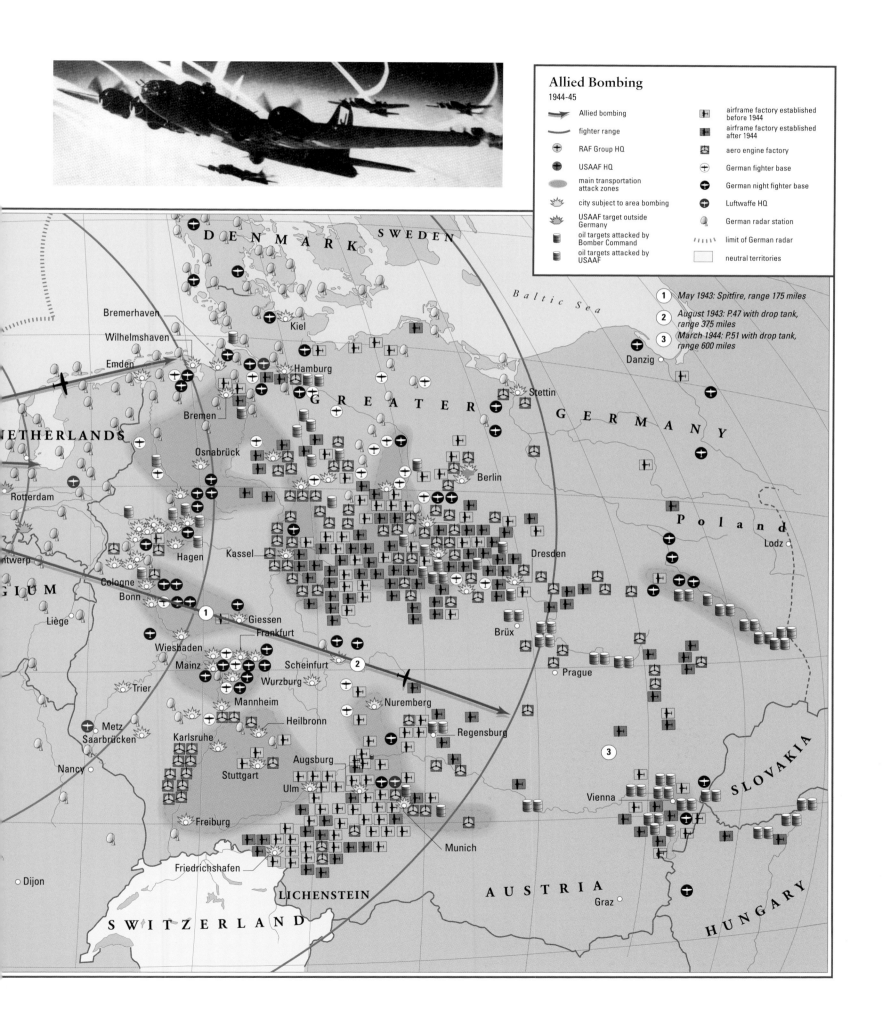

Allied Bombing
1944-45

Symbol	Description	Symbol	Description
✈	Allied bombing		airframe factory established before 1944
⌒	fighter range		airframe factory established after 1944
⊕	RAF Group HQ		aero engine factory
⊕	USAAF HQ	✛	German fighter base
	main transportation attack zones	⊕	German night fighter base
	city subject to area bombing	⊕	Luftwaffe HQ
	USAAF target outside Germany		German radar station
	oil targets attacked by Bomber Command		limit of German radar
	oil targets attacked by USAAF		neutral territories

1 May 1943: Spitfire, range 175 miles

2 August 1943: P.47 with drop tank, range 375 miles

3 March 1944: P.51 with drop tank, range 600 miles

A German 12.8-cm Flak 40 anti-aircraft cannon. These enormous artillery pieces were used in the defense of most major cities in the Reich.

Right: Frankfurt Cathedral miraculously still stands amongst the devastation caused by the Allied Bomber Offensive.

submission. These raids over northern France concentrated on railroad yards, and bridges that would slow or halt any reinforcements being brought up to the battle area. The R.A.F. would also be called upon to "soften up" targets before the army attacked, such as the massive aerial bombardment of Caen, although this proved to be of little use as the enemy was well dug in. The resultant damage to the city inhibited armored advance as well as causing a high civilian casualty rate.

The next targets for the combined bombing offensive, when it returned to its original duty, was to bomb oil refineries and transportation with the aim of again undermining enemy production. The 15th Air Force of the U.S.A.A.F., based in the Mediterranean, carried out raids continuously on the Romanian oil refineries until overrun by the advancing Russian Army. In Germany the rail yards were targeted to hamper troop movement from the different fronts Germany was now fighting on and to halt output from the factories reaching the front.

Throughout 1944–45 the most tonnage of bombs dropped on transport targets was more than 400,000 tons, with the oil industry receiving more than 220,000 tons of bombs. One of the most controversial targets was the bombing of cities, brought to the fore with the bombing of Dresden during 13–15 February 1945. In order to aid the Russian offensive in the east that was now closing in on the borders of Germany, the R.A.F. and U.S.A.A.F. suggested bombing targets that would cause the maximum amount of disruption to German infrastructure and communication, and to destroy transport hubs that would be used by the enemy to move troops from the west to the Eastern Front. These cities included Berlin, Liepzig, Chemnitz, and Dresden. On the night of 13 February, nearly 1,000 Lancaster bombers, aided by pathfinder Mosquitoes, flew to Dresden in two waves and dropped a total of 1,400 tons of high explosive and 1,100 tons of incendiaries. The aim of this technique was to blow the roof off the buildings and set alight the wooden beams that were now exposed. This resulted in a terrible firestorm that reached temperatures of over 2,764°F and the probable death of over 30,000 inhabitants, with 70 percent of the city being damaged. This raid was again followed up by aircraft from the 8th Air Force on 14 and 15 February. The impact of the raid was used by the Nazis for propaganda purposes and made many people on the Allied side feel uncomfortable because of the moral questions that it raised.

The bombing of the Reich by the R.A.F. and the U.S.A.A.F. did not beat Germany into submission on its own, like many of its proponents had promised, but it played a decisive role in holding down resources such as antiaircraft artillery and aircraft, which could be have been used elsewhere. It never broke the will of the Germans, but it did slow down production, and created fear in the workforce with the constant threat of attack.

THE FALL OF ITALY 1945

"WE WERE THRUST OUT ..., IF NOT LIKE THE PROVERBIAL SORE THUMB, CERTAINLY LIKE AN AGGRESSIVE FOREFINGER, REACHING OUT FOR THE ENEMY'S THROAT ALONG THE LINE OF THE SANTURNO."

GEOFFERY COX, NEW ZEALAND INTELLIGENCE OFFICER

Sherman tanks move forward on the right bank of the Foglia River, with infantry in support, August 1944.

After the capture of Rome, followed by the invasion of northwest Europe, the Italian Campaign became somewhat of a sideshow in the eyes of the Allied Commanders. General Mark Clark, obsessed with the capture of Rome before the arrival of the British, lost the chance of capturing the German 10th Army when the U.S. 5th Army broke out of the Anzio beachhead and, as the Allies advanced, they faced yet another line of prepared defense. This would prove just as difficult and as expensive in lives as previous German lines. The Allied armies had also been severely depleted, with experienced units being pulled out of the line in order to take part in Operation Dragoon, the invasion of southern France, these units being replaced by untested troops. The next line the Allies had to break was the Gothic Line, later changed by Hitler to the Green Line in order to underplay its importance. If the line was broken it could not be used by the Allies as a propaganda coup. This defensive line stretched from Persaro on the Adriatic coast, to just south of La Spezia, on the western coast, incorporating thousands of prepared machine-gun nests, antitank guns, and ditches, and hundreds of thousands of yards of barbed wire.

Progress was slow once the Allies had moved up to the Gothic Line, with attacks achieving little. On the 5th Army front, which was now separated from the British and Canadians by the Apennine Mountains, a limited advance was achieved around Mount Fogarito. These hills guarded the entrance to the Po Valley, and all previous frontal assaults had failed. Soldiers of the 442nd Regimental Combat Team climbed up the steep rear slopes of the mountain during April, and managed to take the German positions by surprise, but this was one small victory on a massive front.

The British and Canadians, together with elements of the Polish Army, also attacked on the

This Liberator bomber of the U.S. 15th Air Force has taken a direct flak hit to the wing while providing air support for the final Allied advance in northern Italy.

eastern side of the Apennines. At Rimini, on the night of 25/26 August, an attack following a massive bombardment, even greater than that at Monte Cassino, succeeded after four days of bitter fighting in breaching the Gothic Line. This was not fully appreciated immediately by the Allies, allowing the Germans to reorganize, and it took a further three weeks of fighting before the breakthrough could be exploited. By this time the fall weather had set in, which turned the dust into an impassable muddy quagmire. General Alexander, now Allied Supreme Commander in the Mediterranean, halted all offensives until the spring. A stalemate had once again fallen on the Italian Campaign.

With these two breaches of the Gothic Line, Kesselring was becoming increasingly worried: if the Allies broke out onto the wide, flat Po Valley they could annihilate the German 10th Army, which was already suffering Partisan attacks and was, because of constant bombing of the Alpine Passes and the Italian rail network, almost cut off from the rest of Europe.

This German column tries to negotiate heavy traffic buildup on the Brenner Pass in northern Italy at the end of the war.

During the winter months the Americans received some reinforcements in the form of the first African American combat unit—the 92nd, the 10th Mountain Division, and a Brazilian Brigade. These units would have to wait until spring, however, to enter the offensive.

At the start of April, the Allies eventually broke out of their winter positions and took the Germans by complete surprise. By mid-April they had broken onto the Po Valley and were beginning to move at speed, trapping many Germans against the Po River itself since all the bridges had been destroyed by air attack. However, many Germans escaped by swimming across the river, although at the cost of their heavy equipment. The Po was quickly bridged and the pursuit continued all the way to the Alps, where all the passes were in Allied hands by the close of April. By this time, Kesselring had been replaced to command the armies in northwest Europe by General Vietinghoff, who later would surrender his troops on 2 May 1945.

The fighting up the Italian peninsula had been costly in resources and lives, and was finally at an end. Without this theater of operations many lessons may not have been learned, particularly about amphibious assaults against a prepared enemy. It also held down enemy divisions that could have been used elsewhere, but it was definitely not the soft underbelly of Europe predicted by Churchill.

The End in Italy
April – May 1945

➔ Allied attacks
〜 Allied front line
〜 German defense lines

THE SOVIET ADVANCE 1944

"THERE WAS NO DOUBT THAT AT THIS STAGE OF THE WAR THE RUSSIANS COLLARED FOR THEIR INFANTRY DIVISIONS ANYONE, REGARDLESS OF TRAINING, AGE, OR HEALTH—AND SOMETIMES OF SEX—AND PUSHED THEM RUTHLESSLY INTO BATTLE."

GENERAL FRIEDRICH VON MELLENTHIN

Soviet infantry photographed advancing from their trenches.
By 1944–45 the Soviet Army had grown into the largest fighting force ever created, at its height numbering more than 12,000,000 million men. The Soviet Union conscripted a staggering total of 29,500,000 men into its armed forces. By 1944, the Germans faced this onslaught with some 3,500,000 men.

At long last, as a result of the hard-won victories in the Ukraine, the Soviets were ready to launch an offensive that would drive the German troops from their positions around Leningrad. The city had been under siege continuously since September 1941. The offensive, launched on 14 January 1944, involved the Leningrad, Volkov, and Second Baltic Fronts, supported by long-range aviation (the equivalent of the American and British Strategic Bomber Force). More than 35,000 partisans were also involved, intent on disrupting German lines of supply. By 1 March the Soviets had reached the border of Latvia, and Leningrad's 900-day siege was over.

In the spring of 1944, Soviet planning for the Belorussia operation began. The High Command had come to the conclusion that the next area for liberation was Belorussia itself. The northern part of the German front line in Russia still appeared close to the Russian heartlands. The operation to remove this salient was called Bagration, named after one of the Russian heroes of the Napoleonic invasion of 1812. The operational plan was extended in May to take

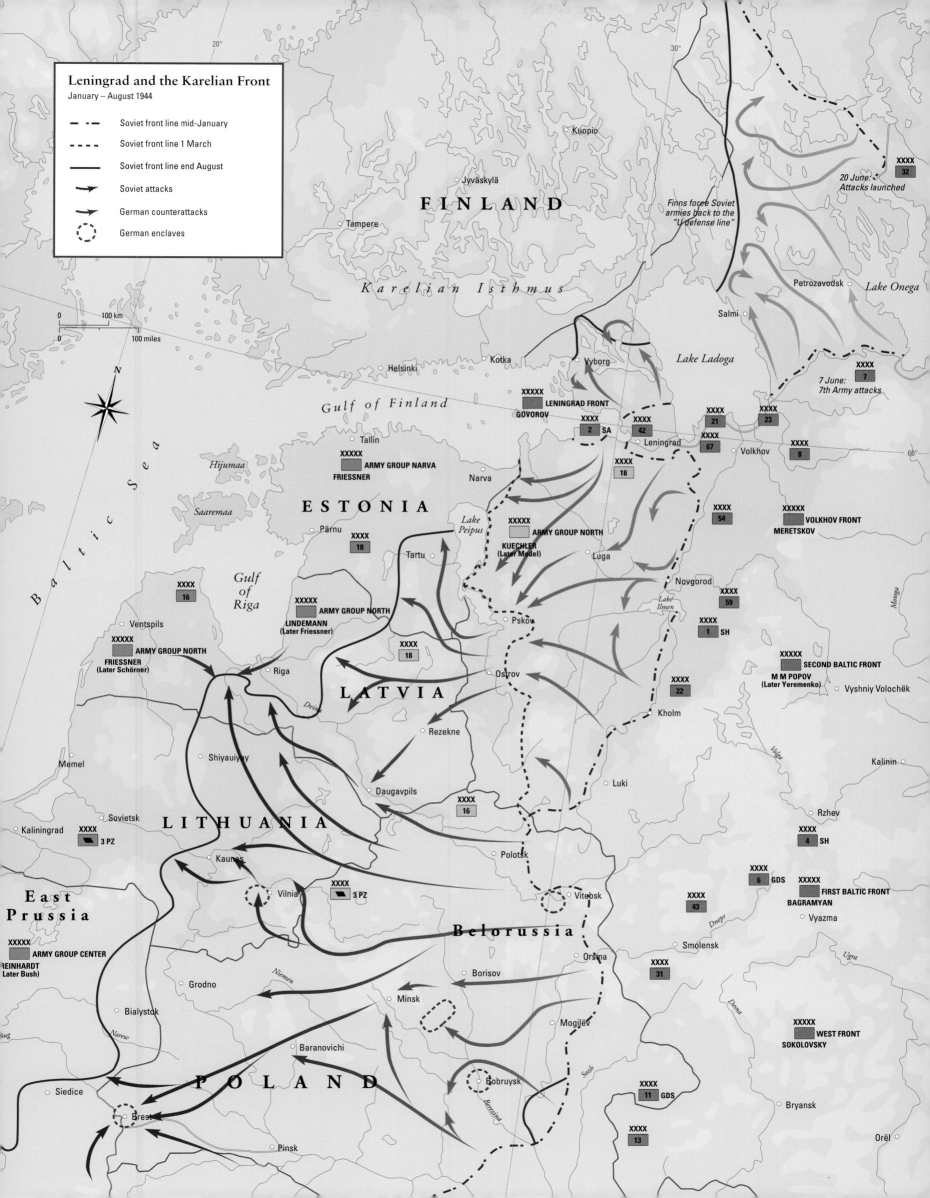

Leningrad and the Karelian Front
January – August 1944

— ·· — ·· — Soviet front line mid-January

— — — — — Soviet front line 1 March

———————— Soviet front line end August

———▶ Soviet attacks

———▶ German counterattacks

⟨ ⟩ German enclaves

FINLAND

Kuopio

Tampere

Karelian Isthmus

Lake Ladoga

20 June:
Attacks launched

XXXX
32

Petrozavodsk   *Lake Onega*

Finns force Soviet
armies back to the
"U defense line"

Salmi

Helsinki   Kotka   Vyborg

Gulf of Finland

7 June:
7th Army attacks

XXXX
7

XXXXX
LENINGRAD FRONT
GOVOROV

Tallin

XXXX
2 SA

XXXX
42

Leningrad

XXXX
67

XXXX
18

XXXX
21

XXXX
23

Volkhov

XXXX
8

Hijumaa

XXXXX
ARMY GROUP NARVA
FRIESSNER

Narva

Saaremaa

ESTONIA

Pärnu

*Lake
Peipus*

XXXX
18

Tartu

XXXXX
ARMY GROUP NORTH
KUECHLER
(Later Model)

Luga

XXXX
54

XXXXX
VOLKHOV FRONT
MERETSKOV

Novgorod

*Lake
Ilmen*

XXXX
59

*Gulf
of
Riga*

XXXX
16

XXXXX
ARMY GROUP NORTH
LINDEMANN
(Later Friessner)

Pskov

XXXX
1 SH

XXXXX
SECOND BALTIC FRONT
M M POPOV
(Later Yeremenko)

Vyshniy Volochëk

Ventspils

XXXXX
ARMY GROUP NORTH
FRIESSNER
(Later Schörner)

Riga

Dvina

LATVIA

XXXX
18

Ostrov

XXXX
22

Kholm

Kalinin

Volga

Rezekne

Velikaya

LITHUANIA

Shiyauiyay

Daugavpils

XXXX
16

Luki

Rzhev

Memel

Kaliningrad

XXXX
3 PZ

Sovietsk

Kaunas

Vilnia

XXXX
3 PZ

Polotsk

XXXX
4 SH

XXXX
6 GDS

XXXXX
FIRST BALTIC FRONT
BAGRAMYAN

**East
Prussia**

XXXXX
ARMY GROUP CENTER
REINHARDT
(Later Bush)

Vitebsk

Belorussia

XXXX
43

Vyazma

Grodno

Niemen

Orsina

Smolensk

Dnepr

Ugra

Bialystok

Minsk

Borisov

XXXX
31

Mogilëv

Narew

Bug

Baranovichi

POLAND

Sozh

XXXXX
WEST FRONT
SOKOLOVSKY

Berezina

Siedice

Bobruysk

XXXX
11 GDS

Brest

Pinsk

XXXX
13

Bryansk

Orël

Scale:
0   100 km
0   100 miles

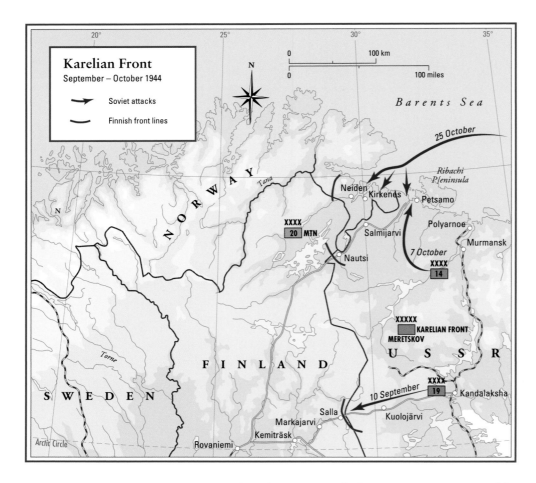

Karelian Front
September – October 1944

→ Soviet attacks

⌣ Finnish front lines

THE KARELIAN FRONT
As well as the gigantic offensive
to retake the western parts of
the U.S.S.R., the Soviets
launched a series of attacks in
the far north, protecting their
ports and installations along the
White Sea coast.

the advance well clear of the Pripet Marshes and to liberate the area between the Dvina and Neman Rivers. This would mean an advance of 400 miles along a front of 360 miles.

The offensive would involve 1,400,000 men, 31,000 guns and mortars, 5,200 tanks and assault guns, with over 5,000 aircraft in support. The main objective was the destruction of German Army Group Center. This army group could still muster 1,200,000 men, 9,500 guns and heavy mortars, 900 tanks, and 1,350 aircraft in its defense.

German radio intercepts picked up increasing traffic, and on 10 June interpreted an order from Moscow to Soviet partisans to increase attacks on rail communications. These were carried out over the next 12 days. On the night of 22/23 June—three years to the day since the German invasion—the Soviet Air Force attacked German rear areas and lines of supply. In the early morning of 23 June, the first part of the offensive began. Meanwhile, on 6 June, the western Allies had landed in Normandy and the Second Front became a reality. Germany was now fighting in the west as well as the east.

On 23 June, the first attacks were launched, made up of operations heading towards Bobrinsk, Vitebsk-Orsha, and Mogilev to Polotsk. There was a determined plan to surround the concentration of German forces at Minsk. Hitler, again, ordered that Vitebsk and Oveha should be "ferte platze" (firm positions) from which a defense line would be somehow created, and held to the last man. By 3 July the Germans, consisting of the 27th Panzer Corps, 110th Division, and other elements at Minsk, were surrounded. These forces were destroyed between 5 and 11 July. The rest of Army Group Center fell back westward from Minsk.

General Walther Model was now in command of Army Group Center. He requested a meeting with Hilter asking to withdraw the garrison at Vilna. Hitler said "No, hold out at all costs." But Model did get some reinforcements from Army Group North to strengthen his remaining resources. While this was happening Vilna fell on 13 July, followed by Pinsk on 14 July, and Grodno on 16 July. Then finally, on 20 July, the Red Army finally destroyed Army Group Center as a fighting force. Of its 67 Divisions, 17 had been annililated and the remaining 50 lost at least 50 percent of their strength.

After this massive achievement, the Soviet advance began to lose momentum, reaching just short of Bialystok and Kaunas. Over the next four weeks, the Soviets captured Kaunas and advanced to the old prewar borders of East Prussia. To the south they managed to advance a further 60 miles almost to the eastern suburbs of Warsaw.

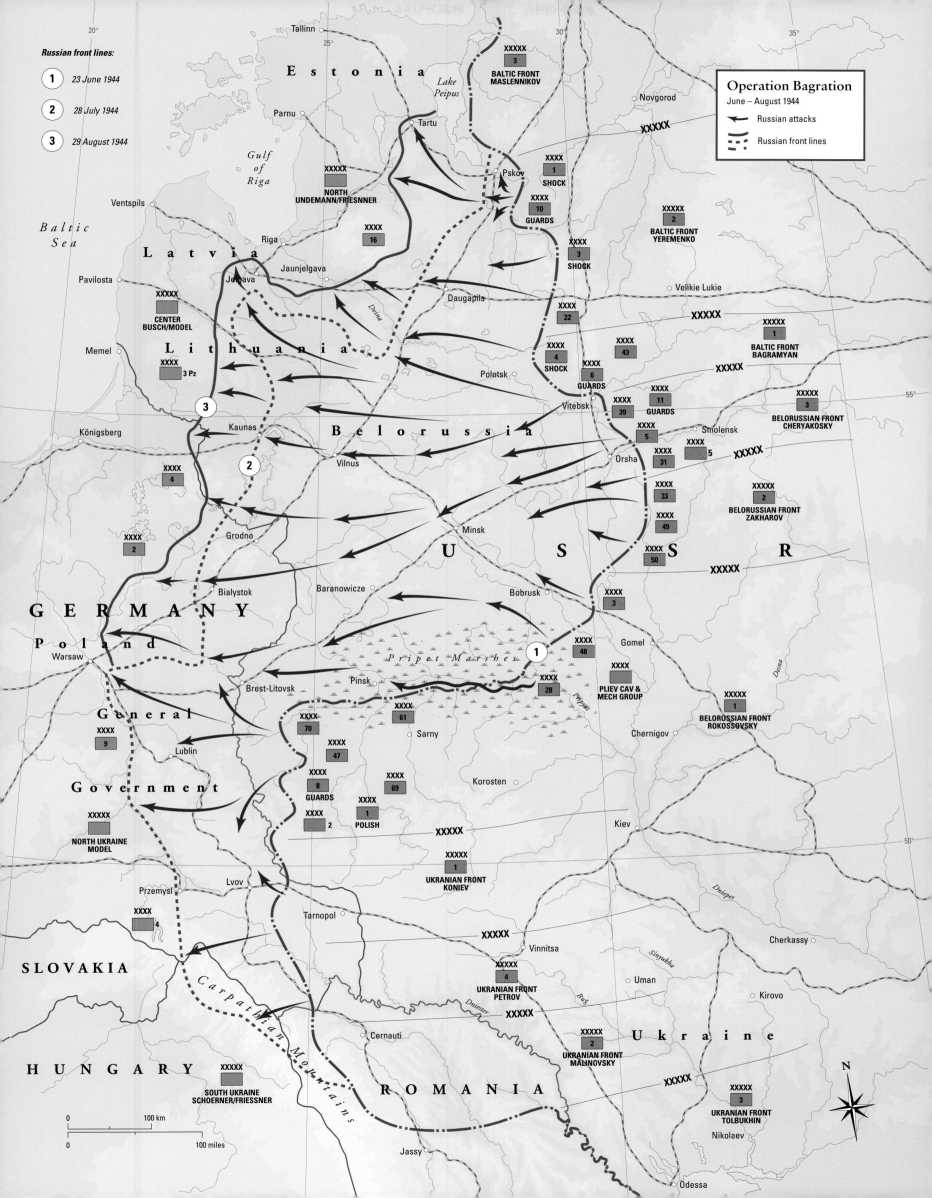

Russian front lines:

(1) 23 June 1944

(2) 28 July 1944

(3) 29 August 1944

Operation Bagration

June – August 1944

⬅ Russian attacks

╍╍╍ Russian front lines

Tallinn

Estonia

Lake Peipus

BALTIC FRONT
MASLENNIKOV — 3

Novgorod

Parnu

Tartu

Pskov

XXXX 1 SHOCK

Gulf of Riga

XXXXX NORTH UNDEMANN/FRIESNNER

XXXX 10 GUARDS

XXXX 2 BALTIC FRONT YEREMENKO

Ventspils

Baltic Sea

Latvia

Riga

Jaunjelgava

XXXX 16

XXXX 3 SHOCK

Velikie Lukie

Daugapils

Pavilosta

Jelgava

XXXXX CENTER BUSCH/MODEL

Daugapils

XXXX 22

XXXXX 1 BALTIC FRONT BAGRAMYAN

Memel

Lithuania

XXXX 3 Pz

Polotsk

XXXX 4 SHOCK

XXXX 6 GUARDS

XXXX 43

XXXX 11 GUARDS

XXXXX 3 BELORUSSIAN FRONT CHERYAKOSKY

(3)

Kaunas

Vitebsk

XXXX 39

XXXX 5

Smolensk

Königsberg

Belorussia

XXXX 31

XXXX 5

(2)

Vilnus

Orsha

XXXXX 2 BELORUSSIAN FRONT ZAKHAROV

XXXX 4

XXXX 33

U   S   S   R

XXXX 49

XXXX 2

Minsk

XXXX 50

Grodno

Baranowicze

Bobrusk

XXXX 3

GERMANY

Bialystok

Gomel

Poland

XXXX 48

Warsaw

Pripet Marshes

XXXX PLIEV CAV & MECH GROUP

Pinsk

XXXX 28

Brest-Litovsk

General

XXXX 61

Pripet

XXXXX 1 BELORUSSIAN FRONT ROKOSSOVSKY

XXXX 9

Sarny

XXXX 70

Chernigov

Government

XXXX 47

Lublin

XXXX 69

Korosten

XXXX 8 GUARDS

XXXX 2

XXXX 1 POLISH

XXXXX NORTH UKRAINE MODEL

Kiev

XXXXX UKRANIAN FRONT KONIEV

Lvov

XXXXX 50'

Przemysl

Tarnopol

Dnieper

XXXX 4

Cherkassy

SLOVAKIA

Carpathian Mountains

XXXXX UKRANIAN FRONT PETROV — 4

Vinnitsa

Bug

Dniester

Sinyukha

Uman

Kirovo

HUNGARY

XXXXX SOUTH UKRAINE SCHOERNER/FRIESSNER

Cernauti

U k r a i n e

ROMANIA

XXXXX UKRANIAN FRONT MALINOVSKY — 2

XXXXX UKRANIAN FRONT TOLBUKHIN — 3

Jassy

Nikolaev

Odessa

0 ___ 100 km

0 ___ 100 miles

N

Soviet Advance into Romania and Hungary

8 August – 15 December 1944

- - - - Soviet front line August
- - - Soviet front line mid-September
——— Soviet front line mid-December
——➤ Soviet attacks
——➤ Romanian attacks
——➤ Bulgarian attacks
——➤ German counterattacks
- - -➤ German withdrawals
✳ Partisan attacks, named

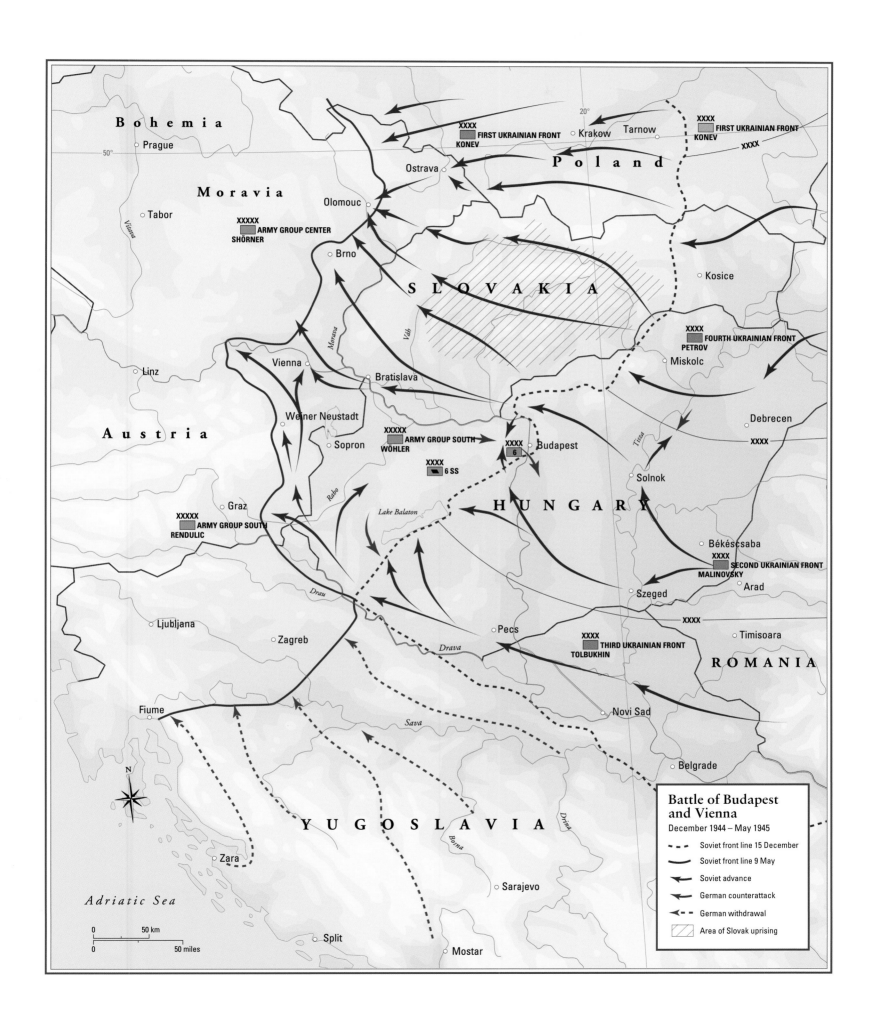

Battle of Budapest
and Vienna
December 1944 – May 1945

- - - -   Soviet front line 15 December
━━━━   Soviet front line 9 May
──►   Soviet advance
──►   German counterattack
◄-- --   German withdrawal
▨   Area of Slovak uprising

ADVANCE INTO GERMANY 1945

"EXCUSE ME MATE, IS THIS THE ROAD TO BERLIN?"

BRITISH TANK DRIVER TO GERMAN CITIZEN

WHILE CROSSING THE BORDER

Right: Canadian troops hitching a ride on a Sherman 'Firefly' tank break the tension briefly during bitter fighting in the Reichswald area of western Germany.

With the last German offensive defeated, the Allied Supreme Commander looked toward a final advance into Germany. Eisenhower decided to keep his "broad front" advance strategy, with Montgomery's 21st Army Group, still incorporating U.S. 9th Army, in the north; Bradley's 12th Army Group in the center; and Dever's 6th Army Group, with Patton's 3rd Army and the French 1st Army, in the south.

First to strike would be 21st Army Group in the north. The Canadian 1st Army was to attack out from the Nijmegen area in conjunction with the U.S. 9th Army to its south to form a pincer movement clearing out the area between the Ruhr and the Rhine. The Germans, anticipating the attack, blew the largest dam on the Ruhr, flooding the plain in front of the U.S. 9th Army, delaying its advance for two weeks, and slowing the Canadians' advance along a very narrow patch of land between the Meuse and the Waal, only after they had cleared the Reichswald Forest. Von Rundstedt hoped the time gained while the valley was flooded would allow him to withdraw his troops to the east bank of the Rhine, a move denied by the Führer. When the U.S. 9th Army started its advance on 23 February, these German forces were trapped, the Allies taking over 290,000 prisoners.

Now the only major barrier in the way of the Allies and ultimate victory was the Rhine River. However, this was crossed at three different places in very different circumstances. The first to arrive at the Rhine was Simpson's 9th Army around the area of Dusseldorf, but all the bridges had been blown by German engineers beforehand. Second to arrive on 7 March was a small armored reconnaissance patrol of Hodge's 1st Army, who found the Ludendorf bridge—built during World War I to bring supplies to the front—still standing, even though engineers had tried to blow it up several times. This bridge was captured and over five divisions crossed under a constant aerial bombardment before it succumbed to its earlier damage and collapsed into the Rhine, taking the 28 U.S. engineers, who had been trying desperately to save it, with it. By the time the bridge fell, pontoon bridges had been assembled allowing the bridgehead to be expanded. The failure to blow the bridge before the arrival of Allied forces led to the dismissal of von Rundstedt by Hitler, who was replaced by Kesselring.

A surprise crossing was made by the men of Patton's 3rd Army at Oppenhiem, south of Mainz, which established a bridgehead to the south, just before Montgomery's massive attack to the north to establish his bridgehead at Rees and Wesel. Operation Plunder was launched on 24 March with a massive artillery and aerial bombardment typical of any of Monty's attacks. The assault would utilize the British 30th and 12th Corps between Rees and Wesel, and the U.S. 16th Corps to the south. The British

Above: American troops bring up a machine gun during the capture of Saarluatern, February 1945.

Below: A group of U.S. soldiers fighting through the German city of Aachen.

crossed the river but soon ran into a concerted defense on the eastern bank with heavily dug in machine-gun posts. The American units faced a lighter defense and soon constructed a pontoon bridge, which was complete by the evening of the 24th. The river crossing was also supported by an airborne drop codenamed "Varsity," utilizing the British 6th Airborne Division and the U.S. 17th Airborne Division. This secured the high ground looking over the bridgehead and bridges over the River Issel. It also became the largest and the most successful airborne operation in history, with almost every one of the drops landing where they should. These troops were then to join up with the 21st Army and continue with them in their advance to the German Baltic Coast.

The 21st Army Group advanced northeast toward Hamburg, losing the U.S. 9th Army as it encircled the Ruhr from the north, heading south to eventually meet up with the U.S. 1st Army, and capturing 300,000 German soldiers in the pocket. The 12th Army Group headed east toward the River Elbe and southward into Bavaria and Czechoslovakia. In the south, 6th Army Group headed to the southeast of Germany to enter Austria and northern Italy. The end of the Third Reich and the war in Europe was close.

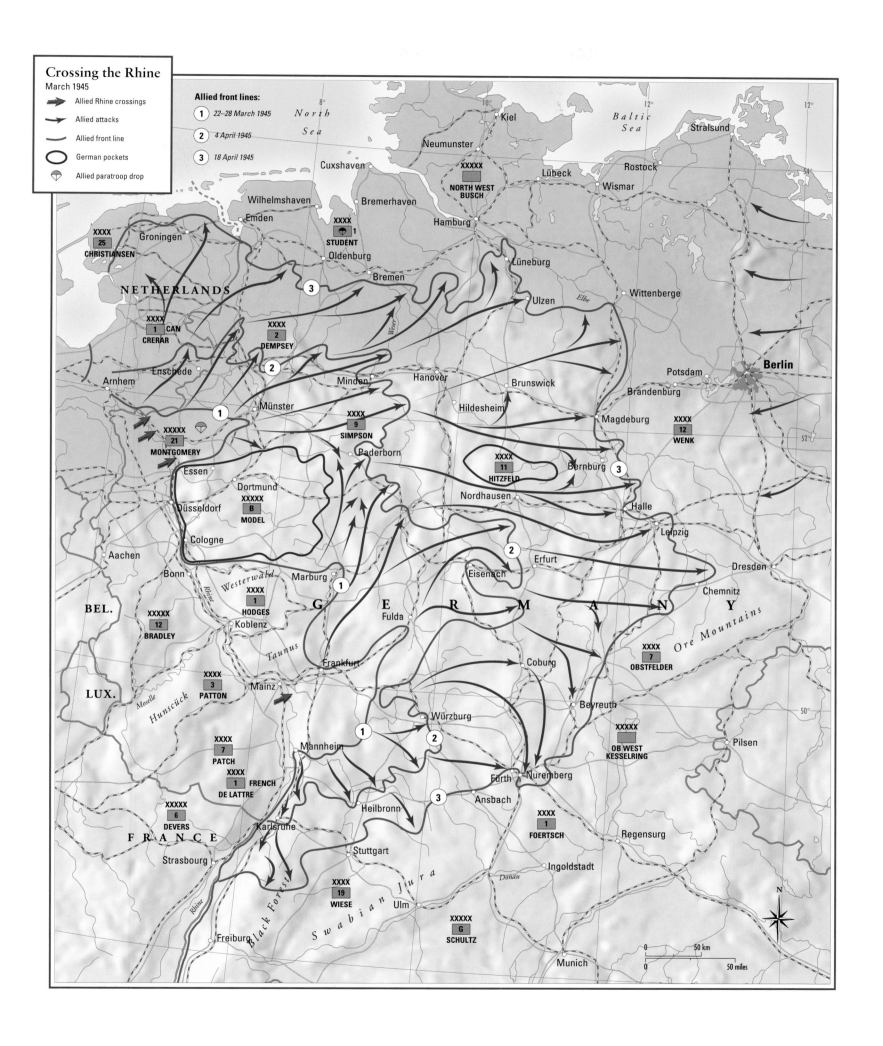

Crossing the Rhine
March 1945

Allied front lines:

- Allied Rhine crossings
- Allied attacks
- Allied front line
- German pockets
- Allied paratroop drop

1 *22–28 March 1945*
2 *4 April 1945*
3 *18 April 1945*

North Sea

Baltic Sea

NETHERLANDS

GERMANY

FRANCE

BEL.

LUX.

Groningen
Emden
Enschede
Arnhem

XXXX 25 CHRISTIANSEN
XXXX 1 CAN CRERAR
XXXXX 21 MONTGOMERY
XXXX 2 DEMPSEY
XXXX 9 SIMPSON
XXXXX B MODEL
XXXX 1 HODGES
XXXXX 12 BRADLEY
XXXX 3 PATTON
XXXX 7 PATCH
XXXX 1 FRENCH DE LATTRE
XXXXX 6 DEVERS
XXXX 19 WIESE
XXXXX G SCHULTZ
XXXX 1 STUDENT
XXXXX NORTH WEST BUSCH
XXXX 11 HITZFELD
XXXX 12 WENK
XXXX 7 OBSTFELDER
XXXXX OB WEST KESSELRING
XXXX 1 FOERTSCH

Wilhelmshaven
Bremerhaven
Cuxhaven
Neumunster
Kiel
Lübeck
Rostock
Stralsund
Wismar
Hamburg
Oldenburg
Bremen
Lüneburg
Ulzen
Wittenberge
Potsdam
Berlin
Brandenburg
Magdeburg
Münster
Minden
Hanover
Brunswick
Hildesheim
Bernburg
Essen
Dortmund
Paderborn
Düsseldorf
Cologne
Aachen
Bonn
Marburg
Koblenz
Nordhausen
Halle
Leipzig
Dresden
Chemnitz
Erfurt
Eisenach
Fulda
Coburg
Frankfurt
Mainz
Würzburg
Beyreuth
Pilsen
Mannheim
Fürth
Nuremberg
Ansbach
Heilbronn
Regensurg
Karlsruhe
Stuttgart
Strasbourg
Freiburg
Ulm
Ingoldstadt
Munich

Westerwald
Taunus
Hunsrück
Moselle
Rhine
Weser
Elbe
Ore Mountains
Black Forest
Swabian Jura
Donau

0 50 km
0 50 miles

N

THE FALL OF BERLIN 1945

"IF THE WAR IS LOST, THE GERMAN NATION WILL ALSO PERISH...
THERE IS NO NEED TO TAKE INTO CONSIDERATION THE BASIC
REQUIREMENTS OF THE PEOPLE... THOSE WHO WILL REMAIN
AFTER THE BATTLE ARE THOSE WHO ARE INFERIOR; FOR THE
GOOD WILL HAVE FALLEN."

ADOLF HITLER TO ALBERT SPEER

Overleaf right: This iconic Soviet painting celebrates soldiers of the Red Army on the roof of Berlin's Reichstag.

Below: A Soviet soldier drags a German solider from his hiding place during the street fighting in Berlin in 1945.

The fall of Berlin was one of the last major battles in the European war. Here two massive Soviet army groups, with the support of another, encircled the city and finally destroyed the capital of the Third Reich. By the end of a huge series of Soviet offensives, Romania and Bulgaria had been overrun and most of Hungary, including its capital Budapest, was in the hands of the Red Army. After waiting for the Warsaw uprising to be crushed by the Germans, the Red Army had pushed across Poland, taking the Baltic coast around East Prussia and Danzig. The Russians were poised on the eastern bank of the Oder, having beaten back a counterattack by Himmler's newly-formed Army Group Vistula and Stalin gave the order for Berlin to be captured by 1 May, May Day.

Before this final push, Russia had to redeploy its armies in line with this operation. This it did with great speed and efficiency, something unheard of four years earlier, placing Zhukov's 1st Belorussian Front due east of Berlin for the main advance, flanked in the north by Rokossovsky's 2nd Belorussian Front with Konev's 1st Ukraine Front to the south. The total number of men reached almost 2.5 million, with 6,250 tanks, 41,600 guns and mortars and 7,500 aircraft. Facing this enormous force was the remnants of the German Army, made up of 33 severely depleted divisions, with 12th Army to the west of Berlin on the east bank of the River Elbe facing the Americans and British. However, General Gotthard Heinrici had been placed in command of Army Group Vistula and set about creating a workable defensive line.

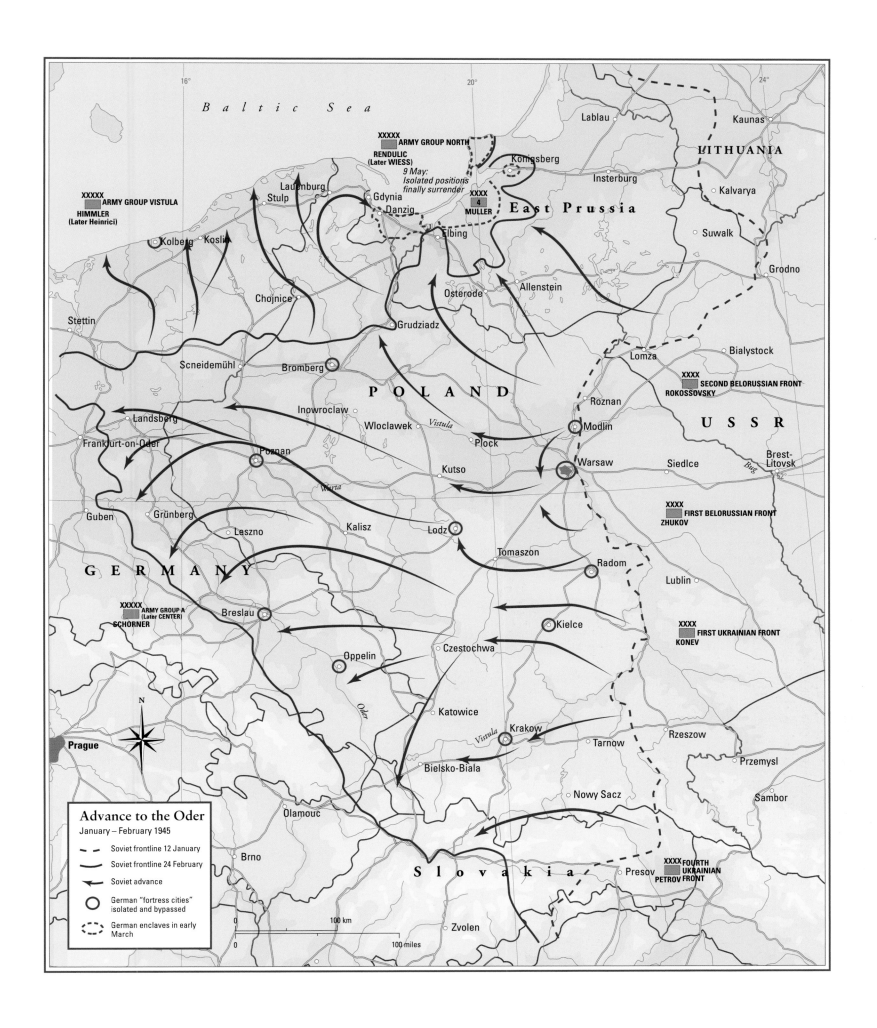

Baltic Sea

XXXXX ARMY GROUP NORTH
RENDULIC
(Later WIESS)

9 May:
Isolated positions
finally surrender

Königsberg

Lablau

Kaunas

LITHUANIA

Insterburg

Lauenburg
Stulp

Gdynia
Danzig

XXXX
4
MULLER

East Prussia

Kalvarya

XXXXX ARMY GROUP VISTULA
HIMMLER
(Later Heinrici)

Kolberg   Koslin

Suwalk

Elbing

Suwalk

Grodno

Chojnice

Osterode

Allenstein

Stettin

Grudziadz

POLAND

Lomza

Bialystock

Scneidemühl

Bromberg

XXXX SECOND BELORUSSIAN FRONT
ROKOSSOVSKY

Inowroclaw

Vistula

Roznan

USSR

Landsberg

Wloclawek

Modlin

Siedlce

Brest-
Litovsk

Frankfurt-on-Oder

Plock

Poznan

Warta

Kutso

Warsaw

Bug

Guben   Grünberg

Leszno

Kalisz

Lodz

XXXX FIRST BELORUSSIAN FRONT
ZHUKOV

Lublin

GERMANY

Tomaszon

Radom

XXXXX ARMY GROUP A
(Later CENTER)
SCHORNER

Breslau

Kielce

XXXX FIRST UKRAINIAN FRONT
KONEV

Oppelin

Czestochwa

Oder

Katowice

Rzeszow

N

Vistula

Krakow

Tarnow

Przemysl

Prague

Bielsko-Biala

Sambor

Nowy Sacz

Olamouc

Brno

S l o v a k i a

Presov

XXXX FOURTH
UKRAINIAN
PETROV FRONT

Zvolen

Advance to the Oder
January – February 1945

- - - Soviet frontline 12 January

——— Soviet frontline 24 February

← Soviet advance

◯ German "fortress cities"
isolated and bypassed

⊂⊃ German enclaves in early
March

0   100 km

0   100 miles

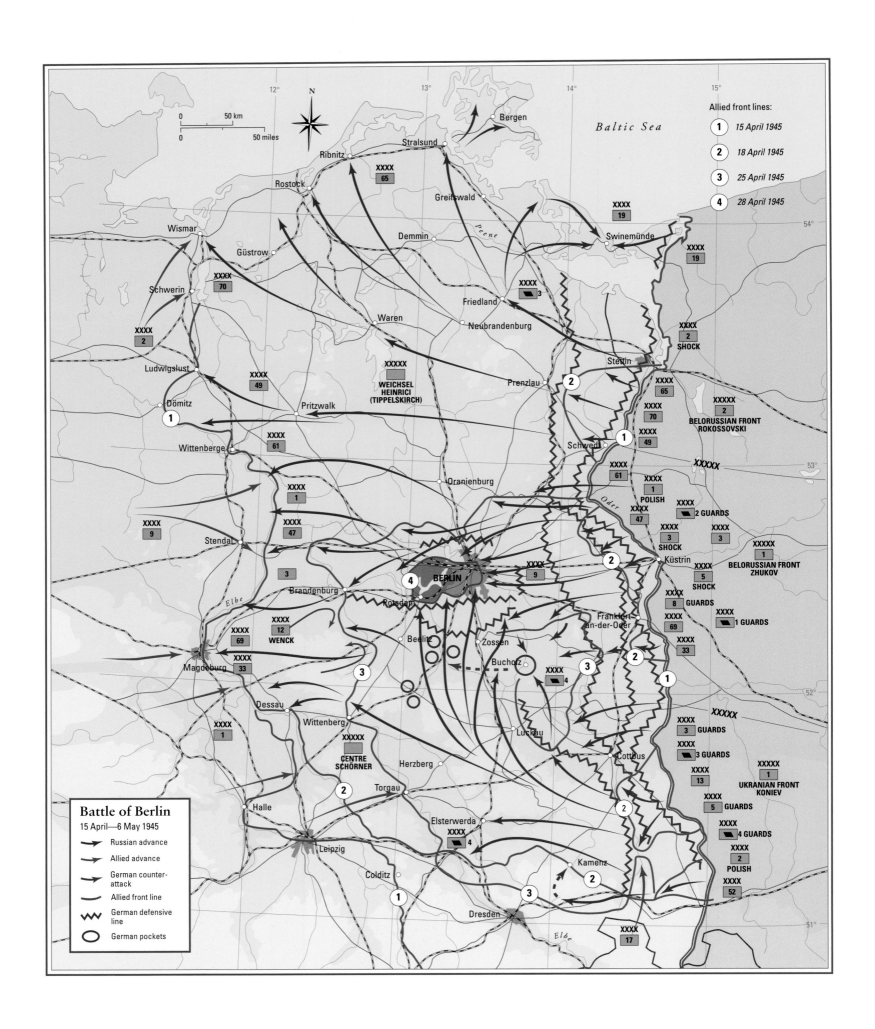

Allied front lines:
- ① 15 April 1945
- ② 18 April 1945
- ③ 25 April 1945
- ④ 28 April 1945

Battle of Berlin

15 April—6 May 1945

- Russian advance
- Allied advance
- German counter-attack
- Allied front line
- German defensive line
- German pockets

A local cart passes through a ruined street in Berlin, evidence of the fighting and bombing that the city had suffered at Hitler's orders.

Anticipating that the main Russian advance would come across the Oder river and along the autobahn heading straight into Berlin, he created three defensive lines around Seelow Heights, incorporating antitank ditches, guns, and bunkers overlooking the river some 70 miles west of Berlin, leaving only a delaying force on the west bank.

The Russian assault went in before dawn on 16 April, following a bombardment that did little to the German defense. Progress was slow against the Germans and the advance began to stall, Zhokov throwing in his reserves in the hope of achieving a breakthrough. To the south Konev's forces were enjoying greater success, especially against 4th Panzer Corps, which was being forced back. Stalin ordered Konev to exploit their gap and once through to swing north for Berlin. With the threat of encirclement Heinrici had to fall back with his divisions. By 18 April the 1st Belorussian Front was at the third defensive line about to burst through, and 1st Ukraine Front had reached Forst. Then the 2nd Belorussian Front launched their attack in the north, holding 3rd Panzer Army on the northern flank, unable to fall back to Berlin. On 19 April the 1st Ukraine Front had beaten its way through 4th Panzer Corps and were now heading north to meet up with the 1st Belorussian Front and west to meet U.S. forces on the River Elbe.

On 20 April, Hitler's birthday, Berlin was greeted by Russian artillery shells raining down on the city center. The Soviets would not stop the shelling until the German garrison surrendered. They moved north and south of Berlin, encircling the city. On 22 April Alfred Jodl, Chief of Staff of German High Command, suggested to an increasingly deranged Hitler that they should move 12th Army away from the Elbe to link up with 9th Army in defense of Berlin. However, on 23 April 12th Army were stopped in their tracks by the advancing 1st Ukraine Front. Hitler appointed General Helmuth Weidling as defense commandant of Berlin. On 25 April Zhukov's and Konev's forces linked up, encircling the city, with Konev's men linking with the U.S. 69th Division near Torgau on the River Elbe.

Inside Berlin, the severely depleted men of the S.S., Wehrmacht, and police, alongside boys of the Hitler Youth and old men of the Volksturm home guard, prepared for the final onslaught. The Russians advanced from all sides and vicious house-to-house fighting continued, many German soldiers fighting on for fear that if they surrender they would simply be shot on the spot. Hitler ordered General Heinrici to hold the city at all costs. He refused this order and was replaced by General Kurt Student. On 30 April, Hitler married his long-time partner, Eva Braun, then committed suicide. Many of his close associates, including Goebbels, with his entire family, followed suit.

General Weidling surrendered Berlin on 2 May but many pockets of resistance held out for some days after. Berlin had fallen, and the end of the war in Europe was within sight.

The Soviet victors proudly stand on their IS-2 tank. After four years of bitter fighting the Red Army had fought its way past the ruins of Stalingrad to the center of Hitler's Reich. In the background is the Siegessäule (Victory Column), named after a historic Prussian victory.

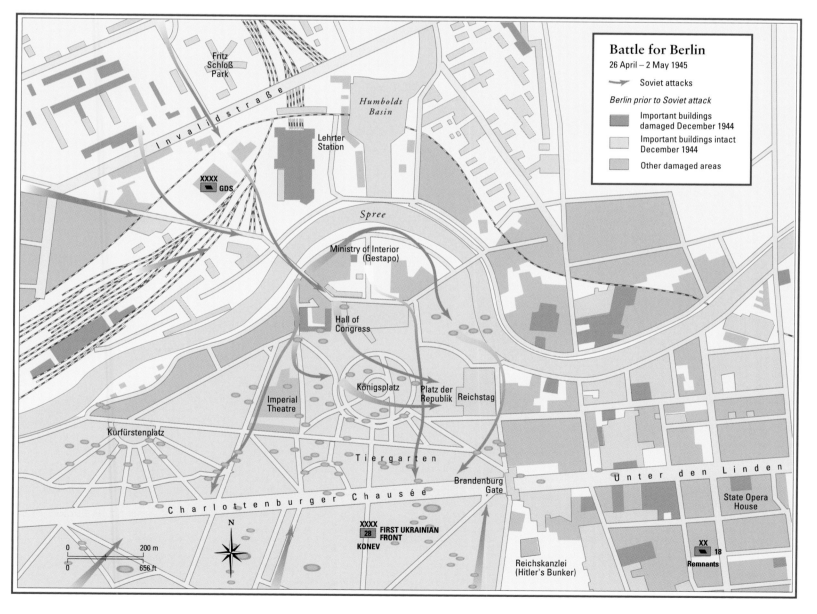

Battle for Berlin
26 April – 2 May 1945

⟶ Soviet attacks

Berlin prior to Soviet attack

Important buildings damaged December 1944

Important buildings intact December 1944

Other damaged areas

VICTORY IN EUROPE

"NORMAN HARRIS CAME IN, TAKING HIS RIFLE OFF HIS SHOULDER
AND NOT QUITE MEETING OUR EYES. HE SAID TIREDLY, WITH HIS
FLAT BOSTONIAN ACCENT, 'WELL, BOYS, IT'S ALL OVER. THE WAR'S
OVER. I JUST HEARD THE ANNOUNCEMENT'."

LESTER ATWELL, U.S. ARMY.

American and Soviet soldiers
exchange handshakes when
their respective units meet at
Torgau on 25 April 1945. Within
a few days the war in Europe
would be over.

Five days after the U.S. and Soviet forces had linked up at Torgau on the River Elbe, Adolf Hitler and his new wife, Eva, committed suicide. In accordance with Hitler's last will and testament, Grand Admiral Carl Donitz was appointed the new Reichspresident. The same day, 1 May, the 10th Army, fighting in northern Italy, under the command of General von Vietinghoff, ordered his forces to cease hostilities in the region, coming into effect on 2 May.

On 4 May, Montgomery took the surrender of all German forces in the Dutch, North-west German and Danish regions from Grand Admiral Hans-Georg von Friedburg and General Hans Linzel on Luneburg Heath. The following day, Grand Admiral Donitz ordered all submarines to cease operations and return to base.

Alfred Jodl, representing German High Command and Reichspresident Donitz, arrived in Rheims on 6 May and on the following day signed the total and unconditional surrender in the presence of General Eisenhower. The news soon broke and Victory in Europe was announced to the western Allies. Soon after the Reich was partitioned, East Prussia being divided between Poland and Russia, as well as the land east of the Oder. The rest of Germany was partitioned into four zones, occupied by the United States, Great Britain, France, and the U.S.S.R. Austria, now politically separated from Germany, was also occupied and divided into four zones.

Five years of war had left Europe in ruins. Hundreds of years of great architectural treasures and art had been utterly devastated. It would take decades to recover, although some villages and towns were never to reappear. Over 43 million people had died, many families grieved for their lost loved ones, and many still do.

Post-war Europe

- → Displaced people, with number in thousands and dates
- ■ NATO member (1949–59)
- ■ Soviet bloc
- □ Soviet sympathy
- □ Non-aligned
- **0.000** U.S. aid per country in millions of $ (Marshall Plan)

ICELAND **29**

Arctic Circle

Norwegian Sea

NORWAY

SWEDEN **107**

FINLAND

Finns 400 (1939–44)

60 (1944)   Estonians   40 (1944–45)

50 (1944)   Latvians   100 (1944–45)   Russians 2500 (1946–50)

50 (1944)   Lithuanians   80 (1944–45)

3,176

North Sea

254

1,079

1,389

271

DENMARK
Germans 8050 (1945–52)

146

IRELAND

UNITED KINGDOM

2,706

556

NETHERLANDS

BELGIUM

L.

Germans 1850 (1945–52)

Berlin

G.D.R.

POLAND

Poles 3500 (1945–52)

U.S.S.R.

Poles 1500 (1945–46)

to U.K., North America, and South Africa

displaced persons (majority Jews) 960 (1947–51)

Germans 250 (1945–47)

CZECHOSLOVAKIA

677

Ukrainians 500 (1945–47)

Germans 525 (1946–47)

ATLANTIC OCEAN

G.F.R. **1,474**

Germans 250 (1945–47)

Hungarians 200 (1946–47)

Slovaks 60 (1946–47)

SWITZERLAND

AUSTRIA

H.

Slovaks 100 (1946–47)

ROMANIA

FRANCE

Croats & Serbs 40 (1946)

Hungarians 40 (1946)

to Israel

Corsica

32

Trieste free state

YUGOSLAVIA

ANDORRA

Germans 250 (1945–47)

Germans 300 (1945–48)

BULGARIA

109

Turks 160 (1950–52)

Balearic Is.

Sardinia

ITALY

ALBANIA

694

50

PORTUGAL

SPAIN

GREECE

Aegean Sea

TURKEY

Mediterranean

Gibraltar to Britain

Tangier international

to Spain

Sicily

Malta to Britain

Morocco to France

Algeria to France

Tunisia to France

Sea

221

Libya to Italy

0   200 km
0   200 miles

N

Burma 1944–45

"WE HAD NO AMMUNITION, NO FOOD, NO CLOTHES, NO GUNS...
THE MEN WERE BAREFOOT AND RAGGED AND THREW AWAY
EVERYTHING EXCEPT CANES TO HELP THEM WALK... AT KOHIMA
WE WERE STARVED AND THEN CRUSHED."

SHIZUO MARUYAMA, JAPANESE FOOT SOLDIER

By August 1943, with the creation of South East Asia Command, the Allies were ready to take the initiative in Burma, with three active fronts. On the Northern Front U.S. General Joseph Stilwell's forces, made up mostly of Chinese soldiers of the 38th Division and supported by Merrill's Marauders and the Chindits, attempted to push north while trying to open the Ledo Road to start supplying Chiang Kai-Shek's forces once again. On the Southern Front, 15th Corps advanced on the Mayu Peninsula with the intention of reaching Rangoon. On the Central Front was Indian 4th Corps, who advanced into the Chindwin Valley.

In the north, Stilwell's forces advanced on Shinbwiyang with the road being constructed directly behind the advance. If a stronghold or Japanese force impeded their progress, Merrill's Marauders, a U.S. Commando unit adept at jungle fighting, having been initially trained by Briton Orde Wingate's Chindits, would plunge headlong into the jungle, outflank the Japanese, and destroy their positions. Also helping the advance, the Chindits launched attacks on the Japanese supply lines experiencing very heavy fighting and achieving tactical victories. They were then moved further north nearer to the advancing Chinese 38th Division and took heavy casualties defending the captured airfield at Myitkyina. The Chinese, by this time, had also started a new offensive from Yunnan on a 200-mile front and the Japanese now had to fight a two-front campaign in the north.

On the Southern Front, the Indian 15th Corps advanced on the Mayu Peninsula along the coast and captured the small port of Maungdaw in January 1944, which aided the supply of the advance as overland routes were still not navigable during the monsoon season. They then went on to capture the rail tunnels leading through the mountains linking Maungdaw with the Kalapanzin Valley. However, this move was foreseen by the Japanese 55th Division, which got around the rear of the attacking Indian Division, the 7th, and cut them off from the rest of 15th Corps. Thanks to air supply the troops managed to hold out in what became known as the Battle of the Admin Box and were relieved when the 5th Division broke through to lift the siege. They then went on to capture the rail tunnels before halting the advance when the monsoon season closed in.

Meanwhile, on the Central Front, the Japanese launched a major offensive using the 15th Army, which was made up of three divisions under the command of Lt-General Renya Mutaguchi. They

Japanese soldiers march along a jungle trail. These men were masters of jungle warfare and always fought with dedication and tenacity.

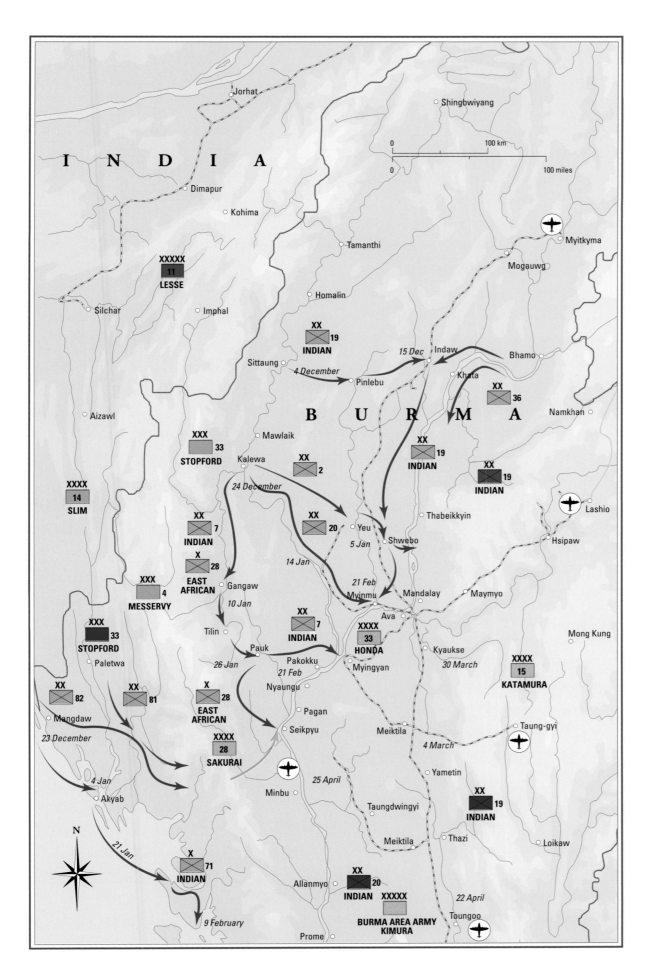

Allied Recapture of Burma
December 1944 – February 1945

Allied advances with dates

Japanese counterattacks

Across the mountains and through the jungle, the mule proved to be the most reliable form of transport.

British soldiers cross one of the many rivers in Burma in the long campaign to recapture the country from the Japanese.

planned to isolate the forward divisions of 4th Corps, go on to capture Imphal, then move to Dimapur. This attack came on 8 March 1944, and the Indian 20th Division fell back to the Imphal Plain on 13 March. The 17th Division was cut off by the Japanese advance, aided by air drops and assisted by the 23rd Division, and managed to fight through the Japanese positions and arrive on the plain in early April. General Slim then decided to reinforce the Central Front by flying in the 5th Indian Division from the south and sending two Brigades to Imphal and one to the Dimapur and Kohima area. On 5 April the Japanese launched a series of vicious attacks against the defenders of the small town of Kohima, the defenders fighting from positions around the District Commissioner's tennis court. The men were relieved by an Indian Brigade on 18 April. After this reinforcement the Allies moved from the defensive to the offensive. By mid-May they had managed to drive the Japanese off the Kohima Ridge. After this defeat, together with health problems affecting the Japanese troops, the Imphal offensive collapsed. By July the Japanese had fallen back behind the line of the Chindwin River.

The Japanese Burma Area Army's new commander, Hyotura Kimura, recognized that his soldiers were at a low ebb and pulled 15th Army back behind the Irrawaddy River, while the 28th Army was to stay defending the Arakan district in the south, while the 33rd Army would continue to harass Stilwell's forces in the north and deny the completion of the Ledo Road. On 21 January 1945, the Chinese Yunnan forces finally linked up with Stilwell's forces and the Ledo Road could be opened but by this time in the war the benefits were debatable. In the south the advance restarted at the end of the monsoon as the Indian 25th Division advanced on Foul Point and Rathedaung, and the West African 81st and 82nd Divisions advanced on Myohaung. With the aid of amphibious commando assaults outflanking the defending Japanese the Myebon Peninsula was cleared by mid-January 1945. Commandos then landed on Daingbon Chaung and after heavy fighting, leaving many Japanese dead, they linked up with 82nd Division coming overland.

After the Japanese retreat to the Irrawaddy, the plan was laid for 33rd Corps on the Center Front to advance to the Shebo Plain and for 4th Corps to cross the Irrawaddy near to Pakokku and capture Meiklia, an important Japanese communications center. During January and February the 33rd Corps successfully captured crossings over the Irrawaddy near Mandalay while, in late February, 4th Corps captured the crossing at Nyuangu. They then captured Meiktila on 5 March after a rapid motorized advance. The Japanese attempted to recapture the town but the 4th Corps was now being constantly reinforced and the Japanese suffered heavy losses, breaking off the attack at the end of March. While the main concentration of Japanese forces had been attacking Meiktila, Mandalay had fallen to 33rd Corps on 20 March, much of the city being destroyed in the process. This effectively cut communications with the 33rd Army in the north, and the 15th Army was reduced to small units that were forced to retreat into the Shan States. The 33rd and 4th Corps then turned to advance down the Irrawaddy and Sittang valleys toward Rangoon. The Japanese evacuation of the port began on 22 April. By 30 April all that was left in the Rangoon area was the rearguard and stragglers that had been left behind in the withdrawal, leaving the Allies to take the port by 2 May. The Japanese attempted another counteroffensive in July across the Sittang River but the plans for this operation were captured and the Allies had time to set up artillery concentrations and ambushes that completely decimated the Japanese attack. Now all that was left to do in Burma was to round up the remnants of the Japanese forces.

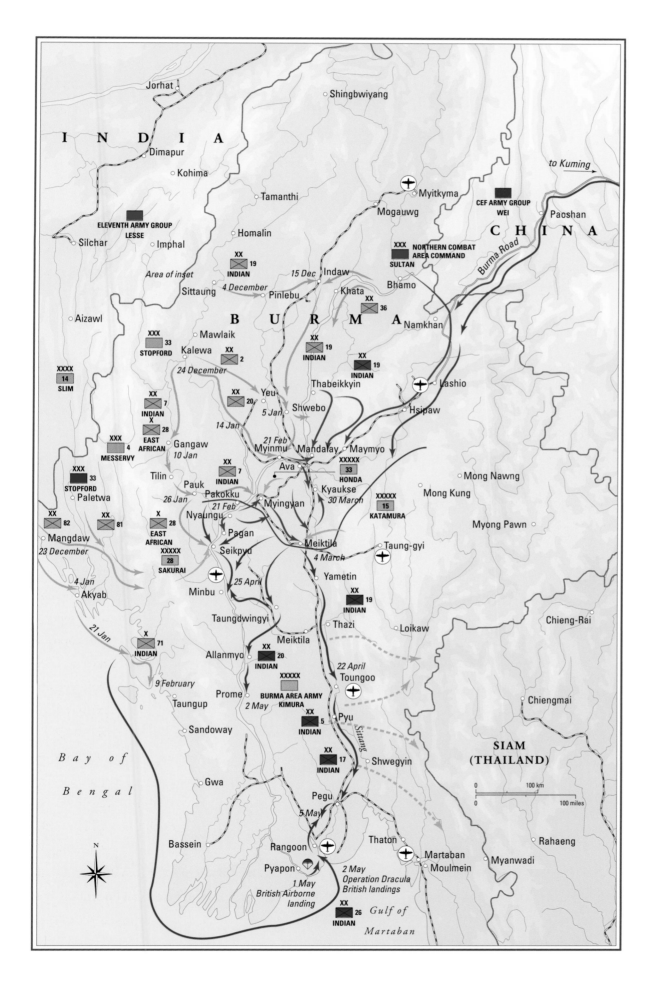

INDIA

Jorhat

Shingbwiyang

Dimapur

Kohima

Tamanthi

Mogauwg

Myitkyma

CEF ARMY GROUP
WEI

Paoshan

to Kuming

CHINA

ELEVENTH ARMY GROUP
LESSE

Homalin

XXX
SULTAN
NORTHERN COMBAT
AREA COMMAND

Silchar

Imphal

Area of inset

Sittaung

15 Dec Indaw

Khata

Bhamo

Namkhan

Burma Road

Aizawl

4 December Pinlebu

XX 19
INDIAN

BURMA

XX 36

Mawlaik

XX 19
INDIAN

XXX 33
STOPFORD

Kalewa

XX 2

XX 19
INDIAN

XXXX 14
SLIM

24 December

Yeu

Thabeikkyin

Lashio

Hsipaw

XX 7
INDIAN
X 28
EAST
AFRICAN

XX 20

5 Jan

Shwebo

14 Jan

XXX 4
MESSERVY

Gangaw

10 Jan

21 Feb
Myinmu Mandalay Maymyo

XXXXX 33
HONDA

Mong Nawng

XXX 33
STOPFORD

Tilin

XX 7
INDIAN

Ava

Kyaukse

30 March

Mong Kung

Paletwa

Pauk

Pakokku

26 Jan

21 Feb

Myingyan

XXXXX 15
KATAMURA

Myong Pawn

XX 82

XX 81

X 28
EAST
AFRICAN

Nyaungu

Pagan

Meiktila

Taung-gyi

Mangdaw

XXXXX 28
SAKURAI

Seikpyu

4 March

23 December

25 April

Yametin

4 Jan

Minbu

Akyab

Taungdwingyi

Thazi

Loikaw

Chieng-Rai

21 Jan

XX 19
INDIAN

X 71
INDIAN

Meiktila

9 February

XX 20
INDIAN

22 April
Toungoo

Allanmyo

Prome

XXXXX
BURMA AREA ARMY
KIMURA

2 May

Taungup

XX 5
INDIAN

Pyu

Sandoway

Sitang

SIAM
(THAILAND)

Chiengmai

XX 17
INDIAN

Shwegyin

Bay of

Bengal

Gwa

Rahaeng

Pegu

5 May

Myanwadi

Bassein

Rangoon

Thaton

Martaban

N

Pyapon

1 May
British Airborne
landing

2 May
Operation Dracula
British landings

Moulmein

XX 26
INDIAN

Gulf of

Martaban

0   100 km
0   100 miles

BOMBING OF JAPAN 1944–45

"UNITED STATES COMMANDERS ... STATED THEIR BELIEF THAT, BY
THE COORDINATED IMPACT OF BLOCKADE AND DIRECT AIR
ATTACK, JAPAN COULD BE FORCED TO SURRENDER WITHOUT
INVASION."

UNITED STATES STRATEGIC BOMBING SURVEY

A view from the control tower of Isley Field, Saipan, shows B-29s of the 73rd Bombardment Group. This crowded airfield provided accommodation for 180 B-29s.

The first raid on the Japanese home islands was carried out by 16 modified B-25 Mitchell bombers in a sortie flown from the U.S. carrier *Hornet* in 1942 and led by Lt-Colonel Jimmy Doolittle. This mission achieved very little damage but was a massive propaganda boost for the United States, also showing the Japanese people that, despite their leaders' claims, their islands could be bombed. The next raids on Japan would not be for another two years, after the introduction of the new Boeing B-29 Superfortress with a 1,500-mile range. Missions could be flown from new airfields constructed on mainland China to attack targets as far as Tokyo. By the end of the war in the Pacific over 90 percent of the bombs dropped on the Japanese mainland would be delivered by these immense four-engined, long-range bombers.

Raids were carried out from Chingdu in China by aircraft from the U.S. 20th Air Force under the command of General Henry "Hap" Arnold, later replaced by Major General

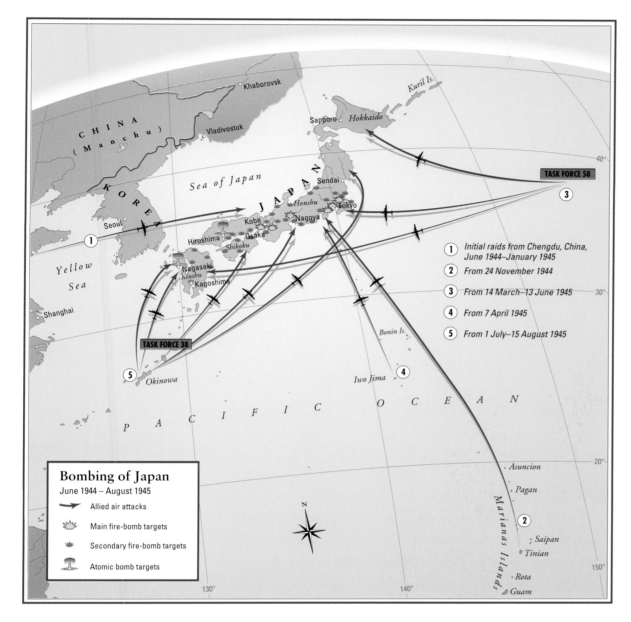

Bombing of Japan
June 1944 – August 1945

→ Allied air attacks

Main fire-bomb targets

Secondary fire-bomb targets

Atomic bomb targets

1 Initial raids from Chengdu, China,
  June 1944–January 1945

2 From 24 November 1944

3 From 14 March–13 June 1945

4 From 7 April 1945

5 From 1 July–15 August 1945

Curtis LeMay, who had personal experience of leading raids over occupied Germany. The aircraft flying from these Chinese bases had to have extra fuel tanks fitted in order to make the return journey, which in turn reduced the bomb load carried and therefore the effectiveness of the raids. The supply route to the new force was flown in over the "Hump" (the Himalayas) from India, so resources were extremely limited. Not until the island-hopping campaign and the capture of the Marianas, would bases be brought into service that were close enough for the B-29s to fly with a full bomb load.

The first of these new bases was on Saipan, and its first mission was launched in late October 1944. The Marianas were ideal bases for the B-29s and their needs were easily supplied by sea from Tinian, Guam, and Saipan. The Marianas were the main hub for all B-29 missions for the rest of the war. The 20th Air Force adopted, as in Europe, a policy of high-level, daylight bombing, but this was soon recognized as untenable due to many contributing factors, such as the weather over mainland Japan, which tended to be cloudy, hampering aiming; when the weather was permissible the high winds over Japan tended to drift the bombs as they dropped off the target. The Japanese air defense system, though woefully inadequate when the U.S. campaign began, started to gain experience and

Seven of the 454 B-29s that flew against Yokohama on 29 May 1945. Over 30 per cent of the city was destroyed in the resulting firestorm.

equipment, such as more antiaircraft artillery and high level interceptors. All this convinced LeMay to follow the example of the R.A.F. against German targets, one of slightly lower level night attacks, often using incendiaries. The major targets chosen for this campaign were to be Tokyo, Nagoya, Osaka, and Kobe, although most Japanese cities would be hit in some way. They were all susceptible to incendiary attack, since many of their buildings were made of wood and paper, resulting in massive firestorms. The first raid was on Kobe on 3 February 1945, which caused massive destruction in civilian areas of the city but also reduced manufacturing production by 50 percent and extensively damaged its shipyards. These successful attacks proved LeMay's theory a viable option and they were continued.

A mission flown on the night of 23/24 February to Tokyo using 174 aircraft succeeded in destroying a square mile of the city. A further raid on the night of 9/10 March, after American pathfinders had marked the target, involved 1,665 tons of incendiaries being dropped. Sixteen square miles of the city were engulfed in an enormous firestorm that resulted in the deaths of over 100,000 people, which was the most destructive and deadly conventional raid ever carried out.

Concerned by the civilian deaths that these raids were causing, the 20th Air Force began dropping leaflets prior to major raids warning the civilians to leave the city, but these were seen by the Japanese as a form of psychological warfare so were played down by their own officials. By the end of the campaign the 20th Air Force destroyed nearly half the built-up areas of all the major cities in Japan, and hundreds of thousands had died.

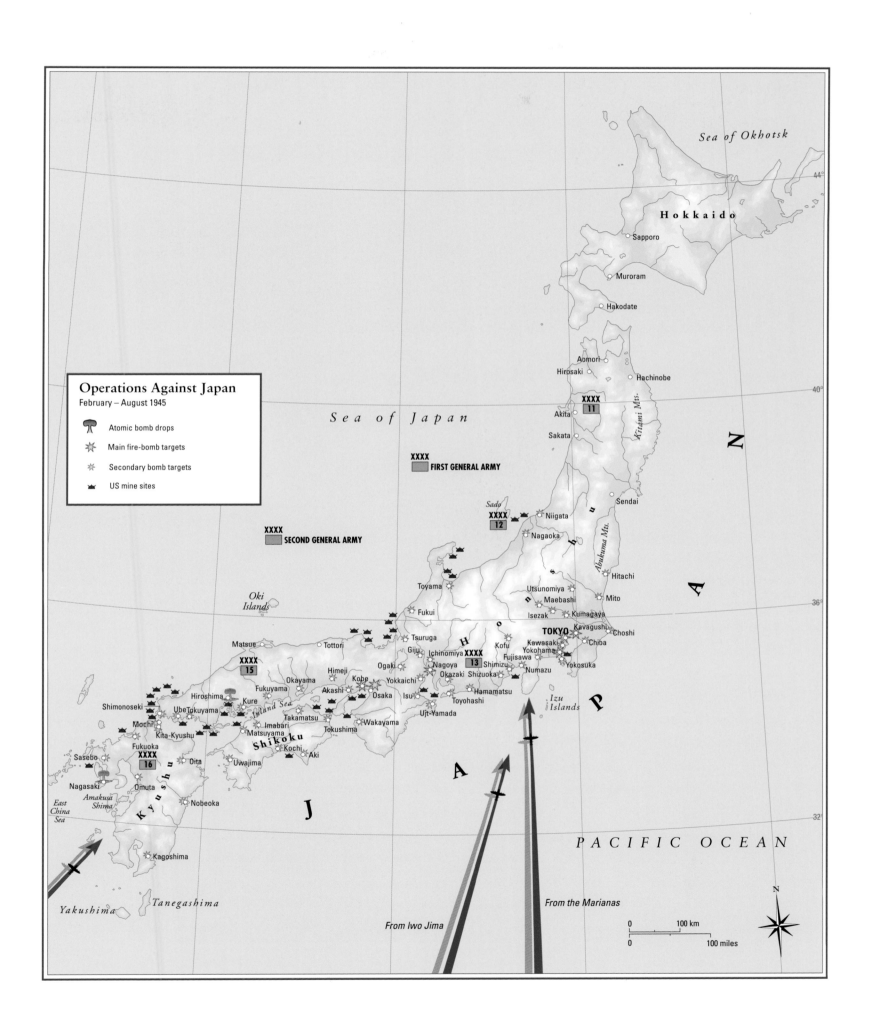

Operations Against Japan
February – August 1945

🍄 Atomic bomb drops

✳ Main fire-bomb targets

✳ Secondary bomb targets

🦇 US mine sites

Sea of Okhotsk

Hokkaido

○ Sapporo

○ Muroram

○ Hakodate

○ Aomori
Hirosaki ○   ○ Hachinobe

XXXX
11
Akita ○

Kitami Mts.

Sea of Japan

Sakata ○

XXXX
FIRST GENERAL ARMY

○ Sendai

Sadọ
XXXX
12
Niigata ○

Abukuma Mts.

○ Nagaoka

XXXX
SECOND GENERAL ARMY

Hitachi ○

*Oki
Islands*

Toyama ○

Utsunomiya ○
Maebashi ○   ○ Mito
Isezak ○
Kumagaya
Kavagushi ○
TOKYO ○   ○ Choshi
Kawasaki   Chiba
Yokohama ○

○ Fukui

Tsuruga
Matsue ○   ○ Tottori

Giju ○
Ichinomiya XXXX
Kofu 13

XXXX
15
Himeji ○
Okayama ○   Ogaki ○
Kobe ○   Nagoya   Shimizu
Yokkaichi ○   Okazaki Shizuoka   Numazu
Akashi ○   ○ Osaka   Isu ○
Fukuyama ○   Takamatsu ○   Hamamatsu ○
Hiroshima 🍄   Kure ○
Inland Sea   Wakayama ○   Ujt-Yamada ○
Shimonoseki ○   Tokushima ○
UbeTokuyama ○   Imabari
Mochi ○   Matsuyama ○
Kita-Kyushu ○   **Shikoku**   Toyohashi

*Izu
Islands*

XXXX
16
Sasebo ○   Fukuoka   Kochi ○   ○ Aki
Oita ○   Uwajima ○

Kyushu
Nagasaki 🍄   Omuta ○
*Amakusa
Shima*   ○ Nobeoka

*East
China
Sea*

○ Kagoshima

Yakushima   *Tanegashima*

From Iwo Jima

From the Marianas

J A P A N

PACIFIC OCEAN

0   100 km
0   100 miles

BATTLE OF THE PHILIPPINE SEA

"THE FATE OF THE EMPIRE RESTS ON THIS ONE BATTLE. EVERY MAN IS EXPECTED TO DO HIS UTMOST."

MESSAGE TO ALL JAPANESE SHIPS

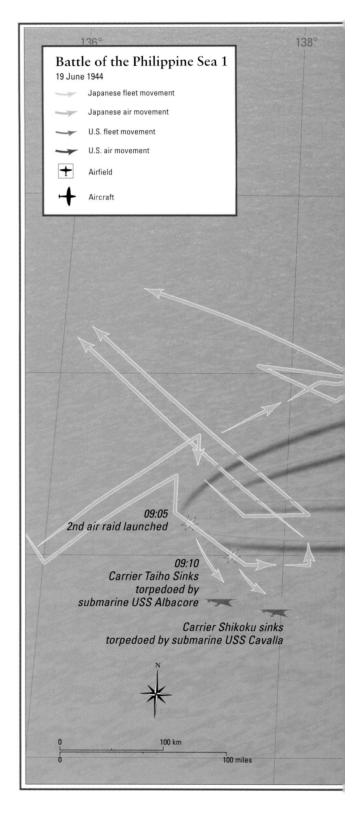

Battle of the Philippine Sea 1
19 June 1944

- Japanese fleet movement
- Japanese air movement
- U.S. fleet movement
- U.S. air movement
- Airfield
- Aircraft

09:05
2nd air raid launched

09:10
Carrier Taiho Sinks
torpedoed by
submarine USS Albacore

Carrier Shikoku sinks
torpedoed by submarine USS Cavalla

0   100 km
0   100 miles

The Battle of the Philippine Sea was to become the largest aircraft carrier action of World War II between 19–20 June 1944 off the Mariana Islands. After the losses suffered at Midway and the Coral Sea, the Japanese Navy was now ready to go on the offensive again after regaining some of its strength. The Naval High Command had developed Operation A-Go, which involved a strike by their carriers and supplementary aircraft from land bases in the northern Philippines, in order to attack the U.S. fleet as it began the next part of its island hopping campaign. Commanding this strike force was Vice-Admiral Jisaburo Ozawa, his fleet consisting of five fleet carriers, including the *Taihu,* which would be his flag ship, and *Shokaku*, four light carriers, five battleships and an accompanying escort of cruisers, destroyers, and oilers. When the U.S. forces launched the invasion of Saipan on 15 June, Ozawa took this as his opportunity to strike, moving into the western part of the Philippine Sea to refuel and prepare.

The Japanese force was spotted by U.S. submarines, and Admiral Mitscher, in command of Task Force 58 covering the Philippine invasion fleet, asked permission to sail and engage the Japanese force. This request was turned down by his superior, Admiral Spruance, who felt the Japanese were attempting to draw Mitscher away from protecting the invasion fleet. The U.S. forces were to fight a defensive battle and allow the Japanese to come on to them. Early on the morning of 19 June the U.S. carriers started launching patrols to search for the enemy fleet, as were their counterparts. Soon a Japanese aircraft spotted Task Force 58 and immediately relayed its position to Ozawa,who ordered aircraft based on Guam to attack. These aircraft were picked up on U.S. radar and a squadron of Hellcat fighters was launched from USS *Belleau Wood*. These aircraft caught the Japanese still forming up and shot down 35 out of 50 aircraft before being ordered to return to their carrier.

These fighters were called back due to another radar contact of approaching enemy aircraft from the west, the first attack from the aircraft of the Japanese carrier force. The U.S. carriers immediately launched all available fighters to attack the approaching Japanese torpedo bombers and escorting Zero fighters, which were regrouping 70 miles short of the U.S. Task Force. The time spent forming up allowed the U.S. fighters to gain height and they began to engage before the Japanese had even reached the Task Force. It turned into a rout of the Japanese, with 41 out of the 68 aircraft launched being shot down by the U.S. Hellcat fighters. Some Japanese aircraft did manage to slip through the fighter screen and attacked the escort ships of the Task Force. However, none of the Japanese planes got through the escorts to attack the carriers.

Later in the morning, the Japanese launched another strike, this time consisting of 109 aircraft. Again, thanks to radar warnings, the U.S. fighters had time to engage the Japanese before they could reach the main carrier group, meeting them 60 miles from the

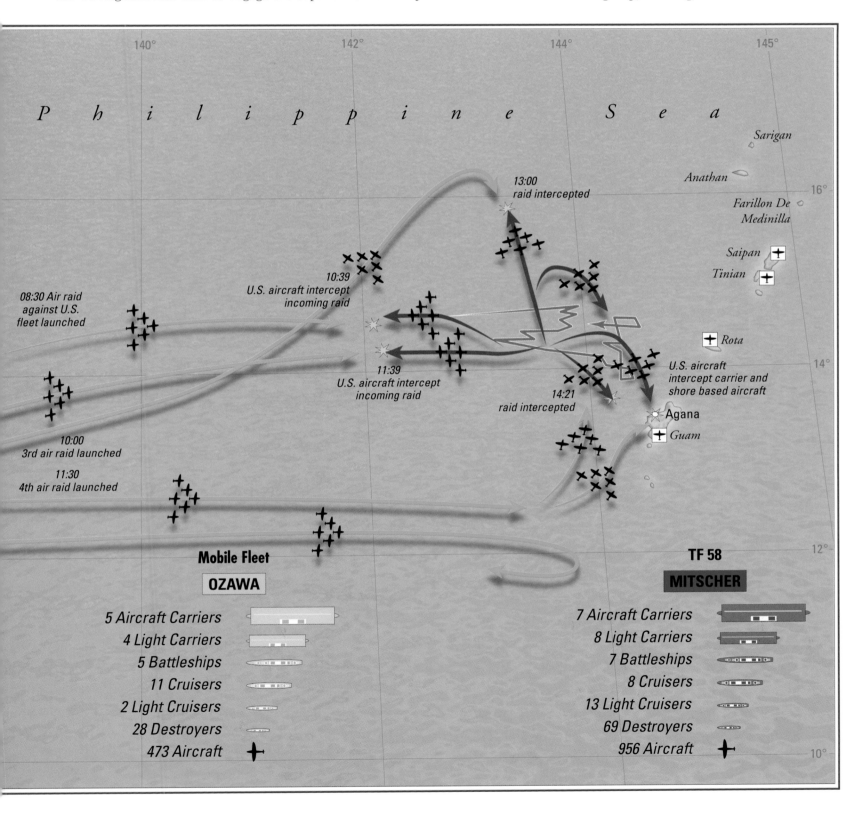

Philippine Sea

140° 142° 144° 145°

Sarigan

Anathan
16°

Farillon De
Medinilla

13:00
raid intercepted

Saipan

Tinian

10:39
U.S. aircraft intercept
incoming raid

08:30 Air raid
against U.S.
fleet launched

Rota

11:39
U.S. aircraft intercept
incoming raid

14:21
raid intercepted

U.S. aircraft
intercept carrier and
shore based aircraft
14°

Agana

10:00
3rd air raid launched

Guam

11:30
4th air raid launched

Mobile Fleet

OZAWA

TF 58

MITSCHER

5 Aircraft Carriers	
4 Light Carriers	
5 Battleships	
11 Cruisers	
2 Light Cruisers	
28 Destroyers	
473 Aircraft	

7 Aircraft Carriers	
8 Light Carriers	
7 Battleships	
8 Cruisers	
13 Light Cruisers	
69 Destroyers	
956 Aircraft	

12°

10°

Task Force. In the engagement 70 Japanese aircraft were shot down, but some slipped through and began to attack the carrier USS *Enterprise*. Almost all were shot down, and *Enterprise* was undamaged. Out of 109 fighters launched by the Japanese, 97 were destroyed.

A third raid was then launched in the early afternoon, comprising 47 aircraft. This was again intercepted but losses were not as great as the previous attacks, when many of the Japanese aircraft broke off the attack. The fourth raid of the day was launched but the Japanese aircrew were given incorrect positions for the U.S. carriers; they flew to Rota and Guam to refuel and begin their search again. On the way to Rota a small number sighted USS *Bunker Hill* and USS *Wasp* and attacked but caused no damage. The aircraft landing on the islands were

The carrier *Zuikaku* under aerial attack. She managed to escape damage, the only remaining survivor of the attack on Pearl Harbor. She was later sunk during the Battle of Leyte Gulf.

spotted and attacked by U.S. Hellcat fighters, further reducing the number of Japanese aircraft. During the air battles U.S. submarine *Albacore* sighted Ozawa's carrier group and proceeded to attack the *Taiho*, disabling her. Ozawa moved his command to a destroyer while his men fought the fires on board. She eventually succumbed, exploded, and sank in the late afternoon. Another U.S. submarine, the *Caralla*, sighted *Shokaku* and fired three torpedoes into her. The fires created by the hits finally reached her bomb store, causing her to blow.

U.S. Task Force 58 then took the initiative on 20 June and started to sail west in search of the Japanese, but failed to find them until mid-afternoon. Mitscher immediately ordered a strike, even though his bombers would have to return in the dark. Two hundred and sixteen aircraft were launched from the U.S. carriers and the attack went in at 6:30 that evening. The Japanese carrier *Hiyo* was attacked by torpedo bombers and damaged, eventually sinking despite her crew valiantly trying to save her. Three other Japanese carriers were also badly damaged. The U.S. aircraft returning to the Task Force had trouble finding it, even when Admiral Mitscher ordered the fleet to operate all its landing lights and for the escort to fire starshell bursts. Eighty aircraft were eventually lost—some from heavy landings on

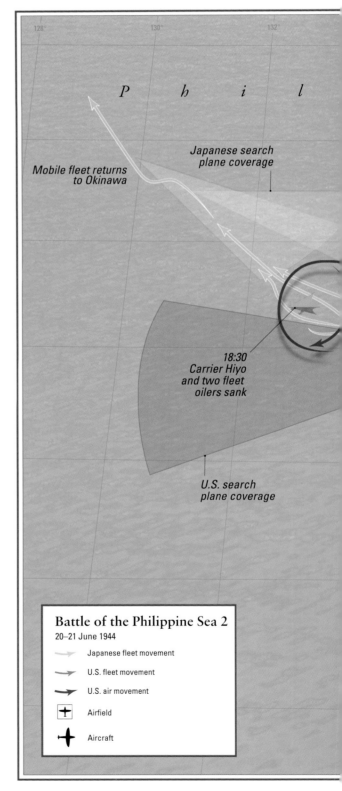

the decks of the carriers and battle damage and some overflying the deck and crashing into the sea, although many of the crew were rescued. The Japanese force was ordered to withdraw. Mitscher desperately wanted to give chase, but was again overruled by Spruance, who assessed that the battle was won and ruled that the Task Force should stick to its role of protecting the invasion fleet.

Admiral Marc A. Mitscher, commander of U.S. Task Force 58, routed the Japanese forces with great skill and tenacity.

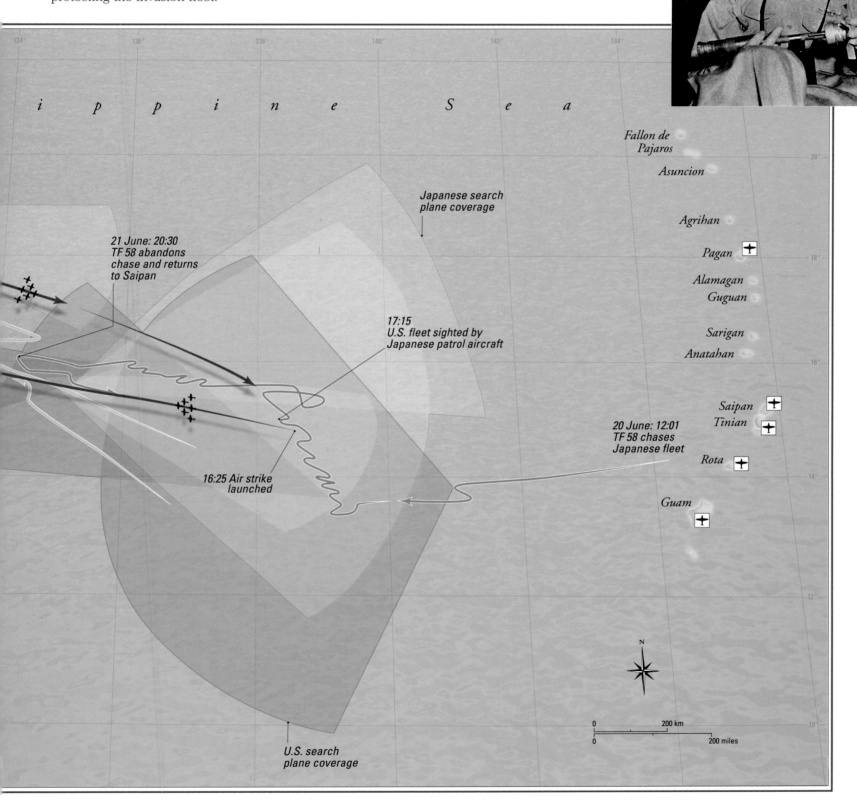

i p p i n e   S e a

Fallon de Pajaros
Asuncion
Agrihan
Pagan ✚
Alamagan
Guguan
Sarigan
Anatahan
Saipan ✚
Tinian ✚
Rota ✚
Guam ✚

Japanese search plane coverage

21 June: 20:30 TF 58 abandons chase and returns to Saipan

17:15 U.S. fleet sighted by Japanese patrol aircraft

20 June: 12:01 TF 58 chases Japanese fleet

16:25 Air strike launched

U.S. search plane coverage

0 200 km
0 200 miles

LIBERATION OF THE PHILIPPINES

"LET THE INDOMITABLE SPIRIT OF BATAAN AND COREGIDOR LEAD

ON ... IN THE NAME OF YOUR SACRED DEAD, STRIKE!

LET NO HEART BE FAINT. LET EVERY ARM BE STEELED."

GENERAL DOUGLAS MacARTHUR, MARCH 1945

Before the invasion of Luzon—the main island in the Philippines—could take place, General MacArthur was keen to establish airfields closer to the northern island. For this he would have to capture Mindoro island. Defenses on Mindoro were minimal, with about 1,000 troops stationed there; the 24th and 19th Infantry Divisions supported by a combat team of 11th Airborne overwhelmed the island within two days. However, there were more assaults on the invasion fleet using the new, unnerving Japanese Kamikaze tactics (suicide attacks from the air), damaging the cruiser USS *Nashville* and several landing ship tanks (LSTs). Within days of the assault on the island, engineers were at work on the airfields and just 17 days later they were ready to receive U.S. aircraft.

G.I.s pass through the still-smouldering suburbs of Manila, the location of the majority of the street fighting in the Pacific campaign.

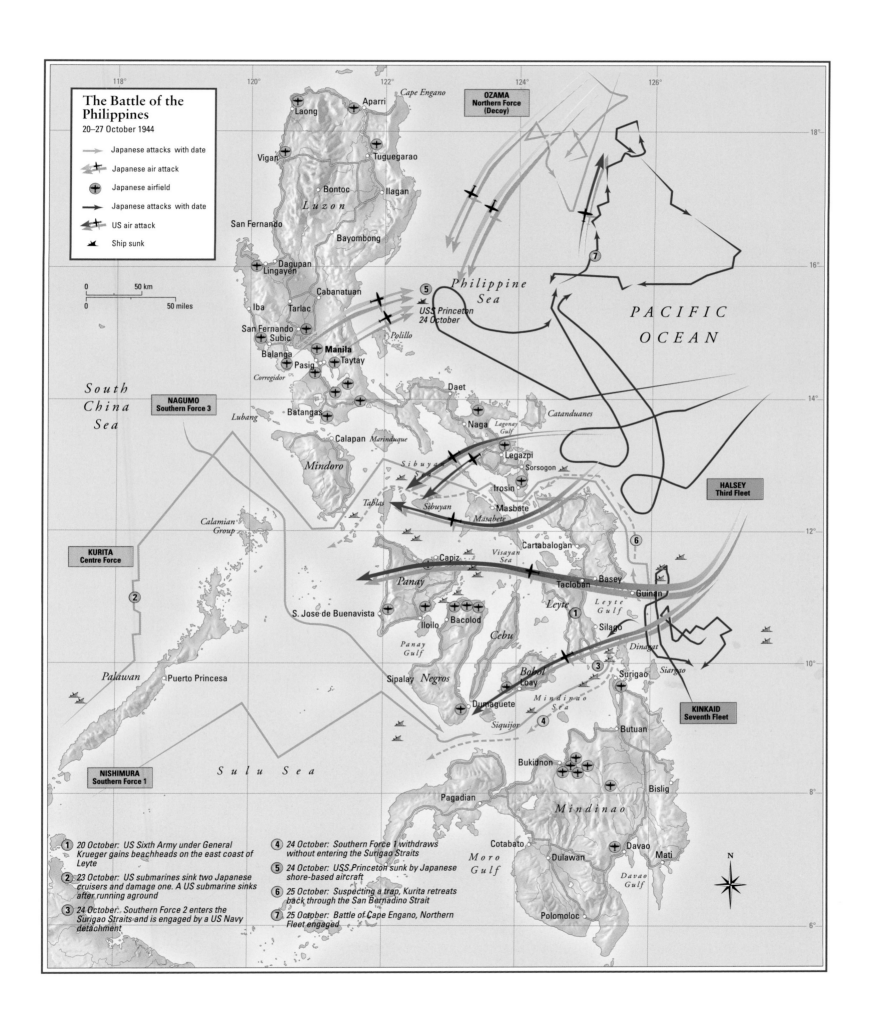

The Battle of the Philippines
20–27 October 1944

→ Japanese attacks with date

✈ Japanese air attack

⊕ Japanese airfield

→ Japanese attacks with date

✈ US air attack

⚓ Ship sunk

0 ——— 50 km
0 ——— 50 miles

OZAMA
Northern Force
(Decoy)

NAGUMO
Southern Force 3

KURITA
Centre Force

NISHIMURA
Southern Force 1

HALSEY
Third Fleet

KINKAID
Seventh Fleet

USS Princeton
24 October

Cape Engano

Laong · Aparri

Vigan · Tuguegarao

Bontoc · Ilagan

Luzon

San Fernando

Bayombong

Dagupan · Lingayen

Iba · Tarlac · Cabanatuan

San Fernando · Subic

Balanga · Manila · Taytay

Corregidor · Pasig

Lubang · Batangas

Calapan · *Marinduque*

Mindoro

Calamian Group

Palawan · Puerto Princesa

South China Sea

Philippine Sea

PACIFIC OCEAN

Daet

Naga · *Lagonay Gulf* · *Catanduanes*

Legazpi

Sorsogon

Irosin

Sibuyan Sea · *Sibuyan* · Masbate · *Masabete*

Tablas

Cartabalogan · Basey

Capiz · *Visayan Sea*

Panay

S. Jose de Buenavista

Iloilo · Bacolod

Panay Gulf

Cebu

Tacloban · Guinan

Leyte · *Leyte Gulf*

Silago

Sipalay · *Negros*

Dumaguete

Bohol · Loay

Surigao · *Siargao*

Dinagat

Mindinao Sea

Siquijor

Sulu Sea

Butuan

Bukidnon · Bislig

Pagadian

Mindinao

Cotabato · Davao

Moro Gulf · Dulawan · Mati

Davao Gulf

Polomoloc

N

① **20 October:** US Sixth Army under General Krueger gains beachheads on the east coast of Leyte

② **23 October:** US submarines sink two Japanese cruisers and damage one. A US submarine sinks after running aground

③ **24 October:** Southern Force 2 enters the Surigao Straits and is engaged by a US Navy detachment

④ **24 October:** Southern Force 1 withdraws without entering the Surigao Straits

⑤ **24 October:** USS Princeton sunk by Japanese shore-based aircraft

⑥ **25 October:** Suspecting a trap, Kurita retreats back through the San Barnadino Strait

⑦ **25 October:** Battle of Cape Engano, Northern Fleet engaged

U.S. soldiers move inland from their beachhead on Luzon, January 1945.

The fighting over, happy U.S. soldiers show off their captured Japanese flag.

Before the invasion of Luzon, the American forces had put in place a massive deception plan, flying reconnaissance and bombing missions over the southern part of Luzon, even dropping dummy paratroops to lure the attention of the Japanese to the south. This deception plan worked so well that when Krueger's 6th Army landed at Linguyan Bay on 9 January 1945 there was no opposition whatever. Within a few days a beachhead of some 20 miles had been established and the coastal town of San Fabian captured, by which time some 175,000 troops were ashore. Again the Kamikaze attacks came, sinking the escort carrier USS *Ommany Bay* and sinking a destroyer, as well as heavily damaging many more transports and LSTs.

General Yamashita, in charge of the defense of Luzon, could do very little to halt the rapid advance of the U.S. forces and decided to opt for a battle on two fronts. He split his forces into two, one retreating into the interior of the island and the other to the defense of Manila, hoping to draw out the fighting for as long as possible. Although his forces outnumbered the Americans, he could do little without the all important air support now almost unavailable to him.

Clark Field airfield was captured on 23 January and the race to capture Manila was on. The U.S. 11th Airborne and 1st Cavalry Divisions, along with 37th Division, advanced from the north with 12th Cavalry being the first to enter the city on 1 February. Two days of hard fighting saw them in the city center but street fighting was set to continue. As the 1st Cavalry entered the city, Yamashita gave orders to Vice-Admiral Denschichi Okochi to destroy all port installations and then declare Manila an open city. This he openly defied and sent his men about the city commiting terrible atrocities on the local population, destroying hospitals while patients were still inside, raping, and pillaging. Over 100,000 Filipinos would die in this cruel Japanese retribution. House-to-house fighting continued throughout February, and by the time Manila was declared secure it had been reduced to rubble.

With Mindanao assaulted by men of the 8th Army on 10 March, where fighting in the jungles would continue until the end of hostilities, the entire Philippines was declared secure on 30 June 1945. Twenty-five Japanese divisions had been all but wiped out, with U.S. losses of 820 men.

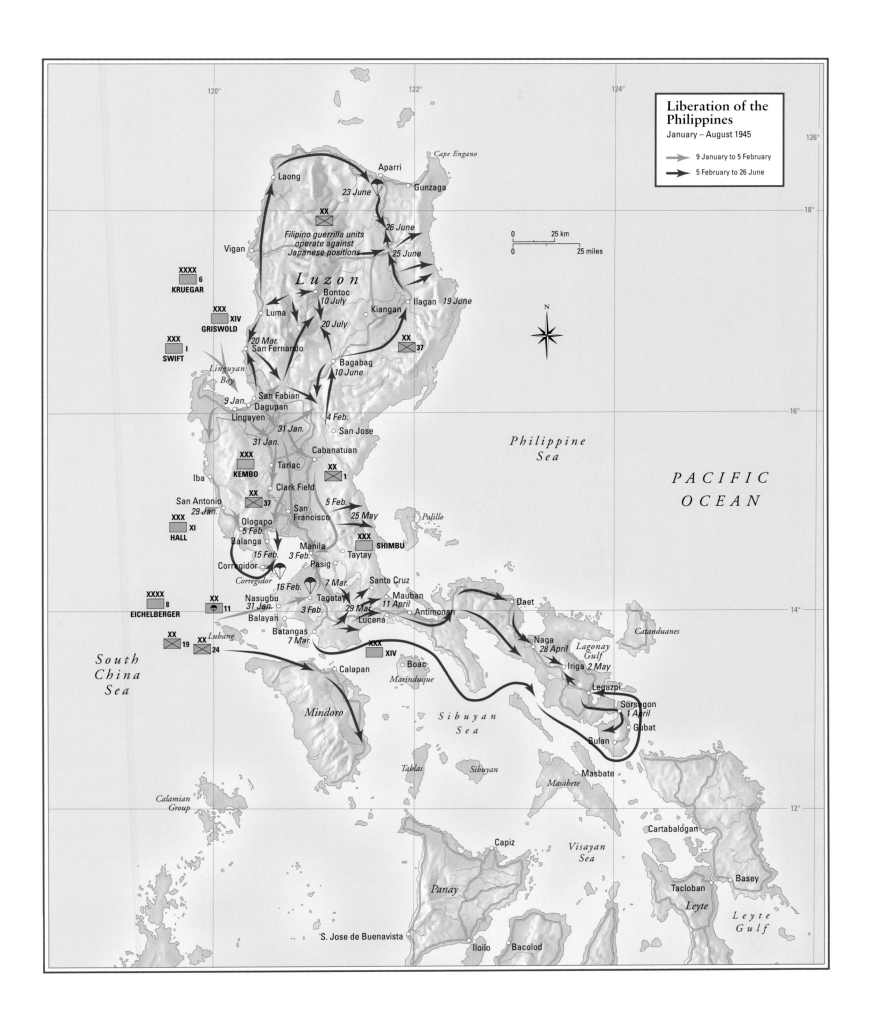

Liberation of the Philippines
January – August 1945

9 January to 5 February
5 February to 26 June

Cape Engano

Laong

Aparri

23 June

Gunzaga

26 June

XX

Filipino guerrilla units
operate against
Japanese positions

25 June

Vigan

Luzon

Bontoc
10 July

Kiangan

Ilagan   19 June

XXXX   6
KRUEGAR

Luma

20 July

XXX   XIV
GRISWOLD

XX   37

XXX   I
SWIFT

20 Mar.
San Fernando

*Linguyan
Bay*

9 Jan.

San Fabian

Bagabag
10 June

Dagupan

Lingayen

4 Feb.

San Jose

31 Jan.

*Philippine
Sea*

31 Jan.

Cabanatuan

XXX
KEMBO

Tarlac

XX   1

Iba

Clark Field

5 Feb.

*PACIFIC

OCEAN*

San Antonio

XX   37

San
Francisco

29 Jan.

25 May

Polillo

Ologapo
5 Feb.

XXX   XI
HALL

Balanga

Manila

15 Feb.

3 Feb.

XXX
SHIMBU

Taytay

Corregidor

Pasig

Corregidor

16 Feb.

7 Mar.

Santa Cruz

XXXX   8
EICHELBERGER

XX   11

Nasugbu
31 Jan.

Tagatay

Mauban
11 April

Daet

*South
China
Sea*

Balayan

3 Feb.

29 Mac.

Lucena

Antimonan

Catanduanes

XX   19

XX   24

Lubang

Batangas
7 Mar.

XXX   XIV

Naga
28 April

*Lagonay
Gulf*

Iriga   2 May

Calapan

Boac

Legazpi

Marinduque

Sorsogon
1 April

Gubat

Mindoro

*Sibuyan
Sea*

Bulan

Tablas

Sibuyan

Masabete

Masbate

*Calamian
Group*

Cartabalogan

Capiz

*Visayan
Sea*

Basey

Panay

Tacloban

Iloilo

Bacolod

Leyte

S. Jose de Buenavista

*Leyte
Gulf*

LEYTE AND LEYTE GULF

"I WILL BREAK INTO LEYTE GULF AND FIGHT TO THE LAST MAN ...
WOULD IT NOT BE SHAMEFUL TO HAVE THE FLEET REMAINING
INTACT WHILE OUR NATION PERISHES?"

VICE-ADMIRAL TAKEO KURITA

The carrier *Zuiho* was sunk along with three other carriers, *Chiyoda*, *Chitose*, and *Zuikaku* during the battle off Cape Engano, destroying Japan's naval air power.

The Battle of Leyte Gulf, in October 1944, was fought as the troops were invading the island of Leyte in the southern Philippines. It would become one of the largest sea battles ever fought and would be the the first time the Japanese first used the Kamikaze as a weapon. Admiral Toyoda planned to draw the powerful U.S. Third Fleet northward with a decoy force led by Admiral Ozawa, while a large pincer movement was executed by three strike forces of Vice-Admiral Kurita, who was approaching through the Straits of San Bernardino, and Vice-Admiral Shima's and Vice-Admiral Nishimura's forces, who were approaching through the Surigao Strait.

Kurito's force was made up of five battleships, 12 cruisers, including his flagship *Atago*, and had the support of 13 destroyers. This force was sighted by two U.S. submarines on the night of 23/24 October and duly attacked. Two cruisers were sunk, including the *Atago,* and one cruiser was damaged, which then limped to Brunei. Kurito moved to the battleship *Yamato.* As Kurito continued his journey and entered the narrow Sibuyan Sea, his force was spotted by aircraft from Task Force 38 and attacked. Over 200 U.S. aircraft attacked the Japanese ships and forced Kurito to withdraw out of range of the U.S. aircraft; in this engagement the battleship *Musashi* was lost. In the late afternoon, Kurito turned to head for the San Bernardino Strait. During the attack on Kurito's ships a force of Japanese bombers had flown from Luzon and attacked Task Force 38, severely damaging the light carrier *Princeton*, which eventually sank.

Nishimura's force, consisting of two battleships, one cruiser, and four destroyers entered the Surigao Strait in the early afternoon of 24 October. Unable to synchronise movements with the other two strike commanders, he ran into a powerful screening force made up of 7th U.S. Fleet Support Force, under

Admiral Thomas Kinkaid. The Japanese force was engaged by PT boats and destroyers, torpedoing and sinking the battleship *Fuso*. The U.S. battleships then opened fire on them with their radar-controlled main armament. Shima's force then arrived behind the damaged and sinking Japanese ships and, realizing the futility of the situation, ordered a withdrawal. Only one ship from Nishimura's force survived. The Americans succeeded in "crossing the T" of the Japanese forces so they could bring all the U.S. guns to bear on the enemy. This was the last time this naval maneuver would occur.

Meanwhile, Ozawa's Northern Force was spotted in the late afternoon of 24 October and Admiral Halsey could not resist the opportunity of attacking and destroying the last remnants of the Japanese Navy, espe-

The USS *Pennsylvania* took part in the last battleship engagement ever fought, at Suragao Strait and famously "Crossing the T," a naval term describing a maneuver in which the maximum number of guns is brought to bear on the enemy ships.

cially as he completely outgunned the enemy. Believing Kurito to be out of the fight, Halsey took the bait offered by Ozawa and headed north with nine carriers, eight light carriers and numerous other fighting craft in pursuit. On the morning of the next day, Ozawa launched 75 planes to attack the pursuing Americans, but few returned. The U.S. carriers then launched the retaliatory attacks against the Japanese, flying over 500 sorties, sinking the carrier *Zuikaku*, the only surviving carrier from the Pearl Harbor attack, and three other carriers, the *Zuiho*, *Chiyoda*, and *Chitose*. As Halsey was about to press home final victory, he heard of the plight of a task group off the coast of Samur and broke off the pursuit.

Kurito had steamed down the San Bernardino Strait and was now sailing along the coast of Samur. In his way were three groups from the U.S. 7th Fleet, commanded by Admiral Kinkaid. Each Task Group, or "Taffy" 1, 2, and 3, consisted of six escort carriers and six destroyers; being lightly armored, they were susceptible to a battleship's heavy guns. Kinkaid thought he had the protection of a Task Force of battleships that had, in reality, gone with Halsey in pursuit of Ozawa. Kiruto stumbled upon Taffy 3, surprised to see the Japanese battleships moving toward them. The commander, Clifton Sprague, sent in his destroyers as a distraction while his carriers beat a retreat. The destroyers broke up the Japanese formation with incredible skill and bravery, as they avoided the torpedoes fired on them, gaining enough time to launch the aircraft from the escort carriers, which then attacked the Japanese ships. But as the carriers retreated, the Japanese continued to fire on them and succeeded in sinking the carrier *Gambier Bay*. Kurito continued his pursuit of the carriers and came within range of the other Taffys before disengaging after the loss of three cruisers. By the time Kurito arrived back in Japan, only *Yamato* was serviceable. The fighting to secure the beachheads had moved in the Americans' favor, but while the sea battle had been raging, the land battle had only just begun.

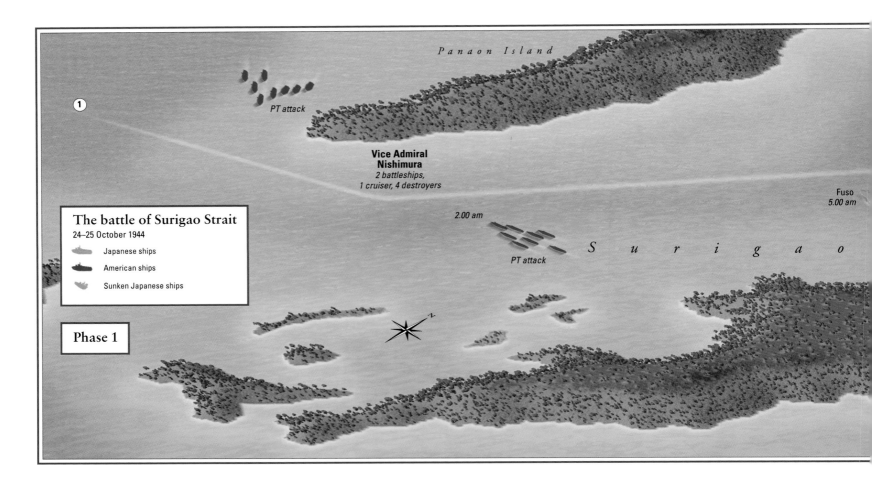

Panaon Island

①

PT attack

**Vice Admiral
Nishimura**
*2 battleships,
1 cruiser, 4 destroyers*

Fuso
5.00 am

2.00 am

S u r i g a o

PT attack

The battle of Surigao Strait
24–25 October 1944

Japanese ships

American ships

Sunken Japanese ships

Phase 1

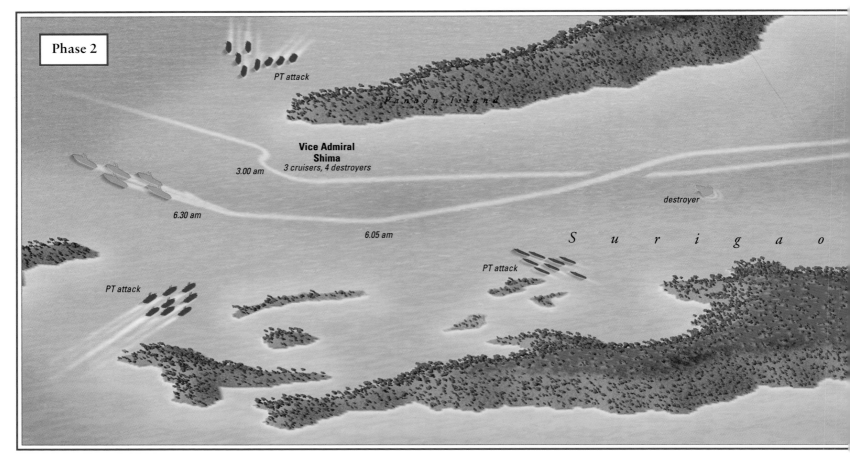

Phase 2

PT attack

Panaon Island

**Vice Admiral
Shima**
3 cruisers, 4 destroyers

3.00 am

destroyer

6.30 am

6.05 am

S u r i g a o

PT attack

PT attack

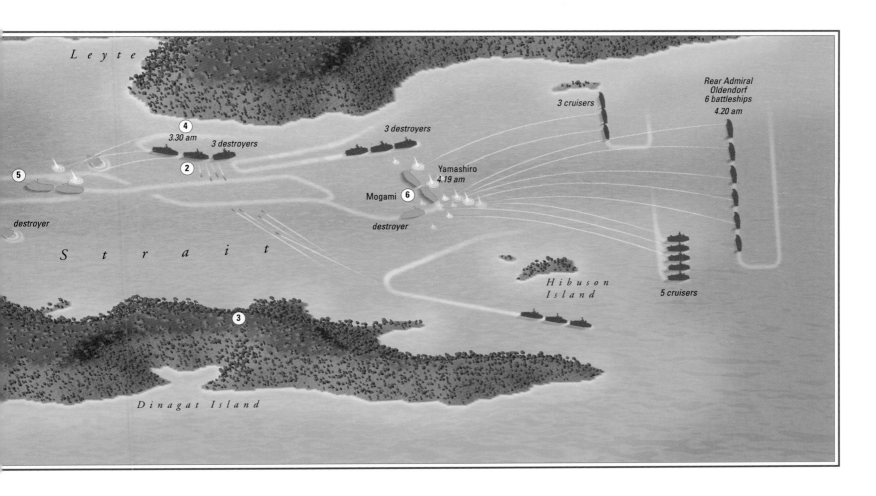

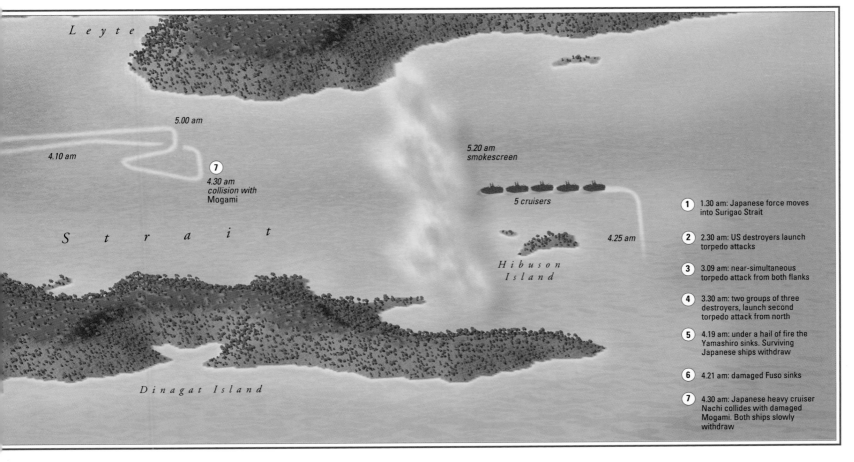

1. 1.30 am: Japanese force moves into Surigao Strait

2. 2.30 am: US destroyers launch torpedo attacks

3. 3.09 am: near-simultaneous torpedo attack from both flanks

4. 3.30 am: two groups of three destroyers, launch second torpedo attack from north

5. 4.19 am: under a hail of fire the Yamashiro sinks. Surviving Japanese ships withdraw

6. 4.21 am: damaged Fuso sinks

7. 4.30 am: Japanese heavy cruiser Nachi collides with damaged Mogami. Both ships slowly withdraw

IWO JIMA AND OKINAWA

"AMONG THE MEN WHO FOUGHT ON IWO JIMA, UNCOMMON VALOR WAS A COMMON VIRTUE."

ADMIRAL NIMITZ, 16 MARCH 1945

The battles for the islands of Iwo Jima and Okinawa, in 1945, would be among the largest and most costly fought in the Pacific area of operations. As the Japanese were retreating nearer to their own sphere of home islands, they became even more fanatical in their defense, frequently fighting to the death rather than face the shame of surrender. Iwo Jima, 650 miles south of Tokyo but inside it's prefecture, was a volcanic island only five miles in length; however, it was the home of three airfields that Japanese interceptors flew from to attack B-29s on their way to the Japanese home islands, as well as an early warning radar station to warn of impending bomber missions. The U.S.A.A.F. saw this island as an ideal base for the planned fighter escort that was badly needed for the B-29s raiding Japan. Plus, bombers could also use the airstrips for emergency landings and refueling. The same applied to Okinawa, which was important to support the future invasion of Japanese home islands.

The task of defending Iwo Jima was given to Lt-General Tadamichi Kuribayashi and a total of 22,000 men, who immediatly set about building and digging a vast array of underground tunnels and fortifications into

A U.S. Marine Corps captain shouts orders to his men over the noise of battle on Iwo Jima.

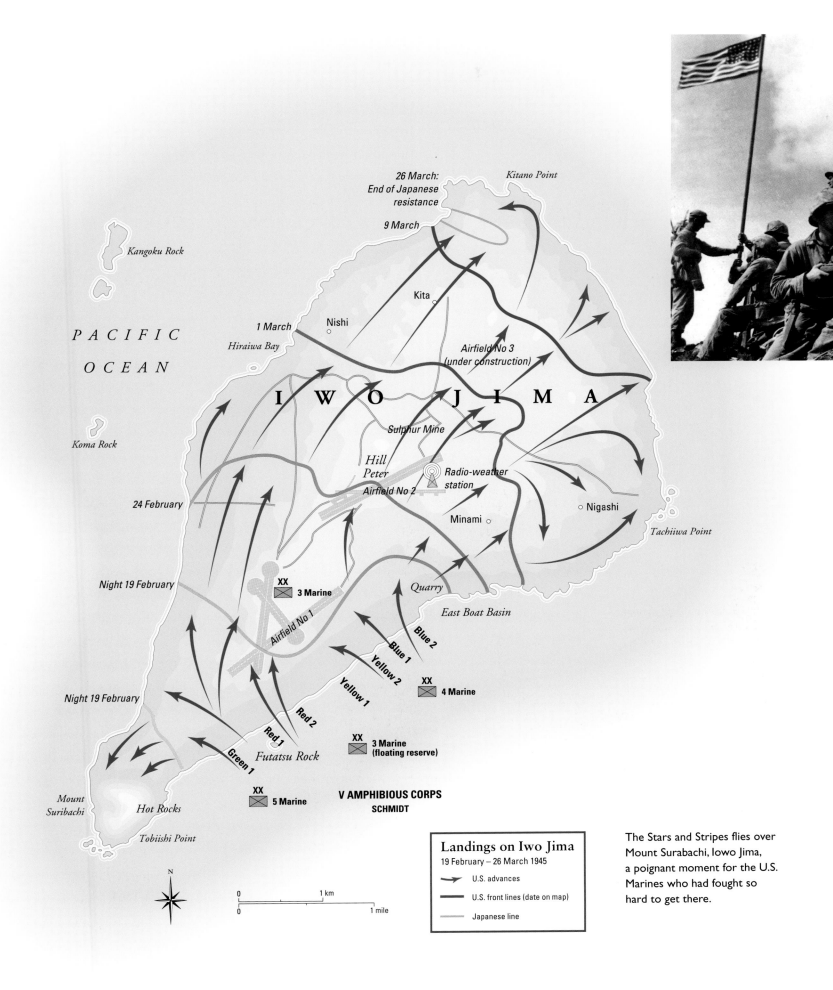

Kangoku Rock

PACIFIC
OCEAN

Koma Rock

26 March:
End of Japanese
resistance

Kitano Point

9 March

1 March

Nishi

Kita

Hiraiwa Bay

I W O   J I M A

Airfield No 3
(under construction)

Sulphur Mine

*Hill
Peter*
Airfield No 2

Radio-weather
station

24 February

Nigashi

Minami

Tachiiwa Point

Night 19 February

Quarry

XX
3 Marine

East Boat Basin

Blue 2

Blue 1

Yellow 2

XX
4 Marine

Yellow 1

Airfield No 1

Red 2

Night 19 February

Red 1

XX
3 Marine
(floating reserve)

Green 1

Futatsu Rock

XX
5 Marine

V AMPHIBIOUS CORPS
SCHMIDT

*Mount
Suribachi*   *Hot Rocks*

Tobiishi Point

N

0 _____ 1 km
0 _____ 1 mile

Landings on Iwo Jima
19 February – 26 March 1945

↝ U.S. advances

▬ U.S. front lines (date on map)

━ Japanese line

The Stars and Stripes flies over
Mount Surabachi, Iowo Jima,
a poignant moment for the U.S.
Marines who had fought so
hard to get there.

A B-24J Mitchell, from the 345th Bombardment Group of the 14th Air Force, attacks the Japanese destroyer *Amatsukazi* off the coast of southern China on 6 April 1945. The destroyer was sunk.

the volcanic rock, which was ideal for these constructions, being soft enough to dig easily but sturdy enough to withstand heavy shelling. Kuribayashi also took a different approach to the defense of Iwo Jima compared to other islands assaulted by the Americans. Instead of attacking the first wave of soldiers as they waded ashore, Kuribayashi would allow the first wave to reach at least 875 yards inland before hidden machine gun emplacements would put them under fire from the rear and flanks. This would be costly on the Marines, who assumed that this invasion would be easy, after seeing the massive preattack bombardment.

Attacking the island would be the 5th Amphibious Corps made up of 5th Marine Division, which would land on the left of the invasion beach; 4th Marine Division, on the right; and 3rd Marine Division as a floating reserve. These units were to be under the overall command of Major-General Harry Schmidt. The divisions were to land on the southeast beaches then strike inland to take the airfields and cut off the dominating Mount Suribachi from the rest of the island, before moving northeasterly to capture the rest of the island.

Following a full 72 days of aerial strikes and a naval bombardment, the first elements of the Marine divisions landed on the beaches on the morning of 19 February 1945. They took heavy casualties as the defenders put their plan into action, and the Marines struggled to dig foxholes on the volcanic ash beaches to escape the withering crossfire. But by the evening of the first day, the Marines had reached the first airstrip and had succeeded in cutting off Mount Suribachi. Three more days of heavy fighting would follow, with the Marines using flamethrowers and explosives to clear the Japanese defenders from their deep bunkers, before Suribachi was eventually taken, and the Stars and Stripes raised. The fighting continued as the Marines moved north, the Japanese always refusing to give up their defenses, fanatical until the end. On the evening of 25 March, the Japanese launched one last attack against the second airfield, with fighting continuing on through the night and both sides suffering heavy casualties. By the morning there were few Japanese survivors and the island was finally in American hands. From the 22,000 Japanese defenders on Iwo Jima before the battle fewer than 200 remained alive, and many of these were badly wounded. The U.S. forces incurred nearly 6,000 killed and over 17,000 wounded.

The invasion of Okinawa would be the largest amphibious assault in the Pacific theater and would also be the last battle fought of World War II. Okinawa, unlike Iwo Jima however, had a large Japanese population and the civilian casualties in the campaign were extremely high. A third were killed, or chose to commit suicide, after being convinced by Japanese propaganda that the U.S. troops were savage killers who would do terrible deeds to them and their families.

The invading U.S. forces totaled 170,000 men, made up from 24th Corps commanded by Major-

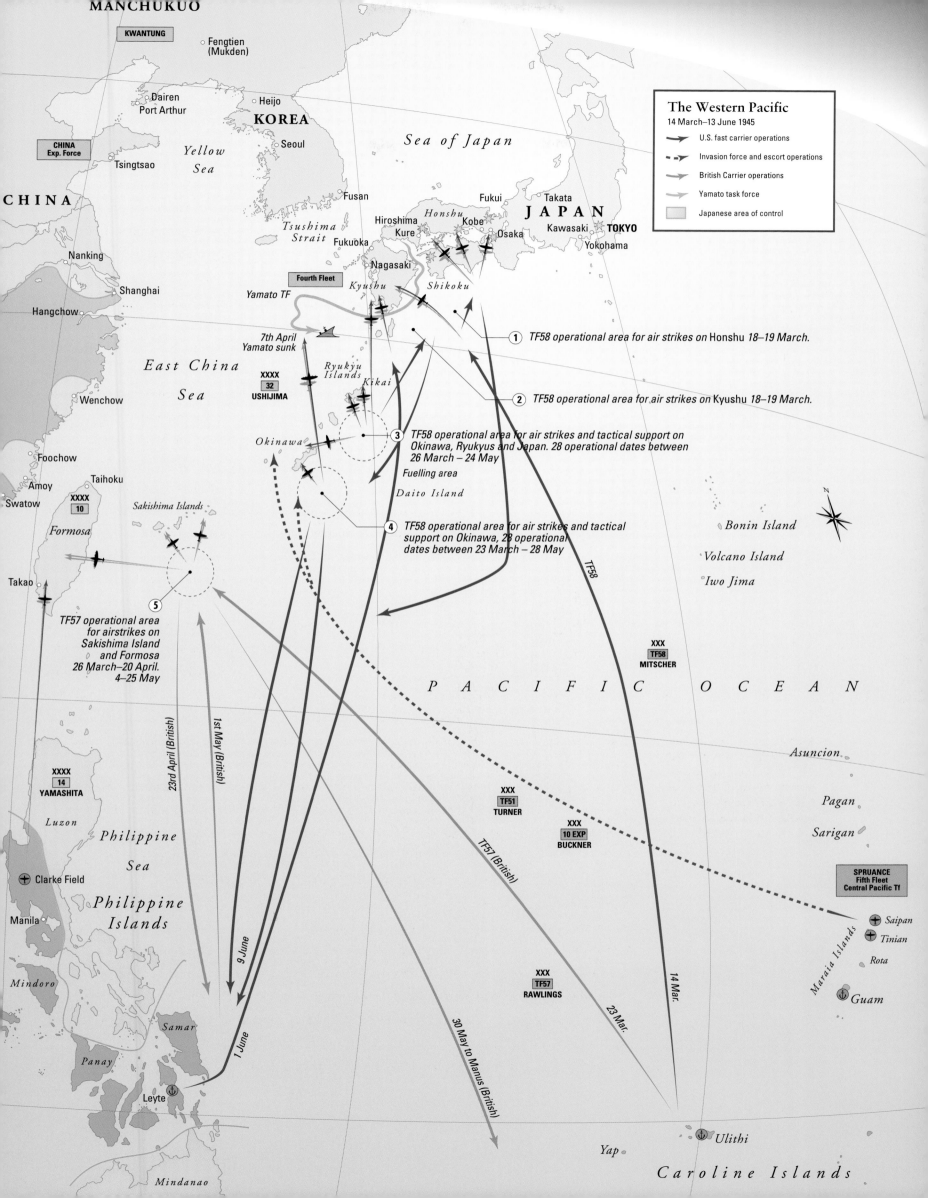

MANCHUKUO

KWANTUNG

CHINA
Exp. Force

CHINA

Fengtien
(Mukden)

Dairen
Port Arthur

Heijo

Seoul

KOREA

Yellow
Sea

Tsingtsao

Nanking

Shanghai

Hangchow

Wenchow

Foochow

Amoy

Swatow

XXXX
10

Formosa

Taihoku

Takao

Sakishima Islands

Sea of Japan

Fusan

Tsushima
Strait

Fukuoka

Fukui

Hiroshima
Kure

Honshu

Kobe

Takata

Kawasaki

TOKYO

Osaka

Yokohama

JAPAN

Nagasaki

Fourth Fleet

Yamato TF

Kyushu

Shikoku

7th April
Yamato sunk

East China
Sea

XXXX
32
USHIJIMA

Ryukyu
Islands

Kikai

Okinawa

Daito Island

Fuelling area

Bonin Island

Volcano Island

Iwo Jima

TF57 operational area
for airstrikes on
Sakishima Island
and Formosa
26 March–20 April.
4–25 May

PACIFIC OCEAN

XXX
TF58
MITSCHER

Philippine
Sea

Clarke Field

Philippine
Islands

Luzon

XXXX
14
YAMASHITA

Manila

Mindoro

Samar

Panay

Leyte

Mindanao

Asuncion

Pagan

Sarigan

XXX
TF51
TURNER

XXX
10 EXP
BUCKNER

XXX
TF57
RAWLINGS

SPRUANCE
Fifth Fleet
Central Pacific Tf

Saipan

Tinian

Rota

Guam

Ulithi

Yap

Caroline Islands

The Western Pacific
14 March–13 June 1945

→ U.S. fast carrier operations

⇢ Invasion force and escort operations

→ British Carrier operations

→ Yamato task force

Japanese area of control

① TF58 operational area for air strikes on Honshu 18–19 March.

② TF58 operational area for air strikes on Kyushu 18–19 March.

③ TF58 operational area for air strikes and tactical support on Okinawa, Ryukyus and Japan. 28 operational dates between 26 March – 24 May

④ TF58 operational area for air strikes and tactical support on Okinawa, 28 operational dates between 23 March – 28 May

⑤

23rd April (British)

1st May (British)

9 June

1 June

30 May to Manus (British)

TF57 (British)

TF58

14 Mar.

23 Mar.

General Hodges, and the 3rd Marine Amphibious Corps commanded by Major-General Geiger. These units would make up the U.S. 10th Army under the overall command of Lt-General Simon Buckner. The Japanese were 100,000-strong, and commanded by General Mitsura Ushijima in the south, and General Takahido Udo in the north. Ushijima took on the most important area of defense around the area of Shuri Castle toward the south of the island and the Motobu Pennisula in the north, ordering his men to hold until the last man and last round; this battle was one he knew he could not win but he wanted to hold the Americans for as long as possible in order to slow the impending invasion of his homeland.

The landings occurred on the thin "neck" of the island toward the center on 1 April. The Marines swept through the north with relative ease and captured the Motobu Pennisula by 20 April. Fighting in the southern part of the island was much more difficult. The islands were honeycombed with caves that leant themselves as natural bunkers. The defenders refused to give up, often leaving the Marines and Infantry no choice but to use flamethrowers or simply blow the cave entrances with explosives, burying the defenders alive. Shuri Castle was eventually taken on 29 May, with Ushijima leading his men to the Oroku Pennisula as a final defensive position. Ushijima committed suicide on 22 June— the same day the island was deemed secure by U.S. forces. The U.S. forces suffered badly from combat fatigue in this bitter, no-quarter struggle. Disease, as well as casualties inflicted by the enemy, numbered 72,000, of which 12,500 were killed in action. A few Japanese were now prepared to surrender, seeing the hopelessness of their situation. Of the Japanese garrison about 7,000 survived to become prisoners of war.

Beach scene on Okinawa, April 1945. Some idea of the scale and complexity of the logistical support needed to keep an island-hopping campaign supplied can be seen here with landing craft and supply ships stretching to the far horizon.

The Fall of Okinawa
1 April – 21 June 1945

→ U.S. attacks

⇢ Demonstrations by
2 Marine Div

— U.S. front lines (date shown)

— Japanese 'Shuri Line'

→ Japanese counterattacks

⊕ Airfield

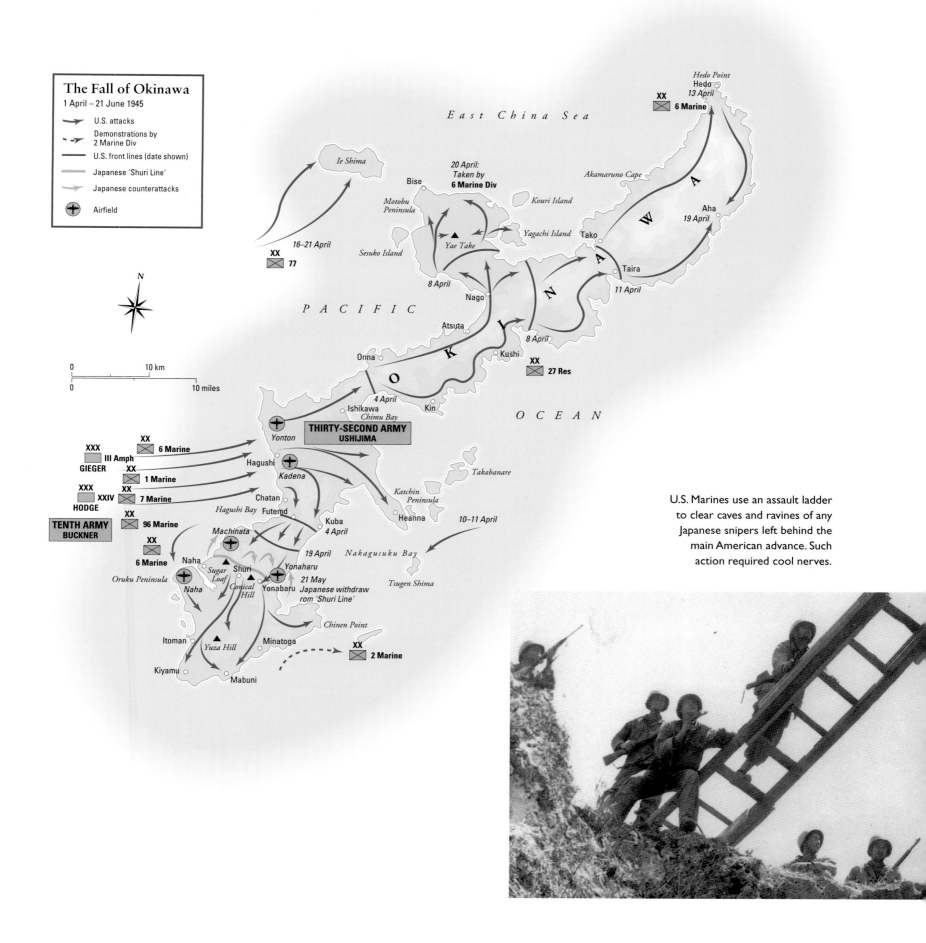

East China Sea

Hedo Point
Hedo
13 April
XX
6 Marine

Akamaruno Cape

20 April:
Taken by
6 Marine Div

Bise

Ie Shima

Kouri Island

*Motobu
Peninsula*

Yagachi Island

▲
Yae Take

Tako

Aha
19 April

Sesuko Island

8 April

XX
77

16–21 April

Nago

Taira
11 April

PACIFIC

Atsuta

8 April

Onna

Kushi

XX
27 Res

OKINAWA

Ishikawa

Kin

Chimu Bay

4 April

OCEAN

⊕
Yonton

**THIRTY-SECOND ARMY
USHIJIMA**

Hagushi

⊕
Kadena

Takabanare

XXX
III Amph
GIEGER

XX
6 Marine

XX
1 Marine

XXX
XXIV
HODGE

XX
7 Marine

Chatan

*Katchin
Peninsula*

Futemd

Hagushi Bay

Kuba
4 April

Heanna

10–11 April

**TENTH ARMY
BUCKNER**

XX
96 Marine

▲
Machinata

⊕

19 April

Nakagusuku Bay

XX
6 Marine

Naha

⊕

Sugar
Loaf

Shuri ▲

Yonaharu

*21 May
Japanese withdraw
rom 'Shuri Line'*

Tsugen Shima

Oruku Peninsula

Naha

Conical
Hill ▲

Yonabaru

Chinen Point

Itoman

▲
Yuza Hill

Minatoga

XX
2 Marine

Kiyamu

Mabuni

0   10 km
0   10 miles

N

U.S. Marines use an assault ladder
to clear caves and ravines of any
Japanese snipers left behind the
main American advance. Such
action required cool nerves.

DAWN OF THE ATOMIC AGE

"NOW, I AM BECOME DEATH, THE DESTROYER OF WORLDS."

J. ROBERT OPPENHEIMER, PHYSICIST

On 6 August 1945 "Little Boy"—the first atomic weapon to be used in war—was dropped on the Japanese city of Hiroshima, instantly killing an estimated 80,000 people. Three days later another bomb, "Fat Man," was dropped on Nagasaki, creating a similar death toll. Much debate has gone into the question: did the Allies need to use such destructive weapons? Many felt the Japanese were already beaten, especially with Russia's entry into the conflict, declaring war on Japan and invading Manchuria. The civilian administration of Japan was already pursuing a peace policy and it was only the military that wanted to continue the fight to the bitter end.

With scientific assistance from Great Britain and Canada, the U.S. government had set up the "Manhattan Project" in the race to build the first atomic weapon, a device so destructive that whoever held it in their possession held the strategic initiative. The Allies had chosen a policy of strategic bombing, and this involved the bombing of civilian targets to break the enemy's industrial infrastructure, as well as lowering morale. This bomb would take destruction to a new level.

Many of Japan's major cities had been hit in the raids carried out by the new B-29 bomber, using fire bombs that decimated the cities. Most of the houses in the cities were wood constructions and this, combined with the narrow streets, meant the bombing caused huge civilian casualties, claiming 100,000 lives in Tokyo. In the invasion of Okinawa and Iwo Jima, the American forces had suffered terrible losses, leading to the speculation of even greater losses of U.S. servicemen in the planned invasion of Japan itself, which the American public would find hard to live with. Casualties were estimated to be in the hundreds of thousands. The atomic bomb offered great force and the lowest amount of U.S. casualties. This is the official reason the High Command and government went ahead.

At Potsdam, President Truman gave the ultimatum to Japan of surrender or, "The alternative for Japan is prompt and utter destruction." The Japanese declined and Truman gave the order for the

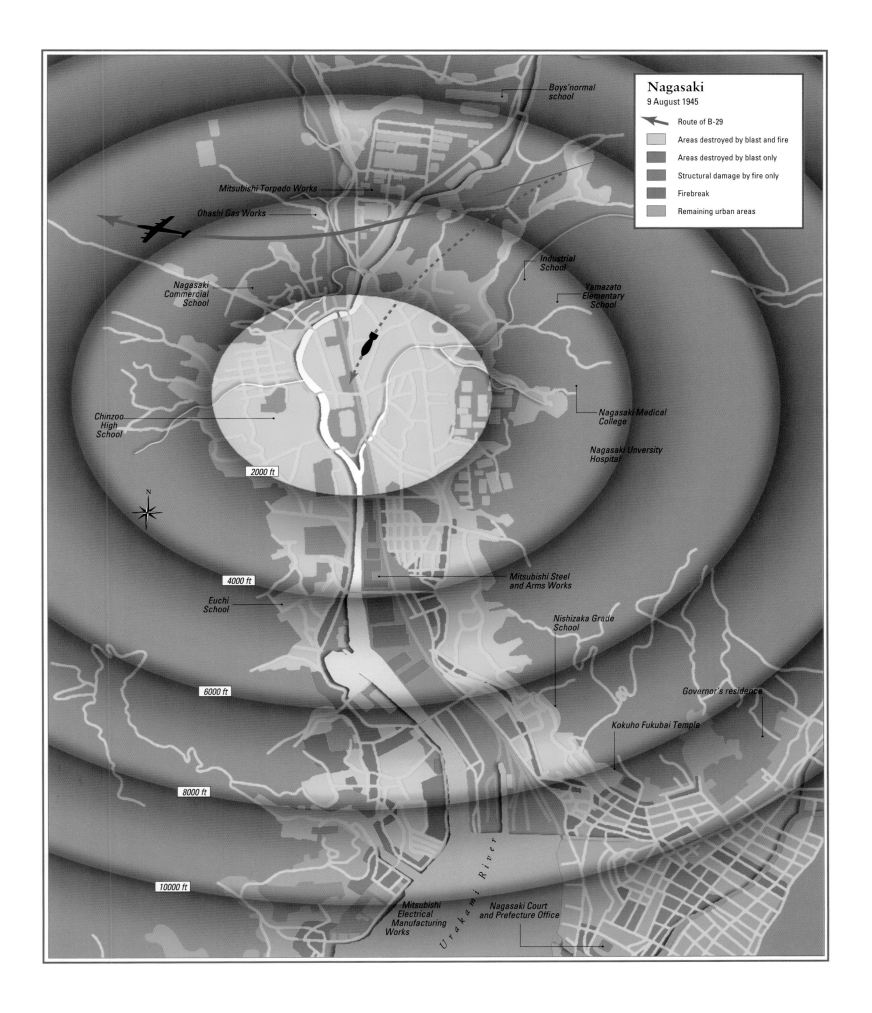

Boys' normal school

Mitsubishi Torpedo Works

Ohashi Gas Works

Nagasaki
9 August 1945

Route of B-29
Areas destroyed by blast and fire
Areas destroyed by blast only
Structural damage by fire only
Firebreak
Remaining urban areas

Industrial School

Yamazato Elementary School

Nagasaki Commercial School

Chinzoo High School

Nagasaki Medical College

Nagasaki Unversity Hospital

2000 ft

N

4000 ft

Mitsubishi Steel and Arms Works

Euchi School

Nishizaka Grade School

6000 ft

Governor's residence

Kokuho Fukubai Temple

8000 ft

10000 ft

Mitsubishi Electrical Manufacturing Works

Nagasaki Court and Prefecture Office

Urakami River

Far right: The atomic explosion over Nagasaki, the second city destroyed by atomic bombs, on 9 August 1945.

bomb to be dropped. The target of Hiroshima was chosen, not just for military reasons, or for its factories and installations, but also for its high population, which would create as large a psychological impact as possible. It had been more or less untouched by the bombing campaign and had a minor logistics base for the military. However, other than the central district, which had several concrete constructions, the main part of the city was of wooden buildings, thus lending itself to utter destruction. *Enola Gay*, the B-29 bomber piloted by the commander of the 509th Composite Bomb Group, Colonel Paul Tibbets, took off from Tinian on the morning of 6 August, accompanied by two other B-29s to record the event. At 08:15 am the bomb was released and then detonated 2,000 feet above the city. Almost all of the city was destroyed and 80,000 people vaporized. Many more would die over the coming months and years as a result of the exposure to radiation. The blast radius was one mile with the resultant fires destroying a further four miles.

Three days later *Bockscar*, flown by Major Charles W. Sweeney, dropped "Fat Man" on the city of Nagasaki, a large port on the south of Japan that was home to several large factories, again largely constructed of wood. The original target was to be Kokura but cloud cover meant that *Bockscar* had to be diverted to Nagasaki. The bomb was released at 11:01 am and killed 70,000 people. This second bomb within days led the Japanese government as a whole to accept the unconditional surrender of their country to the Allies.

The use of these weapons and their destructive power has been the center of much controversy, with many of the U.S. commanders, including MacArthur and Nimitz, believing that the bomb should not have been used at all, and that an invasion was the only option. Others argue that the dropping of the bomb was a show of strength to the Russians who were, at the time, invading Manchuria and already in possession of large parts of eastern-central Europe. The main official reason was to save the lives that would have been lost in the planned invasion of Japan, both U.S., and many more Japanese. Either way, the consequences of using the bomb and the suffering it caused to tens of thousands for many years after the event, highlights why this horrific weapon has not been used again—and hopefully never will be.

Hiroshima, devastated by the first atomic bomb. More people died in conventional bombing raids on Tokyo but the shock effect and destructive power of one single weapon had a massive effect on not only the Japanese but on an equally stunned world.

SOVIET INVASION OF MANCHURIA 1945

"WE CALL UPON THE GOVERNMENT OF JAPAN TO PROCLAIM NOW THE UNCONDITIONAL SURRENDER OF ALL THE JAPANESE ARMED FORCES."

ALLIED ULTIMATUM TO JAPAN, AUGUST 1945

The Soviet Union had agreed at the Yalta Conference between the three major powers, in February 1945, that it would attack Japanese forces three months after the capitulation of Germany in the European Campaign. Three months to the day after the fall of Germany, they carried out their undertaking by attacking the Japanese in Manchuria. It was to be a one-sided battle that would not last long but which was instrumental in bringing Japan to its knees.

The Soviets were to attack in four places, the main attack in Manchuria, with amphibious attacks on northern Korea, the Sakhalin Islands, and the Kurile Islands. Far East Command, under the control of Marshal A. M. Vasilevsky, was enormous, being made up of three "Fronts," the Transbaikel and the 1st, and 2nd Far East. These units totaled 1.5 million men with 5,000 tanks and tens of thousands of artillery pieces. Opposing these forces was the Kwantung Army, severely depleted of heavy weapons and men transferred to the fighting in the Pacific campaign. This army was basically an occupying force made up of light infantry numbering some 600,000 men, which had the capability of fighting small insurgency battles. It was nothing compared to the might of the Red Army that had already gained so much experience fighting the Germans.

A Soviet armored column enters a Manchurian town, possibly Port Arthur, August 1945. The local population seems quite happy to see the end of Japanese rule.

The Russian attack went forward on 8 August 1945, between the two atomic bomb drops, deploying a pincer movement. One side of the pincer came from the west through Mongolia, which was too inhospitable to build the required supply lines required for the Soviet advance. However, the Japanese commanders, believing this would be the case, had left the area poorly fortified and the Soviet advance, therefore, was rapid. During this time airborne troops were also dropped behind the lines to seize vital towns and airstrips in order to fly in further men and supplies if required.

With Soviet forces now penetrating deep into Manchuria (Manchukuo), Japan's Emperor Hirohito declared a ceasefire on 15 August, barely a week after the assault had gone in. With this ceasefire the Russians continued their advance and had reached Mukden and Changchun by 20 August, with Mengjiang also being invaded at the same time.

The Russian amphibious landings to the east went according to plan as well, with the island of Sukhalin and the Kuriles Islands in their hands quickly, which established Soviet Sovereignty in accordance with the Yalta Agreements. The landings in north Korea also went well, but a lack of sup-

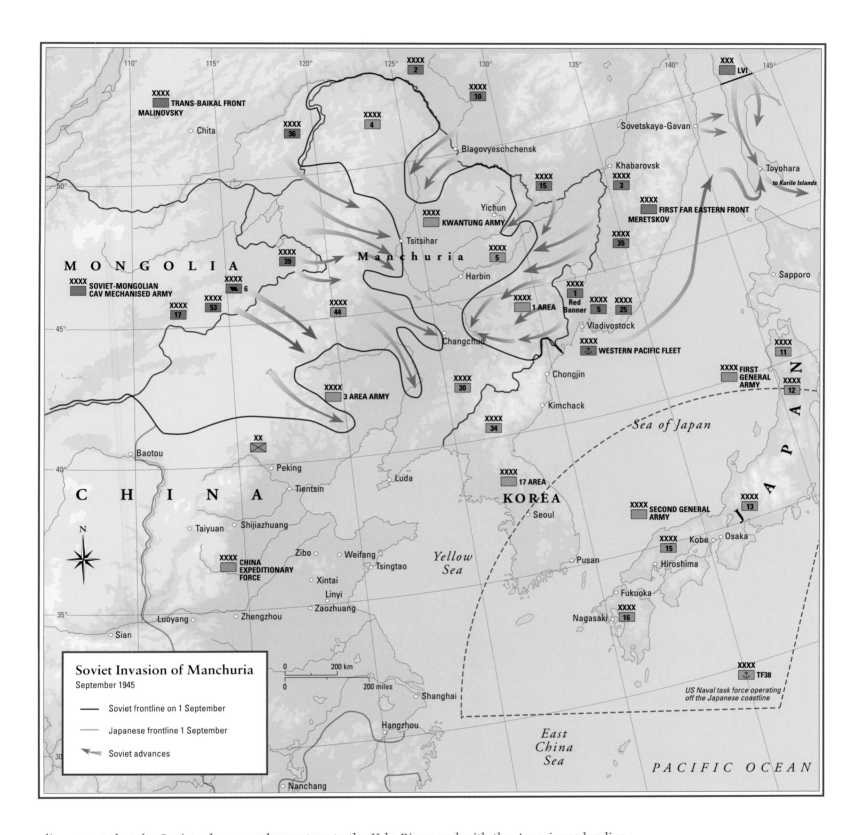

Soviet Invasion of Manchuria
September 1945

— Soviet frontline on 1 September

— Japanese frontline 1 September

←— Soviet advances

plies meant that the Soviet advance only went up to the Yalu River, and with the Americans landing in the south at Incheon after the Japanese surrender, it meant the country was split in two.

There is no doubt that the Soviet invasion of Manchuria contributed massively to the surrender of the Japanese, with the rapid and powerful advance showing clearly to the Japanese that they could never hold out against the combined might of the Allies. However, the division of Korea would eventually lead to the Korean War in 1950–53, a conflict that has not been entirely solved to this day.

MOBILIZATION FOR WAR

Between 1939 and 1945 the largest armed forces ever recorded were raised across the globe. The Soviet Union, which mobilized its entire nation in the fight against Germany, had over 29,000,000 of its citizens in the military between 1941 and 1945. In the United States conscripts and volunteers produced 11,500,000 for its armed forces. These were transported thousands of miles from home to battle fronts across the world. Britain mobilized 4,600,000 with another 4,200,000

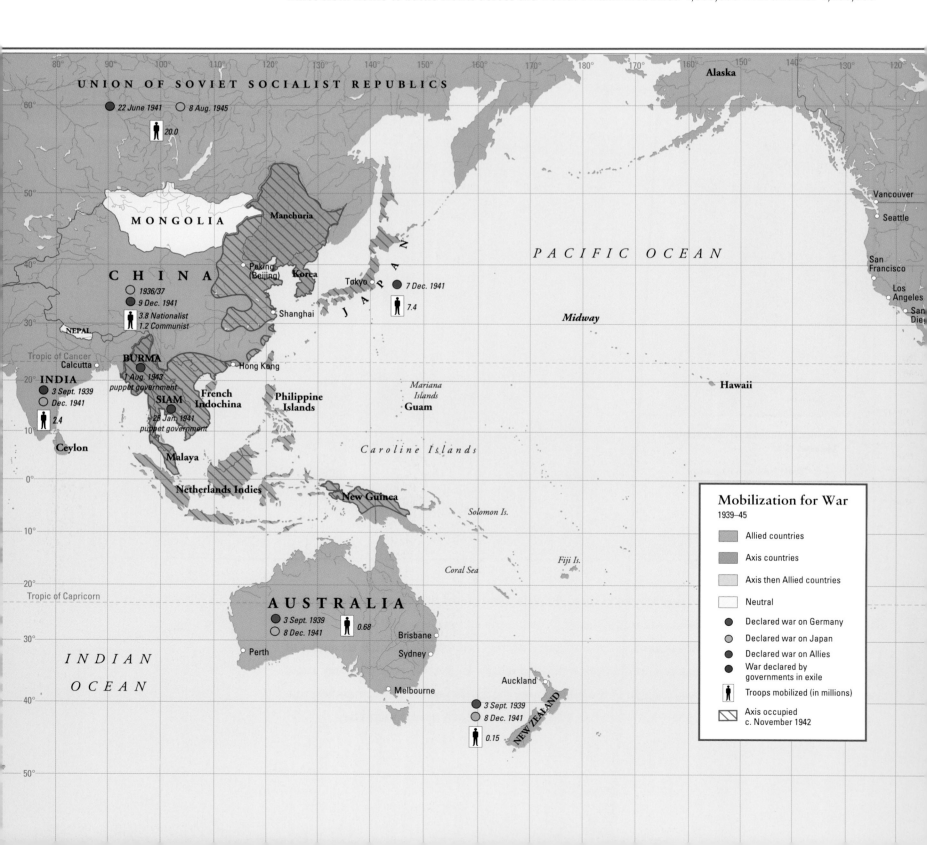

UNION OF SOVIET SOCIALIST REPUBLICS

● 22 June 1941   ○ 8 Aug. 1945

👤 20.0

Alaska

MONGOLIA

Manchuria

Vancouver

Seattle

PACIFIC OCEAN

CHINA

Peking (Beijing)   Korea

Tokyo   ● 7 Dec. 1941

San Francisco

○ 1936/37
● 9 Dec. 1941

👤 3.8 Nationalist
    1.2 Communist

Shanghai

J A P A N

👤 7.4

Los Angeles

San Diego

NEPAL

Tropic of Cancer
Calcutta

BURMA

Hong Kong

Midway

INDIA

● 3 Sept. 1939
○ Dec. 1941

1 Aug. 1943
puppet government

SIAM

French
Indochina

Philippine
Islands

Mariana
Islands

Guam

Hawaii

👤 2.4

25 Jan. 1941
puppet government

Ceylon

Malaya

Caroline Islands

Netherlands Indies

New Guinea

Solomon Is.

Fiji Is.

Coral Sea

AUSTRALIA

Mobilization for War
1939–45

■ Allied countries

■ Axis countries

■ Axis then Allied countries

□ Neutral

● Declared war on Germany

● Declared war on Japan

● Declared war on Allies

● War declared by
   governments in exile

👤 Troops mobilized (in millions)

▨ Axis occupied
   c. November 1942

● 3 Sept. 1939
○ 8 Dec. 1941

👤 0.68

Brisbane

INDIAN

Perth

Sydney

OCEAN

Auckland

Melbourne

● 3 Sept. 1939
○ 8 Dec. 1941

👤 0.15

NEW ZEALAND

coming from the Empire and Commonwealth. Germany began rearming and enlarging its armed forces from the mid-1930s and by 1939 her armed forces stood at 3,180,000 and by the end of the war some 17,900,000 had been conscripted, including Austrians and other nationalities as the Reich increased in size. By the late 1930s, Japan was engaged in a major war in China and had deployed an army numbering over 1,000,000 but by 1944, had over 7,000,000 serving in its forces. Italy, who fought on both Axis and Allied sides, conscripted over 20 percent of its population, some 9,100,000 serving between 1940 and 1945. Besides the full-time military there were millions of part-time militia in many countries, including the National Guard, Volksturm, the Home Guard, and many others. These added many more millions to those mobilized for war, a total that may have reached over 120,000,000.

MILITARY MANPOWER RAISED
BY EACH OF THE MAJOR BELLIGERENT NATIONS, 1939–45

Country		Declaration of War	End of War	Peak Number	Total Mobilized
Albania		13,000	—	—	—
Australia	Armed Forces	91,700	575,100	—	
	Army	82,800	380,700	—	
	Air Force	3,500	154,500	—	993,000
	Navy	5,400	39,900	—	
Belgium		600,000	650,000	—	900,000
Bulgaria		160,000	450,000		1,011,000
Canada	Armed Forces	63,100	759,800	—	
	Army	55,600	474,000	—	
	Air Force	3,100	193,000	—	1,100,000
	Navy	4,400	92,800	—	
China		2,500,000	5,000,000	5,700,000	14,000,000
Denmark		6,600	—	—	6,600
Finland	1939–40	127,800	200,000	—	
	1941–44	400,000	270,000	—	?
France	Sept. 1939	900,000	—	—	—
	1940	4,320,000	—	—	—
	1943–44 Italy	15,000	430,000	113,000	—
Germany	Armed Forces	3,180,000	7,800,000	9,500,000	
	Army	2,760,000	6,900,000	6,500,000	
	Air Force	400,000	1,000,000	2,100,000	17,900,000
	Navy	50,000	700,000	800,000	
Greece	Oct 1940	430,000	—	—	
	April 1941	540,000	—	—	?
Hungary		800,000	210,000	?	?
India	Armed Forces	197,000	2,159,000	—	
	Army	194,900	2,100,000	—	
	Air Force	300	29,200	—	2,581,800
	Navy	1,800	30,500	—	

Country		Declaration of War	End of War	Peak Number	Total Mobilized
Italy	Armed Forces	1,899,000	?	?	
	Army	1,630,000	?	2,563,000	9,100,000
	Air Force	101,000	200,000	—	
	Navy	168,600	259,100	—	
Japan	Armed Forces	1,700,000	7,200,000	—	
	Army	1,500,000	5,500,000	—	9,100,000
	Navy	200,000	1,700,000	—	
Netherlands		270,000	400,000	—	400,000
New Zealand	Armed Forces	13,800	192,800	—	
	Army	11,300	157,000	—	
	Air Force	1,200	c. 27,000	—	?
	Navy	1,300	5,800	—	
Norway		25,000	—	—	90,000
Poland	1939	1,200,000	250,000	?	2,400,000
	1943–45 Italy	8,600	50,000	—	?
	1944–45 N-w E.	28,000	—	—	?
	1941–45 E. Front	30,000	?	?	200,000
Romania	1941–44	686,000	1,225,000	—	?
	1944–45 with Red Army	?	370,000	—	539,000
South Africa	Armed Forces	?	?	?	250,000
	Army	18,000	?	198,000	208,000
	Air Force	1,000	?	?	38,000
	Navy	?	?	?	4,000
U.K.	Armed Forces	681,000	4,683,000	—	
	Army	402,000	2,931,000	—	5,896,000
	Air Force	118,000	963,000	1,012,000	
	Navy	161,000	789,000	—	
U.S.A.	Armed Forces	5,413,000	11,877,000	—	
	Army	4,602,000	5,851,000	—	16,354,000
	Air Force	354,000	2,282,000	—	
	Navy	382,000	3,288,000	—	
U.S.S.R.	Armed Forces	9,000,000	12,400,000	13,200,000	
	Army	2,900,000	6,000,000	—	
	Air Force	?	?	?	?
	Navy	?	?	266,000	
Yugoslavia	1941	150,000	?	—	1,500,000
	1941–45 Partisans	2,000	800,000	—	?

INDUSTRIAL PRODUCTION

Right: In this photograph there are eight of the 2,751 Liberty ships built in the United States during the war years. To construct a Liberty ship 250,000 parts were manufactured and pre-fabricated into 250-ton sections, then welded together in the shipyard. In one famous publicity stunt the ss *Robert E. Peary* was constructed and launched in four and a half days. In the five holds of a Liberty ship she could carry more than 9,000 tons of cargo; this could equate to 2,840 Jeeps, 250 tanks, or 230,000,000 rounds of rifle ammunition.

World War II witnessed the might of the United States' industrial powerhouse. It built ships and filled them with the weapons of war, and it supplied the needs of Britain and its Commonwealth, the Soviet Union, and many others. All this while building its own military strength for war against Japan and Nazi Germany. The Soviet Union also made an heroic industrial effort. After being invaded by Germany, the Soviets moved much of their industry eastward out of Germany's grasp. There they reassembled tank and aircraft factories, one of the greatest industrial efforts ever recorded, then outproduced Germany on almost every necessity of war.

Germany produced relatively slowly at first, the Nazis wanted some consumer goods for "the victor" in 1940, but by 1942 onwards production leapt. Even when heavily bombed by the Allies, they still produced almost 40,000 aircraft in 1944.

Japan, the industrial power house of Asia, could never match the industrial might of its Pacific rival, the United States. It also relied on huge amounts of imports to keep its industry working. By 1945 this was being strangled by Allied attacks on its supply lines.

Britain, despite its somewhat old-fashioned industry and archaic working practices, managed a huge effort, conscripting men and women into industry and men into the coal mines, but by the end of the war Britain's industrial base was utterly worn out.

A U.S. poster calling for greater industrial production, while appealing to all ethnic communities to pull together.

WEAPONS PRODUCTION OF THE MAJOR POWERS 1939–45

AIRCRAFT

	1939	1940	1941	1942	1943	1944	1945
U.S.A.	5,856	12,804	26,277	47,826	85,998	96,318	49,761
U.K.	7,940	15,049	20,094	23,672	26,263	26,461	12,070
U.S.S.R.	10,382	10,565	15,735	25,436	34,900	40,300	20,900
Germany	8,295	10,247	11,776	15,409	24,807	39,807	7,540
Japan	4,467	4,768	5,088	8,861	16,693	28,180	11,066

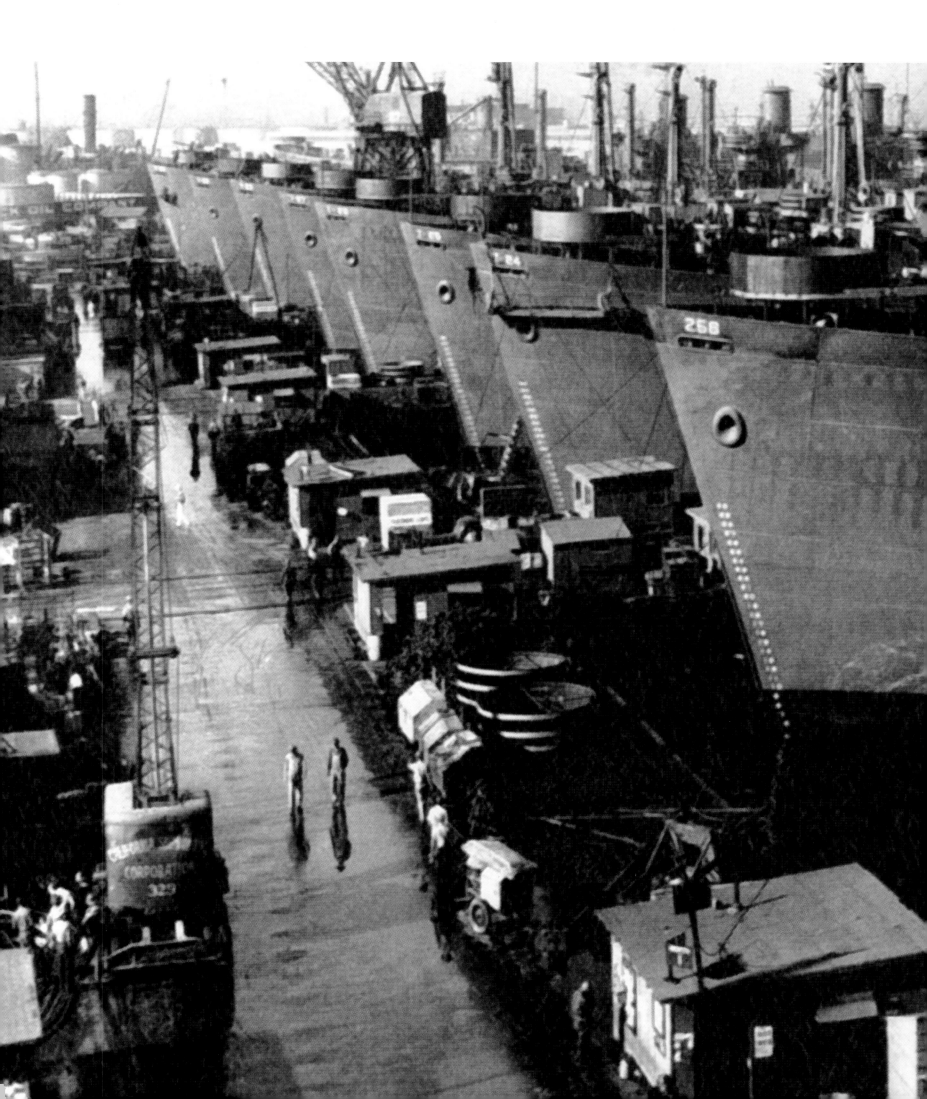

TANKS							
	1939	**1940**	**1941**	**1942**	**1943**	**1944**	**1945**
U.S.A.	—	c. 400	4,052	24,997	29,497	17,565	11,968
U.K.	989	1,399	4,841	8,611	7,476	5,000	2,100
U.S.S.R.	2,950	2,794	6,590	24,446	24,089	28,963	15,400
Germany	c. 1,300	2,200	5,200	9,200	17,300	22,100	4,400
Japan	c. 200	1,023	1,024	1,191	790	401	142

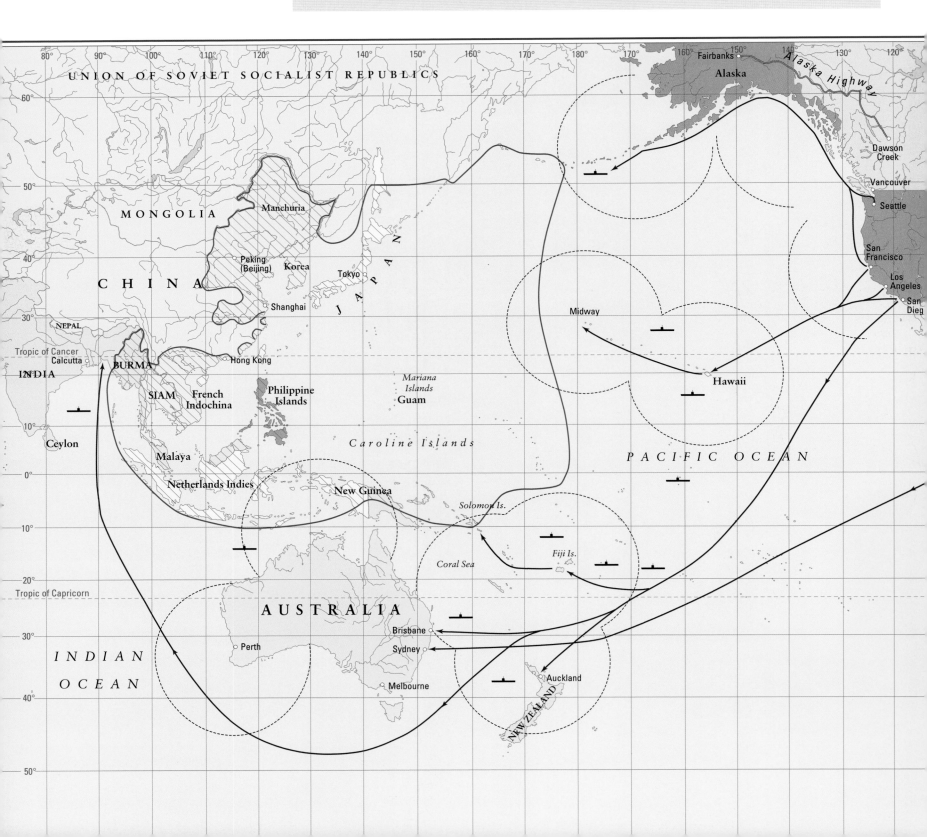

MAJOR WAR SHIPS

	1939	1940	1941	1942	1943	1944	1945
U.S.A.	—	—	544	1,854	2,654	2,247	1,513
U.K.	57	148	236	239	224	188	64
U.S.S.R.	—	33	62	19	13	23	11
Germany (U-boat)	15	40	196	244	270	189	—
Japan	21	30	49	68	122	248	51

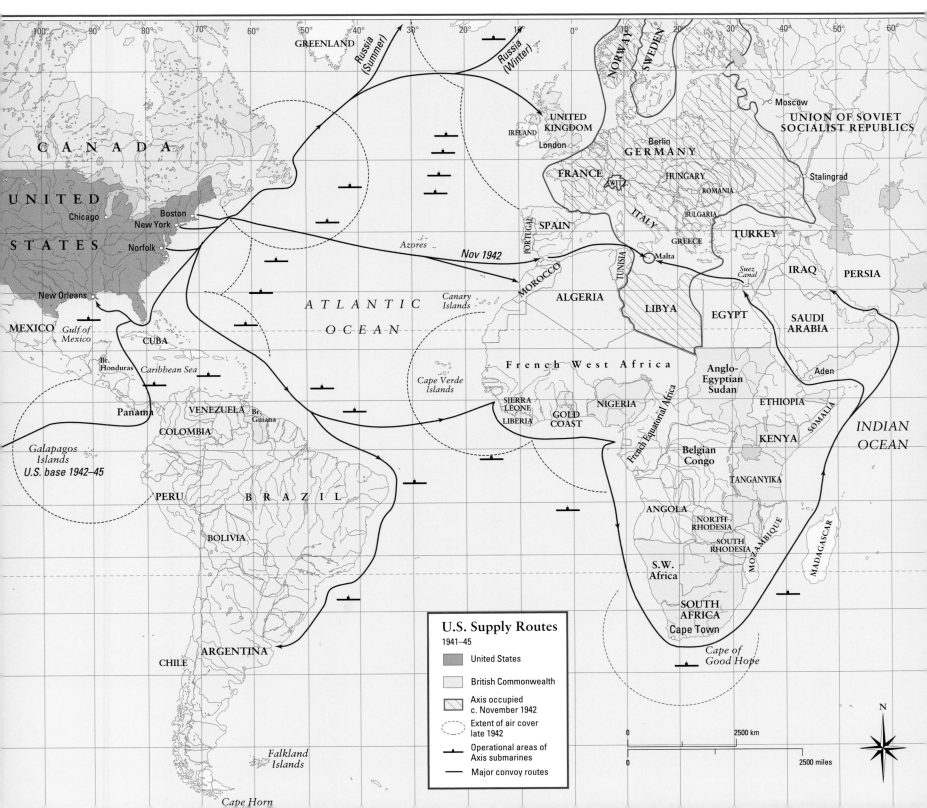

U.S. Supply Routes
1941–45

- United States
- British Commonwealth
- Axis occupied c. November 1942
- Extent of air cover late 1942
- Operational areas of Axis submarines
- Major convoy routes

Casualties of War

The human cost of World War II was noticeably worse for the belligerent states. The statistics on casualties are inexact. Only the official numbers showing those dead, wounded, prisoners, or missing from the United States or the British Commonwealth can be classed as anything like accurate. Elsewhere, there are estimates. The Soviet Union lost more than 20 million military and civilian personnel, including large numbers of prisoners who were deliberately starved to death. Civilian deaths are difficult to calculate but a particularly heavy death toll occurred in eastern Europe, where Poland lost about 20 percent of its population and Yugoslavia and U.S.S.R. 10 percent. Western Europe's losses were modest compared with these excessive death rates. In east Asia, the Chinese suffered from disease and famine, several millions dying along with civilian and military battle casualties. Estimates of the total number of people killed vary from 55 to more than 60 million for the entire war. The estimates based on the latest available figures seem to suggest that it might be as high as 62 million.

UNION OF SOVIET SOCIALIST REPUBLICS

- c. 14,500,000 (c. 9.5 million on the Eastern Front including 3 million as prisoners of war; c. 2 million on Far Eastern Front)
- Over 7 million
- 'Enemies of the state', population of recently acquired territories in Western Soviet Union

MONGOLIA **Manchuria**

CHINA
- 1,324,000
- Up to 10,000,000

NEPAL

INDIA
- 36,092

BURMA

SIAM **French Indochina** **Philippine Islands**

Ceylon

Malaya

Netherlands Indies **New Guinea**

JAPAN
- 1,506,000
- 300,000

Mariana Islands **Guam**

Caroline Islands

AUSTRALIA
- 29,395
- Japanese and Italian origin

NEW ZEALAND
- 12,162

The Casualties of War
1939–45

- Military dead
- Civilian dead
- Large groups of civilian internees

Data for European States

HUNGARY
- ● ● 750,000

AUSTRIA
- 380,000
- 145,000

ITALY
- 279,820
- 17,400 as Allies
- 93,000 Communists and anti-Fascists

BELGIUM
- 9,561
- 75,000

NETHERLANDS
- 13,700
- 236,300

BULGARIA
- 18,500
- 1,500

POLAND
- 850,000 (169,822 as Allies)
- 5,778,200

ROMANIA
- 519,822
- 465,000

CZECHOSLOVAKIA
- 6,683
- 310,000

GREECE
- 16,357
- 155,300

YUGOSLAVIA
- ● ● 1,700,000

ESTIMATED LOSS OF LIFE IN THE SECOND WORLD WAR

Country	Military Losses	Civilian Losses	Total Losses
U.S.S.R. (1941–45)	c. 8.7 million	c. 16 million	c. 25 million
Germany (1939–1945)	3,250,000	3,600,000	6,850,000
U.K. (1939–45)	326,000	62,000	388,000
France	340,000	470,000	810,000
Poland	123,000	* c. 6 million	c. 6,123,000
Yugoslavia	300,000	+ 1,400,000	1,706,000
Hungary			** 840,000
Greece			520,000
Romania			460,000
Austria			480,000
Italy			410,000
Czechoslovakia			400,000
All other European states			425,000
TOTAL ALL EUROPEAN STATES			**c. 43 million**
U.S.A. (All Fronts including the Pacific, 1941–45)			296,000
Japan			2 million
China			c. 15 million
TOTAL ALL FRONTS			**c. 60 million**

Notes: * Of whom c. 3 million were Polish Jews
** Of whom c. 540,000 were Hungarian Jews
+ Including partisans

CANADA
39,319

UNITED STATES
292,100
Japanese origin

Chicago Boston
New York
Norfolk
New Orleans

MEXICO Gulf of Mexico
c. 250
CUBA
HAITI
Br. Honduras Caribbean Sea
HONDURAS
GUATEMALA
SALVADOR NICARAGUA
COSTA RICA
Panama VENEZUELA Br. Guiana
COLOMBIA
ECUADOR
PERU
BOLIVIA
BRAZIL 943
PARAGUAY
CHILE
ARGENTINA

Hudson Bay

ATLANTIC OCEAN

Cape Verde Islands

4,780
(including Merchant Seamen)
NORWAY SWEDEN FINLAND 79,047
271,311
60,595
Recent German immigrants
IRELAND DENMARK
UNITED KINGDOM 4,339
London NETH.
BEL.
Leningrad
Moscow
Königsberg
UNION OF SOVIET SOCIALIST REPUBLICS
Berlin 2,850,000
GERMANY 2,300,000
'Enemies of the state', Jews, Gypsies, Communists and homosexuals
Stalingrad
FRANCE 210,671
173,260 SWITZ. HUNGARY
ITALY ROMANIA
YUGOSLAVIA Sebastopol
BULGARIA
SPAIN ALB.
4,500 (Axis) 7,500 (Allies) GREECE TURKEY
PORTUGAL
10,000 (in concentration camps) SYRIA
TUNISIA Malta Suez Canal IRAQ PERSIA
MOROCCO
ALGERIA LIBYA EGYPT SAUDI ARABIA

French West Africa
Anglo-Egyptian Sudan Aden
SIERRA LEONE NIGERIA ETHIOPIA SOMALIA
GOLD COAST
LIBERIA
SPANISH GUINEA KENYA
Belgian Congo INDIAN OCEAN
ANGOLA TANGANYIKA
NORTH RHODESIA
SOUTH RHODESIA MOZAMBIQUE MADAGASCAR
S.W. Africa
SOUTH AFRICA 8,681
Cape Town
Cape of Good Hope

N

0 2500 km
0 2500 miles

UNITED NATIONS

"IF CIVILIZATION IS TO SURVIVE, WE MUST CULTIVATE THE SCIENCE OF HUMAN RELATIONSHIPS—THE ABILITY OF ALL PEOPLES, OF ALL KINDS, TO LIVE TOGETHER, IN THE SAME WORLD AT PEACE."

FRANKLIN D. ROOSEVELT

On a warship, off the coast of Newfoundland, on 14 August 1941, President Franklin D. Roosevelt of the United States and Prime Minister Winston Churchill of Great Britain signed the Atlantic Charter. This document enunciated several common principles, which the two states would follow in a postwar world. The two men stated that they wanted no territorial, or any other aggrandizement, from World War II. Additionally, all peoples would have the right to select their own style of government and would have no border changes imposed on them. All countries, be they victorious or conquered, would have access to the natural resources of our planet, and it was recognized that economic cooperation between nations was a good policy to follow. The Charter hoped that when Nazi Germany was defeated, that all countries would be secure from aggression, and that humanity would be liberated from fear and need. The freedom of the seas was recognized, and the two leaders maintained that all peoples must renounce the use of force in international relations, and further expressed the desire for disarmament after the outcome of the expected Allied victory.

These principles were very bland because the U.S. President, at that time, was confronting isolationist tendencies in the U.S.A. and walking a tight-rope when, despite an official declaration of neutrality in the war, had, in March 1941, persuaded Congress to pass the Lend-Lease Act transferring war materials to Britain.

In Washington, D.C., on 1 January 1942, the 26 governments at war with the Axis states, stated that they "subscribed to a common program of purposes and principles embodied in the joint declaration ... known as the Atlantic Charter." The signatories were known collectively as the United Nations, a term chosen by Roosevelt. It appealed to Churchill because the term was used in the poet

Byron's *Childe Harold*, which mentioned the Battle of Waterloo when the allies were fighting a previous international tyrant, Emperor Napoleon of France.

> "Here, where the sword united nations drew,
> Our countrymen were warring on that day!'
> And this is much, and all which will not pass away."

Progress on building this new organization was accelerated on 30 October 1942, at an international conference in Moscow. Representatives of the Soviet Union, Great Britain, China, and the United States signed a declaration wherein they foresaw the necessity to establish, at the earliest opportunity, an international organization. One month later, Roosevelt, Churchill, and Stalin met at Tehran and declared that "the supreme responsibility resting upon us and all the United Nations to make a peace which will ... banish the scourge and terror of war."

Representatives of the four powers met at an estate at Dumbarton Oaks in Washington, D.C., in the fall 1944, to draft a number of proposals for a new international organization to replace the League of Nations. Agreement was reached on its purposes, structure, and mode of operation, but there was disagreement on two key issues. There was no consensus on how voting would operate in the new Security Council, the vehicle responsibility for peace and security. Secondly, Stalin demanded seats in the new General Assembly for all 15 constituent Republics of the Soviet Union.

A conference at Yalta between 4–11 February 1945 witnessed Roosevelt, Stalin, and Churchill resolving the issues in Stalin's favor, the other leaders bending over backwards to ensure Stalin was on board. Stalin accepted the Anglo-American view that limited great power prerogatives on procedural matters, but kept the right of veto on serious matters, later much abused during the Cold War.

On 25 April 1945, the Dumbarton Oaks proposals, plus the Yalta modifications, comprised the basis for negotiations at the United Nations Conference on International Organization (U.N.C.I.O.), which was held at San Francisco to draft the Charter of the United Nations Organization. The Charter was signed on 26 June and entered into force on 24 October 1945.

The conference was attended by the 26 signatories that had signed the Declaration of the United Nations and by 20 other states that had declared war against the Axis by March 1945. Four other countries were admitted during the conference: Denmark, the Ukrainian S.S.R., the Belorussian S.S.R., and Argentina. The Soviet Union now had three seats in the General Assembly, Stalin's price for acceding to the United Nations Organization (U.N.O.).

The San Francisco conference was the first major international event not dominated by Europe. Nine western European countries were members, three Soviet republics, 21 American republics, seven Middle Eastern countries, six Commonwealth states, two eastern Asian nations, and two African ones. The U.N.O. recognized all geographical regions of the world. The small states, together with the Asian and Latin American countries, succeeded in altering the Dumbarton Oaks proposals in certain areas. These articles were subject to a compromise, including domestic jurisdiction versus international protection of human rights and promotion of economic and social welfare. Furthermore, a Trusteeship Council was created for supervising 11 territories placed under international trust at the end of the World War II.

GREENLAND

Ellesmere Island

ICELAND

Victoria Island

Baffin Island

ALASKA

NORWAY

UNITED
KINGDOM

DE

CANADA

NETH.

London

G

B.

LU

Paris

Vancouver

Newfoundland

FRANCE

SW

Portland

Montreal

Halifax

San Francisco

New York

PORT.

Madrid

UN Charter signed 26 June 1945

UNITED STATES
OF AMERICA

Lisboa

SPAIN

Casablanca

MOROCCO

ALGERIA

MEXICO

WESTERN
SAHARA

CUBA

MAURITANIA

MALI

HAITI

DOMINICAN
REPUBLIC

BELIZE

JAMAICA

SENEGAL

NIGER

GUAT.

HOND.

BURKINA

NIGER

EL SALV.

NIC.

GUINEA

IVORY
COAST

GHANA

NIGER

C. R.

Caracas

GUYANA

LIBERIA

PANAMA

VENEZUELA

SURINAM

TOGO

COLOMBIA

FRENCH
GUIANA

BENIN

GABO

EQUADOR

PERU

Lima

BRAZIL

BOLIVIA

PARAGUAY

Rio de Janeiro

CHILE

URAGUAY

Buenos Aires

Montevideo

ARGENTINA

**Original Members of the
United Nations 1945**

◼ Original Members

● Security Council Members

Svalbard

*Novaya
Zemlya*

SWEDEN

FINLAND

Stockholm

UNION OF SOVIET SOCIALIST REPUBLICS

Moskva

POLAND

ZECH.

S. HUN. ROM.

YUG. BULG.

ALB. Istanbul

TALY GREECE

Athinai TURKEY

Sakhalin

MONGOLIA

Hokkaido

Beijing

N. KOREA JAPAN

S. KOREA *Honshu*

Tokyo

SYRIA Tehran

LEB.

ISRAEL Baghdad

Cairo IRAQ

JORDAN

IRAN

AFGHAN.

CHINA

Shanghai

PAKISTAN

Delhi

NEPAL BH.

Taiwan

IBYA

EGYPT

SAUDI
ARABIA A. E.

OMAN

Calcutta BURMA

Bombay INDIA BANGLA-
DESH

Hainan

Luzón

LAOS
VIETNAM

THAI.

CHAD

YEMEN

CAMB. PHILIPPINES

CENTRAL
AFRICAN
REPUBLIC

ETHIOPIA

SUDAN

SOMALIA

SRI
LANKA

Mindanao

MALAYSIA

CONGO

UGANDA

KENYA

ZAIRE

TANZANIA

Sumatra

Borneo

Sulawesi

I N D O N E S I A

PAPUA
NEW GUINEA

Java

Timor

NGOLA

ZAMBIA

ZIMBABWE

NAMIBIA

BOTSWANA

MOZAMBIQUE

MADAGASCAR

AUSTRALIA

SOUTH
AFRICA

Cape Town

Sydney

NEW
ZEALAND

FURTHER READING

There have been literally millions of words written on World War II. The works cited below represent some of the more worthwhile studies.

Ambrose, Stephen E.; *The Supreme Commander: The War Years of General Dwight D. Eisenhower*. Doubleday, New York, 1969.

Barnett, Correlli; *Engage the Enemy More Closely: The Royal Navy in the Second World War*, Hodder & Stoughton, London, and Norton, New York, 1991.

Bennett, Ralph; *Ultra in the West: The Normandy Campaign 1944-1945*, Hutchinson, London, 1979 and Scribner, New York, 1980.

Blair, C.; *Hitler's U-boat War, 1939–42 and 1942–45*, Random House, London and New York, 1966 and 1999.

Blumenson, Martin; *The Patton Papers 1940–1945*, Houghton Mifflin, Boston, 1974.

Blumenson, Martin; *Breakout and Pursuit Office of the Chief of Military History*, US Army, Government Printing Office, Washington D.C., 1961.

Chandler, David G. & Collins, James Lawton Jr.; *The D-Day Encyclopedia*, Helicon, Oxford, and Simon & Schuster, New York, 1994.

Dear, I.C.B. & Foot, M.R.D. (eds.); *The Oxford Companion to the Second World War*, Oxford University Press, Oxford and New York, 1995.

Ellis, L. F.; *Victory in the West: The Battle of Normandy*, HMSO, London, 1962.

Erikson, J.; *The Road to Stalingrad*, Weidenfeld & Nicholson, London, 1975.

Erikson, J.; *The Road to Berlin*, Weidenfeld & Nicholson, London, 1983.

Fraser, David; *Knight's Cross: A Life of Field Marshal Erwin Rommel* HarperCollins, London and New York, 1993.

Hamilton, Nigel; *Monty: Master of the Battlefield 1942–1944* Hamish Hamilton, London, and McGraw Hill, New York, 1983.

Lacey-Johnson, Lionel; *Pointblank and Beyond*, Airlife, Shrewsbury, 1991.

Messenger, Charles; *The Last Prussian: A Biography of Field Marshal Gerd von Rundstedt 1875–1953*, Brassey's (UK), London, 1991.

Miller, E.S.; *War Plan Orange*, Naval Institute Press, Annapolis, 1991.

Morison, Samuel Eliot; *History of United States Naval Operations in World War II*, Oxford University Press and Little, Brown, Boston, 1957.

Overy, R.; *Russia's War*, Allen Lane – The Penguin Press, London, 1998.

Stacey, C. P.; *Official History of the Canadian Army in World War II: The Victory Campaign: The Operations in North-West Europe, 1944–1945*, Queen's Printer, Ottawa, 1960.

Strawson, John; *The Battle for North Africa*, Scribner, New York, 1996.

Weigley, Russell F.; *Eisenhower's Lieutenants: The Campaigns of France and Germany, 1944–1945*, Sidgwick & Jackson, London, and Indiana University Press, Bloomington, 1981.

Willmot, H.P.; *Second World War in the East*, Cassell, London, 1999.

Wilmot, Chester; *The Struggle for Europe*, Collins, London, 1953 and Harper, New York, 1952.

INDEX

Figures in *italics* refer to illustrations.

B

ACKNOWLEDGMENTS

For Cartographica Press

Design, Maps and Typesetting: Jeanne Radford, P A B Smith, Alexander Swanston, Malcolm
    Swanston, and Jonathan Young

The publishers would like to thank the following picture libraries for their kind permission to use
    their pictures and illustrations:

Imperial War Musuem: pp. 13, 15, 36, 40, 43, 44, 49, 69, 72, 75, 80, 88, 92, 96, 97, 99, 106, 111, 120,
    124, 133, 138, 156, 176, 177, 188, 197, 198, 199, 207, 222, 232, 236, 247, 286, 297, 316, 318, 319, 344,
    371.
Hulton Getty: pp. 18, 31, 32, 34, 36, 101, 132, 193, 240, 248, 261, 262, 278, 280.
National Archive, Washington D.C.:   p.19, 220, 367.
Private Collection: pp. 20, 22, 73, 74, 79, 87, 112, 118, 122, 152, 158, 161, 162, 223, 234, 270, 271, 276,
    284, 288, 290, 291, 311, 324, 332, 346, 362, 363.
MacClancy Collection: pp. 23, 134, 136, 139, 141, 142, 181, 190, 194, 202, 206, 208, 225, 242, 246, 295,
    338, 370.
A.K.G.:   pp. 24, 26, 27, 309, 364.
Peter Newark Military Pictures: pp. 57, 64, 128, 131, 140, 185.
Tank Museum, Dorset: pp. 59, 83, 90, 205, 331.
Corbis UK Ltd: pp. 61, 127, 209, 219, 254, 263, 298, 308, 337, 372.
Red Lion: pp. 68, 258, 256, 343.
U.S. Army: pp. 98, 230, 282, 289, 314, 342, 354, 356,
Mondadori Archives, Bildarchiv Preussischer Kulturbesitz (Berlin):   pp. 126, 191, 212, 251, 321, 334.
German Archive for Art and History: p. 143.
Keystone Collection: pp. 164, 178, 214, 229, 340.
U.S. Air Force: pp. 187, 259, 317, 322, 348.
U.S. Navy: pp. 146, 150, 167, 213, 216, 292, 293, 352, 353, 358, 359, 379.
Imperial Japanese Navy: p. 170.
U.S. Naval Archive: p. 175.
Et Archive: p. 224.
Charles Messenger: p. 281.
U.S. Marine Corps: pp. 299, 301, 304.
Robert Hunt Library: p. 312.
Novosti Press Agency: p. 339.
Philip Jarrett: p. 366.

Every effort has been made to contact the copyright holders for images reproduced in this book.
    The publishers would welcome any errors or omissions being brought to their attention.